Martin Heidegger:
The Way and the Vision

Martin Heidegger: The Way and the Vision

J. L. Mehta

The University Press of Hawaii
Honolulu

Designed by Penny L. Faron

Library of Congress Cataloging in Publication Data

Mehta, Jarava Lal, 1912-
    Martin Heidegger, the way and the vision.

    Previous editions published under title: The philosophy of Martin
Heidegger.
    Bibliography: p.
    Includes index.
    1. Heidegger, Martin, 1889-   I. Title.
B3279.H49M382   1976   193   76-1832
ISBN 0-8248-0254-3

Die Wanderschaft in der Wegrichtung zum Fragwürdigen ist nicht Abenteuer sondern Heimkehr.

—Martin Heidegger

Contents

Preface

This book is the outcome of a persisting attempt to find my
way into the work of Martin Heidegger, to follow the path his
thinking has taken, and to glimpse what he has seen on his
way. Heidegger's quest—pursuit, pilgrimage, and pathfind-
ing in one—has from the beginning borne, in the words of
Karl Löwith, the stamp of the singularity and solitariness
characteristic of the lone traveler. A major difficulty in the
way of an adequate appreciation of Heidegger's work is the
need to see that this highly individual and unique wayfaring
derives from the nature of the inquiry itself rather than being
the expression of the person Heidegger. In addition, his written work is by no means to be regarded as the documentation
of completed thoughts, as finished reports on what he has seen
along the way. Heidegger's writings present his thinking itself
as the voyage, as a way which is itself the seeing, a thinking
which sees itself as both the way and the vision. In a thought-
voyage of this kind there is no such thing as *the* way, as
Nietzsche saw; there is this one way taken by a thinking that
was lured on and guided by this one star, the question of
Being, appearing just this once on the horizon, there to be seen
if we follow the thinker's track. Although addressed to the
serious student of Heidegger's thought, this is still a beginner's
book, in the sense that it seeks to chart out the totality of
Heidegger's thought rather than follow the thinking, giving

attention more to the content of this thinking than to the way, contrary to Heidegger's own helpful advice to his reader. It has perforce been the report of a voyage of discovery, of what the author found in his effort to form an idea of what Heidegger's writings were all about, of what was going on in them.

As one deriving from the Indian philosophical-cultural tradition, though not unfamiliar with the Western, the author could approach Heidegger's thought only from the outside, seeking to understand it for itself. He was drawn to it by the strangeness and novelty of this questioning voice; baffled and intrigued and challenged in turn by its difficulty; fascinated by its utter difference from the concerns of the other great philosophers in the Western tradition, while yet being so close to them; sensing vaguely that something truly profound was happening here and that a great art was powerfully at work. It was perhaps less difficult for an Asiatic student of philosophy, nurtured in the school of British Idealism and for long under the spell of twentieth-century Analytical Philosophy, to find his way to Heidegger, via Freud and Jaspers, than it has apparently been for those who themselves stand within the Western tradition and are suspicious of and resistant to a deep probing of its absolute presuppositions, as Collingwood called them. But Heidegger's thinking does not permit even the Eastern student of philosophy the luxury of being a detached spectator walking along a tortuous but well-marked trail. The very radicality of his questioning of the foundations of the metaphysical tradition, and the extraordinary sensitiveness of his ear for what still remains unthought in the first thinkers of the West, has a transforming effect on the Indian thinker's relationship to his own tradition and his perception of it. As he proceeds along this course further, even the non-Western reader becomes quite directly involved in Heidegger's path of questioning, is drawn into it as a concerned participant. He begins to sense that the question of Being, as it unfolds itself along this way, is not just a matter of academic curiosity and theoretical knowledge about the foundations of Western culture alone. He begins to see that it concerns all of mankind as it is ineluctably drawn into the history of Being as initially experienced in the West, forced into a participation in its metaphysical tradition as it culminates in the arrival of that uncanniest of all guests, Nihilism, and into becoming a part of what Heidegger calls World-civilization. And the entire path traversed by Heidegger becomes vitally relevant to him as he sees that underneath this menace, this danger, generated by the Western metaphysical experience of Being, there lies hidden "the possibility of a turn," the as yet unthought reality which, by being acknowledged and experienced in thinking, can yet save and heal. The East, an unwitting participant in Western metaphysical history at first, can again turn to the West, freely and with hope, and collaborate in the planetary task of postmetaphysical thinking, questioning, and building.

Heidegger scholars like Walter Biemel have pointed out the inappropriateness of writing on Heidegger from the outside and of trying to provide a summary of his "philosophy." The only legitimate procedure here is to find one's way, as best as one can, into the *movement* of his thinking and make this movement visible, not just to report on the thoughts or on the content of this thinking. For Heidegger's thinking constitutes in essence a movement, a movement from a thought (in the double sense of a *Gedanke* and of something already *gedacht*) to what is as yet unthought in it and so is that which is yet to be thought. His writings embody a thinking, in Eugen Fink's words, that flies ahead "like an arrow of longing to the other shore," not only of what is said there in so many words, but also of itself. "None of his books forms the conclusion of a quest, none also can be called a temporary station; each is a door leading out into the endless beyond and is less an *ergon* than pure *energeia*." This thinking also constitutes a movement away from the pattern, style, and concern of metaphysical thought or "philosophy" as it has developed in the Western tradition, and a movement in the direction of a questioning that is more elemental or primordial. It does not reject metaphysics or "philosophy" because they are wrongheaded, nor set limits to them and restrict their legitimacy as disciplines in respect of method or scope. Taking a step back, he inquires into the dark origins of these thought forms and leaves them aside because their kind of questioning does not and cannot reach into these depths. Deliberately and with determination, he steers his thinking in the direction of this mysterious realm of ultimate simplicities and, while doing so, forges a way leading to this domain and brings this domain itself to light.

Heidegger's subject matter, the *Sache* of his thinking, is not something pre-given but is itself what is sought after; it emerges as we follow the way, and the way takes its determination from what is glimpsed of the *Sache*. Speaking about his way at the Heidelberg Academy of Science, Heidegger said, "In retrospect and prospect, the path shown appears at each halting place in a different light, with a different tone, and calls forth different interpretations." The same is true of the *Sache*, which too appears in a different light, undergoes continuous transformation along the way. In and for thinking, Heidegger repeatedly points out, the way is not merely a method but is part of the matter itself. For thinking, the way is not just a means to the vision; the two belong integrally together. And the path always remains the path of thinking, of incessant questioning and disciplined saying. It does not terminate in the abrogation and supersession of thinking in favor of some kind of mystical illumination, ineffable intuition, immediate experience, or assured knowledge. What is seen on this way, the vision, is not the Platonic *theoria*, not the intellectual intuition of a Schelling, nor the Husserlian *Wesensschau*. It is a vision of what it is to think, of man as a thinking being, and of the way the matter thought about discloses itself as what is sought after. Through the experience of thinking we are offered a glimpse into the unconcealment of what is, and into the concealment underlying all coming into view. Because thinking aims at bringing into view the unthought in what has been thought, because it "plunges into the dark depths of the welling waters in order to see a star by day," what it sees and shows forth in its saying can never be a total disclosure shorn of all mystery. The way, as the way of thinking, always remains a quest, a preparation; it yields no binding, final and encompassing vision at the end, nothing that is of immediate use, no sum of wisdom that can be "applied" to life. The real passion of thinking is the passion for the "useless," Heidegger says, and a thought is then only a genuine thought when it stands in no need of being used and of being considered in terms of utility. And yet, the alert, open-minded reader comes to the end of the journey with a sense of immeasurable riches lying on this path without end, with some awareness of the splendor of the simple, with some understanding of how and why man is today homeless in the world, and of how, in the midst of this homelessness, thinking as meditation is the true and only way to be at home again in the only home there is, the world. "Thinking," Heidegger says, "is indeed an earnest affair, but it is also a festive one." Nietzsche, too, said this, but in Heidegger we see that promise fulfilled, that vision realized in thought.

Just as it is in some ways misleading to speak of Heidegger's "philosophy," it is also somewhat inept to talk about his "vision," for his way of thinking is meant to be a critique of both "philosophy" as traditionally understood and of "vision" as a notion bound up with the terminology of *Lichtmetaphysik*, which Heidegger seeks to overcome. Nevertheless, the conception of thinking as a way of letting what is come into view, of thinking as itself a way of seeing and listening, is crucial here, for it is an essential part of this thinking that on its way to the *Sache* it progressively enables thinking itself to exhibit its hidden, essential nature more clearly. The important thing to see, in our understanding and use of words such as "philosophy," "thinking," "vision," and "way," is that we do not substitute a new terminology for an old one, but rather push beyond to a nonterminological relationship to whatever thinking is about and to a nontechnical attitude to language in general. This, too, we learn only slowly as we follow Heidegger's path of thinking, alternatingly treading on that path, standing back and contemplating it, and while doing so, reflecting on our own. We come to see then that thinking as a way of encountering and experiencing what, through it, comes into view, emerging from the concealment which it never completely sheds, is not the formulation of a world-view, nor the vision of a reality confronting us. It is rather the realization of our belongingness in a reality which is not "other" than ourselves: way and vision and experience together.

In the course of our concern with the thinking and the thoughts of the great philosophers, we never cease asking ourselves, with renewed wonder and constant surprise, what a philosophical thinker is and does. What sort of passion drives a Socrates, a Nietzsche, or a Wittgenstein, and what do they in effect accomplish? In his speech of thanks to the thinker on the occasion of Heidegger's eightieth birthday at Messkirch, Eugen Fink sought, in praise of the Master, to conjure up a composite picture of the philosophical thinker as manifesting in his existence the three aspects of the ecstatic, the ambiguous, and the daimonic. Heidegger's reply is worth quoting, not only as a reply to the sort of praise lavished on him, but as a statement of Heidegger's insight into the basic mark of the way of all thinking: "In your speech you have spoken of many things, perhaps said far too much, concerning me as a person. But to those who know your thinking, one idea did come through, a thought which you have often, and perhaps first among all my students, discerned: my determination of think-ing as something 'finite' and beyond that, the admittedly questionable notion of the 'finitude of Being'. If we reduce everything that you have said here today in my honor and in my 'praise' to this 'finitude', translate it all back to this thought, then we are in agreement with each other." The author's attempt in this book to introduce the reader to the philosophical thought of Martin Heidegger will have suc-ceeded if it enables him to experience for himself the strange consistency and coherence of this thinking: aware of its own ineliminable finitude always, unremitting in its vigilance as regards its course, and yet straining at every step to think what seems to lie beyond the limits of thought.

The first version of this book was written in 1962 and presented as a doctoral dissertation at Banaras Hindu Univer-sity, Varanasi, India. This was slightly revised for publication under the title *The Philosophy of Martin Heidegger* (Varanasi, India: Banaras Hindu University Press, 1967). A revised and abridged edition of this book was published in the Harper Torchbooks in 1971. Further revision of the complete, hard-cover Indian edition, with substantial additions and changes, was made for the present version, which is being published under a new title. In making this change in the title I am thankfully accepting Professor Heidegger's hint in a letter, in which he refers to the Harper paperback as "your book on my 'philosophy'."

This work could not have been written without the benefit of the ten months I spent at the Universities of Cologne and Freiburg during 1957-1958. I am grateful to the *Alexander von Humboldt-Stiftung* for the award of a grant which made this stay possible. I acknowledge thankfully the stimulus I received, in lectures and private conversation, from Professor Ludwig Landgrebe at Cologne and the late Professor Eugen Fink at Freiburg. Special thanks are due my friend Professor Dr. Walter Biemel, not only for the many instructive conversations I had with him at the Husserl-Archiv at Cologne and in his home but also for giving me liberally of his time in explaining, line by line, some very difficult Heidegger texts. Above all, I am profoundly grateful to Professor Martin Heidegger for allowing me the privilege of meeting and talking with him, more than once, in his home, for his cordiality and for his kindness in arranging contacts helpful in my study of his thought. In particular, I recall with gratitude and pleasure the benefits I derived from long conversations with Professor Dr. Heribert Boeder and from Professor Dr. Johannes Lohmann's seminar on comparative linguistics at Freiburg University. I am thankful to Professor T. R. V. Murti, then Director, Centre of Advanced Study in Philosophy at Banaras Hindu University, for encouraging me in my work on the original dissertation, and I am grateful to him and to Professors Kalidas Bhattacharyya, Landgrebe, Biemel, and Heidegger for their encouraging comments on the work. For the many faults and deficiencies that still remain, I am solely responsible. I acknowledge gratefully the help I have received in my understanding of Heidegger from the published work of distinguished Heidegger scholars such as Hans Georg Gadamer, Walter Biemel, Werner Marx, Otto Poggeler, and William J. Richardson. Biemel's *Heidegger* is an indispensable guide, but it appeared too late to be referred to in the body of this work.

My thanks are due to the authorities of the Banaras Hindu University for permission to have this revised version published by The University Press of Hawaii, and to the latter press for its many helpful suggestions. My thanks are also due to my friend Eliot Deutsch for his unfailing helpfulness. I deeply cherish, finally, the encouragement I have received from Professor Glenn J. Gray, and am grateful for the interest he has taken in the availability of my study of Heidegger to readers outside India.

Except where otherwise indicated, all renderings from the German originals are by the author. References to Heidegger's writings in the footnotes are to the German originals. Page references to English translations (E.T.) are given where possible.

J. L. Mehta
Cambridge, Massachusetts
July 1974

I
Heidegger's Way of Thought

I
Heidegger's Way

> The poems composed by every great poet are attempts to
> put into words one single poem. His greatness depends
> on the extent to which he has entrusted himself to this
> unique poem, for it is this which enables him to maintain
> the purity of his poetic utterances by keeping them within
> the ambit of their single origin. This unique poem in a
> poet remains unuttered. None of the individual poems,
> nor all of them together, say everything. And yet each
> poem speaks out of this unique uncomposed poem and
> each time says what is the same.[1]

What Heidegger says about the poet is also true of the thinker,
as he has himself remarked elsewhere,[2] and it is supremely true
of Heidegger himself. All his writings, from first to last,
revolve around one idea, whatever the ostensible theme may
be which at the moment happens to occupy him. This central
thought is the unuttered thought of Being, the hidden source
within him of all that he has said, but which no particular
formulation fully and adequately expresses and which is not
exhausted by all his writings taken together. Heidegger's
'philosophy', therefore, though systematic in the extreme, is
not a system and, by reason of the very task it has set before
itself, cannot be one. It is rather a trail blazed, a path traversed,
a way taken by thought,[3] as he calls it, toward the one goal of
enshrining in language, or rather preparing to do so, the

unuttered thought of Being. It reaches out into the unexpressed future but it does so through a close and devoted
attention to the way this unuttered thought of Being has been
at work in the history of the European philosophical tradition.
The unexpressed and unthought spring of Heidegger's own
thinking is the hidden wellspring of the European philosophical tradition itself and of the course of its unfoldment in
history. One may therefore rightly say, with Otto Pöggeler,
that in Heidegger's thinking "European thought reaches out
beyond its own self and surpasses itself. With unparalleled
energy he leads European thought forward, neither going
back to any of its past forms nor rejecting it out of hand."[4]
Rooted in this tradition and speaking out of it, Heidegger yet
subjects it to deep questioning and in so doing prepares the
way for a new perspective on that tradition and a fresh appropriation of it.[5]

Heidegger's thinking, even more than Hegel's, is profoundly historical in character but, unlike the latter's, its way
is one of questioning rather than of construction. The way
followed by his thought is the way of an inquirer, of one who
is tireless in his questionings, not that of "a dubious prophet
seeking dim and distant goals."[6] In asking or questioning lies
the piety of thought, Heidegger says; in the eyes of faith such
asking is folly, but it is in this 'folly' that the essence of
philosophy is to be found. However, as Heidegger was to
realize, this questioning is itself rooted in a prior 'listening',
which is therefore the primary and proper gesture of thought.[7]
On this voyage of inquiry there are not only no ready-made
answers; the questions themselves have to be creatively formulated afresh. In the light shed by the question itself, the
thinker forges a path towards its answer, travels a little distance, looks back from there to the original question and
reformulates it from the new vantage point. He proceeds thus
from one station of thought to another, giving voice to the
unuttered thought, saying what has not been said before and
yet leaving behind him an inexhaustible 'unsaid' as a task for
posterity. The unity of Heidegger's thought is the unity of a
way taken by thought, not a unity of positions or of doctrine; it
is the unity of a quest and not that of a method followed or of
discoveries made on the way. "To follow one star, only this.

To think is to concentrate on one thought, motionless like a star fixed in the heavens above the world," as he puts it in a little collection of aphorisms.[8] A "wanderer in the neighborhood of Being," Heidegger moves, in his thought, sometimes along what appears to be a well laid-out path, sometimes into forest paths that lead nowhere, but always seeking the adequate word in which Being may find utterance, even when it involves the most radical departure from our accustomed ways of thinking and speaking.

Heidegger's main work, *Being and Time*, is a milestone on this 'way' of inquiry, embodying, in his words, the result of a few steps taken towards the goal of a fresh formulation of the *question* of Being. The book, published in 1927 as *Being and Time*, Part I, still remains a torso and in the preface to its eighth edition (1957) even the promise of a second part is finally withdrawn as being unfeasible unless the whole of the first part is completely recast. This does not, however, mean in any way a rejection and disowning of this early work; on the contrary, as Heidegger remarks there, "the way taken by this book is even today a necessary one, if the question of Being is to move us in our depths." The work has proved epoch-making in contemporary Continental thought and its title, *Being and Time*, has become, as Eugen Fink remarks,[9] the watchword of this century. Because of the sheer originality of its approach, the novelty of its terminological apparatus and its incompleteness, it became a center of heated controversy and its aims were widely and variously misunderstood until, after a quarter of a century, it established itself as a classic in modern German thought.[10] Soon after its appearance, a generation which had lost all its spiritual moorings and to which the central tradition of European philosophical and religious thought had lost its meaningfulness, saw in this work a document which showed the way for extracting the meaning of human existence by an analysis of this existence itself. Its main objective, the problem of Being, was overlooked as inessential and *Being and Time* was appropriated by the Existentialists as one of their major texts. Others, with more academic pretentions, canvassed with equal vigor the view that Heidegger was primarily a thinker of Being, an ontologist. But the ontologists who claimed him as one of their own never cared to inquire whether the 'Being' of which Heidegger was in pursuit was what they understood by this term. Judging his aims in the light of their schooling in the European metaphysical tradition, they completely missed seeing that it was precisely this age-old meaning of Being that he was putting into question. Still others, realizing that Heidegger's thought, going beyond metaphysics, could not itself be interpreted in the sense of traditional ontology, held that his main theme was not a petrified and empty concept of Being but 'world', a new concept of the world to replace the old and outmoded Christian, metaphysical conception as it culminated in the European Nihilism depicted by Nietzsche. Heidegger, for them, was the mythologist and herald of this new world of the future. Finally, the Phenomenologists who were unwilling to go all the way with the Master, hailed this work as striking out a new and more fruitful direction in Phenomenology and gave it the label of 'Hermeneutic Phenomenology'. But, as Pöggeler has well pointed out, what Heidegger actually *thinks* cannot be grasped through any of these catchwords. To label him as an existentialist, the propounder of a heroic nihilism, as a myth-maker, as a metaphysician in the traditional sense or a phenomenologist, or as a pseudo-theologian or a mystic, is to overlook him as a thinker and to miss completely the originality and the profoundly revolutionary character of his thinking.[11]

The Development of Heidegger's Thought

With the publication of *Being and Time* Heidegger achieved a breakthrough into the dimension proper to his own independent thinking and into an explicit awareness of his own intellectual mission as a thinker. But for a right understanding of this work it is necessary not only to keep in view the path taken later by his thought but also to have some idea of the path that led up to it. As he says in "A Dialogue on Language," our past (*Herkunft*) always remains our future (*Zukunft*) and that *from* where we have come is always what comes *toward* us.[12] Hence, a brief account of Heidegger's development before the publication of his main work may appropriately be given here. Born in 1889, Heidegger underwent a Catholic theological education in a Jesuit seminary at Constance. His preoccupation with the problem of the relation between the word of the holy scripture and theological-speculative thought led him to pay close attention to Hermeneutics, a philological discipline developed in the service of biblical exegesis, which was to play, in a widened sense, an important role in the methodology of *Being and Time*. In his closing years at the gymnasium, "in 1907 to be more precise, I came across the problem of Being in the shape of a dissertation by Franz Brentano, the teacher of Husserl, entitled *Of the Multiple Meanings of Being According to Aristotle*, written in 1862."[13] This book was not only the "first guide in my study of Greek philosophy during the gymnasium period" but, in combination with his deep theological studies, it initiated that movement of thought which was to become soon a lifelong passion and bear rich fruits, illustrating Hölderlin's words in the Hymn to the Rhine," . . . for, how you begin is what you will always remain." It was this theological background of his studies—Brentano was a Catholic Aristotelian—that gave the dimension of depth to his philosophical questionings. As he himself says, referring to his theological antecedents, "Had it not been for these theological origins, I would never have come upon the way of thinking."[14] Later, Heidegger was to come into intimate contact with Rudolph Bultmann and the new Protestant theology also at Marburg, during the period when *Being and Time* was under preparation.[15]

The recent publication of a lecture he gave in 1927 on the relation between phenomenology and theology shows how deeply he was concerned about the whole enterprise of theology from the very beginning. This lecture has been published, along with a "Letter" (1964), on the problem of non-objectifying thinking in theology, under the title *Phänomenologie und Theologie*, exhibiting the lifelong persistence of this concern. Quite appropriately, the whole work is dedicated to Bultmann in remembrance of the years 1923 through 1928 at Marburg.

The influence of S. Kierkegaard, the Danish philosopher whose works had recently become accessible in German translation, as providing the existenziell basis for Heidegger's existenzial analytic, is quite patent and acknowledged by him in

Being and Time.[16] Such key terms of the analytic as existenz, anxiety, situation, resoluteness and choice, death, authenticity, repetition, possibility, the anonymous 'one' and the 'moment' have obviously been suggested by Kierkegaard. But, as Heidegger insists, the Dane's contribution to thought does not go beyond the sphere of the existenziell and it has no further relevance to Heidegger's basic problem. In taking over these concepts, therefore, Heidegger modifies them radically for his own purposes.[17] Another experience of the young Heidegger, all-important for his development and destined to play an important creative role in his later work, was the impact of art and poetry upon him, in particular, the poetry of Hölderlin and Trakl. The publication, in 1910, of Hellingrath's edition of Hölderlin's translations from Pindar and, in 1914, of Hölderlin's later hymns, Heidegger says, "had on us students at that time the effect of an earthquake."[18] It appears as if at this time Heidegger was assimilating, with equal avidity and energy, the European cultural heritage in the fields of religion and theology, of art and poetry and of philosophical thought from the Greeks to the present day. In the European religious and literary tradition profound insights into the truth of life and reality find expression which the central metaphysical stream of thought has been unable, strangely enough, to incorporate into itself. Perhaps, as Heidegger was to discover later, the very origin and nature of metaphysics has prevented this, forcing it to move only along a track laid out for it in its beginnings and rejecting as unworthy of thought everything that did not fit in with its conceptualizing, representational ways. Only when thinking goes back into the foundations of metaphysics, to a level deeper than that of metaphysics and theology alike, can it imbibe into itself the truly creative work of religion and poetry, transmuting it and assimilating it in such fashion as to remain loyal, at the same time, to its own path of inquiring and questioning.

It is significant that even while preparing his doctoral thesis, Heidegger was absorbed in extensive logical studies and published a detailed critical survey of recent work in this field ("Neuere Forschungen über Logik"), showing his familiarity with the whole range of logical studies, including even the mathematical logic of Russell and Whitehead.[19] His later rejection of formal-logical argumentation in philosophy and his attempts to probe into the metaphysical foundations of the very concept of logic are obviously not based on total ignorance of what logic is about. By this time Heidegger had come to attach "far-reaching significance to Husserl's circumspect and most felicitously formulated investigations" (that is, *Logische Untersuchungen*) which are credited with breaking the spirit of psychologism in logic. In 1912 he also published an article, "The Problem of Reality in Modern Philosophy," giving an indication of his concern with the problem of Being for the first time, though the approach here is still that of traditional epistemology. The most important personal influence on him during this period, however, was that of the great Neo-Kantian value philosopher Heinrich Rickert, who preceded Edmund Husserl at the university of Freiburg.[20] Heidegger's doctoral thesis, written in 1914 under the supervision of the Catholic philosopher A. Schneider, was entitled "The Theory of Judgment according to Psychologism" ("Die Lehre vom Urteil im Psychologismis") and sought to establish the need for purifying logical theory of all psychological considerations as being completely irrelevant to it.[21] In *Being and Time* and throughout his later work Heidegger resolutely shuts the door upon the psychological and the subjective as only clouding the inquiry, irrespective of whether the inquiry is understood as phenomenology, ontology, or 'essential thinking'.

Heidegger's *Habilitation* thesis, dedicated to Rickert, was published in 1916 and was entitled "Die Kategorien- und Bedeutungslehre des Duns Scotus" ("Duns Scotus' Doctrine of Categories and Meanings"). The main problem which concerns him here is the interrelation between logic, language, and metaphysics, and how the first two lead ultimately into the problem of Being and to the many ways in which Being is expressed. There are foreshadowed thus in this work the twin problems of language and of Being which were to preoccupy him constantly later on, for as Heidegger explains in retrospect,[22] "the *theory of categories* is the usual name for the discussion of the Being of essents[23] and the *theory of meanings* means the grammatica speculativa, the metaphysical reflexion on language in its relation to Being." What seems to have attracted him to this thinker of the Middle Ages is again the dimension of depth in medieval logic, metaphysics, and mysticism, though he also sees clearly the limitations of medieval philosophy, its lack of methodological awareness and the absence of an independent questioning spirit. "The Middle Ages lack what constitutes the characteristic feature of the modern spirit: the liberation of the subject from his ties with his environment, the firm establishment in his own life."[24] This sense of the limits of the medieval consciousness, with all its richness and depth, perhaps accounts for Heidegger's growing interest in Husserl's phenomenology—already evident throughout in this early work—as a possible way out of the limitations, not only of the medieval intellectual approach but also of the dominating epistemological, Neo-Kantian trend in German philosophy during this period. The Duns Scotus book foreshadows, as Herbert Spiegelberg has remarked, Heidegger's preoccupation with the problems that were soon to be central in his own thought, the problems of Being and of Historicity.[25] The need of a 'translogical metaphysics' as the real optics of philosophy, going beyond the logical problems of categories and meanings and the hope of an early, more detailed study about Being, Value, and Negation is here announced by Heidegger. So also is the need of a historical philosophy of the living spirit, as it underlies the whole logico-epistemological sphere, including within it the problems of categories and meanings, a need which becomes acute in view of the pointlessness of mysticism (as mere irrationalistic *Erleben* or experience) and the powerlessness of philosophy as a mere rationalistic structure.

Heidegger's concern with the problem of time is directly testified by the title of the *Habilitation* lecture he delivered at Freiburg University in 1915 (published, 1916): "The Concept of Time in Historiography" ("Der Zeitbegriff in der Geschichtswissenschaft"). The concept of time in history is here "contrasted sharply with that of natural science in a way which shows Heidegger's familiarity with the science of Einstein and Planck."[26] Even at this stage the urgent need for a conception of time deeper than that of chronology is explicitly voiced by Heidegger. Thus the basic themes of Being, Time, and History, as they were to occupy him in *Being and Time* have already appeared on Heidegger's field of vision as of central importance. Nevertheless, he has not yet found his own language; though seeking a "philosophy of the living spirit," he is still shackled in the idiom of traditional metaphysics and expresses himself in terms of eternal values and timeless meanings—ways of speaking later to be attacked so vehemently by himself.

The realization must have soon followed that in order to carry through his project of a "breakthrough into the true reality and the real truth"—as he puts it in the book on Duns Scotus—it was necessary that the metaphysical tradition should not just be taken for granted and accepted uncritically. It has to be examined thoroughly as to its ultimate presuppositions and assimilated afresh by going back to its very origins in Aristotle, Plato and indeed right back to the earliest Greek thinkers before Socrates. The dimension of historicity essential for such an inquiry was opened up to Heidegger through his intense preoccupation, at this time, with the work of Wilhelm Dilthey and his friend Count Paul Yorck of Wartenburg, thinkers who were themselves on the trail that led beyond metaphysics to that level of depth, ever present in the realms of poetry and religion, which has always accompanied metaphysics as its "anti-metaphysical shadow" throughout the European spiritual tradition. But, as Pöggeler has pointed out,[27] even before his contact with the work of Dilthey, Heidegger had been prepared for its philosophical appropriation by his encounter with the dimension of the historical through an intensive study of primitive Christianity and the religious thought of St. Augustine. His lectures on the phenomenology of religion while he was a *Privatdozent* at Freiburg dealt with early Christianity as evidence of the factual experience in life of the dimension of history and it is from his way of understanding the religious consciousness of early Christianity that, as Pöggeler puts it, Heidegger attains the guiding point of view for his own conception of 'facticity' and factual existenz. Taking religion as a matter of factually realized life-experience (*Erlebnis*), Heidegger believes, at this stage, that it should be kept free of all metaphysical conceptualization, very much as Augustine, Luther, Pascal, and Kierkegaard have attempted in different ways to argue. In his unpublished lectures, "Augustine and Neo-Platonism," Heidegger followed Luther in taking up an extreme anti-metaphysical position and attempted to show how in the philosophy of Augustine an original and basic religious experience is perverted by being conceptualized in terms of uncritically accepted metaphysical ideas. According to Heidegger, it is the merit of Augustine that he thinks on the basis of factual life-experience but he goes wrong when, instead of letting this experience come to a natural conceptual blossoming, he tries to impose upon it concepts which have their origin in alien soil. By interpreting the original Christian experience, in other words, in terms of Neo-Platonic metaphysics, Augustine falsifies that experience. To penetrate into its pristine truth once again requires, therefore, first a 'destruction' of the Augustinian conceptualization by means of an analytical interpretation of it. The profound impact upon Heidegger of this realization—how unexamined metaphysical concepts distort and falsify basic life-experience—cannot be overestimated. Seeking to reflect on the reality or Being of Time and of God on the basis of lived experience, Augustine lapses into the representational thinking of metaphysics as it has unfolded itself since Plato, and hence conceives time in Aristotelian terms and Being as 'constancy of presence' in the Greek manner. This conception of Being is the basic presupposition on which the entire tradition of metaphysical thinking in the West rests, a presupposition of which metaphysics itself is aware indeed but not *as* a presupposition. Never subjected to the scrutiny of thought, it has remained up till now the dogmatically accepted foundation of this whole tradition—the Unthought (*das Ungedachte*) of Western philosophy. To understand the character of this foundation, the problem of Being, what it means to be, must be explicitly faced as a *problem* and its consideration taken up at the point where Plato, Aristotle, and the early Greek thinkers left it unexamined and unexplained in all its fateful implications. This is the problem which Heidegger sets himself to explore now, having attained by 1923, if not earlier, a clear awareness of the path he was henceforth to follow.[28]

Before we come to this, however, it will be appropriate to make a brief mention at this point of the role which two schools of thought contemporaneous with Heidegger's development, the philosophy of life and phenomenology, have played in his thinking. Both Dilthey's *Lebensphilosophie* and Husserl's *Phänomenologie* were attempts to extract a meaning out of life and consciousness and build this up conceptually by investigating them from within, immanently, without any presuppositions and without taking any help from the discoveries and constructions of science and metaphysics respectively. Heidegger combines both of these approaches in his analytic of *Dasein* (man), putting them within the framework of the transcendental method of Kant. Reacting, like many other thinkers of his age, against both the absolute spirit of Hegelian rationalism and the claim of natural science to provide a comprehensive conceptual framework for all knowledge, Dilthey sought to base himself on life as the ultimate bedrock from which all philosophy must proceed. Instead of interpreting life in terms of the ready-made abstractions of epistemology or by applying to it concepts derived from the natural sciences, we must start from life as the first and ever present reality. As Dilthey puts it, "Life is the basic fact and it must be the starting point of philosophy. That is what we know from within, something behind which one cannot go. Life cannot be brought before the bar of a Reason sitting in judgment."[29] Life manifests itself in complexes of lived experience (*Erlebnis*), teleological unities of meaning which are objectivized in the cultural productions of man. In an individual, these lived experiences are connected together into the structural unity of his life history. But since the individual's life, as constituted by these unities of meaning, is itself embedded in the wider historical process in which it is only an element, it can only be in terms of the latter that this personal life-experience can be finally understood. "For, man does not understand his own self by means of any kind of rumination upon himself . . . only through an understanding of the historical reality generated by him does he obtain a consciousness of his capacities, for good or for ill."[30]

To know what life means is therefore to understand the essentially historical objectivizations of life as they are studied by the "human sciences" (*Geisteswissenschaften*). Toward the establishment of the epistemological autonomy of these sciences, of history in particular (as against the prevailing epistemology which was solely oriented to the natural sciences), Dilthey in large measure directed his efforts. According to him, the unities of meaning embodied in life-experiences are the ultimate constituents of knowledge in the historical, human sciences, and to get at them what we require is understanding (*Verstehen*) from within rather than causal explanation as practiced in the natural sciences. "Only his history tells man what he is," Dilthey says;[31] human nature is human history and the book of life, to be read, needs, not causal explanation but *Verstehen*, understanding of the way life itself has explicated itself in history. To designate the method by which the book of life may be read and comprehended, Dilthey adopted the term 'hermeneutics', borrowing it from the great religious philosopher, Friedrich Schleiermacher. Traditionally, hermeneutics was conceived as a discipline concerned with the understanding and interpretation of literary texts, in particular the holy scripture, entirely from within and in terms of what is contained within them. This concept was widened by Schleiermacher to include all expression of the human individuality. Every written document or spoken word could be understood, by interpreting its parts in terms of the whole and the whole in terms of the parts, as the expression of the psychology of the writer or speaker, and the aim of the hermeneutic art in the wider sense was to reproduce, through a study of the expression, this inner psychology.[32] Dilthey extended this concept of hermeneutics to the whole of historical reality and in all its manifestations. The historical process, thus interpreted from within and not in terms of thought-constructions imported and imposed from without, reveals itself as made up of meaningful structural unities, ultimately definable in terms of the lived experience (*Erlebnis*) of individuals, but itself a supra-individual meaningful expression of life. Art, religion, and philosophy are direct manifestations of life, part of the objective spirit; it is in their historical unfoldment, not in the speculative knowledge of the Hegelian concept, that spirit progressively attains to self-awareness. Life, in other words, becomes progressively aware of itself, by means of concepts immanently developed, as it unfolds itself in the objectivizations of history. Hermeneutics as it is understood by Dilthey is thus not concerned with the ultimate truth of these historical manifestations of man's self-understanding. It brings to light the finitude of man's knowledge—and this is its great value—but in giving equal validity to the different ways in which man has understood life in different ages, it remains stuck up in a relativism of world-views (*Weltanschauungen*), without any criterion of truth by which they may be judged.[33]

Heidegger rejected the psychological concept of *Erlebnis*, along with all that was subjectivistic in Dilthey's way of thinking and he had no use for the Neo-Kantian epistemological orientation of Dilthey, who intended his main work to be a critique of the historical reason, and the traces of the concept of method in natural science still present in him. But his vision of the historicity of things, his conception of understanding and of hermeneutics as immanent self-interpretation of life were absorbed by Heidegger in his own thinking, not without undergoing profound modification in the process. Historicity and understanding are central operative concepts in *Being and Time* and are also thematically discussed there in considerable detail. In his later writings they continue to play an important role, though in a radically modified form. The concept of hermeneutics is itself further widened by Heidegger, so that it ceases to be merely a theory of the method of interpretation and becomes identical with the basic activity through which man understands and interprets his experience. After *Being and Time*, where the application of this concept is limited to the interpretation of the ontological structure of man, the term *hermeneutics* is dropped by Heidegger, in conformity with the change in his attitude toward the whole conception of method as such. Nevertheless, the hermeneutic approach, in a transmuted, deepened, and still further widened form, is also evident throughout in all his later writings. As the account given later of the remarkable discussion of the 'hermeneutic circle' or the circle of understanding in *Being and Time* will show,[34] this work truly carries forward the work of Dilthey, not merely in regard to the problem of historicity but also in elucidating and developing the notions of understanding and interpretation.[35]

With its intensely questioning spirit and the radicalism of its approach, Edmund Husserl's phenomenology has played a vital role in the development of Heidegger's thought. His keen interest in this discipline even before his personal contact with Husserl in 1916; his intimate association with the latter for more than a decade, during which period Heidegger not only lectured on phenomenological topics but also edited Husserl's *Lectures on the Phenomenology of the Inner Consciousness of Time*; the publication of *Being and Time* in Husserl's *Yearbook of Philosophy and Phenomenological Research* and its dedication, in book form, to the Master—all these are facts which give clear evidence that, for some years at least, phenomenology loomed large in the thoughts of Heidegger.[36] What is more important, in *Being and Time* itself, toward the commencement and again at the end, philosophy is defined as "universal phenomenological ontology" and an illuminating analysis of the meaning of 'phenomenon' is given, along with a discussion of the 'provisional', preliminary concept of phenomenology—the final elucidation of the idea of phenomenology being postponed for later consideration. In *Being and Time*, Heidegger explicitly acknowledges his indebtedness to Husserl: "The following investigations have become possible only because of the ground laid by E. Husserl, with whose *Logical Investigations* phenomenology came into its own."[37] Heidegger adds in a footnote, "If the following investigation takes a few steps forward in the disclosure of the 'things themselves', it is to E. Husserl that the author's thanks are due; he gave to the author during his period of apprenticeship at Freiburg his forceful personal guidance and freest possible access to unpublished studies, thus familiarizing him with the most diverse areas of phenomenological research." What is the extent and scope of Heidegger's indebtedness to phenomenology and to what extent has he appropriated its basic insights into his own work?

Husserl's aim in building up this new discipline was to provide philosophy with a truly secure foundation and establish it as a strict science (*strenge Wissenschaft*) by means of a more radically conceived Cartesian procedure. Suspending all epistemological assumptions and metaphysical presuppositions, he sought to have a glimpse of the "things themselves" (*Sachen selbst*) as they are revealed in pure, primordial experience, uncontaminated by theories and ready-made concepts. To this end, all linguistic expressions and complexes of meaning are traced back to what is ultimately given in conscious-ness and 'constituted' by its own acts, to the exclusion of everything that cannot be described in terms of these acts and is imported from 'without' (that is, the findings of science, ready-made metaphysical concepts). In this phenomenologi-cal reduction, as it was termed, consciousness is studied in respect of its intentionality, that is, of the different ways in which it is directed towards its immanent objects in acts by which these objects are constituted. There is a strict correlation between the modes of consciousness and modes of being (that is, types of immanent objects) as they are connected together in intentional acts. To be, for Husserl, is thus to be a correlate of an act of consciousness, of the pure *ego cogito*; it is to be an object. Unlike psychology, which describes concrete experi-ence in its particularity and is an empirical science, the 'phenomena' of phenomenology, the 'things themselves', are universal essences and it is the purpose of the 'eidetic reduc-tion' to bring these to light by an act of direct intuition (*Anschauung*, looking at). To arrive, through a consideration of the particular and the concrete, at the direct intellectual 'seeing' of the essential structures given in consciousness, the phenomenon in its nonempirical purity, is the primary, not the ultimate, aim in phenomenological inquiry. In the earlier *Logical Investigations* phase of phenomenology it was this primary task that was in the forefront. Later, the problems of a 'transcendental' reduction of all objects of con-sciousness—with all belief in their external reality suspended or 'bracketed'—to its constitutive acts dominate the inquiry.

Husserl's dream was to establish philosophy as a strict science, not indeed in respect of the naturalism and objec-tivism characteristic of the modern natural scientific approach, which he strongly deprecated, but in the sense of bringing to bear upon philosophy a rigor, a clarity as to basic principles and a methodological self-consciousness which would pro-vide it with a new, unshakable foundation, free from all unexamined presuppositions. Such a foundation, Husserl thought, he had found in the subjectivity of the pure ego and pure consciousness, the "wonder of all wonders," on which a rationally grounded system of philosophical knowledge, completely autonomous, could be built. For Heidegger, this quest of a certified, rationally grounded system is a philosophical chimera, the outcome of that subjectivistic, anthropocentric attitude which has come to dominate philosophy since the modern age was ushered in by Descartes and which is itself the mark of an epoch in the history of Being, an epoch characterized by the oblivion, and the all but complete 'withdrawal', of Being. In taking the pure ego or consciousness as the ultimate *fundamentum absolutum inconcussum* and as an allegedly presuppositionless beginning, Husserl fails to be critical and radical enough, for he does not inquire into the mode of Being of consciousness (*Bewusstsein* = *being* conscious), as Heidegger pointed out in his comments on Husserl's drafts for the *Encyclopaedia Britannica* article on Phenomenology.[38] Husserl does not inquire into the subjectivity of the subject; though he has often described the task of phenomenology as the achievement of critical self-awareness and as an overcoming of the naïveté of the natural attitude, his own work does not carry this process through to its end. Heidegger's thought brings to the surface the unexamined presuppositions in Husserlian phenomenology, as Ludwig Landgrebe and Eugen Fink, with their intimate knowledge of both Husserl and Heidegger, have shown.[39] In that sense it may be regarded as carrying the phenomenological start made by Husserl to its logical conclusion. Further, when Husserl takes the 'acts' of consciousness as the acts of a timeless, universal and absolute ego, he falls into the idealistic error of thinking that it can 'constitute' the world solely out of itself, without any anchorage in something factually given, something that it presupposes and cannot spin out of itself. For Heidegger, on the contrary, the factual, existing man is the basic fact and the source of all projects of the understanding. The 'facticity' of man consists in this that the possible ways in which he can understand himself and the world presuppose, and are limited by, the actual historical situation in which man at any time happens to be and the particular tradition he happens to inherit. This is the meaning of the 'hermeneutics of facticity' which Heidegger substitutes, in *Being and Time*, for Husserl's transcendental reduction[40] and the reason why he prefers to employ the method of 'interpretation' rather than that of reflection in his inquiries. The place of the absolute ego of Husserl is taken by the factual, thrown Dasein regarded as the clearing (*Lichtung*) of the disclosure of Being—not the absolute subject but Being is the ultimate ground (looked at from the point of view of man, at least) of all 'constitution'.[41]

Heidegger would agree with much of Husserl's requirements "not to hunt deductively after constructions unrelated to the matter in question, but to derive all knowledge from its ultimate sources, from principles seen authentically and understood as insights; not to be diverted by any prejudices, by any verbal contradictions or indeed by anything in the world, even under the name of 'exact science', but to grant its right to whatever is clearly seen, which thus constitutes the 'original', or what precedes all theories, or what sets the ultimate norm."[42] But the demand for a reduction to pure subjectivity he cannot concede, because such a demand is itself conditioned and determined by the metaphysics of modern subjectivism as it has developed in ignorance of its own roots; its own 'facticity', the givenness of the historical situation out of which it has arisen, remains opaque to it. The historical roots of the concept of subjectivity and the foundations of the metaphysical tradition within which it has arisen remain invisible to Husserl (except, to some extent, in his last phase, when he attempted another new beginning with his *Crisis of the European Sciences*, a work of self-criticism, not perhaps wholly uninfluenced by Heidegger, though still opposed to him). Heidegger does not believe, as Husserl does, in the possibility of a radical start in philosophy, a beginning with a clean slate, by going straight to the 'facts themselves'. Philosophical inquiry for him is essentially historical; wherever one starts, a traditional concept is always presupposed though one may not be aware of it and hence the 'things themselves' never offer a pure, eternal essence. What is purely intuited in the Husserlian *Wesensschau* is always historically determined and therefore penetrating to the essential and original phenomenon always needs going back to the historical beginnings. For this reason philosophy cannot be a science in the sense of an attested, certain, and universally and eternally valid body of objective truths. The compelling validity and objectivity of intuited essences is an illusion, for, as Heidegger shows in *Being and Time*, knowing is a mode of man's own being-in-the-world and a form of the project of understanding, a project (*Entwurf*) which is itself a *thrown (geworfen)* project in the sense that it is determined by tradition and the past. Not pure 'intuition' (deriving from the primacy of 'seeing' in the Greek conception of Being as objective presence) nor the Husserlian intentionality, but care (*Sorge*) as the being of man is what brings about the disclosure of essents.[43] The whole doctrine of intentionality shows itself as untenable, being based on a preconceived notion of a pure cognitive awareness standing over against a world of objective entities. To penetrate into this historical dimension of the presuppositions of thought, to inquire how and why European philosophy is compelled, in the terminal phase of its metaphysical tradition, to formulate its problems within the Cartesian framework and to show how the tenability of this framework itself rests on an unawareness of its own origins, is just the task which Heidegger sets before himself in his thinking.

Heidegger takes from Husserl a method for bringing to light the structures hidden in experience, the 'phenomena' as he himself conceives them, a way of seeing what *is*, without losing sight of all that is presupposed in such 'seeing' and without claiming that such seeing can ever disclose eternal and ultimate 'Truths'. As he makes amply clear in *Being and Time*, phenomenology is for him only a method and even as such it finds application only in the analysis of human existence. For Husserl's conception of philosophy as a strict science, for the transcendental reduction and for the host of 'constitution' problems in phenomenology, Heidegger has no use. After *Being and Time*, even this methodological apparatus is discarded in consequence of a clearer awareness of his own task and of the impossibility of realizing it without giving up the language and concepts of traditional metaphysics and theory of knowledge.

Though in *Being and Time* Heidegger defines philosophy as "universal phenomenological ontology, taking the hermeneutics of Dasein (that is, human existence) as its point of departure," he never identified himself with phenomenology as a school nor accepted any of the 'programmatic' conceptions of this discipline as put forward by Husserl from time to time. The kind of phenomenological description and analysis conducted in this work has been characterized, at one time by Heidegger himself, as 'hermeneutic phenomenology', but this, as he makes clear, does not mean that he was aiming at initiating a new trend within phenomenology.[44] "I attempted, on the contrary, to arrive rather at a deeper conception of the essence of phenomenology in order to give it in this way, on purpose, its place within the framework of European philosophy," Heidegger says, adding that with the help of hermeneutics, understood in a deeper sense than the traditional, "I was enabled to characterize the phenomenological thought that opened for me the way to *Being and Time*."[45] If, following Heidegger's elucidation in this work, we understand phenomenology as a way of bringing into view the being of whatever is, a way of thinking that can lead us to see, and hear, into the nature of things, a way of bringing this to light, then Heidegger is and has always been a phenomenologist. He does not infer, deduce or generalize, offers no 'logical' arguments, 'proves' nothing.[46] Yet, through his analyses and explorations in depth, through the reconnoitering movement of his thought, going in circles around the matter in question, he brings into view coherent structures lying buried under the surface of our everyday experience as well as the presuppositions, the light of Being, implicit in the way we interpret and understand this experience. In *Being and Time*, this is done with some methodological fanfare (though surprisingly little of the technical apparatus devised by Husserl is in evidence). Later, even this is given up as inessential and the manner becomes less academic, simpler and more evocative. But always, from first to last, the one thing that engages Heidegger is the task of bringing into view, through meditative thinking and the employment of language adequate to embody it, what and how things *are* and in what their Being consists. For, as he says, "The one thing that counts, now as before, is to bring to light the Being of the things that are (essents), not, it is true, in the manner of metaphysics but so that Being itself comes out, shining forth, into view."[47]

In a recent autobiographical essay "Mein Weg in die Phänomenologie" (in *Zur Sache des Denkens*, 1969), Heidegger has given a vivid picture of his fascination with Husserl's *Logical Investigations*, from the very first semester of his years as a student of theology at Freiburg, of his unceasing struggles to understand it, and of the manner in which his efforts to grasp the idea of phenomenology were inseparably linked with his interest in Aristotle. As his familiarity with phenomenological seeing deepened, enabling him to interpret the writings of Aristotle more fruitfully, he realized more and more that in essence phenomenology is not so much a new direction in philosophy as rather an ever-enduring possibility of thought. As Heidegger remarks here,

> What happens as the self-exhibiting of phenomena for the phenomenology of acts of consciousness, was conceived even more originally by Aristotle and in all Greek thought and existence as *aletheia*, as the unhiddenness of that which is present, its disclosure, its showing itself. What phenomenological investigations have discovered anew as being the basic stance of thought, turns out to be the distinctive feature of Greek thinking, if not of all philosophy as such.

Once this is clearly realized, one cannot but ask, "From where, and how, is determined that which has to be seen as 'the thing itself' (*die Sache selbst*), according to the principle of phenomenology? Is it consciousness and its objectivity, or is it the Being of beings in its unhiddenness and concealment?" Understood in the sense of such an enduring possibility of thought to seek to respond to the call of what is to be thought, enduring because transforming itself from time to time, phenomenology "can disappear as a title in favor of the matter (*Sache*) of thought, of which the revealment remains a mystery."

Although Heidegger has been profoundly influenced, in certain ways, by the work of Dilthey and Husserl, his own thinking cannot be understood merely as a continuation and radicalization of motives present in these philosophers. He takes these philosophers as contemporary points of departure for his own thinking, as opening for him a 'way'. But having once in this manner launched himself into the main stream of European thought, he goes further back and lines up, as it were, with Nietzsche—the last great thinker of the metaphysical tradition—and, taking up the thread from this herald of "a provisional transition" from this tradition, himself executes the actual transition to another mode of thinking. We can say, in fact, of Heidegger (as he does of Nietzsche) that "in his thinking all motives of Western thought, but all transformed, are skilfully gathered together" *and* transcended so that the entire thought of the West is appropriated in its real truth through the transition. His roots go back into the Greek origins of Western philosophy and there is hardly any major facet of European thought which has not acted as a stimulus to his own development. But to attempt to trace out in detail the variety and extent of the influences that have gone into the making either of his main work or of his later writings would be premature at this stage. Some indication of Heidegger's indebtedness to medieval thought has been given above. The influence of the early Greek thinkers, Heraclitus and Parmenides, is patent in his later writings. The extent to which Plato has stimulated his thinking is evidenced not only by his essay, "Plato's Theory of Truth," by the discussion of the Good (*agathon*) in *Vom Wesen des Grundes* and in *Nietzsche*, but also by the ever-recurring discussion of the Platonic Idea in his later writings. The very formulation of Heidegger's central problem, the meaning of Being, derives from Plato and from Aristotle. A close reading of Heidegger's writings reveals, in fact, the figure of Aristotle as a pervasive presence; the Stagirite, as a thinker who has laid down the basic pattern of the entire tradition of Western metaphysical thought, is, as it were, the invisible partner in the dialog of Heidegger's philosophy. Kant's influence is writ large on *Being and Time* and evidenced further not only by his books on Kant but also by the way he keeps coming back to Kant in his writings. Hegel's importance as a challenge to the thinking of Heidegger is not confined to the problem dealt with in the last chapters of *Being and Time*. How much of Heidegger's philosophizing is a continuing debate with Hegel is made evident by a reference to Heidegger's essays, "Hegel's Concept of Experience," "Identity and Difference," and "Hegel and the Greeks." Heidegger's concern with Schelling, and the importance he has always attached to his work *Über das Wesen der menschlichen Freiheit*, are evidenced by the fact that from 1927 onwards he repeatedly discussed this work at elaborate length in his seminars and lecture courses.[48] Among philosophers who are nearer to our own times, it is above all Nietzsche, with his criticism of the Platonic-Christian tradition and the nihilistic culmination of this tradition in his own thought, that has provided the springboard for Heidegger's quest and which in some measure explains the intensity and the passion with which he seeks to bring into view the thread that runs through the history of Western metaphysics, connecting its beginning (Plato) with its end or consummation in Nietzsche. The powerful impact of the latter on Heidegger's thought and the way in which Nietzsche's philosophy is the key that has enabled Heidegger to lay hold of the inner meaning and significance of the Western metaphysical tradition have become apparent in its full scope only with the publication of his two-volume *Nietzsche* (1961).[49]

The central problem of *Being and Time* is to raise afresh the question of Being, in a sense in which it has never been raised, having been bypassed throughout the whole history of European metaphysical thought. Metaphysics deals with the essent qua essent (*on he on*) and offers a *logos* (statement) about the *on* (the essent; what is). Concerned with the is-ness (*Seiendheit, ousia*) of the essent, it seeks all the time to represent essents as such in their totality. And it does this in a twofold manner, representing, in the first place, the totality of essents as such in respect of their most general features and at the same time, secondly, this totality in the sense of the highest and therefore the most divine essent. Because it seeks to represent the essent qua essent, metaphysics has intrinsically had this twofold onto-theological character ever since Aristotle developed the conception of a "First Philosophy" (*prote philosophia*) in his *Metaphysics*. As Heidegger says,

> Regarded as dealing with the truth of essents as such, metaphysics has a twofold form. But the ground of this twofoldness, let alone its origin, remains unknown to metaphysics, not as a matter of chance or due to negligence but necessarily. . . . As metaphysics, it is by its very nature shut out from a knowledge of Being, for it represents the essent (*on*) as it has become manifest in the light of Being, without being in a position to attend to what has concealed itself in this very *on* as it became

unconcealed. . . . On what has thus concealed itself in the *on* metaphysics remains grounded, in order to be able to devote itself to the representation of the essent qua essent (*on he on*).[50]

The truth of Being, in other words, is the light in and through which beings become manifest, enabling metaphysics to represent them; but in illuminating the essent, Being itself, directing our gaze on the essent, keeps itself hidden.[51] Focusing on the truth of beings but itself grounded on the truth of Being, metaphysics is unable to perceive this latter fact. Further, metaphysics, in inquiring into the nature of what is, is always oriented to essents within the world, to what can be encountered within it and seeks to represent the essent as such and as a whole in terms of that. Its representational thinking takes the Being of essents as 'presentation', that is, it understands it in terms of the present, as sheer presence (*Anwesenheit, ousia*). Metaphysics has always understood Being, therefore, in the light of Time, in terms of a particular mode of it, namely, the present. But it has simply assumed this way of taking Being and taken it for granted, without inquiring into it; nor has it sought to examine its basic presupposition about time itself as an eternal succession of 'nows'. In traditional metaphysics both Being and Time have remained unquestioned presuppositions. Hence, Being as presence is the Unthought (*das Ungedachte*) of metaphysics, the foundation on which metaphysics itself stands and therefore beyond its reach. We must ask, therefore, with Heidegger, "How then does it stand with Being and Time? Must not the one as well as the other, Being as well as Time, must not both, in the way they are related together, become problematical, first of all problematical and eventually questionable? Does this not then show that in the innermost core of what is regarded as the central conception of European metaphysics, something essential in the nature of Being has never been thought about? The question of *Being and Time* is a signpost to this Unthought of all metaphysics. On this Unthought rests metaphysics and therefore what remained Unthought in metaphysics is due to no shortcoming of metaphysics itself."[52]

In *Being and Time*, Heidegger seeks to render problematic what has thus been taken for granted, to think this 'Unthought' of the Western philosophical tradition, to get back into the ground of metaphysics and find out if it is possible to have a more radical and deeper comprehension of Being. The meaning of Being has so long been glimpsed through the veil of a particular modality of time, the present, itself understood in terms of a particular interpretation of Being. Is it possible to break out of this circle or, as Heidegger would prefer to put it, break *into* this circle and comprehend more originally, and formulate in words, what Being itself means?

To answer this question it is necessary not only to examine what time is but to reopen the problem of Being in such fashion as to show its intrinsic connection with time. But since Being is always the Being of beings and, further, since the meaning of Being is manifested only within the comprehension of one essent, man, it is necessary that the inquiry should be anchored to man in his aspect of being open to Being, as the locus where Being and its meaning are disclosed, that is, to *Dasein* (which is Heidegger's technical term for man in his aspect of being open to Being). The traditional way of understanding Being in terms of objective presence, in terms of entities given in the world, must be shown to be one-sided and superficial by demonstrating that man's mode of being is radically different and that it provides us with a deeper conception of Being from which the former can itself be derived. The being of Dasein, of man in his overtness, must be brought into view as also the temporal horizon within which man's being discloses itself. And the way man comprehends Being, the conditions of the possibility of such comprehension, must be laid bare and it must be demonstrated how the comprehension of Being always moves within the dimension of time. The being of Dasein himself, it may turn out, lies in temporality and an 'analytic' of Dasein may yield a way of understanding time that is deeper, more primordial than the common view based on an ontology of objectively given essents. On the basis of time as thus understood in its real, primordial sense, the true meaning of Being itself may then be determined. The analysis of Dasein is thus the path to be gone over in order to arrive at the meaning of Being.

This is the path taken by *Being and Time*. The work, originally published as the first part of a larger study, begins with a general exposition of the question about the sense of Being. This includes a discussion of the necessity, the structure and the preeminence of this question and a statement of the double task—the analysis of Dasein and the 'destruction' (or analytical scrutiny) of the history of ontology—involved in working out the question of Being. An account of the phenomenological method pursued in the inquiry is also given here. The first part of the inquiry proper opens with a preparatory analysis of Dasein. This includes a statement of the general character of the task and an account of the basic constitution of Dasein as being-in-the-world; a detailed analysis of the concept of 'world', including an examination of the Cartesian conception of the world, and of man's togetherness, selfhood and anonymity; an analysis of the different ways in which man is 'in' the world and open to it, that is, an analysis of man's existenzial constitution, including accounts of attunement or mood, understanding, interpretation, judgment, and language; the everyday modes of man's openness to world and his abandonment to it. The preparatory analysis culminates in an exposition of the being of Dasein in terms of care or concern (*Sorge*), to which is added a discussion of the problem of 'reality' and of truth. Then follows an account of Dasein in its temporal aspect, constituting the second Division of *Being and Time*. The problem of the wholeness of Dasein and its relation to death is first dealt with. Heidegger follows this up with an examination of how man can be authentically himself, along with an analysis of conscience; an elucidation of Dasein's ability to be authentically whole in terms of 'resoluteness'; an account of how temporality constitutes the ontological meaning of care. This is followed by an interpretation of the different elements in Dasein's constitution in terms of temporality. Next, an examination of the historicity of man's mode of existence serves to bring out the rootedness of history itself in the primoridal temporality of Dasein. Finally, in the last chapter of *Being and Time*, an attempt is made to bring out the nature of original, primordial time by an account of the vulgar conception of time and a demonstration of its derivative character.[53]

As Heidegger remarks in the introduction to "Was ist Metaphysik?," "The thinking attempted in *Being and Time* sets out on the way to prepare an overcoming of metaphysics," not in the sense of abolishing metaphysics but in the sense of going back to the ground of metaphysics, inaccessible to metaphysics as such, by recalling the truth of Being itself. Because, Heidegger goes on to say, this treatise, in dealing with the question of existenz ultimately aims at penetrating to the truth of Being—the hidden ground of all metaphysics—it is entitled, not 'Existenz and Time' or 'Consciousness and Time' but 'Being and Time'. The 'and' in this title is not to be understood as meaning a juxtaposition of two separate, distinct things. "In *Being and Time*, Being is not something other than time, for 'time' here is the first name (*Vorname*) given to the truth of Being." Time and Being are brought together, Heidegger explains further, because the Greeks, in whose thinking Being first disclosed itself, thought of Being as the presence of what is present, as *einai*, which means "to be present (*Anwesen*)." "The essence of this 'being present' is hidden deep in the earliest names of Being (*einai, ousia*). . . . In 'being present' there prevails, unconceived and hidden, the present duration, that is, time. Being as such is accordingly unconcealed (revealed) through time. Thus time points toward the unconcealedness, that is, the truth of Being." Time in this sense is, of course, not what metaphysics thinks about it; it is to be taken as "the first name, yet to be pondered upon, of the truth of Being, yet to be realized."[54] This hidden presence of time is betrayed not only in the earliest metaphysical name for Being but also in the last, the Eternal Recurrence of the Same. The history of Being, in the epoch of metaphysics, shows a pervasive sway of time which has never been subjected to thinking.

Similarly, in *Kant und das Problem der Metaphysik*, Heidegger explains that the interpretation of Dasein in terms of temporality is motivated solely by the problem of Being as such.[55] The fundamental ontological approach to the foundation of metaphysics in *Being and Time* must be understood in the sense of a repetition, of the renewal of a problem long buried in obscurity and yet ever alive. The opening quotation from Plato's *Sophist* is not meant, Heidegger says, for decoration but as a reminder that in classical metaphysics the battle of the giants over the Being of what is, has already broken out. In this battle, Being is in some sense understood though not explicitly inquired after. The metaphysics of antiquity takes the *ontos on* as *aei on*, that is, as unvarying and permanent, and as *ousia* in the sense of 'presence', a sort of immediate 'having' of the essent. Here the understanding of Being is based on a project in terms of time, as constancy of presence. Thus, from the very beginning the battle over Being is waged within the horizon of time. Why is Being understood, in this spontaneous and self-evident manner, in terms of Time? The conception of time as developed by Aristotle, itself based on a comprehension of Being as presence, and generally taken for granted after him, gives no answer to this question. Hence the necessity, Heidegger says, for raising the old problem again and for an examination of the finitude of Dasein's constitution in such a manner that temporality as its basic transcendental structure comes clearly into view.

As will be evident from a look at the full plan of the projected work given in chapter 2, the published part of *Being and Time* breaks off at a crucial point. Even the analytic of Dasein is not complete, for, as Heidegger repeatedly points out in the course of the text, although the being of Dasein has been found to lie in care and the latter itself shown to be rooted in temporality, the entire analysis leading to this result must be considered as being provisional until a final reinterpretation in terms of a clarified concept of Being is forthcoming. The temporal horizon, within which the new concept of Being was to be determined, has indeed been laid bare. But the next step, the movement back from Time to Being, is not taken and the third Division of *Being and Time*, Part I, entitled "Time and Being" was held back for reasons which Heidegger left shrouded in obscurity for a long time. This has given rise to much misunderstanding as to the intentions and aims of Heidegger and also to the curious result that *Being and Time*, as published, became, even against the wishes of the author, a major contribution to the literature of Existentialism and the main *problem* of the work, in the service of which the analysis of human existence was conducted, was largely overlooked. The second part of the work was, of course, never published. *Being and Time* is thus a fragment; for reasons to be explained later, its continuation was rendered impracticable and yet, since its publication, Heidegger has ceaselessly traveled on the 'way' of his thought, "on his way, a wanderer in the neighborhood of Being."[56] On this 'way' he has left behind him the approach and language of *Being and Time* and, nevertheless, as will be shown in what follows, his thinking does eventually arrive at its destination, that is, at a reawakening of the question of Being and a tentative formulation of a new conception of Being. The project of a 'phenomenological destruction of the history of ontology', the regressive scrutiny of the history of the concept of Being, as planned for the second part of *Being and Time*, has actually been carried out by Heidegger on an extensive scale in writings published since then.

The major part of *Being and Time*, as actually published, comprises the analytic of Dasein, that is, an analysis and interpretation of human nature. The powerful impact that the work had on the related fields of psychology and psychiatry, of philosophical anthropology, especially in its prevalent existentialistic garb, and of theology as newly influenced by the discovery of Kierkegaard, is therefore, quite understandable. But the way an original philosophical work—which, as Nietzsche said, is in its essence always 'untimely'—is received by contemporaries and its immediate impact (or absence of impact, as in the case of Hume's 'stillborn' *Treatise*) has hardly any relation to its real aims and to the basic inspiration behind it. It is a mark of Heidegger's greatness as a thinker that he did not allow himself to be swayed from his central aim by the wide-ranging and epochal contemporary reception of his work. As he has himself remarked,

> If there is such a thing as a catastrophe in the creative activity of great thinkers, it lies not in the fact that they suffer shipwreck and make no advance but rather in that they 'move on', that is, let themselves be influenced by the immediate appeal, which is always the result of a misunderstanding, of their thoughts. What is fatal is always the mere advancing 'further', instead of staying behind at the source where one started.[57]

Unconcerned with the contemporary impact of his work and with the general failure in appreciating its real import, Heidegger has remained loyal to his own initial insight and left, in a real sense, his followers always far behind him. From the point of view of his Being-centered thought, a particular interpretation of man and hence the mode of his existence in history, is only the essential consequence of the nature of truth and of Being itself prevailing at a particular time. For this reason, the nature of man can never be adequately determined in its roots through the metaphysical interpretation of man as a rational animal. "This was the insight," Heidegger explains,

> responsible for the treatise *Being and Time*. The essence of man is determined in terms of the essence (*wesen*, used as a verb, 'be-ing') of the truth of Being by Being itself. In the treatise *Being and Time* an attempt is made to determine the nature of man solely in terms of his relationship to Being, on the basis of the question about the truth of Being and not any more about the truth of essents. This essence of man is described there in a precisely defined sense as *Da-sein*. In spite of the fact that at the same time, as required by the context, a more fundamental concept of truth was developed, the work has not succeeded in the least in awakening even an elementary comprehension of the issue raised here. This failure to understand is due, on the one hand, to the ineradicable and deep-seated habituation to the modern way of thinking. Man is conceived as a subject and all reflection on man is taken as anthropology. On the other hand, the reason for this failure lies in the nature of the attempt itself. Because it has grown out historically and is not something artificial, it derives from what has been hitherto existing. But at the same time it seeks to struggle out of it and therefore, necessarily and continuously, still harks back into the grooves of the past, even calling on it for help, but for the purpose of saying something quite different. Above all, the path thus struck out breaks off at a crucial point. The reason for this breakdown lies in the fact that this path, and the attempt, without intending it, is faced with the threat of itself becoming, once again, a perpetuation of subjectivity and of becoming itself a hindrance to the decisive steps still to be taken by way of completing the account satisfactorily. Any turn towards 'objectivism' and 'realism' is still subjectivism: the question about Being as such stands beyond the reach of the subject–object relation.[58]

Still thinking within the 'fundamental-ontological' framework of *Being and Time*, Heidegger published in 1929 a study of Kant entitled *Kant und das Problem der Metaphysik*, in part fulfillment of the task originally assigned to the projected second part of *Being and Time*. Heidegger seeks, in this book, to interpret the *Critique of Pure Reason* from his own fundamental-ontological point of view and to bring to light, by way of a valuable analysis of Kant's theory of the transcendental power of imagination, the role that Time plays in the Kantian ontology as its implicit and unthought foundation. In the same year was published the widely known inaugural lecture "Was ist Metaphysik?" ("What is Metaphysics?"), to which later (1943) a postscript and then (1949) an introduction were added. This lecture is in the main a discussion of the concept of Nothingness and aims at showing how the Nothing, as the other to all that is, constitutes Dasein's transcendence as experienced in the first instance when we seek to ascend from beings (essents) to Being. Another article published the same year, in a volume presented to Husserl, is entitled "Vom Wesen des Grundes" ("The Essence of the Ground"), where again the direction of the inquiry is from Dasein to its self-transcendence in the project of a ground of everything that is. The main topics discussed are the concepts of ground, freedom, transcendence, and world. In all these writings Heidegger's main purpose is to press forward with the task of forging a path that might lead from the internal ontological constitution of Dasein to Being regarded as sheer transcendence, very much in the manner of *Being and Time*.

After these writings of the first phase (1927-1929), there is a long period of silence until the appearance of the "Brief über den 'Humanismus'" ("Letter on Humanism") in 1947, announcing a shift in perspective, a "change in thinking," and revealing the full scope and the far-reaching character of this change. The few essays actually published during this period give only the barest indications of the change that was coming over Heidegger's thought and of the crisis which made him abandon the path, though not the ultimate objective, of *Being and Time*. The Rectoral Address he delivered in 1933 at Freiburg University[59] reflects Heidegger's involvement, for a brief period, in politics and containing as it does (in

Spiegelberg's words) his "supreme appeal to the will as the lever for shaping man's destiny in his universe," it can hardly be said to mark a change in the basic approach of *Being and Time*. In a sense, as Spiegelberg has remarked,[60] this speech "represents the high-water mark and possibly the turning point of Heidegger's trust in the capacity of human being to force Being to surrender its secret," a trust of which Nietzsche's will-to-power is the symbolic expression.[61] It was with the metaphysical implications of this doctrine that Heidegger's thought was to wrestle in the years to come, with far-reaching consequences to his own thinking about Being and to his whole perspective on the history of Western philosophy. This influence of Nietzsche on his thought was, however, to be apparent only much later, with the writings published since 1950 and, in all its scope, with the publication of his *Nietzsche* in 1961. The new trend in his thought was signaled by the appearance, in 1936, of an essay on the poet Hölderlin, followed by another in 1943, and their publication together in a book entitled *Erläuterungen zu Hölderlins Dichtung* (*Explanations of Hölderlin's Poems*) in 1944 and with two more essays added, in 1951. Heidegger recurs to Hölderlin again and again in his later writings, and published another independent essay on him in 1958-1960, and, finally, gave a lecture on him in 1968. All of these are collected in the latest edition of the *Erläuterungen*.[62] In addition to his preoccupation with Hölderlin, he has also written essays on other German poets such as Rilke, Mörike, Trakl, Hebel and George, as well as an important study, "Der Ursprung des Kunstwerkes" ("The Origin of the Work of Art," in *Holzwege*, 1950).[63] The relevance of Heidegger's interest in poetry and the poetic essence to his thought, and how this interest in integrally bound up with the changed conception of thinking as such, will emerge more clearly in the discussion below of his view on the relationship between thinking and composing (Denken und Dichten).

Also published during this period (1942), the essay "Platons Lehre von der Wahrheit" ("Plato's Doctrine of Truth"), like the book on Kant, pursues the 'phenomenological destruction' proposed originally to be dealt with in the second part of *Being and Time*. Its main purpose is to show how, in consequence of his conception of the Being of things as *idea*, the nature of Truth also undergoes a radical transformation at the hands of Plato, a change of which Plato himself has no awareness. Another essay, published in the following year, "Vom Wesen der Wahrheit" ("On the Nature of Truth"), in certain important respects goes beyond the brief discussion of truth in *Being and Time*. Both of these essays, however, were originally written in the period 1930-1931, though the second one, repeatedly revised before publication, gives some inkling of the necessity behind the change in thought that was taking place in Heidegger at this time. Many courses of lectures which he actually delivered during this period, such as *Einführung in die Metaphysik* (*Introduction to Metaphysics*, 1935) lectures on Nietzsche delivered between 1936 and 1940, on Schelling in 1936, and on Aristotle's *Physics* in 1940, were not published until much later; so also with some articles and essays, such as "The Origin of the Work of Art," "The Age of the World-picture," essays on metaphysics and the history of Being, "Hegel's Concept of Experience," "Nietzsche's saying—God is dead," "Aletheia," "Nihilism and the History of Being," "Serenity," "The Overcoming of Metaphysics," the essay on Anaximander, and "From the Experience of Thinking." During the years following the publication of *Being and Time*, Heidegger seems to have realized with increasing clarity how much of the start made in that work was dependent on the language and approach of traditional metaphysics and how the reversal from Time to Being and back to the reinterpretation of man and the world in terms of a 'clarified' and more basic sense of Being could not be effected without abandoning that language and that approach. By 1936, he seems to have fully realized that metaphysics, as concerned with the truth about essents, is itself grounded in the truth of Being ('truth' being understood in the basic sense of 'unhidden-ness') and is therefore powerless to explore and formulate the nature of this ground. In consequence, Heidegger was forced to move away from the original approach of *Being and Time*; instead of seeking to approach Being through the openness and transcendence inherent in man, he now tries to define man in terms of Being. The language of traditional metaphysics having proved inadequate, and indeed a hindrance, to his basic objective of rethinking the truth of Being, Heidegger is now groping for a new language, a new way of speaking and thinking about Being, about man and about man's relationship to Being. Not until he has found this language and is in secure possession of the new perspective, does Heidegger announce the shift in his approach in the "Letter on Humanism." Because Heidegger published little during the period 1930–1946, the consequent ignorance of the path his thinking had traveled since *Being and Time* led to widespread misunderstanding about the nature of the transition from the earlier to the later position as depicted in the "Letter." But, as will be evident from the following account (see discussion of the 'reversal' in chapter 8 below), this later position is not so much a 'break' in thinking as a continuous development resulting from immanent self-criticism. From the very beginning, the inquiry in *Being and Time* was conceived as circular in character—from the preconceptual comprehension of Being to the analysis of Dasein and its being (that is, care, rooted in time) and from Dasein (time) back to a clarification and determination of the sense of Being. The 'change in thinking' in the second phase of Heidegger's thought, therefore, does not constitute an abandonment of the basic aims of the inquiry; what is abandoned is rather the language of traditional metaphysics, its unavoidably representational and conceptual thinking and its belief in the necessity of a rigid methodology (that is, the final abandonment of the conception of philosophy as a scientific discipline).[64]

The second part of *Being and Time* was to deal with a phenomenological 'destruction' of the history of philosophy, that is, with the task of taking to pieces the whole fabric of Western metaphysics as it has historically developed. The main purpose of this was to show how at each important stage of its evolution it covered up more and more thoroughly the original impulse behind it, the thought of Being as it had flashed into the vision of the early Greek thinkers. To extricate this 'Unthought' out of the intellectual accumulation of the centuries, to recall this original vision and become aware of its inadequacy was the only way to a reopening of the inquiry into this neglected problem and to take it up again for further building where it was left before Plato. This historical inquiry cannot, in fact, be separated from the systematic conceptual analysis of the problem of Being, as will be evident even from the historical discussions in the published part of *Being and Time*. Going back into the ground of metaphysics, Heidegger was to realize more clearly afterwards, is a going back in both the conceptual as well as the historical sense. This kind of regressive investigation of the history of philosophy is conducted by Heidegger both in the *Being and Time* phase (that is, in the studies on Kant and Plato already mentioned) as well as later. Sometimes the historical discussions are included within more comprehensive systematic inquiries, as in the case of *Introduction to Metaphysics*, with its interpretations of Heraclitus, Parmenides, and Aristotle, of *Was heisst Denken?* (*What is Called Thinking?*, 1954), in which the exposition is accompanied by constant reference to past thinkers, and of "Der Satz vom Grund" ("The Principle of Ground," 1957), containing an elaborate discussion of Leibniz. *Vorträge und Aufsätze* (*Lectures and Essays*, 1954) contains interpretations of the concepts of *Logos* and *Aletheia* in Heraclitus, of *Moira* in Parmenides, of Nietzsche's Zarathustra as well as discussions of Kant. *Identität und Differenz* (*Identity and Difference*, 1957) seeks to differentiate Hegel's approach from Heidegger's own and another essay on "Hegel and the Greeks" (1960) is devoted to an examination of Hegel's interpretation of Greek philosophers. "The Nature and Concept of *Physis* in Aristotle" (1960) discusses the Aristotelian concept of Nature and its metaphysical implications. Finally, *Nietzsche* (1961) gives not only a full-scale interpretation of Nietzsche's philosophy but also contains detailed studies of Plato, Descartes, and Kant. Heidegger published, in 1963, important studies on Kant, one an essay (entitled "Kants These über das Sein") and the other a full-sized book (entitled *Die Frage nach dem Ding*) dealing with Kant's doctrine of Transcendental Principles. *Zur Sache des Denkens* (1969) includes two essays which illuminate the historical dimension of his own thinking, and *Heraklit* (1970) contains the full report of a seminar on Heraclitus given jointly by Heidegger and Eugen Fink at Freiburg in the period 1966-1967. Finally, 1971 saw the appearance of Heidegger's 1936 lectures on Schelling's *The Nature of Human Freedom*, along with notes on Schelling written between 1941 and 1943.

For Heidegger, essential philosophical thinking is remembrance (*Andenken*) and hence the analysis of any concept necessarily involves an attempt to recall its genesis—analysis and interpretation are for him inextricably linked together. Moreover, the historical genesis, evolution and transformation of concepts is, according to Heidegger, itself rooted in what he calls the "History of Being," the self-revelation of Being in history. This history, as reflected in the creative thinkers of the West, begins with Anaximander, with whom an 'epoch' of Being is initiated in the West, blossoming forth in its full richness in the thought of Parmenides and Heraclitus. With Plato's interpretation of Being in terms of idea there begins the epoch of the oblivion of Being and the rise of the metaphysical tradition, which is henceforth to dominate European thought. In Aristotle there is again a flash of the original vision, even while 'metaphysics', turned away from Being and busy with the truth of beings, is taking definitive shape. With him, Greek thought comes to its great end. Descartes marks the beginning of the epoch of subjectivism and the complete 'withdrawal' of Being, the era of modern nihilism which unfolds itself steadily through the thought of Leibniz, Kant, and Hegel, culminating finally in the total nihilism of Nietzsche.

As already stated, the aim of Heidegger's historical and critical interpretations is to bring into view what has remained 'Unthought' in the thinking of the great philosophers of the past and to formulate it in words. This work of interpretation—it might well be termed regressive interpretation—is not primarily an affair of historical scholarship but is rather creative in a profound sense.[65] As an explicit repetition (*Wiederholung*) of obscure beginnings, it is at the same time a challenge to think anew and express in adequate language (that is, in language as far as possible free from the terminological fixity and rigid conceptual determination characteristic of later developments, themselves based on these beginnings) something that has never been thought and said but which is the mainspring and the necessary presupposition of the metaphysical thought of the West.[66] For this reason, some of Heidegger's most original formulations of basic philosophical concepts occur in writings which are ostensibly devoted to historical interpretation and criticism. In addition, and above all, he has sought to state in his recent writings his own way of thinking—non-representational and non-conceptual—about Being and its truth, and with that as the basis, to reinterpret in an original manner some of the fundamental concepts of European philosophy such as world, man, ground, identity, thought, language, truth, and historicity. The essays on "The Problem of Technology," "What is Thinking?," "Building Dwelling and Thinking," "The Thing" (all in *Lectures and Essays*) are profoundly and daringly original, difficult to render in another language, driving as they do their own original German to the very limit of its expressive and communicative power. And this is no less true of the essays, "The Principle of Identity" and "The Onto-theo-logical Structure of Metaphysics" (in *Identity and Difference*), the dialogue and essay in *Gelassenheit* (*Serenity*, 1959), the essays on language in *Unterwegs zur Sprache* (*On the Way to Language*, 1959). The verge of obscurity which Heidegger might seem to have reached here and in other previous works (for example, the essay on Anaximander in *Holzwege*), however, by no means implies that it has become either a stylistic mannerism with him or is used as a cloak for obscurantist and mystifying purposes, for even in such late essays as "Zur Seinsfrage" ("The Question of Being"), *Was ist das—die Philosophie?* (*What is Philosophy?*) and the "Dialogue on Language," Heidegger can still be as lucid and simple, as free from academic jargon as one might wish all philosophical writing to be. In these later writings Heidegger has deliberately renounced the conceptual, grasping, exact, 'logical', and calculative thinking characteristic of metaphysics, for such thinking, however adequate it may be to the metaphysical need of keeping a hold on the truth of the essent by representing and objectifying it, is according to Heidegger, deaf to the truth of Being. This renunciation is a sacrifice in the true sense; philosophy, having dreamt out the metaphysical dream and played out that game to its bitter nihilistic end, here bids final "farewell to the essent as such, on the way to preserving and cherishing the favor of Being," a sacrifice in which the might and majesty of metaphysical thinking are at last given up in favor of something much more modest and unpretentious and yet no less difficult and rigorous in its painstaking regard for the right word. This is what Heidegger refers to variously as 'esential' thinking (*das wesentliche Denken*), a thinking that recalls (*Andenken*) 'originative' thinking (*das anfängliche Denken*) or meditative thinking (*das besinnliche Denken*)—an echo of the grace of Being, man's answer to the soundless voice of Being, a still attentiveness to the truth of Being; a patient, responsive putting together in words, and thus bringing into being, of this truth, so that it might become effective in the lives and thinking of men. Such thinking is a slow, laborious process and lays no claim to finality, for it does nothing toward achieving results at one stroke; at best it is a thinking that prepares the ground (*das vorbereitende Denken*), so that one day Being itself may reveal itself in words. It is a thinking that is not *our* doing but is part of the history of Being (*das seinsgeschichtliche Denken*) and entirely under its governance and disposal, a thinking that hears and seeks to catch a glimpse of what is heard.[67]

Heidegger's wayfaring on the path of thinking, his own philosophical itinerary since his student days, has been marked by the presence of the most powerful tensions and by an unrest and movement which have yet borne him along this path with unparalleled singleness of purpose. His journey may be said to come to a close with the publication, in the eightieth year of his life, of *Zur Sache Denkens* (*On the Matter of Thought*). This little book includes his lecture "Zeit und Sein" ("Time and Being"), with which the movement of thought promised and required in *Being and Time* comes full circle. Also included here is a report on the seminar Heidegger gave, for the first time, on a work of his own, "Zeit und Sein," thus in a sense looking back with a questioning glance at his entire completed work. The other two essays in this volume are "Das Ende der Philosophie und die Aufgabe des Denkens" ("The End of Philosophy and the Task of Thinking") and "Mein Weg in die Phänomenologie" ("My Way into Phenomenology"). They describe what happened to philosophy itself, in a historical sense, along his way to the matter (*Sache*) of thinking, and they look forward to the possibilities and tasks the future still holds out and demands.

Hannah Arendt spoke on Heidegger's eightieth birthday

of "the storm that blows through the thinking of Heidegger." But, as she pointed out, this storm, "like the one which blows towards us from the work of Plato even after thousands of years, does not stem from this century. It comes from what is age-old, and what it leaves behind is something finished and perfected, which, like all that is consummated, passes into the realm of the age-old."[68]

Heidegger's Method

Not only in *Being and Time* and the essays of that phase but also in his later writings, Heidegger's thinking is marked by an acute sensitiveness and attention to points of method—later called the 'way'—to the kind of approach and attack demanded by the problem and by an extreme deliberateness and finesse in the use of language. Apart from the second chapter of the introduction in *Being and Time*, which deals systematically with his use of the phenomenological method, scattered reflections on methodology are to be found all over this work. The very first chapter of the introduction, dealing with the necessity, the structure and preeminence of the question of Being, is of central importance as an explicit statement of the considerations that are to determine and steer the whole course of the inquiry. The 'programmatic' discussion of the task of a 'destruction' of the history of ontology in the next chapter is of equal importance because it directs attention to the 'vertical' dimension of Heidegger's methodology which, though not entirely lacking in *Being and Time*, plays an increasingly dominating role in his later writings. In *Being and Time*, Heidegger proceeds from the phenomenal and the 'existenziell' to the phenomenological and the 'existenzial', from the facts of experience to the disclosure of the a priori conditions of the possibility of experience, from the 'ontic' to the 'ontological'. As a footnote in *Sein und Zeit* suggests, Heidegger conceives at this stage the task of philosophy to be one of scientific a priori investigation or research, and the actual method followed by him in *Being and Time* may, therefore, aptly be described as the Kantian transcendental method modified and widened under the influence of the more sophisticated discipline of phenomenology and liberalized by an assimilation into it of the 'hermeneutic' procedure of the human sciences (*Geisteswissenschaften*).

Not logical demonstration but understanding (*Verstehen*), the primary mode of being of man in which all knowing and thinking is rooted, is what Heidegger aims at. As he remarks, ontological investigation is one possible type of explication in which something disclosed in understanding is articulated, worked out and appropriated, that is, in which something is comprehended as *being* this or that.[69] All method, therefore, terminates for Heidegger, not in proof but in an exhibition or disclosure of the underlying phenomenon, in a 'seeing' or 'hearing' of the reality of anything. Hence, the whole treatment of understanding, interpretation, and language in *Being and Time* should also be read as a valuable supplement to the discussion of method in the introduction.[70] The account given here of the nature of possibility and of the projective nature of understanding, the analysis of 'sense', of the circularity of all understanding and of judgment, the discussion of speech and language—these are valuable not only as part of the analytic of existenz but throw a flood of light on Heidegger's own procedure and on the kind of analysis conducted by him. The same is true of the remarks on the 'hermeneutic situation',[71] on sense or meaning[72] and on the necessity, which is again and again emphasized, of 'reepeating' an earlier analysis on higher levels. Heidegger starts with a merely formally sketched but presupposed idea of existenz and in the light of that describes what is phenomenally evident (facts as experienced and observable). What is thus phenomenally described is then phenomenologically interpreted, that is, shown, by means of a phenomenological 'construction' or an existenzial 'projection', to be the expression or manifestation of an underlying ontological structure, the 'phenomenon' in the true sense. The primary phenomenon as thus disclosed is for Heidegger not something absolutely 'given' or an eternally and ultimately valid object of an intuitive vision, but a construct or project of the understanding, which is through and through 'finite' (*endlich*), as Heidegger has particularly emphasized in *Kant and the Problem of Metaphysics*. Its genuineness and validity must, therefore, be established by referring it back to the facts of experience; it must again be phenomenally verified and shown to be concretely exemplified in experience. This to and fro, circular movement in which the ontic, itself understood in the light of an ontological presupposition, leads to the ontological and back again to the ontic, has its parallel in similar other circular movements simultaneously occurring throughout *Being and Time*. For example, from a particular structure, phenomenologically analyzed in the light of an assumed totality, to the whole and back again to the part, until man's ontological structure is grasped in its wholeness; from the inauthentic, described in the light of a presupposed concept of authenticity, to the authentic and back again to the 'everyday' mode of existenz until a clear picture of the way the two modes are related emerges into view; from the preparatory existenzial analysis of man, carried out in the light of a possible temporal interpretation, to the demonstration of the temporal foundations of man's being and back again to a reinterpretation of the existenzial analysis on the temporal level; finally, the movement, which remains uncompleted in *Being and Time*, from the vague natural conception of Being to the analysis of man and his temporal foundations, to a clearer concept of Being as essentially temporal in a deeper sense and back again to a reinterpretation of the results of the existenzial analytic in the light of this clarified sense of Being. What Heidegger has called "the thinking of the reversal" has reference to this movement from 'Being and Time' to 'Time and Being'. This coming-to-pass (*Geschehen*) of the 'reversal' (*die Kehre*), Heidegger says, "is neither something invented by me, nor does it concern merely my thought" but is rather a necessity inherent in the very matter designated by the headings: 'Being and Time' and 'Time and Being'; "the reversal is in play within the matter itself."[73]

An important methodological digression not only offers a justification for this necessarily circular character of the whole inquiry but also brings into focus a characteristic of Heidegger's procedure which has been widely misunderstood.[74] Man is so constituted that, clinging obstinately to the superficial and the outward, he hides from himself, indeed actively resists an attempt to uncover, his ontological depths. Hence, from the point of view of common sense, an ontological interpretation of man, often reversing the truth of what is generally accepted, is bound to have the appearance of proceeding by means of constructions and projections which appear to be forced and which do violence to our ingrained habits of thought. As Heidegger says,

> The ontological constitution of every essent, and that of man in a preeminent sense, is accessible only in understanding insofar as it is of the nature of a project. Because understanding . . .is not merely a kind of knowing but is primarily a basic constitutive element of existenz, the explicit carrying through of its projective activity must necessarily be, especially in ontological understanding, of the nature of construction . . .though this does not mean that it should be arbitrary and fanciful.[75]

Man's finitude as manifested in his understanding of Being lies, Heidegger says, in his obliviousness, a feature which is neither accidental nor occasional but constant and inevitable. Therefore, "all fundamental ontological construction which aims at the disclosure of the inner possibility of the understanding of Being must, in its project, snatch away from oblivion the content of its projection." That this is true not merely about the ontological interpretation of man but of all interpretation whatsoever is exemplified by Heidegger's own interpretations of past philosophers and of the basic metaphysical concepts in the history of European philosophy. The tendency to veil and cover up his own reality does not characterize only man; ultimately, Being as such tends, while revealing itself, to conceal itself and hold itself back at the same time. The same is true of language, the "shrine of Being," which in speaking keeps back what is its very own, and of the great thinkers whose central thought, the nourishing, invisible source of all they have actually said, remains unuttered. That is why, according to Heidegger, all truth or disclosure of Being by its very nature calls for the exercise of a leap of thought and a sensitive, devoted ear, attuned to the true, silent voice of the mystery of Being.

In view of Heidegger's later approach to the history of European thought in terms of the "History of Being," attention may also be drawn to what he says about repetition (*Wiederholung*), tradition (*Überlieferung*), and destiny (*Geschick*) in connection with his discussion of historicity. In the analytic of Dasein (man) these topics may seem to be of peripheral import but in the later Being-centered phase, these concepts assume an ever-growing methodological importance. In fact, the distinguishing feature of the method or way followed by his later thinking has been described by Heidegger himself as a "thinking from the point of view of the destiny of Being" (*Seinsgeschichtliches Denken*), a point of view to which we can attain only through a leap of thought but which brings us to that hidden wellspring of tradition from which, through repetition, we can bring back untold treasures of thought which have failed to enter into this tradition. Brief mention may also be made here of a concept of basic importance which Heidegger has borrowed from Husserl and used in a strikingly original manner throughout the writings of his first phase. This is the concept of 'horizon'.[76] Any object or phenomenon is not only knowable as such but is what it is only within a setting, context or perspective which is itself, in the last resort, not of the character of an object or entity of any sort at all. It is only in the light of this horizon or perspective that it can show itself and be thought about and described. Hence, Heidegger always starts with analyses which prepare the context of meaningfulness and open up a perspective within which a particular phenomenon may then be located and rendered visible. How important a role this concept has played in his approach to the main problems of *Being and Time* is richly illustrated, not only by the statement of the aim of the inquiry at the very beginning,[77] but by the whole analysis of 'world', conceived by Heidegger as not itself an entity or essent but as sheer 'horizon', and, perhaps even more so, by the discussion of temporality. In his later writings, the place of 'horizon' is taken, as explained below, by 'region' (*Gegend*), place or location (*Ort*) and the approach becomes more explicitly 'topological'.[78]

"Any genuine method," Heidegger has said, "is based on adequately viewing in advance the basic constitution of the 'object' to be disclosed, or of the domain within which the object lies."[79] So long as the objective aimed at was an 'object' or essent, namely man, methodological sophistication was quite in place as leading securely to it. But in the second phase of his thought, Heidegger realized that no amount of methodological maneuvering could build a path leading from beings to Being itself. He also came to realize to a more radical extent the fundamental difference between philosophical thinking as the thinking of Being and 'metaphysical' and scientific thinking about essents. The latter is dominated by the concept of system, of representational system-building through concepts in the quest of certainty, of thinking as a kind of grasping (*Begreifen*) and taking secure possession of its object through conceptualization.[80] In a discussion of the concept of method and its role in modern science and philosophy, Heidegger shows how this concept has developed with the rise of modern philosophy in reaction against the medieval conception of truth (*doctrina*) and of the 'assurance' of salvation through faith.[81] Modern man, rejecting faith in salvation as eternal happiness beyond, conceives it as the free unfoldment of all his creative potentialities in this life.

> The problem therefore arises *how* a certainty about his own nature and about the world sought for by man himself (that is, pursued by means of his own efforts) for his this-worldly life, can be attained and justified. Whereas in the medieval world the way to salvation and the manner in which truth came to man (*doctrina*) were firmly settled matters, now it was the *search* for the new way that became decisive. The problem of 'method', that is, the problem of 'striking out a path' for himself, the problem of attaining and justifying a certainty established by man himself, comes into prominence. 'Method' is to be understood here not in the 'methodological' sense as a mode of investigation and research but in the metaphysical sense of a way of determining the essential character of truth, capable of being grounded by the powers of man himself. . . . The problem before philosophy, liberated from the shackles of revealed Church doctrine, is in what way man can attain, by himself and for himself, to an unshakable truth.

It is not surprising, Heidegger adds, that Descartes, who first raised this question and answered it with all explicitness and clarity, should have attached supreme importance to the problem of method, a fact evident from the very titles he gave to his principal writings. *Being and Time*, seeking to go beyond the 'metaphysical' preoccupation with what is to a reopening of the question of the sense of Being itself and aiming at overcoming the subjectivism in which modern philosophy is caught up, still remains embedded in the subjectivistic, man-centered, metaphysical tradition. Going beyond that in his later phase and viewing the development of the metaphysical thinking of the West as itself an epoch in the dispensation of Being (*Seinsgeschick*), Heidegger realized that the whole conception of method is itself a manifestation and an integral part of this subjectivism, that the leap by which alone thought can spring away from the sphere of essents to the dimension of Being must also leave behind the metaphysical concept of method, for in this dimension guidance comes not from man's methodological planning but only from pursuing the ways that open out to an ear that is sensitively and patiently attuned to the unthought and unuttered possibilities latent in the tradition of European philosophical thinking.

This explains why, despite the brilliant and masterly use to which Heidegger had put the Kantian transcendental method in his fundamental-ontological inquiries in *Being and Time*, he abandoned it, along with the title 'Ontology', in his later writings. For Kant, as Heidegger understands him, the Being of objects as experienced by a subject consists in their objectivity. The objectivity of objects is an a priori determination and condition of the possibility of all experience of objects. Hence the method by which we pass beyond objects to their objectivity, their Being, is called by Kant transcendental. But for Kant this transcendence is rooted in Reason, the faculty of ultimate principles which alone certify and warrant their objectivity to objects of experience. Moreover, the Kantian Reason is only a more stringently formulated version of the Cartesian *ego cogito* and a more elaborately articulated and refined form of that ultimate, all-determining Cartesian ground or condition, the subjectivity of the subject. The transcendental method, seeking to discover the conditions of the possibility of objects and their experience, aims actually at disclosing the ontological structure of essents (conceived by Kant in the narrow, specific sense of objects), that is, their

Being, and for this reason Heidegger seized upon it as ideally appropriate to his own task of penetrating into man's ontological constitution.[82] But since this transcendental procedure is itself possible in the light of a particular conception of Being and is applicable only to a thinking that, starting from essents, moves in the direction of Being and since it is inseparably bound up with the subjectivistic need for the grounding and justifying of everything that is, Heidegger abandoned it when he came to realize later that from beings to Being there is no straight passage but only a leap of thought from one dimension to another. The concept of transcendence, like that of horizon, has its origin in the attempt to represent objects, in view of their Being, and as such is 'metaphysical' in character and inappropriate to an attempt to think Being as such, to speak of it, not in terms of essents but as and in itself. As Heidegger has remarked, "Horizon and Transcendence are terms conceived from the point of view of objects and of our representation and are determined only in view of these. . . . In this manner, however (that is, by approaching the Being of anything through these concepts), that which the horizon allows to be what it is, is by no means known as it is in itself."[83]

Heidegger's later reminiscent, meditative thinking of Being has no ready-made paths laid out before it; yet for this 'preparatory thinking' (*vorbereitendes Denken*), as he calls it, there is still the 'way'. Not the modern subjectivistically conceived 'method' but the simple idea of a way is what, according to him, the Greek *methodos* originally connotes.[84] Here thinking and being 'on the way' are identical so that the way cleared and traversed is not left behind but is taken up into and is one with the movement of thought itself. And it is not a smooth and continuous path but involves passing from one level to another in a leap of thought in which there is neither security nor certainty of arriving at a predetermined goal but only a tentative, approximately adequate utterance of Being. The way to Being is indeed no path stretching between two distant places, for Being is what is closest to us; on this path, as Heidegger puts it, "We do not aim at advancing further. All that we want is just really to get to where we-already are."[85] Explaining in some detail his later attitude toward the question of method, Heidegger writes,

The way to knowledge is known in the sciences by the title of 'method' which, particularly in modern science, is no mere instrument in the service of science but has made the latter itself subservient to it. . . . Not only does the method determine the theme but the latter is incorporated into and subordinated to the method. . . . In contradistinction to the procedure of scientific representation, matters stand quite differently in the case of thinking. Here, there is neither method nor theme but only the region or zone (*Gegend*) which dispenses what is thought-worthy and so claims our thinking. Going over the paths of this region, thinking occupies itself with and dwells on the region. Here the way is part of the region, a relationship between the two which, from the point of view of scientific representation, is not only difficult but altogether impossible to see.[86]

For meditative thinking, it is the region itself which as such opens up all access to it, generating and clearing up the paths that lead up to it—the region and the way belong most intimately together. In speaking of this way, Heidegger has in mind something like the *Tao* of Lao-tse which, as he puts it, "perhaps hides within itself the mystery of all mysteries relating to a thinking utterance" (that is, to thinking as inseparable from poetic imagination).[87] Perhaps, Heidegger suggests, even the enigmatic power of the present-day supremacy of method, despite its achievements, itself derives from the fact that these methods are only the backwaters of a large hidden stream, of a way that opens and strikes out the path for everything, of a way that is not so much a static thing but the dynamic source of all way-ing, the coming about of all ways.

It should be obvious from the above that for Heidegger the whole conception of thinking itself, as well as of the nature of philosophy, has changed since he wrote *Being and Time*, where he still speaks throughout of conceptualizing, conceptual formulation, 'bringing to a concept' the sense of Being. Philosophy is there still conceived within the traditional metaphysical framework, as aiming ultimately at providing a new analysis of "what belongs to the concept of a science *of Being as such*, and to its possibilities and its variations."[88] Later, he was to declare that "the thinking of the future is no longer philosophy,"[89] for philosophy aims at conceptualizing, which is a kind of grasping and laying hold of, and at general concepts related together by the purely formal rules of logic, which is only a kind of reckoning or calculating. However useful such grasping and reckoning may be for the sake of achieving certainty in the sphere of essents, they are utterly inadequate when we move in the dimension of Being. Conceptual, representational thinking is itself one way in which the nature of thought, like that of essents and their Being, has been determined through the historical dispensation of Being in the form of European metaphysics. By means of such thinking it is impossible, hence, to think about and enter into the ground and basis, the light of Being, on which metaphysical thinking concerned with the essent as such and in its totality stands.[90] This incapacity of conceptual thought, however, does not mean that the only alternative left is a lapse into irrationalism, the mere shadow of rationalism, or into mysticism, "the mere antitype or counter-part of metaphysics."[91] Another kind of thinking, yet in germ and being developed by Heidegger, still remains, for, as he says, "with the end of philosophy, thinking itself does not also come to an end but passes over to another beginning."[92] Such non-conceptual thinking was, in fact, the prevailing character of Greek philosophizing, as Heidegger shows in a penetrating and highly original interpretation and discussion of the terms *noein* and *legein* in Parmenides' sentence (Fragment VI), *chre to legein te noein t'eon emmenai* ("it is necessary to say and to think that the essent is").[93] The conception of thought as embodied in these twin, root terms of the European philosophical tradition, does not yet imply the modern, subjectivistic, and 'metaphysical' sense of grasping and clutching. Thinking is here not yet understood "as a grasping, neither as a reaching out to grab what lies in front nor an assault upon it. . . . Thinking is here not conceiving (*Be-greifen*, literally, having in one's grip, comprehending). At the pinnacle of the initial unfoldment of its nature, thinking knows no concept. . . . This great thinking of the Greek thinkers in its entirety, including that of Aristotle, thinks without concepts," which by no means implies that its thinking is inexact or primitive.[94]

As already remarked, Heidegger's thinking, from the very beginning, is 'on the way' to an overcoming of metaphysics; by the time of writing "On the Essence of Truth," he had seen that this implied giving up the language of essence (*Wesen*), that is, thinking in terms of essences. (In his later writings, *Wesen* is used in a verbal sense, to denote the process character of Being.) In the terminology of the Platonic, metaphysical tradition, what something is, the 'what' of anything (*to ti estin*) constitutes the nature or essence (the *essentia*) of that thing. The essence as thus understood is, Heidegger says, defined and expressed through what was later called the concept, a representation by means of which we grasp and put at our disposal what something is.[95] As against this, the nonconceptual creative word, instead of enabling us to grasp and lay hold of what is already there before us, instead of serving merely as a means of describing what is present, calls into being. It is evocative of Being; it invokes that presence (*Anwesenheit*), that is, Being, within which (in the light of which) anything can appear before us as an essent.[96] Even in *Being and Time*, Heidegger was alive to the creative character of true, non-representational thinking, which alone is appropriate to Being, as is evident from his whole conception of the projective nature of thought. Later, impressed more and more profoundly with the creative, all-enveloping power of language as the shrine of Being and the dwelling place of man, Heidegger tends to reverse the ordinary conception of the relationship between language and thought—instead of taking language as the medium and instrument for the expression of thought, he now describes thinking itself in terms of language and regards the latter as the fountainhead of all creativity. The place of projective understanding (*verstehen*) is gradually taken by *dichten*, composing in words.[97] Poetic composing (*dichten* in the narrow sense) and thinking, Heidegger says, are the two preeminent modes of saying, rooted in the productive, inventive or creative essence of language. As a mode of creative 'saying', therefore, thinking is itself poetic or inventive in character. "All philosophical thinking, and indeed just the most rigorous and prosaic, is in itself poetic and yet it is never poetry," Heidegger says.[98] All thinking, Reason itself, is of the nature of *poiesis* in the sense of inventing, contriving, making up.[99]

In his book on Hölderlin's poetry, Heidegger says,

> Poetic composition is the act of instituting (*Stiftung*) by
> the word and in the word. What is it that is thus estab-
> lished or instituted? . . .Being, which must be opened
> out, so that the essent may appear. . . .The poet names
> the gods and names all things in that which they are. This
> naming does not consist merely in something already
> known being supplied with a name; it is rather that when
> the poet speaks the essential word, the essent is by this
> naming nominated as what it is. Thus it becomes known
> *as* essent. Poetry is the instituting of Being by means of
> the word. . . .Because the Being and essence of things
> can never be calculated and derived from what is present,
> they must be freely created, laid down and given. Such a
> free act of giving is instituting.[100]

In this wide sense of poetry, of a projective saying as Heidegger also calls it in "The Origin of the Work of Art," thinking
too is projective, poetic or creative.[101] Indeed, he goes even so
far as to say,

> But thinking is composing, in a deeper sense than the
> composition of poetry and song. The thinking of Being
> is the original mode of composing (*Dichten*) . . . .
> Thinking is the utterance of the dictate of the truth of
> Being. Thinking is the primordial *dictare*. Thinking is the
> primal creative composition (*Urdichtung*), which is prior
> to all poesy. . . . All composing, in the wider as well as
> in the narrower sense of the poetic, is at bottom a
> thinking.[102]

And yet this creativity, far from being a property of man, is
itself rooted in his receptivity to the voice of Being, in his
ability to hear the silent chime of the essence of language and in
his dwelling in what Heidegger later calls the *Ereignis*. Going
back, "on his way to language," to the creative word,
Heidegger discovers in it the deeper, root-sense of thinking, at
a level deeper than the traditional contrast between poetry and
thought.[103] Thinking in this sense is identical with creative
utterance, though this creativity comes, Heidegger insists, not
from the assertive will of man but from his surrender to the
voice of Being. Man is capable of speaking the creative word,

of thinking, but only insofar as he first listens, and listening, seeks to echo back in words, as a gesture of thankful corresponding, the voice that addresses and claims him as its very own.[104] As in the case of the sense of Being, so also with the nature of thinking and of language in its indivisible unity with the former,[105] Heidegger is seeking to arrive at a primordial, ultimate sense on which all their historical manifestations may be seen to be so many variations; specific, concrete forms in which they appear historically, determining and dominating the outlook and nature of man in a particular 'epoch' of Being—a sense, itself not a timeless 'universal' and hence capable only of preconceptual description, implied and presupposed in all these forms but inaccessible in terms of any of them.

Heinrich Ott has called Heidegger "the thinker of thinking (*Denker des Denkens*)." As such a thinker he is well aware of the dangers that thinking has to face. "Three dangers threaten thinking. The good and therefore salutary danger is the neighborhood of the singing poet. The malignant and therefore sharpest danger is thinking itself. It must think against its own self, which it can do only seldom. The bad and therefore wild and tangled danger is philosophizing."[106]

Thinking always concerns some matter (*Sache*) which invites and challenges the thinker. But this matter is given to him only by way of what has already been thought, as the unthought in it which calls to be thought. Thinking of the *Sache* is, therefore, at the same time concerned with the interpretation of texts in which the matter has come into view and yet remains hidden as its own unspoken truth. Thinking in its very nature is thus hermeneutics, both interpretation and utterance. An account of Heidegger's 'method' should examine his procedure as an interpreter of texts, not merely his interpretations as we have them in his published class lectures, addresses, essays, and treatises. The recently published report (*Protokoll*) of a seminar on his own "Zeit und Sein" (in *Zur Sache des Denkens*) and the full text of his joint seminar with Eugen Fink on Heraclitus, for the first time give us a glimpse into the secret of this master of the "great, unknown art of selfless thinking," as H.-G. Gadamer has described Heidegger.

Heidegger's Language

As John Wild has remarked about *Being and Time*, "The importance of Heidegger's book lies not in any systematic reformulations of, or in any subtle distinctions between, received meanings. It lies rather in the development of new uses in a living language for the expression of new insights and new meanings."[107] From what has been said above regarding Heidegger's philosophical aims and approach, it is only to be expected that their novelty and the power with which he creates and breaks through into a dimension so long virtually foreign to academic philosophy should be faithfully reflected in his language. The linguistic peculiarities of Heidegger constitute a formidable obstacle not only to his foreign readers, but have evoked bewildered and sometimes deprecatory academic comment from German scholars themselves. But these linguistic difficulties are not generated simply by the gnarled Teutonic genius of the German language in general or by some idiosyncratic mannerism, innate love of obscurantism, or craving for notoriety on the part of the author. The manner in which Heidegger handles language, both in the writings of the earlier phase and in those of the later is inseparably bound up with what he has to say and must therefore be taken as an intrinsic part of the method or 'way' of his thinking. He has repeatedly emphasized that in the realm of thought—which is itself part of the wider realm of 'saying'—the first and basic law is the suitability and 'seemliness' (*Schicklichkeit*) of utterance, the precision and conscientiousness (*Sorgfalt*) of speaking, the economy of words.[108] And in his own writings Heidegger demonstrates the utmost care and deliberation in the use of language appropriate to each of the different stages on his 'way' of thought. A brief consideration of this aspect of his thought will therefore be in place here.

Being and Time has not only established itself as an epoch-making classic of contemporary philosophy by virtue of the profound originality of its thought content, but has also caused quite a stir—as his later writings are doing now—because of its linguistic daring and departures from ordinary German usage. But the boldness and seeming unconventionality with which language is employed by Heidegger, here and in later writings, is intimately determined by the necessities inherent in his thought, as he has himself explained in a passage in *Being and Time* which may here be quoted:

> With regard to the lack of pliancy and the uncouthness of expression in the analyses that follow, we may add the remark that it is one thing to narrate accounts of *essents*, but another to comprehend the essent in its Being. For the latter task we not only lack mostly the words but, above all, the 'grammar'. If it is permissible to refer to earlier, on their level incomparable, researches on the analysis of Being, one may compare the ontological sections of Plato's *Parmenides* of the fourth chapter of the Seventh Book of the *Metaphysics* of Aristotle with a narrative piece from Thucydides; one will then see the unprecedented and outrageous character of the formulations which were imposed upon the Greeks by their philosophers . And where (as in our case) the powers are comparatively feebler and where, moreover, the domain of Being to be disclosed is ontologically far more difficult than that which confronted the Greeks, the circumstantiality of concept formation and the heaviness and roughness of expression are bound to increase still further.[109]

Again, seeking to disclose the original, authentic phenomenon of temporality behind the veil of the vulgar conception of time, Heidegger says, "In finding words by which to define terminologically the primary and authentic phenomena corresponding to the secondary, inauthentic ones, one has to struggle with the same difficulty which grips all ontological terminology. Violence to language is in this field of investigation not arbitrariness but a necessity grounded in the subject-matter itself."[110]

Heidegger's subject matter is not the realm of essents, to which ordinary language is adequate, but the being of essents and, in *Being and Time*, it is the being of man, to be articulated conceptually in all the rich complexity of its structure. But contrary to the hitherto prevailing view, he conceives man not in terms of substantial categories but in terms of *Existenz*. The 'substance' of man, he asserts, is his existenz, the mode or modes in which man is or exists and his task is to find the language which can adequately deal with the ontological and existenzial sphere of the possible, as against the ontic and the existenziell sphere of actual experience and which can lay bare the phenomenological dimension as against the phenomenal. The traditional categories of metaphysics, according to Heidegger, have been developed in the interest of the Greek quest of the nature of essents as such rather than for purposes of discourse about Being as such; and this categorial language has been determined by a specific sense in which Greeks conceived Being, that is, as objective presence. In *Being and Time*, Heidegger seeks, accordingly, to forge concepts of an entirely new order, namely, existenzial concepts (or existenzialia) which will not only do justice to man's specific and distinctive mode of being but which will function as basic ontological concepts in the sense that the categorial concepts about objective entities can be shown to be secondary and derivable from them. In this sense Heidegger may be regarded as concerned, not so much with constructing a system of 'thought' as with building up a basic language from which the languages of the systems, metaphysical or theological, may be shown to be ultimately derivable. In the earlier phase Heidegger conceives this as the language of 'fundamental ontology'; in the later, going back into the ground of metaphysics, he seeks to develop a way of talking which carries discourse to a still deeper level and provides the ultimately basic language, the language of the history of Being (*Seinsgeschichte*) and of its destiny and dispensation (*Seinsgeschick*).

Heidegger is thus compelled to fashion a new language, a new idiom, by moulding the largely categorially patterned language of traditional philosophy into a medium for conceptualizing existenzial structures which, since they concern not static entities but modes of man's be-ing, the *that* and the *how* of his *existenz*, are essentially dynamic and of the nature of process. He achieves this, as Erasmus Schöfer has shown in a careful and detailed study of Heidegger's language,[111] by coining new word-forms, largely through converting words of other parts of speech (especially verbs) into substantive forms, though he is by no means exceptional among philosophers in this practice.[112] The philosopher is engaged in the 'higher order' activity of bringing to light and focusing upon relational structures, complex states of affairs, and relations and processes expressed by the different parts of speech. These are structural features of experience lying hidden in the grammatical structure of the language we use to talk *about* experience and therefore not noticed usually as really being constitutive elements of experience itself. To be able to talk about them he must isolate, define, and conceptualize them, name them and terminologically designate them, without necessarily being guilty, as Ryle seems to think, of the Fido-'Fido' fallacy. To this end Heidegger has coined a whole array of abstract terms, employing circumlocutions, hyphenated phrases, compound terms not in common use, compound words broken up into their component parts and abstract nouns made out of words of almost every other part of speech. These new words serve the purpose of illuminating at one stroke, in the words of Schöfer, a particular phenomenon dug out through analyses and gathered up in one concept. "They sum up, at times awkwardly and in an out-of-the-way manner, the structures and relations first disclosed by a complicated analysis and enable them, by means of the new word, to be grasped and represented as a unified phenomenon."[113] Negatively, these neologisms serve the purpose of enabling Heidegger to avoid, in conformity with the principal philosophical thesis of the work, traditional terms suggestive of the essentialist 'ontology of the *Vorhanden*', as well as the modern epistemological terminology. Not merely these philosophical 'terms of art' but the grammar which, since the Greeks, has determined the basic structure and form of discourse as also the classification of its constitutive elements, is itself rooted in that ontology and the logic in which it has unfolded itself. The attempt to go beyond it, therefore, necessarily involves at least circumventing these grammatical limitations, until there are developed ways of talking of which the grammar has been liberated from its thralldom to logic.[114]

The 'circumstantiality' and 'uncouthness' of expression in *Being and Time*, as also the novel technical vocabulary, is thus meant to force the reader away from the accustomed track of categorial thinking, of thinking in terms of the conceptual framework bequeathed to the Western mind by the

Greeks and by the metaphysicians of modern subjectivism. Heidegger's avoidance of traditional terminology, in other words, is deliberately intended to prevent the reader from lapsing into the use of concepts deriving from the substance-centered as well as subject-centered metaphysics of the Western philosophical tradition. This aspect of the language of *Being and Time* has been well brought out by Hans Lipps in the course of a penetrating discussion of existential philosophy.[115] Contrasting Kierkegaard's and Nietzsche's manner of philosophizing with the compelling, stringent conceptuality (*zwingende Begrifflichkeit*) of Heidegger, Lipps has this to say about the latter's language, "It is just his language at which people have been scandalized, the alleged far-fetchedness and forced character of his expressions. But then, one might think of Aristotle, whose expression *to ti en einai* too, for example, was not found by him ready-made in the language; and we do not find fault with him for having made up this expression. . . ."[116] He alone gets stuck in the language of Heidegger who does not read him the way he needs being read. He requires to be read *literally*. This is a way of reading which cannot be taken as a matter of course, for generally one reads otherwise. Sometimes, we read with a view to orientation so that we may acquaint ourselves with the thoughts of another. Often we skip, even preferring to read just 'in between'. We content ourselves with getting just an idea of what the author is driving at. The writer and the reader meet each other here on a level of average comprehensibility; mostly, things remain half-said, not more being required. And just in the matter of philosophical discussions, the dimension is usually marked out and established by traditions and schools, so that one always somehow manages to get along with terms like 'subject', 'object', 'transcendental', and others. Now, the requirement that Heidegger is to be read literally means just the opposite of such reading. Not that we have to linger at words here as in the case of a piece of writing of which the objective precision motivates a literal reading; here we are required to attend to a word in respect of what, as a *word*, it 'signifies' or conveys. This is something quite different from the objective, the matter of fact, to denote which words are mostly employed. Heidegger appeals for a rediscovery of the potency of words. We must win back the direction in which a word, *of its own self*, suggests its meaning,—as, for example, the allusiveness of a word, still word-bound and not objectively fixed, is always secretly at work in the choice of a word when we are struggling with the formulation of a thought. It is true that words like 'care' (*Sorge*), 'disposition' (*Befindlichkeit*), and others, receive here a special content (*Erfüllung*, filling in of a formal concept by a determinate content of meaning), which is found out above all by following a movement of thought, the adoption of which can only be appealed for. Here we are not simply referred to an already given field of objective relations, in and for the articulation of which language has primarily developed. The unusual and indeed shockingly forced character of the phraseology, and of the way words are compounded, is just what keeps us from slipping into giving to these words 'fulfillments' (*Erfüllungen*) which, being current and factual, come uppermost to our minds. The stringent conceptuality of the existenzial analytic is thus something quite different from the exactness of concepts which belong to a system, for exact means worked out in detail and every systematic concept can be thus worked out in its implications, that is, can be 'realized' *ex definitione*. Through such terms as 'care' and 'disposition', however, we are arrested and compelled into an effort at the articulation of what we had already understood ourselves to be in the depths of our existenz. . . . Nietzsche said, 'To understand me is a distinction that must be earned'. Nietzsche and Kierkegaard both sought their reader. Heidegger, too, seeks him."

In other words, Heidegger deliberately chooses and builds his terminology and his way of putting things not only for the positive purpose of disclosing new 'phenomena' but in studied contrast to traditional philosophical vocabulary. The attempt to go beyond metaphysics and comprehend it in its genesis and essence cannot, Heidegger insists, be carried out in the language of metaphysics.[117] The inquiry into the essence of Being expires unless it gives up the language of metaphysics, in which its representational thinking is crystallized. This is so because language is not a means of expression which may be doffed and changed like clothing, as Heidegger puts it, without making any difference to what has been mentioned in it. "It is in language that there manifests itself first of all, and *is*, that which, in our use of key words, we seem to express only subsequently, making use of expressions which we believe might be discarded at will and substituted by others." Concepts, word meanings, and, primarily, language are not substitutable like 'optical systems' through which we may gaze at a reality existing by itself. Even metaphysical concepts, as Kant saw, are by nature of a different kind than those of science, for that which they grasp and the grasping are here in a basic sense the same. In the realm of the root words of thinking, therefore, it is even less a matter of indifference whether these (metaphysical concepts) are forgotten or whether one goes on using them untested. The attempt to go into the ground of metaphysics and to build afresh implies transforming our way of speaking and a change in our relationship to the nature of language—"inevitably everything here depends on the right way of saying, on that *logos* of which the real nature is beyond the ken of logic and dialectic, themselves offsprings of metaphysics." The utterance of thinking, Heidegger remarks, is not its expression but thinking itself, its movement and its chant.[118] The reader—not excluding the translator!—must therefore be constantly alert and attentive to the precise, literal meaning of almost every word in the text, lest he glide into the usual practice of assimilating the new to the familiar by grasping it in terms of one's own cherished concepts, forgetting that Heidegger's intention is precisely the opposite, that of carrying our thought away from their habitual groves into another dimension, away from "subject, soul, consciousness, spirit, person, life, man" and from idealism and realism, Reality and the Absolute, away from the traditional epistemological and metaphysical concepts as well as from the conceptual framework of theology. On the other hand, Heidegger wants the reader to concentrate on the positive content of the basic philosophical words, old or new, and give them their full weight. To this end, he sometimes takes a word apart, focusing attention upon the component parts of the word, squeezing out of it all its precise, complex meaning and force (for example, in his discussions of *Vor-stellen* and *Gegen-stand*); sometimes as in the later works particularly, he takes recourse to imaginative etymologizing and tries to 'project' or 'compose' the primordial, root meaning of a term, a meaning prior to and underlying the particular meanings a word acquires in actual usage at different times (for example the essays on *Logos* and *Aletheia* in *Vorträge und Aufsätze*). As Ortega y Gasset has remarked, "Heidegger pierces through the common and superficial sense of a word and sets it aside. Under pressure he makes the underlying meaning leap up out of the depths. . . . The common word, with Heidegger, suddenly fills up, it fills up to the brim, with meaning. . . . It seems to us as if we were surprising a word in its *statu nascendi*."[119] Similarly, Beda Allemann describes Heidegger's procedure as one in which "words are spelt out in respect of their component parts, words which are in themselves transparent but of which the constitutive elements, though open to view, are no longer expressly considered or kept in mind in every day use."[120]

In Heidegger's later writings the tendency, already apparent in *Being and Time*, not merely to coin new word forms but to break away from the established syntax and grammatical structure of language, comes clearly into evidence. Heidegger has realized that the grammatical rules which govern a language not only render expression possible but, in constituting and giving form to one possiblity of expressing and disclosing the nature of things, they can also hinder expression by setting limits to it. With the further realization of the 'metaphysically' determined character of logical, conceptual thinking, there arises a different conception of thinking and, correspondingly, the use of language of which the structure is no longer rigidly governed by logic and grammar. The use of paradox, and fusion of heterogeneous linguistic elements, of thought circles, of tautology, the *figura etymologica* (that is, he fights a fight, Nothingness nihilates) and paronomasia—modes of expression common in mystical literature and in Oriental thinking—are clear indications, not so much of the linguistic inventiveness of Heidegger as of the fact that he is laboring to develop a new thought form, *within* philosophy, which alone is adequate to the thinking of Being. The attempt to think without employing the traditional philosophical concepts, indeed to think nonconceptually, and yet to speak meaningfully and illuminatingly about Being is at the root of these linguistic peculiarities of Heidegger. This, and not any sort of flight into irrationalism and mysticism, may perhaps account for the respect with which Heidegger has recently been referring to the 'thinking' of the German mystics Meister Eckhart and Angelus Silesius, as also for his growing interest in the thought of the far East.[121]

In *Being and Time*, Heidegger's thinking, despite his linguistic innovations and departures, is still within the traditional framework and his language and approach typically academic. Still taking language as a neutral 'instrument' of thought and the latter as concept building, Heidegger constructs a large technical terminology to formulate existenzial concepts. Although even here this terminology is largely derived from his native German, he models it, nevertheless, on philosophical Greek, especially Aristotle, and makes free use of the large international vocabulary of scholarship deriving from Greek and Latin.[122] In the later writings he not only abandons the use of technical terms, along with the representational, rigidly conceptual thinking of the earlier phase, but turns definitely away from the foreign vocabulary of the scholarly tradition, deliberately confining himself to words of pure, simple German descent. Schöfer refers to a conversation (in 1959) between Heidegger and Jean Beaufret, in the course of which Heidegger told the latter that in his experiments with language he endeavored to approximate to a condition which would correspond to that prevailing before the Latinization of German.[123] The language of the philosophical tradition of the West has been largely moulded by the Greek thinkers and, later, by the Latinized version of Greek terms in medieval times. In German philosophy the influence of Latin terminology can be traced, after the abandonment of Latin as the medium of creative thought, in Kant and the German idealists. The greatest and most original philosophers of the West have thus been confined in their thinking within a terminological framework inherited, via the Romans, from the Greeks. They have taken it over uncritically and have in consequence remained tied to the Greek way of thinking and of seeing things. But, as Schöfer remarks, "Heidegger, who attempts to think about the nature of Greco-European philosophy, is obliged to dissociate himself from its linguistic mould in order to be able to reflect not in it but about it."[124] Through the elimination of vocabulary deriving from Greek and Latin, Heidegger is able to use a purified language, rooted in the native dialect, free from the philosophical suggestions clinging around that vocabulary and thus capable of uttering the truth of Being in ways that were barred to it.

Critics of Heidegger have complained of the rift in the language of *Being and Time* and of the unevenness of its style. Those parts of the work in which Heidegger discusses traditional doctrines and the views of past philosophers are written in a discursive, descriptive, abstract, complicated *Akademikerdeutsch*; others, where he develops his own original thoughts, as in the analyses of man's modes of being, are analytical, deductive, elaborating. These distinct linguistic levels are present in all writings of Heidegger but, as Schöfer has pointed out, whereas in *Being and Time* they are simply juxtaposed without really fusing together, in the later writings there comes about a greater coherence and unity in style. The reason for the lack of stylistic and linguistic unity in the earlier work is to be found in the fact, already pointed out, that although *Being and Time* represents a turning point in the history of philosophy, "it is a work of transition and bears all the marks of such transition. Both in content and in language, it represents a transition from the thinking within the framework and language of the history of philosophy (of "the Being of beings") to the sphere of the thinking and utterance of 'Being itself' in the later works."[125] It is only in these latter that, with the employment of a purely German vocabulary, a unified style and language are possible and actually attained. In his lecture on Hebel, "the friend of the house," Heidegger describes language—which alone really speaks and not man—as the treasure house of all that is essential. "Whenever and in whatever manner man speaks, he speaks only because he already gives ear to language." This language, the language in which we are born and which is bequeathed to us, is the mother tongue, itself nourished by the dialect out of which it has developed. "The dialect is the mysterious source of every developed language. From it stream forth all those precious gifts which the spirit of a language contains in itself. . . . The spirit of language guards and preserves in itself the invisible but all sustaining relationships to God, to world, to men and their doings."[126] Even when the whole conceptual terminology of the European philosophical tradition is renounced, these riches remain, leaving at the disposal of the thinker as yet unactualized possibilities of utterance and, through giving word to what so far has remained unsaid, of letting what has remained hidden so long come to light and manifest itself.

But whether Heidegger writes in the language of the scholarly tradition of Western philosophy or takes recourse to the simple, pure mother tongue, he is never under the illusion that ordinary language can ever deliver its whole secret, surrender all that lies in it and become completely transparent. As he says in a recent lecture,

> The difficulty lies in language. Our Occidental languages are, each in its different way, languages of metaphysical thinking. Whether the nature of the Western languages is in itself only metaphysical and hence definitively cast into the mould of onto-theo-logy, or whether these languages can offer other possibilities of saying, which means at the same time of saying and yet leaving unsaid, are questions that must remain open.[127]

In a variety of ways, Heidegger has sought to explore creatively the latter alternative, not hesitating to avail himself of the license of linguistic creation generally restricted to poets, delving deep, beyond the purely academic level, into the riches lying buried in the archaic, the literary, the religious and the mystical layers of his native German and drawing into his net the vocabulary of 'German inwardness', as Schöfer calls it, or, as Hans Stoltenberg terms it, the language of the Gothic wisdom of the heart. This, however, by no means implies a lapse into some kind of 'mysticism', an abdication of thinking as such, or that Heidegger is struggling to clothe in words an experience, in itself immediate and ineffable but already given, of which the content is recalcitrant to language. For Heidegger, "The word does not merely name, and so enable us to have in our grasp, our already represented present reality (or essent), it is not merely a means to the depiction of something given. On the contrary, it is the word which first of all bestows presence, that is, Being, in which anything appears as an essent."[128] Language here is one with thought, the project of thinking merges into linguistic composing and both together are creative and evocative of genuine novelty, of a new conception of Being, that is, of new Being.

As compared with the writings of the earlier phase, in which language is still in some measure an instrument for the expression of universal meanings, Heidegger's later thinking is much more intimately language bound. So far-reaching in its consequences for thought is his rejection of the essentialist doctrine—and implied in that, of the conception of meanings as universal essences which may be clothed indifferently in any linguistic symbol—that, in these later writings, what is thought and said becomes inseparable from the individual and unique language and manner of saying it; not only does the thought and the utterance merge into one but the particular language employed and the thought content expressed become indissoluble. Such thinking, like all great poetry, is in a profound sense untranslatable and there is undeniable truth in Karl Löwith's remark that a Whitsun miracle will have to occur, if Heidegger's definition of the love of Being or of the nature of technology were to lend itself to being expressed in English.[129] But this untranslatability, far from being a shortcoming, is not only inevitable but in reality a boon and a challenge to any thinking that concerns itself, not with beings, but with the Being of beings or with Being itself. It compels thought to reflect upon and bring to explicit awareness the spirit of both languages, that of the original and of the translation, and to realize more deeply how Being reveals itself uniquely in the spirit of each language. "Through translation," Heidegger says, "the work of thinking is transposed into the spirit and outlook of another language and thus undergoes an inevitable transformation. But the transformation can become fertile because it makes the fundamental way of posing the question appear in a new light."[130]

Ortega y Gasset has given high praise to Heidegger's language as the perfect example of a specifically philosophical style.[131] Yet, Heidegger has himself, in retrospect, repeatedly characterized the language of *Being and Time* as clumsy and uncouth. On his long 'way' to Being, something in itself ultimately simple, Heidegger's unceasing endeavor has been to gather together language in a simplicity of utterance, to eliminate the circumstantiality and heaviness of expression, as also the technical jargon, of the earlier works. He does this by employing, where he develops his own ideas, an essentially German vocabulary. Without restricting himself to common usage, he exploits the possibilities held out by "the hidden riches of language,"[132] thus creatively transforming his mother tongue itself, in however modest a degree. For, as he says,[133] "Thinking draws inconspicuous grooves in language, marks that are even more inconspicuous than those made by unhurried steps of the peasant walking across a field."[134]

Heidegger's 'way' is a path of which "thinking has an intimation only in the course of being under way; it shows itself and eludes our grasp." Where does it lead? "It is perhaps a way that leads into *the determination of the matter (Sache) of thinking*. This determination brings nothing new. It only takes us to the most ancient of all that is old. It craves the sojourn in the ever sought-after sameness of the self-same." Can we observe this path stretched out before our gaze? "The way leading to this abode disallows it to be described as something lying before us. He who seeks to get on to it is helped only by the unceasing effort to examine (*erörtern*, to find out the locality of) what the word 'being' has once revealed as that which has to be thought about, what it will perhaps one day cover up as something already thought."

What is it that moves the thinker on this path? "He who sets out on the path of the thinking knows least of what, as the determinative thing (*Sache*), moves him towards it, as it were from behind his back and away over him." What about the future of this path? "He who consents to being under way to a sojourn in the most ancient of what is ancient, will yield to the necessity of being later understood differently from the way he meant to understand himself. However, this necessity rests on the possibility that an area of free play still remains granted to the historical heritage . . ."[135]

Notes

1. *Unterwegs zur Sprache*, pp. 37-38 (English Translation [E.T.], p. 160).
2. *Was heisst Denken?*, p. 20 (E.T., p. 50).

3. For an elucidation of Heidegger's philosophy as a "way," see Otto Pöggeler, *Der Denkweg Martin Heideggers*, pp. 7-15.

4. "Sein als Ereignis," *Zeitschrift für philosophische Forschung* 13 (1959):600.

5. See Walter Schulz's well known article, "Über den philosophiege-schichtlichen Ort Martin Heideggers," *Philosophische Rundschau* 1(1953/1954), where a serious attempt is made for the first time to view Heidegger's philosophy in a historical perspective. Schultz sees it as "the inner ending of the process of Western metaphysics," as representing the end of a tradition and therefore incapable of being either assimilated into it or criticized in terms of any phase of that. Western metaphysics, he believes with Heidegger, exhibits a meaningful historical pattern moving toward an end and, secondly, that this culmination is reached in our own times and becomes visible in the philosophy of Heidegger. Attempting as it does to interpret man in his wholeness entirely out of himself and not in terms of any other entity, *Being and Time* is, in this sense only, "a work of the philosophy of subjectivity and indeed its culminating work." This can be explicitly seen in the essay "What is Metaphysics?" in which the metaphysical tradition is shown as culminating in 'Nothing'. Schulz says therefore that this essay is "the metaphysical end work of traditional metaphysics" and that the 'Nothing' of that essay is the "end point of tradition," not only its culmination but its terminal point, after which it passes over into another beginning. Heidegger's philosophy thus represents the historic moment of the self-abrogation, the 'reversal', of the metaphysical tradition and is itself conditioned by this tradition.

See also Werner Marx's *Heidegger und die Tradition*, which shows with particular reference to Aristotle and to Hegel, how Heidegger seeks to go beyond the entire metaphysical tradition and to initiate a new way of thinking about Being and Man.

6. It would therefore be a mistake to approach the philosophy of Heidegger as the work of a solitary Teutonic genius, an 'outsider' thinking profound and original thoughts even though, unlike Wittgenstein, he has fathered no school and is himself part of no 'movement'. Ludwig Landgrebe, Eugen Fink, and Hans-Georg Gadamer, each from a different perspective, have shown how Heidegger's thought is part and parcel of the larger movement of European thought, "an achievement and a part of the progress of philosophy" (to use John Wisdom's words about Ryle's work!). In this respect he is more like Wittgenstein than like Whitehead, though it is only the later Wittgenstein who seems to be at all aware that he is attacking old-established habits of mind, rooted deep in history. The extreme unhistorical attitude of his *Tractatus* phase finds explicit utterance in *Notebooks 1914-1916* (p. 82c): "What has history to do with me? Mine is the first and only world! I want to report how *I* found the world."

7. Cf. *Einführung in die Metaphysik*, p. 5f. (E.T., p. 5f.), where Heidegger discusses the character of "asking as a primordial power," what is implied in real questioning and how the questioning spirit differs from the attitude of religious belief, from the security of faith which has its own particular way of standing in truth. The passion for genuine questioning is for Heidegger the distinctive mark of philosophical thinking, as represented, for example,

by Socrates, "the purest thinker of the West." About the Greeks, Heidegger says, "The Greeks saw in the ability to ask the whole aristocracy of their existence; their ability to question was for them the standard for differentiating themselves from those who were not capable of it and did not want it. These they called barbarians" (*Die Frage nach dem Ding*, p. 32; E.T., p. 42). In Heidegger, however, the passion of questioning is eventually subordinated and made subservient to the sensitivity of 'hearing'. Pure questioning is inspired by the quest for the *radix*, the root, of everything. But this quest itself, that is philosophy, is rooted in the metaphysical conception of Being as Ground. Once this is abandoned, the nature of thinking as questioning is itself modified. As Heidegger says, explaining the statement in "Die Frage nach der Technik" that the devoutness of thinking lies in questioning: "Every question is always raised within (the horizon of) the promise held out by that which is put into question. . . . The primary and proper gesture of thought is not questioning; it is rather the hearing of the promise of that which is to come into question" (*Unterwegs zur Sprache*, p. 175; E.T., p. 71). For Heidegger's "way" of thinking as questioning see Richard Wisser, "Das Fragen als Weg des Denkens" (in *Verantwortung im Wandel der Zeit*).

8. *Aus der Erfahrung des Denkens*, p. 7; E.T., *Poetry, Language, Thought*, p. 4.

9. *Zur ontologischen Frühgeschichte von Raum-Zeit-Bewegung*, p. 42.

10. Some idea of the impact of this work on contemporary European thinkers and of the large polemical literature to which this book and Heidegger's subsequent writings have given rise can be had from the bibliography compiled by Hermann Lübbe (*Bibliographie der Heidegger-Literatur, 1917-1955*, containing 880 titles). A supplementary bibliography (1960; later enlarged into a book) has been brought out by Guido Schneeberger. A "Heidegger Bibliographie, 1917-1966" by M. Dirk Pereboom appeared in the *Freiburger Zeitschrift für Philosophie und Theologie*, 16 (1969):100-161. The standard, most up-to-date work now is Hans-Martin Sass, *Heidegger Bibliographie* (1968), specially valuable for its inclusion of non-German language references.

Brief accounts of early misunderstandings about *Being and Time* and of the stages through which the interpretation of Heidegger has passed are given by Peter Fürstenau (*Heidegger*, 1958), and by Schulz and Pöggeler in articles referred to above. See also Max Müller, *Existenzphilosophie im geistigen Leben der Gegenwart* (2d ed., 1958).

11. The basic precondition for an appreciation of Heidegger, it may be added, is the realization that he cannot be interpreted, and therefore should not be judged, in terms of the thought of any preceding stage in the history of Western philosophy. When approached from a fixed standpoint, whether rationalistic or empiricistic, idealistic or realistic, mystical or positivistic, he can be only 'used or criticized and dismissed' but never truly understood. Further, Heidegger's relationship to the Western metaphysical tradition is in a profound sense, ambiguous. He is critical of his tradition and often 'unfair' to its leading philosophers; leaving it behind, he carries thought forward into a new dimension. But this criticism and overcoming of metaphysics does not, like contemporary positivism, 'prove' it to be an error and so eliminate it (only to restore it in the subtle form of logical analysis!). Far from rejecting

or denigrating metaphysics, Heidegger seeks only to exhibit its limits—though in a different sense and manner than Kant—and bring to light the truth (as he calls it) or basis on which metaphysics itself stands. In this sense he prepares rather for a reappropriation of the whole metaphysical tradition on a deeper level of thinking; his overcoming of metaphysics is really a rejection of its claim to ultimacy.

12. *Unterwegs zur Sprache*, p. 96 (E.T., p. 10).

13. *Unterwegs zur Sprache*, p. 92 (E.T., p. 7). *Von der mannigfachen Bedeutung des Seienden nach Aristoteles*, long out of print, is now available again in a reprint. The title page of this work carries as a motto the sentence from Aristotle: *to on legetai pollachos* ("what *is*, becomes manifest, in respect of its Being, in many ways," in Heidegger's rendering). "Latent in this phrase is the *question* that determined the way of my thought: what is the pervasive, simple, unified determination of Being that permeates all of its multiple meanings? . . . What, then, does Being mean?" (Heidegger's "Preface" to William J. Richardson's *Heidegger*, p. x).

14. Ibid., p. 96 (E.T., p. 10).

15. See Hans-Georg Gadamer, "Heidegger und die Marburger Theologie" (in *Kleine Schriften I*) for a vivid, informative account. Elsewhere ("Introduction" in the Reclam edition of *Der Ursprung des Kunstwerkes*), Gadamer remarks that Heidegger's *opus magnum Being and Time*, grew out of his "fruitful contact, full of tensions, with contemporary Protestant theology after his call to Marburg in the year 1923." How profoundly Heidegger's own work has, in turn, influenced contemporary theology is writ large in the pages of Rudolph Bultmann and Paul Tillich, distinguished theologians who have, however, confined themselves to the existential concepts and idiom of *Being and Time*. For the way the later Heidegger has been appropriated by the theologians, see for example, *Denken und Sein—Der Weg Martin Heideggers und der Weg der Theologie* by Heinrich Ott, successor to Karl Barth at Basel. *The Later Heidegger and Theology* and *The New Hermeneutic*, both edited by James M. Robinson and John B. Cobb, Jr., contain a number of essays discussing the relevance of the later Heidegger to theology. *An Existentialist Theology* by John Macquarrie is a comparison of Heidegger and Bultmann. *Heidegger und die Theologie*, edited with an introduction by Gerhard Noller, is a selection of the most important articles by Protestant theologians on this subject, from the earliest impact of *Being and Time* to 1964.

Heidegger's impact on Catholic theology is attested by Max Müller (*Existenzphilosophie im geistigen Leben der Gegenwart* and several articles), by Joseph Möller (*Existenzphilosophie und Katholische Theologie*), and by Gustave Siewerth (*Das Schicksal der Metaphysik von Thomas zu Heidegger*). Karl Rahner was Heidegger's pupil and his early work *Geist in Welt* shows the influence of Heidegger. As Rahner recently said, "Contemporary Catholic Theology, as it is in actuality, is quite unthinkable without Martin Heidegger" (*Martin Heidegger im Gespräch*, ed. Richard Wisser, p. 48).

16. The distinction between *existenziell* and *existenzial* is basic in Heidegger. The former term refers to the ontic, the factual, and the experienced, whereas the latter refers to its ontological and transcendental condition and

significance. 'Existence' and its derivates are spelled with a *z* in order to indicate their special technical use.

17. About the concept of *existenz* in *Being and Time*, for example, Heidegger says (*Nietzsche II*, p. 476) that here neither the concept in Kierkegaard's sense nor that in the sense of *Existenzphilosophie* is involved.

18. *Unterwegs zur Sprache*, p. 182 (E.T., p. 78).

19. Cf. Spiegelberg, *The Phenomenological Movement*, 1:292.

20. As H.-G. Gadamer has pointed out in his "Introduction" to the German translation of R. G. Collingwood's *Autobiography* (entitled *Denken*), the philosophical climate in Germany during the early years of this century differed in essential respects from that in England. For the background of contemporary German philosophy, characterized largely by a reaction against the dominant Neo-Kantianism, see also Gadamer's "Introduction" to the Reclam edition of Heidegger's *Der Ursprung des Kunstwerkes* and Werner Brock's *Introduction to Contemporary German Philosophy*. The standard histories (by Windelband-Heimsoeth, Stegmüller, Knittermeyer) all contain accounts of Heidegger as also of the contemporary philosophical landscape.

21. For details regarding Heidegger's academic career, see Paul Hühnerfeld, *In Sachen Heidegger*, pp. 40-42.

22. *Unterwegs zur Sprache*, p. 91f. (E.T., p. 6). See also the opening paragraphs of the "Vorwort" to *Frühe Schriften*.

23. This neologism, borrowed from Ralph Manheim, has been used throughout this work to render the German *"das Seiende"* for reasons explained by Manheim in the "Translator's Note" in his English translation of *Einführung in die Metaphysik*. 'Entity', 'what is', 'all that is', 'beings' have also been used in many places alternatively.

24. "Die Kategorien und Bedeutungslehre des Duns Scotus," *Frühe Schriften*, p. 141. Subsequent research has established that the work *de modis significandi* ascribed here by Heidegger to Duns Scotus, was in fact written by Thomas von Erfurt.

25. *The Phenomenological Movement*, 1:296. For this whole paragraph, see the introduction and the conclusion of the Duns Scotus book (*Frühe Schriften*, pp. 135-148 and 341-353, respectively).

26. Ibid., p. 297. See *Frühe Schriften*, pp. 358-375. These three works on the theory of judgment, the doctrine of categories and meanings, and the concept of time, have been published together at last in a volume entitled *Frühe Schriften* (Frankfurt, 1972), with a new "Vorwort" by Heidegger. The latter includes the text of an autobiographical address he gave at the Heidelberg Academy of Science in 1957. An English translation of this *Antrittsrede* will be found in *Man and World* 3, 1 (1970):3-4.

27. See Pöggeler, "Sein als Ereignis," *Zeitschrift für philosophische Forschung*, 13 (1959):604, and *Der Denkweg Martin Heideggers*, pp. 36-45.

28. See *Sein und Zeit*, p. 72 (E.T., p. 490), for reference to his lectures dating back to 1919 on the 'hermeneutics of facticity'; also *Unterwegs zur Sprache*, p. 95 (E.T., p. 95).

Heidegger has explained in his recent "Preface" in Richardson's *Heidegger* (pp. x-xiv) how the way from his first encounter with the question of Being ("whence does Being as such, not merely beings as beings, receive its determination?") in Brentano's dissertation to this clear awareness was a long and devious one, "a tangled process, inscrutable even to me." As he says there, "Meanwhile a decade went by and a great deal of swerving and straying through the history of Western philosophy was needed for the above questions to reach even an initial clarity." Three insights which were decisive in preparing the way to such clarity were: a gradual clarification of the real meaning and scope of the principle of phenomenology, the understanding of *aletheia* (truth) as nonconcealment, based on a renewed study of the Aristotelian treatises (especially Book IX of the *Metaphysics* and Book VI of the *Nicomachean Ethics*) and the recognition of the fundamental character of *ousia* (the Being of what is) as *presence*.

29. *Gesammelte Schriften* VII, p. 359.

30. Ibid., III, p. 210.

31. Ibid., VIII, p. 224.

32. Schleiermacher's *Hermeneutik* has been reedited by Heinz Kimmerle.

33. A thorough discussion of the views of Dilthey will be found in Gadamer, *Wahrheit und Methode*, pp. 205-228. Unlike G. Misch (*Lebensphilosophie und Phänomenologie*) and O. F. Bollnow (*Dilthey*), and like L. Landgrebe (*Philosophie der Gegenwart*), Gadamer brings out the philosophical limitations of Dilthey. See also Pöggeler, *Der Denkweg Martin Heideggers*, chapter 2, entitled "Metaphysik and Geschichte."

34. See chapter 4 below.

35. In the dialog on language in *Unterwegs zur Sprache*, Heidegger explains the deeper sense in which, connecting *hermeneuein* with Hermes, the messenger of the gods, he understands hermeneutics. "Hermeneutics means, in *Being and Time*, neither a theory of the art of interpretation nor interpretation itself, but rather an attempt to determine the nature of interpretation primarily in terms of the essence of the hermeneutical . . . this means primarily not interpreting but rather the bringing of message and tidings." (See *Unterwegs zur Sprache*, pp. 95-98, 120-126; E.T., pp. 9-12, 28-32.)

The concept of a philosophical hermeneutics (philosophy regarded as understanding and interpretation) has recently been worked out on a monumental scale by Hans-Georg Gadamer, an early pupil of Heidegger and a scholar of extraordinary range. His work *Wahrheit und Methode* (1960; third enlarged edition, 1972) inspired by the insights and approach of Husserl, Dilthey, and Heidegger, culminates in a discussion of language as the basis of a hermeneutic ontology. Written in a sober, academic, non-Heideggerizing style, this work is indispensable for a grasp of the aims, methods, and achievements of the type of philosophy which is concerned not so much with argumentation as with understanding. It is no less valuable as providing a perspective for the understanding of Heidegger's thought and for Gadamer's illuminating comments on many aspects of that. Gadamer's *Kleine Schriften* in three volumes and *Hegels Dialektik* contain further studies in hermeneutic philosophy, including essays dealing specifically with Heidegger.

36. For details regarding these facts, see Spiegelberg, *The Phenomenological Movement*, 1:275-283.

37. *Sein und Zeit*, p. 38 (E.T., p. 489).

38. See Walter Biemel, "Husserls Encyclopaedia Britannica Artikel und Heideggers Anmerkungen dazu." The various drafts of Husserl's article, along with Heidegger's comments and a letter to Husserl are published in *Phänomenologische Psychologie*. Heidegger collaborated with Husserl in the preparation of the earlier drafts and the difference between their conception of phenomenology that emerged in consequence can be seen clearly from the material contained in this volume. Cf. in particular, pp. 256-263, 517f., and 600-602. The draft prepared by Heidegger has been translated into English by John N. Deely and Joseph A. Novak in their article, "The Idea of Phenomenology."

39. Landgrebe, *Phänomenologie und Metaphysik, Philosophie der Gegenwart* and subsequent articles; Fink, *Sein, Wahrheit, Welt*.

40. Cf. Landgrebe's article, "Husserls Abschied vom Cartesianismus."

41. Heidegger's dissatisfaction with the notion of the transcendental ego as the source of constitution is clearly expressed in his letter to Husserl (in Husserl's *Phänomenologische Psychologie*, pp. 601-602): "What is the mode of being of that entity in whom 'world' gets constituted? This is the central problem of *Being and Time*. . . . It needs being shown that the mode of being of a human being is totally different from that of all other essents and that precisely because it is such a mode of being that it contains hidden within itself the possibility of transcendental constitution. Transcendental constitution is a central possibility of the factually existing self. . . . The constituting subject is not nothing, hence it is something and has being—although not in the sense of something given. The inquiry into the mode of being of the constituting source is not to be evaded."

42. Quoted in Spiegelberg, *Phenomenological Movement*, 1:128.

43. Cf. *Die Phänomenologische Idee der Intentionalität* by A. de Waelhens in *Husserl und das Denken der Neuzeit*.

44. *Unterwegs zur Sprache*, p. 95 (E.T., p. 9).

45. Ibid., p. 122 (E.T., p. 30).

46. Cf. *Vorträge und Aufsätze*, p. 134: "From the Sciences to Thinking there is no bridge but only a leap. It brings us not only to another side but to a wholly different locality. What it opens up can never be proved, if proving means deriving, on the basis of suitable assumptions, propositions about some state of affairs by means of chains of deductive inference. He who wants to prove or have proved to him that which is known only insofar as it manifests itself while at the same time concealing itself, he who still desires this does not by any means judge in accordance with a higher or more stringent measure of knowledge. He merely *reckons* with a standard and that, too, an inappropriate one. For, to that which lets itself be known only in such a way that in its self-concealment it manifests itself, we can also come up (be equal) only so that we point to it and, with that, enjoin our own selves to let that which shows itself appear in its own unhiddenness. This simple pointing is a distinctive mark of thinking, the way to that which it is given to man to think, once and for time to come. Everything permits of being proved, that is, of being derived from suitable assumptions. But very little is amenable to pointing, to being emancipated into arrival by being pointed to, and

this also very seldom." See also *Der Satz vom Grund*, pp. 40-41, for Heidegger's remarks on "axiomatic thinking."

In a discussion of the problem of a nonobjectifying thinking and speaking in contemporary theology, Heidegger has more recently remarked that it is an error to think that only that which can be objectively calculated and proved as an object in a scientific-technical manner counts as being. "This erroneous view forgets the words written down long ago by Aristotle (*Metaphysics*, IV, 4, 1006a 6f.), "It is uneducatedness not to see in regard to what it is necessary to look for a proof and in regard to what it is not necessary."

47. *Unterwegs zur Sprache*, p. 122; E.T., p. 30. The question whether Heidegger is to be called a phenomenologist has been widely debated. Landgrebe and Fink, both loyal and veteran phenomenologists, both aware of the strains within Husserlian Phenomenology and alive to the need of an inner transformation of it, look upon Heidegger as to a large extent accomplishing this. For a lucid discussion of the whole problem, see Spiegelberg's *The Phenomenological Movement*, Vol. I, and also the excellent review of this work by Richard Schmitt. In various articles published recently, Schmitt has been doing valuable liaison work trying to bring together Continental Phenomenology and English Analytical Philosophy. It still remains, however, to be realized fully how very much off the mark Gilbert Ryle was in his attacks against Phenomenology (beginning with his review of *Sein und Zeit* in *Mind*, 1929). As regards the continuity of the philosophical development from Dilthey through Husserl to Heidegger, see, besides the works of Landgrebe mentioned earlier, Hans-Georg Gadamer: *Wahrheit und Methode*; also, Gadamer's review article on the Phenomenological Movement. But, as Gadamer himself remarks in his book (p. 243), "The true precursor of Heidegger's way of posing the problem of Being and of the opposition to the direction of inquiry in Western metaphysics which it signified, could, therefore, be neither Dilthey nor Husserl but much rather Nietzsche."

48. See Richardson's *Heidegger*, pp. 665-669. Heidegger's recently published *Schellings Abhandlung über das Wesen der menschlichen Freiheit (1809)* contains the text of the lecture course he gave on Schelling in 1936, selections from manuscripts prepared for the Schelling seminar of 1941 and extracts from seminar notes written during 1941-1943. Paul Tillich and Walter Schulz have drawn attention to the parallels between Heidegger and Schelling. See, in particular, the latter's *Die Vollendung des Deutschen Idealismus in der Spätphilosophie Schellings*.

49. Heidegger worked and lectured extensively on some of the dialogs of Plato during the period when he was engaged in writing *Being and Time*, as for example, the *Sophist*, with a quotation from which this work begins, and the *Philebus* which, according to Dr. H. Boeder (personal communication) has had some influence on the analyses of *Befindlichkeit* and *Stimmung* in *Being and Time*. According to Eugen Fink (oral communication), Aristotle's *Nicomachean Ethics*, Book VI, has influenced the analyses in this work, in particular the Aristotelian concept of *phronesis*. In seminars, Heidegger has discussed in detail Augustine's *Confessions*, especially the portions dealing with Memory and with Time, and also Aristotle's *Physics* (oral communica-

tion from Prof. Heidegger), recently published in part under the title *Vom Wesen und Begriff der Physis*. The writings of Heidegger's pupils and followers, such as H.-G. Gadamer (*Wahrheit und Methode*), Volkmann-Schluck (*Plotin als Interpret der Ontologie Platos*), Walter Bröcker (*Aristoteles*), K. Oltmanns (*Meister Eckhart*), and others, give some idea of the concentration with which Heidegger has studied the great Western thinkers. Heidegger has lectured extensively on most of these, from the pre-Socratics to Nietzsche; extracts from some of these lecture courses have been published and a few of them in entirety. It is known that he has occupied himself intensively with the interpretation of Aristotle (Cf. W. Szilasi, "Metaphysik und Geschichte der Philosophie," in *Martin Heideggers Einfluss auf die Wissenschaften*). So far, however, only the exegesis of the introductory chapter of the second book of Aristotle's *Physics*, mentioned above, has been published. For a systematic presentation of the philosophy of Aristotle influenced by Heidegger's lectures, see the book by Bröcker mentioned above. These views have been discussed critically by K. H. Ilting in an article "Sein als Bewegtheit." A commentary on Aristotle's *Peri Hermeneias* remains unpublished.

50. For the whole of this paragraph, see the "Introduction" to "Was ist Metaphysik?" and also "Hegels Begriff der Erfahrung" (*Holzwege*, pp. 161-163; E.T., pp. 105-108) for the ambiguity in *on* and its significance for metaphysics.

51. This is what Heidegger often calls the "oblivion of Being" (*Seinsvergessenheit*). But this should not be understood, he points out, as if Being were an umbrella left somewhere due to the forgetfulness of a professor of philosophy. Forgetting is not exclusively an omission or an act of the human subject. Forgetting is rooted in self-concealment (*Verbergung*) in which what is forgotten is at the same time preserved. ("Zur Seinsfrage," *Wegmarken*, p. 243; E.T., p. 91.)

52. *Was heisst Denken?* p. 42 (E.T., p. 103).

53. Magda King provides a very helpful introduction to the central ideas of *Being and Time* in *Heidegger's Philosophy* (1964). Her lucid and careful 'Guide' stops short, however, with Division One of *Sein und Zeit*. Richard Schmitt's *Martin Heidegger on Being Human* (1969) is a stimulating introduction to *Sein und Zeit* for the reader brought up in an "analytical" climate. *A Commentary on Heidegger's "Being and Time"* (1970) by Michael Gelven is useful for the beginner, but is much too elementary to deserve the title of a commentary.

54. As Heidegger later pointed out (Richardson's *Heidegger*, "Preface," p. xiii), even the delineation of temporality as ecstatic-horizonal which is given in *Being and Time* fails to reach the innermost character of time which can prove adequate from the point of view of the problem of Being.

55. P. 216 (E.T., p. 247f.).

56. "Brief über den 'Humanismus'," *Wegmarken*, p. 175.

57. *Nietzsche I*, pp. 337-338.

58. *Nietzsche II*, p. 194.

59. *Die Selbstebehauptung der deutschen Universität*.

60. *The Phenomenological Movement*, 1:309.

61. This way of putting it, it must be admitted, is not quite fair to Heidegger who has, from the beginning, sought to interpret will in terms of Dasein's openness to Being. I am myself inclined to accept without qualification Heidegger's own interpretation of what he was aiming at in *Being and Time*. The thinking attempted there "remained captive to contemporary modes of representation and language and this also led to inadequate explanations of its own intentions." But as Heidegger adds, "Any one who is prepared to observe the simple fact that in *Being and Time* the problem is set up outside the sphere of subjectivism—that the entire anthropological problem is kept at a distance, that the entire issue is governed solely and emphatically by the experience (that is, the awareness) of man as *Da-sein* (that is, as the place where the disclosure of Being occurs), with a constant eye to the question of Being—he will also see that the 'Being' into which *Being and Time* inquired cannot remain something that is posited by the human subject." (See the "Preface" in Richardson's *Heidegger*.)

This is not the place to enter into the meaning of Heidegger's brief excursion into politics or to discuss the political implications, if any, of his philosophy. The interested reader may refer to the following.

Alexander Schwan, *Politische Philosophie im Denken Heideggers*, 1965; Jean-Michel Palmier, *Les Écrits politiques de Heidegger*, 1968; Beda Allemann, "Martin Heidegger und die Politik," *Merkur* 10 (1967); Beat Sitter, "Zur Möglichkeit dezisionistischer Auslegung von Heideggers ersten Schriften," *Zeitschrift für philosophische Forschung*, 24 (1970); Otto Pöggeler, *Philosophie und Politik bei Heidegger*, 1972; Karl A. Moehling, "Martin Heidegger and the Nazi Party: An Examination" (Ph.D. dissertation, Northern Illinois University, 1972).

62. "Hölderlins Erde und Himmel" (*Hölderlin-Jahrbuch*, 11 (1960), and "Das Gedicht," both included in the fourth, enlarged edition of *Erläuterungen zu Hölderlins Dichtung* (Frankfurt, 1971).

63. Within the scope of the present work it has not been possible to deal at length either with Heidegger's interpretations of Hölderlin, Rilke and other poets or with his views on art. Else Buddeberg's monograph, *Denken und Dichten des Seins—Heidegger/Rilke*, is an excellent introduction to both the thinker and the poet. In his widely read *The Disinherited Mind*, Erich Heller quotes Angelloz (*Rainer Maria Rilke*, 1936) as reporting a remark by Heidegger to the effect that "his philosophy is merely the unfolding in thought of what Rilke has expressed poetically"—which should be taken with considerable qualification. Heidegger's much greater closeness to Hölderlin is brought out illuminatingly in Beda Allemann's monograph, *Hölderlin und Heidegger*, and borne out by Heidegger's own statement (See "Wozu Dichter?" in *Holzwege*) that Rilke's poetry belongs to and expresses the realm of the truth of essents as it has unfolded itself since the consummation of Western metaphysics in Nietzsche; whereas Hölderlin, dwelling in the region of the manifestness of Being, is a harbinger and forerunner, a poet who overflows into the future and molds it.

Heidegger's views on art constitute a radical criticism of traditional aesthetics and are aimed at liberating the philosophy of art from the categories of metaphysics. The essay "Der Ursprung des Kunstwerkes," in which these views are developed, is equally important as marking a significant stage in the growth of Heidegger's own thoughts about World and Thing, Being and Truth. See Gadamer's introduction in the Reclam edition of this essay. In his thorough study of Kantian aesthetics (*Die Bedeutung von Kants Begründung der Aesthetik für die Philosophie der Kunst*), Walter Biemel has shown how 'aesthetics', when thought through to the end, is transformed into a reflection in which art emerges as a 'happening of truth', as Heidegger contends. The whole of Part I of Gadamer's *Wahrheit und Methode* is an elaboration of Heidegger's insights. See also Wilhelm Perpeet, "Heideggers Kunstlehre" and Walter Biemel, "Dichtung und Sprache bei Heidegger."

64. See Heidegger's "Preface" in Richardson's *Heidegger*, where the nature, the inherent necessity and the implications of the 'reversal' are explained at length. Heidegger again insists here, seeking to put an end to "the baseless and ceaseless prattle" about the 'reversal', that "the thinking of the reversal *is* a change in my thought. But this change is not a consequence of altering the standpoint, much less of abandoning the fundamental issue, of *Being and Time*." The basic question of *Being and Time*, far from being abandoned by reason of the reversal, is "fulfilled in a decisive manner in the thinking of the reversal."

65. Inevitably, for this reason, Heidegger's interpretations of past thinkers and of the 'basic words' of philosophy such as *aletheia, logos,* and *physis* have drawn the wrath of classical scholars, orthodox 'academic' philosophers and theologians alike. Only bare mention of a few names in this context can be made here: P. Friedländer and G. Krüger on the interpretation of *aletheia*, of Plato and of Greek philosophy in general; E. Cassirer and H. Levy on that of Kant; B. Liebrucks and van der Meulen on Heidegger's interpretation of Hegel; and W. Marx on that of Aristotle and Hegel; K. Löwith on that of Nietzsche. Heidegger has always acknowledged the 'correctness' of these criticisms but is yet, in a profound sense, left untouched by them. The 'hermeneutic' problem involved is too large to be dealt with here. But cf. Gadamer's comments (*Wahrheit und Methode*, pp. 472-473) on Löwith's criticism and on Heidegger's 'impatience' with philosophical texts. W. Marx's study of the relation between Heidegger and Aristotle (in *Heidegger und die Tradition*) is sympathetic and discerning. Equally valuable for an understanding of Heidegger's way of interpreting the pre-Socratic philosophers is the monograph by George Joseph Seidel entitled *Martin Heidegger and the Pre-Socratics*.

How far the sober, academic fields of classical scholarship, philology, and linguistic science and the interpretation of individual philosophers are themselves being slowly but profoundly influenced by Heidegger's ideas, it is too early to judge. But reference may be made, beside the writings of van der Meulen and Marx mentioned above, to the work of Johannes Lohmann in the field of linguistic science (articles in *Lexis*), that of Gadamer, Krüger and Szilasi on Plato (Cf. E. M. Manasse: "Bücher über Platon" I), of Dieter Henrich on Kant ("Über die Einheit der Subjektivität") and of Otto Pöggeler on the interpretation of Hegel's *Phenomenology of Mind*.

66. In this sense all essential thinking is reminiscent in nature (*Andenken*)

and all philosophical inquiry basically historical in character. As Heidegger explains (*Die Frage nach dem Ding*, p. 32f.; E.T., p. 44), this is so because the historical, as different from the past, is something that is still happening, even if to all appearances it has vanished into the past. What appears to us as such, as a happening or movement that is no longer in existence, may well be just a state of rest. The rest state of happening is not absence of historicity but a basic form of its presence. What is merely past does not exhaust the has-been (*Gewesene*). This is still with us and its mode of being is a peculiar quiescence of happening (*Geschehen*). . . . Rest is only arrested motion, often uncannier than the latter itself. To inquire historically is to set free and to set in motion again the happening that lies resting, frozen and confined, in a question.

67. Cf. *Der Satz vom Grund*, p. 86. Heidegger often uses "das Denken" as qualified in the above manner, to designate his own thought (much as Hegel speaks of *Wissenschaft*), that is, as the name for thought liberated from its metaphysical shackles and no longer conceived as 'philosophy', as it is on its way to a manifestation of its true nature in Heidegger's own thought. Because such thinking is concerned primarily with the truth of Being, and with that of the essent only from the perspective of the former, it is necessarily historical. As he explains in the "Letter on Humanism," Being is (*es gibt*) as its dispensation or destiny, the history of which finds expression in the great thinkers. Hence, the thinking concerned with the truth of Being is as such historical. There is no such thing as 'systematic' thought and beside that, as illustrating it, a history of past opinions. There is also no such thing, despite Hegel, as a system of thought which could make the principle of its thinking the principle of history and at the same time take it up into the system. More profoundly conceived, there is the history of Being, integral to which is thinking as the reminiscence (*Andenken*) of this history, a thinking which is brought to pass by this history.

68. *Merkur*, October 1969.

69. *Sein und Zeit*, p. 231 (E.T., p. 275).

70. Division I, chapter 5.

71. *Sein und Zeit*, p. 232 (E.T., p. 275).

72. Ibid., pp. 151, 323f. (E.T., p. 192f., 370f.).

73. See Heidegger's "Preface" in Richardson, *Heidegger*, p. xviii.

74. *Sein und Zeit*, pp. 310-316 (E.T., pp. 350-364).

75. *Kant und das Problem der Metaphysik*, p. 210 (E.T., p. 240f.).

76. On the concept of 'horizon', cf. Husserl, *Ideen* I, p. 48f.; Landgrebe, *Philosophie der Gegenwart*, pp. 66-67; Gadamer, *Wahrheit und Methode*, p. 332; H. Kuhn in *Philosophical Essays in Memory of Edmund Husserl*, pp. 106-123. Heidegger takes over this concept, transforms it and eventually, along with the 'transcendental' thinking of *Being and Time*, abandons it. For his later criticism of this concept, see *Gelassenheit*, p. 38f. (E.T., p. 63f.).

77. "Our provisional aim is the interpretation of time as the possible horizon for the understanding of Being in general."—*Sein und Zeit*, p. 1 (E.T., p. 19).

78. Heidegger actually speaks of "the topology of Being" in *Aus der Erfahrung des Denkens*, p. 23 (E.T., *Poetry, Language, Thought*, p. 12). Cf. also

"Zur Seinsfrage," *Wegmarken*, p. 240 (E.T., p. 85). It may be pointed out that the concept of *topos*, place or region, was not unknown to Kant. See *Critique of Pure Reason*, A 269, B 325. On this see Pöggeler's "Metaphysik und Seinstopik bei Heidegger" and "Heideggers Topologie des Seins"; also, *Der Denkweg Martin Heideggers*, pp. 280-299.

79. *Sein und Zeit*, p. 303 (E.T., p. 350).

80. Cf. *Was heisst Denken?*, p. 128f. (E.T., p. 211f.).

81. *Nietzsche II*, p. 133f.

82. Even in *Being and Time*, however, 'transcendental' is determined in terms of the existenzial ecstatic temporality of *Da-sein* and has nothing to do with the subjective consciousness. Cf. *Einführung in die Metaphysik*, p. 14 (E.T., p. 15).

83. *Gelassenheit*, p. 39 (E.T., p. 64).

84. *Der Satz vom Grund*, p. 111.

85. *Unterwegs zur Sprache*, p. 12 (E.T., *Poetry, Language, Thought*, p. 190).

86. Ibid., p. 178 (E.T., p. 74f.).

87. Ibid., p. 198 (E.T., p. 92).

88. *Sein und Zeit*, p. 230 (E.T., p. 272). The recently published *Phänomenologie und Theologie* (1970) contains two essays, of which the first ("Phänomenologie und Theologie") dates back to 1927 and the second (a "Letter" on the problem of nonobjectifying thinking and speaking in contemporary theology) was written in 1964. In the first, Heidegger speaks throughout of philosophy as a "science" (*Wissenschaft*). The second examines the notions of thinking, speaking, and objectifying, with full insight into the questionability of what he himself unquestioningly took for granted in 1927.

89. "Brief über den 'Humanismus'," *Wegmarken*, p. 194. See also *Zur Sache des Denkens*, pp. 61-80 (E.T., pp. 55-73).

90. Cf. the Introduction to "What is Metaphysics?"

91. *Nietzsche II*, p. 28.

92. *Vorträge und Aufsätze*, p. 83. Heidegger comes back to this notion of the "end" of philosophy in his great lecture, "Das Ende der Philosophie und die Aufgabe des Denkens" (*Zur Sache des Denkens*, pp. 61-65; E.T., pp. 55-59). The lecture seeks to provide an answer to two questions: "How far has philosophy entered into its end in the present age?" and "Which task is still reserved for thinking at the end of philosophy?" In regard to the first, Heidegger points out that "end" does not mean mere cessation but rather the completion (not perfection) of philosophy as metaphysics. "As completion, end is the gathering together in the most extreme possibilities . . . the end of philosophy means: the beginning of the world civilization based on western European thinking." In regard to the second he asks, "Does, however, the end of philosophy in the sense of its unfoldment in the sciences also mean the full realization of all the possibilities in which the thinking of philosophy was placed? Or is there for thinking, beyond those *extreme* possibilities (the dissolution of philosophy in the technified sciences) still a *first* possibility, from which the thinking of philosophy had indeed to take its rise but which, as philosophy, it could not expressly experience and take possession of? If this were the case, then in the history of philosophy, from its beginning to its

end, a task had to remain reserved for thinking in a hidden way—a task to which neither philosophy as metaphysics nor indeed the sciences deriving from it could have access."

93. *Was heisst Denken?*, pp. 105–109 (E.T., pp. 170–244).

94. Ibid., p. 128 (E.T., p. 211f.). From Plato onwards, throughout the history of Western metaphysics, thinking has been opposed to Being as its object. Hegel indeed identifies the two but he does this by assimilating Being to Thought, thus carrying modern subjectivism to its highest point. Heidegger, going back to the pre-Socratics, seeks to recapture the original unity of Being and Thought, which can still be glimpsed in them and to develop a conception of thought in which the latter is seen as an intrinsic aspect of Being itself. Heidegger says in a revealing passage, "In the apparently unimportant distinction between Being and Thought we must discern the fundamental position and attitude of the Western spirit against which our attack is really directed. This separation can be overcome only by going back to its *origin*, that is, in such a way that its original truth is placed within its own limits and established afresh." (*Einführung in die Metaphysik*, p. 89; E.T., p. 98f.). The conception of thought underlying traditional logic is based on a prior falling apart of thinking and Being since the time of Plato and to overcome that it is necessary to find our way back to the unity of their intrinsic togetherness. Such overcoming of logic, however, "does not mean an abrogation of thought and the domination of mere feeling; it means a more radical and stricter thinking, a thinking that appertains to Being." (Ibid., p. 94; E.T., p. 103.) See also *Identität und Differenz* for Heidegger's account of Being-owned thinking.

95. *Unterwegs zur Sprache*, p. 201 (E.T., p. 94).

96. Ibid., p. 227 (E.T., p. 146).

97. In the writings of the middle period, projecting and composing are used alternatively. Cf. *Einführung in die Metaphysik*, p. 110, (E.T., p. 121), where Heidegger points out that we come to know what man is not through a learned definition but only by the fact that he creatively comes to grips with the essent, through striving to bring it into Being, that is, when he provides it with limit and form, that is, projects something new (not yet present), that is, composes it originally, poetically (imaginatively) grounds it (". . . indem er es in sein Sein zu bringen versucht, d.h. in Grenze und Gestalt stellt, d.h. ein Neues [noch nicht Anwesendes] entwirft, d.h. ursprünglich dichtet, dichterisch gründet"). Manheim's translation of the sentence fails to bring out the synonymity of *entwerfen* and *dichten* in Heidegger's use, as also the fact that, according to Heidegger, through the imaginative project, we seek to let Being exhibit itself in its truth. There is here no suggestion of "creating original poetry."

98. *Nietzsche I*, p. 329.

99. Ibid., p. 582f.

100. *Erläuterungen zu Hölderlins Dichtung*, p. 38 and the entire essay "Das Gedicht," in the 1971 edition; see also Werner Brock, *Existence and Being*, pp. 304–305.

101. Cf. *Holzwege*, pp. 60–61 (E.T., *Poetry, Language, Thought*, pp. 73–74).

102. Ibid., p. 303.

103. As Werner Marx has remarked, "Mankind does remember a time when, in and through such an immediate saying and singing, the whole of a meaningful order arose out of the darkness that had shrouded all-that-is. In and through the mythical song the great and terrifying powers that formed and ruled the cosmos came to light and shone forth—in the brilliance of the beautiful and in the terror of the numinous" ("Heidegger's New Conception of Philosophy").

104. Cf. *Was heisst Denken?*, passim. In *Vorträge und Aufsätze* (p. 183f.), Heidegger remarks about this kind of thinking, "The thinking of Being as such corresponding is a very perplexing, mad affair and, in addition, meager as to results. But perhaps this way of thinking is yet an indispensable one, a way which does not intend to be a road to salvation and which brings no new wisdom. This way is at the most a field path, a path across a field, which does not merely talk of renunciation, but has already renounced the claim to be a binding doctrine and a universally valid cultural achievement or intellectual feat." For thinking as co-respondence, see also *Was ist das—die Philosophie?*, p. 32f. (E.T., pp. 69, 71).

105. Thinking is not something, Heidegger would say, that we do with language; it is language that, as it were, does the thinking with us. "It is language that speaks, not man," as he puts it in *Unterwegs zur Sprache*.

106. *Aus der Erfahrung des Denkens*, p. 15 (E.T., *Poetry, Language, Thought*, p. 8).

107. "An English Version of Martin Heidegger's *Being and Time*." In this detailed review of the English translation by Macquarrie and Robinson of Heidegger's masterpiece, Professor Wild points out a number of basic difficulties in *Being and Time*, difficulties that he traces back to Heidegger's 'error' in leaving undeveloped and confused the notion of *world* in this work. Despite the penetration of Wild's critical remarks and of his own constructive suggestions, one gets the impression that he is judging this work, first, in isolation from the rest of Heidegger's writings and, second, from a perspective that is alien to the author's aims as he himself understands them. (An earlier article of Wild's, juxtaposing Heidegger with Merleau-Ponty, gives some idea of what he is looking for in Heidegger. See "Man and His Life-World" in *For Roman Ingarden*.) The fundamental difficulty in the way of understanding Heidegger's thinking, it seems to be confirmed, comes neither from his language nor from the content of his particular thoughts; it arises, rather, from the demand on the reader to shed, or at least keep in suspension, his own preconceptions, and to keep on the track—which is more like walking on a tight rope, of which the gradient and direction are constantly shifting, than moving along firmly laid out rails—which his thought both builds for itself and follows. As Heidegger has remarked (*Identität und Differenz*, p. 13; E.T., p. 23), "It may happen that when our thinking, set into motion by some particular matter, pursues it, it undergoes a change on the way. In what follows, it is for this reason advisable to pay close attention to the way and not so much to the content." One may also refer to Heidegger's caution about 'way' in the closing paragraph of the epilogue to the lecture "The Thing" in *Vorträge und Aufsätze* (E.T., *Poetry, Language, Thought*, p. 186).

It has been maintained here that *Being and Time* is not to be read as a self-contained system but as a work of transition, "on its way" from the metaphysical thinking of the past to a new way of reflecting about Being—and this is true of Heidegger's thinking as a whole. *"Being and Time* means," as he has said (*Einführung in die Metaphysik*, p. 157; E.T., p. 172), ". . . not a book, but a task. What is truly a task is something we do not know and which, insofar as we genuinely know it, that is, as a task, we know only in asking." See also the illuminating, more elaborate, retrospective com-, ments on *Being and Time* in *Schellings Abhandlung über das Wesen der menschlichen Freiheit*, p. 229.

108. See "Brief über den 'Humanismus'," *Wegmarken*, p. 194; also "Nachwort" to "Was ist Metaphysik?," *Wegmarken*, p. 107 (E.T., p. 391).

109. *Sein und Zeit*, pp. 38-39 (E.T., p. 62).

110. Ibid., pp. 326-327 (E.T., p. 374).

111. *Die Sprache Heideggers*. The author of this work is a student of linguistic science as developed by Leo Weisgerber on lines indicated by Wilhelm von Humboldt. Schöfer has dealt principally with the language of *Being and Time* and other writings of that phase, though he has illuminating things to say about the language of the later writings also. Although his approach is linguistic, the author's principal aim is to throw light on Heidegger's thought in its intimate relation to his language and, in particular, to demonstrate that in addition to being an original thinker, he is also one of the few German philosophers (Meister Eckhart and Nietzsche, to whom may be added Hegel) who are also *Sprachschöpfer*, makers of language, who have creatively participated in developing the fabric of their mother tongue.

112. Such transformation into nouns is, as Justus Schwarz happily puts it in his essay, *Der Philosoph als Etymologe* (in *Philosophische Studien I*, 1949, quoted by Schöfer), "the trace which philosophical thinking leaves behind in a language."

113. *Die Sprache Heideggers*, p. 71. On Heidegger's word synthesis and word analysis and the importance of distinguishing the latter from his much disputed 'etymologizing', see pp. 103-117 of the same work. .

114. See *Sein und Zeit*, p. 165 (E.T., p. 209). Cf. also *Einführung in die Metaphysik*, p. 40f. (E.T., p. 43f.), where Heidegger refers to the deadness of the traditional grammatical forms which have become mere mechanisms and which constitute a steel net in which language and the study of language have been caught fast. Pointing to the necessity of a real revolution in our relation to language, he says, "It does not at all occur to us that what has been known to us so well and so long might be different, that these grammatical forms do not analyze and regulate language from all eternity as if they were something absolute, that they have grown up on the contrary, out of a very definite interpretation of the Greek and Latin languages," itself based on the fundamental view of Being guiding that interpretation. Heidegger points out further that "the determination of the essence of language, the very inquiry into it, is regulated at all times by the prevailing preconception about the essence or nature of essents and about the meaning of essence. But what essence and Being mean expresses itself only in language. . . . These grammatical forms do not suffice for what we are striving after." What is

required, Heidegger suggests, is an essential clarification of the nature of Being in respect of its intrinsic entanglement with the nature of language.

115. In an essay entitled, "Pragmatismus und Existenzphilosophie," reprinted in the volume *Die Wirklichkeit des Menschen*, pp. 52-54.

116. Heidegger has given, in his use, an unfamiliar sense to a large number of familiar words. This practice, bold and shocking though it must appear to contemporaries, has always been a major source of the creative shaping of language by the great philosophers. To the example from Aristotle mentioned by Lipps here, may be added Plato's use of *ousia* and *idea* and Aristotle's *kategoria*, equally radical departures from common usage.

117. Cf. "Zur Seinsfrage," *Wegmarken*, p. 233 (E.T., pp. 71, 73).

118. For examples of the way metaphysical concepts (as embodied in traditional terminology) crop up unawares, see "Zur Seinsfrage" and *Zu Einem Vers von Mörike*. The latter, an exchange of letters between Heidegger and Emil Staiger, is valuable for its discussion of 'appearing' and 'shining forth'.

119. "Heidegger und die Sprache der Philosophie," *Universitas*, 7, 1952, quoted in Schöfer, pp. 110, 115.

120. *Hölderlin und Heidegger*, p. 111.

121. Characteristically, Heidegger refers to Eckhart (*Vorträge und Aufsätze*, p. 175; E.T., *Poetry, Language, Thought*, p. 176) as "this master of thinking." Discussing a line from Angelus Silesius, Heidegger remarks (*Der Satz vom Grund*, p. 71), ". . . one is inclined to think that genuine and great mysticism is characterized by the utmost sharpness and depth of thought. And this in fact is the truth. Meister Eckhart testifies to it."

122. See Schöfer, p. 282 and elsewhere.

123. *Die Sprache Heideggers*, p. 24.

124. Ibid., p. 11.

125. Ibid., p. 280.

126. *Hebel—der Hausfreund*, p. 10. See also the essay entitled "Sprache und Heimat" (in *Dauer im Wandel*, Burckhardt *Festschrift*).

127. *Identität und Differenz*, p. 72 (E.T., p. 73).

128. *Unterwegs zur Sprache*, p. 227 (E.T., p. 146).

129. Cf. *Heidegger—Denker in dürftiger Zeit.*, p. 15.

130. Foreword to the French translation of "Was ist Metaphysik?," quoted in Schöfer.

131. In the essay mentioned in note 119 above.

132. See *Unterwegs zur Sprache*, p. 197 (E.T., p. 91).

133. "Brief über den 'Humanismus'," *Wegmarken*, p. 194.

134. An exhaustive study of Heidegger's prose style still remains to be made, despite Schöfer's book. The style of "Phänomenologie und Theologie," written in conventional scholarly prose, has little in common with that of *Being and Time*, although both were written during the same period. The prose of "Zeit und Sein" and "Kants These über das Sein" is very different from that of his speeches at Messkirch around the same time (for example, "Ansprache zum Heimatabend" and "Über Abraham a Santa Clara"). Class lectures like those on Nietzsche differ from formal compositions and lectures like "Was ist Metaphysik?" and "Der Weg zur Sprache."

As Hans–Georg Gadamer has said ("Der Denker Martin Heidegger" in *Die Frage Martin Heideggers*), "Heidegger is a master of thinking, of the unknown art of self-less thinking. This self-lessness is mirrored in his style, which shapes itself according to the matter seeking utterance, rather than being the expression of his own mind and 'personality'."

135. The above quotations are from the "Vorbemerkung" (1967) to *Wegmarken*, a collection of previously published essays, from "Was ist Metaphysik?" to "Kants These über das Sein."

II
Being and Time

The following account of *Being and Time* follows the order of exposition in that text. For this reason, no page references to quotations from the original are given; however, the corresponding sections in *Sein und Zeit* are indicated by numbers in brackets at the end of each discussion. In rendering Heidegger's terminology into English, I have derived valuable assistance from Walter Biemel's *Le Concept de Monde chez Heidegger*.

2
The Problem of the Meaning of Being

"Obviously you must be quite familiar with what you mean, when you use the word 'being', whereas we, who formerly imagined we knew, are now at a loss." This quotation from Plato's *Sophist*, with which Heidegger prefaces *Being and Time*, indicates the main theme of the work: to formulate afresh the problem of the meaning of Being, to awaken in us once more an understanding of the meaningfulness of the problem itself. The specific aim of the work, Heidegger tells us, is to explicate in concrete detail the problem of the meaning of 'Being' and its preliminary goal, the interpretation of Time as the possible horizon of all understanding of Being.

Necessity, Structure, and Preeminence of the Problem

The work begins with an introductory exposition of the problem of the meaning of Being. In the first of the two chapters that constitute the Introduction, Heidegger discusses the necessity, the structure and the preeminence of the question of Being.

Though today relegated to oblivion, the problem is not indeed a new one. Nor has it been just a peripheral problem in the history of philosophy. It stimulated the labors of Plato and Aristotle, but after them it has ceased to be the subject of real, thematic inquiry. What the Greeks achieved, even though in broken and preliminary fashion, continues to survive in philosophy in some form or other right up to Hegel's *Logic*. But since then a dogmatic prejudice has gradually developed so that the problem itself is not only now regarded as superfluous and trivial, but its neglect is sanctioned by the charge that 'Being' is the most universal and therefore the emptiest of all concepts. What was once the moving power behind the thinking of the Greeks has now become something obvious and crystal clear.

Objections are raised against an inquiry into the nature of Being on three counts. It is objected, first, that the concept of 'Being' is the most universal, as Aristotle[1] and Thomas Aquinas[2] long ago pointed out. However, this universality is not of the sort possessed by a genus, but transcends all generic universality, for which reason it was termed a transcendental in medieval ontology; even Aristotle recognized that the unity possessed by this type of universal was a unity of analogy. The labors of the medieval ontologists, particularly those of the Thomist and Scotist schools, though fruitful in many ways, have, however, hardly succeeded in clarifying the concept. Far from being the clearest, 'Being' remains the most obscure of concepts. Second, it is asserted that 'Being' is indefinable.[3] It is true that 'Being' cannot be defined, like beings (essents), *per genus et differentiam*; it cannot be derived from a higher concept, nor exemplified through lower ones. But from this it follows, not that 'Being' presents no problem, but only that 'Being' is itself not a kind of being or essent. Third, it is claimed that the meaning of 'Being' is obvious and self-explanatory, for in all cognitive acts and propositions, in all our dealings with other things and with ourselves we make constant use of terms like *is*, *was*, *am*, and others. But this apparent obviousness of the verb *to be* is only a screen for a deeper incomprehensibility which envelops it. The fact that we always have a certain understanding of Being, and that, nevertheless, the meaning of Being is shrouded in darkness, only goes to establish the necessity of raising again the problem of what 'Being' means. An analysis of the common and the obvious is precisely the business of the philosopher.[4]

[1]

The answer to any question requires that the question itself be properly understood and articulated. Heidegger, therefore, goes on to discuss the formal structure of the question of Being. Whenever we ask a question, we are seeking for something and this quest takes its direction from a preliminary awareness of what we are looking for—this is what the question is *about*. Then, the question is addressed to, or directed at, something—the *field* of the inquiry. Lastly, in every question there is a central *intention*, a target, the attainment of which sets the question at rest.

Accordingly, the question of Being must start, not with blank ignorance of what we are in quest of, but with some sort of vague and general understanding of what Being means. Such understanding, however shaky and blurred it may be, is, nevertheless, a fact. From this we must start, aiming at attaining full conceptual determination of what is thus vaguely apprehended, and to this we must return and attempt to explain, in the light of the clarified concept of Being, the nature of this vulgar, everyday understanding: its dimness, its indeterminateness, the ways in which it is darkened and overlaid with the theories and doctrines handed down by tradition. In raising the question about Being we must not forget that it is about Being and not beings that we inquire, for, as Heidegger insists, "the Being of the things that are is not itself a being." To realize this constitutes the first step in the understanding of the problem of Being and care should, therefore, be taken to see that we do not ask the question about Being, nor try to answer it, in terms that are adequate only in the realm of beings (essents).[5]

Further, since the question concerns the Being of things, we must direct the question to an essent, to something that is, and it must be such that we may read off the meaning of Being through its investigation. Which essent is preeminently capable of yielding this meaning? In answer, Heidegger points out that the asking of the question about Being is itself a mode of being of a particular kind of being or essent, and only of it, and hence the explication of this question necessarily involves an elucidation of this being, that is, man himself. "The asking of this question, as a mode of man's being, is itself determined by that which the question is about, that is, by Being." To emphasize this unique feature of man and his relation to Being, Heidegger uses for man the term *Dasein* (which in ordinary German usage means "being there" or "existence"), giving to it a new technical sense. An inquiry into the problem of Being must be preceded by an adequate explication of Dasein in regard to its Being and Heidegger claims that this undertaking is neither impracticable nor subject to a circular procedure, for we may well attempt to articulate the character of anything in respect of its Being, even before we are in full possession of an explicit and clear concept of Being itself.

[2]

Having dealt with the general structure of the problem of Being, Heidegger proceeds next to indicate the kind of preeminence possessed by this problem, both in an ontological and an ontic sense. To raise the problem of Being is for Heidegger no act of homage to a hallowed tradition or indulgence in the academic pastime of speculating about abstractions; it is rather to raise the most vital and concrete of all questions. On the basis of our common, prescientific experience we divide the totality of essents into a number of realms, such as history, nature, space, life, human life, language, etc., and the various positive sciences take them up as the fields of their own special research. But, as the present-day crisis in the conceptual foundations of mathematics, physics, biology, history and the cultural sciences, and of theology shows, a proper understanding of the metaphysical presuppositions or the ontological framework and the basic concepts of each of these sciences is of vital importance to their very existence. Such an inquiry is ontological in the widest sense because the different fields of knowledge are marked off from each other so that a particular class of essents may be distinguished and investigated in detail from the point of view of the sort of reality or Being manifested in it. For example, the metaphysically significant point in an inquiry into the nature of history is neither the process of concept formation in history, nor a theory of the historical process itself, but the interpretation of a mode of Being manifested by essents of a certain type considered in the aspect of their historicity. Similarly, the main thing achieved in Kant's *Critique of Pure Reason* is an ontological analysis of the realm of nature and not any kind of theory of knowledge.

The detailed investigations of the positive sciences, each confined to a particular region of the things that are, are termed *ontic* by Heidegger.[6] The study of the conceptual foundations, or absolute presuppositions, or the conditions of the possibility, of knowledge in this region is the corresponding ontological inquiry. These regional ontologies, however, themselves need something more fundamental to stand upon, that is, an explicit elucidation and formulation of what 'Being' itself means. "The question of Being is, therefore, aimed at an a priori determination of the conditions of the possibility, not merely of the individual branches of knowledge which investigate particular spheres of essents as such, but primarily of the ontologies basic to these ontic sciences themselves. Every ontology, articulated in however rich and rigid a system of categories, remains in the end blind and like a cart put before the horse, until it has adequately clarified, as its basic task, the meaning of Being." The ontological preeminence and fundamental character of the question is thus evident.

[3]

Ontically considered also this question is of the utmost importance. The pursuit of scientific knowledge is not the only mode of being of man, nor indeed the primary one. Man holds an exceptional position among all essents on many more counts. Man is not just one more essent among others; the ontic distinction of man is that for him, "in his being, his own being is at stake." The very structure of man's way of being contains in itself a reference to its own being and it is such that man always and already has some understanding of this being. "An understanding of Being is itself a feature of man's mode of being. Man's ontic distinctiveness consists in the fact that he *is* ontological," not in the sense that he constructs systems of ontology, but as possessing, just by virtue of being man, some understanding of Being.[7]

The Being with which man can, and in some way always does, stand in this relation or that, is called by Heidegger *existenz*. The essence of man cannot be described by giving a list of all his attributes and mentioning *what* he is; it consists rather in the fact that "man always has to be (realize) his being as his own." It is to convey this direct reference to Being, constitutive of the essence of man, that Heidegger uses the term *Dasein*. The way man understands himself has its source in his existenz, in a possibility of his own self to be or not to be his own self. Whether he realizes the possibility or misses it, is entirely subject to his own personal decision. The problems of existenz as it is factually (ontically) dealt with in concrete personal life is called *existenziell* by Heidegger, to be distinguished from an analysis of the ontological structure of existenz, for which the term *existenzial* is used. It is because Dasein is ontically existenziell that one can attempt an ontological analysis of its existenziality. Moreover, since the pursuit of science is itself a way of being of Dasein in the 'world', the ontologies which deal with realms of essents which *are* in a different way from man are themselves founded on and arise from the ontic structure of man himself. For these reasons, the fundamental ontology in which all the regional ontologies are rooted must itself be based on the existenzial analysis of Dasein, enjoying as it does a privileged position among essents. The ontic preeminence of the problem of Being is thus sufficiently demonstrated.

It was shown earlier that an elucidation of the problem of Being requires a prior analysis of the ontological structure of Dasein, and now we see that the ontic-ontological preeminence of the question of Being is rooted in the ontic as well as the ontological primacy of the human reality. From this Heidegger concludes that the ontological analysis of Dasein is itself the fundamental ontology we were looking for as basic to the problem of Being. The Dasein is not merely the field to which the question is addressed; it is itself the essent which already stands, in its own being, in the closest relation to that about which the question is asked. Hence, the problem of Being is nothing but a radicalization of a disposition inherent within human nature itself, a systematic conceptual development of the preontological understanding of Being which distinguishes man from all other kinds of essents.[8]

[4]

The Twofold Task of the Investigation

In the second chapter of the Introduction, Heidegger gives a statement of the twofold task involved in the explication of the problem of Being, and this is followed by an account of the method of inquiry adopted in this work and a brief outline of the structure of *Being and Time*.

The first task is the ontological analysis of Dasein as preparing the horizon or context for an interpretation of the meaning of Being. Although, as shown above, Dasein occupies a privileged position among all essents, both ontically and ontologically, this by no means implies that it is itself a transparent datum immediately accessible in its nature in either of the two senses. Dasein is ontically not only close to us—we ourselves *are* this reality. And yet, ontologically, man is farthest away from himself. His preontological understanding of his own being, which as Dasein he always has, is of no use in an ontological interpretation of Dasein, which by its very constitution tends to interpret itself in terms of the 'world' in which it exists and with which its own being is intimately linked. His own ontological structure remains veiled to man; he is "ontically nearest to himself, ontologically furthest, but preontologically not quite a stranger to himself."

The peculiar difficulties besetting an interpretation of Dasein are intrinsic to the very mode of its being. Although disciplines such as philosophical psychology, anthropology, ethics, politics, poetry, biography, and history provide us with rich and varied information about human nature, it is doubtful if they can be regarded as sources of knowledge as important existenzially as they undoubtedly are existenzielly. Existenziell explication is not the same as existenzial analysis. The analysis of Dasein is the principal task before us and the first problem to be dealt with is that of finding out and securing the guiding thread that will take us into the hidden structure of Dasein. We must not approach an interpretation of man dogmatically, with just any ready-made concept of Being and Reality, however self-evident it may seem to be, imposing upon it uncritically a pattern of 'categories' derived from such a concept. The approach and the manner of interpretation must be such that this essent can exhibit itself, from its own self, as it is in itself and that too, in its everyday aspect, as it generally and mostly is. We must next proceed to make explicit the characteristic structure of Dasein in its everyday aspect, so that the being of this essent may then be brought into relief.

Heidegger quite clearly states that the Analytic of Dasein is not intended to provide a full ontology of human nature as a basis for a system of philosophical anthropology. It is solely oriented towards a development of the problem of Being and makes no claim to exhaustiveness. Moreover, even the fragmentary Analytic undertaken here is to be taken as only provisional and preliminary, having for its aim a grasp on the being of man. The explicit interpretation of the meaning of this being can then follow, and this will require a repetition and amplification of the Analytic on the higher and proper ontological level again. It will be shown that the meaning of the being of Dasein lies in its *temporality*, and the provisional analysis of the structure of Dasein will have to be reinterpreted later in terms of temporal modalities. It will have to be shown that it is time which provides the basis for man's tacit understanding and interpretation of Being. This basis, or horizon, as Heidegger calls it, will have to be brought to light and conceptualized. And this can be achieved only by developing originally the notion of time as the horizon of an understanding of Being from the concept of temporality as the Being of Dasein. The new concept of time must at the same time be marked off from the vulgar notion of time which has been traditionally dominant from Aristotle down to Bergson. Finally, the new as well as the vulgar notions of time must both be shown to have their origin in the temporality of Dasein.

Time, in the sense of "being in time," has always functioned as a criterion for distinguishing the spheres of Being, for example the temporal from the eternal. Nature and the processes of history and human discourse are all characterized by temporality, whereas spatial and numerical relationships and the 'meanings' of sentences are said to be timeless. But how and why time has come to assume this preeminent ontological role has never so far been inquired into. Heidegger's aim is to show, on the basis of his study of the problem of the meaning of Being, how and why the central issue of all ontology is rooted in a correct grasp and an adequate explication of the phenomenon of time. Thus, the fundamental ontological task of the interpretation of Being as such includes in itself the working out of the temporality of Being so that the temporal character, not merely of essents, as "being in time," but of Being itself, is clearly brought into view.

[5]

Heidegger next proceeds to discuss the second task involved in the explication of the problem of Being. This is the task of a destruction of the history of ontology. What this means will become evident from the account that follows.

The meaning of man's being, as mentioned above, lies in his temporality, which is also the condition of the possibility of the historicity inherent in man's mode of existence. Man's historicity is prior to his 'being in history' and to what happens in the course of history, for it constitutes his very ontological structure. Man, oriented towards futurity, *is* his past; in the way he *is* at any time and in the way he understands himself, man is determined by the fact that he has grown up within a particular interpretation of human nature that has been handed down from the past. The way he understands himself is based largely on that, and this understanding in turn opens up to him the possibilities within his own being. His own past—and this means always that of his generation—does not follow upon man but is there already, preceding him.

The basic historicity of Dasein may remain hidden from man himself. But, on the other hand, it may also be glimpsed by him, and he may then try to preserve and to cultivate this discovery of what tradition has handed down to him by means of historical research. Such historical inquiry is possible only because man is determined by historicity in the very ground of his being. If, and so long as, this historicity remains obscured from his consciousness, all possibility of historical inquiry remains closed to him. But once his eyes are opened to his own essential historicity, he is bound to see that his questioning about Being is itself characterized by historicity. The analysis of the problem of Being is itself seen to have a history of its own, an awareness of which is essential for bringing oneself into full possession of the innermost possibilities inherent in the question through a deliberate assimilation of the past.

As will be shown later on, man in his natural and usual mode of being is subject to the tendency of forfeiting himself (*Verfallen*) to his world and of interpreting himself in terms of the world. He equally tends to become forfeit to his own tradition, grasped with more or less explicitness, so that in his questioning and choosing he is actually led by the tradition which holds him in its grip, even in regard to the ontological understanding rooted in his own being. Consequently, in handing over to us our heritage, tradition makes it so little available to us in reality that it may rather be said to veil it from our comprehension. This heritage becomes something taken for granted, and access to the original springs of tradition is blocked; the tradition itself prevents, as it were, a recall of its origins. This forfeiture of Dasein to tradition renders us oblivious of our historicity and deprives us of the most basic conditions which make possible a constructive approach to the past and a productive assimilation of it.

The basic concepts of Greek ontology live on, encapsulated, uprooted and taken for granted, throughout the Western philosophical tradition, hardening into systematized doctrine in the Middle Ages and passing over, in its scholastic phase, through the *Disputationes metaphysicae* of Suarez, into the 'metaphysics' and transcendental philosophy of modern times, right down to the *Logic* of Hegel, determining both its aim and its basis. But the original Greek way of conceiving Being, which is the continuous and implicit core and foundation of this tradition, has itself remained unquestioned and unexamined, fading into the light of common day and sinking into oblivion altogether. Hence, in raising this problem afresh it is necessary to bring to the surface and render transparent its own hidden history, and this is possible only through a loosening up of the hardened tradition and a peeling off of the layers of doctrine that it has deposited. This task of boring through the ontological deposit of the ages, by a sort of philosophical excavation, to the original Greek experience which gave rise to that basic conception of Being which became thenceforth definitive for the whole Western metaphysical tradition, this metaphysical archaeology is what Heidegger calls the *destruction* of ontological history by means of the guiding thread of the question of Being. He expressly warns here that this quest of the 'birth certificate' of the original ontological concepts must not be understood as a purely negative enterprise; its purpose is not to get rid of tradition but rather the positive one of uncovering the possibilities and limits inherent in each of the principal stages of ontological history.

Heidegger gives here a brief sketch of the main stages in the history of ontology which were to be subjected to the 'destruction' in the unpublished second part of *Being and Time*. The main instrument for carrying out this operation is the question "whether and to what extent the interpretation of Being has been brought into connection with the phenomenon of Time" in the history of ontology.

The first and only philosopher who went a little way towards exploring the dimension of temporality in the ontological context was Kant, according to Heidegger. A close study of the chapter on schematism of the understanding in the *Critique of Pure Reason* will be helpful, he points out, in grasping Kant's theory of time and simultaneously enabling us to see why Kant was prevented from attaining full insight into the nature of temporality. Kant neglected the problem of Being altogether and never attempted an analysis of the subjectivity of the subject, that is, an ontology of Dasein, on which he remains wholly dependent on Descartes. Secondly, in spite of his 'subjectivization' of time, his conception of the latter is based entirely on the traditional vulgar notion of time. For these reasons, he completely missed seeing the connection between time and the 'I think' (*ego cogito*).

Although Descartes claimed to provide a firm basis for philosophy with his *cogito sum*, yet even his supposedly radical start leaves unexamined the mode of being of the *res cogitans* or, more precisely, the ontological sense of *'sum'*. The second stage in the 'destructive' digging for the origins would thus be an inquiry into the ontological basis of *cogito sum*. Further, Descartes takes over the central conception of medieval ontology in his view of the *res cogitans*, which as *ens* is *ens creqtum*, as opposed to God who alone is uncreated. This view of the creatureliness of all that is, is thus taken over uncritically by Descartes.

The far-reaching influence of medieval ontology on later philosophy can, however, be fully realized only when the meaning and limits of Greek ontology have been made clear. Such a study of the foundations of Greek ontology will show that the classical interpretation of the Being of the things that are (beings or essents) gets its orientation from the 'world' or 'nature' in the broadest sense and that it is indeed an interpretation in which Being is understood through Time. The clearest evidence of this is the determination of the meaning of Being as *parousia* or *ousia*, which has the ontological-temporal sense of 'presence'; here the Being of everything is conceived in terms of a particular temporal mode, namely, the *present*. Already, we find Parmenides taking *noein*—the simple awareness of something just there (*vorhanden*) in its pure givenness—as the guiding principle of his interpretation of Being. It has, like *legein*, the temporal structure of pure actuality or 'being in the present' of something. The essent is thus interpreted as having its being in pure presence or *ousia*.

Heidegger also promises a detailed exegesis of the chapter on Time in Aristotle's *Physics*, which, he says, may be chosen as distinctive of the basis and limits of the Greek science of Being. This treatise on Time is the first detailed exposition of this phenomenon that has come down to us, and it has in essence determined all later views of time. An examination of the Aristotelian view will show that Kant's theory of time also moves within the Aristotelian framework, which implies that Kant's ontological outlook remains basically Greek.[9]

[6]

The Nature of the Phenomenological Method

The statement of the two fold task in the explication of the problem of Being is followed by a detailed account of the phenomenological method of investigation adopted by Heidegger. This includes general remarks on the nature of "phenomenology," analyses of the concepts of *phenomenon* and *logos* and a preliminary exposition of his own notion of phenomenology.

The main object of the inquiry for Heidegger is, as we have seen above, the Being of beings (or of the things that are) and the meaning of Being as such in general. Since he is seeking to formulate the question itself afresh, no ready-made discipline such as ontology in the old narrow sense, nor the traditional methods of inquiry, can be unquestioningly taken over for the purpose. On the contrary, it is only from the compulsions factually inherent in the particular question and from the mode of treatment required by "the things themselves" that an adequate discipline or method can be built up. In his treatment of the fundamental problem of philosophy, namely, the problem of Being, Heidegger adopts the phenomenological method. *Phenomenology* means for him neither a particular 'standpoint' nor a particular 'trend' in philosophy but primarily a *method*, a method which is rooted in the nature of the facts themselves, rather than a technical tool which may be applied generally without regard to the subject matter in question. Its motto is "to the things themselves," as against all fanciful construction and lucky finds, as against the adoption of concepts which are only seemingly evident, as against pseudo-problems which pass, through generations, for genuine questions. Taking his clue from the fact that the expression 'phenomenology' is derived from two Greek terms, *phainomenon* and *logos*, Heidegger goes on to offer a valuable analysis, first, of the concept of phenomenon and then, of the concept of *logos*.

The Greek word *phainomenon* is derived from the verb *phainesthai* which means "show oneself," "come to light." It, therefore, signifies "what shows itself," what makes itself manifest as it is in itself, what stands revealed or what can be brought into the light of day—which Greeks sometimes identified simply with *ta onta*, the things that are. What *is*, an essent, can show itself in various ways; it can even show itself as what it is not in itself. In showing itself in this manner, the essent 'looks or seems like. . . .' This is seeming or illusion, appearing to be, something that in reality is not what it seems to be. *Phenomenon* thus has the double sense of 'appearance', one positive (showing itself) and the other negative (seeming). The two senses are logically interconnected, for only insofar as something claims to show itself, or to be a phenomenon, *can* it show itself as something that it is *not*. Hence the primary and original sense of 'phenomenon' is the positive one and the second (seeming) must be regarded as a privative modification of that.

Different from both these senses there is a third sense of 'appearance', which is logically unconnected with them—manifestation in the sense of *Erscheinung*. Signs, indications, representations, symptoms and symbols, for example, in showing themselves indicate or point to something that itself does not appear. In this sense appearance means, not showing itself, but the announcing of something that does not show itself or appear through something that does appear. It is thus a sort of not showing itself, but one which is different from the privative sense of appearance mentioned above. Not showing itself, it can also not *seem* to be. Yet, appearance in the sense of *Erscheinung* presupposes and is possible only on the ground of something that shows itself though it is itself not the *Erscheinung*. It is obvious, therefore, that the first, primary sense of phenomenon as showing itself or appearing is the basic one.[10]

The main purpose of Heidegger's elaborate analysis of the ambiguities of phenomenon, appearance, and other related terms (exemplified in Kant's use), is to bring out the basic sense of 'showing or exhibiting itself', so that all the other senses may be seen to be derivative and definable in terms of this fundamental meaning of phenomenon. But, as he points out, 'showing itself as it is' defines only the *formal* sense of the term, which may find application either in the *vulgar* or common usage of the term (as, for example, when sensible things, or essents are described as phenomena), or in the proper *phenomenological* usage. For example, Kant's space and time, which, though themselves a priori forms under which the manifold of sense is grasped, may be made 'to show themselves' and become phenomena in this usage.

In his discussion of the concept of *logos*, Heidegger begins by pointing out that in Plato and Aristotle this concept has a variety of meanings which they never reduce to a common denominator. If we say that the basic meaning of *logos* is speech we must go on to indicate what speech itself is. Its plain and simple meaning remains completely hidden from view when *logos* is translated, and this always means interpreted, as reason, judgment, conception, definition, ground, or relation and then explained in terms of these. *Logos* as speech, according to Heidegger, means rendering manifest the thing spoken about. This is what Aristotle means by describing the function of speech as *apophainesthai*, letting something be seen, letting what is spoken about come to light.[11] In speech as *apophansis*, what is said fulfills its function in making manifest, thus rendering available for oneself and others, that about which it is said. *Apophansis* finds its concrete embodiment in actual uttered speaking. It is only because *logos* has this apophantic function of showing forth or exhibiting that it can have the structural property of *synthesis*, which primarily consists, not in the joining together of ideas in a judgment, but in letting something be seen *as* something, in this togetherness.

Further, it is because *logos* is a 'letting something be seen' that it can be true or false. The truth of the apophantic *logos*, its *aletheia*, consists in taking out of its hiddenness that which is spoken about so that it reveals itself and lets itself be seen in its truth or uncoveredness—in 'dis-covering' it. Similarly, falsity consists in covering up, masking something, so that it is seen as something that it is not. And just because 'truth' means 'dis-covering' and because *logos* is a particular mode of 'letting something be seen', we must not speak of *logos* as the locus of Truth. In ascribing to Aristotle, as is sometimes done, the doctrine that truth resides in judgment, we not only do injustice to him but thoroughly misunderstand the Greek concept of truth. In the Greek sense, truth resides basically in *aesthesis*, the pure sensible taking in or perception of something (*vernehmen*). 'True' in the purest and most original sense, that of discovering, is the pure *noein*, the straightforward perceptual awareness of the simplest sense qualities and "determinations of the Being of the things that are as such." Such awareness can neither mask itself nor be false, but at the most remain uncognized.

Gathering together the results of the foregoing analyses of *phenomenon* and *logos*, Heidegger formulates the meaning of phenomenology as the *legein* (speaking, laying out, exhibiting), that is to say, the *apophainesthai* of the *phainomena*—"letting that which shows itself, just as it shows itself by its own self, be seen from its own self." This formal sense of the term amounts to the same as expressed by the maxim, "To the facts themselves!" But, as pointed out earlier, phenomenology, unlike all other "logies" (such as theology), does not have reference to any particular subject matter of which it is the science, but indicates only the *how* of treating whatever may be studied by this science. Phenomenology is a science *of* phenomena in the sense that it grasps its objects and treats them in such a way that they are directly exhibited and demonstrated, ruling out all determinations that cannot be directly validated.

This formal concept of phenomenology must next be 'deformalized' to yield the phenomenological concept, and the latter must be distinguished from the vulgar. What sort of phenomena does phenomenology aim at bringing to light? What is a phenomenon in the preeminent sense? Heidegger's answer: What by its very nature necessarily demands being expressly 'shown forth' obviously can only be something that precisely does *not* generally show itself at the first glance, but rather remains hidden from view, in contrast with what mostly does show itself directly. Of course, this hidden something must be such that it bears an essential relation to what is patently self-exhibiting, something that in fact constitutes the real significance and ground of the latter. What can thus remain hidden, or lapse back into covertness, or show itself deceptively, is indeed not any particular essent, but the Being of the things that are. Phenomenology is the proper way of approach to problems which ontology claims as its own. In fact, ontology is possible only in the form of phenomenology, for the phenomenological notion of phenomenon (what shows itself) refers to the Being of beings (essents), its meaning, its modifications and derivatives. This notion of phenomenon implies, moreover, that there is nothing further 'behind' it, though it is always possible—hence precisely the need for phenomenology—that what may become a phenomenon should remain hidden and submerged. The opposite of phenomenon, in this sense, is not 'noumenon', as Heidegger says with pointed though tacit reference to Kant, but hiddenness or covertness.

The hiddenness of phenomena may be of various sorts. A phenomenon may never have come to light, may remain undiscovered; it may be lost from view, even after it has once emerged from hiddenness; it may be partially visible in a veiled manner, in the form of illusion. Further, the covering up may be due to chance or it may be inevitably bound up with the nature of the facts themselves. Phenomenological concepts stand in particular danger of the latter, because a notion that has come to life in the course of actual phenomenological investigation, when torn from this context and made common currency, hardens and degenerates into an empty phrase, losing its power to reveal and 'dis-cover'. Since phenomenology, in its concern with the 'originary' and 'intuitive' grasp and explication of phenomena, has nothing to do with "the naïveté of chance, sudden and unthinking visionary flashes," special care must be taken, methodologically speaking, to guarantee the proper starting point for the analysis, the access to the phenomena and the possibility of cutting through the coverings that overlay the phenomena.

The vulgar notion of phenomenon, as we have seen, is applicable to essents, and since it is from an essent that we must start in our quest for the Being of beings, it is the first task of phenomenology to secure the right 'entry' to the exemplary essent, the Dasein. Though in essence phenomenology is the science of the Being of the things that are, yet it must start, for reasons explained earlier, with fundamental ontology, that is, the analytic of Dasein. The significance of such an analytic or phenomenological description lies in the fact that it is essentially a kind of *interpretation*. Heidegger's description of the analytic of Dasein as hermeneutic, or science of interpretation, and his characterization of its relation to ontology and to philosophy in general are so important as to justify a full reproduction of what he says in this connection.

> The *logos* of the phenomenology of Dasein has the character of *hermeneuein*, through which the real meaning of Being as well as the basic structures of its own being are made known (or rendered explicit) to Dasein on the basis of the awareness of Being which already belongs to Dasein as such. The phenomenology of Dasein is hermeneutic in the original sense of the word, according to which it denotes the work of interpretation. But, inasmuch as it is through the disclosure of the sense of Being and the basic structures of Dasein that the horizon is at all

brought out for all further ontological investigation of essents other than human, this hermeneutic becomes at the same time 'hermeneutic' in the sense of a working out of the conditions of the possibility of every ontological inquiry. And, finally, so far as Dasein, as a being with the possibility of existenz, has an ontological priority over all other essents, hermeneutic obtains a specific third sense, which is philosophically the primary one, of an analytic of the existenziality of existenz. In this hermeneutic is rooted the 'hermeneutic' which is concerned with the working out, as the ontic conditions of the possibility of history, of the ontological implications of the historicity of Dasein. Such a study of the methodology of the historical sciences is hermeneutic only in a derived sense.[12]

Being as the basic theme of philosophy is not itself a class of beings, and yet it concerns every being. Its 'universality' is to be found on a higher level. Being and the structure of Being lie beyond every essent and every existing property of beings. Being is *transcendence pure and simple*. . . . Every disclosure of Being as transcendence is *transcendental* knowledge.[13] *Phenomenological truth (disclosure of Being) is* veritas transcendentalis.

Ontology and phenomenology are not two different disciplines belonging, among others, to philosophy. The two titles characterize philosophy itself according to its object and to its mode of treatment. Philosophy is universal phenomenological ontology, based on the hermeneutic of Dasein, which as the analytic of *existenz*, has tied fast its guiding thread to that from which it *takes its rise* and to which it finally *returns*.[14]

The elucidation of the preliminary concept of phenomenology indicates, Heidegger adds, that its essential character does not lie in its *actuality* as a trend in philosophy. Higher than actuality stands *possibility*. The right way to understand phenomenology is to grasp it in its possibility.[15]

[7]

Heidegger's Introduction concludes with a brief outline of the work as originally planned. Corresponding to the two principal tasks involved in the inquiry into the problem of

Being, the whole work was to be divided into two parts. Part One, dealing with the interpretation of Dasein by way of temporality and the explication of Time as the transcendental horizon of the problem of Being, was to have three divisions: the first containing the preparatory fundamental analysis of Dasein; the second on Dasein and Temporality; and the third on Time and Being. Part Two was to deal with the main features of a phenomenological destruction of the history of ontology, with the problem of temporality as the guiding principle. It was also to have three divisions: the first dealing with Kant's doctrine of Schematism and Time, as the first stage in the study of temporality; the second was to discuss the ontological foundations of the *cogito sum* of Descartes and his carrying over of the medieval ontology into the problems concerning the *res cogitans*; the third was to be a study of Aristotle's treatise on Time as distinctive of the phenomenal basis and the limits of Greek ontology.

It may be pointed out that the published part of this work contains only the first two divisions of the first part of the work as originally planned. *Being and Time*, as it is now before us, thus consists only of the Introduction and the first two divisions of Part One on "The Preparatory Fundamental Analysis of Dasein" and "Dasein and Temporality" respectively. In the following account, the first topic is dealt with in chapters 3 and 4 and the second in chapters 5 to 7.

[8]

Notes

1. Aristotle, *Metaphysica* B 4, 1001a 21.
2. Aquinas, *Summa Theologica* II 9492.
3. Pascal says, "We cannot undertake to define Being without falling into the same absurdity: for we cannot define a word without beginning with the word *it is*, either expressed or understood. To define Being therefore, it is necessary to say *it is*, and thus to employ the word defined in the definition." (Blaise Pascal, *Thoughts, Letters and Minor Works*, p. 426, Harvard Classics.)
4. Heidegger speaks here of the necessity of an 'explicit repetition (*Wiederholung*)' of the question about Being. For the concept of 'repetition', see chapters 1, 6, and 8. As he remarks in retrospect (*Unterwegs zur Sprache*, pp. 130-131; E.T., p. 36), "The apparently revolutionary intention (of his own thinking) seeks before anything else to win back what 'has been' in a still more radical form. On the very first page of *Being and Time*, there is deliberate mention of 'repetition'. This does not mean the uniform rolling

on of what is ever the same but to retrieve, recoup, gather together what lies hidden in the ancient."

5. Traditional metaphysics is concerned, Heidegger points out (*Einführung in die Metaphysik*, p. 14f.; E.T., p. 16f.) with the essent as such, that is, with beings in regard to their Being (conceived as *physis* by the Greeks). But the inquiry into Being as such is quite different in nature and origin from this. In the current sense, "the question of Being" signifies inquiring into the essent as such (metaphysics). But regarded from the standpoint of *Being and Time*, it means inquiring into Being as such. "The question of Being" in the sense of the metaphysical question regarding the essent as such just does *not inquire* thematically into Being. Being as such is just what remains hidden from metaphysics and lies so utterly in oblivion that this forgetfulness of Being, which itself falls into oblivion, is the unknown but constant impetus to metaphysical inquiry. Heidegger distinguishes between the *fundamental* question of Being from the *leading* question of metaphysics. See *Nietzsche* for an elaboration of this distinction.

6. Explaining the terms 'ontic' and 'ontological', Heidegger says, "The expression ontic, based on the Greek *to on*, the essent, signifies 'concerning the essent'. But the Greek *on*, the essent, involves its own essence or character of being an essent (*Seiendheit, ousia*) which by no means remains the same in the course of its history. . . . Ontological means the coming about of the gathering together of essents in respect of their character of being essents. Ontological refers to that reality which by its very nature stands within this history (that is, the history of Being which underlies ontology), going through that according to the way essents become unconcealed in it." ("Hegels Begriff der Erfahrung," in *Holzwege*, pp. 161-163; E.T., pp. 105-108).

7. This 'understanding' however, amounts to nothing more than a vague and general awareness and is by no means conceptually articulate. As Heidegger remarks (*Der Satz vom Grund*, p. 154f.), "It is no empty sound, when we speak of 'Being', when we say 'is'. We understand what we are talking about. At the same time, we are perplexed when we try to express, that is, to bring into view, *what* we think. We remain at sea when we seek to reach an agreement as to the historical identity of what we think about, despite the multiplicity of the ways in which it is conceived, experienced, and expressed. We are glad to sidestep this perplexity and escape into what is commonly believed. With the perplexity there is joined the failure to see that what we think, when using the word 'Being' and without having any thoughts about it, is the most thoughtworthy of all. The habitual and common way in which we understand and speak of 'Being' cannot, however, be criticized or dismissed as just a piece of negligence and carelessness. This habitual mode of our relationship to 'Being' is necessarily implied in the way in which, in the first instance and mostly, man, hanging around in the midst of essents, co-responds to the destiny of Being.". Such understanding, is not only an actual fact but is necessary. "Without opening up of Being we could not be 'human beings' at all. That we *are* is, of course, not absolutely necessary. . . . But once man enters into existence, it is a necessary condition of his being-there that he understand Being" (*Einführung in*

die Metaphysik, p. 64; E.T., p. 71). Man, as Heidegger was to say later, is the opening or clearing (*Lichtung*) of Being.

8. In *Kant und das Problem der Metaphysik*, where the problem of metaphysics is conceived as being a problem of fundamental ontology, Heidegger defines fundamental ontology as "that ontological analytic of finite human nature which aims at providing the basis for the metaphysics 'inherent in the nature of man'. Fundamental ontology is the metaphysics of man's Dasein as a necessary requisite for rendering metaphysics (as such) possible" (p. 13; E.T., p. 3f.). The problem of Being as raised in *Being and Time* is conceived by Heidegger at this stage as the basic problem of providing a foundation for metaphysics through a demonstration of the temporal character of the understanding of Being inherent in Dasein. The metaphysics of Dasein has for its aim the disclosure of the ontological structure of Dasein so as to lay bare the conditions of the possibility of an understanding of Being within Dasein, on which all express inquiry into Being is based. Such an inquiry is ontology because it investigates the being of Dasein and it is fundamental ontology because by exhibiting Dasein's understanding of Being, it provides the foundation of the possibility of metaphysics. But fundamental ontology is only the first stage of the metaphysics of Dasein which is always historically rooted in the factual *Dasein*. Fundamental ontology, motivated solely by the problem of Being as such, aims at the interpretation of Dasein as temporality; and it is inspired by the will to show that philosophizing is itself nothing but the transcendence of Dasein occurring in an explicit manner.

The "Introduction" to "Was ist Metaphysik?" explains why the terminology of fundamental ontology, employed in the earlier works, was later abandoned by Heidegger. "The inquiry which goes back into what lies hidden in the *on* is concerned thus, from the point of view of metaphysics, with the ground of ontology. Hence, the procedure adopted in *Being and Time* is called 'fundamental ontology'. But this title, like all terms in this case, was found to be inappropriate. To be sure, from the metaphysical standpoint it expresses what is correct; but just for that reason it is misleading. The important thing is to achieve the transition from metaphysics to recalling the truth of Being. So long as such thinking still conceives itself as fundamental ontology, it bars and obscures its own way. In other words, what this title tends to suggest is that the attempt to think about the truth of Being and not, like all ontology, the truth of beings, is itself a kind of ontology. Meanwhile, the thinking which seeks to recall the truth of Being by a return into the ground of metaphysics has, with the very first step, abandoned the whole sphere of ontology. On the other hand, every philosophy which attempts to represent 'transcendence' directly or indirectly, necessarily remains ontology in a real sense, whether it tries to build a foundation for ontology or whether it claims to reject ontology as a conceptual petrification of the immediacy of experience."

9. Heidegger points out in retrospect (Cf. *Nietzsche II*, p. 415) that at this stage the 'destruction', like 'phenomenology' and the hermeneutic-transcendental type of inquiry, is not yet conceived in terms of the history of Being. As he explains later (Cf. *Was ist das—die Philosophie?*, pp. 33-34; E.T.,

pp. 71, 73), the term 'destruction' is meant not in the sense of a break with history, a denial of it, but rather as the assimilation and transformation of its legacy. 'Destruction' does not here mean destroying but pulling down and clearing away the merely historical (*historischen*) assertions about the history (*Geschichte*) of philosophy. Destruction means opening our ear, making it free for what addresses itself to us in our heritage as the Being of what is. (Cf. also "Zur Seinsfrage," *Wegmarken*, p. 244f.; E.T., p. 43.)

10. Cf. Heidegger's discussion of being, appearing, and seeming in his account of the Greek view of Being (*Einführung in die Metaphysik*, pp. 75-83; E.T., pp. 83-98).

11. Aristotle, *De Interpretatione*, chapters 1-6; *Metaphysics Z 4*; *Nicomachean Ethics Z*.

12. As mentioned in chapter 1, the term 'hermeneutic' was dropped by Heidegger after *Being and Time*. In the "Dialogue on Language" (*Unterwegs zur Sprache*, p. 121f.; E.T., p. 29f.), he explains the reasons for doing so and also how he wants the term to be understood now: *hermeneuein* as listening to and bringing a message. The essence of the hermeneutic relation between man and Being is Language.

13. From the standpoint of his later phase, Heidegger comments on this statement about Being as sheer transcendence as follows ("Brief über den 'Humanismus'," *Wegmarken*, 167-168): "Just as the openness of spatial nearness transcends every near and distant thing, from the point of view of the latter, similarly, Being is by its very nature farther than all that is, for it is the clearing, the openness itself. Besides, in accordance with the at-first-unavoidable starting point in the prevailing metaphysical way of thinking, Being was conceived from the perspective of the essent. Only from such a point of view does Being show itself in a transcending and as that. The introductory determination of Being as sheer transcendence recapitulates in a simple statement the way in which the essence of Being hitherto dispensed itself to men. This backward-looking determination of the nature of Being remains indispensable for the forward-thinking attempt to raise the question about the truth of Being. . . . But whether the determination of Being as pure transcendence adequately describes the simple nature of the truth of Being is of course the main problem for a thinking concerned with the truth of Being."

14. Heidegger's quest for the phenomenon must not be understood, as his treatment of the preliminary conception of phenomenology here might suggest, in the Platonic, Kantian, or Husserlian sense of a search for eternal, universal, formal essences and structures. As Otto Pöggeler has pointed out (in the article "Sein als Ereignis"), "When in *Being and Time* Heidegger unearths a structure, it appears at first to be a phenomenon in the sense of Kant's 'condition of the possibility of experience' or of Plato's *eidos*. The preliminary concept of phenomenology, as Heidegger develops it at the beginning of *Being and Time*, is sure to give the false impression that Heidegger's investigations are eidetic investigations like those of Husserl's phenomenology. But any one who understands *Being and Time* in this sense must feel himself banged on the head when (he comes to) a statement of Count Yorck which Heidegger cites in this work: because of the inner

historicity of self-consciousness, a 'systematic' treatment in isolation from history is bound to be inadequate. The purely 'systematic' aspect of method must be supplemented by the temporal or historical aspect as it emerges only towards the end of *Being and Time*. The essence (*Wesen*) or phenomenon which concerns Heidegger is never a timeless entity or meaning but essentially process (*wesen*, understood as a verb), the historical unfolding of the truth of Being."

15. These remarks on phenomenology are again quoted by Heidegger at the end of "Mein Weg in die Phänomenologie." Along with "Das Ende der Philosophie und die Aufgabe des Denkens," this essay may be read as a commentary, from the perspective of his later thinking, on what he says here. These essays (both in *Zur Sache des Denkens*) explain how and why Heidegger later abandoned the notion of phenomenology as a "method," along with the whole conception of philosophy as a "science," without, however, relinquishing what was most significant in phenomenology: the call, "To the thing itself" (*"zur Sache selbst"*). What phenomenology is in its possibility, Heidegger seeks to realize in his practice by way of inquiring into "What remains unthought in the cry, 'To the thing itself'." See also the "Dialogue on Language" in *Unterwegs zur Sprache*, passim, and the "Preface" in W. J. Richardson, *Heidegger*.

3
Man and World

Division one of *Being and Time* contains six chapters and is devoted to the preparatory fundamental analysis of Dasein. This chapter presents an exposition of the first four of these and deals, respectively, with the following topics: the nature of the task; being-in-the-world in general; the concept of the world; being-with, self-hood, and everyman. Being-in as such and care as the being of Dasein, topics dealt with in chapters 5 and 6 of this division, are taken up in the next chapter of the present work.

The Nature of the Task

In his exposition of the task of a preparatory analysis of Dasein, Heidegger sharply differentiates the Dasein's mode of being from that of things that are simply present in the world. In contrast with them, Dasein possesses two distinctive features. Firstly, Dasein is not a 'thing' whose nature can be exhausted by stating its essence (the *essentia*, the 'what'); its reality consists rather in the fact that it has to be. "The 'essence' of Dasein lies in its existenz."[1] Hence, its characteristic features are not to be described in terms of 'properties' or qualities possessed by objectively present (*vorhanden*) things, but are solely to be thought of as possible ways in which Dasein has to be. The term Dasein is thus meant to signify, not the 'what', as house, tree, and others do, but the 'that', the way in which it is. Secondly, Dasein is characterized by ipseity, 'my-ownness'.[2] In the case of things that are just there, their own being is of no concern to them. For Dasein, on the contrary, its own being is at stake. Man has always 'to be', he *is* his possibility or, as Heidegger puts it, "he is related to his being as to his very own possibility." The choice of what he is to be is unavoidably his own, he can and must choose himself in his very Being, win himself or lose himself, have an authentic mode of being or an inauthentic one.

From the above considerations it follows that the ontological interpretation of Dasein must be developed out of the existenziality of its existenz and that, too, not from any special mode of its existence but from its indifferent everyday aspect. This 'indifference' of the everyday mode of existence, its *averageness*, is a positive characteristic of man, and on it alone can an ontology of human nature be built up. Just because this characteristic is ontically the 'first and foremost' which Dasein mostly exhibits, it is always passed over, for "the ontically closest and most intimate is ontologically the farthest, the least known and, in its ontological significance, the most frequently overlooked." It is just through a consideration of what is ontically the *ordinary*, everyday mode of man's existence that his deepest ontological structure can be discovered.

The concepts through which the being of Dasein is to be described are called by Heidegger "existenzials" because they are generated from a consideration of the structure of man as existenz. They must be sharply distinguished from "categories," the application of which Heidegger restricts solely to the description of essents other than human. Greek ontology was developed on the basis of an interpretation of Being for which essents as we encounter them in the world were the model, and the categories were the a priori determinations of the Being of such essents. Man's being is, however, of a different order, as we have seen, and is characterized by existenz. The a priori determinations of existenz are the existenzials. An essent is either a *who* (existenz) or a *what* (just being present as object); the being of the former is describable in terms of existenzials, that of the latter in terms of categories.

The existenzial analytic of Dasein aimed at by Heidegger is something quite different from anthropology, psychology, and biology, each of which attempts, in its own way, to give an account of man. However valuable these sciences may be, they do not and cannot answer the basic philosophical question as to what man truly is. In its philosophical aspect, the problem was raised by Descartes when he made the *cogito sum* the starting point of philosophy. But though he dealt, to a certain extent, with the *cogitare* of the *ego*, he has nothing whatever to say, Heidegger points out, about the *sum*. The analytic of Dasein is concerned just with the being of this *sum*; only when this is determined can we say anything about the mode of being of the *cogitationes*. Moreover, in starting with the 'I' or the subject as something given, Descartes completely misses the phenomenal complexity of what *is* given, the Dasein. Further, "every idea of a 'subject', however carefully safeguarded ontically against the assumption of a soul substance or the reification of consciousness, necessarily involves the ontological assumption of a *subjectum* (or *hypokeimenon*)." Unless the notion of a 'thing' is itself clarified as regards its ontological origins, it is impossible to attach a positive meaning to the being of 'subject', 'soul', 'consciousness', 'spirit', 'person', and others, even when they are acknowledged to be no 'things'. Hence, these terms, along with 'life' and 'man', are avoided by Heidegger in thinking about the being that we ourselves are.

The philosophy of life (*Lebensphilosophie*), as represented by such thinkers as Bergson, Dilthey, Scheler, and in a sense Husserl,[3] does indeed show an implicit tendency to grapple with the being of Dasein, though, remarkably enough, it never raises the question of the ontological sense of 'Life' itself. Wilhelm Dilthey, in his attempts to grasp the significance of life experiences (*Erlebnisse*) from the totality of that life itself, was on the way to this question, but he never succeeded in explicitly formulating what he dimly perceived. Even the much more fundamentally radical and penetrating phenomenological investigations of personality made by Husserl and Scheler do not go far towards an elucidation of what the *being* of a person consists in. Neither Scheler nor Husserl goes beyond the purely negative characterization of a person as not a thing, substance or object, as not being merely psychological or even a mere subject of rational or intentional acts.[4]

What really blocks the way to a new formulation of the problem of the being of Dasein is the Greek-Christian philosophy of man, and neither Personalism (Scheler) nor Life-philosophy (Dilthey) takes note of the inadequate ontological foundations of that philosophy. This traditional theory of human nature has two aspects. Firstly, it defines man as *zoon logon echon*, the rational animal. The mode of being of the *zoon*, however, is taken as that of something objectively present (*vorhanden*), and the way of being of the *logos* remains as obscure as when they are both taken together. The other element in the traditional theory is theological in character, originating from the Biblical statement, "And God said, let us make man in our image, after our likeness." (Genesis 1 : 26.) Christian theology combines this with the Greek definition of man and formulates its conception of the being of man as the *ens finitum*, like its conception of God, on the basis of Greek ontology. In modern times the Christian definition was de-theologized, but the idea of the 'transcendence' of man, as a being who reaches out beyond himself, has remained. But in all this the problem of the *being* of man remains unnoticed; as in the case of all created things, this being also is understood as something objectively present. And the same is true of those modern theories of man which start with the *res cogitans* or consciousness or the system of 'life experiences' (Dilthey), so long as the way in which they *are* itself remains unexamined and they are taken as something obvious and ultimately 'given'.[5]

[10]

It hardly needs to be added that modern psychology and biology give us as little information about the being of man—though ontological presuppositions are necessarily implicit in all their empirical accounts—as we have found to be the case with philosophical anthropology above. Ethnology and the study of primitive life are similarly guided in the selection, classification, and interpretation of the facts they discover by tacit ontological presuppositions about human nature on which they themselves can throw no light.

[11]

Being-in-the-world

Heidegger takes, as the most suitable starting point for the analytic of Dasein, the explication of the fundamental constitution of this essent as *being-in-the-world*. As the hyphenated expression suggests, this should be viewed as a unity of which the elements are indissolubly linked together, so that if we consider any one of them the others are necessarily implied. The three elements which comprise this single phenomenon are 'in the world', the essent which has this mode of being and 'being-in' as such. Heidegger discusses these constituents of the basic structure of Dasein—the ontological structure of 'world' and the nature of mundaneness, the 'who' of this essent in his average everyday character and the ontological constitution of 'in-ness' itself—in three separate chapters. Before undertaking this, he gives a preliminary analysis of the concept of being-in or in-ness.

What do we mean when we say that something "is *in* . . ." ? Obviously, the 'in' here characterizes the mode of being of an essent which can be 'in' another in the way water is in a glass or clothes are in a wardrobe and so forth. These are all things which have the mode of being *vorhanden*, of things which present themselves as objects within the world. The 'in' characteristic of them is one of the ontological features called *categorial* above, features which belong to essents other than those of the nature of Dasein. Being-in or in-ness, on the contrary, must be understood as an *existenzial*, constitutive of Dasein, and not as referring to a type of relation subsisting between two *vorhanden* objects. Heidegger even adduces etymological evidence to show that the existenzial sense of 'in', as compared to the categorial, is the more original one. 'In' originally does not connote a spatial relation between two simply given things at all but derives from 'innan', dwelling, *habitare*. Being, as the infinitive of 'I am' understood existenzially, means dwelling with, being familiar with. Being-in is thus "the formal existenzial expression for the being of Dasein, which has being-in-the-world as its essential constitution."[6]

In order to exemplify one aspect of the ontological structure of Dasein, Heidegger chooses existing in the world, being with it (*sein bei*), as an existenzial deriving from being-in. It is important, he says, to consider closely such commonplace phenomena of experience in order to be able to *see* the basic ontological features of our existence, features that can never be adequately brought to light so long as we remain confined to the traditional ontological categories. Existenzially considered, the intimate way in which Dasein lives *with* the world, by it, never means anything like the being together of two *vorhanden* things. Dasein and World are not two things juxtaposed together, in the way we speak of a table standing by the door or a chair touching the wall. In a case like the latter, one cannot speak of a 'touching' at all, not because on closer inspection we can always find empty space between the chair and the wall, but because the chair cannot in principle touch the wall, even if there were no empty space between the two. Such touching would be possible only if the wall were something 'for' the chair, which it could encounter in the world. "An essent (man) can touch another essent presenting itself within the world only if by its very nature it has in-ness as its own mode of being—if by its very being there (*Da-sein*) it has such a thing as world disclosed to him, out of which essents can manifest themselves to him through touch and thus become accessible in their objective presence." Two entities, each *vorhanden* in the world but neither 'having' a world, can neither 'touch' nor be 'by the side of' each other.

This is, of course, not to deny that Dasein has its own way of being *vorhanden* in the world. But this matter-of-fact presence of Dasein must be distinguished ontologically from the factuality of a piece of stone. The former is termed by Heidegger the *facticity* of Dasein, to be discussed in greater detail later on. Similarly, though being-in as an existenzial must be distinguished from internality or within-ness as a category, this does not mean that Dasein possesses no 'spatial' character. Dasein, in fact, has its own 'being-in-space' which in turn is ultimately possible only because of its being-in-the-world. "Only when we understand being-in-the-world as the essential structure of Dasein can we have an insight into the *existenzial spatiality* of Dasein."

The being-in-the-world of Dasein manifests itself, owing to the latter's facticity, in various ways of being-in, such as having to do with something; producing, cultivating, and fostering something; using or giving up something. All these ways of being-in, including their *deficient* modes (having nothing to do with, omitting, neglecting, and so forth), are ways of being which Heidegger terms 'taking care', concern or preoccupation (*Besorgen*). Understood in its ordinary usage it may mean executing something, providing or apprehending something (take care -that, -of, -for). This ontic usage is distinguished by Heidegger from its technical ontological use to signify the way of being of any possible being-in-the-world. *Care*, it will be explained later, is the very being of Dasein as ontologically understood. It is because being-in-the-world is an essential character of Dasein that its being for the world is in essence 'caring'. Heidegger points out, however, that this 'being-in' should not be understood as a 'property', which Dasein may or may not have. Dasein can, on the contrary, relate itself to the world in one way or another only because in its very nature it is constituted by being-in-the-world. Similarly, what present-day biology says about man's *having* a world or possessing his environment can be explained ultimately only on the presupposition of Dasein's ontological structure as being-in-the-world.

Being-in has so far been characterized in negative terms. But this predominance of negative characteristics is not just by chance; it points to a peculiar feature inherent in the phenomenon and is thus something positive in a real sense which is appropriate to the phenomenon itself. For Dasein itself, being-in is a phenomenon that is always in certain fashion 'seen'. But because mostly it is misinterpreted or inadequately understood it becomes the negative task of phenomenological analysis to remove these misinterpretations and inadequacies. The main thing that veils the phenomenon from view is the fact mentioned earlier that man tends to understand his own self ontologically in terms of the essent, which he himself is not but which he first and mostly encounters within the world. Man, instead of recognizing being-in as his own ontological structure, thinks of it as a 'relation' between one entity (world) and another (soul). Hence, "although Dasein always has a certain prephenomenological acquaintance with it, its being-in-the-world remains *invisible*, owing to an inadequate ontological interpretation." This latter is generally given in terms of the subject-object relation, on the basis of which the entire structure of a theory of knowledge is then built up.

[12]

The 'relation' between man and world cannot be defined in terms of 'knowledge' of an object by a subject, because knowing is itself one mode of Dasein's being-in-the-world and thus presupposes the latter. So long as knowing is not recognized to be itself a mode of being in and toward the world, all kinds of insoluble problems arise as to how a subject, possessing its own inner sphere of immanence in which knowledge is supposed to reside, can transcend this inner sphere and reach out to the object.[7] As against all such phenomenally unprovable constructionistic approaches, therefore, we must start with Dasein's already being-in-the-world as constitutive of its being. Dasein's being-in-the-world, however, is not in the first instance a kind of "fixedly staring at something purely *vorhanden*," as Heidegger expresses it, but involves being wholly absorbed into the cared for world. There must be a lack in the preoccupied having-to-do-with the world, a suspension of the active, interested attitude, to make it possible for man to have a purely cognitive relation to the world, so that an essent he encounters within this world can show itself to him in its pure *eidos* or look.

Such looking at things, in a kind of 'dwelling upon' them, is what is meant by the perception of *vorhanden* things. In our calling something, or talking about it, *as* this or that thing, perception finds its culmination; such talk or judgment, like perception, is a way of Dasein's being-in-the-world and not just a process going on 'within' a subject. Dasein is not shut up within its inner sphere to begin with and then going out of itself in the act of perception; in its very mode of being it is ever 'outside', in the midst of essents within a world which from the beginning stands disclosed to it. Similarly, perception of an object does not mean that Dasein, so to speak, goes out of its lair hunting for the object and afterwards returns to the cabinet of its consciousness with its knowledge as a kind of booty, as Heidegger graphically puts it; even in merely thinking of an essent or imagining it we are as much 'outside' ourselves as in original perceptual knowledge. Knowledge thus is a mode of Dasein's being, founded on its being-in-the-world. "Knowing does not itself *produce* a *commercium* of the subject with a world, nor does it *arise* from an action of the world upon a subject."[8]

[13]

The Concept of the World

Having given a preliminary analysis of 'being-in', Heidegger proceeds with the task of discussing in detail each of the three elements comprised in being-in-the-world, beginning with an ontological analysis of 'world'. In what does the worldliness (or 'worldishness', as Magda King suggests) of the world consist? What is the world? A description of the essents contained in the world and an account of events connected with them will not do, for "such a description remains stuck up among essents, it is ontic," whereas we are looking for the being of the world, as a phenomenon in the true sense, rather than the beings in the world. The things within the world are natural things and value-charged things, the latter themselves founded on the former. What is the being of natural things, of nature? What is the ontological significance of the substantiality of natural substances? Even these questions, says Heidegger, though in fact ontological, do not bring us nearer the 'world', for nature itself is an essent within the world. And so also are the things charged with value. Hence, neither the ontic description of intramundane essents, nor the ontological interpretation of the being of these essents get at the phenomenon of 'world'. 'World' is ontologically speaking not at all a name for essents of the other than human type but a character of Dasein itself. Worldliness is an ontological concept forming a constitutive element of being-in-the-world, which we have seen above to be an existenzial character of Dasein.

The word 'world' has four senses, Heidegger points out, which must be kept distinct. Taken in an ontic sense it means the totality of essents *vorhanden* within the world. In the ontological sense it refers to the being of this totality of essents, or to regions or wholes within this totality (for example, the world of mathematics). Thirdly, it may mean, again in an ontic sense, not the totality of *vorhanden* essents within the world, but the sphere 'in which' a particular Dasein actually 'lives'. This is the preontological existenziell meaning (for example, 'a woman's world'). Lastly, 'world' may have the ontological existenzial meaning of *worldliness* as an a priori concept.

The phenomenon of worldliness has been overlooked thus far in the history of ontology because of a failure to grasp the existenzial constitution of Dasein as being-in-the-world.[9] Instead, attempts have been made to interpret world in terms of the being of essents *vorhanden* within the world, that is, of nature. But as we have seen Dasein discovers essents as nature only in a particular mode of its being-in-the-world, which, far from being equivalent to a disclosure of world, in fact involves a deprivation of the world character of the world. It is only through an existenzial analysis of Dasein, taking its start from the average quotidian existence of Dasein as its primary mode of being, that we can have a glimpse of the phenomenon called world. The immediate everyday world of Dasein consists of its surroundings or milieu, hence an ontological analysis of the kind of essents to be met with in Dasein's immediate surroundings is taken by Heidegger as the starting point for his analysis.

[14]

Our everyday being-in-the-world consists of our commerce with things in our environment, in the manner of 'taking care' (preoccupation) mentioned earlier. The primary character of this commerce lies, as we have seen, not in a purely theoretical or contemplative knowing, but in active, manipulative, and practical concern with them, which, Heidegger points out, has its own kind of 'knowledge'. The question he now proceeds to discuss is, what is the being of things as thus 'known' by Dasein? The phenomenological explication of this has nothing to do with a description of the actual properties of these things, but with a determination of the structure of their being, which is accessible only in the attitude of practical concern. For this purpose, however, it is important that we do not take them in their aspect as *things*, which are ontologically characterizable by such properties as substantiality, materiality, extension, etc. By speaking of these as immediately given 'things' we at once go wrong ontologically. The Greeks had a name for 'things'—*pragmata*—which adequately suggests the connection with *praxis* mentioned above. Heidegger uses the term 'utensil' (*Zeug*) for things as immediately encountered in the everyday attitude of 'caring'. The task now is to find out what constitutes the being of a utensil. What is the nature of utensility?

A utensil is essentially 'in order to', 'for the purpose of', and hence always carries a reference to something else. In fact, it always belongs to a whole utensilar system in the context of which alone it exists as a utensil. Further, a utensil shows itself in its true being only in the process of being used; the less it is merely looked at as an object and the more it is only utilized, the more fully does it reveal itself for what it truly is—a utensil. The mode of being of the latter is called by Heidegger its 'handiness', which is something that belongs to the utensil as it is in itself but which no amount of mere gaping at the 'look' of a thing can enable us to discover. The manipulative use of a tool is not a blind activity but has its own kind of awareness, an awareness of the multiplicity of references involved in the 'in order to' of the utensil. Such 'seeing', by which the user becomes aware of the being of the utensil, is called by Heidegger *circumspection* (*Umsicht*), taken in its literal etymological sense. What is handy (*zuhanden*) is not only not theoretically grasped; even for the circumspect glance it is not in the focus of attention. "The peculiar thing about what is directly handy is that precisely to be really handy it withdraws itself in its handiness, as it were." What is in the focus of attention is the product, the 'what for?' of the utensil.

This product, the thing made, is in its turn a utensil having its own 'what for?' The hammer is for making shoes, and the shoes are for walking. But the hammer is made out of iron which is not itself something made but found in nature. Thus, in the course of using the hammer we are led to 'nature'. But this 'nature', as implied in the total utensilar context, is nature under the aspect of handiness, as it is seen in the light of its products, not nature as simply there, or as a pervasive force, or as the poet contemplates it. The referential context in which a utensil is embedded connects it not only with an entire utensilar system and with nature as something exploitable but also with the user; in the production of an article of use Dasein itself is implied. The system of utensils thus involves a whole world, the handy environing world (*Umwelt*) of man's everyday practical life. It may be objected that the handiness which has been described here as the way of being of essents is merely a subjective coloring projected on to a world that must first be simply present (*vorhanden*). But this objection overlooks the fact that for such subjective projection to be possible, essents must have been discovered as purely *vorhanden* first of all. That this is not possible should be clear from what has been said earlier regarding knowledge as ontologically grounded in being-in-the-world, of which it is a derivative mode. The handy world is the world as it discloses itself in the first instance, and the world as simply given is derivative. Handiness is the ontological-categorical determination of an essent as it is 'in itself'.

Heidegger next proceeds to consider how the world phenomenon, which seems to be presupposed in what has been said above, can itself be shown to arise out of our experience of the 'handiness' of things. "Is there," he asks, "any way at all that leads from the being of these handy essents to an exhibition of the phenomenon of world?"

[15]

World is itself not an intramundane essent, and yet it is so far determinative of such essents that they can be discovered and show themselves in their being only insofar as there is already a disclosure of world. Heidegger seeks to show that in his practical concern with utensils handy around him, Dasein at the same time discovers the 'worldliness' attaching to these essents, that in the course of Dasein's preoccupied commerce with these essents, world 'flashes out'. He points out three modes of preoccupation belonging to Dasein's everyday being-in-the-world which let the essents cared about so meet it that their mundane character, the whole within which they exist, comes into view. Sometimes, in our practical concern with essents we come across one that cannot be put to use, for example, a utensil that is damaged. It is still a utensil that is handy, but its unutilizability makes it stand out with a certain conspicuousness that brings its character of simply being present to our notice. Sometimes, on the other hand, in our practical concern we come up against a situation where something has not merely lost its handiness, but is not at all there. A utensil that *should* have been handy, but is not, acquires a certain obtrusiveness, in its absence, that deprives it of some of its handiness—standing helpless in front of the lacking utensil, we become aware of the fact that the utensil is not merely something that can be handy but is something which may simply be there (*vorhanden*) or not. Finally, while thus practically oriented, we may come across something that is there and yet is not handy, something that stands in our way, being there to no purpose. This is the importunity of an essent that, just by not being handy and disposable, announces its character as sheer, brute presence. These three modes of preoccupation or concern, namely, conspicuousness, obtrusiveness, and importunity, have the function of bringing into view the character of being *vorhanden* implicit in handy essents.

The utensilar nature of handy things is, as we have seen, determined by a network of references which remain implicit and submerged in the natural practical attitude. When a utensil turns out to be unusable, in the manner described above, the constitutive reference of 'in order to' is broken and this snapping of the referential link brings to the fore, and renders explicit, the matrix of references in which the utensil is embedded. We now see that in our preoccupied commerce with things we were all the time concerned with a whole, a totality of which our circumspect awareness always had a glimpse. Similarly, when a utensil which should have been, but is not, actually there, our circumspect vision encounters an emptiness that renders explicit a totality. Through this whole or totality the world 'announces itself' in the midst of our practical concerns; what is thus glimpsed is itself neither a handy object nor indeed a thing existing objectively in the manner of something *vorhanden*. Our circumspect vision moves within a whole and all handy things are comprehended within it, but this whole itself is not accessible to circumspection, nor is it built up out of handy things. It 'flashes out', opens up, in the course of our quotidian dealings with things, marginally, as it were, but as something always presupposed as a reality.

What the handy things are in themselves is to be found in the inconspicuousness, unobtrusiveness, and nonimportunity in which they lie submerged so long as world does not announce itself, in the sense indicated above; when this happens they shed their handiness and emerge as *vorhanden* things. The latter aspect, being thus derivative, can never yield an ontology of the being-in-itself of things. This can only emerge from a better understanding of the phenomenon of world as opened up through the totality of references constitutive of the utensilar whole. Heidegger is thus led to a detailed discussion of the nature of Reference and Signification insofar as they are relevant to this problem.

[16]

In order to carry further the investigation of the phenomenon of reference as already revealed in the foregoing analysis of utensils, Heidegger selects a particular type of utensil, the sign, for detailed ontological analysis. Signs, such as signposts, signals, flags, and others, are themselves utensils having the specific utensilar function of showing or pointing, which may be regarded as one type of referring. For example, in an earlier time, the arrow on a motor car used to stick out, at the driver's command, to indicate which way the car was to turn. As a utensil, this sign is a constituent in the network of references which make up the sphere of traffic. This pointing function of the sign can be understood as a sort of 'referring' though it must be remembered that this 'referring', in the sense of pointing, is not the specific ontological nature of the sign as a utensil. The general ontological character of a utensil lies in its serviceability, in what it is for. On this is grounded the kind of reference termed 'pointing' which characterizes a sign. The specific being of the sign can be grasped if we consider how we react to the pointing arrow of a car. We do this either by turning aside or by standing still, and these are both ways of being-in-the-world of Dasein, continuously adjusting itself and on the move, be it by turning in one direction, be it by restraining such motion. It is through this adjustive behavior and the consequent practical circumspect cognition (*Über-sicht* or 'global view') that the being of the sign manifests itself and not to any direct gazing either at the sign itself or at the object to which it points. The circumspect surveying look does not seize on the sign as such, but is a way of gaining orientation in the environing world. "A sign is not a *thing* that stands to another thing in the relation of pointing but a utensil which expressly lifts up into our ken a utensilar whole and with that brings into view the 'worldly' dimension of handy things."

To provide further evidence of the uniqueness of a sign as a utensil, Heidegger enters into an interesting discussion of the way we 'set up' a sign and into the function of signs in the life of primitive man, as for example, in fetishism and magic. Without going into this, it should be sufficient to indicate how the study of signs throws light upon the nature of reference. Signs, Heidegger points out, bear a threefold relation to referring. Firstly, pointing, as a possible concrete exemplification of the what-for of utility, is founded on the structure of a utensil in general, that is, on the in-order-to of referring. Secondly, the pointing sign, as a utensil, belongs to a utensilar whole, to a referential system. And thirdly, the sign is not merely one handy thing among others but is handy in such a way that it explicitly brings the environing world into our circumspect view. "It is an ontic handy object which, as this particular utensil, at the same time functions as something that is indicative of the ontological structure of handiness, the referential whole and worldliness together." The preferential status of the sign as a utensil thus lies in the fact that it preeminently reveals the phenomenon of reference as the ontological presupposition of handy essents.[10]

[17]

It has been shown above that the being of a handy utensil is to be found in its referential structure and this means that the handy essent has in itself the character of being relative to, of being destined for, something. The ontological character of what is handy lies in *destination*, object or end (*Bewandtnis*), which contains in itself the suggestion of letting something take its destined course or reach its end (*bewenden lassen*).[11] That intramundane essents have a destination is meant by Heidegger to be an *ontological* determination of the being of these essents and not an ontic proposition about them. Since that for which something is destined is in its turn destined for something else and so on, the destination of a particular essent is bound up with the 'totality of destination' (*Bewandtnisganzheit*) which is presupposed in the former. This totality culminates in "a for-what (*Wozu*) which itself has no further destination, which is itself not an essent having the mode of being of something handy within a world but which is an essent whose being is determined as being-in-the-world, to the very constitution of whose being belongs the character of worldliness." This is the primary what-for, which is itself not a means to some further end and which is, therefore, termed 'for-the-sake-of-whom' (*Worum-willen*) by Heidegger.[12] A consideration of the structure of destination thus leads us finally to the being of Dasein, in its very being concerned with its own being.

The term '*bewenden lassen*'—to let what is at hand *be* as, and for what, it now is—used above is meant to be understood in an ontological sense, in the sense of rendering possible an encounter with essents in their character of being at hand, and as possessing a destination. This 'letting be' is an a priori, "a prior making free or releasing of essents in their handiness within the environing world," thus making them available for encounter. So far as essents at all manifest themselves or are discovered in their being by the preoccupied Dasein, they are already, from the very first, handy essents and not things that are simply there.

The being of essents at hand is their destination, but to discover this implies a prior disclosure of the 'totality of destination'. In the discovery of handy essents the disclosure of their world character is thus presupposed. The 'totality of destination', in view of which (*Woraufhin*) the a priori 'rendering posssible' frees essents for an encounter, must have already somehow revealed itself in some fashion 'prior' to such encounter. This is the world, the whole in view of which essents at hand in the environing world are set free for an encounter, and it is itself not the kind of entity that can be encountered in the world. This prior disclosure of world, in view of which intramundane essents are released for encounter, is the comprehension of world which always inherently characterizes Dasein. "Dasein comprehends itself in terms of a whole system of connections to which its existence is referred (that is, the what-for, the for-whose-sake and so forth comprehended under the 'totality of destination'), as being *in* that which is constituted by the in-view-of-what of the a priori rendering possible, that is, the prior permitting of an encounter with essents. The in-what of the referential comprehension as the end (the in-view-of-which) which allows the encounter with essents in the mode of being of destination is the phenomenon of world." Heidegger's main purport, in his extremely difficult discussion in this section of the work, is to show that the being-in-the-world of Dasein is not to be understood in a spatial sense. The above account is meant to describe how Dasein is yet in the world, in a nonspatial, noncategorial sense, embedded in a referential network of ends and purposes which are *his* ends and purposes, and to explain how, correlatively, the world, disclosing itself to man as a mode of his own being, is also made up in essence of a totality of 'destinations' or ends which ultimately refer back to the final end-in-itself, which is man himself. Heidegger's main concern, it must not be forgotten, is to exhibit the Dasein's mode of being, the way it is *in* the world, and to show that its being-in-the-world is an ontological feature of its own being, that world itself is an existenziality characterizing man's ontological structure.

Heidegger has explained, as described above, in what manner Dasein exists in some sort of familiarity with world, a preontological comprehension which does not mean an explicit theoretical knowledge of it but which is rather the basis which makes the latter possible. This familiarity depends upon the fact that Dasein, in its referential character, has some awareness of its being referred to the various relational structures explained above. This complex of relations in the midst of which man lives, and from which he draws all the meaningfulness of things, makes up the meaningful context in terms of which he understands himself and his world. This meaningful complex is what Heidegger terms *Bedeutsamkeit* or significance. "In its familiarity with this complex of a significant relationality, Dasein constitutes the ontic condition of the possibility of the discoverability of essents which meet it in a world in their mode of being as 'destination' (being at hand) and are thus able to manifest themselves as what they are in themselves." And Dasein, in turn, by the very fact of its being, is dependent upon, or referred back to, the system of essents which are at hand; this dependence (*Angewiesenheit*) is an essential ontological feature of Dasein's being.

The significance complex, with which Dasein is always in some measure familiar, contains in itself the ontological condition of the possibility that Dasein, as one who tries to comprehend and interpret its world (as a 'knower'), can become aware of or disclose meanings. And the disclosed 'significance', considered as the existenzial constitution of man, his being-in-the-world, is the ontic condition of the possibility of the 'totality of destination' being discovered by him. Keeping in mind the structural distinctions made earlier, we may sum up by pointing out, as Heidegger expressly does, the ontological distinctions that obtain here. We have, first, the being of the essents as encountered immediately and in the first instance, that is, their at-handness. This is a *categorial* determination and so is, secondly, the *Vorhandenheit*, the character of simply being given, which is a secondary, derivative feature of things as encountered in the world. Thirdly, there is the being of the ontic condition of the possibility of the intramundane essents in general being discovered, that is, the 'worldliness' of the world. This is an *existenzial* determination of the being-in-the-world of Dasein. It would, therefore, be a mistake to think of the system of references which, in its character of significance or meaningfulness, makes up the mundaneness of the world, in terms of a purely formal system of relations. The latter has reference solely to essents in their character of simply being given and this has been shown to be a feature triply derivative in the ontological sense.[13]

[18]

The Cartesian interpretation of the nature of the world has been so overwhelmingly influential in determining the whole modern outlook and way of understanding things that Heidegger has considered it necessary to examine it at length here. By contrast, this examination of the Cartesian ontology also clarifies the intentions of Heidegger himself and brings into relief the revolutionary character of his own approach. He seeks, in what follows, not only to give a brief account of Descartes' position but also to inquire into the presuppositions of the Cartesian doctrine so as to bring into view the unexamined ontological foundations on which the whole Cartesian legacy rests. For this purpose, he discusses Descartes' ontology under the following three heads: (1) the determination of 'world' as *res extensa*, (2) the foundations of this ontological determination, and (3) the hermeneutic discussion of the Cartesian ontology of 'world'. Heidegger postpones for the present (to the unpublished Part Two of *Being and Time*) the 'phenomenological destruction' of the *cogito sum* which alone can provide the final justification and completion of the criticism offered here.

The modern ontological dualism of nature and mind, with all the problems to which it has given rise, is traceable to the Cartesian distinction between the *ego cogito* and the *res extensa*. For Descartes, the term *substantia* denotes the being of anything. Like the Greek concept of *ousia*, this term is also ambiguous, sometimes meaning 'substantiality', the being of an essent conceived as substance, and sometimes the 'substance' or the essent itself—an ambiguity which is not a matter of just sheer chance. The ontological determination of *res corporea* or body, therefore, requires an elucidation of what substantiality means. According to Descartes, substances are known by their attributes and, in the case of body, it is through the attribute of *extensio* or extension that the substantiality of physical substances is known. The being of what we call 'world' is thus to be found in extension, for, as Descartes says, "Every other thing that can be attributed to body, presupposes extension and is only some mode of an extended thing."[14] Figure is a mode of extension, as also motion and, as Descartes adds, in continuation with his analysis of 'hardness', "in the same way, it may be shown that weight, color and all the other qualities of this sort . . . may be taken from it, itself meanwhile remaining entire: it thus follows that the nature of body depends on none of these."[15] The being of *res corporea* thus consists of extension, which remains unaltered, the same in the midst of all change, and hence constitutes the substantiality of this substance.

[19]

According to Descartes, the ontological determination of *res extensa* is based on the concept of substantiality, which is what Being means for him. "By substance," he says, "we can conceive nothing else than a thing which exists in such a way as to stand in need of nothing beyond itself in order to its existence."[16] Substantiality in this sense of independence can be possessed only by God, the *ens perfectissimum*, for as Descartes says, "all other things can exist only by help of the concourse of God," being produced and thus dependent. The being of everything other than God consists in being *ens creatum*, in creatureliness. Between the two kinds of existents, creator and creature, there is an 'infinite difference', and yet both *are*. Hence, though the term substance may be used for both—for even created things are in a sense independent, being not dependent on human production—"the term substance does not apply to God and the creatures *univocally* . . . no significance of this word can be distinctly understood which is common to God and them." What meaning, then, is to be attached to 'Being' as used for each of the two kinds of substances, the one finite and the other infinite? As Heidegger points out, Descartes here touches on a problem with which medieval ontology was constantly preoccupied. Realizing that 'Being' could not univocally apply to both and also that it could not be taken as just a name applied indifferently to both without itself possessing a general meaning, they attempted, following Aristotle, to meet the difficulty by the doctrine of 'analogical' meaning. In this respect Descartes remains far behind the scholastics and he in fact evades the problem inherent in the conception of Being understood as substance.

Descartes not only evades the ontological problem in the concept of substantiality but even expressly declares that "substance cannot be first discovered merely from its being a thing which exists independently, for existence by itself is not observed by us (*per se nos non afficit*)." Substantiality (Being), being inaccessible in the way that essents are, can thus be determined only in terms of substantial essents, bodies and minds and their attributes of extension and thinking. This accounts for the ambiguity of 'substance'. As Heidegger explains,

> What is intended or meant here is substantiality but it is understood in terms of an existent property of substance. Because the ontic is made to underlie the ontological, the

expression *substantia* is used sometimes in the ontological sense and sometimes in the ontic, but mostly carries a hazy and blurred onticontological sense. Behind this apparently trivial difference there lies concealed a failure to cope with the fundamental problem of Being. Its proper treatment requires that the equivocations be tracked down in the *right manner*; he who attempts this does not merely 'busy himself' with 'mere word meanings', but has to venture forth into the most basic problems inherent in the 'things themselves', in order to get clear about such 'nuances'.

[20]

Descartes' ontology of the 'world' as made up of essents whose being lies in extension is neither concerned with the phenomenon of world nor does it succeed in so determining the nature of essents within the world as to reveal at least their world-implying character. His very method of approach prevents him from raising the problem of world. It is not merely that he gives an account of the world which is ontologically mistaken; the very basis of his interpretation is such as to make him miss the phenomenon of world as well as the mode of being of handy things as first encountered within the world. Keeping in mind the importance of always first getting the right approach to a phenomenon, Heidegger asks, "Which mode of being of Dasein is fixed upon as the adequate channel of approach to that essent with whose being, determined as extension, Descartes identifies the being of 'world'?" For Descartes, the only proper mode of access to it is the faculty of knowing, *intellectio*, in the sense of mathematical-physical knowledge, a way of comprehending essents which alone, according to Descartes, ensures certain grasp of their being. In Heidegger's words, "What is such, in its mode of being, that it satisfies the conception of Being as accessible to the mathematical way of knowing alone counts as something that *is* in the proper sense. Mathematical entities are such that *they always are what they are* and hence the being of essents in the world must lie in something that is *permanently enduring*, as *remanens capax mutationum*." Thus, from a predetermined idea of Being implicit in the concept of substantiality and from the idea of this specific type of knowledge, Descartes imposes upon the 'world' the kind of being that it must have. Proceeding on the basis of an idea of Being (permanent *Vorhandenheit*, simple givenness) which remains obscure as to its origins and unvalidated as to its legitimacy, Descartes prescribes to the world what kind of being it must have, instead of letting the mode of being of intramundane essents emerge from a consideration of these essents themselves.

Descartes is very well aware that essents do not directly show themselves in their true being; for him things as immediately given, with all their sensory qualities, are of no significance ontologically. According to him, "the perceptions of the senses do not teach us what is in reality in things . . . do not present to us these objects as they are in themselves," and further, "the nature of matter or body considered in general does not consist in its being hard, or ponderous, or coloured, or that which affects our senses in any other way. . . ."[17] Descartes' interpretation of hardness shows quite clearly his complete inability to grasp in their own peculiar mode of being things as they present themselves to sense. Interpreting as he does the experience of resistance in terms of a relation between two *vorhanden* objective entities, Descartes fails to see that hardness and resistance could not manifest themselves at all if there were no essents of the type of Dasein or at least that of living beings. Descartes is dominated by the concept of Being as permanent, as simple givenness. He therefore identifies world with essents having a particular mode of being within this world, thinks of the being of Dasein in terms of substance and, in consequence, fails to see that both sensible and rational understanding are themselves derived modes of being-in-the-world. Descartes' basically traditional ontological orientation made it impossible for him to find his way to a deeper grasp of the problem of an ontology of man, turned his glance away from the phenomenon of world, and drove him to an ontology of 'world' conceived in terms of one particular type of essent within the world.[18]

It was pointed out earlier that the distinction between the 'being-in' (as an existenzial) characterizing Dasein and the 'internality' or insideness (as a category) denoting a relation between two physical things simply there does not imply that

Dasein does not possess a spatiality of its own. Heidegger now turns to the task of showing to what extent spatiality is constitutive of Dasein, in what sense space is a constituent of the world (which itself has been shown to be an element in the total structure of being-in-the-world), and how, in particular, the specific spatiality of the essents that are encountered in the environing world is itself based on their character of belonging to a world. He begins with a discussion of the spatiality that attaches to intramundane handy things.

[21]

The things that are at hand in our everyday dealings are not only such as to be encountered first and foremost but are characterized by a certain *nearness*, as the term 'at hand' itself suggests. This nearness is not something that is determined by a measurement of distance, but is regulated by the circumspect estimating that occurs in the course of our practical occupation with these things. What is in this sense near is also fixed in regard to its direction by the circumspect glance of our concern, so that the utensil does not just have a position in space but has its own *place*, a place where the utensil has its own 'in-order-to' in the totality of the utensilar system. As part of a utensilar whole, the utensil has always a place where it belongs. And the particular utensilar system has its own location which, as the context in which a utensil has its place, constitutes the general condition of the possibility of belonging here or there. This is what Heidegger calls the *region*, which must first be disclosed if there is to be any possibility of assigning places within it to a utensilar manifold. This regional orientation of the complex of places where utensils belong constitutes the 'around-ness', the environing character (*das Umhafte*) of the surrounding world (*Umwelt*). The measurable three-dimensional manifold of possible positions, that is, space in the scientific sense, is based on and derived from this primary experience of the spatiality of things at hand. The regions in which things in their utensilar character take their places, are discovered through the totality of destinations which at the same time renders available the encounter with utensils. Heidegger illustrates the primary disclosure of places and regions thus:

The Sun, whose light and warmth are in our everyday use, has his distinctive places, as discovered by our circumspect vision and determined by changes in the way we can utilize what he bestows: sunrise, midday, sunset and midnight. . . .The house has its sun-and weather-sides, according to which the different rooms are oriented, and within them, again, the furnishing is suitably arranged. Churches and graves are, for example, laid out according to the directions of sunrise and sunset, the regions of life and death.

In connection with the at-handness of regions, it is worth noting that it possesses the character of inconspicuous familiarity in a more fundamental sense than that possessed by things at hand themselves. It makes itself felt in the privative mode of our preoccupation with handy essents by emerging into conspicuousness; when we fail to find something in its place, the region in which it is situated acquires a conspicuousness which thrusts the region as such into our awareness. Space, as we discover it through our circumspect being-in-the-world in the form of the spatiality of the utensilar whole, belongs always to the essents themselves as their place. As yet, 'bare space' is still hidden, being split up into places.

[22]

Heidegger next takes up for consideration the spatial character of being-in-the-world. The encounter with utensils in their environing space is ontically possible only because Dasein itself as being-in-the-world, is 'spatial' in character. But this spatiality of Dasein must be conceived in consonance with the mode of being proper to Dasein, a mode of being 'in' the world in the sense of preoccupied and familiar commerce with essents encountered with the world. Grounded in its particular mode of being-in, Dasein's spatiality exhibits the twofold character of rapprochement (*Ent-fernung*) and situating (*Ausrichtung*), which Heidegger goes on to discuss in that order.

He uses the term *Ent-fernung* (literally, de-distancing, bringing near) in a special sense, in the active and transitive sense of "making the distance disappear," that is, bringing something near. Dasein "is intrinsically 'de-distancing'; as the essent that it is, Dasein lets things encounter it in a certain nearness." Unlike distance, the stretch of space separating two objects, which is a categorial determination of nonhuman essents, rapprochement is an existenziality and a condition of the possibility of spatial intervals between two things being discovered at all. Not only in the circumspection of our practical concern with things but also in the purely cognitive attitude, we bring about a nearness of things; in fact, such nearness characterizes all our relations with things. As Heidegger says, "In Dasein there lies an intrinsic tendency to nearness." This is shown, for example, not only in our everyday life but by the different ways and devices for the modern conquest of space which has, by extending the horizons of our environing workaday world, brought about an extraordinary shrinkage of the world as such. Rapprochement, in the sense of the spatiality inherent in Dasein cannot be expressed in terms of pure distance. Even when we seek to indicate how far something is from us, we do it in a way which has reference to our everyday practical concerns, for example, when we say, "It is just a short walk to that place," or, trying to be more precise, "It is half-an-hour's walk to that house." The half-hour here is not equivalent to thirty minutes, but a duration which has no 'length' at all in the measurable quantitative sense; this duration is always interpreted in terms of our accustomed quotidian preoccupation. The objective distances between *vorhanden* things do not coincide with the 'near' and 'far' of intramundane handy things. This way of understanding distance in terms of rapprochement should not be dismissed as merely 'subjective'. This is a subjectivity which "discovers what is most real in the reality of the world. . . . The circumspect rapprochement of the everyday life of Dasein discovers the being in-itself of the 'true world', of the essents in the nearness of which Dasein as an essent already always finds itself."

Our exclusive orientation in terms of measurable distances tends to conceal from our view the basic spatiality of our being-in. What is 'nearest' to us is hardly ever that which has the least distance from us, but is rather something that is 'within reach' and available for our preoccupied grasp and glance. What is at the shortest distance from us, for example, the spectacles on our nose, the street under our feet, may be, for our preoccupied, seeking glance, very much farther from us than that picture on the wall or that friend waiting for us round the corner. To be in our nearness means to be within the circle of what is first and foremost handy for our circumspect look. In a similar way, the place occupied by Dasein is not to be understood as a location of the sort characteristic of a physical object or of an essent at hand occupying a place in a certain region. Dasein occupies a place in the sense of being a center of 'rapprochement' by which handy essents in the environing world are brought within a region disclosed to the circumspect look. As a de-distancing center of rapprochements, man carries his own space with himself, a space which he can never cross over himself.

In addition to the rapprochement which characterizes his way of being-in, Dasein also possesses the character of *Ausrichtung* or situating.[19] "The circumspect preoccupation," Heidegger says, "is a situating rapprochement," so that the nearness into which things come always has a direction in a region. Like rapprochement, this directedness (for example, right and left) is also part of the 'space' which Dasein carries with it. The de-distancing in Dasein's way of being-in-the-world is always, in other words, direction giving. Right and left are not, for example, something subjective but are directions of situatedness within a world already at hand. In his discussion of the phenomenon of orientation,[20] Kant realized that the 'mere feeling' of right and left is, in the absence of a 'subjective principle', powerless to enable us to orient ourselves in space; he failed to see, however, that the a priori principle he was looking for lies in Dasein's being-in-the-world, with its constitutent character of directed rapprochement.[21]

[23]

On the basis of the preceding, Heidegger sums up his view of the general nature of space in its relation to the spatiality of Dasein, indicating how categorial space emerges from this primary existenzial space. As being-in-the-world, man has always a 'world' disclosed to him, within which essents become available to him by virtue of the totality of destination. The circumspect awareness which enables him to comprehend the referential complex, and the matrix of significance presupposed by it, at the same time reveals the spatiality of being-in-the-world. Essents at hand are encountered not only as embedded in a totality of destination but their *bewenden lassen* (that is, the rendering possible of essents in their destination) is at the same time seen to involve the spatial characteristic of directed rapprochement of handy essents in a region. A region is the 'where' to which every possible utensilar whole must belong in order to enable utensils to be encountered as being 'placed' in the nearing-situating manner described above. The totality of destination, which constitutes the being of essents at hand in the environing world, involves a spatial destination characterized by regionalness. This discovery of the spatiality of being-in-the-world then becomes itself the basis which makes possible the further knowledge of space as such.

In regard to space itself, Heidegger says, "*Space is neither in the subject, nor is the world in space. Space is rather 'in' the world, being disclosed by the being-in-the-world constitutive of Dasein.*" Space is not something that inheres in a subject, nor does the latter see the world 'as if' it were in space. It is the subject itself, in the sense of Dasein, that is spatial in character and it is in this sense that space is an a priori. A priori does not mean a prior inherence in subject which, to begin with, is without a world and which then projects space out of itself. "Apriority means here the priority of encountered space (as region) in the course of our encounter with essents at hand in the environing world." Once space itself has thus emerged, we may contemplate it for itself, in a noncircumspect, unpreoccupied way; such mere looking at "neutralizes the regions of the environing world to mere dimensions." The places occupied by handy essents sink into mere positions and the spatiality of intramundane handy essents loses with them its character of destination. The world, deprived of its environing character, turns into the 'natural' world.[22]

[24]

Being-with, Selfhood, and Everyman

It has been shown above that man (Dasein) in his everyday mode of existence, from which point of view he is always the central theme of the analysis, is not only *in* a world but in such a way that he is, first and foremost, abandoned to the world, taken up with it and absorbed in it. How this happens is explained by Heidegger in connection with the question regarding the 'who', the carrier of this everyday mode of existence. This question regarding the 'who' of the average, quotidian Dasein is a question about the ontological structure of Dasein, about its modes of being in the world, and as such an existenzial question. The aim of this existenzial inquiry is to disclose the phenomenon of the 'who' of Dasein's quotidian existence, the anonymous 'they', or 'everyman' or 'one' (*das Man*); it also throws light on certain other features of man's way of being-in-the-world, such as 'being-with' (*Mitsein*) and 'fellow-man' (*Mitdasein*), which are no less essential aspects of the structure of man's being-in-the-world than those described earlier.

A formal indication of who Dasein is has already been given: I myself am this essent, its being is my own being. But though this does suggest, ontically and ontologically, where we should look for this 'who', it does not offer us anything more. Further elucidation of this 'who', in both these respects, is therefore required. Ordinarily, the 'I' is regarded as that which remains identical in the midst of our varied behavior and experiences, thus standing as a point of reference for this manifold. Ontologically speaking, it is something that lies at the basis, the *subjectum*, which, as remaining the same in the midst of change, has the character of a *self*. This traditional account, comprehends the 'I' in the sense of something *vorhanden* or simply given, however much it may try to guard itself against the conception of a soul substance, of consciousness as a thing, of the person as an objective entity. Implicitly, Being is here conceived as substantiality and Dasein as something *vorhanden*, though, as we have seen, *Vorhanden*-ness is a mode of being characteristic of nonhuman essents. Ontically also, the proposition "I am myself this Dasein" does not provide an unambiguous basis for an ontological explication of this 'I', for, as Heidegger says, "It could be, that the who of the everyday Dasein is precisely *not* always I myself."

It may be objected, in favor of the traditional interpretation, that the 'I' is an immediately self-evident datum, based on "a simple, formal and reflective self-awareness" which it would be unjustifiable to ignore while trying to answer this question about the 'who'. To this Heidegger's answer is that the above mentioned way in which the 'I' is said to be directly given does not reveal Dasein in its everyday character. "Is it," he asks, "a priori self-evident that the access to Dasein must be through a simple, reflexive awareness of an I as the center of acts of consciousness?" This kind of givenness may prove misleading for the analytic of Dasein, for it may turn out that in the very constitution of man, which is always my own, there is some basis for the fact that he is first and foremost *not his own self*, that when asked who he is, he promptly claims to be a self or an 'I', all the more loudly, as Heidegger expresses it, when he is precisely *not* that. The 'I' here must be understood in the sense of a purely formal indication of something which may phenomenally manifest itself by way of just its opposite, as, for example, in the case of loss of self, thus calling for further ontological elucidation. Further, we have seen that there is no such immediately given thing as a mere subject without world, or an isolated 'I' without other selves.[23] Man is in the world *along with* others, and the ontological structure of being-with must also not be left unexamined.

In his discussion of these problems connected with the 'who' of Dasein, Heidegger takes his clue from the principle formulated earlier, "the essence of Dasein lies in its existenz." If the 'I' is an essential determination of Dasein, it must be interpreted in an existenzial sense, that is, as a particular mode of being of Dasein. To object that the conception of the self as 'only' a way of being of Dasein completely volatilizes the real 'core' of Dasein is to insist on presupposing that Dasein's mode of being is at bottom that of a *vorhanden* entity and to forget that "the 'substance' of man is not spirit as the synthesis of soul and body, but existenz."[24]

[25]

Man exists in a world in which he finds not only essents at hand (*zuhanden*) and on hand (*vorhanden*) but also essents which, differing in their mode of being from these, are like himself in being themselves in-the-world. Man encounters another Dasein within the world, which is neither *zuhanden* nor *vorhanden* but exists in a mode the same as his own; it is encountered as being *also* there *together with* himself. This 'also being there along with' is not to be taken in the sense in which a *vorhanden* essent may be there together with us. Both the 'also' and the 'with' must be understood not in the categorial but in an existenzial sense, as a mode of being specifically characteristic of Dasein. It is this character of necessarily being in the world as being-together-with possessed by Dasein which makes this world always a shared one; the world of Dasein is a together-with world (*Mitwelt*) and Dasein's being-in is always a way of being-together (*Mitsein*) with others. The others are encountered not by first being distinguished as other subjects from one's own self as already simply given, but are disclosed directly to our preoccupied circumspect look in the environing world, as being encountered from and within the world. Man finds even himself, in the first instance and for the most part, not by looking within himself but "primarily in *what* he pursues, uses, awaits or prevents, in the essents at hand in the environing world with which he is in the first instance occupied." Dasein knows itself first, and mostly, in terms of its world and the others also are encountered as being-with in terms of the handy objects within the world engaging them, in terms of their own preoccupations and pursuits. Dasein is in itself intrinsically being-with, not an isolated essent unrelated at first with others. That man's being-in-the-world is intrinsically constituted by his being-with is an existenzial and ontological feature of man, even though ontically, in a particular case, there may not be anybody else in fact there with him. Being-with determines Dasein existenzially even when actually another Dasein is not present or to be seen. Even Dasein's being alone is being-with in the world; loneliness being a privative mode of the latter, its very possibility is evidence of being-with. Conversely, the fact of my being alone cannot be removed by the mere presence of one or many other men in my vicinity. But just as being-with determines my own

Dasein, so being a fellow-Dasein (*Mitdasein*) is a determination of the Dasein of another. Hence, when I am lonely in the midst of many, they do not cease to have the character of being-there with me but are only encountered in the privative mode of indifference and strangeness.

Dasein's relation to utensils at hand within its world has been expressed by the term 'preoccupation' (*Besorgen*) and, corresponding to the difference in the mode of being of other human beings, Heidegger uses the term 'solicitude' (*Fürsorge*) to indicate our relation to these. Both terms, it will be noticed, derive from *Sorge* or 'care' which, as will be shown later, constitutes the being of Dasein. Just as the reality of utensils at hand is disclosed to our preoccupation, similarly, the being of other people as being together with us in our world is disclosed to our solicitude. This term is also to be understood as an existenzial, since it refers to a mode of being of Dasein which renders the reality of others accessible to it. Characteristically, in actual social life, this solicitude manifests itself in its privative and indifferent modes, as, for example, in attitudes of being for, or against, or doing without, one another, of passing each other by, of having no concern with one another, which are all deficient and indifferent modes of solicitude characterizing our quotidian, average way of being-with-others.

Heidegger distinguishes between two possible ways in which solicitude can manifest itself positively. On the one hand there is the solicitude in which a person, as it were, takes away the worries of the other and, putting himself in his place, takes upon himself the tasks of the other, stepping in to deputize for the other. Such solicitude very often renders the other dependent and subordinate even though this fact may remain implicit and outside his awareness. But there is also the possibility of a solicitude that, instead of jumping in for the other, rather jumps ahead, "*anticipating* the other in his existenziell ability to be (*Seinkönnen*), not in order to relieve him of all 'care' but really to give it back as such to him, as his own 'care', for the first time." This is the real solicitude which enables the other "to become transparent to himself *in* his care, and to become free for it." These manifestations of solicitude, the one interfering and dominating and the other anticipating and liberating, are the two extreme possibilities between which our everyday being-with-others oscillates. It may be noted at this point that just as preoccupation has its own way of being aware of what is at hand, that is, circumspection, so solicitude, has its own 'eye', taking cognizance of the other through 'consideration' (*Rücksicht*) and 'indulgence' (*Nachsicht*). Further, the being of Dasein is, as being-in-the-world, the final terminus for the 'totality of destination', the ultimate 'for whose sake'. But since to Dasein's being there also belongs being with others, it follows that the way Dasein 'is' contains in itself an intrinsic element of being for the sake of the other. This makes it possible for the other to stand revealed as Dasein existing together-with, and as emerging out of the total context of 'significance' or of belongingness to a world.

Since being-with is constitutive of the being of Dasein and the latter has always a certain comprehension of Being, Dasein also always has understanding of the other, an understanding which is not any sort of conceptual knowledge but "an original existenzial mode of being, which first makes (conceptual) knowledge possible." It is a mistake to interpret our 'knowledge of other minds' on the basis of empathy (*Einfühlung*), as if Dasein first had a preconceptual knowledge of itself as an isolated subject and then projected this cognitive relation to itself upon the other. Dasein's relation to (being-toward) itself is not the same as to others—the latter mode of being-to is "an independent, irreducible relation of being; it has already come into existence along with the being-with of Dasein." Empathy is not an original existenzial phenomenon and, far from constituting the being-with, is itself possible only on the basis of that. By the very fact of its existence Dasein is with-others-together. Being-together-with others should not be conceived as a summation of many 'subjects' happening to exist at the same time. The plurality of subjects as mere 'numbers', says Heidegger, is itself disclosed through a particular mode of being-with and being-toward one another. The unregarding being-with, as a sort of mere coexistence, indeed 'reckons' with the others but without seriously 'counting upon' them or even wanting to have anything to do with them.

[26]

Man, in his everyday mode of being merges, goes out into, the world of his preoccupation, including his being-with the others, and is thus not 'himself'. *Who* is it, then, that functions as the being of this everyday being-with-others? The others are encountered in what they are (and they *are* what they pursue) in the course of our preoccupation with essents in the environing world. In the preoccupation with what engages us, with, for, or against the others, we are constantly worried about keeping ourselves distinct from others, either wanting to iron out the disparity with others or to establish some kind of superiority over them. "The being-together-with others is—in a way hidden from itself—anxious about this distance." This character of 'aloofness' or distantness (*Abständigkeit*) pervades all being-with; the more persistently and deeply at work in our everyday life the more unobtrusive it is. Man is possessed with this concern about maintaining a proper distance from other people, yet in his everyday being-with-others, he stands under the domination of the others. "He *is* not himself, the others have deprived him of his being. . . . The whim of the other disposes of the everyday possibilities of being inherent in Dasein." Such is the unobtrusive domination of the other under which man, as being-with, comes unawares. Giving himself up to the others, who are themselves nothing more than people he is with, he acquires for himself the status of anonymity, however much he may try to conceal his intrinsic belongingness to them by calling them 'others'. Who is this anonymous entity of the everyday being-with-others? "Not this man nor that man," says Heidegger, "not oneself and not a few and not the sum of all. The 'who' is the neutral *they* or *one* (*das Man*).[25]

As Herbert Spiegelberg has said, Heidegger's description of this everyday, impersonal mode of being is "one of the most impressive accounts of everyday personal existence in its tendency to escape from itself and to fall into inauthentic being."[26] In what follows, therefore, Heidegger's own words are freely translated at length.

In the use of public vehicles and employment of media of communication such as the newspaper, one person is like the other. Dasein's own existence is wholly dissolved in this mode of being of 'the others'; in its unobtrusive, impalpable presence the impersonal 'one' establishes its own dictatorship. We enjoy and amuse ourselves as *one* does; we read, see, and judge literature and art as one sees and judges; we dissociate ourselves from the crowd as *they* do; we find revolting what they find revolting. This *one*, who is nobody in particular and is yet everybody, prescribes what the everyday mode of being of Dasein is to be. He, everyman, has his own ways of being of which the concern with 'disparity' has been already mentioned. This is itself based on the 'averageness' characterizing everyman's preoccupations, and the latter in turn is the basis for the tendency of 'leveling down' which, on the lookout for every exception to the rule of mediocrity, quietly suppresses every sort of preeminence. In consequence, everything original is overnight flattened out into something long known; what has been won by being fought for becomes common and handy; every mystery loses its power. These three characteristics describe the mode of being of the 'one'. They constitute the 'public' character of his existence which governs all interpretation of the world and of man and which, having a say in everything, wins in everything its point, not because it has any specially favored access to the nature of things but because it never penetrates beneath the surface to the things themselves. The 'one' is present everywhere; he spreads himself all over, but in such a way that wherever Dasein pushes on to a decision, the 'one' has already slunk away somewhere else. The 'one' can take all responsibility most lightly because there is no one in particular who need be answerable for anything. The 'one' takes over the load of Dasein's personal everyday existence and in thus accommodating and obliging Dasein constantly, he establishes more unshakeably his dominion over it. Each man is the other and nobody his own self. This everyman, this 'who' of the quotidian Dasein is the *Nobody* to whom Dasein, in its being-together with others, has delivered itself up. The 'permanence' of Dasein in such everyday being-together lies in the distance, averageness, leveling down, publicity, relieving the load of existence and obligingness mentioned above as the modes in which it exists. The self of Dasein, or that of the other, has not yet found (or lost) itself; its mode of existence is still dependent and inauthentic.

The 'one' is as little *vorhanden* as Dasein, nor can it be

explained as a 'general subject' hovering above the plurality of individuals. No account can be given of the 'one' in terms of the traditional logic which is rooted in a crude ontology of essents simply given. The 'one' is an existenzial and as a primary phenomenon is part of the positive constitution of Dasein. The self of everyday Dasein is *oneself*, to be distinguished from the *authentic* self. As 'oneself', Dasein is dissipated in the 'one' and has to find itself first. Further, Dasein comprehends itself and the world, in the first instance, in terms prescribed by the 'one'. This is the world as disclosed to one's everyday being-with, its referential system of meaningfulness being articulated by the 'one' himself; and it is not 'I', in the sense of being my own self, who 'am', but rather the others in the form of the 'one'. Dasein is in the first instance everyman and mostly it remains so. When, however, Dasein does discover the world and when its own real self reveals itself to it, this disclosure of 'world' and revelation of Dasein always occurs first as a sweeping away of all that has so far veiled and obscured it, as a smashing down of the fence of dissimulations with which Dasein hedges itself against its own self.

Dasein's preontological interpretation of its being is based on this mode of being as 'one'. Its ontological interpretation also tends at first to be in terms of the 'world' as made up of simply given substantial entities; even the meaning of Being is first grasped in terms of the mode of being of such *vorhanden* essents. Because of Dasein's tendency to go out and be absorbed in the world, the phenomenon of world itself is passed over and ignored. The very constitution of man's being-in-the-world is such that, in the first instance and in his everyday mode of being, world tends to cover itself and be missed wholly. Dasein's being an authentic self, conversely, does not depend on an exceptional state completely cut off from the 'one', but is an existenziell modification of the 'one' regarded intrinsically as an existenzial. This also means that the self-sameness of an authentically existing self is ontologically something very different from the identity of an 'I' that remains permanent in the midst of a multiplicity of experiences.[27]

[27]

Notes

1. Elucidating this statement ("Brief über den 'Humanismus'," *Wegmarken*, pp. 156-157), Heidegger says: "What man is, his nature or essence, in the traditional language of metaphysics, rests on his ek-sistenz. But ek-sistenz in this sense is not identical with the traditional concept of *existentia*, which means actuality, as distinguished from *essentia* or possibility." What the statement intends to say is that man's mode of being is such that he is the 'there (*Da*)', that is, the clearing of Being. The ecstatic nature of man lies in ek-sistenz, standing out in the truth of Being, to be distinguished from the metaphysical conception of *existentia* (conceived as *actualitas* in medieval philosophy, as objectivity of experience by Kant, as the self-knowing Idea by Hegel, as the Eternal Return of the Same by Nietzsche). Further, the question about the 'nature' or 'essence' of man is inappropriately posed when we ask what (or who) man is, for in doing so we take for granted that the 'what' or the 'who' is something in the nature of a person or object. Nature or 'essence' (*Wesen*) is to be understood here in the sense neither of *esse essentiae* nor of *esse existentiae* but rather in terms of the ek-static character of Dasein. Lastly, the statement should not be understood in the sense of a secularized transference to man of what Christian theology says about God (*Deus est suum esse*), for ek-sistenz means neither the realization of an essence nor does it generate or posit an essence itself.

Sartre's assertion that existence precedes essence, on the contrary, takes the terms *existentia* and *essentia* in the sense of metaphysics, according to which, ever since Plato, essence precedes existence. Sartre merely converts this sentence; but the converse of a metaphysical statement itself remains metaphysical and as such oblivious of the truth of Being. This principal statement of 'existentialism' thus has nothing at all in common with the above statement in *Being and Time*. The point of determining the humanity of the human being as ek-sistenz is that it is not man that is important but Being as the dimension of the ecstatic character of ek-sistenz. Fundamentally different from all *existentia* and 'existence', 'ek-sistenz' is the ek-static dwelling in the neighborhood of Being. It is the guardianship of, that is, the concern (*Sorge*) for, Being. Heidegger insists (Cf. *Nietzsche II*, p. 473f.) that the term existenz was 'temporarily' employed in *Being and Time* as preparatory to an overcoming of metaphysics, conceived from the point of view of Da-sein's ecstatic relationship to Being and as such lying outside the scope of a philosophy of existence as well as being "separated by an abyss" from the basically theological passion of Kierkegaard.

2. Elsewhere, Heidegger explains this as follows: "To say that Dasein is in each case my own (*je meines*) means that I am thrown into Dasein, so that I may be, as myself, Dasein . . . it means neither that it is posited by me nor that it is separated off into an isolated ego. Dasein is *itself* only by virtue of its intrinsic relationship to Being. This is what is meant by the oft-repeated sentence in *Being and Time*: "The understanding of Being is inherent in Dasein" (*Einführung in die Metaphysik*, p. 22; E.T., p. 23f.).

3. *Ideen II*. See also the analysis of the '*Lebenswelt*' in the *Krisis* work. For the whole problem see Gadamer, *Wahrheit und Methode*, pp. 229-240.

4. Heidegger, at this stage, is in close sympathy with the transcendental method of phenomenology, that is, insofar as it seeks to be a science dealing with the transcendental constitution of everything known by us. The transcendental ego which, according to Husserl, brings about this constitution is, however, itself left undetermined as to its mode of being by Husserl. The analytic of Dasein seeks to accomplish just this. As Heidegger writes in a letter to Husserl (see Walter Biemel, "Husserls Encyclopaedia-Britannica Artikel und Heideggers Anmerkungen dazu"), the central theme of *Being and Time* is the problem of the mode of being of that essent in whom the 'world' gets constituted, the task of showing that human existence as a mode of being is utterly distinct from all other essents and it is man as an essent who comprises in himself this possibility of transcendental constitution; the transcendental constitution is a central possibility of the existenz of the factual self. For Heidegger the transcendental ego responsible for the constitution is neither the Cartesian *cogito* nor the 'pure consciousness' of Husserl but the existenz of Dasein. The mode of being of Consciousness itself is unquestioningly presupposed by Husserl (at least before the last phase of his 'farewell to Carteseanism' in his work on *The Crisis of the European Sciences*) and this is where Heidegger refuses to follow him.

5. The analytic of Dasein is not an empirical investigation or any sort of psychology but is an ontological inquiry into the a priori conditions of the possibility of factual human existence. But, Heidegger points out in a footnote, "The disclosure of the a priori is not 'aprioristic' construction. Through the work of Husserl we have not only learnt to understand the meaning of genuine philosophical empiricism but also to employ the tools necessary for this. Apriorism is the method of every scientific philosophy that understands itself. Because it has nothing to do with 'construction', a priori research requires a properly worked out phenomenal basis." See also what Heidegger says about "the a priori of the factual subject" (close of chapter 4 below).

For the phenomenological conception of the a priori, see Max Scheler, *Der Formalismus in der Ethik und die materiale Wertethik*, Part I, chapter 2A. Scheler discusses thoroughly the Kantian conception of the a priori and on the basis of this criticism develops his own doctrine of the "material a priori." He defines the a priori in terms of unities of significance which are not conceptually constructed but immediately intuited prior to and without regard to their actual exemplification in experience. What is thus cognized through an intuition of the 'essence' (what-ness) can never be confuted by observation and induction, since the identification of every actual instance as this or that through observation is itself dependent upon a prior intuition of the essence which is 'fulfilled' in this instance. The phenomenological a priori is thus based, according to Scheler, on immediate experience and not on the constructions of a capricious 'understanding'; it has no need of the wholly mythological assumption of a chaos of sensations which have to be then given form through the instrumentality of 'synthetic functions' and 'powers' of the mind. The a priori-a posteriori distinction has nothing to do with the opposition of formal and material and the identification of the a priori with the formal is a basic error of the Kantian theory. It is equally erroneous, according to Scheler, to equate the a priori with the rational and the a posteriori with the sensible. There is also such a thing as an apriorism of the emotional which is as much independent of inductive procedures as the logical a priori. Scheler likewise rejects the subjectivistic interpretation of the a priori as flowing from the acts of a transcendental 'subject' or consciousness in general and hence possessing universality and necessity.

6. Commenting later ("Brief über den 'Humanismus'," *Wegmarken*, pp. 188-189) on this description of 'being-in-the-world' as dwelling (that is, dwelling in the truth of Being), Heidegger says that the reference to 'being-in' as 'dwelling' is no play with etymology. See the essays," . . . dichterisch wohnet der Mensch . . ." and "Bauen Wohnen Denken" (both in *Vorträge und Aufsätze*, E.T., *Poetry, Language, Thought*) for a development of this conception.

7. Cf. *Nietzsche I*, p. 569, "The knowable and the knower are together determined in their essence by a common essential basis. . . . Knowing is not a kind of bridge that happens to connect the two banks of a river, already existing as objective entities, but is itself the river which, through its flow, brings into existence the banks and brings them together more intimately than any bridge can ever do."

8. Commenting on the charge that his conception of being-in-the-world is purely this-worldly and atheistic, Heidegger says ("Brief über den 'Humanismus'," *Wegmarken*, pp. 180-181) that this view does not assert that man is just a 'worldly' entity in the Christian sense, turned away from God and cut off from transcendence or, more correctly, the Transcendent, that is, the super-sensible, highest essent or God. 'World' in being-in-the-world, however, does not mean the earthly essent as distinguished from the heavenly, nor the 'worldly' as distinguished from the 'spiritual'. 'World' here means the openness or clearing of Being in which man ek-sists as thrown. From the point of view of man's ek-sistenz, the 'world' is in a sense just the Beyond, in and for ek-sistenz, but not beyond in the sense that man is, to start with, a pure subject, on 'this side' of the beyond. Man's ek-sistenz in the openness of Being, constitutive of his essence, is what first illuminates the 'between', within which the relation of a subject to an object then becomes possible.

The determination of man as being-in-the-world, further, implies nothing as to whether man is purely this-worldly or other-worldly, nothing about the existence or nonexistence of God, nor about the possibility or impossibility of gods. It is, therefore, hasty and wrong, Heidegger says, to brand this interpretation of man as atheistic and to ignore the pointed remark in "Vom Wesen des Grundes" (*Wegmarken*, p. 55n; E.T., p. 91n): "The ontological interpretation of Dasein as being-in-the-world judges neither positively nor negatively as to man's possible being in relation to God. But the elucidation of Transcendence has provided us with an *adequate concept of Dasein* in terms of which we can now *ask* how it stands with man's relationship with the Divine ontologically." The thinking which is based on the truth of Being inquires more deeply than is possible for metaphysics. "Out of the truth of Being alone can the nature of the Holy be thought. Only on the basis of the essence of the Holy can the nature of Divinity be thought.

Only in the light of the nature of Divinity is it possible to think and say what the word 'God' should name." We must first gain access in thought into the dimension in which alone the question about the relationship of God to men can be asked, the dimension of the Holy which remains closed to us, even as a dimension, so long as the openness of Being has not lit up and in this illumination is close to men. In this nearness to Being alone can a decision be arrived at, if at all, Heidegger says earlier in this essay, whether and how God and the gods deny themselves and the night persists, whether and how the day of holiness dawns, whether and how in the dawn of the holy a manifestation of God and the gods can begin afresh. But the holy—which is only the open space for the coming (*Wesensraum*) of divinity, which in turn provides only a dimension for the gods and for God—can shine forth only when previously and after long preparation Being itself has opened itself up and been realized in its Truth.

9. In "Vom Wesen des Grundes" (*Wegmarken*, pp. 38-52; E.T., pp. 47-81), Heidegger gives a brief history of the world concept. In early Greek philosophy *kosmos* meant not so much the essents themselves as 'how' they *are* as a whole, this 'how' as a whole being regarded in a way as a prior determinant of essents and relative to man. With the new ontic understanding of existenz that emerged in Christianity, the relation of *kosmos* with human existence was taken in a more intimate sense, so much indeed that *kosmos* came to be used as a term for a particular basic mode of human existenz. (*Kosmos houtos* in St. Paul denotes the human state in general, with its distance from God; for St. John also *kosmos* denotes the human state which is turned away from God. This, as Heidegger points out, is a wholly anthropological concept of the world.) The New Testament conception of *kosmos* becomes more explicit in Augustine and Thomas Aquinas. In Augustine, *mundus* or world has the double meaning of the totality of created beings (*ens creatum*) and of absorption in worldliness (*habitare corde in mundo; amare mundum*). Similarly, for Aquinas also *mundus* means both *universum* as well as *saeculum* (worldliness, in the sense in which *saecularis* is the opposite of *spiritualis*). In pre-Kantian rational metaphysics, the study of the systematic unity of the whole of simply given entities, the whole of created beings (rational cosmology), became an important part of *metaphysica specialis*, being put next to Ontology. Right from his dissertation of 1770, *De mundi sensibilis etc.*, Kant was preoccupied with the concept of the world in the 'cosmological' sense; in his *Anthropology*, the existenzial, human meaning of world also comes in for discussion, though without the specifically Christian coloring. In the *Critique of Pure Reason*, the concept of the world is an Idea of the pure reason, a transcendental concept of synthesis embracing the totality of all appearances or objects of possible experience. Thus, with Kant the world concept of traditional metaphysics undergoes a transformation; it receives a deeper ontological interpretation, world being no longer regarded as an ontic totality of things strung together. At the same time world means, for Kant, the totality of the finitude of the *human* state, a meaning which emerges clearly in the existenziell connotation which the world concept has in Kant's *Anthropology*, where world is regarded as the 'game' of life all of us play and is not a merely regional title referring either to the totality of natural

entities or to the community of human beings, but to man in his relationship to the whole of essents.

World as the whole within which man lives and in terms of which he understands himself, thus becoming a self, 'is' itself not an essent to which he is externally related. It is subjective, but not in the sense of being confined to the 'inner sphere' of Dasein misconceived as pure subject; it is objective, but not in the sense of being one among other existing objects. It is in fact a manifestation of Dasein's transcendence, its being-in-the-world, which alone renders possible both subjectivity and objectivity. The existenzial concept of world, Heidegger says, far from being arbitrary, as the historical account above shows, "seeks to bring into the explicitness and sharpness of a *problem* a phenomenon of Dasein which has always been familiar but not ontologically grasped in a comprehensive manner."

10. In a footnote, Heidegger refers the reader to E. Husserl's analyses of relation, reference, signification and so forth, in his *Logische Untersuchungen* and *Ideen I*, 10. The former in particular is still valuable as providing concrete examples of the phenomenological approach to problems of logical analysis.

11. *Bewandtnis* is translated by Walter Biemel (*Le Concept de Monde chez Heidegger*, pp. 47-49) as 'destination' (end, object), because, as he points out, this term has the advantage of having the same constitutive elements as contained in *Bewandtnis*, that is, on the one hand, *that which* is destined and, on the other, that *for which* the object is destined. This corresponds to what Heidegger calls the *womit* and the *wobei* of *Bewandtnis* respectively. That *which* is destined is the utensil which is used and the *for-what* is the operation for which it is destined, its *raison d'être*. And the operation can itself be employed *for* something else, can become the *that* employed *for*, that is, the hammer is *for* hammering and the latter itself may be *for* driving a nail. In the English translation of *Sein und Zeit*, the term is translated as 'involvement'. This hardly makes for intelligibility.

In regard to *bewenden lassen*, Biemel explains that the preoccupied Dasein always discovers essents as having a destination. Heidegger designates this fact by the expression '*bewenden lassen*' and Biemel suggests that this may be translated by 'to render possible' in the sense of admitting the encounter with a being. Only when an entity is disclosed as having a destination, is it possible for it to be encountered as something at hand. Letting an essent have a destination or be relative to an end is an a priori condition, therefore, which renders possible an encounter with essents as handy.

12. *Umwillen*, 'for the sake of' (*à quoi final* = the final 'for what'—Biemel). Heidegger's discussion of the *Umwillen* in "Vom Wesen des Grundes" suggests the closeness of this concept to Aristotle's *hou heneka* (*Metaphysics*, 2 1013b 16), the *causa finalis*, end or final where-fore, that is, the *arche*, both in the sense of cause and of the principle of intelligibility. Discussing the *agathon* of Plato, Heidegger says, more explicitly (p. 38; E.T., p. 45), "Das Wesen des *agathon* liegt in der Mächtigkeit seiner selbst als *hou heneka*—als das *Umwillen* von . . . ist es die Quelle von Möglichkeit als solcher."

13. In *Being and Time*, the analysis of the 'utensil' is provisional and partial only. For a consideration of the utensil as it is in its own being, see "The Origin of the Work of Art" in *Poetry, Language, Thought*. Here the utensil ar

character of a utensil is shown to lie in its 'reliability', as springing from the utensil's rootedness not only in a 'world' but also in the 'Earth'.

14. *The Principles of Philosophy*, Everyman's Library, p. 185.

15. Ibid., p. 201.

16. Ibid., p. 184.

17. Ibid., p. 200.

18. See chapter 9 for Heidegger's general estimate of Descartes. According to Werner Marx, Heidegger's thought constitutes a massive attack against Cartesianism. "Almost every one of Heidegger's positive statements or compositions has a negative or antagonistic side, for they are all born out of his life-and-death struggle with his arch-enemy Cartesianism. . . . I see his new conception of philosophy as his final triumph over Descartes, the end of a long struggle beginning in the works of his first period and ending in those of the second" ("Heidegger's New Conception of Philosophy").

19. As Biemel translates it; De Waelhens renders it as 'structuring', but perhaps 'directedness' suggests the meaning better.

20. In the essay, "What does it mean to orient oneself in thought?"

21. A penetrating discussion of Kant's doctrine of space will be found in *Die Frage nach dem Ding*, pp. 153-157 (E.T., pp. 196-201). Heidegger remarks here that the chief difficulty of Kant's view lies, not in his formulation of the problem of space, but rather in his assigning space as pure intuition to a human subject, the being of which has been inadequately determined. How the problem of space develops in consequence of a "radical overcoming of its connections with a subject," can be seen, Heidegger points out, in *Being and Time*, sections 19-24 and 70.

For Heidegger's later description of man's relationship to space in terms of 'dwelling' see "Bauen Wohnen Denken" in *Vorträge und Aufsätze*, pp. 154-158 (E.T., *Poetry, Language, Thought*, pp. 154-158). See also "Art and Space," where Heidegger seeks to think space as space, in its very own character and manner of being.

22. As Heidegger has pointed out ("Vom Wesen des Grundes," *Wegmarken*, p. 52n; E.T., p. 81n), the analysis of the environing world in sections 14-24 is meant solely to lead on to an account of the world phenomenon and, as being itself not this, remains of secondary importance. The notion of world indeed remains undeveloped in *Being and Time*, as John Wild remarks (*Review of Metaphysics* 16, 1962), but in view of Heidegger's statement and of his discussion of the world concept in "Vom Wesen des Grundes" (1928), it can hardly be called an 'error'. The account there constitutes an indispensable supplement to the preparatory approach to the problem of world in *Being and Time*. See the summary included in chapter 8 of this work. That a complete account of the structure of world must await clarification of the sense of Being is explicitly stated by Heidegger towards the end of section 69.

Describing ("Der Ursprung des Kunstwerkes" in *Holzwege*, pp. 33-34; E.T., *Poetry, Language, Thought*, pp. 44-45) how a work of art sets up and opens out a world, Heidegger indicates, again only partially, the nature of world. It is not merely a collection of all things, known and unknown, not an imaginary framework holding them together. World comes to pass, worlds (*weltet*), and is more real than the realm of the tangible and the perceptible in which we feel so much at home. World is never an object; it is the ever unobjectifiable. "When a world opens out, all things acquire their own pace, their leisureliness or haste, their remoteness and nearness, their breadth and narrowness." In "Brief über den 'Humanismus'" (*Wegmarken*, p. 180), Heidegger speaks of world as "not an essent nor the realm of essents, but the openness of Being." For Heidegger's latest account of world, see *Vorträge und Aufsätze*, pp. 178–181 (E.T., *Poetry, Language, Thought*, pp. 179–182).

23. This has been amply shown by Max Scheler in his phenomenological studies of sympathy. (See his book *The Nature of Sympathy*.) For an excellent account of Scheler's views and his place in the phenomenological movement, see H. Spiegelberg, *The Phenomenological Movement*.

24. As Heidegger remarks later ("Brief über den 'Humanismus'," *Wegmarken*, p. 161), though this statement still employs the language of the metaphysical tradition, its main point is to bring out the ek-sistent character of man. From the point of view of the history of Being, 'substance' is itself the misleading translation of *ousia*, which denotes the presence of the present and which mostly, in its mysterious ambiguity, also means what is present itself. If we take the metaphysical term 'substance' in this sense, which is already suggested in *Being and Time*, in conformity with the 'phenomenological destruction' executed there, then the statement that "the 'substance' of men is ek-sistenz" says nothing other than this: that the mode in which man in his own essence is in relation to Being, is the ecstatic inherence in the truth of Being.

25. Cf. Kierkegaard's penetrating remarks on such impersonal and anonymous modes of being in *The Present Age*.

26. H. Spiegelberg, *The Phenomenological Movement*, p. 329; see also J. Wild's essay, "Man and His Life-World" in *For Roman Ingarden*.

27. Heidegger's account of world here is provisional and incomplete, as already pointed out. In accordance with the fundamental-ontological procedure of *Being and Time*, world is conceived as an existenzial, that is, from the point of view of Dasein. Only in the later phase does he give an interpretation of world in terms of the truth of Being, for which see the last chapter of this work.

A lucid exposition of the concept of world in Heidegger is given by Walter Biemel in his little book, *Le Concept de Monde chez Heidegger*. See Ludwig Landgrebe's *Philosophie der Gegenwart* (chapters 1 and 2) for a succinct and systematic account of Heidegger's views on the nature of man and the concept of world in the context of contemporary German philosophy and, in particular, of the doctrines of Husserl. Taking the ideas of Husserl and their critical development by Heidegger as his basis, the phenomenologist Eugen Fink has made "world" the central concept in his philosophy. Cf. *Zur Ontologischen Frühgeschichte von Raum-Zeit-Bewegung* (1957); *Sein, Wahrheit, Welt* (1958); *Alles und Nichts* (1959); *Spiel als Weltsymbol* (1960); *Nietzsches Philosophie* (1961), *Epilogue zur Dichtung* (1971).

Following Eugen Fink, Vincent Vycinas has recently given an account of Heidegger's philosophy (*Earth and Gods*) from the perspective of the phenomenon of world, in which Heidegger's thinking converges according to him. As will be obvious from the interpretation offered in the last chapter of this work, the present writer cannot agree either with Vycinas' view of the 'three phases' of Heidegger's thought or with his assumption that Heidegger's philosophy culminates in a return to the Greeks only. Vycinas' work is, however, valuable for its extensive treatment of Heidegger's conception of the world as the Fourfold (*Geviert*, the Foursome, as Vycinas happily renders it).

4
Man's Existential Structure

Having given a preliminary account of the constitutive elements in the unified structure of being-in-the-world, Heidegger returns to a deeper-level thematic inquiry into the nature of being-in as such, at the same time preparing the way for an understanding of care as the real being of Dasein. It has been shown that being-in is not the same as the 'within-ness' of one *vorhanden* essent in another, nor the projection of a property of the subject, but that it is an intrinsic mode of being of Dasein itself. It will not do, Heidegger points out, to try to retain the traditional philosophical schema of subject and object and explain being-in as a relation between the two by describing Dasein's being as this 'between' itself. Such an account splits up the primary phenomenon of being-in and seeks to rehabilitate the basic subject-object schema which it has been his intention to avoid by taking the unified phenomenon of being-in-the-world as his starting point. It is in order to avoid this unserviceable and worn-out conceptual framework of subject-object that Heidegger employs the term *Dasein*, giving to it the sense of human existence and playing upon the two constituent parts of the word: *Da* (there) and *sein* (to be).[1] The essent who is intrinsically constituted by being-in-the-world *is* itself its 'there' (*Da*), having its own existenzial spatiality (upon which depends the possibility of locating anything as 'here' or 'there') and disclosing this as an area of openness. "This essent carries in its very being the character of disclosedness. The expression 'there (*Da*)' indicates this intrinsic opened-up-ness." The old doctrine of *lumen naturale*, the natural light in men, refers to this existenzial ontological feature of man, that he *is* in such a way as to be his 'there'. He is 'illumined' in the sense that he has cleared, lighted or opened up (*gelichtet*) by himself, not through another essent, but in such a way that he is himself the 'clearing' or opening."[2] Dasein is its openness, and the problem to be discussed now is: what are the ways in which Dasein is its 'there', what is the existenzial constitution of this 'there' (*Da*)? The three constituent ways, all equally primary, in which Dasein is its openness are: the way Dasein is 'placed' or disposed in life and the world (*Befindlichkeit*), understanding (*Verstehen*), and speech or discourse (*Rede*). But since these are modes of Dasein's being, the ways in which Dasein by its very being there brings a 'clearing' with it, Heidegger also deals with them as they are manifested, first and foremost, in its everyday mode of existence.[3]

[28]

Disposition, Understanding, Interpretation, and Speech

The ontological term *Befindlichkeit*, "being placed, or disposed, in a situation," refers to something that is ontically a matter of common, everyday experience: our moods, how we feel at the moment, the various ways in which we are attuned to our environment. Whether in a state of undisturbed equanimity or of ill humour, whether bored and out of tune, we are always in some fashion 'attuned' to the world. These moods (*Stimmungen*) constitute the primordial mode of disclosure in which Dasein is brought to an awareness of its own being as '*Da*'. Mood and feeling have their own peculiar modes of disclosure and, in John Wild's felicitous rendering, give access to much that is opaque to pure theory; constantly fluctuating but ever present in one form or the other, they reveal the situation in which we find ourselves at the moment.[4] In such nontheoretical awareness of mood and feeling, man is revealed to himself as an essent who is delivered up, as sheer fact, to his being as something that he has to be in his actual existence; he is brought to an awareness of the naked fact *that* he is, and of this being of his as something that he has to realize. The sheer 'that he is' is revealed in such a mood, the whence and the whither remain in the dark. This naked 'that' of existence, of the Dasein in it (*'Da'*), is called by Heidegger 'thrown-ness' (*Geworfenheit*), the fact that man always finds himself there, thrown into life, into the openness of his *'Da'*, in one situation or the other. This expression is meant to indicate the *facticity* of being delivered up, conceived as an existenzial determination of Dasein as being-in-the-world. This facticity is not the brute factuality of something simply given but a character of its own being, which Dasein appropriates in its existence, even though at first as something thrust upon it. It is not the factuality of "an object from which I am detached, and at which I can stare," but an existenzial facticity concerned with itself, either turning back to take over its factuality or turning away from this as a burden. Mostly it is the latter, "a finding that originates not so much in a direct seeking as in an effort to escape."

The first ontological characteristic of "finding ourselves in a situation" thus is that it "reveals Dasein in its thrown-ness, in the first instance and mostly, in the mode of avoidance and evasion." Secondly, a mood just overtakes us, coming neither from 'outside' nor from 'within', but grows out of our being-in-the-world, as a mode of existence in the world.[5] It is not primarily a mental state 'within' us, which is then projected on to persons and things, but is a basic existenzial mode of the simultaneous disclosure of world, being-together and existence. Through our moods, the whole complex of our being-in-the-world already, always, stands primordially disclosed. Thirdly, the primary disclosure of world through Dasein's way of being-in (as described earlier) must now be understood in terms of "the attuned finding ourselves in a situation" which characterizes our way of being in the world, so that when essents encounter us from within the world, we do not just take notice of them but are *affected* in various ways; they touch and concern us. They matter to Dasein because of its already being in an attuned way in its situation. Dasein, in other words, is open to the world and receptive for an encounter with essents within it because of this attuned mode of being in the world. Only because a man is fearfully, or fearlessly, attuned to his situation, can he discover an essent at hand in his environing world as something threatening, for example. Our senses affect us because, as attuned through moods, we are already receptive and accessible. Ontologically, therefore, our moods and dispositions must be considered as being the basic condition of the possibility of discovering the world, for they alone render us open to what comes from the world. A pure looking at, "even though it may pierce into the inmost veins of the being of a *vorhanden* entity," can never discover such a thing as a threatening object confronting it in the world. Even the purest *theoria* or contemplation has its basic mood of "a quiet tarrying with."[6]   [29]

Keeping in view the interpretation of anxiety as a fundamental disposition which follows later, Heidegger further elucidates the structure of *Befindlichkeit* by an analysis of fear regarded as one of its modes. Like other feelings, fear may be considered under three aspects—that *of* which, or before which (*wovor*), we are afraid; the feeling, the fearing, itself; and that *for which* (*worum*) we are afraid. That of which there is fear, the frightening thing, may be an essent at hand, or on hand, or a fellow-man. What arouses fear is something that is threatening, that is destined to harm, that approaches us from a neighboring region known to us as such, that comes ever closer, yet never quite close enough to be within grappling distance. Fearing itself is a kind of letting the threatening thing be free to matter (be of concern) to us, it is what discovers the approaching threat as something fearful; the circumspect look sees the fearful thing because it is already fearfully disposed. It is because our attuned being-in-the-world carries within it, "the slumbering possibility of 'fearfulness' that the world becomes open to us in such a way that anything in the nature of a frightening object can emerge and approach us out of it." The different modifications of fear due to variations in the constitutive elements of the feeling, such as fright, horror, or shock, are all existenzially possible ways in which Dasein "finds itself in a situation," ways of being-in-the-world attuned in a 'fearful' manner.   [30]

Another way, equally original with disposition, in which Dasein is 'there', is 'lit up', revealing itself and the world, is understanding as a fundamental existenziality, the basic mode of Dasein's being. As an existenzial, understanding (which, for Heidegger is primarily *phronesis* in Aristotle's[7] or 'knowing how' in Ryle's sense) refers to an ability, not to do something particular but to *be* in the sense of existing. A human being is not a *vorhanden* entity which has additionally the gift of being able to do something, but is primarily possibility, an ability to *be*, in this way or that. His being is in some measure always already open to him, and to say that man 'understands' is to refer to his comprehension of his being in terms of possibilities of being, of a disclosure of his ability to be, of his potentiality of being, Dasein is what it can be, and how it actualizes its possibility. The existenzial possibility of being characteristic of Dasein must be sharply distinguished from the empty logical possibility as well as the sheer contingency of the factual. "As the modal category of the existence of the simply given thing, possibility denotes what is not yet actual and what is never necessary, being ontologically lower than actuality and necessity. Possibility as an existenzial, on the contrary, is the most primordial and ultimate ontological determination of Dasein." Possibility as an existenzial does not mean the ability to be no matter what one likes (*libertas indifferentiae*), for man is already thrown into a situation not of his own choosing; he is already handed over to himself as possibility and hence is "thrown possibility, through and through." Because he has some comprehension of the way he is in the world, which means an awareness of his 'ability to be', he can go astray or be mistaken about himself; and in this power to be, he is also "delivered up to the possibility of finding himself again in his possibilities." Dasein's understanding, the awareness of its ability to be, is always in terms of possibilities, whether it refers to its own self or to the world in which it exists.

Understanding delves into possibilities, in all the essential dimensions of what can open itself for it, because in itself it has the structure of what Heidegger calls a 'project' (*Entwurf*).[8] The projective character of understanding implies that the possibilities, in view of which Dasein does the projecting, are themselves not thematically grasped, for then they would cease to be possibilities and turn into something given. "Understanding, regarded as projective, is the mode of being of Dasein in which it *is* its possibilities as possibilities." Further, as existenzially projective in his way of being, man is always 'more' than what he as a matter of fact is. However, he is never more than what is implied in the facticity of his ability to be, and never less, for existenzially he *is* what in his ability to be he is *not yet*. It is because his mode of being is so constituted that he *is* what he will be (or fail to be), that he can with understanding say to his own self, "Become, what thou art!" Finally, understanding has its own possibilities of being authentic, if it orients itself toward Dasein's being as the ultimate end and arises from its own self as such, or of being inauthentic, if it attaches itself primarily to the disclosure of the world, interpreting Dasein's own self in terms of the world. Of course, since understanding is concerned with a comprehensive disclosure of Dasein's being-in-the-world, the choice of either of these possibilities does not involve exclusion of any term in this complex whole—in every understanding of the world, existenz is also understood and vice versa.

Just as preoccupation has its circumspect seeing, and solicitude its regardful look, so there is a 'sight' which concerns Dasein's existenz as such, the transparency of 'seeing through' (*Durchsichtigkeit*). This is what renders 'self-knowledge' possible, not in the sense of spotting out and contemplating a point called the self in ourselves, but of comprehending the full disclosedness of being-in-the-world through all its constitutive elements. Man's own self is visible to him only insofar as his being with the world and with his fellowmen, as constitutive factors of his own existenz, have become transparent to him. All seeing, understood in this broad sense of enabling the disclosure of essents of any kind as they are in themselves and including not merely the seeing of what is simply given (perception) but also circumspection, regard and transparent penetration, is based on understanding as the primary mode of awareness. And from this it follows that the traditional primacy of intuition (looking at, having a view of—*Anschauen*) in the noetic sphere is as untenable as the corresponding preeminence of being as something simply given in the ontological sphere. Intuition (that is, direct cognition of something objectively given) as well as thought, Heidegger asserts, are both remote derivatives of understanding and even the phenomenological 'intuition of essence' is based on existenzial understanding. What exactly is the nature of this kind of 'seeing' can only be determined after the concept of Being has first been elucidated, for the being of anything alone is a phenomenon, in the phenomenological sense, which the 'intuition of essence' aims at disclosing.

[31]

The two existenzials, "finding oneself in a situation" (disposition) and understanding together constitute the basic openness of being-in-the-world, such that the attuned Dasein is aware of the possibilities from which it exists and, opening up possibilities through its projects, is already attuned to them. Understanding, as projecting one's being on possibilities, elaborates itself through 'interpretation' or explication and in this manner possesses itself explicitly of what is understood. Heidegger explains the nature of interpretation by dealing at length with its exemplification in the understanding of the world. On the basis of the significance or meaningfulness presupposed in the disclosure of world, the preoccupied Dasein becomes cognizant, through the circumspect look, of the what-for of the handy utensils it encounters. Such cognizance lifts the utensil out of its vaguely comprehended background of meaningfulness, so that it is now explicitly known *as* something 'in order to'. Understanding something in this manner *as* something is 'interpreting' it. "The 'as' is what renders something explicit; it constitutes interpretation." This may occur on a pre-predicative level, in the simple cognition of an essent at hand, for example, without necessarily being formulated into a proposition. The pre-predicative articulation of what is understood by means of the 'as' of interpretation is implied in the mere seeing of a utensil, which can be perceived as such only on the basis of a utensilar whole in which it is an element—the implicit utensilar system attains explicitness in the simple perception of a utensil as such. An 'as-free' cognition of something, far from being a primary cognitive mode, can only mean an experience of merely having something in front of oneself, staring at something without understanding. It is thus a privative and derived mode of the primary and originally simple and direct interpretative perception.

Interpretation, or judging something as something, not only in everyday circumspect articulation of our cognition of utensils but generally, is always based on a prior intention or 'prepossession' (*Vorhabe*), foresight or 'preview' (*Vorsicht*) and anticipation or 'preconception' (*Vorgriff*). There is already in us some comprehension of a totality of destination or purpose from which we take our orientation when we try to interpret and appropriate explicitly what is thus dimly understood—this is the *prepossession*, on the basis of which interpretation proceeds. Further, this interpretative assimilation takes place always under the guidance of some consideration in respect of which what is understood is explicated—this is the foresight or *preview*. Lastly, the interpretation occurs in terms of a conceptual scheme which is already fixed upon, whether as foreshadowed in the thing to be understood itself or imposed from without—this is the *preconception* or conceptual anticipation determining all interpretation. Interpretation is thus never a presuppositionless grasping of something already given. When, in interpreting a text, for example, the interpreter appeals in the name of what is 'in there', generally this alleged what is 'in there' is nothing else but the preconception of the interpreter himself, taken for granted and unexamined, a preconception which is necessarily implied as its very condition in all interpretation. How can we account for this *fore-* or *pre*-structure of understanding, this a priori element always present in it, and for the *as* structure of interpretation? Do the two together constitute a single unified phenomenon, connected existenzially with the phenomenon of project, and pointing to something basic in the ontological constitution of Dasein? A consideration of the nature of sense or meaning may throw some light on these questions. Projective understanding reveals an essent in its possibility. In the case of an intramundane essent, understanding projects it against the background of the world, that is, of a totality of significance to which Dasein's preoccupation has already anchored itself. When an essent is thus disclosed we understand it, that is, it has meaning or 'sense'. The concept of sense refers to the formal framework of what is disclosed by understanding and then articulated through interpretation. "Sense is the final end or purpose (*Woraufhin*) of a project, structured through prepossession, preview and preconception, on the basis of which something can be understood as something." There is, in other words, first the projection of an essent against the background and in the manner mentioned above; this puts it in a meaningful context which gets structured through the three elements in the *pre*-structure of understanding; from this the essent acquires its sense or meaning.[9]

The fact that interpretation functions within the *pre*-structure of understanding means that all interpretation, which is supposed to generate understanding or knowledge, must itself be based on prior understanding of what is to be known through interpretation. This has been in a way always recognized, at least in the spheres of textual and historical understanding. But if, in these spheres, one must already presuppose what is to be established (since interpretation presupposes prior understanding and is 'nourished' by it), are we not involved in moving in a circle which, according to the most elementary rules of logic is a vicious circle, and does it not mean a decrement in the scientific status of these inquiries? It is sometimes thought that the ideal state of affairs in interpretation, whether historical or textual, would be reached if the circle could be avoided completely and objective knowledge, as independent of the standpoint of the observer as it presumably is in natural science, could be attained. But this would be a complete mistake. "To see anything vicious in this circle and to be on the lookout for ways and means to avoid it, and indeed even to look upon it as an unavoidable shortcoming, is radically to misunderstand the nature of understanding." It is to measure understanding and interpretation by the yardstick of a particular ideal of knowledge, that of natural science, which is itself a degenerate species of understanding that has depleted itself to the verge of incomprehension. The basic conditions of any possible interpretation can be fulfilled, not by getting out of this circle but by entering into it in the right manner. The circle of understanding is not a circle in which some arbitrarily chosen mode of knowledge revolves but is an expression of the existenzial *pre*-structure of Dasein itself. Far from being vicious, the circle conceals in itself possibilities of a deeper knowledge, provided it is understood that "the first, last and constant task of interpretation" is to assure itself that its prepossession, preview and preconception do not come from inspired flashes and popular notions, but have been worked out on the basis of the 'things themselves'.

[32]

Heidegger treats statement (*Aussage*) or judgment as being grounded in understanding and a derivative form of interpretation. An analysis of the nature of judgment is important because it occupies a central place in the problems of fundamental ontology. It does so because, since the decisive beginnings of classical ontology, *logos* has provided a unique mode of access to everything that really is and to the Being of all essents and also because judgment has always been regarded as the ultimate and proper 'seat' of Truth, a phenomenon most intimately linked up with the whole problem of Being. Heidegger distinguishes three interconnected senses of statement which together make up the full structure of judgment. Primarily, judgment signifies exhibiting, in the original sense of *logos* as *apophansis*, letting essents be seen as they show themselves by themselves. For example, the assertion, "the hammer is too heavy" is meant to enable the disclosure, not of a 'sense', but of this essent (the hammer) itself in a certain mode of handiness, nor has it anything to do with any sort of 'representation' or with some mental state of the speaker. Secondly, judgment is predication, involving the assertion of a 'predicate' about a 'subject', which thus becomes determined by the former. What was exhibited in the judgment in the first sense has here been narrowed down by undergoing a determination through the predicate, but the judgment in this sense still has its basis in exhibiting. "The parts of the predicative articulation, subject and predicate, are an unfoldment within the function of exhibiting. The determination as such does not itself disclose but, as a mode of exhibiting, limits our seeing to what shows itself—the hammer—as such, so that what stands in overtness (or is disclosed) may be explicitly disclosed in its determinate character through an express restriction of our vision." A statement in the sense of predication also remains basically apophantic in character. In the third place, statement is communication in the sense that it lets others also see what is exhibited as thus determined. What is shared through communication here is a common mode of being-in-the-world in its relation to or in its being-toward what is exhibited. Communication as understood in this existenzial sense of partaking may take the form of a propositional utterance, which can be repeated and passed on from one to another. Thus 'objectified', an utterance widens the area of shared disclosure, though this always exposes the utterance to the possibility of becoming merely repetitive. What it purports to exhibit may once again sink back into partial or total obscurity. The nature of a judgment can be thus summed up by saying that it is a communicative and determining showing forth or exhibiting.

The statement can exhibit because something has already been revealed to understanding or disclosed to circumspection; it is not "a free floating process which by itself can at all disclose anything but occurs always on the basis of being-in-the-world." It represents a mode of interpretation having, like it, an intention or prepossession (what is already disclosed); its preview (the determinative predicate, which the judgment detaches from its fusion with the subject), and a preconception (the concept of the predicate as a separate entity). Further, the judgment or statement is a secondary (modified) form of interpretation. The proposition, "the hammer is too heavy," for example, formulates what is already disclosed and understood through preoccupied circumspection and what is already interpreted, even without the use of words, by the appropriate action of laying the hammer aside or exchanging it with another. The absence of words does not imply that there has been no interpretation; and even when the interpretation is accompanied by words such as "too heavy!" or "another hammer!" this is obviously not a proper judgment in the sense defined. Judgment, itself a form of interpretation, always modifies the original interpretation. In the original circumspect interpretation, what is intended is the hammer as a handy utensil, but in becoming the 'object' of a judgment the intention undergoes a change. The handy essent as something *with* which we want to accomplish some purpose becomes something *about* which an ostensive assertion is made. The preview sees something simply there in what was a utensil, something to-do-with, so that its handiness retreats in favor of the objectivity of something *vorhanden*, something present as an object, possessing such and such attributes. The as structure also undergoes a modification, because now the predicative determination of the subject takes the latter as simply given. "The 'as', in its function of appropriating what is understood, no longer reaches out into a totality of destination. As regards its possibilities of articulating the referential relations, it is cut off from the complex of significance which is constitutive of the environing world. The 'as' is pushed back into the uniform level of the simply given. It dwindles into the structure of merely letting a determinate *vorhanden* thing be seen." It should be noted that it is in this leveling down of the original 'as' of circumspect interpretation to the 'as' which determines what is simply given that the special virtue of judgment consists, for thus alone does it become capable of functioning as a purely theoretical judgment and of exhibiting something in the mode of being purely looked at.

Judgment, thus, has its ontological genesis in interpretative understanding. The original 'as' of the interpretation (*hermeneia*) of circumspect understanding must be distinguished from the *apophantic* 'as' of judgment. Between the two extremes of the judgment embodying interpretation as it occurs implicitly in preoccupied understanding and the purely theoretical judgment there is a wide range of statements, such as those reporting events in the environing world and descriptions of essents at hand, which simply cannot be assimilated to the purely theoretical judgment without radically distorting their sense. Heidegger also points out in this connection that 'Logic', as it has developed out of the Platonic and Aristotelian views of *logos* (sentence, statement), is itself ultimately rooted in the existenzial structure of Dasein. In accordance with the ontological bias of the Greeks in favor of the *Vorhanden*, the *logos* was itself treated as an entity of the simply given type: a number of words juxtaposed in a certain order, like things. The unity behind the words as thus strung together in a sentence was to be found, according to Plato, in the thing disclosed by them; for him all *logos* is *logos tinos*. In Aristotle's more advanced view, *logos* is at the same time *synthesis* and *diaresis*, connecting and separating at once, and in this manner revealing a reality as such. Aristotle's view foreshadows, though without realizing its full ontological implications, the 'as' structure of judgment which, as we have seen, has its origin in the hermeneutic 'as'. A failure to grasp this origin has led to the development of the Aristotelian doctrine into what Heidegger calls a superficial 'theory of judgment'. According to this theory, judging consists in the connecting together and separating of representations and concepts. Judging is then further formalized into a system of 'relations', so that propositions become, in corresponding measure, instruments of calculation rather than media of ontological interpretation. The *copula*, for example, becomes in this process, a mere connecting link and it is forgotten that in the basic sense it has nothing to do with links and bindings. Since making statements and ontological understanding constitute the possibilities of being of Dasein itself, the 'is' leads back ultimately to problems connected with the existenzial analytic. A more adequate analysis of *logos* in terms of the ontological phenomenon of Being inherent in it, and not merely in terms of its 'logical' powers as has so far been done, can alone bring into view the hidden ontological presuppositions of logical theory.[10]

[33]

Only after having dealt with *Befindlichkeit* and understanding, with the possibility of interpretation inherent in it, does Heidegger turn to speech or discourse (*Rede*), the third of the fundamental existenzialities of Dasein which constitute together the being of the 'there', the openness of its being-in-the-world. He does this in order to point to the fact that the phenomenon of language (*Sprache*) is rooted in the existenzial constitution of the openness of Dasein and that the existenzial-ontological basis of language lies in speech. Interpretation and judgment presuppose understanding as articulated through speech. Sense, as mentioned earlier, is what undergoes the articulation and it is speech which articulates it into a whole of meanings. The attuned comprehension of being-in-the-world expresses itself as speech. The complex of meanings 'comes to word', so that it is not words that are provided with meanings but "the words accrue to the meanings." Language is the spoken-out form of discourse or speech; the latter is an existenzial, while the former is a fact, an essent at hand within the world. Speech, as the meaningful articulation of the attuned understanding of being-in-the-world, including being-together-with others, is part of the existenzial constitution of the openness of Dasein and is constitutive of its existenz.

The structural components of speech are: What is spoken about (*das Beredete*), what is spoken (*das Gerdete*), communication, and expression. Not only categorical statements but all forms of speech, such as assenting, denying, inviting, warning, and others, are *about* something, because speech, as partly constituting the openness of being-in-the-world, shows in its own structure the basic pattern of Dasein's mode of being. And in all speech, whether it is request, question, or statement, something is said through which it becomes capable of being commonly shared. In the third place, speech is communication, not merely in the narrow sense of conveying information, but in the wider existenzial sense of an articulate sharing of the attuned "finding oneself in a situation" and understanding. "Communication is never anything like a transportation of experiences, such as beliefs and wishes, from the inside of one to that of another." Speech only renders explicit the shared *Befindlichkeit* and understanding that are implied in the being-together-with others which characterizes Dasein's being-in-the-world. Lastly, through speech we express ourselves, which does not mean that at first we are shut up and encapsulated within ourselves. Dasein, as being-in-the-world, is already 'outside' there by virtue of its attuned understanding and the expressive function of speech is a manifestation of just this aspect of Dasein's existenz. These components of speech are not empirically determined properties of language but constitute a totality of "existenzial characteristics rooted in the ontological structure of Dasein which make such a thing as language ontologically possible." They are all essential to language, though the attempts to comprehend the 'nature of language' have nevertheless always taken their orientation from one particular element in this total structure and conceived language in terms of 'expression', of 'symbolic form', of communication as 'statement' or proposition, of giving 'information' about personal experience, or of 'giving form' to life. To understand the full nature of language it is not enough even to take all of these together; "the essential thing is first to work out the ontological-existenzial totality of the structure of speech on the basis of the analytic of Dasein."

How speech and understanding are interconnected becomes clear when we consider *hearing* which is an existenzial possibility belonging to and constitutive of speaking itself. "Just as the vocal utterance is grounded in speech, so the acoustic perception has its basis in hearing. Giving ear to is the existenzial openness of Dasein for others and also for its own potentiality of being . . . Dasein hears because it understands." The ability to hear, in this primary existenzial sense, is the basis of listening or 'harkening' (*Horchen*), which is phenomenally more primary than what is described as 'hearing' in psychology, that is, the sensation of tones and sounds. "What we hear in the first instance are never noises and sound complexes, but the rattling carriage, the motorcycle. What one hears is the column on the march, the north wind, the tapping woodpecker, the crackling fire." As being-in-the-world and understanding, Dasein is already, from the first, *with* what it understands, namely the intramundane essents at hand. When we listen to somebody speaking, what we hear in the first place is what he says and not the sounds he utters. "We are from the beginning already by the side of (with) the essent talked about, along with the other."

Another important possibility of speech is *silence* and, like the former, it also has its basis in understanding. He who keeps silent in conversation can contribute more substantially to understanding than one who never "runs short of words." Incessant talk about something does not in the least promote its understanding, but on the contrary veils what is understood with an illusion of clarity, reducing it to "the incomprehension of triviality." But to be silent does not mean to be dumb. The dumb, lacking the ability to talk, want all the more to speak and are in no position to give evidence of an ability to keep silent. "He who never says anything is also unable, at a particular moment, to keep silent. Only in proper speaking is authentic silence possible. To be capable of silence, one must have something to say."

Dasein possesses language because speech is constitutive

of the being of its 'there', that is, the attunement and under-standing which make up its openness and its vocal manner of being-in-the-world. It is not surprising, therefore, that the Greeks should have defined man as *zoon logon echon*, an animal that talks. To say that man is an essent that speaks, means not just that he possesses the ability to make vocal utterances, but that he exists in the world in the mode of discovering the world and himself. Speech is an essential aspect of man's openness to the world and to himself. Heidegger points out that the Greeks possessed no word for language, understand-ing it primarily as speech (*logos*) and in philosophical thought taking it as statement or judgment. Grammar as originally developed by them was based on 'logic', that is, on *logos* understood as statement and as grounded in the ontology of the *Vorhanden*. In linguistic science also the doctrine of seman-tic categories has been based on speech understood as state-ment. Once the nature of speech is grasped in its full existenzial depth and scope, the necessity of providing a sounder ontolog-ical basis to linguistic science and of liberating grammar from logic becomes quite apparent. As regards the nature of lan-guage itself, the important question which still remains ob-scure, and indeed has not properly been raised at all, despite the achievements of linguistic science, concerns the mode of being of language. Is language an intramundane handy utensil, or does it have the mode of being of Dasein, or is it neither of the two? Is there any ontological significance in the fact that, semantically, language has primarily a "worldly," indeed a predominantly spatial orientation and that its "meanings" mostly bear the mark of the complex of meaningfulness at-taching to the world?[11]

Since, as has been explained earlier, Dasein in its everyday mode of being tends to surrender itself to the 'one' and be absorbed into him, Heidegger proceeds to inquire if there is any specific mode in which the three existenzials—disposition, understanding, and speech—manifest themselves in Dasein's everyday manner of being. What are the kinds of understand-ing, speech, and disposition appropriate to the mode of being of the 'one' and what specific possibilities of being open out for him? What is the basic mode of Dasein's everyday existence? Heidegger answers these questions by giving first an account of chatter or gossip (*Gerede*), curiosity or inquisitiveness (*Neugier*), and ambiguity (*Zweideutigkeit*), and then discussing Dasein's thrownness and forfeiture (*Verfallen*).

[34]

Man's Everyday Being and Forfeiture

The term 'chatter' or gossip is meant by Heidegger to be taken in a neutral, nonderogatory sense and as denoting a positive phenomenon, the mode of interpretation and understanding characterizing Dasein in its everyday life. Man's quotidian, average talk is carried on in a language that embodies a certain understanding and interpretation of existenz. In the first instance and within certain limits, he is permanently delivered up to this prior interpretedness (*Ausgelegtheit*) in the language that he speaks and which governs his understanding of the world, of himself, and of his fellowmen. Language as a repository of understanding (that is, meanings) contains within it the deposit of the already attained disclosure of essents and comprehension of Being which we inherit and thus also the possibilities available and the horizons open for further interpretation and conceptual articulation. But precisely because of this, it becomes possible for speech as communication to be generally understood without making the hearer turn with understanding to the thing talked about. In such a case, one does not so much understand the reality talked about as only hear what is spoken as such; only the latter is understood, the former being noticed only vaguely and superficially. Communication, as a mode of being-together-with, no longer brings about a participation in the basic relationship to the being of the things talked about. In the everyday mode of being-together, speech becomes its own end and the diction, the pronunciation and the style of speaking become the criteria which determine its genuineness and relevance. It is spread around and repeated, acquiring in this process an authoritative character; "the thing is so because 'one' says it." Such chatter is not confined to the spoken word but occurs also in the written, so that the average understanding of the reader is never in a position to decide—indeed it does not need to, for it 'understands everything'—what is originally creative and achieved by effort and what is merely repetitive.

Speech, as constitutive of Dasein's being and its openness, has thus the possibility of turning into chatter and thereby closing up Dasein's being-in-the-world and covering the intramundane essent from its view. Whatever is said is understood as 'saying' something, disclosing something, but because of a failure to go back to the bottom of what is spoken, it only closes up what it pretends to disclose. Speech in the form of chatter is not so much a mode of disclosure as of closure and concealment. Much of what we know is learnt through the meanings contained in everyday speech, and a great deal never goes beyond such average understanding. Man grows up in the midst of such everyday interpretedness and is powerless to escape its grip. "In it and from it and against it is accomplished all genuine understanding, interpretation and communication, redisclosing and fresh appropriation. It is never as if man were at any time placed in front of the open land of a 'world' in itself, untouched and uncorrupted by this interpretedness, just to contemplate what he encounters." Even the possibilities of his attuned disposition, the way he finds himself in his situation, the way he 'sees' things, are determined by the meanings incorporated in the chatter of the 'one' and its everyday interpretedness. Chatter, casting a veil on what is, thus constitutes a mode of being of man's uprooted understanding which "cuts him off from the real and primary ontological relationships (*Seinsbezüge*) to world, to fellow-men, and to his being-in itself." Suspended in this uprooted condition, but taking shelter under the obviousness and self-assurance of the interpretation inherent in average existence and talk, he remains unaware of the weirdness of his own suspended state.

[35]

The second characteristic of Dasein's everyday mode of being is 'curiosity' or inquisitiveness, which Heidegger describes with reference to the phenomenon of 'sight' attaching to, and dependent upon, Dasein's openness or 'clearing'. Like the different modes, described earlier, in which Dasein is open, its everyday existenz also has its own sight, its own way of seeing. It has, in fact, a strange tendency to 'see' (for which Heidegger uses the term 'curiosity') which is not limited, characteristically, to seeing but denotes generally the peculiar tendency to make perceptual contact with everything. In Greek philosophy knowing was conceived in terms of the desire for seeing, as is evident from the very first sentence of Aristotle's *Metaphysics*.[12] This interpretation of the existenzial genesis of knowledge was already implicit in Parmenides' statement that only what manifests itself to pure contemplative perception is Being, that only such seeing discovers Being. Since then the thesis that real truth is to be found only in pure contemplation becomes the foundation of Western philosophy down to Hegel. The preeminence of 'seeing' has been noticed above all by Augustine in connection with his discussion of *concupiscentia*, where he speaks of 'the lust of the eyes' to include the general experience of the senses in their search for knowledge.[13] As being-in-the-world, man is ordinarily preoccupied with the world, concerned with the handy essents disclosed through circumspection. Having disposed of the things at hand, his preoccupation may come to rest and his circumspect look become free to wander to "the distant and unknown world," to explore the possibilities of seeing, in a relaxed and lingering manner, just what the 'world' looks like. His glance turns to the mere *look* of things, thus bringing what is far to a closeness with himself. In the case of curiosity, however, one wants to see not so that one may understand but just for the sake of seeing. Curiosity flits, says Heidegger, from one new thing to another and is thus characterized by what he calls not abiding or tarrying with what is nearest. This constant unrest and agitated quest of the novel leads, in consequence, to a dissipation or scattering into ever new possibilities. In curiosity there is nothing of the admiring beholding of things, of the *thaumazein*, the wonder that makes us aware of our own ignorance. A third constitutive element in the phenomenon of curiosity or inquisitiveness is its *abodelessness*, for curiosity, not 'dwelling' anywhere, is everywhere and yet nowhere. Chatter and curiosity, the two everyday modes of speech and sight respectively, function together, one dragging the other along with itself. "Curiosity, to which nothing is any longer closed, and chatter, to which nothing remains un-understood," give themselves, that is, to Dasein in this mode of being, the guarantee of a supposedly genuine 'full life'.

[36]

The third characteristic of Dasein's everyday openness is ambiguity, which envelopes not merely the world, but equally Dasein's being-together-with others and even the way it understands its own self. When everyone has access to all things and everyone can say anything he likes about them, it is no longer possible to decide what has been disclosed in genuine comprehension and what not. "Everything seems as if genuinely understood, grasped and spoken and is yet at bottom not so, or it does not seem so, but is yet at bottom so." Not only what is and happens, but what should or can be, including what ought to be done, is infected with ambiguity. Everyone has already from the first surmised and noticed what others think of and notice, but when it comes to the execution of what one was 'on the track of', the being-together of the 'one' vanishes and each is thrown back upon himself. Curiosity and chatter, always on the move, have long since lost interest in the matter and if something genuine and new is achieved, it is for them already antiquated by the time it gains publicity. In this ambiguous mode of existence Dasein is always 'there', in the openness of public togetherness, "where the loudest chatter and the most resourceful curiosity keep the 'business' going, when daily every sort of thing, and at bottom nothing, happens." This ambiguity pervades also man's relationships with others so that each is watchful of how the other will react, what he will say, a being-together-with marked by "a tense, ambiguous spying on each other, a furtive mutual overhearing."

[37]

The three characteristics of the openness of being-in-the-world described above are existenzial determinations which together constitute the basic mode of Dasein's everyday being and which Heidegger terms the 'forfeiture' (or fall) of Dasein. The latter exists, as explained earlier, first and mostly *with* the 'world' of its preoccupation, goes out into it, losing itself in the publicity of the 'one'. "Dasein has from the very start already fallen away from the authentic potentiality of being itself and fallen for the 'world'. This not-being-himself is a positive phenomenon, being man's immediate and usual mode of being, and hence it should not be understood in the sense of a 'fall' from a purer and higher original state of which "we have not only ontically no knowledge but ontologically also no possibilities and guiding principles of interpretation." Forfeiture is not a bad and lamentable ontic property of man which would some day be eliminated, but an existenzial feature of man who by the very fact that he is in the world, becomes forfeit, not to another essent simply given, but to *world* which, as an existenzial, itself belongs to his being.

The phenomenon of forfeiture is characterized by a complex 'agitatedness', the various elements of which Heidegger next goes on to explicate. Through chatter and the 'interpretedness' of public existence, man offers to his own self the possibility of losing himself in the 'one' and thus himself brings upon himself the constant temptation of forfeiture. Being-in-the-world is in itself seductive or tempting, making man a temptation to himself. Chatter, curiosity, and ambiguity give to him a guarantee of the trustworthiness, genuineness and fullness of all possibilities of being. The self-assuredness and determination of the 'one' absolves him from the need for authentic understanding, thus exercising a profoundly appeasing influence upon him, "as if everything was in the best order and all the doors were open." The forfeiture of being-in-the-world is at the same time appeasing or reassuring. But this appeasement, far from bringing stillness and rest, only intensifies the forfeiture, driving man to restless activity and bringing him into a state of self-estrangement in which his own innermost potentiality of being becomes concealed to him. Being-in-the-world as forfeiture is therefore also self-alienating, thrusting Dasein into inauthenticity, a possible mode of its own being. The inner movement characteristic of forfeiture, tempting, appeasing, and alienating, leads Dasein, finally, to be caught up and entangled in itself. This agitatedness of forfeiture as manifested in the above mentioned four ways, is called by Heidegger the sudden and rapid plunge or crash in which Dasein, unknown to itself "falls from itself, in the bottomlessness and futility of inauthentic everydayness." The mode of movement in this fall, in which man's understanding is constantly torn away from projecting authentic possibilities and plunged into the sham existence of the 'one', into the comforting illusion of knowing everything, is characterized as the whirl (*Wirbel*) by Heidegger. This whirl reveals man's thrownness in its moving and throwing character, for thrownness is not something that has occurred once for all or a finished fact at any time, but man, so long as he is, remains in the state of being thrown and is whirled into the inauthenticity of the 'they'.

Forfeiture is not to be conceived as if Dasein were an isolated ego point or subject, which becomes displaced from itself to the world as an object and is contained within it as an essent simply given. It is a mode of being of Dasein's being-in, in which its own potentiality of being-in-the-world is at stake, even though in the mode of inauthenticity. Man becomes forfeit because of this inauthentic concern for his being-in-the-world and he can gain authentic existence through a transformation of this original everyday state of forfeiture. Further, forfeiture denotes an intrinsic ontological structure of Dasein itself, not an ontic property attaching to it. Nor is it meant to be "an ontic judgement about the 'corruption of human nature', not because means to prove this are lacking, but because the problems to which it refers lie prior to all judgement about corruption and innocence, . . . about whether man is 'steeped in sin', is in *status corruptionis*, or changes himself into the *status integritatis*, or finds himself in the intermediate stage of *status gratiae*." All such theories of man's state, whether they are based on religious faith or on a philosophical 'world-view' must be ultimately rooted, as ontic pronouncements, on the ontological comprehension of Dasein's existenzial constitution.[14]

[38]

Care as the Being of Man—Reality and Truth

Having exhibited the total structure of Dasein's being-in-the-world in its full complexity, Heidegger goes on to ask how this unified structure can be conceived in its unity and wholeness. It has been shown that Dasein's average everydayness consists of a being-in-the-world which is forfeited and open, thrown and projecting. Also, in Dasein's existence with other essents and fellow human beings, its very own potentiality of existence is at stake. Is it possible to find a way that will enable us to grasp this complex structure in its wholeness so that it can be seen to spring from a single unifying principle of the being of Dasein? Neither by putting together the elements of the whole exhibited above, nor by adopting any particular feature of our experience, which by nature is oriented to intramundane essents of the simply given kind, nor by deducing the being of Dasein from any particular ideal image of man, can we be led to this underlying principle. We can reach it only by looking *through* the whole so as to have a glimpse of the original unity of the phenomenon as it pervades and conditions every element in this whole. The ontological structure of Dasein is such that, through attunement and understanding, its own being is disclosed to it in some fashion. If we can find a specific kind of comprehending attunement that opens man's own being to him in a distinctive and simplified way, we shall have at our disposal one of the most far-reaching and basic possibilities of disclosure, and of access to his being, lying within man himself. Heidegger finds in Anxiety (*Angst*) such a fundamental attunement and, taking that as the ontic and phenomenal basis, offers his ontological interpretation of the being of Dasein in his wholeness as Care (*Sorge*).

After showing how and why anxiety is a specially suitable mode of attunement from which to start, Heidegger proceeds to describe the preontological interpretation of himself which man has already given, even in ancient times, in terms of care. Since the analytic of Dasein is aimed at preparing the ground for the problem of the sense of Being in general, Heidegger next considers the way care is related to 'worldliness', handiness, and simple givenness as modes of being and the problem of Reality arising out of this. Finally, since the problem of Being and Truth are closely interwoven, the phenomenon of Truth is discussed in detail. "An essent *is*, independently of the experience, knowledge and conceptual grasp through which it is revealed, known and determined. But Being 'is' only in the understanding of essents to whose being there belongs such a thing as the understanding of Being." There is thus a necessary connection between Being and understanding, requiring, for an adequate preparation for the problem of Being, an ontological elucidation of the phenomenon of Truth.[15]

[39]

In order to demonstrate how anxiety or dread is preeminently suited to disclose the being of Dasein and with the intention of penetrating deeper into a grasp of the wholeness of the structure described above, Heidegger takes the foregoing analysis of forfeiture as his point of departure. The absorption in the 'they' and the world of his preoccupation reveals a flight of man from his potentiality of being authentically his own self. This phenomenon of the flight of Dasein from its own self and its authenticity, this turning away from authentic self-hood, in which the latter becomes closed to view, is an ontic, existenziell characteristic of Dasein which provides the clue for an ontological, existenzial interpretation. The fact that it is man's flight from himself, with the consequent veiling of authentic self-hood, indicates that it is a privation of an original openness. "Only insofar as ontologically Dasein is brought into the openness intrinsically belonging to it, can Dasein also fly *from* it." In this turning away, the 'from what' it is a turning away is disclosed as being there, even though not explicitly grasped. What is ontically a flight thus offers a phenomenal basis for an ontological conception, by means of phenomenological interpretation, of that from which it is a flight. Such an interpretation is least exposed to an arbitrary and artificial conception of the being of Dasein because it represents only the carrying out of an explication of something that is revealed ontically by Dasein itself and is not a meaning imported from without.

The examination of fear earlier has shown that the 'before what' or object of fear is always an intramundane menacing entity approaching us from a particular region. In anxiety there is no such object. All flight is flight from something threatening, and in the flight characteristic of its forfeiture also there must be something threatening before which Dasein has to fly. Further, since it is from its own self that Dasein turns away in forfeiture, that from which it flies cannot be described as fearful, for the object of fear is always an essent within the world. The turning away of forfeiture, therefore, is no flight from an essent within the world; it is, on the contrary, a turning towards and being absorbed in essents within the world. Heidegger concludes, hence, that "the turning away of forfeiture is grounded rather in anxiety, which in turn makes fear possible." Unlike fear, anxiety or dread has no definite object and its 'of what' is not an essent within the world, whether at hand or simply given. Anxiety encounters nothing determinate and tangible that threatens it; the 'totality of destination' of essents sinks into insignificance and loses its meaningfulness and importance. That in face of which we are anxious is being-in-the-world as such, which is no 'object' or thing at all. For this reason, in anxiety the threat comes from no particular region, is nowhere, which does not mean, however, that this 'nowhere' is nothing at all but only that it envelopes all region and openness of world in general. It is already 'there', everywhere—"and yet nowhere, it is so near that it oppresses and suffocates and yet it is nowhere." The absence of a determinate object, the nothing and the nowhere of anxiety, the utter unmeaningness into which intramundane essents lapse, have an importunity which makes the world as such obtrude itself in its worldly character, showing that the 'of what' of anxiety is the world as such. The nothingness before which there is anxiety is the nothingness of handy essents, not total nothingness, for it is grounded in the most primary 'something', the *world*. And since this is itself intrinsically an ontological element of being-in-the-world, it is really the latter that is the 'before what' of anxiety. Anxiety thus reveals, originally and directly, the world *as* world, not as itself an essent or the sum of intramundane essents but as the existenzial in-what of all possible essents.

As a disposition, anxiety is not merely 'in face of' something but also for the sake of someone, that is, for Dasein, not as to any specific and determinate possibility of its being but about its being-in-the-world itself. Because in anxiety intramundane essents sink into insignificance and the 'world', including the togetherness with others, "has nothing more to offer," man is thrown back upon himself, upon his authentic potentiality of being-in-the-world, for whose sake he has the anxiety. Isolating him, revealing him as *solus ipse* and leaving him to his own innermost ability of being-in-the-world, anxiety takes away from man the possibility of understanding himself, in his forfeiture, in terms of the 'world' and of the commonplace interpretation of public existence. "Anxiety reveals in Dasein its *being toward* (that is, its being in relation to) its very own potentiality of being, that is, its being *free for* the liberty to choose and take hold of itself." In anxiety both the 'of what' and the 'for what' of anxiety is being-in-the-world and the anxiety, as a disposition, is itself a mode of being-in-the-world. This existenzial identity of the disclosure and what is disclosed, revealing the world as world and the being-in as isolated, sheer, thrown potentiality of being, makes it evident that the phenomenon of anxiety is a preeminent disposition on which to base the interpretation of the being of Dasein.

In contrast to the everyday smug and self-assured attitude of feeling at home in the world, the sense of uncanniness (*Unheimlichkeit*) going with anxiety, its nothing and nowhere, makes one feel at the same time ill at ease and not at home. The everyday intimacy of being-in vanishes and Dasein is brought back out of its forfeited absorption into the 'world'. This makes it evident that the flight of forfeiture is a flight *from* the menacing uncanniness of the Dasein, thrown and delivered up to itself in its Being, in this everyday mode of being-in-the-world, and that it is a flight *to* intramundane essents with which its preoccupation, lost in the 'one', can busy itself in comforting familiarity. Anxiety is thus the basic disposition of Dasein and "the smug familiarity of (everyday) being-in-the-world is itself a mode of the homelessness of Dasein and not the other way round. The sense of not feeling at home must be conceived as being the more original and primary phenomenon, existenzially and ontologically." It is because anxiety is already latent in being-in-the-world that fear can arise in connection with essents within the world. "Fear is anxiety forfeit to the world, inauthentic and unaware of itself as such." Although every disposition or attunement is capable of revealing the full character of being-in-the-world, with its constitutive elements of world, being-in, and self, yet anxiety is thus unique and preeminent in this respect because it isolates man and, bringing him back out of his forfeiture, reveals to him the possibilities of being authentic and inauthentic inherent in himself.[16]

[40]

The quest for the ontological wholeness of the total structure of Dasein, which prompted the foregoing analysis of anxiety, has shown that being anxious is a mode of Dasein's being-in-the-world, that its 'before what' is the thrown being-in-the-world and, thirdly, that its 'for whose sake' is the potentiality of being-in-the-world. Disclosing Dasein phenomenally in this manner, as factually existing being-in-the-world, it has brought to light features of Dasein which are comprised in the three ontological characteristics of existenziality, facticity (thrownness), and forfeiture. Together they constitute the total structure of Dasein. Heidegger now comes back to the problem of determining the ultimate unity underlying this whole structure, "the basic connection that weaves them together." How, he asks, is this unity itself to be characterized? Man is an essent who, in his own being, is concerned about his own being and, being free for his own innermost potentiality of being and thus for the possibility of authenticity and inauthenticity he has always already, in his being, chosen and 'lined up' with a possibility of his own self. Ontologically this means that man is, in his being, always already in advance of himself, beyond himself, in relation to his own potentiality of being. This is what Heidegger calls Dasein's being-ahead-of-itself, its self-anticipation which, as a characteristic of its being-in-the-world, has also the character of thrownness. Dasein is always already in a world, thrown into it and left to its own resources and ahead of itself. Finally, the factual existenz of Dasein is not merely a thrown potentiality of being-in-the-world but is such that Dasein has at the same time already gone out into the world of its preoccupation, spending itself in it, in flight from the uncanniness of latent anxiety. The formal existenzial wholeness of the ontological structural totality of Dasein, its Being, is summed up by Heidegger as being-ahead-of-itself-already-in-(the world-) as-being-with (essents encountered within the world).[17] This structural formula is 'filled up' and given a content by giving it the title of *Care*, which, Heidegger points out, must be understood in a purely ontological and existenzial sense, excluding all ontic suggestions as, for example, the cares and anxieties of life, and others. The preoccupation characteristic of Dasein's relation to handy essents and the solicitude of its encounter with fellow-men are both based on care as the ontological condition of their possibility.[18] Further, care underlies not only existenziality, in isolation from facticity and forfeiture, but encompasses all these ontological characteristics in their unity, and it underlies equally Dasein's relationship to itself and to other persons and things, in the being-ahead-of-itself of both authenticity and inauthenticity. Care is an existenzial a priori presupposed in all behavior and state of Dasein as factual and hence does not imply any preeminence of the practical over the theoretical attitude. 'Theory' and 'practice' are both "possibilities of being of an essent whose being must be determined as care." For this reason it is also a mistake to try to reduce the intrinsically indivisible wholeness of the phenomenon of care to particular mental acts or impulses like willing and wanting or urge and propensity. These are not just processes which are "ontologically indifferent" but are necessarily rooted ontologically in Dasein as care. Since the fundamental ontology pursued by Heidegger is not aimed at constructing a complete ontology of Dasein and much less a concrete philosophical anthropology, he contents himself with giving brief, but very illuminating, indications of how such existenziell psychological processes are existenzially grounded in care, how they arise as ontic modes of being-in-the-world in which the full ontological structure of care is manifested and presupposed.

Though care thus represents a fundamental existenzial and ontological phenomenon, it is not simple in its structure but, as the formula stated earlier indicates, complex and articulated. "The ontologically elementary wholeness of the structure of care cannot be reduced to an ontic 'ultimate element', as certainly as Being cannot be 'explained' in terms of beings. It will be evident at the end that the notion of Being generally is as little 'simple' as that of the being of Dasein." This complexity of the structure of care suggests that the ontological inquiry must be pushed still deeper so as to disclose the underlying unity and wholeness on which this complex structure is itself ontologically based. This is taken up by Heidegger in the second Division of *Being and Time* dealing with temporality.

[41]

Heidegger next offers confirmation of the existenzial interpretation of Dasein as care through Dasein's preontological interpretation of himself in the form of an ancient fable, exemplifying how the comprehension of Being lying within Dasein utters itself preontologically. Such testimony, in which man speaks out about himself 'originally' and with no theoretical prepossessions, is of particular importance because it originates from man's historic past which, in view of the historicity intrinsic to his being, determines his present understanding of himself and of Being in general. The Latin fable which Heidegger quotes, narrates the story of *Cura* (care), who, while crossing a stream, picks up a lump of clay and moulds it into the shape of a man. Jupiter, who happens to arrive there, gives it a soul. When it comes to giving it a name, however, there ensues a quarrel in which Care, Jupiter, and Earth (who has given to this creature a piece of her body) each insists on his or her own name being given to this form. Eventually, they make Saturn the arbitrator, whose judgment is that it should be named *Homo* because it is fashioned out of earth (*humus*) but that when the creature dies, Jupiter, who has given it the soul, shall receive back the soul, and Earth, who has given the body, shall get back the body; but since Care has first brought it into being, it shall be in her possession so long as it lives. It is significant that the decision as to man's being and how it is to be conceived comes from Saturn, who stands for Time. Even on this ontic level, the concept of care possesses, as a quotation from Seneca which Heidegger adduces shows, the double sense of causing Dasein to be free to realize its possibilities through its projects and at the same time indicating its abandonment or thrownness in the world of its preoccupation. In connection with the ontic testimony given above, it must be kept in mind that the existenzial-ontological concept of care is not just a theoretical generalization from such ontic understanding of experience, but is general in the sense of being a priori, as the existenzial condition of the possibility of all ontic caring and abandoning oneself to projects in life. The transcendental 'generality' of the phenomenon of care and all fundamental existenzialia has a width of range which offers a field within which every possible ontic interpretation of Dasein finds scope.

[42]

The history of philosophy shows that, even when on-tological understanding and not merely ontic experience is concerned, the interpretation of Being is oriented to the being of intramundane essents conceived solely as a system of *vorhanden* entities (*res*). Being in general, not excluding the being of Dasein, is given the sense of Reality, with substantiality as its basic determination. Since this traditional concept of reality has thoroughly blocked the way to an adequate analytic of Dasein, to an understanding of the nature of intramundane essents as encountered in their handiness and to that of Being in general, Heidegger proceeds to a detailed discussion of the whole problem of reality, including a treatment of reality as a problem of Being and the provability of the external world, of reality as an ontological problem and of the relation between reality and care.

Traditionally, intuitive knowing (that is, knowing as a kind of contemplating or looking on) as a function of the soul or consciousness, has been thought to be the proper way of grasping the real. Since the real possesses the character of being 'in itself' and independent, the problem of what it means to be real has been linked up with "the possible independence of the real from consciousness and with the possible transcendence of consciousness in the 'sphere' of the real." What reality means ontologically can be determined only when we have first elucidated, as to its being, *that from* which the real is independent and *that which* is supposed to be transcended; and the claim of 'knowing' to be the primary mode of access to the real must itself be examined. The foregoing existenzial analytic has already made it clear that knowing is a derived (*fundierter*) mode of access to the real, which is available only as an intramundane essent, and that it is based on Dasein's being-in-the-world, of which the basic ontological constitution is care.[19] The question whether there is at all a world and whether its existence can be proved is "as a question put by Dasein as being-in-the-world—and who else could put it?—senseless." It is also ambiguous because it does not distinguish between world as the in-what of being-in and 'world' as made up of intramundane essents. With the existence of Dasein, world is inevitably disclosed, and with the disclosure of world there goes the discovery of 'world' in the sense of intramundane essents, although the latter may still remain undisclosed in their character as real, that is, as *vorhanden*. And even this is discoverable only on the basis of a world already revealed.

The attempts to solve the problem of the reality of the external world without prior clarification of the world phenomenon have led to confusions such as those apparent in Kant's 'Refutation of Idealism'. According to Kant, "it still remains a scandal to philosophy and to human reason in general that the existence of things outside us . . . must be accepted merely on *faith*, and that if anyone thinks good to doubt their existence, we are unable to counter his doubts by any satisfactory proof."[20] In the proof that he himself offers, Kant seeks to establish that "the mere, but empirically determined, consciousness of my own existence proves the existence of objects in space outside me," existence being understood by Kant in the sense of being *vorhanden*.[21] I am conscious of my own existence, that is, of a manifold of representations, which are changing, in inner sense, as determined in time. But such determination presupposes something permanent, which cannot be in me—since it is only through this permanent something that my existence in time can itself be determined—but must be outside me. Taking his start from the empirically given change 'in me' and his basis as the general idea of a being in time, which is also 'in me', Kant takes a "demonstrative leap" into the 'outside me'. All that Kant proves, granting the validity of his proof and its basis, is the necessary copresence of changing and permanent essents, both simply given or *vorhanden*. Even if he had established that these two juxtaposed simply given entities are subject and object, which he does not, the decisive ontological point, the being-in-the-world of this 'subject', the Dasein, would still remain obscure. "The coexistence of the physical and the psychical is ontically and ontologically wholly different from the phenomenon of being-in-the-world." The difference *and connection* between the 'in me' and the 'outside me' is presupposed by Kant in his proof. If he had been aware of this structural totality as thus presupposed and grasped the ontological implications of this, the very possibility of thinking that "the existence of things outside me" stands in need of proof would have collapsed.

The "scandal of philosophy" consists, Heidegger says, not in the fact that this proof has so long not been forthcoming, but in this that such proofs are ever again expected and attempted. These expectations and aims arise due to the inadequacy of the ontological starting point with something inde-pendent *of* and external *to which* a 'world' simply given is supposed to be proved. Once the nature of Dasein is correctly understood, such proofs are seen to be futile and unmeaning. Nor are the attempts to base, in the absence of a proof, the existence of the external world 'merely on faith' or to take it as necessarily presupposed by a subject, any more acceptable. "Having *faith* in the reality of the 'external world', justly or unjustly, *proving* this reality, sufficiently or insufficiently, *presupposing* it, expressly or not, attempts such as these take for granted, in their inability to see through to their own basis, a subject who is *worldless* to start with, or is not certain of his world and must first be in principle assured of it." Being-in-the-world is thus made dependent on a grasping (presuming, ascertaining and believing) which itself is a derived mode of being-in-the-world. The problem of reality, in the sense dis-cussed above, is an impossible one, not because it leads to insoluble difficulties, but because the essent in question itself "as it were repels" this way of posing the problem. The problem is not to prove that and how an 'external world' exists as *vorhanden*, but to exhibit *why* Dasein as being-in-the-world has the tendency first to bury the 'external world' into nullity 'epistemologically' and then to prove that it exists. The reason for this lies, as should by now be obvious, in the forfeiture of Dasein which leads it to displace its primary comprehension of Being to an understanding of it as something simply given.

The epistemological attempts to solve the problem of reality in the form of realistic and idealistic theories, though not without a core of real philosophical questioning, are fruit-less, not because they fail epistemologically, but because they lack, owing to their neglect of an existenzial analytic of Dasein, a secure phenomenal basis on which to build. The existenzial-ontological assertion, that with the being-in-the-world of Dasein intramundane essents are already revealed, agrees with the thesis of Realism insofar as the simply given existence of things in the world is not denied, but it differs from all Realism insofar as the latter takes the reality of the 'world' to be in need of proof and also capable of it. What, however, completely distinguishes it from Realism, which attempts to explain reality ontically in terms of real causal connections between reals, is its failure in ontological understanding. As regards Idealism, however untenable in the end it may be, it is superior to Realism in insisting that Being and Reality are only 'in consciousness' and thus giving evidence of its realization of the impossibility of explaining Being in terms of beings. But to recognize, as Idealism does, that Being cannot be explained in terms of beings and that Reality can lie only in an understanding of Being, is not yet to inquire into the Being of consciousness, the *res cogitans*, itself. This is just what Idealism does not do. Heidegger, therefore, concludes that

> if Idealism is a term which implies grasping that Being is never explicable in terms of beings but is ever something 'transcendental' for every essent, then there lies in Idealism the one and only right possibility of dealing with philosophical problems. Then Aristotle was no less an Idealist than Kant. But if Idealism means tracing back all essents to a subject or consciousness which are distinguished only by remaining undetermined as to their Being, at the most being negatively characterized as not being 'thingly', then this Idealsim is in point of method no less naïve than the crudest Realism.

Heidegger's discussion of the presuppositions underlying all attempts to solve the problem of Reality 'epistemologically' makes it evident that it can be adequately dealt with only as an ontological problem by being taken up within the existenzial analytic of Dasein.[22]

If the term 'reality' means the being of simply given essents within the world (*res*)—and it cannot mean anything else—an adequate analysis of that must lead through an elucidation of the phenomenon of intramundaneness, of world, to being–in–the–world as intrinsic to the constitution of Dasein and ultimately to care as the structural unity of the being of Dasein. Of course, to some extent a phenomenological account of the reality of the real can be given even without express reference to its existenzial, ontological basis. In his treatise on "the origin of our belief in the reality of the external world," Dilthey has attempted this, explaining how reality is of the nature of resistance and is known through impulse and will.[23] "The willing as well as its obstruction appear within the same consciousness," says Dilthey, confining himself to his principle of phenomenality. Here, however, the ontological significance of the 'appearing', of the 'within', and of the relation of consciousness to the real is left completely undetermined. This drawback is ultimately due to the fact that 'life', 'behind' which, as Dilthey holds, one cannot go, is allowed to remain in ontological indifference by him. The same holds true of Scheler's voluntaristic theory of existence developed on the basis of Dilthey's valuable analysis of resistance, according to which "the being of objects is immediately given only as something correlative to impulse and will." Resistance is experienced as not being able to get through, as a hindrance to the impulse to get through, but with this there is already disclosed something which is the objective of impulse and will, the final purpose with reference to which alone there can be any coming up against resistance. This goal itself opens up a totality of destinations which in turn is grounded on the disclosure of the referential totality of meaningfulness (significance). "The experience of resistance, that is, discovering something as resistant to our striving, is ontologically possible only on the basis of a disclosure of world." Impulse and will are themselves modes of care, and hence resistance can refer only to the 'external world' in the sense of essents within the world, but never in the sense of world. "The consciousness of reality is itself a way of being-in-the-world."

Reality as an ontological title can have only a restricted application to intramundane essents, including essents at hand and simply given, and even among them, if taken in the traditional sense, only to the simple givenness of things, not to all kinds of simple givenness. And Dasein and world it cannot ontologically characterize at all. Reality is thus ultimately referred back ontologically to the phenomenon of care. But to say that reality is grounded in the being of Dasein does not mean that the real can exist only as what it is in itself, if and only so long as Dasein exists. Not the existence of the real but its reality depends upon the existence of Dasein. "Only as long as Dasein *is*, that is, only so long as there is the ontic possibility of understanding Being, is there (*es gibt*) Being.[24] When Dasein does not exist there 'is' also no 'independence' and no 'in itself'. Such a thing is then neither capable of being understood nor not understood. Then intramundane essents are neither discoverable nor can they remain hidden. *Then* one can neither say that essents are nor that they are not." Being, not beings, reality, not the real, are dependent on care as the being of Dasein, and hence the latter itself cannot be interpreted in terms of reality (or of substantiality), a conclusion which Heidegger has expressed through the thesis that *the substance of men is existenz*.[25]

[43]

The above considerations finally lead Heidegger to the problem of Truth, which is ontologically closely linked up with the problem of Being and the understanding of Being. Parmenides, reflecting on the Being of things, identified Being with its perceptual apprehension (*noein*), and in Aristotle one can find numerous expressions of this intimate relationship. The ancients, Aristotle says, were led to their inquiries by the compulsion of truth itself; they philosophized about truth (*philosophein peri tes aletheias*). Philosophy itself is characterized by him as the science of truth (*episteme tes aletheias*) and at the same time as a science which investigates beings as beings (*episteme he theorei to on he on*), that is, in view of their Being.[26] Is it possible to demonstrate this necessary connection between truth and Being, why one necessarily 'goes together' with the other and to show the ontological and the ontic connection between truth on the one hand and man and his understanding of Being on the other? In answer, Heidegger discusses first the traditional concept of truth and its ontological foundations. He then goes on to an account of the primary, original phenomenon of truth which is thus disclosed, laying bare the derivative character of the traditional concepts. In conclusion, he elucidates the mode of being of truth and the necessity of presupposing that truth *is*.

The traditional view of the nature of truth, as already indicated in Aristotle's statement that the experiences of the soul are approximations to things (*pathemata tes psyches ton pragmaton homoiomata*), is that truth has its locus in judgment and that the nature of truth lies in the 'agreement' of the judgment with its object.[27] This view, which goes back to Aristotle, was formulated later in the definition of truth as *adequatio intellectus et rei* (the approximation of intellect or knowledge and thing) by Thomas Aquinas who also uses the terms *correspondentia* and *convenientia* (accord) for such adequation. Even Kant holds fast to this view, as is evident, for example, from his statement, "The nominal definition of Truth, that it is the agreement of knowledge with its object is here assumed as granted"[28] or from what he says in the introduction to the Transcendental Dialectic, "Truth or illusion is not in the object, insofar as it is intuited, but in the judgment about it, insofar as it is thought."

Considering the important role that the concept of agreement or correspondence has played in the most varied theories of knowledge, Heidegger seeks to penetrate into the fundamentals of this 'relation' obtaining between one thing (*intellectus*) and another (*res*). Instead of just taking for granted this relational whole (*adequatio intellectus et rei*), we must inquire into its ontological basis. Since the two terms of this whole, knowledge and thing, agree, though not in the sense of being the same, there must be something in view of which they can agree. Further, since knowledge must *so* 'give' something *as* it is, this 'so-as' constitutes the nature of this relation of agreement. To discover how such a relation is ontologically possible, Heidegger first discusses judgment, for truth, according to common opinion, is an attribute of knowledge which consists in judgment. A distinction must be made in judgment between the real psychic process of judging and the judged ideal content, the latter alone being that to which truth can be ascribed. It is this ideal content which stands in the relation of agreement with the real thing which the judgment is about. Is the agreement itself, in its mode of being, real or ideal or neither? How shall we conceive ontologically the relation between the ideal entity and the real simply given? And how about the relation between the ideal content and the real process of judging itself? In face of these difficult questions, "should we not raise the problem of the mode of being of this relation between the real and the ideal (*methexis*) itself? Is it just a chance that for more than two thousand years this problem has not advanced a step further? Or is it that the question has taken a wrong turn already with the initial ontologically unclarified separation of the real and the ideal?" It is evident that in order to get the whole problem into proper perspective, the mode of being of knowledge itself must be examined so as to bring into view the phenomenon of truth.

Truth is exhibited phenomenally within knowing when knowledge evidences itself as true. If some one with his back to the wall says truly that the picture on the wall hangs slanting, his statement is verified when on turning round, he perceives the picture hanging slantingly. In judging thus the speaker does not refer to any representations in the sense of a psychic process in his mind nor even in the sense of an ideal image or of an 'idea' of the picture on the wall. The 'merely representing' judgment, according to its innermost intention, refers to the real picture on the wall. This is what is meant and nothing else. Every interpretation that brings in something else here, supposed to be meant in a representative judgment, falsifies the phenomenal state of affairs spoken about in the judgment. To state (judge) something is a mode of being in relation to the existing thing itself. What perception establishes is nothing other than *that* it actually *is* the essent itself which was meant in the statement, that the statement–making relation to what is stated is a showing forth of the essent, that it *discovers* the essent about which it is. What is evidenced is the discovering character of the statement. The essent meant in the judgment shows itself so as it is in itself; it is in itself so as the statement shows forth or discovers it to be. What is subject to verification is not an agreement between knowledge and object or between the psychical and the physical or an accord (coherence) among the 'contents of consciousness'. "What stands to be evidenced is solely the being discovered (*Entdeckt-sein*) of essents itself, *that* in the 'how' of its discoveredness. Its verification is achieved when that which the statement is about, that is, the essent itself, shows itself as being the *same*. Verification or confirmation (*Bewahrung*) means the self-exhibition of the essent as identical."[29] Such confirmation is possible only because knowledge, as verified statement, is, ontologically regarded, a discovering way of being in relation to the real essent itself. To say that a statement is true means that it discovers the essent in itself. It gives utterance to, exhibits, 'lets be seen' the essent in its discovered-ness and has nothing to do with the correspondence between knowing and its object in the sense of the approximation of one essent (subject) to another (object). The being true (truth) of a statement must be understood as *being discovering* (*Entdeckend-sein*) and this is itself ontologically rendered possible on the basis of being-in-the-world, which thus constitutes the fundament of the original phenomenon of Truth.

The above interpretation of truth as being discovering is neither arbitrary nor does it throw overboard the good old tradition, as it might at first appear, but is only the necessary explication of what was foreshadowed in it. "The truth of *logos* as *apophansis* is *aletheuein* in the mode of *apophainesthai*; bringing essents out of hiddenness, to let them be seen in their unhiddenness (discoveredness)." For Aristotle, *aletheia* denotes 'the things themselves', what shows itself, the essent in the how of its discoveredness, and the first of the fragments of Heraclitus, the oldest philosophical writing to deal expressly with *logos*, gives us a glimpse of the conception of truth as discoveredness (unhiddenness). This conception of truth as *a-letheia*, taken for granted in their prephilosophical understanding, underlies the terminological use of '*aletheia*' by the Greeks.[30] Anticipating, as it were, the vehement criticism of this etymological interpretation which later actually came from classical philologists, Heidegger remarks here, "In adducing such proofs, we must guard ourselves against unrestrained word mysticism; yet it is in the end the business of philosophy to save *the power of those most elemental words* in which man gives utterance to himself from being leveled down by the common (vulgar) understanding into unintelligibility, which in turn becomes a source from which pseudo-problems are generated." Truth, hence, in its most primary and original form is being discovering. This is a mode of being of Dasein and is what makes any kind of discovery at all possible. And what is discovered, in this mode of Dasein's being in the world, is truth in a secondary sense. "What is 'true', that is, discovering in the primary sense, is Dasein. Truth in the second sense means not being discovering but being discovered, not discovering but discoveredness." As has been explained earlier, the discoveredness of essents in the world is based on the disclosed character of the world, which is itself grounded in the overtness (*Erschlossenheit*) basic to

Dasein's mode of being. It is in this openness that the phenomenon of truth in its most basic form is to be found. It is primarily Dasein that has its being, *is*, 'in truth', though, of course, this does not mean that ontically Dasein has always or at any time "entered into the whole truth."

The full existenzial sense of the statement that Dasein is in truth is summed up by Heidegger, with reference to what has been said before about the structure of Dasein, as follows. Dasein's intrinsic overtness or openness in general, comprehending the whole structure of its being as it has become explicit in the phenomenon of care, is the basis of the disclosure of the world and of essents within the world. Secondly, this openness is intrinsically factual or 'thrown'. In the thrownness of this overtness, Dasein is disclosed to itself as being already in a particular situation in this particular world. Further, the project character of Dasein, as being related to the potentiality of its being, opens to it the possibility of either understanding itself, inauthentically, in terms of the essents in the world or, authentically, in terms of its own innermost potentiality of being. The authentic openness, exhibiting the phenomenon of truth in its most original form in the mode of authenticity, constitutes what Heidegger calls the truth of existenz. Finally, because of the forfeiture inherent in man, he is by his very constitution, at the same time in 'untruth'. Because he has lost himself in his 'world', what he discovers is at the same time turned into sham and covered up by chatter, curiosity, and ambiguity. "Dasein's being in relation to essents is not extinguished but uprooted. The essent is not completely hidden, but is on the contrary discovered, though at the same time turned into a sham; it shows itself—but in the mode of illusion or seeming. . . . To the facticity of Dasein belong closure and covertness. The full existenzial ontological sense of the statement that Dasein is in truth implies at the same time that Dasein is in untruth. But only insofar as Dasein is overt, is it also closed." For this reason, anything new is discovered not on the basis of complete hiddenness but from what is already disclosed in the form of illusion; and what is once discovered has to be guarded by Dasein against lapsing into illusion and dissimulation. "Truth (discoveredness) has always to be first wrenched from essents. The essent is snatched out of hiddenness. At any time a particular discovery is always as it were an act of depradation. Is it just a chance that the Greeks gave utterance to the nature of truth in a privative expression (*a-letheia*)?"[31]

Turning now to the task of showing the derivative character of the traditional interpretation of the phenomenon of truth, we must recall the derivation earlier of propositional truth, as a mode of circumspect interpretation, from the primary overtness of Dasein. This is confirmed by the express and specific considerations which Heidegger now brings forward. The openness of Dasein in virtue of which it discovers intramundane essents is manifested in speech, which is a way in which Dasein gives utterance to its discovering-being in relation to essents. In stating or judging, man expresses himself as such about the essent discovered, communicating to others the "how of the discoveredness" contained in the statement and henceforth preserved in it. Embodied in a statement, it becomes itself an essent at hand or simply there in the world, at the same time containing in itself a relation to the essent spoken about. Even in repeating such a statement, without any direct discovering experience of the essent, we bring ourselves into relation with the essent spoken about. In the mode of being of the 'they', in our forfeiture to what is said, statement takes over the place of being in direct discovering relation to the essent. To appropriate the essent again in its discoveredness it becomes necessary to confirm the discovering character of the statement, by verifying the relation which the statement, as an essent at hand or simply there, claims to have, in its capacity as discovering, with the essent. This relation itself, obtaining between two simply given essents, is then conceived as being of the nature of an essent simply given. In consequence, "the discoveredness of anything becomes the *vorhanden* (simply given) conformity of a *vorhanden* essent, the spoken out statement, to another *vorhanden* essent, which the statement is about. . . and when the mode of being of the terms of the relation are taken indiscriminately as being merely *vorhanden*, this relation shows itself as a *vorhanden* agreement between two *vorhanden* essents.

Truth as overtness and as being discovering in relation to discovered essents thus gets transformed into truth as agreement between essents simply given (*intellectus* and *res*) within the world. Because Dasein, going out into the world of its preoccupation, understands, in the first instance and mostly, truth (discoveredness) also in terms of statement, that is, in terms of *vorhanden* being, what is derivative in the existenzial-ontological sense becomes ontically and factually the only 'real' truth. Thus Dasein's normal understanding of Being (that of itself and other essents) as something *vorhanden*, itself hides from view the original phenomenon of truth. The Greeks, who were responsible for developing systematically and scientifically this way of understanding Being, which became thenceforth dominant, in terms of simple, objective givenness, nevertheless had a living, though preontological, understanding of the original sense of truth. Aristotle, in fact, tried to maintain the original sense of truth as against the derivative meaning. "Aristotle has never advocated the thesis that the original locus of truth is judgment. He says rather that *logos* is that mode of being of Dasein which can be discovering *or* veiling. The distinctiveness of the way *logos* is true lies in this *dual possibility*, in the fact that it *can* also *veil* and cover up. It is not judgment which is the primary locus of truth but, on the contrary, statement itself, as a mode of being-in-the-world, is grounded in the overtness of Dasein." Truth in this sense is an existenzial and the ontological condition of the possibility that statements can be true or false.

If, as explained above, truth in the original existenzial sense is an intrinsic aspect of the constitution of Dasein, it follows that, as Heidegger challengingly says,

> The essent is only *then* discovered and *so long* overt as Dasein at all *is*. The Laws of Newton, the Principle of Contradiction, every truth in general, these are true only so long as Dasein *is*. When there was no Dasein at all and when there will no longer be, there was no truth and will be none, because as overtness, discovery and discoveredness it *cannot* then be. . . . Before the Laws of Newton were discovered they were not 'true', from which it does not follow that they were false. . . . That before him the Laws of Newton were neither true nor false cannot mean that the essent, as discovered and exhibited by them, was

not there before. Through Newton, the Laws became true, making the essent as it is in itself accessible. . . . To discover thus is the mode of being of 'truth'. That there are 'eternal truths' will only then be adequately established when it is successfully proved that in all eternity Dasein was and will be. . . . [Until then it] remains a fantastic assertion.

To say that all truth is relative to the being of Dasein does not mean, however, that it is 'subjective' in the sense of being left to the whim of the subject. Since discovering is rendered possible by, and is a mode of, the openness of Dasein to what *is*, it discloses to him the essent as it already is itself, independently of his 'subjective' whims. This also enables truth to possess universal validity.

From the above it should be clear why we must necessarily presuppose that there is truth. Truth must be presupposed because we *are* 'in truth'. "It is not we who presuppose 'truth', but it is truth which at all makes it ontologically possible that we can do such a thing as presupposing." To presuppose something means to understand it as the ground of the being of another essent, and such ontological understanding is possible only on the basis of the overtness or discovering character of Dasein. To presuppose 'truth', accordingly, is to understand it as something for "the sake of which" Dasein is. As has been shown before, Dasein, constituted by care and ahead of itself, is in its being concerned about its innermost potentiality of being, of which its overtness and ability to discover are intrinsic aspects. In this being ahead of itself lies the ultimate 'presupposition', that is, of Dasein itself in its openness. "Because presupposing itself belongs to the being of Dasein, 'we' must also presuppose 'ourselves', as determined through overtness. . . . We must 'make' the presupposition of truth because with the being of the 'we' it *is* already 'made'." It lies in the intrinsic thrownness of man that he must presuppose himself and his openness, and thus Truth, for there is no possibility of his ever choosing himself freely to come into existence or not.[32]

Because it ignores the inevitability of this presupposition, the usual refutation of scepticism, the denial of Being or of the knowability of truth remains halfway from the mark. All that it proves is that judgment presupposes truth, that exhibiting something is to discover it. It leaves unexplained the ontological ground of this necessary connection between statement and truth, the mode of being of truth, the sense of presupposing it and the fact that even when nobody judges, truth is presupposed, so far as Dasein at all is. A sceptic, says Heidegger, cannot be confuted, as little as the being of truth can be proved; so long as he factually *is*, negating the truth, he also does not need to be refuted, for, "so far as he is and has understood himself in this being he has extinguished Dasein, and with that Truth, in suicidal despair." It is as little possible to establish that there has ever been a 'real' sceptic—whose existence all refutations of scepticism take ultimately for granted—as to prove that there are 'eternal truths'. Perhaps sceptics are commoner, Heidegger comments, than the "harmless formal logical maneuvers of surprise attack (*Überrumpelungsversuche*) against scepticism are willing to admit."

Heidegger rejects all attempts to set up an 'ideal subject' to solve the problem of truth and knowledge. Though justified in their demand for an apriori in the solution of philosophical problems, they fail to see that an ideal subject does not really satisfy this demand, missing, with this "fantastically idealized subject," the apriori of the factual subject, the apriori inherent in the facticity of Dasein. "The ideas of a 'pure I' and of a 'consciousness in general' contain so little the apriori of 'real' subjectivity, that they pass over or do not at all see the ontological characteristics of facticity and the ontological constitution of Dasein. Rejection of a consciousness in general does not mean negating the apriori any more than starting with an idealized subject guarantees an apriority of Dasein that is justified by facts." To maintain that there are 'eternal truths; and to confuse the phenomenally based 'ideality' of Dasein with an idealized absolute subject, declares Heidegger, belong to those remaining shreds of Christian theology within the sphere of philosophical problems which have not even yet been weeded out radically enough.

The preceding analysis of truth is intended by Heidegger to show how thoroughly and indissolubly Being, Truth, and

Dasein are bound up together. The understanding of anything like Being is possible only because Dasein is overt and capable of understanding. " 'There is' Being, not beings, only so far as there is Truth. And Truth *is* only so far and so long as Dasein is. Being and Truth 'are' equally basic and 'arise' together." What it means to say that Being—as distinct from beings—*is*, can only be discussed when the sense of Being and its understanding are fully clarified.

[44]

Notes

1. Explaining in retrospect (Introduction to "What is Metaphysics?") the significance of the term *Dasein*, Heidegger says, "To characterize with a single term both the relationship of Being to the nature of man and the essential relation of man to the openness ('there') of Being as such, the name of 'being there' (*Da-sein*) was chosen for that essential realm in which man stands as man." The term *Dasein* is not used just as an arbitrary substitute for 'consciousness' in *Being and Time*, Heidegger further points out, but was rather meant to suggest a way of thinking about man's essence which could be adequate to the leading problem of the inquiry—the relationship in which Being stands to the essence of man. "*Dasein* is a name given to that which should, for once, be realized and then thought out accordingly, as a place—namely, the locus of the truth of Being." See also Heidegger and Fink, *Heraklit* (pp. 200-203), where the relation between "Dasein" and "consciousness" is examined again.

2. *Lichtung* means a clearing, that is, the open space within a thick forest, with its suggestion of openness, light, free space, in the midst of surrounding darkness and inaccessibility. In Heidegger's later thinking the notion of *Lichtung* becomes more and more central and is subjected to continued revision and deepening, in conformity with the change or turn in his thinking. The following comments from *Heraklit* (p. 260) may be helpful in understanding the discussion of *Lichtung* in the last chapter of this book. "Do *Lichtung* and light have anything at all to do with each other? Obviously not. *Lichtung* means: to clear, to lighten, to weigh anchor, to clear land by rooting out. This does not imply that where a clearing (*Lichtung*) occurs there is light. The cleared is the free, the open, and at the same time what is cleared or opened up of something that conceals itself. . . . Light and fire can have a place only in a clearing. . . . Darkness is indeed without light, but it is cleared, opened up. For us the important thing is to experience unhiddenness as *Lichtung*. This is the unthought in what has been thought in the entire history of thought." See above all, *Zur Sache des Denkens*, pp. 71-80 (E.T., pp. 65-73), for a more elaborate clarification.

3. Werner Marx elucidates this conception of Dasein as follows ("Heidegger's New Conception of Philosophy"): "The basic insight of *Sein*

und Zeit in my opinion, is the insight into the awe-inspiring fact that man is not only a 'being' like all other beings, not only 'is', but is so constituted that through most of his acts he stands in some awareness of 'that and how he is' and other human and nonhuman beings 'are'. Every one of man's acts is an act in some awareness of the Essence of 'Being'. Heidegger developed at length the constitutive forces or the conditions of the possibility of man's awareness of Being. In two of these I find the true source of Heidegger's new conception of philosophy. In the sixth book of *Nicomachean Ethics* and the ninth book of the *Metaphysics*, Aristotle explained how certain basic human acts unconceal the truth of Being. I believe that Heidegger was greatly influenced by Aristotle's notion of the truth discovering ways of man, by this version of Truth and of *nous*, when he developed how the transcendental human reality breaks itself open. In and through understanding, moods, and speech—it discloses or illuminates 'itself'. In and through these ways-to-be, that strange lucidity is brought about in the realm we now commonly call our 'consciousness'—a name that Heidegger avoids not only because of its Cartesian implication but because it prevents us from realizing that each individual lucidity or overtness is part and parcel of a wide and general overtness, of an elementary sort of Truth or *aletheia*. It has not been sufficiently recognized, in my opinion, that Heidegger, even in his first phase, insisted on this overtness as an a priori, as a prior condition for any subject-object relationships."

4. J. Wild, *The Challenge of Existentialism*, p. 87.

5. See also: "Was ist Metaphysik?" *Wegmarken*, p. 8; E.T., p. 364) for further discussion of the revelatory function of moods (boredom and joy); *Erläuterungen zu Hölderlins Dichtung*, p. 119f. (intoxication as the elevation of mood which alone makes us receptive to the voice of the attunement-dispensing celestials); and *Nietzsche I*, p. 53f., on affects and feelings.

6. Historically, feelings and affects have always drawn the attention of philosophers, beginning with Aristotle's account of *pathe* in the second book of his *Rhetoric*. But, as Heidegger points out, their ontological interpretation has hardly advanced a step further since Aristotle, feelings being now dealt with only as a class of psychological phenomena, by the side of knowing and willing. It is to the credit of phenomenologists such as Max Scheler to have brought to light, under the influence of Augustine and Pascal, the philosophical relevance of affective phenomena. In illustration, Heidegger quotes as follows from Augustine and Pascal respectively: "We cannot enter into truth except through charity"; "The saints on the contrary say, while speaking of things divine, that we must love them in order to know them."

In *Der Formalismus in der Ethik und die Materiale Wertethik* (Part II, chapter 5, 2), Scheler points out that even the alogical, emotional activities of the mind (feelings, will, love, and so forth) have an a priori character not borrowed from thought—the aprioristic *ordre du coeur* or *logique du coeur* of which Blaise Pascal speaks in his *Pensées*. The prejudice in favor of the rational and the logical, going back to Greek thought, has led to a clear-cut separation of Reason and Sensibility and to the identification of the latter (comprising the affective and conative aspect of the mind) with the empirical sphere. The heart is not just blind feeling but has its own *reasons*, as Pascal says, which means, according to Scheler, that there is a mode of experience of which the objects are as inaccessible to understanding as color is to the ear, a mode of experience which brings before us genuinely 'objective' objects and an eternal order obtaining among them (that is, values). Feeling, preference, love, and hate open our eyes to the world and its value content. See also N. Hartmann: *Ethics I*, pp. 176–180. John MacMurray puts forward a forceful protest against the bifurcation of mind into rational and irrational powers in his *Reason and Emotion* and, from another point of view, W. M. Urban discusses the 'logic' of affective discourse in *Language and Reality*. Paul Tillich has interesting observations to make on emotional cognition in his *Systematic Theology* (Vol. I, pp. 86, 109, 127) and discusses these in their ontological implications in *Love, Power and Justice*.

On this whole problem see Bollnow (*Das Wesen der Stimmungen*, 3d ed.), whose approach, however, is determined by the aim of assigning a place to moods and feelings in a complete philosophical anthropology.

In *Was ist das—die Philosophie?* Heidegger describes philosophy as the expressly accomplished correspondence which speaks insofar as it heeds the appeal, and listens to the voice, of the Being of what is. "This correspondence is necessarily and always attuned, not just by chance and occasionally. It is in an attunement. And only on the basis of the attunement (disposition) does the language of correspondence obtain its precision and its tuning. . . . The Greek thinkers Plato and Aristotle drew attention to the fact that philosophy and philosophizing belong to that dimension of man which we call mood (in the sense of being attuned and disposed). Plato says (*Theat.* 155 d), "This is specially the *pathos* of a philosopher—wonderment. There is no other *arche* for philosophy." Aristotle says the same (*Met.* A, 982b 12 sq.), "Astonishment is *arche*—it pervades and dominates every step of philosophy, not merely the first." With Descartes, the Greek *thaumazein* changes into doubt. Trust in an ever attainable certitude of knowledge is the *pathos* and so the *arche* of modern philosophy.

7. Aristotle, *Nicomachean Ethics*, Bk. VI.

8. In *Kant und das Problem der Metaphysik* (p. 210-211; E.T., pp. 240-242) Heidegger explains that "the constitution of the being of any essent, including Dasein, is preeminently accessible only in understanding so far as it has the character of a project. Because understanding—as fundamental ontology shows—is not merely a kind of knowing but primarily a basic element of existenz in general, the express carrying out of a project, particularly that involved in ontological conceptualization must necessarily be a construction. Construction, however, does not mean a free-floating concoction of something but is rather a projecting with a previously determined and assured guiding thread as well as starting point. . . . Every fundamental ontological construction is verified through what its project brings into view, how it brings Dasein to a manifestation of itself. . . such construction may be understood as an assault by Dasein, originating in Dasein itself on the primordial metaphysical fact in Dasein, (that is, its finitude) an understanding of Being that is enveloped in oblivion and which has to be wrenched away from that through Dasein's thrown project."

From his later perspective, Heidegger says ("Brief über den 'Humanismus'," *Wegmarken*, p. 168) that though Being is lit up for man in ecstatic project, it is not the project that generates Being. The project, moreover, is intrinsically a thrown one. In projecting, the propulsion comes not from man but from Being itself which allots to man his ek-sistenz as *Da-sein*.

9. Sense, Heidegger adds, is an existenziality of Dasein, not a property adhering to an essent, or lying 'behind' it or floating somewhere in between. Only Dasein 'has' meaning. Therefore, he says, "when we inquire into the meaning of Being, we are not indulging in any profound speculation about what may lie behind Being, but only inquiring about Being itself so far as it enters into and stands within the comprehension of Dasein. The sense of Being can never be contrasted with beings or with Being as the underlying 'ground' of beings because 'ground' is accessible only as meaning, even though it may be itself the very abyss of senselessness."

Commenting later on the approach to the sense of Being in *Being and Time* via the understanding of Being inherent in Dasein, Heidegger says (Introduction to "What is Metaphysics?"), "An attempt which, starting from the representation of the essent as such, seeks to effect a transition to the thinking of the truth of Being must, in a certain sense, still represent the truth of Being also. Such a representation is bound to be of a different kind and, as representation, inadequate to what is the real goal of thinking. In *Being and Time*, the relation, originating in metaphysics and making a transition to the relationship of the truth of Being to human nature, is called understanding. But understanding is regarded here also from the point of view of the unconcealedness of Being. It is the ecstatic (that is, standing within the sphere of the overt), thrown project. The sphere which, in projecting, offers itself as open, in order that something (Being) may exhibit itself as something (Being as itself in its unconcealedness), is the sense. 'Sense of Being' and 'Truth of Being' mean the same."

10. A detailed analysis of *logos* was undertaken later (1944) by Heidegger in a course of lectures (unpublished) on Logic. See the essay on *Logos* in *Vorträge und Aufsätze*.

11. In later writings Heidegger returns again and again to the question which is merely touched upon here: the mode of being of language. Reflection on language from the point of view of the truth of Being, he says ("Brief über den 'Humanismus'," *Wegmarken*, p. 149), can no longer be merely philosophy of language, moving within the confines of the metaphysics of subjectivity. On language and its relation to Being, see the last chapter of this work.

12. *Pantes anthropoi tou eidenai oregontai physei* (All men by nature desire to know). Heidegger renders this as: *Im Sein des Menschen liegt wesenhaft die Sorge des Sehens.*

13. *Confessions*, X 35, Everyman's ed., p. 238.

14. Explaining this from his later perspective, Heidegger says, "The forgetfulness of the truth of Being in favor of the pressure of essents, themselves without being considered in their essence, is the sense of the 'forfeiture' or fall mentioned in *Being and Time*. This word does not mean the fall of man in the secularized sense of moral philosophy, but denotes an intrinsic aspect of man's relation to Being, within the relationship of Being

with the nature of man. In accordance with this, the terms 'authenticity' and 'inauthenticity', employed in an introductory fashion, do not mean either a moral, existenziell or 'anthropological' distinction, but the 'ekstatic' relationship of human nature with the truth of Being, which is something yet to be brought within the purview of thought, being hitherto hidden to philosophy." ("Brief über den 'Humanismus'," *Wegmarken*, p. 163).

15. Later, Heidegger was to describe this in terms of man's standing within and his belongingness to the clearing (*Lichtung*) of Being. Commenting on what is said here about the 'understanding of Being' (*Seinsverständnis*) characteristic of Dasein, Heidegger says, "In the as yet clumsy and provisional language of the treatise *Being and Time*, this was expressed by saying that the basic feature of the Dasein that is man is determined by the understanding of Being. Understanding of Being here does not mean at all that man as subject possesses a subjective representation of Being and that Being is a mere representation, as Nicolai Hartmann and many of my contemporaries have tried to interpret the attempt made in *Being and Time*. Understanding of Being means that man by nature stands in the openness of the project of Being and endures the understanding as thus meant. When the understanding of Being is conceived in this way, the representation of man as a subject is, to speak with Hegel, brushed aside." (*Der Satz vom Grund*, p. 146). See *Sein und Zeit*, p. 208 footnote (E.T., p. 493) for Heidegger's comment on Hartmann's conception of ontology.

Hartmann has discussed Heidegger's views in his *Zur Grundlegung der Ontologie* and occasionally referred to them in other essays. For a critical examination of Hartmann's ontology from the point of view of Heidegger's thought, see Katharina Kanthack, *Nicolai Hartmann und das Ende der Ontologie* (1962).

16. Characteristically, Heidegger points out in a footnote, the phenomena of anxiety and fear first drew the attention of Christian theologians—Augustine and Luther and, most penetrating in his analysis, S. Kierkegaard (*The Concept of Dread*).

Like most critics of Heidegger, Bollnow (*Das Wesen der Stimmungen*) takes exception to the central position accorded by Heidegger to the mood of anxiety. He overlooks, however, that for Heidegger a basic mood is so not in the sense of a universal and eternal feature in man's make-up but is basic in a particular historical epoch, varying from one epoch of the historical self-revelation of Being to another. As Pöggeler has pointed out ("Das Wesen der Stimmungen"), the existenzial structures disclosed in *Being and Time* are not unhistorical and eternally universal 'conditions of possibility' in the Kantian, or 'Ideas' in the Platonic sense, but are historically determined. The key mood of anxiety, further, is distinctive in that it alone reveals Nothingness, loosening the grip of the essent on us and enables us to hold ourselves in what is the other to all essents. Nothingness, in revealing the bare 'that' of things, becomes the condition of the possibility of the overtness of the essent as such, as also of transcending it. See chapter 8 below for Heidegger's treatment of anxiety in *Was ist Metaphysik?* In *Kant und das Problem der Metaphysik* (p. 214; E.T., p. 246), Heidegger points out that in *Being and Time*, anxiety is discussed solely from the point of view of the possibility of understanding Being and of the question of Being as such. In the Postscript (1943) to "What is Metaphysics?," Heidegger refers to the widespread misunderstanding that the lecture elevates an isolated and, what is more, a morbid mood, namely, dread, to the status of the one key mood, preaching thus a 'philosophy of anxiety' that paralyses the will to act. Such a misunderstanding arises, he remarks, when anxiety is taken, in isolation from its relationship to Nothing, as a merely psychological process. "An experience of Being as what is 'other' than everything that is comes to us in dread, provided that we do not, from dread of dread, that is, in sheer timidity, shut our ears to the soundless voice which attunes us to the horrors of the abyss. . . . The lecture, attentive to the voice of Being, thinks beyond it into the attunement occasioned by the voice—an attunement which takes hold of man in his essence so that he may learn to experience Being in Nothing." In the Introduction (1949) to this lecture, Heidegger specifically refers to the historical character of the attunement of anxiety—the present is an epoch of the 'withdrawal' of Being and, therefore, any attempt to think Being must lead through Nothingness and be itself anxiously attuned.

17. To illustrate the extent to which this account can be misunderstood, Wyschogrod quotes (*Kierkegaard and Heidegger*, 1956) from an article by Marjorie Glicksman (Grene) in the *Journal of Philosophy* 35:4 (1938). Commenting on Heidegger's definition of care, she writes: "Paraphrased, this guarded definition states the platitude that human nature participates through anticipation in the future and through memory in the past; and at the same time is bound by indissoluble ties to the insistent cares of the present." The mistake here, Wyschogrod points out, is that Heidegger is not saying that there is first a 'human nature' which then 'participates' in the past and the future; but that human nature is in the past and in the future by its essence and no matter how thin it is sliced it already is extended. Such 'misunderstanding', it may be added, is itself an illustration of the general tendency to assimilate a new thought and level it down to the prevailing mode of understanding by interpreting it in terms which are hallowed by tradition and which have the sanction of common usage.

18. In *Kant and the Problem of Metaphysics* (p. 244f.), Heidegger describes care as "the unity of the transcendental structure of the innermost neediness (the need for the understanding of Being evidenced in Dasein's transcendence) of Dasein." Confusion prevails, Heidegger points out, if 'care' is understood as expressing a view about human life and as an ethical evaluation instead of as a term denoting the structural unity of the transcendence, in itself finite, of Dasein.

19. For an explanation of the conception of 'founded' modes in phenomenology, see Marvin Farber, *Foundations of Phenomenology*, p. 261.

20. *Critique of Pure Reason*, N. K. Smith's translation, p. 34.

21. Ibid., p. 245.

22. Commenting on Nicolai Hartmann's views in a footnote (*Sein und Zeit*, p. 208; E.T., p. 493), Heidegger points out that a consideration of the ontological foundations on which all epistemology rests necessarily leads to a thoroughgoing revision of traditional ontology and cannot rest satisfied with a mere critical improvement on it.

23. *Beiträge zur Lösung der Frage vom Ursprung unseres Glaubens an die Realität der Aussenwelt und seinem Recht*, in Wilhelm Dilthey, *Gesammelte Schriften*, Vol. V. Also see Hodges, *The Philosophy of Dilthey*.

24. On this circumlocution (*es gibt Sein*) for "there is being," see "Brief über den 'Humanismus'," *Wegmarken*, p. 165; also *Was heisst Denken?*, p. 116 (E.T., p. 189). The meaning of '*es gibt*' is further deepened in "Zeit und Sein" (*Zur Sache des Denkens*) and discussed in its full sweep.

Commenting on this sentence in "Brief über den 'Humanismus'," (*Wegmarken*, p. 167), Heidegger remarks: "To say that only when Dasein is, is there Being means that only while there occurs the clearing of Being does Being deliver itself to men. But that the 'there', the clearing as the truth of Being, itself occurs, is brought about by Being itself. The statement does not mean that Being is made or produced by man."

25. Explaining, in the Introduction (1949) to "What is Metaphysics?," the use of the term 'existenz' in *Being and Time*, Heidegger remarks that it is used exclusively to denote the being of man, his Dasein, "in the overtness of which Being reveals and conceals itself, vouchsafes itself and withdraws," though this truth of Being neither exhausts itself in Dasein nor is simply identical with it. 'Existenz' in *Being and Time* denotes the mode of being of the essent who remains open to the overtness of Being in which he stands by enduring this overtness. This enduring is expressed by the term 'care' which also leads into the ecstatic essence of Dasein. The ekstatic character of *existenz* lies in this enduring (*Ausstehen*), which is not so much 'standing out' in the sense of stepping out of the immanence of consciousness (this would be to conceive existenz from the point of view of subjectivity and substance) as rather a 'standing in', an instancy (*Inständigkeit*) in the 'out' and 'there' of the unconcealedness of Being—in this lies the stasis of the ecstatic. "Standing within the openness of Being, holding on to it (care) and holding out in the utmost extremity (being toward death)" together constitute the full essence of existenz. To say that man alone exists is to say that "man is the essent whose being is characterized by an openness such that it stands within the unconcealedness of Being, from Being, in Being." Because man is characterized by existenz he can represent beings and have consciousness of what he thus represents. "Consciousness presupposes the ecstatically conceived existenz as the *essentia* of man. . . . Consciousness by itself neither creates the openness of essents nor does it bestow on man the ability to stand open for essents." The "intentionality of consciousness" would not have the scope to operate, Heidegger points out, if man's essence were not already constituted by his 'instancy'. Further, being a self follows from existenz; the latter itself is neither identical with self-hood nor definable in terms of it.

In his notes on *Existenz* (1941) in *Nietzsche II*, (pp. 475-476), Heidegger says that it was 'temporarily' used in *Sein und Zeit* to refer to the ecstatic instancy (*Inständigkeit*) in the illumination of the clearing of the 'there' (*Da*) of Da-sein. "Here, neither Kierkegaard's concept nor that of existentialism is involved. Existenz is rather conceived in terms of the ecstatic character of Dasein and with the aim of interpreting Da-sein in terms of his preeminent relationship to the truth of Being. The temporary use of the term is determined solely from the point of view of this problem, which serves only as preparatory to an overcoming of metaphysics. And this is outside the scope of the philosophy of existence and existentialism; it is separated by a deep gulf from the basically theological passion of Kierkegaard, but, on the other hand, is concerned with the attempt to come fundamentally to grips with metaphysics." To differentiate his sense of the term from that in Existentialism, Heidegger later spells it as *ek-sistenz*.

26. Aristotle, *Metaphysics A and T₁*.

27. Aristotle, *De Interpretatione* 1, 16a 6.

28. *Critique of Pure Reason*, Kemp Smith's translation, p. 97.

29. See Husserl, *Logische Untersuchungen*, Investigation VI (sections dealing with *Evidenz und Wahrheit* and the corresponding chapter in Farber's *Foundations of Phenomenology*). See Ernst Tugendhat's important study, *Der Wahrheitsbegriff bei Husserl und Heidegger* for a thorough and critical examination of Heidegger's concept of truth, comparing it with that of Husserl. A briefer version of Tugendhat's critique, "Heideggers Idee der Wahrheit" is included in *Heidegger*, Otto Pöggeler, ed.

30. Commenting on this in *Heraklit* (p. 259f.), Heidegger says, "About *aletheia* as *aletheia*, there is nothing said in the whole of Greek philosophy. . . . *Aletheia* thought about as *aletheia* has nothing to do with 'truth' (*Wahrheit*), but means unhiddenness. What I then said in *Being and Time* on *aletheia* tends already in this direction. *Aletheia* as unhiddenness has always engaged me, but 'truth' got in between. *Aletheia* as unhiddenness tends toward (approximates the meaning of) what clearing (*Lichtung*) is. . . . In the essay, "On the Essence of Truth" I had, at the place where I speak of 'freedom', the *Lichtung* in view; only, here also 'truth' crept up from behind." See also *Zur Sache des Denkens*, pp. 74–79 (E.T., pp. 67–71), for the relation between *aletheia* and *Lichtung*.

31. In "Platons Lehre von der Wahrheit" (written about 1930 but published in 1942), Heidegger discusses Plato's transformation of the original Greek conception of truth as *aletheia* or unhiddenness as a basic character of essents into correctness of thought or knowing. For the Greeks, what is unconcealed is not merely something that manifests itself; it is rather an unceasing conquest of hiddenness in which what is unconcealed is torn out and wrenched away from hiddenness. Because for the Greeks, hiddenness, as self-concealment, pervades the nature of Being and thus determines also the essent in its presence (*ousia*, being) and availability ('truth'), therefore, Heidegger says, the word for what the Romans called *veritas* and we call 'truth' is for them qualified by an *alpha privativum* (*a-letheia*). Because Plato conceived the being (*ousia*, presence) of essents as Idea, and no longer as the emergence of what is hidden into unconcealedness (as in early Greek thought), he transformed the conception of truth from the unhiddenness of essents to the correctness of knowing. The conception of truth, Heidegger asserts, must be liberated from the 'yoke of the Idea', under which Plato has placed it, thus harnessing it with perceiving, thinking, and judging. "No attempt to ground the essence of unconcealedness in 'reason', in 'spirit', in 'thought', in '*logos*', in any sort of 'subjectivity' can ever retrieve the essence of truth." (*Wegmarken*, p. 143). For this it is necessary that we first become aware of what is positive in *a-letheia* as a character inherent in Being itself rather than in essents.

See the account of "Vom Wesen der Wahrheit" in chapters 8 and 10.

Heidegger's interpretation of Plato's views and of *aletheia* has been severely criticized by Gerhard Krüger ("M. Heidegger und der Humanismus") and also by Paul Friedländer (in *Platon* I, 2d., 1954; see also the chapter on *Aletheia* in the English translation). For Heidegger's reply to the latter see his essay "Hegel und die Griechen" (in *Die Gegenwart der Griechen im Neueren Denken*, p. 55 and *Wegmarken*, p. 271). Heidegger's final position on the matter is stated in "The End of Philosophy and the Task of Thinking" (*On Time and Being*, pp. 70-71). He admits here that "the assertion about the essential transformation of truth, that is, from unconcealment to correctness, is also untenable." *Aletheia* comes, rather, under the perspective of correctness from the very beginning.

32. Drawing the full implications of what is said in *Being and Time* about man's thrownness and being ahead of himself, Heidegger writes ("Brief über den 'Humanismus'," *Wegmarken*, pp. 161-162): "Man is rather 'thrown' by Being itself into the truth of Being in order that, eksisting thus, he may tend the truth of Being, so that in the light of Being the essent may manifest itself as the essent that it is. It is not man who decides whether and how it appears, whether and how God and the gods, history and nature enter into the clearing of Being, present or absent themselves. The arrival of essents rests in the dispensation (*Geschick*) of Being. The problem for man, however, is whether he discovers the appropriate feature of his essence which corresponds to this dispensation; for it is in conformity with this that he, as ek-sisting, has to guard the truth of Being. Man is the shepherd of Being. *Being and Time*, with its realization of ecstatic existenz as 'care', is straining after this thought alone."

5

Wholeness and Authenticity

The aim of the preparatory analysis of Dasein, as carried out in the first division of *Being and Time*, was to find within the ontological structure of Dasein itself a clue that would lead eventually to an answer to the main question, namely, the question about the meaning of Being. The basic assumption necessary for the investigation has been that to ask what the meaning of Being is, is to ask how, and as what, Being can be understood and interpreted. "To clear the horizon in which such a thing as Being can be understood at all is the same as the elucidation of the possibility of the comprehension of Being in general which itself belongs to the constitution of the being we call Dasein." The clue thus is to be sought in the understanding of Being already inherent in Dasein. If it is pursued until we reach a point where the being of Dasein emerges in its primal unity and wholeness, we shall have in our hands the guiding thread that alone can lead us to the answer to the question of Being. The existenzial analytic has thrown light on Dasein's mode of being-in-the-world and shown that intrinsic to man is his overtness, his openness to other essents, to world and to himself. It is this which makes it possible for him to have always a certain understanding of his own being and, as being 'in Truth', to some extent of Being in general. As 'thrown' into the world and concerned in his very being with his being itself, man is characterized by a potentiality of being which makes him be ahead of himself and try to understand and interpret what *is*, including his own being, through projects of understanding. The existenzial analytic has deepened our comprehension both of the nature of understanding itself and of the being of Dasein as care.

But, Heidegger now asks, have we attained, with the characterization of Dasein as care, to an understanding of the ultimate and primal interpretation of the being of this essent and do we have in our grasp the Dasein in *its wholeness*? An interpretation that goes back to the origins, the primal foundations, must have in its possession a fully assured 'hermeneutic situation', that is, the prepossession (purpose or aim), the preview and the preconception taken together, and also be certain of having taken into account the phenomenal wholeness and unity of the essent in question. But the existenzial analysis of Dasein carried out so far cannot lay any claim to completeness because the prepossession and preview of the interpretation have been confined till now to the average, everyday character of Dasein, that is, to its potentiality of being as manifested only in its *inauthentic* aspect; and also they do not have the wholeness of Dasein in their grip.

Although it was claimed that the wholeness of Dasein is to be found in care, it is obvious that man's everyday existence lies 'between' life and death. Further, if the being of Dasein is determined as existenz and the latter consists of the potentiality of being, it is evident that so long as Dasein exists, with its potentiality of being, there must be something that it *is not yet*. An essent whose essence consists in existenz is intrinsically resistant to any attempt to grasp it as a whole; the very nature of this essent renders an ultimate ontological interpretation of Dasein a doubtful undertaking. If the attempt is at all to succeed, the being of Dasein in its wholeness and authenticity must be brought within the 'prepossession' or aim of the inquiry, and this means raising the problem of the ability of Dasein to be a whole. So long as man exists, there is always something that still remains, something that he can and will be. His own end, that is, death, remains 'outstanding', something that is yet to be. "This end, belonging to its potentiality of being, that is, to its existenz, circumscribes and determines the wholeness that is ever possible to Dasein." The end of

Dasein in death can be brought within the purview of the potentiality of being possible to Dasein when an ontologically adequate, existenzial concept of death is arrived at. But death can *be*, in a sense conformable to the mode of being proper to Dasein, only in an existenziell being 'toward' or in relation to death (*Sein zum Tode*). The existenzial structure of such being in relation to death gives the ontological constitution of Dasein's ability to be whole. Similarly, the potentiality of being a whole authentically must be found from within Dasein itself. "Obviously, Dasein itself must show within its being the possibility and manner of an authentic existenz, if it is not to be a conception either forced on it ontically or an ontological invention." Such attestation of authentic existenz is provided by conscience, which, like death, is a phenomenon demanding a genuinely existenzial interpretation.[1]

The primal ontological ground of the existenziality of Dasein, according to Heidegger, is temporality. Hence the articulated structural totality of the being of Dasein as care can become fully intelligible only when referred to that basis. In fact, all the elements in the ontological structure of Dasein will have to be considered again from the point of view of their temporal meaning, and the nature of time itself will have to be examined in all its aspects, before we are in a position to venture upon a project of understanding in which the sense of Being in general emerges within the horizon of time. All these different topics connected with the temporality of Dasein, namely, being in relation to death, the authentic potentiality of being, temporality, and the vulgar concept of time, are discussed by Heidegger consecutively in the six chapters comprising the second division of *Being and Time*. They are here dealt with, in that order, in this and the next two chapters.

[45]

Man's Wholeness and the Existential Concept of Death

At the first glance it seems as if, by the very nature of the case, access to Dasein in its wholeness is impossible, not because of any theoretical difficulty, but because its very mode of being prevents it. The being ahead of itself implied in care as the structural totality of Dasein means that so long as Dasein is, it is in relation to its ability to be—even when it has "nothing more to hope for and has 'closed his account'." Even in total hopelessness, or in the disillusioned 'being prepared for anything', Dasein is not severed from its possibilities and does not cease being ahead of itself. "In Dasein something always still *remains* which, as the potentiality of its own being, has not yet become 'real'. In the nature of Dasein's basic constitution there lies, accordingly, *a constant inconclusiveness*. The incompleteness signifies that something is left outstanding in the matter of its potentiality of being." The moment man 'exists' in such a way that nothing more remains outstanding, he ceases to exist as Dasein. So long as he *is* he never attains wholeness and when he does possess it, the gain turns into sheer loss of being-in-the-world. Dasein cannot be ontically grasped in experience as an existent whole and, hence, it seems, cannot be ontologically determined in its wholeness. But the latter conclusion does not necessarily follow, for in this "merely formal argumentation" the Dasein is unconsciously understood in the sense of a *vorhanden* entity and it is forgotten that no-longer-existing and being-ahead-of are to be taken here in a genuinely existenzial sense and not as categorial descriptions. In order to gain a truly existenzial concept of death and to understand both the existenziell potentiality of being whole as well as the existenzial problem of Dasein's ontological wholeness, it is necessary to discuss in detail the problem of *existenz* (that is, Dasein's 'ability to be') which has been neglected so far. Heidegger does this in connection with the treatment of death which follows.[2]

[46]

It may be argued that though it is denied to man to experience his own passage into nonexistence as Dasein and thus to understand himself in his wholeness, yet in the death of another he can, by virtue of his being-together-with, know 'objectively' what death is and thus make an ontological determination of Dasein's wholeness possible. But this is just an illusion, for what we experience, when we are with another who loses his being-in-the-world, is not his death, not the real "having come to an end" or the loss of being as such, that the dying person suffers. When another dies, "we may experience the strange ontological phenomenon of the sudden change of an essent from one mode of being (Dasein) to another (an essent simply given). The *end* of the essent qua Dasein is the beginning of this essent qua *vorhanden* entity." But then, the essent that still remains is not pure bodily thing—the corpse is something no longer alive, not just a material thing that never had life. The 'deceased', as different from the dead, is an object of concern to those left behind, as shown by their rites of funeral and burial. Surely, he is something more, in his mode of being, than a utensil at hand. Moreover, though the deceased *himself* is not there factually, yet we can be *with* him in the sense of still sharing in the common 'world' from which he has departed. From all this it should be clear that being with the dead in such manner just does not bring within our experience the real coming to an end of the deceased. Even if it were possible to understand through 'psychological' insight the dying of another, this would not be relevant to the ontological sense of death as the dying person's *own* possibility of being. The death of the other, hence, cannot provide us, ontically or ontologically, with what is claimed for it. The claim itself rests on "the thoroughly unjustifiable assumption that one's own Dasein can be substituted as one likes by another, so that what remains outside my own experience is accessible in that of others." It is true that in the ordinary being-togther-with in the world, the substitutability of one Dasein by another plays a large role, particularly in matters of our everyday preoccupation. In the being-together-with in the world of one's preoccupation, substitutability is not only possible but is even constitutent of the being-together. No such deputizing is, however, possible when it comes to that possibility of being which consists of the coming-to-an-end of Dasein and which endows it with its wholeness. "*No one can relieve another of his dying.*" One may indeed sacrifice oneself by dying for another, and this always as concerns some particular matter (principle or cause), but this does not in the least relieve the other of his death. "Death is something which each Dasein has to take upon its own self. Death is, so far as it 'is', always intrinsically my own, a peculiar possibility of being in which the very being of one's own Dasein is at stake. . . . Ontologically, ipseity or my-ownness (*Jemeinigkeit*) and *existenz* are constitutive of death. Dying is no event but a phenomenon to be existenzially comprehended." In this 'ending' which constitutes the wholeness of Dasein there is no deputizing possible and hence this attempt to reach the wholeness of Dasein must also be considered a failure. To ensure a truly existenzial approach to this problem, it is necessary first to arrive at an adequate ontological determination of End and Wholeness as phenomena constitutive of death.

[47]

The concepts of wholeness and end, which can be exhaustively and adequately dealt with only when we have at our disposal a regional classification of the various modes of Being on the basis of a clarified notion of Being as such, are here discussed only so far as they are pertinent to an ontological interpretation of Dasein. Heidegger seeks to distinguish only the existenzial sense of these concepts from the categorial and to show that when applied to Dasein in the latter sense they are utterly inadequate to its ontological status. The existenzial concepts, further, are arrived at, not by way of deduction but by "gathering from Dasein itself the existenzial sense of this coming to an end and to show how such 'ending' can constitute the being-whole of an entity that has existenz."

Dasein is infected with an ever present incompleteness, which cannot be annulled and which finds its end in death. To describe this not-yet clinging to Dasein, as long as it is, in terms of something 'outstanding', some lack that remains to be made good—as in the case of an outstanding debt which is made good by payment—may be misleading, for it is about essents at hand that we generally speak of a lack which can be made up by an addition. But the not-yet of Dasein's possible death cannot be ontologically determined in this manner, for Dasein is not a sum of handy essents pieced together. "Dasein *is* not made complete and 'all together' when its not-yet has been made good, so little that just then it no longer is. Dasein ever already exists just so that its not-yet *belongs* to it." It may be said that there are other essents, not of the character of Dasein in which also the not-yet is inherent. But, though one may say, for example, of the moon, partly covered by shadow, that a quarter still 'remains', this is only because of our inability to perceive it whole, not because the moon itself lacks wholeness. The not-yet of Dasein, on the contrary, is not merely not accessible to experience but is itself nonexistent and refers to something that Dasein, lacking it, has to become. But, it may be objected again, the unripe fruit also *becomes* ripe, its ripeness being not externally added to it but something to which it attains from within its own self. As ripening, it *is* its unripeness. As in the case of Dasein, the not-yet is incorporated into its own being as constitutive of it. But the similarity between ripening as end and death as end ceases here. With its ripening the fruit attains its perfection but not so man, who has indeed "run out his course" in death but cannot, with that, be said to have exhausted necessarily his specific possibilities—which are rather snatched away from him at death. Thus, ending does not necessarily mean consummation. In none of the ordinary senses of ending, as they apply to simply given or handy essents, is death in fact the end of Dasein—neither in the sense of becoming perfect, nor of simply vanishing, nor of being there as a finished product, nor that of being available in its entirety as an essent at hand.[3]

Just as the not-yet of Dasein's wholeness cannot be conceived as 'outstandingness', so also its end is not to be conceived either as consummation or as cessation. But, "just as Dasein, so long as it is, *is* its not-yet, constantly and already, so also *is* it ever already his end. The ending implied in death does not mean the being-at-an-end of Dasein but a *being toward (in relation to) the end* of this essent. Death is a mode of being which overtakes Dasein as soon as it is. 'As soon as man comes into life he is old enough to die'." What is therefore needed is an existenzial explanation of 'being toward the end' which will throw light on the not-yet inherent in existenz itself and also provide an adequate basis for an understanding of Dasein's wholeness in relation to death.

[48]

Before proceeding to an existenzial analysis of death, Heidegger points out how it must be kept distinct from other types of interpretation. Death in the widest sense is a phenomenon of life, understood in a biological, ontic sense.

The coming to an end of an animate being is its perishing (*Verenden*). Since man also dies in the physiological, vital sense, but as determined at the same time by his primary mode of being as Dasein, he does not just perish but suffers decease (*Ableben*). Dying (*Sterben*), on the other hand, refers to *the mode of being* in which Dasein *is* in relation to its death (*Tod*, the general term for death). The existenzial interpretation of death is presupposed in all biology and ontology of life, in all biographical and historical as well as ethnological and psychological accounts of death. "A psychology of dying provides information rather about the 'life' of the 'dying' person than about his dying itself," for Dasein's dying cannot be equated with an experience of factual decease. The existenzial analysis of death, conceived as the 'end' of Dasein, has nothing to do with an ontic decision as to whether Dasein lives on beyond death in another world, though it remains purely 'this-worldly' insofar as it interprets this phenomenon simply with a view to comprehending how it enters into Dasein as a possibility of its being. "Even to ask, meaningfully and rightfully, what comes after death is possible only when one has arrived at a conception of what death is in its full ontological character. . . . The this-worldly ontological interpretation of death lies prior to every ontic and otherworldly speculation." For the same reason, a "metaphysics of death," seeking to determine how and when death "came into the world" and what significance it possesses, as evil and suffering, in the cosmic order, lies outside the scope of the existenzial analysis of death. These questions require a prior ontological understanding, not only of death but of the universe in general and of evil and negativity in any form, in particular. "The questions arising out of a biology, psychology, theodicy and theology of death methodically presuppose the existenzial analysis of death." Its sole aim here is to lay bare the ontological structure of Dasein's being *toward* the end.[4]

[49]

It has become apparent that the phenomenon of death as being toward the end, and consequently also the wholeness of Dasein, can be adequately grasped only in terms of Dasein's basic ontological constitution, that is, care. Care has been 'defined' as Dasein's "being already ahead of itself in (the world) as being with the (intramundane) essents encountered." This formulation brings out the fundamental characteristics of the being of Dasein, existenz being expressed through 'being ahead of', facticity through 'already being in' and forfeiture through 'being with'. Heidegger gives a preliminary sketch of the way these three are disclosed in the phenomenon of death by way of introducing the existenzial analysis. As explained before, Dasein's being-at-an-end means existenzially being toward the end, its not-yet being something to which it is related. The end awaits Dasein as something impending, for death is not a simply given essent yet to be, not an outstanding due (*Ausstand*) but rather something imminent (*Bevorstand*). There are other things that may also await man and be impending, for example, events in the world, such as a thunderstorm or the arrival of a friend, and possibilities of his own being, such as a journey or the giving up of something he would like to be. Unlike these, death is the innermost potentiality of his own being, awaiting him, before which he stands. It is a possibility in which his very being-in-the-world is at stake, in the imminence of which he is, therefore, thrown back completely upon his innermost potentiality of being, with all his relations to another Dasein broken off. "This possibility, its very own and unrelative (that is, absolute), is at the same time the extremest. As able to be, Dasein is incapable of getting ahead of (or overtaking) the possibility of death. Death is the possibility of Dasein's utter impossibility of being. Thus death discloses itself as the innermost, unrelative, unsurpassable possibility." This disclosure is grounded in care as constituted by Dasein's *existenz*, its openness in the mode of being ahead of itself.

Further, this possibility is one in which man by the mere fact of existing is already thrown. He may have no theoretical knowledge of this state of being delivered up to his death, as an aspect of his being-in-the-world. Yet, this thrownness into death is revealed to him all the more profoundly and compellingly in the disposition of anxiety. "The dread of death is anxiety before one's innermost unrelative and unsurpassable potentiality of being. . . . It is not an incidental, chance weakness of mood in a particular individual but, as the basic disposition of Dasein, a disclosure of the fact that Dasein exists, as thrown into being, *toward* its end." Finally, the fact that most people do not, in the first instance and mostly, know anything of death cannot be brought forward as proving that being toward death does not universally belong to Dasein. It only shows that, first and foremost, Dasein, in flight before its innermost being toward death, keeps this hidden from itself. "Dasein dies factually, so long as it exists, but first and mostly in the mode of forfeiture." The forfeited absorption into the 'world' of its preoccupation is a flight from the homelessness of its own being toward death. Thus, existenz, facticity, and forfeiture characterize Dasein's being toward death. This existenzial concept of death means, of course, that from the point of view of its ontological possibility, dying is grounded in care.

[50]

The connection between being toward death and care, sketched above, finds its concrete expression in man's everyday mode of being. In being toward death, he is related to his own self as a preeminent potentiality of being. But the self of Dasein's quotidian existence is the 'one', constituted by the vulgar understanding and interpretedness as it expresses itself in chatter. Hence the way everyday Dasein interprets its being toward death should be evident from its chatter and from the kind of attunement in which it becomes aware of such being. For the public everyday being-together, death in the sense of decease is a matter of constant occurrence—someone or the other, known or unknown, is all the time dying. 'Death', as a familiar event within the world, with its characteristic inconspicuousness, is already provided with an interpretation which takes its sting away from it and is leveled down to an occurrence which indeed affects Dasein but which yet appertains to nobody in particular. "The public interpretation of Dasein says, 'one dies', so that everyone else as well as oneself can persuade himself that it is not precisely myself, for this 'one' is the nobody." In the ambiguity of everyman's chatter, "death, undelegatable and my own, is perverted into a public event which 'one' encounters." Losing himself in the 'one', man remains unaware of a preeminent potentiality of being belonging to his own self, justified and strengthened by the 'one' in this temptation to hide from himself his own innermost being toward death. The veiling and evasive attitude towards death in everyday life leads, further, to an attempt at appeasing, in our solicitous being-together, every anxious concern with death. Condoling and consoling, the 'one' manages to bring about a constant appeasement and reassurance about death. For public life even the death of others is not infrequently a social unpleasantness, if not sheer tactlessness, from which society should be carefully protected. The 'one' tacitly regulates the everyday attitude to death, condemning all "thinking of death" as cowardly fear and morose flight from the world. "The 'one' does not let the disposition of anxiety before death rise up. . . . The 'one' manages to transfer this anxiety (in which Dasein is confronted with the unsurpassable possibility of death) into the mere fear of an approaching event, a weakness unworthy of Dasein's self-assurance." The cultivation of such an attitude of 'superior' indifference estranges Dasein from its innermost, unrelative potentiality of being-toward-death into a constant flight before it and a dodging of it, by giving it a new interpretation, and understanding it inauthentically and covering it over and disguising it. But this flight shows that even the everyday 'one' is determined by being-toward-death. "Even for the average everyday Dasein, this innermost, unrelative and unsurpassable potentiality of being is constantly at stake, even though only in the mode of a concern manifesting itself in the form of an unperturbed indifference towards the most extreme possibility of its existenz." Having brought to light Dasein's flight before death phenomenally, Heidegger proceeds to the task of explicating phenomenologically the understanding of death implicit in Dasein's every evasion of it.

[51]

The preliminary sketch of the ontological structure of death led to an analysis of its concrete expression in the everyday attitude to death. Heidegger now takes us, after completing his interpretation of the vulgar conception of death, back in the reverse direction, with a view to providing the full existenzial concept of death. The chatter of the 'one' says,

"One dies also some day but, for the present, not yet." What the 'one dies' means we have already seen. The everyday interpretation admits some kind of certainty of death, an ambiguous and spurious kind of certainty which covers up and waters down the reality of death, lightening the burden of being delivered up to death. By its very nature Dasein's forfeited being-toward-death cannot be authentically 'certain' of death, and yet *is* so, in a way. To be certain of anything means to *hold* something true to be 'true'. Like truth, which in the primary sense means the discovering character of Dasein and, secondarily, the discoveredness of things, certainty also, being co-original with truth, has the double sense of Dasein's being certain and of things as certainties. Conviction is one mode of certainty in which "Dasein lets itself be determined in its comprehension of an essent solely through the testimony of the disclosed (true) thing," so that in such a case holding something to be true is, as holding oneself 'in truth', self-sufficing. But everyday man, veiling from himself his own innermost possibility of death, is factually 'in untruth' and hence his certainty must also be an incongruous, inappropriate kind of holding something to be true, in which he is not uncertain in the sense of doubting, but holds that of which he is certain in hiding and in obscurity. As an undeniable 'fact of experience', Everyman says, death is inevitable. "*One* says it, but the 'one' overlooks that, in order to be certain of death, Dasein must be certain, within its own self, of its own innermost unrelative potentiality of being. Everyman says that death is certain, and with that plants into Dasein the illusion, as though it were itself certain of its death." The way everyday man understands the certainty of death is betrayed in his critical, sober 'thinking' about death, a thinking for which death is a highly probable fact, "being only *empirically* certain," and thus falling behind the highest apodictic certainty attainable in certain forms of theoretical knowledge. This shows again the vulgar misunderstanding of the mode of being proper to Dasein and its being toward death, for the empirical certainty of death has nothing to do with death as it truly *is*.

Even though Dasein talks, in the publicity of the 'one', ostensibly only of this 'empirical' certainty of death, *yet at bottom* it does not really keep exclusively and primarily to the cases of death that occur (around it). *Evading its death*, even the everyday being in relation to death is yet certain of death in a way different from what it is itself prepared to admit in pure theoretical reflection. . . .The forfeited everydayness of Dasein knows death as a certainty and yet evades *being* certain of it. But this evasion is phenomenal evidence, through the very thing it avoids, that death must be conceived as the innermost, unrelative, unovertakable, *certain* possibility.

Further, in saying of death that it will come certainly "but for the present not yet," everyman casts a veil over the peculiar character of the certainty of death, that it is possible any moment. Together with the certainty of death there goes an indefiniteness as to its when. Everyday being toward death evades this by investing it with definiteness, not by calculating the moment of decease, but by bringing it into proximity with the foreseeable emergencies and possibilities of our daily concerns, through which it seems to become something tangible and temporally localizable.

The full existenzial-ontological concept of death, therefore, may be summed up by saying that "death as the end of Dasein is the innermost, unrelative, certain and as such indefinite, unsurpassable possibility of Dasein. As the end of *Dasein*, death *is* in the being of this essent *toward* his end." In conformity with man's mode of being, death lies in, or means existenzially, his being in relation to his end. Inasmuch as he exists as being in relation to his death, his own most extreme not-yet is incorporated into himself. Far from disproving Dasein's possibility of existing as a whole, it is the structural complex of care, with its being-ahead-of-itself and the consequent not-yet, that renders possible ontologically this being toward the end in Dasein. But the evasion in face of death characteristic of man's everyday state of forfeiture represents an inauthentic being in relation to death. The problem now is whether he can grasp his innermost possibility of death, as characterized above, in an authentic manner, whether he can take his stand in an authentic being toward his end. "Inauthenticity is grounded in a possible authenticity. Inauthenticity is a mode of being in which Dasein can mislay itself, and generally has already done so, but in which it need not necessarily and constantly place itself." An authentic being toward death is thus existenzielly a possibility and the question Heidegger next takes up is how this is existenzially possible and what the existenzial conditions of such possibility are.

[52]

In view of the fact that Dasein factually exists mostly and primarily in an inauthentic mode, it is important to make sure that a project of understanding aimed at grasping the existenzial structure of authentic being toward death is not just a 'fantastic undertaking', a merely arbitrary imaginative construction, and that it is guided by indications lying within Dasein itself. Heidegger therefore, takes as his basis the existenzial concept of death already worked out along with the nature of the inauthentic being toward death elucidated above. From what has been said about the latter it follows that an authentic being toward death cannot lie in evading the innermost, unrelative possibility, nor in covering it up and giving it a new interpretation intelligible to everyman. Further, being toward death is a being in relation to a possibility, a preeminent possibility of Dasein itself. But, unlike the way we contemplate a possibility in the sense of a concern for realizing something in the sphere of essents at hand or simply given, it does not annul the possibility (that is, its character as possible) of the possible by converting it into something that, as realized, lies at our disposal. "Death as something possible is not a possible handy or simply given entity but a possibility of being of *Dasein*." A realization of that possibility, bringing about Dasein's decease, would be to take away from Dasein all possibility of existing in relation to its death. Nor does being toward death lie in 'brooding' over death and, taking it as something that can be dealt with, in softening it down as a possibility, so that "as something possible it may show as little of its possibility (that is, its possible character) as possible." In the authentic being toward death, on the contrary, "the possibility must be grasped *as* unmitigated *possibility*, cultivated *as possibility* and, in (our) attitude towards it, *endured as possibility*." Authentic being in relation to possibility should also not be understood in the sense of an attitude of expectation, which by its very nature regards the possible from the point of view of "whether and when and how" it would be actually there and is intrinsically a waiting for that. "In expecting also there lies a breaking away from the possible and securing a footing in the actual." In expectation, with its concern for the actual, the possible is drawn into the sphere of the actual. Being toward the possibility which is death, on the other hand, must be so related to it as to disclose it, in this being and for it, as pure possibility, a way of being related which Heidegger terms "running ahead (*Vorlaufen*) to the possibility." This reaching forward or anticipation does not bring about a nearness to the possible in the sense of realizing it and thus annulling it as possibility but rather intensifies its character as possibility. "The closest proximity of being in relation to death as a possibility is as far removed from the actual as possible. . . . Death as possibility offers Dasein nothing to realize and nothing that it can itself actually *be*." To the anticipative running toward it, death reveals itself as possibility, growing ever greater, measureless and absolute, and as the possibility of the boundless impossibility of existenz.

In being toward death, man reaches out anticipatively to a potentiality of his own being and is thus disclosed to himself in his extremest possibility. Understanding himself thus, he becomes aware of the possibility of his own authentic existenz, showing all the five existenzial characteristics of death mentioned above. Death, as man's innermost possibility, reveals to him his own innermost potentiality of being, in which he can cut himself off from the 'they', an ability which indeed first makes manifest his factual forfeiture to the everyday 'oneself'. Anticipation of death also reveals his innermost possibility as unrelative, a potentiality of being which he alone can take upon himself and in which he is thrown back upon his own solitary self. "Death does not just indifferently 'belong' only to one's own Dasein but it *claims* it as single and *alone*. . . . It renders evident the fact that all being with the objects of our concern and every being-together-with others fail when it comes to our own innermost potentiality of being. Dasein can only then *be authentically itself* when it enables itself, solely by itself, to become so." Thirdly, the innermost, unrelative possibility is unovertakable; in anticipative being toward it, man learns to face, in free self-surrender, the most extreme possibility of existence, that of giving up his own self. Becoming anticipatively free for his own death, he is liberated from being lost in the chance possibilities that keep obtruding and is thus enabled to grasp truly and to choose from the factual possibilities before him in the perspective of the final, unovertakable one. His own existenz is revealed to him as a perpetual task. Further, since his own possibilities are grasped in the perspective of the end, that is, as finite, he also avoids the danger of misinterpreting them in terms of the possibilities of existing open to others. And since the possibility thus anticipated is one that cannot be overcome, it includes all the possibilities preceding it, thus making possible an anticipation of Dasein in its *wholeness* and enabling it to exist as the potentiality of being whole. This innermost possibility, further, is certain. It discloses Dasein as a possibility only in such fashion that, anticipating it, Dasein *enables* this possibility as its innermost potentiality of being. "The disclosure of possibility is grounded in the anticipative *enabling* (rendering possible)." The certainty of death does not take its stand in the truth of simply given essents and apodictic evidence is of no relevance to it; it has nothing to do with the graded order of evidence about *vorhanden* essents. "Holding death, which can only be mine, to be true exhibits a certainty different in kind, and more primordial, than any certainty concerning essents encounterable within the world, or that of formal entities; it is certainty attaching to being-in-the-world (itself). As such it . . . claims Dasein in the full authenticity of its *existenz*," assuring him of his unsurpassable wholeness. Hence, the evidence of an immediate datum of our inner experiences, of the I and of consciousness as immediately given, lags far behind the certainty of this 'running ahead' in anticipation. Lastly, this certain possibility is indeterminate, so that its 'when' always remains indefinite, in the anticipation of which man opens himself to a threat, constant and springing from his own 'there' or overtness; a threat in which he must hold himself, cultivating rather than obscuring the indeterminateness of this certainty. An attuned understanding of this is existenzially rendered possible to man by the mood of anxiety which discloses to him the constant, sheer menace rising up from his own innermost isolated being and in which he finds himself facing the nothingness of the possible impossibility of his existence.[5] "The (anticipative) 'running forward' renders Dasein utterly isolated and in this isolation of itself enables it to be certain of the wholeness of its potentiality of being. For this reason, the basic mood of anxiety belongs to this self-understanding of Dasein in its very depths."

Heidegger sums up the existenzial concept of authentic being toward death as follows: "The (anticipative) 'running ahead' discloses to Dasein its being lost in the 'oneself' and brings him before the possibility, without any support in concerned solicitude, of being its own self, a self existing in passionate, factual and anxious freedom toward (in relation to) death, delivered from the illusions of the 'they' and sure of itself." Being toward death, in essence, consists in discovering, developing, and holding fast to the anticipative 'running forward' as something that renders possible the extremest possibility of Dasein itself. The *ontological* possibility of an existenzielly authentic being toward death (that is, potentiality of being whole) has thus been elucidated, though this does not mean much so long as the corresponding ontic potentiality of being is not existenzially established as arising from the nature of Dasein itself. Heidegger, therefore, turns next to the task of showing how Dasein testifies, out of its innermost potentiality of being, to a possible authenticity of its existenz and whether this existenziell phenomenon fits in with the ontological possibility 'projected' above.

[53]

Authenticity, Conscience, and Resoluteness

Is there any evidence, rooted in the being of man himself, of an authentic potentiality of being his own self? Since the self of everyday Dasein is the 'oneself', as we have seen, and authentic selfhood is an existenziell modification of this everyday state, it remains now to be determined what such modification existenzially means and how it is ontologically possible. Dasein, in being lost to the 'one' has already put off the load of authentically choosing a potentiality of its being and surrendered it to the everyman, a lapse into inauthenticity which can only be reversed when Dasein expressly pulls itself out of its forfeiture to the 'one' and back to its own self. This pulling back, further, must concern the very point of which the omission caused Dasein to lose itself in inauthenticity, and this means that it must retrieve and take back upon itself the act of choosing, which itself implies that it must first choose to take this choice upon itself. "In choosing this choice, above all, Dasein makes possible for itself its authentic potentiality of being." The possibility that man can find his way back to himself is to be found within his own self as an ability to be something that, in a sense, he already *is*. Such testimony Heidegger finds contained in the phenomenon popularly called the voice of conscience, which, in spite of, and indeed by reason of, the ambiguities and controversies attaching to its meaning, is to be regarded as a primordial phenomenon of Dasein's existenz.

The ontological analysis of conscience that follows lies prior to any psychological description and classification of conscience as subjectively experienced and it is equally remote from a theological interpretation of conscience. Conscience, as a phenomenon of Dasein, is not a *vorhanden* fact or event which sometimes occurs and to which an inductive empirical proof might be relevant, but is an aspect of Dasein's mode of being manifesting itself in its factual existenz. In its cognitive function, conscience is an expression of the overtness of Dasein which as we have seen, is constituted by mood, understanding, forfeiture, and speech. Conscience is of the nature of a 'call' (*Ruf*), which is a mode of speech. The call of conscience is an appeal (*Anruf*) to Dasein's innermost potentiality of being itself and a summons (*Aufruf*) to an acknowledgement of guilt in the depths of its being. Corresponding to the call, there must be a hearing of the call, depending upon a will to have conscience which in turn involves the 'choosing of choice', the ultimate choosing which Heidegger calls resoluteness (*Entschlossenheit*). In what follows, these different aspects of conscience, guilt, and resoluteness are discussed in their existenzial import.

[54]

Conscience in some fashion gives Dasein "something to understand," is an intimation of something, and is thus connected with the way Dasein is its 'there', that is, is overt. Lost in the publicity of the 'one' and his chatter, man has ear only for the 'oneself' and in consequence fails to listen to his own self. If he is to be brought back, through no other agency but himself, from this lost state, this listening to the 'they', binding him to them as with a chain, must be terminated and that too through a possibility existing within his own self of a kind of hearing that can accomplish this. The possibility of such a suspension lies in his responding to a direct unmediated call from within himself that can cut through his self-forgetful surrender to the 'one' and awaken in him a 'hearing' which, in contrast to the clamor of the manifold ambiguities of everyday gossip, responds to a call that is "soundless, unambiguous, giving no opportunity for curiosity to fasten upon." Through such calling, conscience gives intimation of something to Dasein. Vocal expression presupposes, and is therefore not essential to, speech. This is also true of the call, popularly the 'voice', of conscience, which is no 'voice' in the literal sense but a "giving something to understand," an intimation or disclosure that causes a jolt, an unsettling shake-up. "Calling is from afar and in the distance. The call reaches him who wants to be retrieved." This way of describing the phenomenon of conscience has the merit of avoiding the usual types of interpretation of conscience in terms of mental faculties, intellect, will or feeling, or of 'acts' of a person, thus clearing the way for an analysis of its existenzial structure.

[55]

In speech something is said of or about something, and in the call of conscience this is the average, everyday Dasein itself, the 'oneself' of preoccupied being-with-others. It is a call that reaches the 'oneself' and calls him back to his own *self*, passing over Dasein in its forfeited, everyday aspect, so that "only the self of the 'oneself' is appealed to and made to hear, with the result that the 'one' collapses into himself" and everyday Dasein is recalled to its self. "Precisely in this passing over, it thrusts into insignificance the 'one' keen on 'appearances'. The self, deprived of this shelter and of this hiding place is, however, brought back to itself through this call," the self understood in the existenzial sense of a mode of being-in-the-world and not in the sense of something inside us and shut off from the 'external world'. *What* is said in the call, the content of the appeal as such, is strictly speaking nothing. "The call speaks out nothing, gives no information about happenings in the world, has nothing to tell," least of all is it an appeal of the self to start a "dialogue with itself." Nothing is conveyed *to* the self in the call which is rather a summons, not bringing the self to trial, but recalling it to itself and its innermost potentiality of being and thus inspiring it forward to its innermost possibilities. "Conscience speaks solely and always in the mode of silence" and, without thereby losing in distinctness, forces Dasein wordlessly into the secrecy of its own self. What the call discloses is something unequivocal and, despite the vagueness of its content, certain as to the direction it takes.

[56]

The next problem to be discussed, towards an ontologically adequate interpretation of conscience, concerns the 'who' of this call, how the Dasein called is related to the caller and how this 'relation' is to be ontologically grasped. Not merely is the receiver of the call indefinite but the caller also is shrouded in a peculiar indeterminateness and indefinability. It cannot be known, as things in the world are known, by "name, station, origin and appearance" and is nothing one can be acquainted with, or observe, or talk about. But this negative characterization expresses a positive feature of the caller, namely, that he goes out, and is absorbed without remainder, into his function of calling. Further, though it would be true to say that in the call of conscience it is man (Dasein) who calls to his own self, he is not only the called but also the source of the call, yet this answer as to the 'who' of the call is too simple. It ignores the peculiar impersonal character of the call which 'comes', unexpected and unwished for, independently of our agency, and yet not from anybody else. "The call comes *out* of me and yet *upon* me from beyond me." This phenomenal characteristic of the voice has led to its interpretation as an alien power entering into us, a power either extraneously owned or the revelation of God Himself within us. Alternatively, the phenomenon itself may be explained away by means of a biologically oriented theory. Both interpretations base themselves upon the implicit ontological assumption that "what *is* must be *vorhanden*; what cannot be shown objectively to be simply given *is not* at all," thus completely disregarding the principle that conscience as a phenomenon of Dasein can only possess a mode of being appropriate to the latter's existenzial constitution.

The analysis of the facticity of Dasein has shown that Dasein is to be conceived as thrown into existenz, as an essent which has to be what and how it is and can be. In this mode of existing, "*that* he factually is may remain hidden as to its '*why*', but the '*that*' *itself* is open to Dasein," being the thrownness which is revealed to it in its moods and to which Dasein mostly reacts by flight, a flight before the uncanniness of its isolated being-in-the-world. "The fundamental mood of anxiety discloses this uncanniness and, as the most elementary form of the thrown Dasein's overtness, brings its being-in-the-world face to face with the nothingness of the world, before which it is tormented with the anxiety for its innermost potentiality of being." Heidegger suggests that the source of the call of conscience is this anxious Dasein, determinable by no 'worldly' attribute, the naked 'that' in the nothingness of the world, unfamiliar to the everyday 'oneself' and so an alien voice. Nothing could be more foreign to the 'one', lost in the multifarious concerns of the 'world', than this self, alone in the uncanniness of being thrown into nothingness. " 'It' calls and yet for the preoccupied ear of curiosity it offers nothing to hear that can be repeated and publicly talked about. And what indeed has Dasein, in the uncanniness of its thrown being, to report? *What* else remains to it but its own potentiality of being which anxiety discloses? How else can it call except in the form of a summons to this ability to be, which is solely at stake for it?" Recalling Dasein to the privacy of its potentiality of being, the call speaks in the uncanny mode of silence. Conscience, with its source in man's thrownness, its appeal to him in his innermost potentiality of being and its summons recalling him from his forfeiture, thus shows itself as the call of care in its full structure of already-being-in, ahead-of-itself and being-with essents. Care as the being of Dasein is the ontological condition of the possibility of conscience. To seek for its source in an extraneous power only shows a failure to understand the nature of Dasein's mode of being. To interpret conscience as an objective universal force, far from ensuring an independent, objective status to conscience, is rather "a flight before conscience, a way out for Dasein, through which it sneaks away from the thin wall which, as it were, separates the 'one' from the uncanniness of his being."

So far, the analysis of conscience has sought to trace it, as a phenomenon of Dasein, back to its roots in the latter's ontological constitution, thus preparing the way for an understanding of conscience as an attestation, from within Dasein itself, of its innermost potentiality of being. What is attested by conscience and indeed the full nature of conscience itself, however, can be determined only after a consideration of how the call is heard or understood. "Only from the way the call is understood and together *with* it, is it possible to comprehend the experience of conscience in its entirety." The analysis of the understanding of the call, and of guilt to which the voice of conscience always somehow refers, may then lead to an explicit discussion of what the call intimates or gives Dasein to understand.

[57]

With its source in the homelessness of man's thrown solitude and recalling him to his own self, the call of conscience summons him forward to his ability to be. Conscience is a "calling forward recall." Though it 'says' nothing and gives no 'knowledge', yet the call discloses, along with its character as a summons, its source and its objective. It also offers Dasein something to understand and is an intimation, according to all accounts of the experience of conscience, whether the 'good' conscience or the admonitory conscience, of its own guiltiness. The various existenziell accounts, however, leave the existenzial concept of guilt obscure. Since it is from Dasein itself that the claim to guilt arises, such a concept must be drawn out from an interpretation of the being of Dasein, not arbitrarily concocted and forced upon it. "If it is at all possible to understand the nature of guilt, indications of its possibility must be found within Dasein," and that, too, in the everyday, forfeited mode of its existence. "All ontological investigation of phenomena such as guilt, conscience, death, must start from what the everyday interpretation of Dasein has to 'say' about it." Even though the interpretation offered by Dasein in its everyday, forfeited state is inauthentically oriented and fails to go to the ontological root of the matter, yet "seeing anything wrong always contains within itself, at the same time, the disclosure of an indication of the original 'Idea' of the phenomenon concerned."

In everyday understanding, being guilty (*schuldig*) is understood in the sense of owing something to somebody who has a claim over it, a sense which attaches to objects of concern involving a claim to ownership by another. Another sense of guilt (*Schuld*) is incurring blame for something, or committing a fault. Common to both senses is failure to fulfill a requirement, through omission or commission, being responsible for endangering, misleading or ruining another in his existenz. The formal concept of guilt may thus be determined as "being the ground of a deficiency in the Dasein of another and in such a way that this 'being the ground for' is itself in turn determinable as deficient." This deficiency or want is the inadequacy in face of a demand issuing to Dasein by virtue of its being-with others. Being guilty, whether in the sense of making oneself culpable or of being indebted or of being to blame for something, is a mode of being of Dasein. Hence, an elucidation of the phenomenon of guilt is possible only if the idea of 'guilty' is derived from the mode of being of Dasein. For this purpose, it is necessary that this idea must be *formalized* to such an extent as to lift it out of the sphere of the calculating preoccupations of everyday being-with and eliminate all references to moral and legal concepts. Even in the moral sphere, guilt is regarded as a deficiency, a lack of something that should and can be. But lack in the sense of not being there can refer only to something *vorhanden* and thus guilt, as a mode of being of Dasein, cannot be understood in terms of the kind of lack implied in the moral ought. "In this sense, there can be no intrinsic deficiency in existenz, not because it is perfect, but because its mode of being is distinct from all *vorhanden* existence."

Nevertheless, the character of a 'not' inheres in the idea of 'guilty' which must be existenzially elucidated. Also, as mentioned before, guilt contains within it the idea of 'being the ground of'. Guilt may, therefore, be described as "being the ground of a being determined through a 'not'." Since the 'not' contained in guilt as existenzially conceived has no reference to anything *vorhanden*, there is no reason to mistake, in regard to being the ground of a deficiency, this being who is the ground as itself 'deficient'. From a deficiency caused by Dasein, for example the failure to fulfil a demand, we cannot infer back to a deficiency in the 'cause'. Hence, "being guilty does not result, in the first instance, from a fault or offense committed but, on the contrary, the latter is itself 'grounded' in a more original being-guilty of Dasein." Such an original being-guilty in the very being of Dasein and its existenzial possibility are demonstrated by Heidegger in the following manner. The being of Dasein is constituted by care, with its elements of facticity (thrownness), existenz (project) and forfeiture. As existing, Dasein is thrown, not brought into its 'there' by itself and as existing, it is already determined as a potentiality of being. Its thrownness is always "at its back," not as an event which has befallen it once for all but as a constant mode of its being. As existing thus, man is the ground of his ability to be, without having himself laid this foundation; he exists as the thrown ground—a fact revealed to him as a burden in his moods—solely by projecting himself upon the possibilities into which he is thrown. In becoming a self, and as such to lay the ground for his own self, he can never have command over it and yet as existing has to undertake 'being the ground of'. "To be its own thrown ground is the potentiality of being that is at stake for care." Being the ground and existing as thrown, man always remains 'behind' his possibilities, never existing ahead of his ground but only out of it and *as* that. Being the ground accordingly means for him never being master over his own being in its ground. It is this 'not' which is implied in the existenzial sense of thrownness, for Dasein, existing as ground, is itself a nullity of itself, a nullity which does not mean not being *vorhanden* or not existing but a 'not' which constitutes the very being of Dasein as thrown. This 'not' refers to man's thrown existence *as* self, emerging from the ground not through himself but (given over) *to* himself, in order that he may exist *as that* (that is, as ground). "Dasein is not itself the ground of its being insofar as this arises from its own project, but as being a self it may well be called the *being* of the ground. This is always ground only of an entity whose being has to undertake being-the-ground." Man exists as his ground by projecting himself into possibilities, but his projects are, ontologically speaking, doubly infected with nullity. Firstly, they are always thrown projects, thus incorporating the nullity in his way of being his ground, and secondly, because in choosing one possibility he is not able to realize another. Such nullity characterizes Dasein's freedom in the choice of its existenziell possibilities. In the existenzial structure of throwness and of project there lies thus an intrinsic nullity, which also accounts for the inauthenticity of Dasein's forfeiture, its invariable factual state. Thus care, the being of Dasein, is in its very nature shot through and through with nullity. As a thrown project it may be characterized as "the being-the (null)-ground of a nullity." And this means that Dasein is *as such* guilty.

Nullity in this existenzial sense is thus constitutive of Dasein's very being, though the ontological sense of the 'not' of this nullity still remains obscure. This is in fact true of the ontological nature of 'not' in general, for although ontology and logic have occupied themselves intensively with the 'not', they have hardly looked into its ontological character, assuming as they have done that every 'not' has the negative sense of a lack or deficiency. Even the problem of the ontological origin of 'notness', of the conditions of the possibility of the 'not' has never been raised. For the ontological interpretation of the phenomenon of guilt, the concepts of privation and lack do not suffice. Least of all can this phenomenon be approached by way of the idea of evil, of *malum* (the bad) as *privatio boni* (privation of the good), both *bonum* and *privatio* having their origin in an ontology of *vorhanden* being, to which the concept of 'value' can also be traced. The fact that Dasein is guilty in the very root of its being is the ontological condition of the possibility that in its factual existence it can incur guilt as well as of the possibility of moral goodness and evil, that is, of morality in general. Since morality presupposes guilt as its ontological condition, it cannot itself define the nature of the primary being-guilty. To object that we have no such consciousness of a primary guilt is hardly relevant, for the existence of guilt does not imply its consciousness. "More primary than its *knowledge* is *being*-guilty. And only because Dasein is guilty in the ground of its being and, as thrown and forfeited, shuts its eyes to this, is conscience possible and so alone can its call give to Dasein to understand the fact of its being-guilty at the roots." The call of conscience calls man forward to his inner capability of being, recalls him to the nullity of being his own thrown ground. It gives him to understand that, taking his stand in the possibility of his being, the 'not'-infected ground of his 'not'-infected projects, he has to pull himself out of being lost to the 'one' and come back to himself, to the fact that this is a debt he owes himself, a responsibility he has yet to discharge, that he is guilty. This call of conscience is the call of his own being as guilty, that is, of care. Rightly and authentically understood, it is a summons to Dasein to acknowledge and take authentically upon itself this being-guilty.[6]

The summons to being guilty, far from inviting man to heap guilt upon himself by acts of commission or omission, only calls upon him to be authentically what he already is. To hear and to understand this call rightly means to choose the potentiality of being authentically guilty. It means becoming free for the call and being ready to receive it and thus to submit to his innermost possibility of *existenz*. The 'oneself', to whom his own profound guiltiness remains hidden and which he does his utmost to evade, is thus called back to his own being-guilty. "To understand the call is to choose, not conscience, which, as such cannot be chosen, but *having* conscience in the sense of being free for the innermost being-guilty. *Understanding the call* means *having* the will to have conscience." Such will is the most fundamental existenziell presupposition for the possibility of factual guilt, for only thus does Dasein let its innermost self *act* in itself, out of its chosen potentiality of being, and be responsible. Although the call conveys no information, it is yet not to be regarded as merely critical in its function but as something positive, in the sense that it discloses Dasein's most primary potentiality of own being. Conscience thus is an attestation, coming from Dasein's own being, of an authentic potentiality of being. The last step in the interpretation of conscience that remains is to show how the existenzial interpretation of conscience squares with its vulgar understanding and with the common everyday experience of conscience.

[58]

The ontological interpretation of conscience as the call of care which recalls Dasein to its innermost potentiality of being guilty and the understanding of conscience as the will to have conscience do not seem to harmonize with the vulgar interpretation of conscience. Forfeited Dasein, understanding itself in terms of the objects of its concern, is bound, naturally, to give to itself a 'corrupt' interpretation consonant with its own mode of being. But the ontological interpretation cannot disregard the vulgar experience of conscience and must be in a position to explain how, even in misinterpreting the basic phenomenon, it remains yet ontologically rooted in the nature of this phenomenon itself. Heidegger adduces four objections that might be brought forward against the foregoing ontological explanation of conscience from the point of view of the vulgar interpretation. In the first place, it might seem that the ontological interpretation does not take account of the basic forms of conscience, the 'bad' and the 'good', the 'censuring' and the 'warning' conscience. All interpretations of conscience rightly take it as primarily 'bad', indicative of guilt. But in the vulgar interpretation, the experience of conscience occurs after the commission or omission of an act, the voice referring back to that and not summoning forward as in the ontological account. The voice of conscience is regarded as an event in the succession of our experiences, occurring subsequent to the experience of the act, that is, as belonging to the order of *vorhanden* mental processes. As we have seen, however, the call of conscience is not a process of this kind but has the mode of being of care. It is only when mistaken as a process that it can be taken as occurring later than the act and thus as referring back to it. It does have a retrospective reference but this is a reference back, beyond the act committed, to the thrown being-guilty which is 'prior' to any particular guilty act. At the same time, it calls forward to *being*-guilty as something to be taken up in one's existenz, so that being-guilty rather 'follows' the call than otherwise. The order in which processes of experience follow each other does not give the phenomenal structure of the way we exist. As for the 'good' conscience, which is supposed to intimate man's own being good to him, it "reduces what was once conceived as the effluence of divine power to a slave of pharisaism" and contradicts the very meaning of goodness. To take the 'good' conscience as a privation of the 'bad', as the experienced absence of a bad conscience, is no better. Here the call is not experienced at all but, on the contrary, by assuring himself that he has done no wrong, man "steps out of the very possibility of being addressed by the call."[7] The 'good conscience' is not a phenomenon of conscience at all. This also disposes of the distinction between the 'censuring' conscience—which, as referring backwards, is also open to the above criticism—and the forward-referring 'warning' conscience, which again is oriented to the willed act, that is, something *vorhanden*, and as such is possible only on the presupposition that the call is first directed to Dasein's potentiality of being itself.

In the second place, it might be objected that the alleged rootedness of the voice, as a call to being-guilty, in the being of Dasein is never testified in experience. This, Heidegger says, must be admitted, from which it by no means follows that the full nature of this call of conscience is revealed in vulgar experience. On the contrary, man in his forfeited, everyday mode of being, understands himself ontically in terms of what preoccupies him, and, ontologically, takes Being in the sense of being *vorhanden*, and so doubly veils the phenomenon from himself. For him conscience appears as a mental 'process' and as a judge and mentor, something to be reckoned with practically. Kant's view of conscience as a kind of court of justice, following from his conception of the moral law, and his value theory, presupposing the view of Dasein as an object of practical concern (an entity that has to realize a value or a norm) are both illustrations of such veiling of the phenomenon of conscience. A third objection is that the existenzial interpretation overlooks the fact that conscience is experienced only in connection with some particular act done or willed. This common sense interpretation takes its stand on 'facts' but, however right within certain limits, it unduly narrows the scope of the call by restricting it to particular acts. It treats Dasein as if it were "a kind of 'establishment' of which the accounts only need being balanced properly to enable the self to stand as an unconcerned spectator 'by the side of' the succession of experiences." Finally, it might be objected that conscience has an essentially critical function only, which is again true in the sense that its voice issues no positive demands. But the popular view takes the missing positiveness, and therefore denies it, in the sense of giving concrete and utilizable suggestions for action. Conscience cannot give such 'practical' guidance for the simple reason that basically it is a summons calling Dasein to its inmost potentiality of existenz, which is very different from running a business, as the vulgar consciousness tends to understand it. "The call reveals nothing which could be positive or negative *to be concerned about*, because ontologically it bears upon a mode of being of an entirely different kind, that is, *existenz*." Taken in this existenzial sense of a call to one's inmost possibility of existenz, conscience has the most positive function conceivable. The above ontological criticism of the vulgar interpretation of conscience, showing how existenzially it falls short of grasping the original phenomenon, offers no judgment on the existenziell moral quality of Dasein's conduct, though it is true that a deeper existenzial interpretation always opens out possibilities of a deeper existenziell understanding.

[59]

The existenzial interpretation of conscience is aimed at a discovery of testimony existing within man himself of his inmost potentiality of authentic existenz. This testimony, the voice of conscience, manifests itself phenomenally, as a mode of his being, in the way the call is taken up and grasped authentically by him, that is, as the will to have conscience. The existenzial structure of the latter is explained by Heidegger as follows. The will to have conscience is the way Dasein understands itself in its authentic potentiality and is therefore a mode of its overtness, with its three marks of understanding, mood, and speech. Dasein's comprehension of the call of conscience is accompanied by the attunement of anxiety, which is "a phenomenal proof of the fact that in understanding the call Dasein is brought before the awesomeness of its own self." Further, hearing and understanding the silent call, which is Dasein's primordial speech, it responds, not by a vocal utterance, but by speech in the mode of silence. "Conscience calls only silently, that is to say, the call comes out of the silence of this awesomeness and recalls the Dasein, summoned by it to become still, in the stillness of its own self." To the 'one', hearing and understanding nothing but chatter, conscience naturally appears dumb and therefore obviously nonexistent.

The preeminent and authentic overtness of Dasein, attested by its will to have conscience, is constituted by the disposition of anxiety (dread), by understanding (through projecting itself in its inmost being-guilty) and by speech in the mode of silence. This wordless, anxious self-projection is called by Heidegger "resoluteness (*Entschlossenheit*)." Dasein's overtness (*Erschlossenheit*) has been described earlier as the original, primary Truth and the way Dasein is 'in truth' as the truth of existenz. Resoluteness, as defined above, is the *authentic* Truth of Dasein. It has been shown earlier that the overtness of the 'there' of Dasein brings about the disclosure of being-in-the-world (including world, being-in, and self). The disclosure of world makes possible the discovery of essents within the world. This is based on a comprehension of the 'totality of destination', itself deriving from an understanding of 'significance', which in turn depends upon the ultimate for-whose-sake or end, that is, the self-projection of Dasein upon its possibilities. Thrown Dasein projects itself, first and foremost, in its factual existence, into the forfeiture to the 'one' and the world of everyday preoccupation. The call of conscience, if understood through resoluteness in the sense defined above, recalls man to an authentic openness, which in turn transforms his awareness of the 'world' and of others. "The 'world' at hand does not become another in 'content', the circle of the others is not changed, and yet now the [Dasein's] comprehending and preoccupied being-toward handy essents and its solicitous being-with the others is determined from [the depths of] its innermost potentiality of being itself." Nor does this authentic self-hood mean that Dasein, becoming an unattached 'I', is cut off from his world; authentic openness, on the contrary, consists of being-in-the-world authentically. Resoluteness frees man for his world and enables him to let other fellow-men 'be' themselves in their inmost potentiality of being and to cause disclosure of this potentiality through its anticipative, liberating solicitude.

Resoluteness manifests itself only in comprehending, self-projecting resolution in face of factual possibilities. In itself it possesses no particular content and has nothing to do with the actual grabbing of possibilities that may offer themselves. Resolution in the existenzial sense is the "revealing projection and determining of the particular factual possibility." As authentic overtness, resoluteness means letting oneself be summoned out of the state of being lost in the 'they', and thus discovering, for the first time, the factual possibility as one's own possibility.[8] The existenzial definiteness of resoluteness (which existenzielly might appear vague and indefinite, being resoluteness about nothing in particular) is further elucidated by Heidegger with reference to the existenzial phenomenon of 'situation'. As shown earlier, Dasein, being its 'there', has its own spatiality and just as this spatiality is grounded in its general overtness, so also resoluteness, as a mode of overtness, has its situation. Situation is the 'there' of an existing man as disclosed by his resoluteness. It is not an objectively existing framework or setting in which he happens to exist or into which he puts himself, a simply given conglomeration of circumstance and chance. On the contrary, situation has its being only through and in resoluteness, which alone discloses to the resolutely existing self the specific factual destination character of circumstances, that, and how, they have relevance and 'matter' to it. Everyman, on the other hand, aware only of "the general position," is intrinsically blind to situation in the existenzial sense. Through resoluteness man comes to have existenz in his situation and this means that the call of conscience, summoning him to his ability to be, holds up no empty ideal of existenz before him but rather calls him forward in his situation and is thus something positive and definite. The existenzial interpretation of the understanding of the call as resoluteness shows that conscience, arising from the very foundations of man, is that mode of being in which he himself enables his factual existenz, thus testifying to his innermost potentiality of being.

Throughout this discussion, terms like 'action' and 'practice' have been avoided in order to eliminate the suggestion that there is anything specifically practical about resoluteness as against the theoretical attitude. But care, of which resoluteness is the authentic manifestation, encompasses the being of Dasein so basically and wholly that it must be taken as already presupposed as a whole in (that is, as prior to) the distinction between the theoretical and practical attitudes and cannot therefore be itself built up in terms of them.[9]

With the concept of resoluteness as explained above, we have reached a point where a definite ontological sense can be attached to Dasein's potentiality of being whole.[10] Yet, its ability to be whole, the existenzially deduced authentic being toward death as the authentic potentiality of being whole, remains a purely existenzial project, lacking in attestation from within Dasein. Only when the latter is found and Dasein has "become accessible phenomenally in its authenticity and wholeness can the problem regarding the meaning of the being of *this* being, to whose existence alone there belongs an understanding of Being, be regarded as placed on a sound basis."

[60]

Notes

1. In a footnote here Heidegger credits Kierkegaard with having dealt with the problem of existenz on the phenomenal level. As he says, "In the 19th century S. Kierkegaard explicitly grasped the problem of existenz as an existenziell one and thought it through penetratingly. The existenzial problem is so foreign to him, however, that in the ontological respect he is completely under the sway of Hegel and the classical philosophy as seen through him. Therefore more is to be learnt philosophically from his 'edifying' writings than from the theoretical—with the exception of the treatise concerning the concept of dread." (See also *Was heisst Denken?*, p. 129; E.T., p. 213). Unlike Jaspers, who tends to bracket Kierkegaard with Nietzsche as a forerunner of modern existentialistic thinking, Heidegger evaluates him more discriminatingly. In *Nietzsche II* (p. 472), Heidegger speaks of "Kierkegaard, who is neither a theologian nor a metaphysician and yet is of greater importance than both." In *Holzwege* (p. 230), Kierkegaard is described as "no thinker but a religious writer, not just one among others but unique in his appropriateness to the destiny of his age."

In his *Kierkegaard and Heidegger*, Michael Wyschogrod has made a comparative study of these two as concerned with the "ontology of existence."

Wyschogrod sees that Heidegger's primary concern, as opposed to that of Kierkegaard, is ontological. However, in comparing the implicit ontological basis of Kierkegaard's existenziell thinking with the explicitly ontological orientation of Heidegger's existenzial inquiry, he overlooks the fact that the latter has no finished, ready-made concept of Being at all, but is rather in the quest of one. And Heidegger's quest is not religious but philosophical, a quest inspired and guided not by faith but by a questioning that, by the intensity of its concentration, creatively brings Being itself 'to speech'.

Because of a failure to grasp the essentially circular or spiraling character of Heidegger's thinking, Wyschogrod finds the "reversal" in Heidegger's later thought as constituting a break with the standpoint of *Sein und Zeit*, what he calls a "basic dichotomy in the ontology of the early and later periods." In the early work, Being is not thematically discussed at all and even the analysis of the being of Dasein is explicitly stated by Heidegger to be incomplete and provisional, an analysis which must be gone over again after a clarified concept of Being is attained.

2. Marjorie Grene has remarked in connection with Heidegger's conception of being toward death: "This is, so far as I know, the first time since Plato that death has been given central philosophic significance in the interpretation of life. In the case of Lucretius, for example, the fear of death, and in that of Hobbes, the fear of violent death, are hinges, so to speak, on which their philosophic systems are hung; but they are not, like Heidegger's 'resolve to death', internal to the analysis of life itself " (*Martin Heidegger*, p. 44).

3. In a footnote Heidegger points out that the distinction between a Whole and a Sum, *holon* and *pan*, *totum* and *compositum* has been well known since the time of Plato and Aristotle, though the categorial differences implied in the distinction are by no means explicitly recognized and conceptualized. The beginnings of an analysis of these structures, he says, may be found in Husserl's *Logische Untersuchungen*, II, 3.

4. The conception of death as determinative of the structure of life, that is, of human existence, Heidegger points out in a note, is age old. Not only has Christian theology recognized this, but so also have recent philosophers like Dilthey. See also G. Simmel, *Lebensanschauung* and K. Jaspers, *Psychologie der Weltanschauungen*, p. 229f. and pp. 259-270.

5. As Wyschogrod points out (*Kierkegaard and Heidegger*, pp. 61-62): "Heidegger's work on Kant, where he develops the analysis of Dasein from the point of view of its finitude, the negativity inherent in Dasein is made the source of the possibility of the three questions that are the basic interest of reason: What can I know? What shall I do? What can I hope? Each of these questions, Heidegger claims, is made possible by the fact that there is something which Dasein is not, which constitutes its finitude."

6. In what manner and sense the philosophical concept of guilt can function as a guideline for the theological explication of sin, which is revealed only in faith, is explained by Heidegger in *Phänomenologie und Theologie*, p. 30.

7. Max Scheler says, "When we say, 'the conscience is aroused', this simply means that it offers resistance against the behavior concerned; it can

never be construed as judging it to be good. For this reason, even the 'bad conscience' is as decidedly positive a phenomenon as the 'good conscience', which is really only the experienced absence and the experienced lack of the 'bad conscience' regarding a particular action of which the morality is in question." (*Der Formalismus in der Ethik und die Materiale Wertethik*, 3d ed., p. 334.)

8. Cf. *Einführung in die Metaphysik* (p. 16; E.T., p. 17), where Heidegger points out that to will is to be resolved and, like the latter, it is rooted in the overtness of Dasein for the illumination or clearing of Being and does not in any way consist of gathering up energy for 'acting'. All relationship to Being is one of letting-be and all willing is grounded in 'letting'. In *Holzwege* (p. 55; E.T., *Poetry, Language, Thought*, p. 67) he remarks, "Resoluteness as thought in *Being and Time* is not the (unvacillating) decided action of a subject but the opening up of Dasein (releasing it) from its prepossession with essents to the overtness of Being." In *Gelassenheit* (p. 61; E.T., p. 81), Heidegger points out, "One must . . . think the word 'resoluteness' as it is thought in *Being and Time*, as the *expressly* undertaken opening up of itself by Dasein for the overt (that is, truth as overtness itself)."

As shown in later chapters of this work, the metaphysical thought of the modern period is dominated by the conception of Being, man and thought (that is, the relationship between the first two) as essentially of the nature of Will. The attempt to 'overcome' the metaphysical conception of Being and to get at its 'sense' or truth necessarily involves, therefore, not only a metaphysical interpretation of Will (so long treated as only a 'psychological' faculty) but, beyond that, its interpretation in terms of the truth of Being (that is, the *Ereignis*. See the last chapter of this work), so that the essence or true nature of Will is seen to lie in a 'letting' (*Lassen*) in relation to that Truth. In his later writings, Heidegger returns again and again to this problem. Cf. *Nietzsche I*, pp. 44-79; the Reclam edition of *Der Ursprung des Kunstwerkes*, *Zusatz*, pp. 95-97 (E.T., *Poetry, Language, Thought*, pp. 82-84); also *Holzwege*, p. 55 (E.T., *Poetry, Language, Thought*, p. 67), and *Gelassenheit*, passim.

9. Since his inquiry is aimed at the fundamental ontology of Dasein, Heidegger contents himself with the existenzial analysis of conscience. To give an account of the various existenziell possibilities, their principal features and interrelations and to interpret them in respect of their existenzial structure is the task, he says, of a thematic existenzial anthropology. Karl Jaspers' *Psychologie der Weltanschauungen* may be considered the first attempt in this direction.

10. Heidegger's account of authenticity, according to Marjorie Glicksman [Grene] (*Martin Heidegger*, pp. 46-47) provides "the unique contribution of existentialism to ethical theory. . . . The stress on authenticity puts the traditional concept of responsibility in a new light." She goes on to explain how the concept of authenticity is rooted in the existential interpretation of freedom as both a venture and a fact: "We live from birth to death under the compulsion of brute fact; yet out of the mere givenness of situation it is we ourselves who shape ourselves and our world. And in this shaping we succeed or fail. To succeed is not to escape compulsion but to transcend

it—to give it significance and meaning by our own projection of the ab-surdly given past into a directed future. But such shaping of contingency, such imposing of meaning on the meaningless, is possible only through the very recognition of meaninglessness—of the nothingness that underlies our lives. Thus authenticity is a kind of honesty or a kind of courage . . ."

It is strange that having seen so much—and having summed up Heidegger's argument with such clarity—Grene completely fails to grasp the 'ontological' import of the analytic of Dasein, the fact that all understand-ing implies a project of Being. She does not boggle at the 'nothingness' that underlies our lives but feels compelled to hold "that the analysis of human being cannot properly be called 'ontology' " (p. 85) and to ask, "What, in all honesty, can a writer mean when he talks about an a priori account of human being?" (p. 83). The answer, of course, is that the existenzials, in the unity of their complex structure, constitute the conditions of the possibility of the *being* of man, of his factual characteristics and his experience, very much as the Kantian categories are the a priori conditions of the possibility of his knowledge of *vorhanden* entities. Grene's entire treatment of the ontological aspect of Heidegger's thought betrays a lack of sympathy which is perhaps due to the fact that, taking its point of departure from a different philosophi-cal background, it employs language which has become unintelligible in the current philosophical climate in Anglo-Saxon philosophy. Almost every point of criticism she brings forward may be traced to lack of sympathetic understanding and to a failure of communication.

6
Man and Temporality

The existential project of an authentic potentiality of being in Dasein has brought to light the phenomenon of being toward death as the 'running ahead' of Dasein on the one hand and that of its authentic ability to be resolute on the other. Is it possible to bring these two together, not merely externally but in such a manner that they show themselves to be intrinsically related, and to ensure that the attempt to do so does not merely remain an ontological project without any phenomenal basis? The only possible way, from the point of view of method, is to start from the existenzielly attested phenomenon of resoluteness and then to find out whether there is not something within the nature of resoluteness itself which exhibits anticipativeness as its inmost authentic possibility and whether it does not attain to its true nature and its authenticity and certainty only when it projects itself into the extremest possibility, that is, only in the anticipative 'running forward' in relation to death. Both the existenzial phenomena of anticipation and resoluteness will have to be considered in view of the existenziell possibilities foreshadowed in them and then "thought through to the end." Only through such existenzial interpretation can the concept of anticipative resoluteness be worked out into an existenzielly possible authentic potentiality of being whole without laying itself open to the charge of being an arbitrary construction.

In the next place, in order to safeguard the further development of the existenzial interpretation of Dasein, culminating in the final elucidation of the ontological meaning of care, more explicit clarification of the methodological aspects of the analytic of Dasein than was hitherto possible has to be given. Thirdly, a more detailed existenzial analysis of the phenomenon of self-hood—incapable, as we have seen, of being defined in terms of substance or subject—is called for, so that its connection with care may become clear. Having sufficiently elucidated the phenomenon of care in all its aspects, Heidegger takes up, fourthly, the inquiry into its ontological sense, that is, temporality as phenomenally manifested in Dasein's anticipative resoluteness. Further, since the vulgar notion of time does not necessarily correspond with the ontological conception of temporality, an account must be given of the way it necessarily arises from the latter. Finally, in view of the temporal character of care as the being of Dasein, the entire analysis of Dasein must be recapitulated in terms of time and the principal elements of the ontological structure of Dasein must be reinterpreted from the point of view of their temporal character. Each of these topics is now discussed, in this order, with a view to preparing the ground for the detailed discussion of time and historicity that is to follow.

[61]

Resoluteness, Selfhood, and the Temporal Sense of Care

The first point needing elucidation is how to conceive the connection between the existenzielly demonstrated phenomenon of resoluteness as the will to have conscience and the existenzial project of an authentic potentiality of being whole. As has been explained, to be resolute means to project oneself on one's own innermost being-guilty, not once in a while, but as long as one exists. This 'guilt', lying in the very core of Dasein's being, can be said to be appropriated, fully and authentically, only when Dasein, revealed to itself in full transparency by resoluteness, comprehends itself as being permanently guilty. Such transparency is possible only when Dasein in its resoluteness is revealed, in respect of its potentiality of being, "up to its very end," which means existenzially, revealed in its being *toward* the end. "Resoluteness really becomes what it can be when it is *an understanding being in relation to the end*, that is, as anticipating death." Resoluteness is thus not merely connected with anticipation as something external to it but "contains within itself authentic being-toward-death as the possible existenziell modality of its own authenticity." Resoluteness means responding to the call to take one's inmost guilt upon oneself and really to appropriate it is an existenziell possibility of being authentically or inauthentically guilty. This must, therefore, be conceived as the ability to be guilty factually. Resoluteness projects itself into, that is, understands itself in terms of, this potentiality of being, which is a primordial possibility of Dasein. But man's being in relation to his supreme possibility is his being toward death which, as a possibility, is revealed to him in his 'running ahead'. For this reason, only as anticipative can resoluteness become a basic mode of being in relation to the innermost potentiality of being of Dasein. Resolute Dasein incorporates authentically in its existenz the realization, rendered possible by care as the being of Dasein, that it is the null ground of its own nullity, that is, death. "Anticipation discloses first (Dasein's) being-guilty on the basis of the *whole* being of Dasein. Death and guilt are implicit, equally originally, in care. Only anticipative resoluteness comprehends the ability to be guilty *authentically* and *wholly*, that is to say, from its very *origins*." Only thus also does the authentic existenz of Dasein become unrelative and unsurpassable.[1]

Resoluteness, as a mode of overtness, is the original truth of existenz. The holding-to-be-true of what resoluteness discloses, that is, the situation in the existenzial sense, its being certain in the sense of taking one's stand in this, is characterized not by sticking obstinately to the situation but by a freedom and openness for the factual possibility of the moment. Certainty of resolution means keeping oneself free for its possible and, in view of facts, necessary, retraction. But since untruth is equally inherent in man's mode of being, the anticipative resoluteness gives him also a certainty of the possible closure and irresoluteness through a lapse into the 'they', of the indefiniteness of his potentiality of being, of the indeterminateness that pervades all existenz but which is revealed in authentic disclosure. This is indeterminateness as to his own potentiality of being—though certain as regards his particular decisions—which first manifests itself wholly in being toward death, certain and yet indeterminate as to the particular moment when it will come, and which is originally revealed in the disposition of anxiety.

The above analysis has made it clear that the authentic being toward death, as the inmost, unsurpassable, certain and yet indeterminate possibility is the mode in which resoluteness manifests itself, attaining its full nature only as anticipative resolution. On the other hand, it has also led to a fuller existenzial understanding of anticipation itself, so long only an ontological project, but exhibited now to be "no concocted possibility thrust upon Dasein, but the *mode* of an existenziell potentiality of being attested in Dasein." Anticipation does not exist in the form of a free-floating attitude but "must be conceived as a possibility, implicit in the existenzielly attested resoluteness and thus attested along with it, of its own authenticity." The problem of Dasein's potentiality of being whole is thus not merely a theoretical or methodological problem of the analytic of Dasein but a factual and existenziell question, with its origin in an ontic possibility of Dasein, and it finds its solution in the concept of resoluteness as Dasein's authentic potentiality of being. Further, anticipative resoluteness is not an expedient devised for "vanquishing" death but a realization, responsive to the call of conscience, that first enables death to establish its full power over Dasein's existenz, tearing off all frivolous masks. It does not mean seclusion and flight from the world but rather a resolute readiness, free from illusions, for action; nor does it spring from any 'idealistic' demand, soaring beyond existenz and its possibilities but arises rather from a sober comprehension of the basic factual possibilities of Dasein. "Together with the sober anxiety, which brings (Dasein) before its isolated ability to be, there goes the joy of being well prepared for this possibility."

But, it may be asked, does this ontological interpretation of existenz not presuppose a particular ontic conception of authentic existenz, a particular ideal of Dasein? This, Heidegger answers, is indeed so, and is a fact which must neither be denied nor half-heartedly accepted but recognized to be necessarily implied in the very object of the inquiry. Philosophy does not deny its 'presuppositions', but neither should it merely accept them; the presuppositions must be explicitly grasped so that, in harmony with them, that of which they are presuppositions may be developed in a more compelling and effective manner.

[62]

Anticipative resoluteness has brought Dasein phenomenally into view in respect to its possible authenticity and wholeness and thus the 'hermeneutic situation', formerly inadequate, has been brought into contact with the desired foundations. Dasein in its authentic potentiality of being has been brought within the prepossession or intention, the guiding preview of the idea of existenz has been made determinate and the preconception of the existenziality of Dasein has gained in articulation. It has also been demonstrated how this essent, which we ourselves are, is ontologically the farthest, because forfeited, everyday Dasein covers up ontically its own authentic being by interpreting itself in terms of the 'world' of its preoccupation. An ontological interpretation of the being of Dasein must obviously be *extorted* in deliberate opposition to the everyday tendency. "Dasein's very mode of being requires that an ontological interpretation aiming at depth must take by force the being of this essent in opposition to its own tendency to hide and veil itself. Hence, from the point of view of the claims, and of the self-sufficient and complacent obviousness, of everyday interpretation, existenzial analysis has always the character of doing *violence*." Though in the ontology of Dasein this is particularly prominent, all interpretation, being of the nature of a project, has this character of being violent.

What, it may be asked, is it that guides ontological interpretation as the project that attempts to grasp the being of an essent with a view to conceptualizing its structure? What are the fingerposts that can direct the project towards Being? Heidegger's answer is that such guidance is to be found within Dasein's mode of being itself, that is, in the self-interpreting character of Dasein, which always already has some comprehension, explicit or not, adequate or otherwise, of existenz.

This ontic understanding necessarily implies some understanding of Being, however vague, nontheoretical and 'preontological' it may be. But then, it may be asked further, from where is the criterion of 'authentic' existenz derived and is there any existenziell and ontic basis for this existenzial analysis and ontological interpretation? Heidegger admits that existenzial interpretation can never arrogate to itself the right to legislate over the existenziell possibilities and necessities but, on the contrary, must justify itself in the light of those existenziell possibilities which provide the ontic foundation for its ontological project. Since Dasein's being is intrinsically potentiality of being and Dasein can exist as free for it, or unfreely against it, there is no other way for ontological interpretation except to base itself on ontic possibilities (modes of the ability to be) and to project them on (understand them in the light of) *their* ontological possibility. Everyday, forfeited Dasein interprets itself in terms of the 'world', of its preoccupation. Hence, the only adequate procedure is to arrive at existenziell and ontic possibilities in direct opposition to that and base the existenzial analysis on them. The 'violence' of the interpretative project is thus turned into a true 'emancipation' of the undisguised phenomenal existence of Dasein. The existenzielly authentic potentiality of being which manifests itself in man's attitude towards death, arising out of the depths of his existenz, cannot by any means be regarded as an arbitrary basis for the existenzial interpretation.

But the existenzial interpretation itself, including the account of inauthentic, everyday forfeiture—is it not carried out, one may ask, under the guidance of a clue deriving from a presupposed concept of existenz? "Is not everything here illumined, even though dimly, by the light of the 'presupposed' idea of existenz?" Heidegger admits that such an idea of existenz is here taken as the starting point, but as already made clear before, this is supplied by the understanding of himself as being-in-the-world inherent in man himself, who is I myself in my ability to be. "This assumed idea of existenz," Heidegger says, "is the existenzielly informal indication of the formal structure of all understanding of Dasein in general." Beginning with this idea of existenz, the analysis proceeds to the structure of care and the ontological distinction between existenz and reality, leading up to the thesis that the substance of men is existenz. But implicit in this idea of existenz, it may be objected further, there is an awareness of Being, which is thus presupposed, even if not explicitly. But since this was exactly the goal of the analytic of Dasein, is it not apparent that the entire fundamental ontological procedure moves in a circle, seeking to understand Being through an analysis of Dasein's existenz and grounding this analysis itself in the understanding of Being inherent in Dasein? Though it has been explained already how the 'circle' belongs to the nature of understanding itself, Heidegger again takes up for discussion the circle argument, pointing out that 'presupposing' the idea of existenz and Being does not mean assuming a proposition in order then to deduce from it, in accordance with the formal rules of inference, other propositions about the being of Dasein. The 'presupposition' here is of the nature of a project of understanding, such that its interpretative explication "itself lets what is to be interpreted (that is, the Dasein) become articulate, so that it may decide for itself whether, as this essent, it yields the ontological structure which it was disclosed, in the sense of a formal indication, as having." Existenzial analysis cannot avoid this circularity in proof—and there is nothing here to avoid—for it does not, by its very nature, prove anything in the manner of deductive logic. As care, Dasein, always ahead of itself, is constantly projecting itself existenzielly on determinate possibilities and so, preontologically, on existenz and Being. Like all inquiry, philosophical inquiry is itself a mode of being of Dasein and is the supreme expression of such projection, aiming at giving form and articulation to the understanding of Being inherent in existenz. The 'circle objection' is itself the manifestation of a resistance on the part of the 'good sense' of Dasein forfeited to the 'one'. It is a resistance against the recognition that over and above the 'real' beings with which it is at home, there is also Being to be understood and in a way always is understood, for it is only in the light of the comprehension of Being that beings can be 'really' experienced. The talk of the circle of understanding is the expression of a failure to realize that understanding itself is a mode of being of Dasein and that this being is constituted by care. To deny the circle or to try to overcome it is to perpetuate this failure. Our efforts, therefore, should be directed rather at "leaping radically and wholly into this circle so that a full view of the circular being of Dasein may be assured at the very start of the analysis of Dasein."[2]

[63]

After this methodological digression, Heidegger proceeds to an elucidation of the relation between care and selfhood. We have seen that the phenomenon of care is a whole possessing a complex structure, with existenziality, facticity, and forfeiture as its elements. Dasein's character of being-ahead-of-itself as being toward the end and the anticipative resoluteness rendered possible by it, along with the phenomena of death, conscience and guilt have been shown to be anchored in care. What gives unity to the whole of this complex structure unified in Dasein's existence? Obviously, such unity can come only from Dasein itself being, as a self, this wholeness. The 'I', which has always been considered in traditional ontology as the supporting ground (substance or subject) seems to 'hold together' the wholeness of this structural totality. The previous discussion of the self has shown that it is an intrinsic determination of Dasein. Since, however, Dasein's 'essence' lies in existenz, the 'I' and the self must be existenzially conceived. The categories of objective reality (*Vorhandenheit*, substance) cannot be applied to man, whose being has been determined as care. The phenomenon of selfhood is included in the concept of care, though the existenzial relationship between the two still remains a problem to be tackled.

The explanation of the self as an existenzial may be approached by way of the interpretation which everyday Dasein gives to the self and which expresses itself in the way it says 'I', meaning thereby just itself and nothing more, no attribute or predicate but just the absolute subject, which always remains the same. The attributes of simplicity, substantiality, and personality which Kant takes as basic in his discussion of "The Paralogisms of the Pure Reason" spring from a true prephenomenological perception, though it is doubtful, Heidegger says, if this ontic perception can be adequately interpreted ontologically by means of these 'categories'. Kant, of course, demonstrates the untenability of applying them to the soul substance but this merely amounts to a rejection of the ontic theses describing the 'I' in terms of these categories and is in no way helpful in arriving at an ontological explanation of self-hood. "Although Kant seeks to hold fast more firmly than his predecessors to the phenomenal content of 'I' propositions, yet he lapses back into the *same* inadequate ontology of the substantial, the ontic foundations of which he has theoretically denied to the 'I'." In justification of this criticism and also to bring out the ontological significance of 'I' propositions, Heidegger discusses in some detail the Kantian analysis of the 'I think'.[3]

According to Kant, the 'I' is a mere consciousness accompanying all concepts, a transcendental subject of thoughts, a mere form of representations in general, "the form of apperception, which belongs to and precedes every experience." The phenomenal content of the 'I' lies for Kant in 'I think', that is, in the *res cogitans*. When he speaks of the 'I' as a 'logical subject', this means the subject of the logical activity of connecting, so that all connecting is 'I think' in the sense of 'I connect'. In all connecting and relating, the 'I' is thus always the basis, the *hypokeimenon*, for which reason the subject is consciousness in itself, not a representation but the 'form' of that, that is, the formal condition of representation as such. What Kant's analysis positively achieves is "first, that he sees the impossibility of ontically tracing back the 'I' to a substance and, second, that he holds fast to the 'I' as 'I think'." Nevertheless, he conceives this 'I' again as subject, that is, in an ontologically inadequate sense, "for the ontological concept of substance does *not* characterize the self-hood of the 'I' qua self but the sameness and permanence of what is all the time (taken as something) *vorhanden*." To determine the 'I' ontologically as subject is to take it as *vorhanden*, that is, to take the being of the 'I' in the sense of the reality of the *res cogitans*.[4] Why, Heidegger asks, does Kant fail to follow up ontologically the right phenomenal start he makes with the 'I think' and is forced to fall back on subject and the substantial? The 'I' is not only 'I think' but 'I think something'. Kant himself repeatedly emphasizes that the 'I' is relative to its representations and is nothing without them, yet for him these representations are something empirical, which the 'I' 'accompanies' and 'belongs to'. He never worries about the mode of being of this 'accompanying' and 'belonging to', at bottom taking the 'I' as being invariably simply given together with its representations. Had Kant realized the necessity of this 'something' in the 'I think something' and tried to determine it ontologically, he would have seen that the 'something', as intramundane, presupposes *world*. But Kant did not see the phenomenon of world and hence failed to perceive that 'I' propositions refer always to an essent that, as 'I', is-in-the-world.[5]

In saying 'I', man gives expression to himself as being-in-the-world, though in his everyday forfeited state this means only the essent that he himself is and not *how* he is. Fleeing from itself into the 'one' and saying 'I', Dasein voices a self that it is authentically not. In its self-concerned obliviousness of its own self, the self manifests itself as ever the same single entity but as indeterminate and empty. And, as being concerned with this empty self, everyday Dasein *is* that. The ontological interpretation of the 'I', proceeding in a direction contrary to that of everyday understanding, must take it as being-in-the-world and this involves the whole structure of "being-already-ahead-of with-essents-in-the-world," that is, care. "In the 'I', it is care that finds utterance, in the first instance and mostly, in the 'flighty' I-saying of preoccupied concern. The 'oneself' says, oftenest and most loudly, 'I-I' because he is at bottom *not authentically* himself and evades this authentic potentiality of being." The self is not the permanently *vorhanden* ground of care but must be existenzially understood in terms of the authentic ability to be a self, that is, of the authenticity of the being of Dasein as care. From this comes the constancy or permanence of self, misinterpreted as the persistence of a subject, as also constancy in the sense of having firmly taken one's stand. "The permanence of the self in the double sense of constancy and steadfastness of one's stand is the *authentic* possibility as against the unautonomous state of irresolute forfeiture. Steadiness and constancy of self (*selbst-ständigkeit*) means existenzially nothing else than anticipative resoluteness. Its ontological structure discloses the existenziality of the selfhood of the self." Dasein attains its authentic self in the radical isolation of wordless, anxious resoluteness, not saying 'I-I' but *being* in silence the thrown being that it authentically can be. Self in this sense is the original phenomenal basis for all questions regarding the being of the 'I'. Care thus does not need to be founded on self; existenziality as a constituent of care can explain the ontological nature of the autonomy ('self standingness') of Dasein of which, corresponding to the structure of care, the lack of independence is an aspect. "The comprehensive structure of care includes in itself the phenomenon of self-hood."[6]

[64]

The above discussion was partly aimed at preparing the ground for the explication of the sense of care as the being of Dasein, which is the task now, needing, Heidegger says, an unwandering eye on the existenzial nature of the inquiry. By sense is meant, as explained earlier, the background, itself not thematic, on which something becomes comprehensible. The in-view-of-what of the primary project is that through which something can be conceived in its possibility. To explicate the in-view-of-what of a project means to reveal that which makes possible what is projected and requires that the project, the implicit basis of interpretation itself, be focally looked into, so that what is projected becomes evident and comprehensible in respect of its in-view-of-what. To bring out the sense of care hence means to lay bare the project underlying and guiding the original existenzial interpretation of Dasein, so that the in-view-of-what of that which is projected becomes visible. What is projected here is the being of Dasein, revealed as to its authentic potentiality of being whole and its in-view-of-what; the being as thus revealed is what itself renders possible the constitution of this being as care. To ask for the sense of care is to ask what makes possible the wholeness and the articulated unity of the systematic structural totality of care. Dasein is, authentically or inauthentically, disclosed to itself, as to its being, as care. What is it that renders this being of Dasein as care, and so its factual existenz itself, possible?

What is projected in the original existenzial project has been disclosed as anticipative resoluteness, which is rendered formally possible, in respect of the unity of its articulated structural totality, by being-toward the inmost and supreme possibility of Dasein's being. This is itself possible only because Dasein can at all come up towards or approach (*Zukommen*) itself in its inmost possibility and endure this as possibility. Such letting oneself come towards oneself is the primary phenomenon of 'the coming', the future (*Zukunft*). It is only in this sense of what is coming that being toward death is possible as toward something future, which means here not a now which, not yet actual, will be sometime, but the 'coming' (*Kunft*) in which Dasein comes to itself in its inmost potentiality of being. Anticipation is possible only because Dasein as existing is already in its being oriented toward the future. In the next place, anticipative resoluteness involves taking up into existence one's inherent being-guilty, to *be* the thrown ground of a nullity, which in turn implies becoming what one already was. And this is possible only if man, oriented toward the future, can *be* his 'has been', that is, as appropriating his past into his existenz. "Only insofar as Dasein *is* its 'has been', can it so come to its own self in the future as to come *back* to it. . . . The 'running ahead' into the extremest and inmost possibility is the comprehending coming back to one's inmost 'has been'. Dasein can *be* its 'having been' only insofar as it is prospective." Man, in other words, can take up his past into himself only because he is already inherently 'futuristic' in his mode of being. Thirdly, anticipatory resoluteness discloses the momentary situation so that it can be factually dealt with through an encounter with the essents that may happen to be present in it. Such encounter is possible through a 'presentation', a rendering *present*. "Prospectively returning to itself, resoluteness enters the situation through rendering present." The 'has been', appropriated into existenz through its orientation towards the coming, gives rise, together with the latter, to the present, and the three together constitute in their unity the primary phenomenon of temporality. Only insofar as Dasein is determined by temporality is it possible for him to be anticipatively resolute, that is, capable of authentic wholeness. Temporality manifests itself as the sense of authentic care.[7]

It is through the concept of temporality that the structure of care can be grasped in its primary unity, ahead-of-oneself being based on future, already-being-in on the 'has been' and being-with on 'presentation' (*Gegenwärtigen*, rendering present). Here the 'ahead' and 'already' are not to be understood in the vulgar sense of 'not yet' and 'no longer', which would be to take care as something *vorhanden*, a process *in* time. The 'ahead' refers to a futurity which alone can make it possible for Dasein to exist so as to be concerned about its potentiality of being; projecting itself on the latter, in consequence of its futurity, is an intrinsic feature of Dasein's existenziality. Its primary sense is the future. Similarly, the 'already' refers, not to the bygone, which term Heidegger reserves for application to simply given entities, but to the 'has been' in the sense of *being* one's 'has been'. Thrown Dasein, so long as it exists, can be only as already having-been—this is its facticity. Finally, encountering essents in the world and being with them, Dasein effects their 'presentation', though in primary temporality this means not forfeiture but rather a withdrawal from it into the authentic present, that is, the Moment; forfeiture being based on the inauthentic form of 'presentation'. Temporality is what renders possible the unity of existenz, facticity, and forfeiture and thus constitutes the primary wholeness of the structure of care.

Temporality, Heidegger points out, does not arise from joining together the past, present, and future, which are themselves derivative modes of primary temporality. Temporality 'is' not at all an entity, but is rather sheer process. It 'times' or temporalizes itself (*sich zeitigt*) in its various modes, rendering possible the different modes of Dasein's existenz. Future, past, and present, involving as they do the movements, respectively, of 'toward oneself', 'back to', and 'encounter with' show temporality to be the *ekstatikon* pure and simple, the primordial 'standing outside itself' in and for itself. Future, past, and present in this sense are therefore called by Heidegger the 'ecstasies' of temporality, which 'temporalizes' itself in the unity of these ecstasies, as against the vulgar understanding of time in which, as a result of its existenzial inauthenticity, these ecstasies are leveled into a uniform succession of 'nows'. Temporality in this sense, as against the vulgar conception of time, is the original, basic time. It should be noted further that in primary and authentic temporality the future possesses a preeminence. Further, existing authentically toward his end or death, man does not 'come to' an end but rather exists finitely (*endlich*), with his end taken up in his own existenz. It is not the unavoidable termination of his life but the anticipative appropriation of death in his own existenz that makes him finite. Hence, the authentic future, manifested in anticipative resoluteness, is itself finite. So is temporality itself. The finitude of this root temporality does not mean that after Dasein's decease time does not 'flow on' but rather concerns the way Dasein's 'coming to or arriving at itself' can be ultimately determined as such. The 'coming to himself' which characterizes man's existenz in the unsurpassable possibility of his nullity closes his potentiality of being and is therefore what existing in one's inmost nullity means. The thesis of the fundamental finitude of temporality is simply a consequence of holding fast to the phenomenal character of primary temporality as it manifests itself in what is projected in the primary existenzial project of Dasein itself. The failure to recognize the finite character of primary temporality, or even its a priori rejection, is due to the obtrusiveness of the vulgar conception of time, for which time can only be endless. The problem is to show, not how the common infinite time is transformed into the primary finite time, but, on the contrary, how inauthentic time arises out of the authentic temporality proper, converting finite temporality into infinite, endless time. "Only because original time is finite can the derived form of it temporalize itself as *in-finite*." The upshot of the above analysis may be summarized as follows: Time is fundamentally the 'temporalization' of temporality, which renders possible the constitution of the structure of care; temporality is intrinsically ecstatic; temporality 'times' itself primarily out of the future; primary time is finite.

[65]

The next task is to show how the phenomenon of time as thus understood applies to and renders possible the ontological constitution of Dasein, including its inauthenticity and the temporal meaning of its everydayness; how it explains the nature of autonomous selfhood and of its lack; how it accounts for Dasein's historicity; how primary temporality is the condition of the possibility and necessity of the everyday experience of time, including reckoning with and measuring time; how

intramundane existents are 'in time'. The accomplishment of
this task will not only demonstrate the comprehensive sweep
of Time's might but also deepen our understanding of the
existenzial phenomenon of temporality itself, even though
this repetition of the analytic of Dasein at the temporal level
will still remain incomplete as long as the meaning of Being
itself is not fully elucidated. The analytic, meant to provide
access to the meaning of Being, can itself be completed only on
the basis of a clarified meaning of Being itself.

[66]

In regard to its ontological origins, the being of Dasein
has been revealed in the preparatory analysis to possess a
complex and articulated structure, consisting of a multiplicity
of phenomena as described in previous chapters. In his temporal interpretation of Dasein, Heidegger begins with the
temporal aspect of the overtness of Dasein in general, with its
three modes of understanding, disposition, and speech along
with the forfeiture of everyday Dasein. The temporal aspect of
Dasein's authentic overtness has been described already as
resoluteness, the way Dasein in its existenz can really be its
'there' and, in connection with the discussion of care, the
temporal constitution of the latter has been briefly sketched.
This is now taken up by Heidegger to be worked out in detail.

[67]

The Temporality of Man's Overtness

Understanding in the primary existenzial sense means being
projecting in relation to a potentiality of being, for the sake of
which Dasein exists. In understanding, its own ability to be is
disclosed to Dasein while holding itself in an existential possibility, as an awareness of 'where it stands'.[8] At the basis of such
projective comprehension there lies the future as a coming to
or arriving at oneself out of a possibility of existenz. Future
ontologically renders it possible for an essent (man) to be such
that he can exist in comprehension of his potentiality of being.
Projecting, oriented to the future, grasps a possibility, not
theoretically but by flinging itself into it as possibility. Only
through such understanding Dasein *is* what it can be. The term

'anticipation' (*Vorlaufen*) is used only for the authentic future, in which man reaches forward to himself in his inmost potentiality of being. Ahead-of-it (*sich vorweg*), which Dasein always is, is used for the existenzial future generally and indifferently as an aspect of care. In inauthentic understanding, which projects itself on objects of preoccupation, man comes to himself, not primarily in his inmost potentiality of being but by way of his practical concern with them, tended toward or ad-tending to what he gets, or fails to get, out of the objects of his preoccupation. Inauthentic future is thus of the nature of expectancy or ad-tension (*Gewärtigen*). Only because factually Dasein is expectant of or tended toward his ability to be, in terms of what practically concerns him, can he expect or await something. Hence, expectation (*Erwarten*) is a modality of future, founded on ad-tension, of which the authentic temporalization is anticipation.[9]

Understanding as a mode of existenz involving some kind of projection of one's potentiality of being is thus primarily oriented toward the future, but no achievement of understanding would be possible if it were not determined at the same time by the past and the present. Everyday preoccupation, in which one becomes aware of one's ability to be in terms of the practical concern with the objects of preoccupation, involves, corresponding to the ad-tension of inauthentic future, a being *with* these objects, that is, the 'ecstasy' of the present. Anticipative resoluteness involves a present in which resolution discloses the situation. "In resoluteness the present is not only pulled out of the dispersal into objects of immediate concern but is held firmly in the future and past. The present as thus maintained in authentic temporality and hence itself authentic, we call the Moment," which must be understood in the active sense as an ecstasy.[10] This phenomenon of the Moment cannot be explained in terms of the 'now', which appertains to intratemporality (that is, being within time), the time 'in which' something comes into being, passes away or is simply there. As the pure presence of encounter it is itself the condition of the possibility of anything being in time. As against this authentic present, Heidegger terms its inauthentic manifestation as presentation or making present (*Gegenwärtigen*), to be further explained in connection with the temporal interpretation of forfeiture, in which inauthentic understanding projects the potentiality of being on the basis of what practically concerns it. Inauthentic understanding has also its aspect of the past. In authentic understanding, Dasein *is* its 'has been' and such being one's 'has been' Heidegger calls 'repetition'. Inauthentic self-projection, however, is only possible when Dasein, taking its possibilities from the objects of its preoccupation, becomes oblivious of its inmost thrown potentiality of being. "This forgetting is not nothing nor just a failure to remember, but a special, positive ecstatic mode of the past." It is a disengaging and closing oneself in face of one's own 'has been', such that in it one shuts out from awareness also this disengaging and closing. Oblivion as an inauthentic relationship to one's past thus concerns one's own thrown mode of *being* and is what makes it possible to hold and retain, in a presentation, essents encountered in the world. "Just as expectation is possible only on the basis of ad-tension, similarly remembering is grounded in forgetting and *not the other way round.*" Oblivious of his relationship to his own past and cut off from authentic potentiality of being, man can remember only the superficialities of the objects of his preoccupation.

Attunement or mood, which always accompanies understanding, is also based on temporality. As a finding itself in some state (disposition), it brings Dasein before its thrownness which, being prior, is the ground of such attunement. Man can be brought to face the fact of his thrownness only if in his being he *is* his 'has been'. Just as understanding is primarily based on future, so disposition is grounded primarily in the past, by which its other two ecstasies are conditioned. The basic existenzial character of disposition is a "bringing back to," which is itself not produced by the past but is grounded in it and discloses it. The purpose of the temporal interpretation of disposition is not to deduce moods from temporality and thus resolve them into pure phenomena of temporalization but to show that moods, in what they existenzially signify, are not possible except on the ground of temporality. Heidegger carries out the temporal interpretation of moods mainly in connection with the phenomena of fear and anxiety, with a view to further elucidating their existenzial significance.

Fear, disclosing to the everyday circumspect look an approaching threat, is expectation of coming evil (*malum futurum*) and is not only related to something 'in' the future but is itself a reaching out into the future, the ad-tension which gives it the character of inauthentic temporality. But mere expectation is not necessarily fear, the specific attunement character of which consists in the fact that the ad-tension of fear lets the threat come back to or react on the factually preoccupied ability to be and is thus a fear for the fearing Dasein itself. Fear intrinsically involves, further, self-forgetfulness, "the confused state of being thrown out of gear in face of one's own factual potentiality of being," or as Aristotle characterizes it, a depression or confusion.[11] Flung back by that upon his thrownness, which remains hidden from him, and confused because of his forgetfulness, man clings to possibilities of saving himself which have already been disclosed to his circumspection and jumps from one of these to the other. The self-forgetfulness of fear leads to a bewildered presentation of wavering possibilities, distinguishing it thus from pure expectation. The specific ecstatic unity which renders fear possible is thus based on forgetting which as a mode of the past, modifies the way the other two temporal elements in fear, the present and the future, are temporalized. "The temporality of fear is an ad-tending presentative forgetting." Fear, in other words, is grounded in a forgetting that leads to ad-tension towards and presentation of its object, as well as of the means of escape.

Anxiety, the fundamental disposition, confronts Dasein with its inmost thrownness and discloses the uncanniness of everyday familiar being-in-the-world. In anxiety the 'before what' and the 'for what' coincide, both referring to Dasein, and the threat comes not from essents within the world but rather from the fact that they no longer 'say' anything to us, that the world in which I exist has become unmeaning. The nothingness of the world which fills us with dread does not signify the absence of things simply given in the world; they must, on the contrary, be encountered in order to show themselves in their emptiness and relentless lack of purpose. "The preoccupied presentation finds nothing in terms of which it can understand itself, it clutches at the nothingness of the world; lighting upon the world, understanding is brought through anxiety to the being-in-the-world as such," which is both the 'what for' and the 'before what' of anxiety. Being anxious is neither of the nature of expectation nor of ad-tending in general and yet contains the elements of the future, though not in the inauthentic form of ad-tension. In disclosing to Dasein its own weird nakedness, anxiety brings it back to the pure 'that' of its inmost, isolated thrownness. It is not indeed a bringing back to evading forgetfulness but also not to remembering and to resoluteness. Anxiety rather recalls Dasein to its thrownness as something which it is possible to repeat, to an authentic potentiality of being which, as repetitive, must come back to the thrown 'there'. Such bringing of Dasein to a confrontation with this repeatability is the specific ecstatic mode of the past that is constitutive of the disposition of anxiety. As against the fluctuating presentation of fear, the present of anxiety is held steadily in the return to one's own thrownness, though this must not be confused with the Moment, the temporal condition of resoluteness. Anxiety brings one in the attunement of a *possible* resoluteness, ready for the emergence of the Moment. The characteristic temporality of anxiety is primarily rooted in the past and this gives it the power of driving man back from his 'worldly' possibilities to his naked uncanniness and revealing to him at the same time the possibility of an authentic ability to be. Fear is occasioned by an essent in the environing world of preoccupation, while anxiety arises out of Dasein itself. Something from within the world overwhelms it with fear, whereas anxiety wells up from being-in-the-world as thrown being toward death. Anxiety can mount up only in a resolute Dasein. The resolute person knows no fear, his proper attunement being that of anxiety, which does not hinder and confuse but rather liberates him from vain possibilities and renders him free for authentic ones. Though both anxiety and fear are grounded in the past, yet, from the point of view of their respective temporalizations, the one originates in the future of resoluteness, the other in a shadowy present.

Not merely fear and anxiety but other dispositions also, like disgust, sorrow, melancholy, and despair are existenzially grounded in the temporality of the past and this is no less true of affects and moods like hope, joy, and enthusiasm. Even hope, which appears to be wholly based on the future and is often characterized as the expectation of a *bonum futurum* (good future), must be explained with reference to the ecstatic temporal relationship of Dasein to its thrownness, the load of which, as the assumption of one's 'has been', is experienced as lightened in the elevation of hope. Similarly, the dull, unattuned character of the mood of indifference, "which clings to nothing and urges to nothing and resigns itself to whatever the day brings," demonstrates most trenchantly the power of *forgetting*, the oblivious resignation to one's thrownness, a mood so utterly different from the equanimity that has its origin in resoluteness. Heidegger concludes, therefore, that only a being "who exists as already 'has been' and in a constant mode of the past can be affected" and be brought back into a present that has taken up the past into itself.

Just as understanding is based on the primary ecstasy of the future and mood on that of the past, so the third constitutive element in the structure of care, forfeiture, is existenzially determined by the present. Heidegger illustrates the temporality of forfeiture with reference to the phenomenon of curiosity. The tendency to see, in the wider sense of perception in general, is, as explained earlier, characteristic of curiosity. Such perception enables essents at hand and simply given to be encountered, in respect of how they look, and so be grounded in the present which provides in general the ecstatic horizon within which essents can be present bodily. But for curiosity, essents simply given are presented not so that, in 'tarrying' with them, they may be comprehended. Curiosity rather "seeks to see just for the sake of seeing and of having seen." Such presentation, caught up in itself, renders the relationship of curiosity to the future thoroughly inauthentic. Its ad-tension, failing to take the future in its character of possibility, hankers after it as if it were something actual. Its unsustained presentation seeks constantly to slip away from the ad-tension in which it is yet in its unsustained way 'sustained' or held. The present escapes from the ad-tension, producing the 'not abiding or tarrying with' characteristic of curiosity. Further, this escaping is an ecstatic mode of ad-tension which hastens after the presentation and constitutes the existenzial temporal condition of the possibility of scattering or dissipation. This, together with the untarrying in the present, becomes the basis of the abodelessness which is the extreme opposite of the authentic present, the Moment. The way in which this escaping present of forfeiture temporalizes itself exhibits also the various characteristics, mentioned earlier, of tempting, appeasing, estrangement, and entanglement implied in forfeiture. The mode of temporalization of 'escaping' the present is grounded in the finite nature of temporality. Thrown into being toward death, Dasein first and mostly flies from its thrownness into the forlornness of forfeiture, in which the authentic present ever escapes it, until resoluteness pulls it back, if at all, to face its thrownness and thus to authentic existenz in the Moment, as really being toward death.[12]

Since speech (*Rede*) is the articulation of the full overtness of the 'there', as constituted by understanding, mood, and forfeiture, it has no specific dominant temporal ecstasy of its own. However, since speech is mostly concerned with the 'environing world' of preoccupation, presentation has a preferential role in it. The tenses of verbs and other temporal aspects of speech do not owe their origin to the fact that speech 'also' refers to processes in time, nor to the fact that it is itself an activity that occurs in time. Speech, rather, is in itself temporal, being grounded in the ecstatic unity of temporality. Because speech is always speech about what *is*, the analysis of the temporal constitution of speech and the explication of the temporal character of linguistic structures can, however, be taken up only when the problem of the fundamental interconnectedness of Being and Truth has been properly developed. Also the ontological significance of 'is', which a superficial 'theory of judgment' has reduced to a mere copula, can then be adequately dealt with.

Understanding is grounded primarily in the future (manifesting itself through anticipation or its inauthentic counterpart, ad-tension), disposition in the past (repetition or forgetting), and forfeiture in the present (presentation or the Moment), though in each case the other two ecstasies are also present as modified by the dominant ecstasy. It is in the ecstatic unity of the full temporalization that the unity of the whole structure of care, including existenz, facticity, and forfeiture, is ultimately grounded. The overtnesss of the 'there', as shown above, is thus based on temporality but since its overtness concerns at the same time the whole of being-in-the-world, an account of the temporal constitution of the overtness of Dasein must show also how, from the point of view of temporality, being-in-the-world is possible. This is what Heidegger now takes up for discussion.

[68]

The Temporal Structure of Being-in-the-world

From what has been said above it is clear that the ecstatic unity of temporality, with its modes of the future, the past, and the present, is the condition of the possibility that an essent (such as, Dasein) can exist in such a way as to be its 'there', that is, as overt or 'lit up' (*gelichtet*, cleared). The light which constitutes this lit-up character of Dasein is not any ontic simply given force and a source of luminosity occasionally irradiating this essent. What renders Dasein open and luminous, as explained earlier, is care, in which the full overtness of the 'there' is grounded and which alone makes all illuminating and every perception of or receptivity to anything possible. The light that makes Dasein into an opening or clearing is to be understood not as a *vorhanden* power planted into Dasein but as its total ontological structure. This is comprised in care, itself grounded in ecstatic temporality. This is the ultimate condition of Dasein's overtness. The complex phenomenon of being-in-the-world also is rendered possible, in its unity, by Dasein's rootedness in temporality. Heidegger begins his consideration of the temporality of being-in-the-world with an analysis of the temporal determination of its everyday mode, that is, of the preoccupied practical concern with handy essents. He then shows how the purely contemplative attitude of scientific investigation develops out of the former. This demonstration of temporality as the condition of the possibility of being-in-the-world in general is followed by a discussion of the temporal being of the world and its possibility, and of the problem of its transcendence.

In connection with the account of our preoccupied practical commerce with things in the environing world, we have seen that this preoccupation or concern is not produced by the object of the concern (utensil) nor can the latter be derived from the former. Yet there is a connection between them, such that an understanding of the 'wherewith' of the concern throws light on the preoccupied commerce itself and also the other way round. The object with which we are so concerned is of the character of a utensil. Moreover, this concern is not confined to an isolated utensil but involves a whole utensilar system. The relational character of destination is presupposed in the circumspect encounter with essents at hand. Letting a handy essent be in its destination as existenzially implied in concern or preoccupation and the latter, as being-with, is part of the constitution of care. And since care is in turn grounded in temporality, it follows that the existenzial condition of the possibility of 'letting be in its destination' must lie in a mode of temporality. Handling a utensil implies a prior awareness of its destination and any understanding of the 'what-for' has the structure of ad-tension. It is this tending toward through which, by backward reflection, that which has the destination is revealed as possessing the destination. "The ad-tension to the what-for, together with the retention of that-which-is-for, renders possible in its ecstatic unity the specific manipulative presentation of the utensil." Neither the expectancy (ad-tension) of the what-for nor the retention of what has the destination are here focal and thematic activities. They constitute, as it were, the background of the presentation in which the characteristic preoccupied absorption into the utensilar world occurs, a background of a unity of relations already fashioned by the temporality of destination within which preoccupation has its circumspect functioning. Further, in order that one may lose oneself in the utensilar world and really go to work in it, a specific forgetfulness, the forgetting of oneself, is essential.

The temporality of preoccupation is further elucidated by Heidegger with reference to its different modes of conspicuousness, obtrusiveness, and importunity. Ordinarily, the handy utensil as it is in itself is encountered in the inconspicuousness of something obviously and simply there. What must be the existenzial structure of "letting something be in its destination," so that anything may be drawn into the focus of attention and be encountered as conspicuous? A utensil emerges into conspicuousness when, in the course of its use and to it, it shows itself as unworkable or damaged. In consequence, the ad-tending, retaining presentation is then held up or obstructed, bringing the practical aim (of Dasein) and the what-for (of the utensil) expressly to the surface and in juxtaposition with each other. Emergence into conspicuousness is ontologically possible only in this manner. Hence, the awareness of destination, its letting be, is grounded ultimately in the ecstatic unity of ad-tending retaining presentation. Similarly, the discovery, to the circumspect look, that something is missing or not at hand is possible only on the basis of an ad-tending that 'temporalizes' itself in unity with a presenting. Without such ad-tending presentation, Dasein would never be in a position to find out that something is lacking. The possibility of being surprised is similarly grounded in the fact that in the ad-tending presentation of one handy essent we may be inad-tentive to another that is possibly connected with it as regards its destination. The temporality on which, as explained above, the "letting be in its destination" of concern is based, is still wholly preontological and unthematic as regards our comprehension of destination and handiness. How it enters into focal comprehension is taken up for consideration at a later stage of the inquiry by Heidegger.

The scientific, theoretical attitude to the 'world' arises on the basis of the circumspect preoccupation with essents at hand. Heidegger now proceeds to offer an existenzial account of the rise of the scientific consciousness on this basis. This demonstrates further the temporality of being-in-the-world as basically constitutive of Dasein and of its practical as well as theoretical relationship to the 'world'. Heidegger's concern here is not with the ontic aspect of the development of science but with the ontological genesis of the theoretical attitude, that is, with the existenzial conditions of the possibility of Dasein's existenz in the mode of a scientific investigator. What is attempted here is an existenzial concept of science as against the 'logical' concept which takes science from the point of view of its final result, as a system of true or valid propositions. The following existenzial interpretation of science is limited in its scope. A fully adequate interpretation can be given only when the meaning of Being, as well as its relation to truth, is fully cleared up on the basis of the temporality of existenz. It is limited, secondly, to the immediate aim of exhibiting the transformation of circumspect preóccupation with essents at hand into theoretical investigation of simply given essents so as to bring out fully the temporal constitution of being-in-the-world.[13]

The changeover from the practical, circumspect attitude to the theoretical may at first sight seem to arise from a mere withholding of all active manipulation in the course of preoccupied dealing with things, leading thus to pure contemplation of them. 'Theory', on this account, would be ontologically based on absence of practice, that is, on a privation. But the circumspection that is part of the preoccupied dealing with things, with its own manner of 'tarrying with' them, such as observing, examining, inspecting, and so forth, is by no means the same as theoretical contemplation. " 'Practical' dealing has its *own* ways of tarrying with. And just as practice has its specific sight—'theory'—so also theoretical inquiry is not without its own practice." It is evident from the use of various techniques, preparations, and apparatus in the pursuit of scientific research that the scientific attitude as a mode of being-in-the-world is not merely a purely 'intellectual' activity.

It might be maintained that all practical activity in science is ultimately in the service of pure observation and disclosure of "the things themselves," that is, 'seeing' in the widest sense. As Kant has said, "In whatever manner and by whatever means a mode of knowledge may relate to objects, *intuition* is that through which it is in immediate relation to them, and to which all thought as a means is directed."[14] This idea of *intuitus*, Heidegger remarks, has been the guiding principle of all interpretation of knowledge from the beginnings of Greek ontology till today. As befits the preeminent role thus given to 'seeing', the demonstration of the existenzial genesis of science must take its start from the specific 'seeing' of circumspection by which the 'practical' concern with things is guided. Circumspection operates within the referential framework of the destination of the system of utensils at hand. It is guided by a more or less explicit global view of the totality of the utensilar environing world, involving a primary comprehension of the totality of destinations. The global view itself receives its light from Dasein's potentiality of being, the 'final for whom' of his concern, and it brings the handy essent, in the course of its practical manipulation, closer to Dasein by way of an interpretation of what is seen by means of the global circumspection. Such bringing closer of the object of preoccupation through circumspect interpretation is called by Heidegger "deliberation" (*Überlegung*), with the scheme of 'if-then' peculiar to it. The circumspect deliberation brings the environing world close in the existenzial sense of presentation, of which bringing something to one's mind or representing it is only one mode.

Such circumspect presentation is an aspect of the full ecstatic unity of temporality, being grounded in a retention, in memory, of the utensilar system in the preoccupation with which Dasein ad-tends to a possibility. The presentation that is implied in deliberation brings close what is disclosed through the ad-tentive retention. Deliberation can function in the scheme of 'if-then' only when a system of destinations is already comprehended in the global view of preoccupation. What the 'if' refers to must already be understood as this or that particular thing. For such understanding explicit predication is not essential, for the schema of 'something *as* something' is implicit in pre-predicative understanding. This as-structure is ontologically grounded in the temporality of understanding. Only when Dasein, ad-tentive to the 'what for', retains an essent at hand, can it explicitly bring it closer through presentation and thus grasp it *as* this particular essent. The rootedness of the present in the future and the past is thus the existenzial-temporal condition of the possibility of such interpretation in terms of the 'as' schema. Every project of the understanding becomes necessarily subject to the as-structure in the course of its explicit development, the 'as' itself being grounded, like all understanding and interpretation in the ecstatic, horizonal unity of temporality.

The foregoing discussion of circumspect deliberation and its temporality is intended by Heidegger to put in clear light the human existenzial situation in which the shift from circumspect preoccupation to theoretical discovery takes place. How the change itself occurs is explained by Heidegger with reference to a proposition expressing circumspect deliberation. While circumspectly using a tool, we can say deliberatively, for example, "The hammer is too heavy," or just, "Heavy!" meaning that it is difficult to manipulate, that it requires great strength to use it. The sentence can, however, also mean that this thing, the hammer, lying before me, possesses weight, the 'property' of heaviness, a way of speaking from which the context of the ad-tending retention of a utensilar totality and references to destination have vanished. The hammer as thus seen is no longer a tool but has become just a material body subject to the laws of gravity. The essent as so encountered has now nothing about it with reference to which it could be found 'too heavy' and such circumspect talk about the hammer being 'too heavy' has, in fact, no longer any sense. This latter mode of talking exhibits the hammer differently, not because one abstains from manipulating it or because its utensilar character is disregarded. "The handy essent as encountered is now looked at differently—as something simply given. The comprehension of Being governing the preoccupied commerce with intramundane essents *has undergone a sudden change*." The theoretical attitude, in other words, arises in consequence of a different way (the theoretical) of grasping intramundane essents which is itself the result of a shift in the comprehended mode of being of these essents. In the 'physicalistic' proposition, "The hammer is too heavy," not only is its tool-character disregarded but also another character that every handy utensil has, its place, which now becomes irrelevant, just a point in space-time. The utensil's place-manifold, formerly restricted to the surrounding world, is not merely modified into a manifold of positions but becomes unbounded, including in its purview the whole universe of simply given essents.

The classical example of the genesis, not only historical but ontological, of a science is the rise of mathematical physics. What is crucial to its development is not the importance attached to the observation of facts, nor the 'application' of mathematics to the processes of nature but the mathematical project of nature itself. Such a project discloses a realm of what is permanently *vorhanden* (matter) and opens up a dimension in which its quantitatively determinable aspects, such as motion, energy, space, and time, come into view, rendering possible the disclosure and investigation of such things as 'facts'. What is of decisive importance in the mathematical project of nature is not its being mathematical as such but the fact that it discloses an apriori, namely, the prior project of Being as *vorhanden*. Mathematical physics "is a model science not because of its exactitude and universal necessity but because in it the thematic essent is disclosed in the way in which alone anything that is can be disclosed: in a prior project of its ontological constitution" (that is, of its being). From this a priori comprehension of Being follow the methods, the conceptual structure, the possibility of truth and certainty appertaining to it, the manner of validation, the sort of bindingness, and the mode of communication distinctive of the scientific enterprise. These factors, taken as a whole, constitute the full existenzial concept of science.[15]

The mathematical project of nature, taken in all its aspects, involves what Heidegger calls "thematization," which makes possible an objectivization of essents within the world such that they can now freely become objects for the pure discovering, investigating attitude. The mode of being-with-intramundane simply given essents in which the latter are objectivized is preeminently a presentation. But it is a presentation which is distinguished from the present of circumspection in that in physical science discovering is solely ad-tentive to the discoveredness of simply given essents, being grounded existenzielly in the resoluteness of Dasein projecting itself upon its ability to be in 'truth'. The thematization or objectivization of the simply given essent presupposes a transcending of this essent by Dasein. Since this thematization is itself a transformation of the circumspect mode of discovering essents as at hand, such transcendence must be implicit in the practical mode of being with handy essents as well. The transcendence is itself made possible by the disclosure of world occurring along with Dasein's factual existenz as being-in-the-world. Finally, since Dasein's being is grounded in temporality, the latter is presupposed in Dasein's being-in-the-world, and so in the transcendence which in turn is presupposed in the preoccupied being with essents, both in the practical as well as the theoretical attitudes.

It has been explained in chapter 3 how circumspect preoccupation involves the comprehension of a totality of destinations based on a prior comprehension of 'significance' or
meaningfulness, the latter being in its unity what Heidegger
calls the world. The question now to be dealt with is, what
must be the mode of being of the world so that Dasein might
exist as being-in-the-world? Dasein, existing for the sake of a
potentiality of its own being and as thrown among essents,
understands itself in terms of the connection between the 'for
the sake of' itself and the 'in order to' (of these essents).[16] That
in which Dasein understands itself as thus existing is its 'there',
the world, which, therefore, has the mode of being of Dasein
itself. Dasein's being is care and its ontological sense consists
of temporality, which constitutes the overtness of the 'there',
including the world. Hence, the unity of significance (that is,
the relational complex of meaningfulness, consisting of the
what-for, for-the-sake-of-whom, to that purpose), that is, the
ontological constitution of the world, must also be grounded
in temporality. "The existenzial-temporal condition of the
world lies in this, that temporality as ecstatic unity possesses
something like a horizon. The ecstasies are not just transports
in which one is carried away (*Entrückung*) but also include the
'where to' of the transport," which is termed by Heidegger the
"horizonal schema" and which is different in each of the
ecstasies. The schema in which man reaches out in the future is
'for the sake of himself'. That in which he is disclosed to
himself through attunement as thrown is the 'before what' of
thrownness, characterizing the horizon of the past. Existing
for his own sake and as thrown, he is with existents and,
therefore, presentating; the schema of this horizon of the
present is 'in order to'. The horizon of temporality, in the
whole of its schemata, determines that in view of which the
factually existing Dasein is disclosed. In the horizon of the
future a potentiality of being is projected, in that of the past the
'already being' is disclosed, and in the horizon of the present
objects of preoccupation are discovered. This shows how, by
virtue of the horizonal constitution of the ecstatic unity of
temporality, there is disclosed to this essent who is his own
'there', such a thing as the world. "Insofar as Dasein temporalizes itself *is* there also a world. . . . The world is neither

simply given nor at hand but temporalizes itself (that is, brings itself about) in temporality. It 'is' with the 'outside itself' of the ecstasies, 'there'. If no *Dasein* exists, 'there' is also no world." Preoccupied being with essents at hand as well as the thematizing, objectivizing discovery of simply given essents already presuppose the world, being themselves modes of being-in-the-world. As thus presupposed in all encounters with intramundane essents, the world, grounded in the horizonal unity of ecstatic temporality, is transcendent. The world, in other words, is the transcendental condition of the possibility of encountering essents within it as objects. Such possibility is the real problem of transcendence and not how a subject comes out of itself to meet objects, supposed, falsely, to constitute in their totality the world. The relational complex of significance which makes up the structure of the world is not a network of forms cast over some given material by a worldless subject. "The factual Dasein comes rather, ecstatically comprehending itself and its world in the unity of the 'there', back out of these horizons to the essent encountered within them. This comprehending 'coming back to' is the existenzial sense of the presentating encountering of the essent which is, for this reason, called intramundane." As an existenzial, the world is 'subjective' but as temporal and transcendent, it is more 'objective' than any possible object. The existenzial, ontological possibility of Dasein's being-in-the-world is thus rendered intelligible by being explained in terms of the ecstatic horizonal unity of temporality. The full working out of the structure of the world in general, however, can be undertaken only when an ontology of intramundane essents securely based on a clarified idea of Being is developed.[17]

[69]

Earlier, it has been found that Dasein, as being-in-the-world, possesses a spatiality of its own. Like every other aspect of Dasein's constitution and mode of being, the specific spatiality of Dasein is also grounded in temporality. The demonstration that Dasein's spatial character is based on its temporality, of course, does not mean reducing space to time or deducing it from the latter. Nor does it mean giving priority to time over space, in the sense of Kant, who offers only an ontic determination of all psychic processes as necessarily occurring 'in' time. Dasein never exists as something simply given in space, filling up a part of it like a physical body or a utensil, but rather, in a literal sense, takes up space (better, takes space in). With his very existenz man brings with him an area of free play around him, a locality or region within which he takes his 'place'. This 'occupying room' is constituted, as we have seen, by situating and rapprochement and the former presupposes a region to which an essent at hand must belong, as already discovered. Further, the preoccupied being-in-the-world has an orientation and direction.

> Belonging to a region has intrinsic reference to destination, being always determined factually through the system of destinations connected with the utensil of concern. The relational complex of destinations can be understood only in the horizon of a disclosed world. Further, it is its horizonal nature that renders possible the specific horizon of the 'where to' of belonging to a region. The disclosure of the region to the oriented Dasein is itself grounded in an ecstatic retentive ad-tension to the possible 'over here' and 'over there'. This oriented ad-tension to a region is at the same time a bringing close or de-distancing of essents at hand and simply given.

Such rapprochement, and likewise all measurement of distances, is grounded in a presentation, on which situating also depends. It is because Dasein in its being is ecstatic-horizonal that it always carries with it a space that it 'rooms in' for itself. The 'here' of this space, of course, does not mean a position in space but the area opened up through situating in which the utensilar whole of immediate concern has free play. Manipulating and becoming absorbed in the object of preoccupation is based on rapprochement in the mode of forfeiture, a closeness that is characterized by an ad-tentive forgetting of the present.

> In the presentation which brings something near, from its 'over there', the presentation loses itself in itself, forgetting the 'there'. Hence it is that when the 'observation' of intramundane essents occurs on the level of such presentation, the illusion arises as if there were, to begin with, only

a thing before us, here indeed but indefinitely in a space in general. Only on the ground of ecstatic-horizonal temporality is it possible for Dasein to break into space. The world is not simply given in space; the latter, however, is discoverable only within a world.[18]

[70]

The existenzial analytic as worked out so far has been oriented toward the inconspicuous, average mode of existence in which Dasein first and mostly maintains itself, in other words, its everydayness. And yet the concept of everydayness itself in its ontological, existenzial, and temporal sense has so far remained unexamined and obscure. It is even doubtful if the concept of temporality as so far explicated can suffice to define the existenzial sense of everydayness. This term denotes the quotidian mode of man's existence, the prevailing 'how' of his existenz. The phrase, 'first and mostly' is also meant to suggest this. "'First' means the manner in which Dasein is manifested in the togetherness of public life, even though 'in reality' it may in fact have 'overcome' this everydayness existenzielly. 'Mostly' means the manner in which Dasein manifests itself to everybody, not always but 'as a rule'." Everydayness means the way man whiles away his time, his living at ease with his habitual and customary ways, the monotony of 'the same today as yesterday'. These are not just aspects manifested in his life but constitute the mode of *being* implied in the way he manifests himself publicly, though one which is not without its private, individual expressions.

The inadequacy of the preceding explication of temporality becomes obvious when we consider the perplexing phenomenon of everydayness, in particular, the fact that man, in passing his days, *stretches* through the succession of the days of his life. The monotony, the life of custom and habit, the 'mostly' of everydayness, cannot be understood except in terms of this fact of Dasein's stretching through, or extension in, time. Further, an interpretation of Dasein's temporality and of the ontological sense of everydayness must take into account the fact that Dasein, in spending its time, reckons 'with' time and reckons it by means of astronomical calendars. But since everydayness means at bottom nothing else than temporality, on which Dasein's being is grounded, a fully adequate understanding of everydayness can be achieved only in the light of a clarified sense of Being in general.

[71]

Notes

1. Heidegger points out in a footnote that the guiltiness inherent in the ontological constitution of Dasein is to be distinguished from the theological conception of a *status corruptionis* which is based on a factual guilt having a distinctive character, and a testimony, of its own, but of which philosophy as such can have no cognizance. Guiltiness as existenzially defined may, however, be taken by theology as providing the ontological condition of the factual possibility of such a *status*. The existenzial analysis of being guilty proves nothing either *for* or *against* the possibility of sin; as a philosophy that inquires, the ontology of Dasein cannot, in principle, 'know' anything about sin.

2. To say that all projects of the understanding are thrown projects, or to speak of the finitude of Dasein, is the same as recognizing the inherently circular character of understanding or the reciprocal dependence of man and language upon one another. In other words, while attempting to understand (and rational knowledge is only a mode of understanding) himself, the world, and 'Reality', man can never attain to an unconditioned or absolute standpoint outside this 'circle' and above its historical manifestations. With the circularity of understanding goes also its historicity. The concept of "the circle of understanding" has been worked out in detail, elaborated as to its implications and made the basis of a theory of philosophical knowledge conceived as hermeneutics by Hans-Georg Gadamer in his *Wahrheit und Methode* (1960). See, for "the hermeneutic circle" in particular, p. 178f., 250f., and 275f. and, in addition, p. 240f. for illuminating comments on Heidegger's hermeneutic phenomenology.

3. In *Kant und das Problem der Metaphysik* (III *Abschnitt*), Heidegger has approached the analysis of Transcendental Apperception and its ontological significance from another angle. See chapter 9 below.

4. In a footnote Heidegger points out that even if one interprets, like Heimsoeth, Kant's doctrine of the Self in the *Critique of Pure Reason* in the light of his view of the practical Reason and its primacy, eliminating all naturalistic and rationalistic suggestions, the fact remains that Kant's thought moved basically within the horizon of an inappropriate ontology of the *Vorhanden* and the substantial. Kant's conception of the 'I' has been criticized by Max Scheler from a personalistic, phenomenological point of view in *Der Formalismus in der Ethik und die materiale Wertethik*, where he points out that positing the 'I' as a correlate of acts (of consciousness) turns it into an object and as such it can in no possible sense of the word be a condition of the possibility of objects. Not the pure 'I' but the Person is the agent of all acts (including cognitive acts) in the phenomenological sense, according to Scheler.

5. In *Kant and the Problem of Metaphysics*, Heidegger seeks to interpret Kant's transcendental philosophy from the 'fundamental ontological' point of view, showing how the foundation of transcendental philosophy gives way and an abyss opens up, once the transcendental ego is seen in its basic relationship with time. See the account in chapter 9 in this book.

6. Commenting on the discussion of self-hood in *Being and Time*, Heidegger remarks ("What is Metaphysics?," Introduction) that although existenz neither consists in being a self nor is definable in terms of self-hood. yet, since metaphysical thought describes self-hood in terms of substance or subject, the first attempt to strike out a path that leads away from metaphysics to the ecstatic existenzial nature of man, has to lead through the metaphysical conception of man's self-hood.

7. The root temporality of Dasein, Heidegger points out, must be understood here in a strictly existenzial sense, excluding all suggestion of future, past, and present as applied to *vorhanden* processes in the vulgar conception of time, which is derivative and secondary, being a manifestation of the inauthentic self-interpretation of Dasein.

Wyschogrod (*Kierkegaard and Heidegger*, pp. 64-65) draws attention to Heidegger's "thoroughgoing dissolution of Being into a field," the efforts to "dissolve any entity into extended componentiality" or "the field concept of Being," which is also evident in his treatment of Time.

8. As Heidegger explicitly points out here (*Sein und Zeit*, p. 336; E.T., p. 385), the term understanding (*Verstehen*) is used by him in the sense of a fundamental existenzial and not as a particular mode of knowing, as distinguished, for example, from causal explanation and conceptualization, nor indeed in the sense of knowing as thematically grasping anything. This marks a radical departure from the usage of Dilthey and of Jaspers, for whom understanding is one particular mode of knowing, exemplified in the human sciences, as against causal explanation, which is the characteristic mode of knowledge in the natural sciences.

9. In the English translation of *Sein und Zeit*, *Gewärtigen* is rendered as 'awaiting' and *Erwarten* as 'expecting'.

10. In connection with the Moment, Heidegger refers in a footnote to S. Kierkegaard. The latter, he says, "has seen the existenziell phenomenon of the Moment most penetratingly, which does not, however, mean that he has succeeded equally in the existenzial interpretation. He adheres to the vulgar concept of time and defines the Moment with the help of 'now' and eternity. When Kierkegaard speaks of 'temporality', what he means is the 'being-in-time' of man. Time as intratemporality knows only the 'now' but never the Moment. When, however, this is existenzielly experienced, temporality in a more fundamental sense is presupposed, even though not in an existenzially explicit manner."

For an account of Kierkegaard's conception of the Moment, see Karl Jaspers: *Psychologie der Weltanschauungen*, p. 109f. As Jaspers shows, Kierkegaard thinks of the Moment as a synthesis of the temporal and the eternal, as the meeting point of time and eternity, in deliberate contrast with the Platonic, heathen conception of the moment as an atomistic abstraction from which the past and the future are wholly shut out, leaving only the abstract present. The concrete present, on the other hand (in the Christian as opposed to the Greek view of time), is the "fullness of time," the eternal in which the past and the future are incorporated, a present which, being sufficient and complete in itself, annuls time and lifts man above the stream of atomized time. As Wyschogrod points out (*Kierkegaard and Heidegger*, p. 126), for Heidegger the Moment is 'futuristic' whereas Kierkegaard, lacking the conception of primordial temporality, thinks of it in terms of the present.

    11. *Rhetoric*, B5, 1382a 21.

    12. When time is conceived as a flow of 'nows', the present can appear only as any arbitrary point in this series, 'flowing' in the direction of the past, *going* away in an endless chase of one 'now' by another. In the authentic, existenzial present—the Moment—both the future and the past *come* towards each other and meet at the overt *Da* ('there') of Dasein. For him who stands in the Moment, past and future run *towards each other*, as Heidegger puts it (*Nietzsche I*, p. 311).

    13. The lecture on "Wissenschaft und Besinnung" (1953) in *Vorträge und Aufsätze* may be read, along with the lecture, "Die Zeit des Weltbildes" (1938) in *Holzwege* as supplementing the present account. See also "Die Frage nach der Technik" (1953) in *Vorträge und Aufsätze*.

    14. *Critique of Pure Reason*, B33.

    15. The origin of modern natural science in the mathematical project of nature, the metaphysical significance of the latter and its implications for the *Critique of Pure Reason* have been dealt with at length by Heidegger in *Die Frage nach dem Ding*, pp. 49-83 (E.T., pp. 65-108).

    In a series of notable articles, the phenomenologist Oskar Becker has criticized Heidegger for the one-sideness of his hermeneutic approach in general and of his existential interpretation of science in particular. Primarily concerned with the phenomenology of the mathematical, logical, and aesthetic spheres of experience, he makes an energetic plea for the claims of "paraexistenz" and of a complementary discipline of "Paraontology." See, in particular, his *Dasein und Dawesen*. Becker's views have been discussed critically by Gadamer (*Wahrheit und Methode*, note, pp. 91-92) and Pöggeler (*Der Denkweg Martin Heideggers*, note, pp. 306-307). Cf. also the latter's article, "Hermeneutische und mantische Phänomenologie."

    16. As Heidegger remarks in "Vom Wesen des Grundes" (*Wegmarken*, pp. 53-54; E.T., p. 86), to say that Dasein exists 'for the sake of' itself is not to assert any egoistic-ontic thesis about man nor does it imply any solipsistic isolation of the individual. It rather draws attention to the condition of the possibility of man's conducting himself either egoistically or altruistically. "Only because Dasein as such is characterized by self-hood can a person relate himself as 'myself' to a 'thyself'. Self-hood is the presupposition of the possibility of the 'I' which is revealed always in relation to a 'thou'. Self-hood, however, is never relative to a 'thou' and is neutral in respect of being an 'I' or a 'thou', being presupposed in them.

    17. This has been attempted by Heidegger later in the lecture "Das Ding" in *Vorträge und Aufsätze*. See the last chapter for an account of World and Thing in Heidegger's later language.

18. In the context of his later thinking about Time in terms of *Ereignis*, Heidegger points out (*Zur Sache des Denkens*, p. 24; E.T., p. 23) that the attempt to derive the spatiality of Dasein from Temporality in *Being and Time* is not tenable.

7
Historicity and the Concept of Time

The Nature of Historicity

The single aim that has guided the existenzial analytic as developed so far by Heidegger has been that of discovering a possibility of answering the question of the sense of Being in general. The explication of the question itself has required an analysis of the phenomenon of the comprehension of Being, within which alone Being is accessible and which is part of the constitution of Dasein. Only when this last is fully grasped, along with the comprehension of Being inherent in it, will it be possible to formulate adequately the problem of Being itself. The elucidation of temporality as the ultimate condition of the possibility of care and the analysis of Dasein's authentic potentiality of being whole seem to provide us with a complete understanding of Dasein in its ultimate nature. But it is still doubtful whether the whole of Dasein in regard to its authentically being whole has really been brought within the scope of the existenzial analytic. Man's wholeness has been thoroughly dealt with in respect of his being-toward the end, that is, his death. But death is, formally speaking, only one end of man, the other end being his beginning, his birth. In his wholeness he exists 'between' birth and death, but so far he has been dealt with as if he existed only in a 'forward' direction. "Not only (its) being-toward the beginning remained unnoticed but also, above all, the fact of its stretching or *extending between* birth and death. Just this 'continuity of life' (*Lebenszusammenhang*) in which Dasein always in some manner exists has been over-looked in the analysis of its being-whole." How this problem can be tackled on the basis of the concept of temporality as so far developed is shown by Heidegger in the course of his discussion of temporality and historicity.

At the first glance the 'continuity of life' between birth and death appears to be a simple matter, the continuity being supposed to be due to the succession of experiences 'in time'. A deeper look into what is ontologically assumed here, however, reveals the remarkable fact that in this succession of experiences only the experience of a particular 'now' is actually 'real', the past and the future experiences being no longer 'real' or yet to be so. Dasein, real only in the momentary 'now', hops through, on this view, the 'time' of its life. Through this succession of experiences, the self in some way remains the same, though what it is that remains the same and its relation to what changes remains uncertain. The underlying assumption here is that this is an entity simply given 'in time', though, of course, not of the nature of a 'thing'. In view of what has been said earlier regarding temporality as the ontological meaning of care, it is obvious that this popular conception of Dasein is of no value for an ontological analysis of the exten-dedness of Dasein between birth and death. Dasein does not exist as the sum of the momentarily real experiences coming into being and perishing in succession. Basically, the vulgar conception of a 'continuity of life' seeks, rightly, for a framework for this continuity within Dasein itself rather than as stretching out beyond it. But it fails to reach an ontological comprehension of this continuity because it tacitly assumes Dasein to be of the nature of something *vorhanden* 'in time'.

Dasein does not fill in an already laid out track or stretch of life in the course of its existence from moment to moment but rather extends or stretches itself, its own being from the very first being constituted as an extending. "*In the being* of Dasein lies already the 'between' in relation to birth and death." It is not the case that Dasein '*is*' at any one point of time, being, in addition, encompassed by the no-longer or not-yet actual moments of birth and death. Birth is not something past in the sense of being no longer *vorhanden*, just as death is not something yet to be *vorhanden*. The factual Dasein exists as being born (*Gebürtig*), both death and birth being modes of Dasein's being as made up of care. In the unity of thrownness and being toward death lies the continuity of birth and death and, "as care, Dasein *is* the 'between'." Since the ground of the unity of the structure of care lies in temporality, the ontological elucidation of the continuity of life must be sought in Dasein's temporal constitution. The specific movement of existenz—to be distinguished from the motion of a simply given essent—characteristic of Dasein's 'extended self-extending' is called by Heidegger the happening or occurrence (*Geschehen*) of Dasein. This 'happening' character of Dasein is the real ontological problem involved in the 'continuity' of Dasein and to explicate its structure and the existenzial-temporal condition of its possibility means comprehending ontologically the nature of historicity. On the other hand, the persistence of the self which, along with the movement of Dasein, is part of this 'happening', also leads back to the way temporality 'temporalizes' itself. But the problem of historicity has nothing to do with history (*Historie*) as the science of what happens in history (*Geschichte*), neither with the epistemological problem of historical knowledge (Simmel) nor with the logic of historical concepts (Rickert), for both of which the historical past is only the object of a science.

If historicity itself is to be elucidated on the basis of temporality, ultimately of authentic temporality, then, from the very nature of the task it can be done only by way of a phenomenological construction, by deliberately wresting it from the veils of the vulgar interpretation of Dasein's historicity. The latter must naturally be the starting point. The existenzial construction of historicity must be guided by the interpretation, already arrived at, of Dasein's authentic potentiality of being whole and by the analysis of care as temporality. What lay implicit in the way temporality temporalizes itself (brings itself on) will become explicit in this project of historicity and it will also become clear that the everydayness with which the existenzial analytic was immediately concerned is the inauthentic historicity of Dasein. Further, since man exists historically, he can thematize this mode of existence itself and build up on this ontological basis a science of history. Man is not 'temporal' because he 'stands within history' but that, on the contrary, he can exist historically only because in the very depths of his being he is temporal. Lastly, since Dasein is not merely historical but also exists 'in time' (both historicity and existing 'in time' being manifestations of his temporality), a discussion of the nature of this intratemporality will also be essential. Each of these points is discussed in turn by Heidegger in the last two climactic chapters of *Being and Time*. Heidegger explicitly disavows any intention of trying to solve the problem of historicity by some kind of *coup de main*. "The inadequacy of the available 'categorical' means and the uncertainty of the primary ontological horizon become all the more glaring, the more the problem of history (*Geschichte*) is carried to its ultimate roots." The following discussion contents itself with indicating the ontological position of the problem of historicity. After all, what matters in the analysis that follows is that "it attempts, on its part, to prepare the way for the assimilation, yet lying ahead, of the investigations of Dilthey by the present generation and thus to carry them forward."

[72]

The term history, as pointed out earlier, is ambiguous, standing both for the historical reality (*Geschichte*) as well as for a possible science of it (*Historie*). The latter sense has already been ruled out, for the time being, as irrelevant in the present context. But the vulgar interpretation of Dasein includes a number of other meanings to which Heidegger draws attention. In the first place, history may be understood, not as the object of a science or as this science itself but as something that is past and gone, belonging to a past time and no longer existing. What thus belongs to the past may in turn be either still effective in the present or, even though physically present in the form of a relic, of no influence on the 'now'. Secondly, history may mean the past, not so much in the sense of what is bygone but as something originating from it. "What 'possesses a history', stands in a continuity of becoming. . . . History here means a 'continuity of events or of action which runs through 'past', 'present' and 'future'." In the third place, history means, not a mode of being but the sphere of human existence, as distinct from that of Nature, with the transformations and vicissitudes to which it is subject. Lastly, the historical means what is handed down by tradition irrespective of whether it is historically acknowledged or just taken for granted without awareness of its origins. These four meanings are linked together by the fact that they all refer to man as the 'subject' of events. How, Heidegger asks, should their occurrent character be determined? Are they just a succession of events cropping up and then vanishing? How is the occurrence of history related to Dasein and is the latter first factually given and then happens to "land itself into history?" Does Dasein become historical by a combination of circumstances and events, or is it because it is already in its being historical that such things as circumstances, events, and vicissitudes become ontologically possible? Why does the past have a predominant function in Dasein's 'temporal' existence?

Preparatory to his exposition of the fundamental structure of historicity, Heidegger first takes up the last question. An article of antiquity preserved in a museum belongs to a past time and yet it is there in the present. This article, not yet gone into the past, is not historical merely because it is an object of historical interest, for it can be such only if in itself it somehow possesses historical reality. What is past about this present article and what *was* it that it no longer is, even if it is now again used as a utensil? What it was and is no longer, what is gone from it, is "nothing else than the *world* within which, as part of a utensilar system, it was encountered as a handy essent and was utilized by a preoccupied Dasein existing in-the-world. The *world* is no longer. What was formerly intramundane in that world is, however, still there." And since the world *is* only as a mode of being of an existing Dasein, the passing away of a world means the passing away of Dasein. This, however, would imply that only the past Dasein is historical and not the present. Moreover, Dasein cannot be past in the sense of no longer being there, for he never is *vorhanden* but rather possesses *existenz*. What has ceased to have existenz is not something that has gone into the past but what Heidegger calls (to distinguish the existenzial from the categorial past) the 'has-been-there' (*Da-gewesen*). What is past about such articles thus is the fact that they derive from a world that was and which belonged to Dasein who once 'has-been-there'. This is the primary historical reality and hence Dasein is historical, not as something past but precisely as existing factually, not as something that has-been-there but as being its has-been, at the same time presentating and reaching out into the future. The above analysis, however, only renders still more acute the riddle as to why the past, in the sense of the has-been, predominantly determines historicity. In the primary sense it is Dasein that is historical and intramundane essents, including objects at hand as well as Nature, are so only in a secondary sense. The latter, as also belonging to a world, Heidegger includes in the sphere of what he calls world history. "What is world-historical has historical reality not because it is historically objectivized but as, encountered within a world, the essent that it is in itself. The temporality of historical reality, it is clear, cannot be understood in terms of the intratemporal *vorhanden* essents and, therefore, the mere distance 'in time' has no significance for the historicity of an essent, which is much more fundamental than the mere 'antiquity' of a relic. It is, however, not sufficient merely to assert the ontic fact of Dasein's historicity. More important is the ontological problem of the conditions of the possibility of the historical constitution of the subjectivity of the historical 'subject' and it is to this problem that Heidegger now turns.

[73]

Dasein's being, as we have seen, consists of care which is itself grounded in temporality. The latter determines man's authentic existenz in the mode of anticipative resoluteness in which, looking at death full in the face, as it were, he takes upon himself his own thrownness and exists resolutely in his situation, projecting himself on this or that factual possibility of existenz. Although it is not within the competence of the analytic of existenz to say anything about factual possibilities and about what is and about what is resolved in resoluteness, yet "we must ask from where these possibilities on which Dasein factually projects itself can *at all* be drawn and conceived." The anticipative self-projection on death, the unsurpassable, innermost possibility, only guarantees the wholeness and authenticity of the resoluteness and discloses no factual possibilities. But in its throwness and being delivered up to its own potentiality of being, Dasein, as being-in-the-world, is thrown as dependent on a 'world', factually existing with others and understanding itself in terms of the prevailing 'average', publicly interpreted character of Dasein. It is from the latter, against it and yet for it, that it grasps in resolution its own chosen possibility. Resoluteness thus discloses the particular factual possibilities of existing authentically out of the heritage which, as thrown, man takes over. The resolute assumption of his thrownness involves the inheritance of possibilities that have come down as a legacy, even though not explicitly recognized as such.

The more unambiguously man anticipatively grasps the extreme possibility of death the more resolute he is and the more unequivocal his choice of the possibility in which to exist. "Only being free for death gives to Dasein an aim and thrusts it into existenz in finitude. Grasping the finitude of existenz, Dasein is torn away from the endless multiplicity of the possibilities of pleasure, of taking things lightly, of evasions that immediately suggest themselves and is brought into (an awareness of) the simplicity of its fate (*Schicksal*). This is the original, root occurrence of Dasein, implicit in authentic resoluteness in which, free for death, it surrenders itself to an inherited but at the same time chosen possibility." Fate does not spring from a clash of circumstances and events, for even the irresolute person may be tossed about by them, even more than he who has chosen, without 'having' a fate. Further, taking upon himself the powerlessness of being left to himself, but with the power of his own finite freedom, man exists with others in the world. His 'happening' is a joint happening with them, a collective fate which Heidegger calls destiny (*Geschick*), the 'occurrence' of community and of the people.[1] The fateful destiny of Dasein in and with his 'generation' makes up the full authentic occurrence of Dasein. Fate is possible only on the basis of care, that is, temporality, as ontologically constituted by death, guilt, conscience, freedom, and finitude. Only an essent who intrinsically reaches out into the future and has simultaneously appropriated the past with its legacy of possibilities, can exist, in possession of his own thrownness and authentically in the Moment, for 'his time'. Only authentic temporality, which is at the same time finite, renders possible such a thing as fate, that is, authentic historicity. The resolute taking over of an inherited possibility of existenz, when explicit, is repetition. "Repetition is the explicit (taking over of) tradition, that is, the return to the possibilities of Dasein that has once been." This repetition of the possible means, however, neither a restitution of what is past nor a tying of the present to what is 'obsolete'; it is rather the return of the past possibility in resoluteness which, as existenz in the Moment, is at the same time a disavowal of that past (as distinguished from the "has been") which is still operative in the today. "Repetition neither abandons itself to the past nor aims at progress. For the authentic existenz in the Moment both are immaterial."[2] Since repetition is a manifestation of resoluteness, through which Dasein exists explicitly in the ultimate historicity of fate, it follows that historicity is rooted not so much in the past or in today as in the future. "History as Dasein's mode of being has its roots so intrinsically in the future that Death as a possibility flings its anticipative existenz back to its factual thrownness and thus lends to the 'has been' its peculiar preeminence in historicity. *The authentic being toward death, that is, the finitude of temporality is the hidden ground of the historicity of Dasein.*" Through repetition, destiny is explicitly disclosed as being in the grip of the legacy coming down from the past; repetition first reveals to Dasein its own history. The 'happening' of Dasein, as thus based on anticipative resoluteness, is the authentic historicity of Dasein.[3] How this 'happening', or fate, makes up the continuity of Dasein from birth to death, however, still remains a riddle on which light may be thrown by a consideration of the inauthentic historicity of Dasein. This, therefore, is next discussed by Heidegger.

[74]

Primarily, man comprehends himself in terms of what he encounters in the environing world and of the objects of his circumspect preoccupation. It is not possible to determine the 'continuity' of Dasein in terms of these, and the occurrence of history likewise does not consist in the isolated flow 'of streams of experience' in individual subjects. If history is to be defined neither in terms of a series of changes in the objects nor of a succession of experiences within the subject, can it be described in terms of the connection between subject and object? If yes, what would be the mode of being of this linkage itself? The thesis of the historicity of Dasein, however, does not refer to a worldless subject but to an essent who exists as being-in-the-world. "*The occurrence of history is the occurrence of being-in-the-world.*" Dasein's historicity means the historicity of world and, with that, the historicity of what is encountered within it; things at hand and simply given, even nature "as landscape, a place to settle in and exploit, battlefield and place of worship." The history of intramundane essents, which is not something merely 'external' as against the 'inner history of the soul', is called by Heidegger world history, meaning both the occurrence of world in its intrinsic unity with Dasein as well as that of things at hand and simply given within the world. Heidegger draws attention to the peculiar movement characteristic of what 'happens' with utensils and other things in the world, a movement not to be explained in terms of change of place but part of the general 'ontological riddle' of the movement of 'happenings' in general, to which this exposition of historicity is intended to lead.

Because of the temporally grounded transcendence of the world, the occurrence of being-in-the-world implies that world-historical essents are already 'there' objectively, without being actually grasped as historical. But since factual Dasein, as forfeited, goes out into the objects of its preoccupation, it understands its history in terms of world-historical essents. Taking Being in the sense of substantial existence, it interprets them as simply given things appearing and passing away, without raising the problem of the mode of being of what is world-historical and of the movement characteristic of happenings in general. Everyday man takes his fate as lying in the multifariousness of the daily affairs in which he is 'scattered'. In order to come back to his own self, he must pull himself out of the scattering and discontinuity of this inauthentic existenz. Thus the question of building up the continuity of Dasein, in the sense of the unity of a chain of 'experiences' between birth and death, arises out of the horizon of understanding characteristic of inauthentic existenz. The question is not how man acquires the unity and connectedness of a chain of 'experiences', but in which mode of his being does he so lose himself that he must, only as an afterthought as it were, pull himself out of his dispersion and invent for himself a unity that can give cohesion to his existenz. This is the forfeited mode of being from which Dasein comes back to authentic existenz through anticipative resoluteness. As repetition of the legacy of possibilities, the occurrence of such resoluteness is authentic historicity and in this lies the ultimate and basic extendedness of the whole of existenz, needing no connecting together.

> The resoluteness of the self in face of the impermanence of dispersion is in itself the *extended continuity* (*erstreckte Stätigkeit*) in which Dasein, as fate, contains birth and death and their 'between' incorporated into its existenz in the Moment, open to what is world-historical in its particular situation. In the fate-ful repetition of past possibilities Dasein brings itself back into immediate temporal-ecstatic relation with what has been. This self-surrender to the legacy of the past, recalling Dasein from the unsurpassable possibility of death, retrieves its 'birth' and draws it into its existenz. This, of course, only enables it to take up the thrownness of its own 'there' in a manner which is less infected with illusion.

Resoluteness, which is not just a mental 'act' lasting for the moment but has an existenziell permanence presupposed in all 'acts' of resolution, constitutes the loyalty of existenz to itself. Its preparedness for anxiety is at the same time awe before the unique authority that a free existence can command in face of the repeatable possibilities of existenz. In inauthentic historicity, the primary 'extendedness' of fate remains closed from view. Everyman, blind to possibilities and incapable of repeating what has been, is aware only of the remnants of what has been. He takes them alone as 'real' and, lost in the presentation of today, understands the past in terms of the present. Authentic historicity, on the contrary, means a de-presentation of the today and a weaning from the conventionalities of everyman. For it, history is the 'recurrence' of the possible and it is aware that possibilities recur only when existenz is open for them in resolute repetition. The existenzial interpretation of the historicity of Dasein cannot be cleared of all obscurities so long as the enigma of Being and of movement continue to haunt the inquiry. Nevertheless, an ontological project of the genesis of history as a science out of the historicity of Dasein may be attempted, to the limited extent that is required for throwing further light on the nature of historicity and its rootedness in temporality and as preparatory to the later elucidation of the problem of a 'destruction' of the history of philosophy.

[75]

Since Dasein's being is fundamentally historical, every factual science is dependent on this historicity. But the science of history presupposes it in a more specific and intimate way. Of course, history as the study of the history (Geschichte) of Dasein must presuppose the latter as its possible object. But historical science presupposes historicity not only in this sense or in the sense that such knowledge is itself part of the history of Dasein's attitude to what is. "*Historical (historische) disclosure of history (Geschichte), whether it is factually carried out or not, is in itself, in accordance with its ontological structure, rooted in the historicity of Dasein.*" To grasp how this is so is to arrive at an understanding of the existenzial origin of history from the historicity of Dasein. It is to project ontologically the idea of history as a science which makes the disclosure of historical essents its specific business. Thematizing historical existence in its specific mode of being, it delimits a region of essents, builds up a methodology appropriate to it and a conceptual structure for its interpretation. The thematization of historical reality presupposes that the 'past' as such should already be disclosed and the access to it be open for historical science.[4] This is rendered possible by the historicity of Dasein's being, so that, by virtue of its ecstatic, horizonal temporality it is open in its 'has been'. Further, since only Dasein is at bottom historical, the object of historical science must have the mode of being of Dasein that has been and with that, everything that is world-historical. Relics of the past, such as monuments and records, can function as material for the historian only because they are already world-historical in their mode of being and are understood in terms of their intramundane character by the historian whose being toward what has been is itself determined by his own historicity. It follows that the proper object of history, its basic theme, must be derived from the authentic historicity of Dasein as manifested in the repetitive disclosure of what has been. Repetition comprehends Dasein that has been in its past authentic possibility. Hence history thematizes its objects by a project of past Dasein in relation to its inmost possibility of existenz. But how can history, the science of 'facts' have the *possible* for its object? If Dasein really *is* only in its existenz, Heidegger answers, then its 'factuality' consists just in the resolute self-projection on a chosen potentiality of being. What has actually been is nothing else than the existenziell possibility in which fate, destiny, and world history have been determined. "Since existenz can only be as factually thrown, the more simply and concretely history comprehends and 'merely' depicts the has-been-in-the-world in terms of its possibility, the more profoundly will it disclose the silent power of the possible."[5]

In bringing to light past Dasein in its possibility, history at the same time sees the universal in the particular. "The theme of history is neither what has happened only once nor some universal hovering above, but the factually existent past possibility. This cannot be repeated as such, that is, authentically grasped historically, if it is perverted into the colorlessness of a supratemporal ideal pattern. Only factual authentic historicity is capable, as resolute fate, so to reveal the past historical reality that in repetition the 'power' of the possible strikes home into factual existenz, that is, approaches it in futurity." In other words, the possible, though a legacy from the past, approaches present existenz by way of its ecstasy of the future, as something coming towards it. History thus has its starting point not in the 'present', proceeding thence backward to the past but, like historicity, it also temporalizes itself out of the future.[6] A historian who straightaway occupies himself with the 'world view' of an age, does not grasp his object historically but rather takes it only 'aesthetically'. Similarly, an age in which a highly differentiated interest in historical investigations is dominant does not necessarily manifest authentic historicity. "In the end, the emergence of a problem of 'historicism' is the clearest evidence of the fact that historical science seeks to alienate Dasein from its authentic historicity. The latter does not necessarily stand in need of history. Unhistorical ages are not as such necessarily lacking in historicity."[7]

Referring to Nietzsche's essay "The utility and disadvantage of history for life," Heidegger points out that history can be useful or disadvantageous to life only because Dasein is historical in the very roots of its being. The three types of history distinguished by Nietzsche, though without going into the question as to why they are just three or into the ground of their unity, are the monumental, the antiquarian, and the critical. This tripartite character of history is foreshadowed in the historicity of Dasein, which is itself rooted in temporality. Reaching out into the future in the resolute repetitive disclosure of a chosen possibility, Dasein is open for the 'monumental' possibilities of human existenz. Monumental history corresponds to this kind of historicity. History is also antiquarian because repetitive appropriation of the possible at the same time involves the reverent preservation of past existenz through which the possiblility is itself revealed. And since Dasein's temporality authentically manifests itself in the Moment, authentic history, de-presentating the today and liberating man from the forfeiture of its publicity, is also a criticism of the present. The possibility as well as the structure of historical truth must be dealt with on the basis of the authentic overtness (truth) of historical existenz. Further, since the basic concepts of the historical sciences are existenzial concepts, the theory of the human sciences (*Geisteswissenschaften*) presupposes a systematic existenzial interpretation of the historicity of Dasein. The significance of Wilhelm Dilthey's investigations lies in their ceaseless effort to push forward to this goal, as does also that of Count Yorck of Wartenburg's profounder thoughts on the nature of historicity.

[76]

Heidegger's own views, as he acknowledges, were developed through a study of Dilthey's work and were confirmed and strengthened by the ideas of Count Yorck, to be found scattered in his letters to Dilthey.[8] Heidegger refers to the widespread picture of Dilthey as the sensitive interpreter of intellectual and literary history who also happened to occupy himself with demarcating the fields of the natural and human sciences, giving a prominent role to history and to psychology in the latter and combining all these interests into a loose-jointed relativistic 'philosophy of life'. This picture, though superficially correct, misses the substance of his achievement. Dilthey's work can be divided into three domains: studies in the theory of the human sciences; inquiries concerning the history of the human sciences; preoccupation with the con-struction of a 'psychology' which can comprehend man as a whole. There is much that is tentative, hesitant, and conflict-ing in these studies, but this, Heidegger says, expresses only the elemental unrest driving him onward to the one goal of 'bringing life to philosophical comprehension' and of securing a hermeneutic foundation for this understanding of life 'out of life itself'. Everything turns round a psychology which can explain life in its historical continuity, regarded as the mode in which man *is*, as the object of the historical sciences and as the root of these sciences all in one. For him hermeneutics is primarily the self-elucidation of the activity of understanding and only secondarily concerned with the methodology of history. Though Dilthey manifests, in conformity with the tendency of his age, a bias in favor of natural scientific modes of explanation, yet his innermost philosophical tendency lay in the attempt to comprehend the nature of historicity. Instead of dilating further on Dilthey's work, Heidegger refers the reader to the valuable account already given by Georg Misch and passes on to discuss some of the central ideas of Count Yorck, to the originality of whose reflections on history, it may be added, Heidegger was the first to draw the attention of scholars.[9]

Yorck adopted a critical attitude towards the role Dilthey assigned to analytical psychology, without seeing through its inner contradictions, and towards the excessive importance he attached to the theory of knowledge. This finds expression in remarks that amount to a demand for a logic and theory of method not derived from science but presupposed in it in the

form of an ontological theory of the different categorial structures of nature and of history as two distinct realms of being.
Yorck criticizes Dilthey for using the comparative method in
the human sciences because, as he puts it, "comparison is
always aesthetic, clinging always to the outward form." The
aesthetic category of form is out of place in Dilthey's much
more profound conception of history as a nexus and unity of
forces. He finds fault with Dilthey for not sufficiently em-
phasizing *the generic difference between the ontic and the
historical.*" The traditional approach to history, confining itself
to what is tangible and capable of being grasped in a visual
image—Ranke is called a great 'ocular' and the historical
school is charged with not being historical at all but operating
with antiquarian, aesthetic construction—has no access to the
living, impalpable reality of history. This manner of thinking,
Yorck points out with his sure insight into history, with its
cult of form and natural scientific bias, is itself a product of
history and is determined by a particular metaphysical attitude
underlying it. Historical knowledge is "knowledge of the
hidden springs. . . . In history, what makes much sound and
strikes the eye is not the main thing. Its nerves are invisible, as
all that is significant is invisible." He speaks of his communion
with the Spirit of History, "a spirit which did not manifest
itself to Faust in his cell, nor to the master, Goethe. Do not run
from him in terror, however stern and impressive the appari-
tion may be, for he is really brotherly and kindred in a different
and deeper sense than the dwellers of bush and field." The
effort to commune with this spirit is similar, Yorck says, to the
struggles of Jacob, a sure gain for him who engages in it.

Yorck's clear insight into the fundamental nature of history comes from his awareness of the ontologically distinctive
mode of man's being, inaccessible to the objectivizing approach of natural science or of history modeled on that. For
him the core of historicity lies in the fact that man is not just a
natural object but *lives* (*exists*, in Heidegger's sense) and is not
an abstract 'I' but a self in all its fullness. The inherent historicity of man (of self-consciousness, in Yorck's language) implies
that philosophy cannot be separated from historicity. There is
no real philosophizing that is not historical and hence, as
Yorck adds, "the separation of systematic philosophy from

historical exposition is inherently mistaken." Philosophy must be conceived as a manifestation of life, not just as the expectoration of bottomless thought, arising from nowhere. Seeking to grasp historicity and life conceptually in non-ontic, non-ocular categories, Yorck realized the difficulty of expressing in words what is revealed by an analysis that tries to go deeper than what can be visualized: "What penetrates into the ground of life eludes exoteric representation." Yorck sees that a comprehension of historicity is faced with the task of working out "the generic difference between the ontic and the historical," which must be the final goal of the Philosophy of Life. Nevertheless, the problem needs a more radical formulation. For the historical (as distinguished from the ontic) to be conceptualized philosophically, it is necessary that both the historical and the ontic should be comprehended under a more original unity, making it possible to compare and contrast them with each other. This can be done only when it is realized that the question of historicity is an *ontological* question about the way historical existence is constituted, that the problem of the ontic is likewise an ontological problem about the constitution of nonhuman essents, of *vorhanden* entities in a wide sense and that the ontic comprises only one domain of what is. Both classes of essents are comprehended in the idea of Being and it is this that must be 'generically differentiated'. Yorck applies the term ontic to nonhuman reality because he is still in the grip of the traditional ontology for which Being is just the simply given. The problem of the 'generic difference' can be developed only when the question of the sense of Being in general has first been elucidated through a fundamental-ontological inquiry.[10] It is in this sense that the preparatory existenzial-temporal analytic of Dasein is prompted by the determination "to foster the spirit of Count Yorck, in order to further the work of Dilthey."

[77]

The Vulgar Conception of Time

As evidence of the temporality of Dasein's being, it has been shown by Heidegger how the historicity of existenz is grounded in temporality. But the interpretation of historicity

took no account of the fact that, to the ordinary man's understanding, history is made up of happenings 'in time', and of the
'passage' of time as it concerns man in his day to day life. This
is an incompleteness in the analysis of Dasein's temporality as
carried out so far. Heidegger, therefore, seeks to make it good
by discussing at length in the last chapter of *Being and Time*
what he calls 'intra-temporality', that is, being 'in time', how
man concerns himself with time, the genesis of the vulgar
conception of time and Hegel's view of the relation between
time and spirit. The question whether and how time can be
said to *be* can be taken up only "when it has been shown how
far temporality itself in the wholeness of its temporalization
renders possible anything like an understanding of Being and
speaking about beings."

[78]

Constituted by care and existing in the unity of a forfeited, thrown project, Dasein is always preoccupied and concerned about essents in the world. This concern is grounded in
temporality in the mode of ad-tending, retaining presentation.
In his preoccupied calculating and planning, in the precautions
and preventive measures he takes, man constantly uses,
whether in so many words nor not, the terms 'then', 'be-
forehand', 'now', 'at that time'. Preoccupation expresses itself
ad-tentively in 'then' (future), retentively in 'at that time'
(past), presentatively in 'now'. 'Then', with the sense of 'not
yet' implicit in it, expresses ad-tending, retaining presentation;
'at that time' with 'no longer now' implicit in it, expresses a
retaining that is ad-tentively presentating. In both, presentation, the 'now', has a special importance, for in saying both
'this' and 'at that time', the point of reference is the 'now'.
Every 'then' is a 'then, when' and so with 'at that time' and
'now', with their implicit reference to '—when'. This seemingly obvious structure of 'then', 'at that time', and 'now' is
called by Heidegger datability, which does not necessarily
imply any reference to the dates of a calendar. What is that, it
must be asked, to which such datability intrinsically appertains
and in what is it grounded? Obviously, 'then', 'now', 'at that
time' refer to a point of time—apply to time itself. But do we
really understand what we mean by these terms? From where

do we get this 'now, when'? We never find it amidst in-tramundane simply given entities, nor do we 'acquire' it at all. Yet we make use of it, unavoidably, in everything we say. "Even the most trivial, everyday casual talk, saying, for ex-ample, 'it is cold', includes the sense of 'now, when'." Why is it that, whenever Dasein speaks of an object of its preoccupation, a reference to 'then, when' and so forth is always implied? This is so because in interpretatively speaking of something, Dasein also gives expression to itself, that is to say, to its circumspect, comprehending being with essents at hand, which enables them to be encountered, and because this 'speaking about', explicating itself also at the same time, is itself grounded in, and possible only as, a *present-ation*. It is the ad-tending-retaining presentation that makes itself explicit through in-terpretation. And this in turn is possible only because—ecstatically open in itself—it is already overt to itself and capable of articulation through comprehending, verbal interpretation. Because temporality constitutes ecstatic-horizonally the lit-up character of the 'there', therefore it is ultimately in its 'there' always already capable of explication and hence known. The self-explicative presentation, that is, what is explicated in being spoken of as 'now', is what we call 'time'. This is the form in which primary temporality is im-mediately known to us, as explicated in our attitude of preoc-cupied concern. The fact that what is explicated in terms of 'now', 'then', and 'at that time' possesses the structure of datability, proves that it has its origin in self-explicating tem-porality. In saying 'now', the 'there' is implicitly contained because 'now' is an explication of the presentation of essents. Datability, in terms of 'now', 'then', 'at that time', is a reflec-tion of the ecstatic constitution of temporality and therefore intrinsic to any expression of time. And, since the ecstatic unity of temporality implies the overtness of Dasein and the discovery of intramundane essents, explicated time is dated with reference to these essents as, for example, 'now, when the door bangs', 'now, when I don't have the book'. If the ad-tending which expresses itself in 'then' explicates itself and, through the presentation that this involves, comprehends that to which it ad-tends in terms of its 'now', then it follows that saying 'then' already implies 'and not now'. Similarly, terms indicating duration express the way temporality explicates itself in the form of a span of public time, corresponding to the ecstatic extendedness of temporality.

The ad-tending, retaining, presentating preoccupation 'takes' its own time, even in the absence of specific methods of determining time, and dates it in terms of the object of concern. When ad-tending man goes out into and becomes absorbed in what preoccupies him, he forgets himself, and the time that he takes, his time, also remains unnoticed and hidden. The different ways in which he takes his time and represents it to himself depends primarily on the way he *has* his time, corresponding to each particular mode of his existenz. Authenticity and inauthenticity of existenz depend, as shown earlier, upon the manner in which temporality manifests itself. The irresoluteness of inauthentic existenz temporalizes itself in the mode of an inad-tentive, forgetful presentation, such that irresolute Dasein, always occupied with and lost in the object of its preoccupation, loses its time on it and therefore always says, "I have no time." And just as inauthentically existing Dasein 'has' no time, so the resolute, authentic man, whose present is the Moment, always has time. In resoluteness the 'there' is disclosed as situation and therefore what he meets in it is never such that he could irresolutely lose his time on it. Factual, thrown Dasein can 'take' its time and 'lose' it only because, as ecstatically extended temporality and the overtness of the 'there' grounded in it, it is allotted a 'time'. Dasein's factual existenz includes being with others in an everyday, general, public kind of intelligibility, in which everybody says 'now', each dating it differently and yet understanding each other quite well. Time as explicated and stated by Dasein as being-in-the-world with others is necessarily time made public. And since everyday concern grasps everything in terms of the 'world', it takes time not as *its* time but rather uses it up, as it were from a public fund.

[79]

The phenomenal character of this public time is further elucidated by Heidegger in connection with an account of intratemporality. Dasein, in the overtness of its ecstatic temporality, is concerned with its time, converting it explicatively into public time and being guided by that. Because Dasein exists as thrown and forfeited, it understands its time as an object of preoccupation and explicates it in terms of something measurable and public. "The thrownness of Dasein is the ground of there being a common, public time." Public time is *the* time; in it intramundane essents, at hand and simply given, are encountered, for which reason Heidegger calls them intratemporal. The nature of public time and the sense in which it can be said to *be* is further clarified by the interpretation of intratemporality which follows. Thrown Dasein, left to the 'world' of its preoccupation and dependent on it, ad-tends to the potentiality of its being–in–the–world so as to count *with* and *on* that which is particularly required for its ability to be—the possibility of seeing, the light needed by its circumspect commerce with handy essents. Such orientation is found in the natural alteration of day and night, sunrise providing Dasein with the means of dating the time of its concern. The day becomes the natural measure of his time and is itself subdivided into morning, midday, and evening, according to the sun's movement. A common, public measure of time is thus at hand for everyone living under the same heavens and, along with it, the possibility of a means of measuring it, the clock. The temporality of Dasein, thrown and abandoned to the 'world', inevitably leads to the discovery of a clock, that is, a regularly recurring handy essent that has become available in ad-tending presentation. "The thrown being with (*sein bei*) essents at hand is grounded in temporality. This is the ground of the clock. As the condition of the possibility of the factual necessity of the clock, temporality is also the condition of its being discovered; for only the ad-tentive-retentive presentation of the sun in his course, encountered along with the discovered intramundane essents, enables and also requires, as self-explication, dating in terms of what is publicly at hand in the environing world." The production of more handy clocks, themselves regulated by this primal clock, follows naturally.

Dating, the specification of the 'then', is based on a concerned ad-tending and always has reference to some kind of appropriateness. Time as explicated in concern is always 'time for' or 'not the time for' something. The ad-tending, retaining presentation which characterizes preoccupation (concern), comprehends time in relation to a what-for which, in turn, is ultimately anchored to the final for-whom of Dasein's potentiality of being. Public time thus manifests, in this relation of in-order-to, the structure of meaningfulness characteristic of world. Hence, time as it is temporalized in the form of public time is called by Heidegger world-time, not as something *vorhanden* within the world but as an aspect of world itself, understood in the existenzial, ontological sense explained before. Time as manifest to preoccupation "is datable, spanned or stretched out and public and, as thus structured, belongs to world itself." The time of preoccupation is rendered explicitly public through the development of methods of measuring time which, as Heidegger goes on to explain, is itself grounded in a particular mode of temporalization. Calculation of time cuts itself gradually loose from a direct reference to the sun so that, as in the case of primitive man, time is read off directly from the length of one's own shadow and later, from handmade sundials. How is it, Heidegger asks, that we are able to read off time directly from the sundial, or from a pocketwatch, things which are not of the nature of time as such? Looking at a watch and taking note of the time is not merely to observe the change of the hand but to say, explicitly or not, "*now* it is so much time, *now* it is time to—," which means that looking at the watch and being guided by it is intrinsically saying 'now', an explication of the 'now' in its full structural character of datability, span, publicity, and worldliness. This 'now'-saying is the verbal articulation of a presentation, temporalizing itself in unity with retentive ad-tension. "Dating, as it occurs in the use of a clock, shows itself to be a preeminent presentation of a simply given essent." Measuring time by means of a clock means presentation of a series of measures in a stretch of present space on the dial and expressing them as measures of time by a series of 'now'-saying. In its measurement, the publicizing of time thus reaches its culmination, so that time can now "be met with by anybody at any time as 'now and now and now'. This 'general' time, accessible on clocks, is to be found as it were in the form of a simply given manifold of 'nows' without the measurement's being directed thematically at time as such." Since both clock and time-measurement are based on the temporality, and consequently the historicity, of Dasein, it can be shown how far the use of a clock is ontologically itself historical in character.

Dating in terms of spatial relationships, as is done in time-measurement, by no means spatializes time. The ontologically essential feature of time-measurement does not lie in the fact that in it time is determined in terms of spatial lengths and movements of the hand in space but rather in the specific presentation which makes measurement possible. Dating in terms of a 'spatially' simply given essent is hardly to spatialize time. The alleged spatialization means nothing else than the presentation of a simply given essent (the clock hand) as it is present in each 'now'. What we ordinarily call time thus first comes to be known by way of time-measurement. In preoccupation everything is said to have its time, which is possible only if things are at all 'in time'. This time, within which intramundane essents are encountered, is world-time, possessing the same transcendence as world. Along with the disclosure of world, world-time is also disclosed, so that for all preoccupied being with intramundane essents the latter are necessarily comprehended as being 'in time'. This time is neither 'objective', in the sense of something *vorhanden* within the world, nor 'subjective', in the sense of a process within a subject. World-time is more objective than any possible object, being, along with world, the condition of the possibility of all objects. It is to be found, contrary to Kant's view, as immediately in the physical as in the psychical, manifesting itself as it does first in the heavens, with which it is even identified in primitive consciousness. But world-time is also more subjective than any possible subject because it is the condition of the possibility of care as the very being of the factually existing self. If time is thus neither subjective nor objective, neither within nor without, and is prior to all subjectivity and objectivity, in what sense can it be said to be? "Is it then a phantom, or does it exist more really than any possible essent?" This question, like that concerned with the connection between Truth and Being, must await elucidation till the final stage in the inquiry into the problem of Being and Time.

[80]

Ordinarily, in his everyday mode of existence, man builds up his concept of time in terms of the way it immediately enters into his experience, and this stands in the way of his comprehending its real nature as temporality. Heidegger next proceeds to give an account of how this vulgar conception of time is derived from Dasein's concern with intramundane essents and the intratemporality that characterizes them. Dasein's circumspect concern encounters time explicitly in the use of a clock, which involves, existenzially speaking, a presentation of the moving pointer, such that in following it, its changing positions are counted.

> This presentation temporalizes itself in the ecstatic unity of an ad-tentive retaining. To retain the 'at that time' ad-tentively means to be open, while saying 'now', for the horizon of the 'before', of what is 'now' no longer. To ad-tend to the 'then' presentatively means being open, while saying 'now', for the horizon of the 'after', of what is not yet 'now'. That which manifests itself in such presentation is Time. . . . It is what manifests itself as that which is counted in the presentating, counting pursuit of the moving pointer, in such fashion that presentating temporalizes itself in its ecstatic unity with the retaining and ad-tending which are horizonally open towards the 'before' and 'after'.

This definition of time is nothing but an existenzial-ontological explication of the definition of time given by Aristotle: "For time is just this—number of motion in respect of 'before' and 'after'."[11]

Aristotle's definition of time is based on a 'natural' comprehension of Being. However, since for Heidegger this is just what is problematic, a full discussion of the Aristotelian analysis of time can be taken up only after the problem of Being is solved.

Aristotle's definition provides the basis for all later discussions of the concept of time. They all take time as it is manifested in circumspect concern, world-time as disclosed in the use of a clock and made up of a series of 'nows'—"now-time," as Heidegger calls it. In the natural attitude preoccupation is wholly taken up with its object. Its temporal aspect as such is not thematically grasped and is therefore taken as merely made up of now, then, at that time. For the vulgar comprehension time thus becomes the 'river of Time', a flow of simply given 'nows'. The time of concern, world-time, is characterized, as explained earlier, by datability and meaningfulness. But when, as in the vulgar interpretation, time is taken as pure succession, neither of these structures emerges into view. Both are covered up by the vulgar understanding of time and, in consequence, the ecstatic-horizonal constitution of temporality is lost sight of. The 'nows' are understood as if they were, like essents in general for the everyday understanding of Being, also simply given; those which are gone are taken as making up the past and those that are still to come as the future. "The vulgar interpretation of world-time as now-time lacks the horizon in which world, meaningfulness, and datability can be accessible to it." Ontologically, the idea of simple givenness as the fundamental mode of Being is the way the 'nows' are understood. In the succession of 'nows', even though particular 'nows' appear and vanish, the 'now' character is permanently present because the flow of the 'nows' is uninterrupted and without a gap. This is what Plato meant by calling time the image of eternity: "wherefore He planned to make a movable image of Eternity which abides in unity. He made an eternal image, moving according to number, even that which we have named time."[12] On the basis of this conception of time as made up of moments understood as ultimately indivisible *vorhanden* entities, attempts are then made to tackle the problem of the continuity of time. The spanned character of time, deriving from the horizonal extendedness of the ecstatic unity of temporality, remains hidden. The leveling and covering up of world-time, and hence of temporality in general, involved in the vulgar interpretation of time becomes compellingly obvious in its main thesis that time is endless, infinite. Once time is conceived as primarily a series of 'nows', it is clear that it must be 'endless on both sides', every 'now' being preceded by another without any ultimate first term and followed by another without a last term in the series. A thesis like this is possible only on the assumption of time as a free-floating course of *vorhanden* 'nows', real in itself.

This leveling of world-time and covering up of temporality has its origin in Dasein's being itself, in care. Thrown and forfeited Dasein is lost in the objects of its preoccupation, betraying through this a flight before its own authentic existenz, that is, from the disclosure of death in anticipative resoluteness. Dasein averts its eyes from the end of its being-in-the-world, a 'looking away from' which is itself a mode of the ecstatic futurity of its being toward the end. "The inauthentic temporality of forfeited, everyday Dasein must as such look away from the finitude of authentic futurity and in consequence misconceive temporality in general." And this self-forgetful conception of the 'infinity' of public time is further strengthened by the fact that the vulgar understanding of Dasein is governed by the anonymous 'they' and the way everyman interprets death. Unaware of the finitude of time, he takes the leveled up succession of 'nows' as if it had no relation to the temporality of the individual Dasein in its everyday being-together-with, from which it originates. Dasein knows only the public time which, as leveled off, belongs to everyman, that is, to no one in particular. But as in the case of death, which is in some way glimpsed even in evasion, this endless succession of 'nows', harmlessly running its course, carries with it, in its own mysterious way, a reminder of true temporality. We say, time passes away, but not that it arises, when, on the public view of time, we could with equal right say both. This shows that the temporality of world-time is not wholly shut off from man's view and that he is aware that time does not let itself be halted. Such awareness implies a desire for the halting of time which itself presupposes the presentating, forgetful ad-tending of inauthentic existenz. "Because Dasein, being ahead of itself, is tended towards the future, it is bound to understand the sequence of the 'nows', while ad-tending to it, as a slipping away and passing. Dasein knows the fugitive time in terms of the 'fugitive' knowledge of his death." The vulgar understanding, in its emphasis on the passing away of time, reflects the finite futurity of Dasein's temporality. The 'irreversibility' of time's flow, as vulgarly understood, shows that public time has its origin in temporality, "of which the temporalization, primarily futuristic, 'goes' to its end ecstatically in such a way that it 'is' already towards its end."

The vulgar conception of time as an endless, passing, irreversible sequence of 'nows'—which at the same time gives rise to the public view of history as an intratemporal happening—has its justification in the everyday mode of being of Dasein and forfeits its legitimacy only when it claims to be the ultimately true conception of time. Only on the basis of the temporality of Dasein is it possible to explain why and how world-time is implied in its temporalization and to expose the covering up and leveling that is inevitably involved in the vulgar conception. On the other hand, temporality itself is inaccessible within the horizon to which the vulgar conception is limited. A consideration of the latter, therefore, provides justification for the claim that temporality is time in the primordial sense. Ecstatic, horizonal temporality temporalizes itself in terms of the future, whereas the vulgar understanding comprehends it in terms of the 'now'. From this 'now', it is impossible to explain or derive the genuine present, the Moment, the genuine future or the genuine past as they arise from the primordial ecstatic unity of the temporalization of temporality.[13] Heidegger points out in a footnote that the traditional concept of eternity as *nunc stans* (the 'now' standing still) is evidently derived from the vulgar comprehension of time and of Being as permanent simple givenness.

Even though the vulgar experience of time is limited, for the most part, to world-time, it also gives to it a preeminent relationship to soul and Spirit. Hence, in principle even the interpretation of Dasein as temporality does not lie outside the horizon of the vulgar conception of time. Aristotle, for example, says, "But if nothing but soul, or in soul, reason, is qualified to count, there would not be time unless there were soul."[14] Similarly, Augustine declares, "Whence it seemed to me, that time is nothing else than protraction; but of what, I know not; and I marvel, if it be not of the mind itself?"[15] Hegel has even attempted expressly to establish a connection between spirit and time as commonly conceived. Kant thinks of time as 'subjective' but lets it stand, without any connection, by the side of the 'I think', though, as Heidegger proposes to show later, in another respect there emerges in Kant a deeper understanding of time than in Hegel.

[81]

Heidegger concludes his discussion of time by giving an account of Hegel's view of time and its relation with spirit. According to Hegel, history, which is essentially the history of spirit, unfolds itself within time. He seeks, not merely to lay it down as a fact, but to inquire into the conditions that make it possible for spirit to 'fall into time'.[16] By way of elucidating further the interpretation of Dasein as temporality through a comparison with Hegel's view, Heidegger first discusses Hegel's concept of time, which, as he says, represents the most radical conceptual expression of the vulgar understanding of time. He examines, next, the relation between time and spirit. The first explicit discussion of time in the history of Western philosophy, Heidegger points out, occurs in Aristotle's *Physics* in the context of an ontology of Nature, alongside an account of place and movement. Hegel's analysis of time also is carried out in the second part, entitled "the philosophy of Nature," of his *Encyclopaedia of the Philosophical Sciences*. The first section of this part deals with space and time, both of which are for Hegel "the abstract external-to-one-another." The treatment of space is followed by that of time because, for Hegel, space itself passes over into time, that is to say, when thought through dialectically in respect of what it *is*, it reveals time to be its own truth. Space, being the abstract multiplicity of points distinguishable in it, points which are themselves spatial in nature, is itself without any distinctions. Yet, insofar as the point distinguishes, Hegel calls it the negation of space, though a negation which itself remains in space. In this difference-less external-to-one-another of a manifold of points consists the 'punctuality' of space. "The negativity," Hegel goes on, "which, as point, relates itself to space and which develops in space its determinations as line and surface, is, however, just as much *for itself* in the sphere of being-external-to-itself and its determinations therein, though as positing in the sphere of being-external-to-itself it appears indifferent as regards the tranquil side-by-side (of 'punctuality'). As thus posited for itself, it is time."

Commenting on this sentence, in which Hegel thinks space in its truth as time, Heidegger explains that when space is merely represented, and so not yet grasped in its being, the negations are, as it were, simply given. But when it is subjected to thought, through thesis, antithesis and transmuting synthesis, and thus grasped in its being, these negations do not remain lying in their indifference but are transmuted, that is, are themselves negated. Through this negation the point posits itself *for itself* and emerges from its indifference, differentiating itself from others, no longer being this one and not yet that one. The punctuality of indifference is itself annulled and the points no longer lie side by side in 'paralysed restfulness'; the point asserts itself against other points. This negation of the negation (punctuality) is time, according to Hegel. The positing itself for itself of a point is a now–here, now–here, and so on. As posited for itself, every point *is* a now–point, for the 'now' is that *through* which any point can posit itself for itself and thus is the condition of the possibility of such positing. The being of the point as it is grasped in pure thought is thus time, the 'now', which itself is determined by Hegel as follows: "Time, as the negative unity of self–externality, is likewise something purely abstract, ideal. It is the being which, in that it is, is not, and which, in that it is not, is: it is intuited becoming." Becoming for Hegel is the passage from being to nothingness or from nothingness to being and in terms of time this is just what the 'now' is. Further, time is 'intuited' becoming, a passage that is not thought through but simply contemplated as a sequence of 'nows'. Hegel thus understands time in the vulgar sense, in terms of 'now', as something simply given and hence with the structure of the 'now' covered up and leveled. Heidegger points out that though Hegel occasionally speaks of time as "the abstraction of consuming," yet, if time is taken as intuited becoming, neither arising nor passing away can have any priority in time. Even while characterizing time as 'becoming', Hegel understands this becoming in an abstract sense so that, as Heidegger remarks, Hegel's view of time is most adequately expressed in his definition of it as "the negation of negation" (of punctuality, that is) in which the sequence of 'nows' is formalized and leveled to the last degree. This shows, Heidegger points out in an important footnote, how much Hegel's conception of time is based on the vulgar understanding of time, that is to say, on the traditional concept, deriving, in fact, directly from Aristotle's *Physics*. The section on time in Hegel's *Jena Logic* is virtually a paraphrase, Heidegger says, of Aristotle's treatise on Time, agreeing with the latter on such points of detail as the determination of time as 'now', its characterization as 'boundary', as 'points', as the 'absolute this', the view of time as cyclic. To be sure, the main thing in Aristotle, the exhibition of a fundamental connection between the 'now' and the other characteristics, eludes Hegel. Heidegger says further that Bergson's view of time, despite the difference in the way he establishes it, agrees with Hegel's thesis that space 'is' time; only Bergson reverses it into, "Time is space." Bergson is also, Heidegger points out, indebted to Aristotle in his view of time, as shown by the fact that his book on Time was published at the same time as a study on Aristotle entitled, *Quid Aristoteles de loco senserit*, discussing his account of time.

Coming to Hegel's interpretation of the relation between time and spirit, Heidegger asks in what sense spirit is understood when its actualization is said to fall into time defined as negation of negation. The essence of spirit is, for Hegel, the *concept*, understood not as an intuited universal, the form of something thought, but as the form of the very thinking which thinks itself, the conceiving of *itself as grasping the not-I*. And since grasping the not-I means distinguishing, the pure concept involves, as a grasping of this distinguishing, distinguishing the distinction. Spirit is thus for Hegel the negation of a negation, the absolute negativity. The concept is the self-conceiving conception (conceived-ness) of the self, which is how the self is authentically itself and free. The negating of the negation is at the same time the 'absolute unrest' of the spirit as well as the self-manifestation intrinsic to it. The progress of the spirit as actualizing itself in history carries with it a principle of exclusion, through which what is excluded is not just cut off from spirit but surmounted. Progress, therefore, is never merely quantitative but is essentially qualitative, conscious and aware of its goal (the attainment of its own concept), and in which at every step the spirit has to overcome itself as its own enemy and obstacle in a hard, unending battle against itself. Because this unrest of the spirit striving to reach its own concept is negation of the negation, it falls in time. As Hegel says, "Time is just the notion definitely existent, and presented to consciousness in the form of empty intuition. Hence spirit necessarily appears in time, and it appears in time so long as it does not grasp its pure notion, that is, so long as it does not annul time. Time is the pure self in external form, apprehended in intuition, and not grasped and understood by the self, it is the notion apprehended only through intuition."[17]

Drawing attention to the inadequacy of Hegel's view, Heidegger points out that he demonstrates the possibility of the historical actualization of spirit in time by going back to the identity of the formal structure of spirit and time as negation of negation, that is, by reducing them both to empty abstractions. Since time is conceived by Hegel as utterly leveled world-time, its origin remains completely hidden and it is left as something *vorhanden* standing over against spirit. For this reason, first and foremost, spirit has to fall 'into time', though what this 'falling' and 'actualization' of spirit, in reality existing outside time, ontologically signifies, is left obscure by Hegel. Hegel neither explains the origin of the leveled off time nor does he examine whether the essential constitution of spirit as negation of negation is at all possible except on the basis of primordial temporality. Without entering into the ontological tenability of Hegel's view of time and spirit at this stage, Heidegger says that his very attempt to 'construct' a relationship between the two suggests such a deep-lying kinship. Hegel's 'construction' was prompted, according to Heidegger, by his struggles to conceive the spirit in its concreteness, as the following sentence from the last chapter of *The Phenomenology of Mind* shows: "Time therefore appears as spirit's destiny and necessity, where spirit is not yet complete within itself; it is the necessity compelling spirit to enrich the share self-consciousness has in consciousness, to put into motion the immediacy of the inherent nature (which is the form in which the substance is present in consciousness); or, conversely, to realize and make manifest what is inherent, regarded as inward and immanent, to make manifest that which is at first within—that is, to vindicate it for spirit's certainty of self."[18] Heidegger's own existenzial analytic of Dasein, on the contrary, starts, as he remarks, with the 'concrete', factually thrown existenz itself and goes on to show how temporality constitutes the primordial condition of its possibility. 'Spirit' does not have to fall in time, for it *exists* fundamentally as the temporalization of temporality; the latter temporalizes world-time, within the horizon of which history can 'appear' as intratemporal happening. 'Spirit' does not, Heidegger says, fall into time; it is rather the factual existenz that, as forfeited, falls *out* of the primordial authentic temporality, a 'falling' which is itself a mode of temporalization.[19]

[82]

The preparatory existenzial analytic of Dasein in division one (sections 9–44) exhibited Care as the being of Dasein and, in division two (sections 45–82), Care itself has been shown to be ontologically grounded in temporality. This exposition of the ontological constitution of Dasein, Heidegger points out in conclusion, is only *one way* that might lead to what is the basic aim of the inquiry, the working out of the question of Being, and a way which, if it leads to this goal, must be thematically traversed again in the light of the clarified idea of Being. As universal phenomenological ontology, philosophy cannot rest content with the distinction, yielded by the analytic of Dasein, between the being of Dasein and that of nonhuman entities. Neither the domination of classical ontology by thing-concepts, nor the ever-recurring tendency towards reification of consciousness, nor the distinction, valuable in itself, between consciousness and thing, can be adequately explained so long as the *question* of the meaning of Being remains unformulated and unclarified. It is impossible, Heidegger asserts, to inquire into the origin and possibility of the 'idea' of Being in general by means of the 'abstractions' of formal logic, without securing first an adequate horizon in which the question may be raised and an answer attempted. The essential thing is "to seek a *way* for the elucidation of the fundamental ontological question and to *follow* it. Whether this is the *only* way, or at all the *right* one, can be decided only *after one has travelled along it*. The dispute regarding the interpretation of Being cannot be composed, for *it has not yet been even enkindled*." Such enkindling must first be prepared for, and the investigation conducted in *Being and Time* is on the way to that. As so far carried out, the investigation stands at the point where something like 'Being' has been disclosed, in a preliminary and nonconceptual way, in the understanding of

Being which is part of the understanding implied in Dasein's existenz. How, Heidegger asks, is this understanding that discloses Being at all possible for Dasein? Is it possible to answer this question by going back, as has been attempted here, to the basic ontological constitution of man, who has such understanding of Being? Is it possible to make a project of Being on the basis of a primordial mode of the temporalization of temporality? "Is there a way leading from primordial Time to the sense of Being? Does Time itself reveal itself as the horizon of Being?"

[83]

On this note of interrogation, this openness to further questioning, *Being and Time* comes to a close.[20] More correctly, it breaks off at this point, before the completion of even Part One of the work as planned originally. The third division of this part, it may be recalled, was to deal with "Time and Being" and thus bring the first part to a conclusion. This, however, could not be done, for reasons explained in the next chapter (in the section entitled "The Reversal of Thought and the *Letter on Humanism*"). This failure was due, as we shall see, to the gradual emergence of a deeper, newer insight into the nature of his own questioning. This required a reformulation, in language and approach more adequate to the new insight, of the questioning (*Fragestellung*) of *Being and Time*, and then dealing with the topic of the third division from this perspective. This last task was accomplished, after over thirty years of unceasing work devoted to the former, in Heidegger's lecture "Time and Being" (published 1968). Explaining the connection between the original plan and its eventual execution Heidegger remarks, "At that time the author was not equal to the task of adequately working out the theme named in the title 'Time and Being'. The publication of *Being and Time* was broken off at this point. What is contained in the text of this lecture, composed now three and a half decades later, can no longer be tacked on to the text of *Being and Time*. The leading question, nevertheless, has remained the same, which only means, however, that the question has become even more question-worthy, and even more alien to the spirit of the age."[21]

Notes

1. The notion of *Geschick*, momentous in Heidegger's later thinking is attached in that phase, to Being. See the following definition (*Vorträge und Aufsätze*, p. 32): "To dispatch, or give a start to, someone—this is called in our language, *schicken* (sending forth). That comprehensive "sending forth" which first of all brings man on a path of disclosure we call the *Geschick*. It is in terms of this that the nature of all history (*Geschichte*) is determined. The latter is neither only the object of history (*Historie*) nor is it merely brought about through the doings of man." See also *Der Satz vom Grund*, passim.

2. "A tradition," Heidegger says elsewhere (*Der Satz vom Grund*, p. 171), "when petrified, can degenerate into a burden and a hindrance. This is possible just because tradition in the proper sense, as the word *Überlieferung* suggests, is a delivering (*liefern*) in the sense of *liberare*, deliverance. As liberating, tradition brings hidden treasures from the 'has been' into the light, even though this light may at first be only that of a hesitant dawn."

3. Historicity is inherent in Dasein's existenz or, in Heidegger's later language, in his ek-sistenz in the clearing (*Lichtung*), the dispensation (*Geschick*) of Being, which is the real source of all historicity. "As ek-sisting he stands in the destiny (*Geschick*) of Being. The ek-sistenz of men is as ek-sistenz historical, not primarily and merely because all sorts of things take place in the course of time with man and his affairs. Because our concern is with the ek-sistenz of *Da-sein*, therefore so much emphasis was placed on a realization of the historicity of Dasein in *Being and Time*." ("Brief über den 'Humanismus'," *Wegmarken*, p. 167.)

4. See *Einführung in die Metaphysik*, p. 33 (E.T., p. 36): "Historical science, as science, in no way determines man's fundamental relationship to history, but always presupposes such a relationship. For this reason alone man's relationship to history, a relationship which is itself always a historical one, can either be distorted, misinterpreted, and degraded into mere antiquarian information by historical science or, on the other hand, the latter may open up important fields of vision for the already established relationship to history. A historical relationship of our historical existence to history may become an object, and represent a cultivated state, of knowledge; but it need not be so necessarily. Moreover, all our historical relationships cannot be scientifically objectified and 'neutralized', especially the essential ones. Historical science can *never create* the historical relationship to history but only illuminate a relationship once set up and ground it in an informed way . . ."

5. As Heidegger remarks in the language of the later phase ("Brief über den 'Humanismus'," *Wegmarken*, p. 148), "Admittedly, we think of our words 'possible' and 'possibility', under the domination of 'logic' and 'metaphysics', only in contrast with 'reality' or actuality, that is, in terms of a specific—the metaphysical—interpretation of Being as *actus* and *potentia*, which distinction is identified with that between *existentia* and *essentia*. When I speak of the 'silent power of the possible', I do not mean the possible of a merely imagined *possibilitas*, not the *potentia*, as the *essentia* of an *actus* of *existentia*, but Being itself which inclines toward (*mögend*) and has power over thinking and so over the nature of men, that is, over his relationship to

Being. To have influence or power over something (*vermögen*) means here to guard it in its nature, to keep it within its element."

See also *Hölderlin*, p. 107; *Nietzsche I*, p. 393; *Vorträge und Aufsätze*, p. 98, where Heidegger speaks of "guarding the mystery of Being and keeping watch over the inviolability of the possible." As a critic has remarked, the principle that "higher than actuality, stands possibility" (quoted in chapter 1 above) pervades Heidegger's work from beginning to end. Cf. W. Müller-Lauter, *Möglichkeit und Wirklichkeit bei Martin Heidegger*, p. 1, a work in which Heidegger's thinking has been assessed (adversely) in terms of the problem of modality.

6. The paragraph from which the above lines are quoted is characterized by Thomas Langan as "a paragraph that may well become a classic in the philosophy of history." Cf. *The Meaning of Heidegger*, p. 62.

7. As Heidegger was to express it later (*Holzwege*, p. 301), "History (historical science) always figures out what is coming in terms of the images of the past as they are colored by the present. History ceaselessly annihilates the future and the historical relationship to the arrival of destiny."

8. *Briefwechsel zwischen Wilhelm Dilthey und dem Grafen Paul Yorck v. Wartenburg 1877-1897*. With the publication of *Bewusstseinstellung und Geschichte*, 1956, edited by I. Fetscher from the philosophical remains of Count Yorck, the latter's views have become available in a more systematic and comprehensive form. For Gadamer's estimate of this work as accomplishing something (throwing a bridge across the gulf that divides speculative Idealism and the empirical standpoint of the century) which neither Dilthey nor Husserl could do, see *Wahrheit und Methode*, p. 237f.

9. In his "Introduction" to vol. 5 of Dilthey's collected works. See also *Lebensphilosophie und Phänomenologie* (1930).

10. In his later phase, Heidegger seeks to explain history (*Geschichte*) in terms of Being, making it virtually identical with Being itself. The usual conception of historicity is based on the metaphysical interpretation of essents as such, he asserts, and history as Being remains unthought. The historicity of history still remains hidden because the objectivization of all essents characteristic of modern subjectivity necessarily excludes the unobjectifiable happening character of what *is* as such. As Heidegger puts it (*Nietzsche II*, p. 388), "What is, is what happens. What happens is what has already happened. This does not mean that it is past and gone. What has happened is alone that which has gathered itself together into the essence of Being as the has-been, from which and as which, is the coming of Being itself—even though it be in the form of a withdrawal and a staying away. . . . What happens is the history of Being, Being as the history of this staying away."

11. Aristotle, *Physics* IV 11, 219b 1f.

12. *Timaeus* 37d; trans. R. G. Bury.

13. For the Moment, see *Nietzsche I*, pp. 311, 356, 398f. and 438-447—passages which throw light on both Nietzsche's doctrine of the Eternal Return and Heidegger's conception of primordial time. See also Walter F. Otto's remarkable essay, "Die Zeit und das Sein" (Time and

Being) in *Anteile-Martin Heidegger zum 60. Geburtstag*. In the true present, things are revealed to us in their depths, so that, as Otto says, what is truly present is always something that we experience as looking at us, as holding us in its gaze. To gaze upon the mortals is an inherent character of the gods (as both Heidegger and Otto remark) and hence the true present not only embodies the fullness of time but also the presence of a divinity glancing at us. Otto's discussion thus throws some light on Heidegger's cryptic statements about the gods and their mode of being in his account of the World quadrate. See chapter 9.

14. *Physica*, trans. Ross, IV. 14, 223a, 25.

15. *Confessions*, XI, 26. Everyman edition, p. 271.

16. *Die Vernunft in der Geschichte*, ed. Hoffmeister, p. 153.

17. *The Phenomenology of Mind*, trans. J. B. Baillie, p. 800.

18. Ibid.

19. See the last chapter for Heidegger's later reflections on time.

20. This note of interrogation, it should be noted, is not just rhetorical. It reflects rather the unremitting stance of Heidegger as a thinker towards what is questionable and question-worthy, towards what has already been thought and what is still to be thought, towards the path he has taken so far—right from the initial opening of the question—and the path still to be cleared and followed. What has already been thought by himself also becomes forthwith something questionable, including the manner in which he has posed his question, though the matter (*Sache*) in question always remains question-worthy. Even his own completed lifework has become for Heidegger something to be questioned, as is shown by his frequent references to his own thought in the third person (for example, in Martin Heidegger and Eugen Fink's, *Heraklit*) and by the questions he proposed, as his own small contribution, for a symposium on his philosophy at Duquesne University in 1966 (see Heidegger's "Letter" in John Sallis, *Heidegger and the Path of Thinking*). The questions he submitted for consideration regarding *Being and Time* were: "Has the question posed in *Being and Time* regarding the 'meaning of Being' (as Being) been at all taken up as a question? If so, in what manner has the question been discussed, and in which respects? Have critics ever asked whether the question posed is possible or impossible? What consequences do the answers to the above questions have for the characterization of the relation in which Heidegger's thinking stands to the tradition of Western philosophy? Where do the limits of the question posed (including the way of posing it) in *Being and Time* lie?"

21. *Zur Sache des Denkens*, p. 91 (E.T., p. 83).

III
The Roots of
Metaphysical Thinking

8
Early Essays and the "Reversal"

Being and Time had as its objective the reopening and elaboration of the question of Being. This involved, as the plan was initially conceived by Heidegger, a double task: first, that of giving a temporal interpretation of Dasein and the explication of Time as the transcendental horizon of the question about Being and second, the working out of the main features of a phenomenological destruction of the history of ontology in the light of temporality. The published part of *Being and Time*, of which an account has been given above, contains only the preparatory fundamental analysis of Dasein, followed by an account of Dasein and temporality, but without the promised third division of Part One on "Time and Being" in which the inquiry was to proceed in the reverse direction. In the "Letter on Humanism," Heidegger refers to this 'reversal' (*Kehre*) of the approach from Being and Time to Time and Being as an essential part of the spiralling inquiry into Being and explains why the part dealing with it was withheld from publication along with the rest of the first part of *Being and Time*. As he there says, "Here the whole thing undergoes a reversal. The division in question was withheld because thought failed in giving adequate utterance to this reversal and did not come through with the help of the language of metaphysics. The lecture, "On the Nature of Truth," thought out and communicated in 1930 but printed only in 1943, gives a certain glimpse into the thinking of the reversal from *Being and Time* to *Time and Being*."[1] What this reversal means and what implications it had for the development of Heidegger's thought in its second phase as he has explained it in the "Letter on Humanism," we shall consider below. The second part of *Being and Time* containing the 'destruction' was never published, also perhaps because of the change of perspective and approach which occurred in Heidegger's thinking in connection with the 'reversal'. A beginning in this direction, however, was made with the publication in 1929 of *Kant and the Problem of Metaphysics*, and in his later writings Heidegger has constantly returned to this historical destruction, discussing for this purpose the great figures in the history of Western philosophy from the Pre-Socratics to Nietzsche. This aspect of Heidegger's thought will be dealt with in the next chapter. Soon after the publication of *Being and Time*, there appeared Heidegger's much discussed inaugural lecture, "What is Metaphysics?" and, in the same year (1929) an essay, "On the Nature of Ground." Another essay, entitled "On the Nature of Truth," was also conceived in this period and made public in the form of lectures, though not published, after repeated revision, until 1943. These essays give some idea of the way Heidegger sought to approach the problem of Being in the first phase of his thought, and exhibit both the unity and the integral character of his thinking as well as its inner dynamism and mobility. Because of their intrinsic importance and also because they prepare the way for the development of Heidegger's thought in the second phase, a brief account of these is first given here.[2]

A lecture, "Phenomenology and Theology," delivered in 1927 but not published until 1970, is valuable for the light it throws on Heidegger's conception of philosophy and theology as sciences, one ontological and the other positive, but it contributes little to the central question of Being.

The Early Essays

"What is Metaphysics?" is concerned not with expounding any thesis about metaphysics but with the unfoldment, elaboration, and solution of a metaphysical problem—the problem of Transcendence which is here taken as being identical with the problem of Nothingness. The various sciences, Heidegger begins by pointing out, are engaged in investigating the different fields of essents; the pursuit of science means that a particular essent, man, breaks into the totality of what is in such a manner that essents manifest themselves as and how they are, becoming, through the in-break of science, *what* they are. But in its mode of relationship, its attitude and in the way of its breaking into, science is concerned solely with what is, the essent, and nothing beyond it. Science has no use for this nothing beyond what is and turns away from this Nothing as from "a horror and a phantasm."[3] What, Heidegger asks, is this Nothing beyond essents? To define Nothingness is impossible, for that would be to treat it as itself an essent. Nor can it be derived from negation, a form of logical judgment, for negation presupposes the Nothing which is "more fundamental than the 'not' and negation." Despite the formal impossibility of an inquiry into Nothingness, however, we may still attempt, Heidegger asserts, to determine whether it is at all 'given' in experience and how it is encountered and recognized as such on the basis of a preconceptual familiarity with it implied in our everyday use of 'is not'. Nothingness is the complete negation of the totality of essents not merely in the formal sense of negating in imagination the idea of such totality, but in reality. This totality, though never cognitively in our grasp, is what we find ourselves placed in the midst of and of which we always have some awareness. The totality of what is, is disclosed in our moods and feelings and among these the attunement of anxiety is distinctive in that it brings us face to face with Nothing itself. This is an event in Dasein which, though rare and fleeting, is of fundamental importance (being the ontic manifestation of what, in the ontological sense is always implicitly there), for it transforms man into his *Da-sein*. Anxiety reveals the Nothing, not as an essent, not as an object, not as something detached from the totality of essents, but as at one with this totality as it slips away from us. The encounter with Nothingness in anxiety does not mean that the totality of essents is either annihilated or negated in judgment. The essence of the Nothing consists rather in a total relegation to the vanishing totality of essents—Nothingness repels Dasein, referring it back to the totality as it slips away (*abweisende Verweisung*). This is a nihilation which discloses the totality for the first time in its sheer otherness to Nothing. "The essence of the primordially nihilating Nothing lies in the fact that it alone brings Dasein face to face with what is as such," for the primordial disclosure of Nothingness alone renders possible the revelation of beings. To be *Da-sein* means to be suspended and held within Nothingness and this means being beyond, transcending, the totality of essents, a transcendence which alone renders self-hood and freedom also possible. This Nothing is not an entity but an event, a nihilating which occurs in the Being of beings.[4] Because mostly we are lost in essents and held fast to them, we are ordinarily not aware of Nothing which yet unceasingly nihilates, manifesting itself in the guise of judgments of negation. This, however, is neither the sole nor even the chief mode of nihilation manifesting itself in Dasein—the harshness of opposition and the violence of loathing, the pain of refusal, the mercilessness of an interdict and the bitterness of renunciation are more abysmal and oppressive, as Heidegger says, than the mere adequacy of rational negation. Dasein's suspension in Nothingness makes man the stand-in (*Platzhalter*) for Nothing and at the same time constitutes his transcendence, his metaphysical character, by virtue of which Dasein goes beyond what is, the totality of essents. Classical metaphysics as well as Christian dogma had their own conception of the Nothing, each implying a view of Being, according to which Nothing was the conceptual opposite of what truly is, that is, its negation. According to Heidegger's analysis, Nothing ceases to be the vague opposite of what is and reveals itself as integral to the Being of essents. Being and Nothing belong together, not because they are at one in their indeterminateness and immediacy, as Hegel thought, but because Being itself is essentially finite and reveals itself only in the transcendence of Dasein suspended in Nothingness.[5]

The problem of Nothing thus embraces the whole of metaphysics as concerned with the question of Being, at the same time forcing us to face the problem of the origin of negation, that is, to a decision as to the legitimacy of the rule of 'logic' in metaphysics. Science itself, it has been shown, is rendered possible as the investigation of essents by the overtness of Nothing, that is, by Dasein's going beyond essents in their totality. Because Nothing manifests itself in the very depths of man, he is struck with wonder that things are and how and why they are, and so gives birth to science. Philosophizing itself is possible only as a leap that launches us into the Nothingness which sets us free from the idols we all carry with us and to which we all cling, making us return again and again to the fundamental question of metaphysics: "Why are there essents at all, rather than Nothing?"[6]

In *Kant and the Problem of Metaphysics* also, Heidegger speaks of Nothingness as the transcendental horizon of the disclosure of essents in the course of his discussion of the Transcendental Deduction: it is the projection into Nothing, which is not to be conceived as a *nihil absolutum*, that constitutes the transcendental condition of the possibility of objects in general.[7] The transcendental, nonempirical object or X of which Kant speaks is not an essent and yet a 'something', that is, according to Heidegger, Nothing conceived as pure horizon within which essents can appear and be known.[8] Heidegger explicitly states that anxiety and Nothingness are discussed by him solely with a view to elucidating the possibility of an understanding of Being, adding that "the Being of beings can at all be understood only if in the roots of its nature Dasein holds itself suspended in Nothingness—therein lies the deepest finitude of transcendence."[9]

"What is Metaphysics?" formulates a solution of the problem of transcendence, showing how going beyond the essent occurs in the very essence of Dasein, and concludes that this going beyond is metaphysics itself. But, as Heidegger says in the postscript, the main question—what is metaphysics?—remains unanswered because the question itself goes beyond metaphysics in the traditional sense, arising as it does from a thinking which is already on the way to an overcoming of metaphysics but which is compelled, by the very nature of the case, to speak the language of what it seeks to overcome. Traditional metaphysics is concerned with the truth about essents and seeks to determine what essents are by way of conceptualizing the beingness (*Seiendheit*) of what is. It inquires into the truth about beings in the light of the truth of Being, which is the ground on which it functions and which provides the horizon within which it moves, but which remains unknown and unfathomable to itself. To ask, "what is metaphysics?" insofar as it involves asking what its own ground is, is thus already to rise beyond metaphysics, while yet remaining partly caught up in it.

Closely linked with this implicit motivation (that is, a realization of the questionability of metaphysics) behind the lecture is the attack against the primacy of logic in metaphysics, for its helplessness in face of the problem of Nothing. As Heidegger suggests in the postscript, the thinking of Being—"essential thinking," as not only concerned with Being but as itself an occurrence of Being—which only follows the thinking whose forms and rules constitute 'logic' cannot remain faithful to the law of its own truth. " 'Logic' is only *one* of the possible explications of the nature of thinking and one which, as its name shows, is based on the experience of Being as attained in Greek thought. The suspicion cast upon 'logic' . . . arises from a knowledge of that thinking which has its source not in the observation of the objectivity of essents but in the experience of the truth of Being." The exactest thinking, Heidegger adds, is never the most stringent thinking, for the former merely subserves the reckoning of and with essents, whereas the latter seeks strenuously to keep in view the essential nature of its subject matter.[10] As against such 'calculative thought', the thinking that is primarily determined by what is the other to essents is called by Heidegger 'essential thinking'.

Written in the same year as "What is Metaphysics?" the essay "On the Nature of Ground" ("Vom Wesen des Grundes") discusses the problem of *arche* and tries to show how the metaphysical quest for an ultimate ground of things—and the scientific quest for the causes of things—springs from the very nature of Dasein's existenz as constituted by Transcendence. The concept of *arche* or Ground is a central concept of metaphysics and its analysis goes back to the *Metaphysics* of Aristotle, 1013a-1014a, where three types of ground are distinguished, namely, the ground of the 'what', of the 'that', and of the truth of anything. The principle of ground or sufficient reason as enunciated by Leibniz (*nihil est sine ratione*, there is nothing without a reason or ground), Heidegger points out, does not throw any light on what ground itself is; in its positive formulation (*omne ens habet rationem*), it speaks of the essent, saying that everything that is must have a ground but says nothing about the nature of ground as such. Leibniz's discussion of the origin of this principle (in *Primae veritates*) makes it evident, however, that propositional truth always needs 'grounding' and shows how the concept of truth is intrinsically linked up with that of ground. A consideration of truth in the ontic sense (the pre-predicative manifestness of essents, in which propositional truth is rooted) as well as in the ontological (the overtness of Being which renders ontic truth itself possible) shows the same inner connection and suggests, further, that basic to both truth and ground is Dasein's transcendence, which alone renders these possible. Ontic truth and ontological truth are concerned, Heidegger says, with the essent in its Being and with the Being of essents, respectively. "They are intrinsically bound up with each other because of their relationship with the distinction between Being and beings (Ontological Difference). Along with the emergence of this distinction, and based on it, there appears truth in this bifurcated form." Since Dasein, with the comprehension of Being inherent in it, relates itself to essents, the ability to make this distinction (that is, the factual occurrence of the Ontological Difference) must be grounded in an essential character of Dasein.[11] This ground, Heidegger says, lies in its transcendence and it is, therefore, in the domain of transcendence that an elucidation of the nature of ground or *arche* must be sought. As existenz, Dasein is inherently transcending, going beyond the essent as such, beyond everything that is, including itself. "With the fact of *Da-sein* this rising up beyond is already there," as Heidegger says. That *towards* which the transcendence occurs is the world, which is itself no essent but a constitutive element in the structure of transcendence (for which reason the world-concept must be regarded as a transcendental one). Dasein's transcendence is thus constituted by its being-in-the-world, not in the sense that it factually exists in the world but in the sense that its very existence as Dasein depends upon its being ontologically constituted as being-in-the-world. Dasein's existenz as transcending renders it possible that essents should manifest themselves by "entering into a world." "Only when in the totality of essents one essent emerges as Dasein, there comes the hour and the day of the essent's entry into a world (*Welteingang*). Only with this primordial occurrence of transcendence, when an essent of the nature of being-in-the-world breaks into the totality of essents, there arises the possibility of essents manifesting themselves."

It is in the context of Dasein's transcendence as being-in-the-world that Heidegger now proceeds to elucidate the nature of ground. As an existenzial, the world is the totality of the 'for the sake of' (*Umwillen*, the *hou heneka* of Aristotle) or the ends of Dasein. In willing these ends, that is, in projecting himself on possibilities of his own self, man goes beyond himself, thereby becoming a self. The willing, however, which projects forward this 'for the sake of' and is its basis, is not an act of will in the usual sense, for all such acts themselves presuppose transcendence. As the primary projection of the 'for the sake of' it is freedom itself. When, in consequence of transcendence, freedom holds projected before it, as its correlate, the 'for the sake of', there comes about world—"the world dispenses itself and 'worlds' (*weltet*)." Freedom is thus the ground of the world, in a transcendental sense.

This interpretation of freedom as based on transcendence, Heidegger points out, goes deeper than the Kantian determination of freedom as spontaneity (in the sense of causing itself), for freedom is not just one sort of ground but the source of ground in general. "Freedom is freedom in relation to ground," a relation which Heidegger calls grounding. Rooted in the freedom of transcendence, grounding manifests itself in three modes: instituting or founding (*Stiften*); providing a basis or rooting (*Boden-nehmen*); establishing or justifying (*Be-gründen*). Grounding in the first sense is the projection of the 'for the sake of', the free, transcendental act of letting a world dispense itself, the world-project (*Weltentwurf*). But man's reaching up beyond in the project of a world implies, at the same time, finding himself in the midst of essents, attuned to them and wrapped up in them (*Eingenommenheit vom Seienden*). By virtue of being taken up with essents, Dasein secures a ground to stand upon, becomes rooted in essents. This is grounding in the second sense. Establishing himself in the midst of essents, man thus sets up a world, projecting possibilities of his own self. Thirdly, Dasein relates itself to essents (the 'intentionality' of Dasein), not being merely in the midst of them or in a world. Grounding in the above two senses renders such intentionality possible, giving rise, at the same time, to grounding as establishing or justifying. Grounding in this sense is necessarily bound up with the manifestness of essents as its transcendental condition and it renders ontic truth possible. With such grounding there comes into being the problem of 'why?' But the transcendental possibility of the 'why?' lies in the fact that all why-asking presupposes a preconceptual comprehension of Being (what, how, that, and not) without which no 'why?' would be possible. This primary comprehension of Being, therefore, "contains the first and last primordial answer for all questioning" and constitutes thus the ultimate grounding (as establishing or justification). This is transcendental grounding in the sense of ontological truth, for it lays bare the ontological constitution of what is. And because ontic truth (manifestness of essents as and how they are) is based on ontological truth, all disclosure and discovery of essents must in its way be concerned with grounding, must seek to find out causes, to prove and validate itself. Grounding, as manifested in the three senses of Ground, namely, possibility (projection of world), basis or fundament (being taken up with essents), and justification (ontological grounding of essents), has thus its origin in Dasein's transcendence, that is, in the finite threefold freedom to ground (corresponding to the three modes of grounding); it alone renders possible, in its unity, that whole—essents in their totality—within which Dasein can exist. As to the question whether the three modes of grounding have any common feature which links them together in a basic unity, Heidegger only throws out a hint here that each of these, in its own way, springs from the concern (*Sorge*) for perdurability and continuance, which in turn is possible only as temporality.[12]

The principle of ground or sufficient reason says that every essent has its ground. The above account of the nature of ground explains why this is so.[13] Because of the prior comprehension of Being already present in all our dealings with essents, Being is, to start with, of the nature of grounding.

"Because 'ground' is an essential transcendental feature of Being in general, therefore the principle of sufficient reason applies to essents. And ground is implied in the nature of Being because Being (not beings) is there only for a transcendence," a transcendence that is triply grounding in the above manner. Freedom, finite because in projecting certain possibilities it deprives itself of others, is thus the source of the principle of ground. "Freedom is the ground of Ground," not as itself one of the modes distinguished above but as their transcendental unity. In this sense, however, this ground is the abyss (Ab-grund) of Dasein; in projecting world, man rises up beyond essents and beyond himself and through such rising up knows himself as this abyss, finite in his thrownness and in his world-project, finite in his transcendence and in his freedom to ground, finite and, therefore, a being that goes into remote distances (ein Wesen der Ferne), for "only through such primeval moving beyond to the distant, which he accomplishes in transcending all that is, can he achieve the true nearness to things."

In all the writings of the first phase, Heidegger seeks to approach the problem of Being through the comprehension of Being inherent in Dasein, through an analysis of man's capacity to go beyond himself and beyond essents as such. The problem of transcendence is thus central to this approach. Being and Time, as Heidegger points out in "Vom Wesen des Grundes," has no other aim than to offer a concrete demonstration of a project of transcendence with a view to the attainment of the 'transcendental horizon of the inquiry into Being', the preparation of the ground on which the problem of Being may be raised.[14] An elucidation of the nature of transcendence was attempted there in order to win a horizon within which the concept of Being could be philosophically grounded and ontologically interpreted. "Was ist Metaphysik?" approaches the problem of transcendence by way of an inquiry into Nothingness understood as the other to what is. In "Vom Wesen des Grundes" also the nature of ground is discussed, much more explicitly, in terms of transcendence, for as Heidegger says there, "It is only through transcendence that the essent as essent can come to light and it constitutes, therefore, a preeminent domain for the discussion of all problems concerning the

Being of essents." This essay does not merely discuss the nature of ground in the context of transcendence but also aims, through this discussion, at elucidating the nature of transcendence itself.[15]

Heidegger defines transcendence as the ground of the Ontological Difference; it is by virtue of his transcendence that man can distinguish between Being and beings and so relate himself to essents in the light of his comprehension of Being. In transcendence, Dasein goes out beyond all essents as such, including itself, reaching up to world, which is part of the structure of transcendence, of Dasein's being-in-the-world, itself. In order to clarify further the conception of transcendence, Heidegger enters into a discussion of the concept of world.[16] Further, transcendence is dealt with here as the basis of the freedom through which Dasein's project of the world is rendered possible. As manifesting itself in freedom, Dasein's transcendence is the source of the threefold grounding. Man, as thrown, establishes himself in the midst of essents, at the same time setting up a world through the limited projection of his possibilities—both by virtue of his transcendence, which also renders possible the intentionality of his relationship with essents. Transcendence conceived as the source of the threefold grounding is thus what being-in-the-world means.

In *Kant und das Problem der Metaphysik*, Heidegger is naturally very much concerned with the problem of transcendence. The central problem of the *Critique of Pure Reason* is the problem of the possibility of ontological knowledge: How can finite human Dasein go beyond what is, transcending the essent which it has not only not itself created but on which it is dependent for its very existence as Dasein? This is the problem of the nature and basis of the transcendence involved in the prior comprehension of Being within Dasein. Essents can present themselves to Dasein only if it is already capable of this preontological comprehension of Being and is 'turned towards' and open to what may confront it. This primary 'turning towards' and 'letting things confront' it, which alone can bring into being a horizon, an area of freeplay (*Spielraum*) for essents to manifest themselves in, constitutes the transcendence of Dasein. Such transcendence is called by Heidegger Dasein's "holding itself suspended in Nothingness," for the 'object in general' of the a priori 'turning towards' is no essent but a Nothing (that is, Being itself as the other to 'what is'). The main purpose of the Transcendental Deduction, in both its forms, is thus, according to Heidegger, to demonstrate the possibility of transcendence, a transcendence which is essentially finite in character, and to elucidate its complex structure as constituted by pure understanding and pure intuition, with the synthesis of the pure imagination playing the dominant mediating role. The pure imagination or 'transcendental Schematism' in fact constitutes, according to Heidegger, the basis and indeed the very essence of the finitude of Dasein's transcendence. And since the Schematism, as Heidegger interprets Kant, necessarily operates with pure images of Time, it is temporality that ultimately renders transcendence possible, as *Being and Time* seeks to demonstrate. Kant's highest principle of all synthetic judgments, that "the conditions of the *possibility of experience* in general are likewise conditions of the *possibility of the objects of experience*," expresses, according to Heidegger, the basic unity of the full structure of transcendence or ontological knowledge. This consists, not in the knowledge of essents, but in the prior projection of a horizon (the X or object in general; the Nothing, as Heidegger calls it) within which essents may be encountered in the light of an a priori project of their Being. In place of the traditional "proud name of an ontology" which presumes to supply a priori synthetic knowledge of things in general, Kant substitutes a 'transcendental' philosophy which is content to investigate the nature of man's finite transcendence, that is, of the subjectivity of the human subject in all his finitude. This is also Heidegger's aim in his first 'fundamental ontological' phase, though with the explicitly recognized objective of reawakening the problem of Being and of conceptualizing the nature of Being as it enters into man's preontological comprehension by virtue of his transcendence.

"On the Nature of Truth" ("Vom Wesen der Wahrheit") marks a significant advance in Heidegger's thinking and points forward to the second phase of his thought after the reversal (*Kehre*). It will, therefore, be appropriate to deal with it here briefly. In *Being and Time*, the relevance of the notion of truth to the problem of Being was barely hinted at; "Vom

Wesen des Grundes" made it more explicit how the problem of truth was closely involved in any discussion of transcendence, ground, and Being. The present essay, dealing with truth not merely from the point of view of Dasein's overtness, his discovering character and the discoveredness of essents, but with truth in its own essence, leads, through the compulsion of its own inner logic, from the metaphysical view of truth as concerned with essents as a whole to a deeper conception of truth as an occurrence in Being itself, from the truth of essents in their totality to the truth of Being.[17]

Heidegger begins with an examination of the conventional view of truth as agreement or correspondence. Whether truth is understood as the truth of things (*Sachwahrheit*), in which a thing really is what it is taken to be, or as propositional truth (*Satzwahrheit*) based on the former, in both senses it means agreement or correctness—*veritas est adaequatio rei et intellectus*. According to the medieval theological conception, the truth of (created) things consists in their conformity with an idea in the divine intellect and therefore the truth of the thoughts and propositions of the human intellect, that is, their conformity with things, has its ultimate sanction in the divine intellect. In later philosophy the Creator is replaced by Reason but the basic conception remains the same, giving rise to the impression that the determination of the nature of truth has nothing to do with the problem of Being. This way of conceiving the nature of truth is taken for granted and the nature of untruth, failure to agree, is simply dismissed as falling outside truth in its essence, for untruth is the very opposite of truth. When, however, propositional truth is understood, in the Greek sense, as the correspondence (*homoiosis*) of a statement (*logos*) with a thing (*pragma*), the question arises as to the inner possibility of such correspondence. In order that a proposition should correspond with a thing or state of affairs, the two should be in some respect similar, as these two are not. The possibility of comparing them must therefore be sought in the way a proposition is 'about' the thing. The proposition is related to the thing by way of representation, it represents (*Vor-stellen*, literally placing in front of, presenting) the thing *so as* it is. "The representative statement speaks of the thing represented, stating it to be *such as* it is. This 'such—as'

(*so—wie*) applies to the representation and what it represents."
To represent something means here, as Heidegger explains,
letting something stand over against us as an object
(*Gegenstand*, literally, what stands opposite).[18] "What thus
stands opposite to us must, as thus placed, come to us traversing an area of openness (or an open 'towardness'—*ein offenes
Entgegen*) and yet stand in itself as a thing, manifesting itself as
an invariable entity. This manifestation of the thing, by
traversing an open 'towardness', is accomplished within an
area of overtness, which is not itself created by the representation but is only taken over and occupied by it as a realm of
relationships." All the activities and relationships of man
occur in an area of overtness, standing within which he relates
himself to essents manifesting themselves in it. Making a
statement about an essent, by representing it and giving it the
status of an object, is at the same time to submit to the
requirement of representing it *so as* it is in the statement made.
Such a statement is true in the sense of being correct, for it has
taken the essent as manifest in the area of overtness as its
measure, being itself based on a relationship of overtness to the
essent. A statement can be true in this sense only because the
speaker, open to what manifests itself as an essent, has freely
accepted it as a binding criterion. Hence, Heidegger concludes,
the essence of truth lies in freedom, for it is the freedom of
man's openness on which truth in the sense of correctness is
grounded.

It may be objected that to ground truth, allegedly something eternal, independent of man and above him, on freedom
is to debase it and turn it into a property of the human being,
into something subjective and arbitrary. This, Heidegger declares, is a prejudice which can be dissipated, provided we are
ready to alter our manner of thinking about freedom and the
nature of man. Once we do this and try to grasp the essential
connection between freedom and truth we shall be led to a
realization of the hidden ground of man's own nature, itself
rooted in a more profoundly conceived truth. Freedom, which
has been described here as freedom for what is manifest in an
area of overtness, is what lets a particular essent be the essent
that it is. "Freedom is the letting be of essents"; it is to yield
oneself to the essent, to accede to what is manifest and to its

overtness, conceived by the Greeks as *aletheia* or unconcealedness. Letting-be, that is, freedom, is in itself exposing, eksistent; it is exposing oneself to the uncoveredness of essents. It is through such ek-sistent yielding and letting oneself into the uncoveredness of the essent as such that this uncoveredness, the overtness of what is manifest, that is, the *Da*, is itself maintained as such. Freedom, as identical with such ek-sistenz and letting-be, is not a property possessed by man but, on the contrary, itself 'possesses' man as his *Da-sein* and renders man's historicity itself possible.[19] Truth is that unconcealedness of the essent through which an overtness comes to prevail, an overtness within which all man's attitudes and activities then operate.

When man does not let the essent be what it is, illusion and untruth arise. But since ek-sistent freedom as the essence of truth is not a property of man, who is, as *Da-sein*, himself 'owned' by it, untruth cannot arise merely due to the incapacity and negligence of man. Untruth must come from the essence of truth itself and hence any inquiry into the nature of truth which aims at reaching the core of the problem must show how untruth also has its origin in the essence of truth. Through his attuned ek-sistenz man is let into the uncoveredness of the essent in its totality—which is not just the sum of the known essents—and all his behavior vibrates with this manifestness of the essent in its totality. Yet this whole eludes his grasp and cannot be understood in terms of manifest essents, remaining something indeterminate and indeterminable, though itself determining everything. What is in totality remains hidden and it is just the letting be which, in letting each particular essent be and so manifest itself, at the same time covers up, hides, essents as a whole. "Letting things be is in itself also a concealment." Da-sein's ek-sistent freedom thus simultaneously both reveals (particular essents) and conceals (essents in their totality). This concealment is a keeping back, a nonrevelation and hence untruth in the authentic sense. "The hiddenness of essents in their totality, the authentic untruth, is older than all manifestness of this or that essent, more primordial than the letting be itself," the mystery that attaches to the essent as such and pervades the *Da-sein* of man. In letting things be, ek-sistent *Da-sein* keeps this hiddenness itself hidden. The essence of truth thus comprises within itself its own dis-essence (*Unwesen*) in the form of untruth—a paradox pointing to the unexplored dimension of the truth, not of beings but of Being.[20]

Holding fast to what is practicable and controllable, man bars from himself an awareness of this concealment of the hidden, and this ground phenomenon of Dasein is lost in oblivion. What is thus forgotten, however, is not abolished out of existence by being forgotten but rather acquires a mysterious presence of its own. Denied all access to it, man falls back on his own resources and abandons himself to the realm of the practicable, planning, and scheming and taking himself as the measure of all things. Oblivious of the essent in its totality and its concealment, man clings to his own measures for his self-assurance. Dasein not only ek-sists but at the same in-sists, sticking obstinately to the multiplicity of essents and to what it can practically do with them. The ek-sistent turning away from the mystery of concealment and the insistent turning towards the practicable, one in origin and essence, constitute that aberration (*Irre*, going astray, confusion) into which man does not just incidently lapse but within which, in-sisting ek-sistently, he always already stands. Aberration, erring, is part of *Da-sein's* inner constitution. "In the uncovering of particular essents, the concealment of the hidden whole of essents has its sway and, as the oblivion of this concealment, it takes the form of aberration or loss of bearings." All the ways in which man falls into error are due to this but so also is his ability, in his very faltering and fumbling, to shed error by experiencing his aberration as aberration. In his in-sistent ek-sistenz man is particularly subject, even in his oblivion, to the sway of the mystery of concealment and to the pressure of this aberration, being afflicted by the compulsion of both. Truth in its full nature, comprehending its own opposite or dis-essence within itself, holds man under the sway of this affliction, this need, which makes him turn his gaze again towards the mystery and ask what the essent in its totality is, what the Being of essents is.

In tracing the inner possibility of propositional truth back to the ek-sistent freedom of letting be as its ground and suggesting that this ground itself has its essential origin in concealment and erring, Heidegger's aim was to show that the nature of truth is not an empty and abstract generality but is strangely complex in its structure. A reflection on this leads beyond the confines of our accustomed conceptions regarding the nature or essence of anything, beyond the problem of the essence of truth into the problem of the truth of essence (*Wesen*), that is, that of Being itself. In fact, as Heidegger adds in a concluding note appended later, the problem of the essence of truth was prompted by the question about the truth of essence or Being.[21] But the attempt to answer the latter question cannot succeed, and could not be carried through, without abandoning the language and approach of traditional metaphysics and effecting a reversal in the mode of thinking. "The question about the essence of truth has its answer in the statement: the essence of truth is the truth of essence" (*Wesen*, to be taken as a verb, that is, in the sense of being). But to say this, and to show how the nature of truth is inseparably bound up with the truth of Being needs a complete alteration of perspective and a change in the way Being reveals itself to us. "The answer to the question of the essence of truth is the utterance of a reversal within the history of Being," an utterance for which the metaphysical terminology of 'essence' (*Wesen*) is no longer adequate.[22] In the present lecture the crucial question regarding the meaning (*Sinn*), that is, the overtness or the truth of Being and not merely of beings, is deliberately left undeveloped, Heidegger says, and "the thinking proceeds to all appearances on the lines of metaphysics. Yet in its decisive steps, which lead from truth as correctness to ek-sistent freedom and from this to truth as concealment and error, it accomplishes a change in the direction of the inquiry which involves the *overcoming* of metaphysics."

The Reversal of Thought and the "Letter on Humanism"

The principal aim of *Being and Time* was to reawaken the problem of Being in the fundamental sense in which it had lapsed into obscurity in the Western metaphysical tradition since Plato and Aristotle. In the necessarily 'representational' thinking of this tradition, the essent is indeed investigated in regard to its Being but Being itself, its meaning and the way it unfolds and reveals itself, that is, its truth, is taken for granted and presupposed. At the very start of this tradition Being was understood in the sense of objective presence and this conception of Being, oriented to what is objective and simply given (*vorhanden*) and to the temporal mode of the present, itself never became a problem. Hence the sense of Being, what Being itself is, has remained buried in oblivion as the Unthought (*das Ungedachte*, that which has never been subjected to thinking) of the Western metaphysical tradition. *Being and Time* reopens the question, bringing it for the first time in the history of Western philosophy (as Heidegger himself claims) into the focus of explicit inquiry. The sense of Being is to be disclosed through an elucidation of the comprehension of Being that is part of Dasein's ontological constitution. This is achieved in *Being and Time* by exhibiting, by means of the preparatory analytic of Dasein, the conditions of the possibility of such comprehension within Dasein itself. This is followed by an explication of the true character of temporality (as against the vulgar conception of time as an unceasing flow of 'nows', in terms of which Being was hitherto understood) and of the temporal structure of Dasein. A path has been laid out to lead the inquiry right up to Time as the 'transcendental horizon' within which and through which Dasein's understanding of its own Being functions—entirely from within Dasein itself and in terms of Dasein's own overtness and comprehension of Being. The question that still remains to be answered is whether a path can also be built that may lead from primary Time to the sense of Being itself.

The whole inquiry, conducted in the manner of traditional, transcendental metaphysics and conceived as universal phenomenological ontology, based on the hermeneutic of Dasein, was nevertheless inspired by a sense of the inadequacy of traditional metaphysics and was calculated to discredit it. The aim of replacing it by a Fundamental Ontology also inspired *Kant and the Problem of Metaphysics* and the essays discussed above in which fundamental metaphysical concepts such as those of Nothing, Ground, Transcendence, and Truth were discussed so as to lead, beyond the limits of traditional metaphysics, into the fundamental ontological dimension, that is, to the problem of Being itself. The first essay—"What is Metaphysics?"—showed that if we seek, from within Dasein itself, to pass from the overtness inherent in it to Being (which, as Heidegger says in *Being and Time*, is sheer transcendence) we have to stop short at Nothing, for that is what reveals itself as Dasein's transcendence. This was also the conclusion of the book on Kant. The essay on the nature of Ground also made it evident that the conception of freedom, based on Dasein's transcendence as the source of all grounding, leads to the discovery that this freedom itself is the 'abyss' of Dasein, with its source in the 'not' between beings and Being, the Ontological Difference. The essay on the essence of Truth, lastly, led to the brink of the problem of Being, to the problem of the truth of Being as the nodal problem on which everything hinges and where the direction of the inquiry must turn round so that Being is no longer approached by way of Dasein but proceeds from the truth of Being to the nature of man. This is the reversal to which Heidegger's thought was led by the necessity inherent in its own movement.[23] What prevented its being carried into effect was the language of traditional metaphysics, it was metaphysics itself. *Being and Time*, seeking to go beyond it, was itself seen to be in the grip of the subjectivity characteristic of metaphysical thought and of its concern with the truth of essents. It was therefore powerless to lead to the truth of Being. It was not possible to think adequately about Being, on the basis of the primary temporality as it had emerged at the end of the inquiry into Being and Time, by means of the methodology and the conceptual framework of *Being and Time* as initially planned. The chapter which was to deal with "Time and Being" and in which Being was to be thought of in terms of primary temporality, along with numerous problems which were postponed earlier for treatment in this chapter, was dropped.[24]

The whole project had to be abandoned as incapable of being carried through, as a path that could indeed bring us to the verge of the problem and give a glimpse of its real nature but which, by its very nature, was incapable of leading *into* the heart of the main objective, that is, the sense or truth of Being itself. Before the inquiry could proceed further on its goal it was necessary to have a closer look at the credentials of metaphysics, to go down into its roots and thus to shed the remaining vestiges of its hold on the inquiry. As Heidegger remarks in the introduction, added in 1949, to "What is Metaphysics?" "A thinking that seeks to reflect on the truth of Being, but which is itself rooted in the agelong habit of representing the essent as such, itself gets entangled in such representation. Under these circumstances, both by way of a preliminary reflection as well as in order to lead on to the transition from representational thinking to the thinking that recalls, nothing becomes more important than raising the question, What is metaphysics?" When one penetrates, as Heidegger does in this introduction, into the ground of metaphysics, the foundation it stands upon, it becomes evident that metaphysical thinking is only concerned with the truth of the essent as essent. In its representation of what is, it has the latter focally in its sight. But this sight itself is dependent on the light of Being, which as such remains beyond the range of metaphysical thinking. Every interpretation of the essent occurs on the basis of an illumination of Being, its unconcealedness. "But whether and how it manifests itself in and as metaphysics, remains obscure. Being in its revelatory essence, that is, in its truth, remains unconsidered. . . . The truth of Being may thus be called the ground (of metaphysics)." A thinking, therefore, that sets out in quest of the ground of metaphysics, the truth of Being itself, instead of merely representing the essent as essent, has, Heidegger says, in a way given up metaphysics, which can no longer retain the first place in a thinking concerned with the truth of Being. From the point of view of metaphysics, such thinking goes back into the ground of metaphysics. But, as Heidegger here only suggests, what still appears from this point of view as ground is presumably something different, as yet unformulated, when considered in itself.

Although operating with a prior conception of Being, metaphysics does not discuss Being itself, "for it does not reflect on Being in its truth, nor on truth as unconcealedness, nor the latter in its essence." This essence of truth is beyond the reach of the representational thinking of metaphysics and has remained concealed from it during its long history from Anaximander to Nietzsche. Throughout this history, Heidegger points out, confusion has prevailed in its statements about Being, for though metaphysics speaks of Being, what it really means is sometimes the essent as essent and sometimes essents in their totality. What is at stake in this quest for the truth of Being is the "nearness and remoteness" of that from which philosophy itself, as the representation of the essent as such, derives. This is the occurrence, brought about by Being itself, of the original relationship of Being with the nature of man, a consummation to which metaphysics has itself become the barrier. Metaphysical thinking, which is projected, set up, by an essent as such, that is, man in his will to grasp Being in the network of his concepts, is basically representational in nature and must be supplemented, Heidegger asserts, by a kind of thinking "which is brought to pass by Being itself and, therefore, subserves Being."

The realization of this incapacity of metaphysical thought to go back into its own ground, the truth of Being, and to think about the Unthought of this truth, is what prevented the promised third division of *Being and Time* from appearing. The reversal promised there was rendered impracticable by this reversal in Heidegger's own way of thinking. But this 'turn' in thinking was itself, in turn, brought about by Heidegger's ceaseless effort to think about *that* reversal, the reversal from 'Being and Time' to 'Time and Being'. A "change in thinking," a total shift of perspective, prevented the carrying through of the plan of *Being and Time* on its own terms and according to its methods. The nature of this change, which was only hinted at in some essays on the poetry of Hölderlin, was indicated explicitly, after a long period of silence following the publication of *Being and Time* and the early essays, in the "Letter on Humanism" (1947), though it was not until the publication of the two-volume *Nietzsche* (1961) that a full view of the way of thought traveled by Heidegger during the period of transition (1930-1946) became available. This change, Heidegger explains in the "Letter," is "not an alteration in the standpoint of *Being and Time* but is a change through which the thinking attempted there at last emerges into its location in the dimension out of which the experience (or awareness) behind *Being and Time*, the experience of the oblivion of Being, developed." This change is thus not a break in the voyage of Heidegger's thought nor an abandonment of one goal for another. Even in its radical shift of perspective and alteration in style and approach in the second phase, Heidegger's thought remains loyal to its one and only objective, following it as "a star fixed in the heavens."[25]

What is the nature and scope of this change? It is a change, first, in the basic mood, a change of attitude toward the whole quest. In his early work on Duns Scotus, Heidegger expresses his determination to effect a "breakthrough into the true Reality and the real Truth."[26] This Promethean, aggressive attitude, in which man thinks of himself as destined to take truth and reality by storm, as it were, pervades all Heidegger's early writings.[27] This attitude of man's self-assertion (*Selbstbehauptung*), however, is not to be understood as peculiar and personal to Heidegger in the early phase; it is rather an attitude inseparably bound up with the whole of the Western metaphysical quest, at least since the rise of modern subjectivism with the philosophy of Descartes and not absent among the Greeks. In its modern form it is crystallized in the conception of the human spirit (*Geist*) as intellectual will, of which a classical expression may be found in Hegel's inaugural lecture at Berlin University:

> The courage of truth, the faith in the power of the spirit, is the primary condition of philosophy. Man, since he is spirit, can and should respect himself as worthy of the highest; he cannot think too highly of the greatness and power of his spirit and with that faith there can be nothing so unyielding and hard as not to open itself to him. The nature of the Universe, hidden and closed to start with, has no power to withstand the boldness of man's search for knowledge; it must open itself before him and disclose to his eyes its riches and its depths, offering them for his gratification.[28]

In lectures delivered in 1935 at the University of Freiburg,[29] Heidegger, too, describes spirit or *Geist* as "a fundamental knowing resolve toward the essence of Being" and as "the mobilization of the powers of the essent as such and as a whole" and speaks of the debilitation or emasculation of the spirit characteristic of the modern age, quoting with approval the definition of spirit given by him in his address, in 1933, "The Self-assertion of the German University." In "The Origin of the Work of Art" (1935), he says, still within the grip of the language of metaphysics: "Knowing, which is a willing and willing, which is a knowing, is the ecstatic entry of the existing man (that is Dasein) into the unhiddenness of Being."[30] The way Dasein understands itself and its relationship to Being before the 'reversal' is, as Walter Schulz puts it,[31] the self-assertion of Dasein in its impotence and finitude, a kind of 'heroic nihilism', incarnated in the figure of Prometheus, to whom Heidegger refers, in his address of 1933, as the first of the philosophers.

Around 1935, this mood (*Stimmung*) changes. There is an abdication of this will, of this self-assertion in the face of Being. The study of Nietzsche, with whom Heidegger intensively occupied himself, by way of lectures delivered during 1936-1940, seems to have brought home to him the devastating, shattering realization that Nietzsche's philosophy of the will-to power was only the nihilistic culmination of something inherent in the very nature of the metaphysical tradition of the West as it had developed from Plato onwards. The realization that in his own philosophy, deliberately seeking to 'overcome' metaphysics, this will, this nihilistic canker, was still a powerful driving force, standing between him and Being—the goal of his entire quest—seems to have led to the collapse of this will and to a complete surrender to the 'Voice of Being'. It is of this supreme renunciation of the metaphysical will by thought that he speaks in the *Feldweg*. "Renunciation does not take. Renunciation gives. It gives the inexhaustible power of the simple." This is the sacrifice, the offering of thankfulness and homage for the grace of Being, of which Heidegger speaks in the postscript to "What is Metaphysics?" This is not a failure of the courage to think but an acknowledgment that it flows, not from the assertive will of man but through a demand of Being itself.[32] The dominant mood now is not anxiety in the face of Nothingness but one of tranquil detachment (*Gelassenhèit*).

In the second place, there is a change in the conception of the task of philosophical thinking, its nature and its purpose.

Not only is 'metaphysics', as constituting the core of such thinking, abandoned as a game that has finally been played out, but even the Fundamental Ontology of *Being and Time* is dropped as a possible discipline.[33] The term 'philosophy' itself becomes suspect; as Heidegger says, "the thinking of the future is no longer philosophy because it aims at thinking on a level deeper than metaphysics, which term also means the same."[34] This thinking, Heidegger continues, without intending to discard the name of "love of wisdom" and become, as Hegel desired, wisdom itself in the shape of absolute knowledge, is on its way to "a descent into the poverty of its preliminary, provisional nature." Thinking is no longer conceived as an activity centered in man and reaching out toward Being. "Thinking unfolds and realizes the relationship of Being with the nature of man. It does not itself produce this relationship. . . . All efficacy rests in Being, flowing down from there toward the essent. Thinking, in turn, lets itself be claimed by Being, in order to give utterance to the truth of Being."[35] To realize the essential nature of thinking and thus make it in practice what it truly is, it is essential that we liberate ourselves from the technical interpretation of thought, a way of understanding the nature of thought going back to Plato and Aristotle, for whom thinking was a *techne*, the activity of deliberation in the service of doing (*praxis*) and making something (*poiesis*), also characterized as *theoria*. In this technical interpretation of thinking, sanctioned by 'logic', which also emerged at this time, Being as the true element within which thought moves and has its sustenance is sacrificed. Thinking expires, like a fish out of water, when it abandons its element, for it is this element which enables thinking to be what it is. "To put it simply, thinking is thinking of Being, where the 'of' has a double meaning. Thinking is of Being insofar as, being brought to pass by Being, it belongs to Being. At the same time it is thinking of Being insofar as, belonging to Being, it listens to Being."[36] It is Being which constitutes that "silent power of the possible" which enables, renders possible, thinking, bestowing upon it its own proper essence.

A thinking which concerns itself with the truth of Being and is therefore no longer representational, cannot, like metaphysics occupy itself with the construction of concepts.

But the abandonment of conceptual thought, that is, philosophy in the traditional sense, is not an abdication of thinking as such. Liberated from the fixity of concepts and the straitjacket of logic, thinking for the first time comes into possession of its own essential nature as "thinking that recalls" (*Andenken*), by immersing itself in the historical revelation of Being as it speaks through the language of the ancient philosophers and of poets, ancient and modern, in whom it has found utterance. Such thinking is, therefore, inherently historical in character. As Heidegger says,[37] the mystery of reminiscent thinking (*An-denken*) lies in the fact that in such thinking, as it peers down into what has been, this 'has been' itself comes back to us from the opposite direction, comes toward us as a task set for us by the future; "suddenly, thinking, as remembrance of the past, is compelled to think of what has been as something that has yet to unfold itself." This is the task of thinking and expressing in words that which still lies as the Unthought (*das Ungedachte*) in what has been already thought in the past.

The language and the terminology which has been developed by metaphysical thinking through the ages is utterly powerless to enable us to reflect on its own foundation, on the truth of Being itself, and give it utterance in words. But, as Heidegger says, "The one and only thing that is of supreme concern is that the truth of Being should find utterance and that thinking should find the proper language for that." *Being and Time* was on the way to this but, as a pioneering attempt, it was still held fast in the tradition and language of metaphysics. The inadequacy of this language and the need to find a more suitable way of expressing the truth of Being, that is, what Being means, seems to have led Heidegger to immerse himself in the poetry of Hölderlin and to occupy himself, afresh and more intensively, with the nature of language.[38] Language is regarded now not as a manifestation of the overtness of Dasein but rather as the locus and vehicle of the self-revelation of Being itself. "Language is the house of Being," a house in which man, too, has his dwelling. It is here that Being is to be sought for and found through the patient creative effort of raising in words a temple in which Being may shine forth in its truth. Language is 'brought to pass' by Being, a house put together by Being, ek-sisting within which man is aware of Being and of his relationship with it. In its concern for the words in which Being itself may 'come to word' and enshrine itself, thinking thus stands in the neighborhood of poetizing or composing (*Dichten*). In his essay "Hölderlin and the Nature of Poetry," Heidegger says, "The poet names the gods and he names all things in respect of what they are. This naming does not merely consist in bestowing a name on something that is already known; the poet, in uttering the essential word, rather nominates the essent to be, for the first time, what it is through this naming. Thus it becomes known *as* an essent. Poetry is the verbal instituting (*Stiftung*=founding, setting up) of Being."[39] The nature of language and, as rooted in that, the relationship between thinking and composing is a topic to which Heidegger returns again and again in his later writings.

In the course of the analytic of Dasein in *Being and Time*, Heidegger says, time and again, that this analysis is provisional and incomplete and will have to be carried out all over again, in respect of each of the main features of Dasein emerging from the analysis, in the light of a clarified idea of Being. This is what he does in his treatment of man after the reversal. The direction of the inquiry is now no longer from man to Being but from Being to man, who is now interpreted in terms, or in the light of, Being.[40] In the introduction to "What is Metaphysics?" Heidegger explains why man had to be taken as the point of departure in *Being and Time*, despite the fact that even that work had as its ultimate aim "to lead our thinking on the way on which it may find the relationship between the truth of Being and the nature of man, to open up a path for our thinking on which it may expressly ponder upon Being itself in its truth." No express reference to the oblivion of Being could be made in *Being and Time* because it had still to be demonstrated. "A realization of the true nature of such oblivion led to the crucial conjecture that the conception of the unconcealedness (that is, truth) of Being requires that the relationship of Being to the essence of man be conceived wholly as a feature of Being itself, rather than of man. But this conjecture, though already entertained, could not be raised explicitly as a problem in *Being and Time* until the determination of man's essence was first extricated from the traditional subjectivistic and rationalistic approaches."[41] From the changed perspective in thinking after the reversal, man is regarded "no longer as the master of what is. Man is the shepherd of Being."[42]

Replying to Jean Beaufret's suggestion of a revival of humanism and to his interpretation of *Being and Time* with its analysis of human nature, as the document of a humanistic, man-centered philosophy, Heidegger discusses the metaphysical roots of humanism as it has developed since Roman times. All humanism, including the humanistic interpretation of man as a rational animal or as person, he says, is as such based on a preexistent and presupposed metaphysical doctrine about the totality of what is. "Every determination of the nature of man which takes for granted a view of the essent, without inquiring into the truth of Being, is consciously or unconsciously, metaphysical. . . . Humanism, in determining the humanity of man, not only fails to inquire into the relation of Being to man but is even a hindrance in the way of such inquiry."[43] Metaphysics, oblivious of man in his relationship to Being, fails to take notice of the simple fact that man comes into possession of his true nature only insofar as he is responsive to the claim of Being. Man stands in the clearing or light of Being and in this consists his ek-sistenz; the 'there' (*Da*) of Da-sein is this clearing of Being, where he stands in the proximity or nearness (*Nähe*) of Being. This is a nearness in which man is not externally related *to* something other, but is itself the dimension of Being, from which all 'nearness' in the ordinary sense flows. Man, as man, has his dwelling in the neighborhood of Being.[44] Thrown into existence by Being itself, man ek-sists so as to guard the truth of Being, cherish and make it manifest by giving it utterance in words. It is in this sense that man is the shepherd of Being. Man's 'project' of Being is not generated by his fancy or self-will but is brought about by Being itself. And the historicity that characterizes Dasein is itself the manifestation of a temporality that inheres in Being primarily, entering into Dasein because of its intimate involvement in the history of Being itself (*Seinsgeschichte*). Thus, what principally concerns Heidegger, as it emerges more clearly in the second phase of his thought, is not so much man, as Sartre and his followers thought, as the 'nature' or essence of

man. This is not itself something 'human' but is wholly determined by Being. Hence any description of man in his
essence can be only in terms of the way Being has entered into
relationship with man, that is, in terms of man's *Da-sein*.[45]

Heidegger admits that in the *Being and Time* period, when
new ground was to be broken and a start made towards a
dimension of thought counter to that of metaphysics, his
language and thought had to retain a foothold on metaphysics.
Being, approached through Dasein, had to be described in
terms hallowed by the metaphysical tradition, for example,
transcendence and ground. In the phase after the '*Kehre*',
Heidegger is extremely careful of the language he employs in
speaking of Being and tries to eliminate every trace of
metaphysically tinged expressions. In order to guard against
the misunderstanding of his own use of the term "Being"
(*Sein*) in the sense sanctioned by tradition, he sometimes spells
it as "*Seyn*" in the nineteenth century manner, sometimes
writing it with a cross over it (*Sein* crossed out) and even going
so far as to suggest the abandonment of the term altogether.
With this there goes a radical change of style and of the
vocabulary. The trappings of erudition, the weight of learning
and the gestures of scholarship fall away, without prejudice to
an unceasing concern with what has been thought in the past.
As against the thickness and intensity of the earlier writing,
there appears an artful simplicity and freshness of style in the
later works, but without loss of expressive power. The thinking becomes evocative and poetical but is none the less pointed
and steered by the inner logic of its movement. Correspondingly, the vocabulary also alters and the formidable apparatus
of technical terminology is dropped in favor of the natural
resources of a language rich with the associations of its own
literary heritage. Instead of coining technical terms with well
defined 'logical powers' and thereby achieving conceptual
articulation, Heidegger seeks now to lay bare, and to utilize for
thought, the richness of meaning hidden in common words,
words which have been worn out and denuded of their force
by ordinary usage. While the 'definition' of a term empties it of
all but the bare minimum of meaning, the 'topological' interpretation (*Erörterung*) of basic words, with which Heidegger now engages himself, enables us to have a glimpse of the

entire expanse of meaningfulness out of which the single word speaks to us. By disclosing to our view the 'region' in which the word has its genesis, he enables us to draw from it meanings which have remained obscure and so far unuttered by it.[46] This is the simple explanation of the 'verbal jugglery', the 'play with words' and the 'forced etymologizing' of which Heidegger is often accused.

The Western metaphysical tradition culminates in the subjectivism of modern philosophy, bearing, in its end phase, nihilistic fruits in the thinking of Nietzsche. *Being and Time* is an attempt to shake off the hold of this tradition, for it is based on an uncritically assumed conception of Being. But as a first attempt it succeeds only partially in its manner of posing the question, in its approach to it and in its language. Attempting to step out of the sphere of subjectivity, it still proceeds from man (and the understanding of Being immanent in him) to Being, with undiminished trust, characteristic of metaphysics, in a methodology that can lead securely to port. But once it was realized that the impulse behind the thinking in *Being and Time* was one that inevitably led toward an overcoming of metaphysics by going back into its foundation, the truth of Being itself, it became equally obvious that this could not be achieved through the language and the methodological devices at the disposal of metaphysics. And where the language of tradition could not be avoided, new meanings had to be given to, though not arbitrarily imposed upon, some of the basic philosophical terms in that language.

By the time the "Letter on Humanism" was written, Heidegger had emerged clear of the vestiges of the metaphysical approach, with full consciousness of the necessity behind the change in the manner of posing the question and conducting the inquiry. Without having traversed the path taken by *Being and Time* and the early essays, the explicit realization of the need for a new approach and a new way of speaking would never have come. The impulse and the basic philosophical experience behind his thought, in the first as in the second phase, is the same.[47] The 'way' taken by Heidegger's thinking, probing forward and moving occasionally into blind 'forest trails', is continuous and pushes ahead towards its one and only goal, the utterance of the truth of Being. At different stations or halting places on this way, he has sought to formulate the truth of Being in what appeared to him the most adequate fashion, which in retrospect he has sometimes thought to be clumsy. As he has said recently, "I have abandoned an earlier standpoint, not so that I might adopt a different one in its place, but because even that earlier standpoint was a halting place in a thinking that is on its way. The way is what is enduring in thought."[48] That is why Heidegger, even after having moved beyond *Being and Time* in the sense indicated above, can say in the "Letter on Humanism" that the thinking which attempted to take a few steps forward in that work has not even today gone beyond Being and Time. That is why he comes back, again and again, to this work in his later writings, reinterpreting its basic concepts in terms of his advance along each milestone in the journey of his thought, insistently reminding the reader of the continuity of his thought and the singleness of his purpose. His writings after the reversal are both a criticism and a commentary on *Being and Time*.[49] "Perhaps," Heidegger remarks, "the basic shortcoming of the book *Being and Time* is that in it I have ventured out too far too soon."[50] The treatment of most of the topics dealt with there is not only explicitly provisional but opens out vistas which are explored and investigated more adequately only in Heidegger's subsequent writings.

Notes

1. "Brief über den 'Humanısmus'," *Wegmarken*, p. 159.
2. Ampler analyses of these essays, as also of *Kant und das Problem der Metaphysik* and *Die Selbstbehauptung der deutschen Universität* will be found in Richardson, *Heidegger*.
3. On the feasibility of an inquiry into Nothing, see *Einführung in die Metaphysik*, pp. 18-22 (E.T., pp. 19-24).
4. "Brief über den 'Humanısmus'," (*Wegmarken*, pp. 189-190): "Because nihilation is present in Being itself (which is not a given property of and discoverable in essents), therefore we can never observe it as something given and adhering to essents." It is equally impossible, Heidegger points out here, to derive Nothing from no-saying. Because the Nothing never appears as an object, it is falsely concluded that it must have its origin in the no-saying of a subject. Such a conclusion is, of course, only a manifestation of modern subjectivity. "Nihilating is in Being itself and by no means in the Dasein of men, insofar as this (Dasein) is conceived as the subjectivity of the

ego cogito. . . . Being nihilates—as Being. That is why in the Absolute Idealism of Hegel and Schelling, Nothing appears as the negativity of negation in the nature of Being. The latter, however, is then conceived as unconditioned will, in the sense of absolute actuality, which wills itself in the form of the will of knowing and of love. In this will, Being still lies hidden as the Will to Power."

5. In the "Postscript" of 1943, Heidegger explicitly states that Nothing which "never and nowhere is, unveils itself as that which is distinguished from all essents, that is, what we call Being." Only the essent, but not Being is accessible to science, for the latter is neither an existing quality of essents nor capable of being conceived and established objectively. "This, the sheer other to all essents is what is not, the non-entity." Instead of dismissing Nothing as the merely nugatory we should try, Heidegger says, "to experience in Nothing the vastness of that which gives every essent the warrant to be. This is Being itself. Without Being, whose unfathomable but still not unfolded essence is vouchsafed us by Nothing in essential dread, everything that is would remain in a state of Beinglessness. But then, even this, regarded as abandonment by Being (*Seinsverlassenheit*), is not sheer Nothing, assuming that it is of the truth of Being, that there never is Being without the essent, that there never is an essent without Being. . . . Nothing as the other to what is, is the veil of Being."

In the earlier editions of this essay, Heidegger had said, "There is indeed Being without the essent . . . ," whereas in later editions this reads, "Being never is without essents. . . ." The emendation was noted and commented upon by Max Müller, (*Existenzphilosophie im geistigen Leben der Gegenwart*, 2d edition, pp. 45-46) and discussed by Schulz "Über den philosophiege-schichtlichen Ort Martin Heideggers." See also Richardson's discussion of what he calls "the case of the altered epilogue." (*Heidegger*, pp. 563-565.)

6. For a full discussion of the significance of the question, "Why are there essents rather than nothing?," see *Einführung in die Metaphysik*, chapter 1. Heidegger explains here how this is the basic question of metaphysics, the foremost of all questions in respect of comprehensiveness, depth, and primordial character. To take the leap of asking this question, with its recoil upon itself, is to philosophize. The question not only asks for the ground of what is but, by confronting the essent with the alternative of Nothingness, deprives it of its obviousness and renders it questionable in its totality.

In the "Introduction" to "What is Metaphysics?" Heidegger expresses surprise that it has never occurred to his critics to consider why a lecture seeking to think the truth of Being by way of the Nothing and thence to the nature of metaphysics, should claim that this is the basic question of metaphysics. Why does this attempt to think of Being by way of the Nothing return in the end to a question concerning the essent again, asking "why?" in the traditional causal manner of metaphysics, very much as the metaphysician Leibniz, in his *Principles of Nature and Grace*, asked, "Why is there anything rather than nothing?" Is the question at the end of the lecture a metaphysical question, like that of Leibniz, about the supreme cause of everything that is? As Heidegger explains, the question here is asked in an entirely different sense; for, not being concerned with essents and their first cause, it starts with that which is not an essent, that is, Nothing, which is the sole theme of the lecture. From a point of view that has passed beyond metaphysics to its own ground, that is, from the point of view of the truth of Being itself, to raise this question is to ask, "How is it that essents take precedence everywhere and lay claim to every 'is', while that which is not an essent, the Nothing—which in this sense is Being itself—remains forgotten?"

7. Pp. 71, 113–115 (E.T., pp. 125–128).

8. *Critique of Pure Reason*, A 108, A 235f., B 204f.

9. P. 214. J. P. Sartre has discussed Heidegger's view of Nothing and compared it with Hegel's (*Being and Nothingness*, pp. 16–20). In *Nietzsche I* (p. 73), Heidegger himself points out how German Idealism, conceiving Being as will also had the daring to think of the negative as comprehended in Being. A penetrating examination of the concept of finitude in the philosophy of Heidegger will be found in Henri Birault's article, "Heidegger et la pensée de la finitude." Birault, following Kojeve's interpretation of Hegel, refers to the similarities between Hegel and Heidegger as philosophers of finitude, seeking to interpret human existence in finitistic and atheistic terms. Birault also gives a historical account of the concept of finitude and negativity, differentiating Heidegger's conception of *Endlichkeit* from the views of Plato and Sartre and from the Christian doctrine.

10. For a critical discussion of Heidegger's attack on logic and an elucidation of the sense in which it should be understood, see Walter Bröcker's, "Heidegger und die Logik."

11. In the foreword to the 3d edition (1949) of this essay, Heidegger says that both "Vom Wesen des Grundes" and "Was ist Metaphysik?" were written in 1928 and remarks on the link connecting the two as follows: "The latter reflects on the Nothing, the former mentions the Ontological Difference. The Nothing is the 'not' of essents and is thus Being as understood from the point of view of the essent. The Ontological Difference is the 'not' between the essent and Being. But just as the 'not' of essents is not sheer nothing, so also the Difference as the 'not' between the essent and Being is not a mere *ens rationis*, a mere construct of the understanding that distinguishes." The 'not' of the Nothing and the 'not' of the Difference, though not one, are yet connected together in the sameness of the essence of the Being of essents. The two essays seek, without explicit awareness of it, to bring into view this 'sameness' as a problem for further reflection.

Heidegger's exploration of the sense of Being and his critical inquiry into the ground of metaphysics both revolve round the "Ontological Difference," which is thus a basic concept in his philosophy. See the last chapter of this work for Heidegger's growing concern with this notion. In his study *Transzendenz und Differenz*, Alberto Rosales has dealt with the problem of the Ontological Difference in the early Heidegger and shown how this notion is presupposed in the entire project of *Being and Time*.

12. "Vom Wesen des Grundes" was written about the same time that Heidegger gave his first seminar on Schelling's treatise on human freedom, and his views on freedom and ground here are clearly influenced by Schelling. Heidegger's lecture course on Schelling's treatise, given in 1936 and

included in his *Schelling*, not only contains a thorough discussion of the metaphysics of freedom but shows him clearly moving away from the *Being and Time* phase to his later approach and perspective. Pointing out that Schelling's treatise has nothing to do with what is generally called the problem of the freedom of the will, he says, "For, here freedom is regarded not as a property of men but, on the contrary, man is thought of as the property of freedom. Freedom is that encompassing and pervasive reality (*Wesen*) standing within which only does man become man. That is to say, the nature or essence of man is grounded in freedom. Freedom itself, however, is a determination of real Being (*Seyn*) in general, over-arching the being of man. So far as man *is* as man, he must participate in this determination of Being, and man *is* insofar as he accomplishes this participation in freedom."

13. In this essay, Heidegger discusses the Principle of Ground as saying something of the essent only (namely, that every essent has a ground) and as uninformative about the nature of Ground itself. In a full-scale study devoted to this principle much later (*Der Satz vom Grund*, 1957), Heidegger realized that he had been too hasty in arriving at the above conclusion. As he says there (pp. 84–85), "That account, though correct, led to confusion, firstly, in respect of the possible ways and openings suggested by the Principle of Ground for dealing with the particular problem of the nature of Ground and, secondly and above all, in respect of the basic question (that is, the question of Being) which has inspired all (my) thinking, and towards the service of which that essay was also a contribution." All grounding comes from Being and it is by virtue of its grounding character that beings always have a ground.

Beginning with the Greek concepts of *arche* and *aition*, ground has been variously conceived in the history of thought as *ratio, causa*, principle, justification, and condition of possibility. The word denotes the basis, the *fundus*, on which something rests. Ground (principle) and Reason are translations of the Latin *ratio*—a translation which also bifurcates the undifferentiated *ratio* into the twofold sense of Reason (*Vernunft*) and ground or cause. *Ratio* itself is the translation of the Greek *logos*, containing within itself the implicit double sense of Being as presence and as ground, both together in their unity with speech. The literal meaning of the term *Logos*, according to Heidegger, originally refers to Being and Ground in one without, however, distinguishing between the two and hence without also an awareness of the unity which they form together. Because of this unity of Being and Ground, the conception of Being as Ground remained implicit; later thought, seeking to represent Ground, 'displaced' it to the essent, as belonging to that rather than to Being. Really speaking, it is to Being that ground and grounding belong; Being and Ground are the same in the sense of belonging together in a unity of essence, not fusing together in bare identity but held apart in their togetherness. But so long as *logos* is interpreted in terms of the later *ratio* and *Vernunft*, this is bound to remain hidden. As the source of all grounding, Being itself is without ground and to speak of it as self-grounding would be to treat it as if it were itself an essent. Being itself rests, not on anything that can be described in terms of ground, reason, or cause but in the mystery of play (*Spiel*), that highest and profoundest play of which Heraclitus speaks, the play of *aion*, of world as the dispensation of Being, in the later language of Heidegger. Implicit in the way Being revealed itself to the Greeks is the conception of Ground, which became explicit later in the European attitude to essents and in the definition of man as the rational animal; it has culminated in the complete domination of our lives by the Principle of Sufficient Reason in the form of the omnipotence of technology in the Atomic age of today. "Is this the last word that can be said about Being," Heidegger asks in conclusion, "that it is Ground?" Does the nature of Being not need deeper reflection and a more adequate formulation?

14. P. 39n (E.T., p. 97n).

15. As Heidegger points out (p. 37; E.T., p. 93), the first express mention of transcendence occurs in Plato's doctrine of the *agathon* as *epekeina tes ousias*, "beyond Being," in the *Republic* (VI, 509B). The *agathon* is conceived by Plato as the primordial ground of the possibility of truth, understanding, and Being as connected together in the unified conception of the ultimate end, the *hou heneka* or the 'for the sake of'. In later tradition, however, the emphasis on the separate existence of Ideas in a celestial region, the *hyperouranios topos*, has tended to overshadow the transcendental conception of the *agathon*. For Heidegger's interpretation of the Idea of the Good, also see "Platons Lehre von der Wahrheit" and *Nietzsche II*, pp. 223-228.

16. "Vom Wesen des Grundes" (*Wegmarken*, pp. 38-51; E.T., pp. 47-80). This supplements the elaborate analysis of this concept in *Being and Time*.

17. A clear exposition of this essay is given, along with an English translation, by Werner Brock (*Existence and Being*, pp. 142-183, 319-351). Like some of Brock's other renderings, however, his translation of a 'key term', as he calls it, like *das Seiende im Ganzen* by "the things that are *within the whole*" does not make sense.

As Heidegger explains (*Nietzsche I*, p. 277), the phrase "essents in their totality" is used by him to denote all that is not sheer nothing: Nature, inanimate and living; history and its manifestations and those who fashion and carry it; God, the gods and half-gods. And it includes what is in becoming, what is originating and what is passing away; appearance, semblance, delusion, and falsity; even nothingness as the limit of this whole of what is.

A. de Waelhens and W. Biemel have provided a very helpful commentary on the essay in their article, "Heideggers Schrift 'Vom Wesen der Wahrheit'."

18. For a detailed discussion of *Entgegenstehenlassen* see *Kant und das Problem der Metaphysik*, pp. 69-82 (E.T., pp. 74-89), and elsewhere.

19. See also *Vorträge und Aufsätze*, pp. 32-33.

20. As Heidegger explains (*Nietzsche II*, p. 362), this statement is not a formal general proposition belonging to an essentialistic ontology in which 'essence' is represented metaphysically, appearing as 'Idea' in its historically decisive form. The statement, meaning the word 'essence (*Wesen*)' in a verbal sense (be-ing), is about Being itself in regard to the way It, Being, is. How Being is, consists in the 'staying out' (*Ausbleiben*) or withdrawal of its own self.

21. "Vom Wesen der Wahrheit," *Wegmarken*, p. 96. The first two paragraphs of this note were added in the second edition (1969) and are not included in Brock's *Existence and Being*.

22. Arguing against the concept of essence as something invariable, Heidegger says (*Nietzsche*, pp. 173-174) that the nature or essence (*Wesen*) of something is traditionally taken as the universal which is common to many particulars. But the fact that the essence of anything is in certain contexts—not always—what is common to many particulars is a consequence of the essence and not its intrinsic character. The identification of essence with the property of universality has blocked the way into the all-important problem of truth for centuries. Particular truths are different from each other and are many; but the essence is universal and, as valid for many, one. This universal, that is, what is valid for the many in question is, however, then taken as the universally valid in an absolute sense. Universality now means, not what is valid for these particulars but what is in itself and in general and forever valid, the immutable, the eternal, the timeless. This is how the principle of the immutability of essence, and so of the essence of truth, arises. This principle, Heidegger asserts, is logically correct but metaphysically false. From the point of view of the particular 'cases' of truth, the essence of truth consists of what is common to the many and as such one and identical. But from this it does not by any means follow that the essence in itself cannot change. For, admitting that the essence of truth changes, the changed essence can, despite the change, still be the essence which is valid for the many. What persists through the change is the immutable within the essence which, as such, is ever changing. This, Heidegger claims, is an affirmation of the essential character of the essence, its inexhaustibility and of its real self-hood and identity, in sharp contrast with the vacuous identity of sameness, as which alone the unity of the essence can be conceived so long as it is taken merely as a universal. From the point of view of traditional logic, the conception of a changeable essence is bound to be judged as leading to sheer relativism. But this objection against the changeability of essence is valid only under a preconceived notion of unity and identity and of what is called the Absolute; it stands and falls with it and with the validity of the conception of essence as what is valid for many.

For an account of Heidegger's conception of Identity, see the essay in *Identität und Differenz*. Essence (*Wesen*) in the sense of *essentia* is, according to him, the 'metaphysical' interpretation, based on its concern with the 'what' of essents, of the more fundamental *wesen*, be-ing, taken as a verb.

See also *Vorträge und Aufsätze*, pp. 37-39, where *Wesen* is explained in terms of *währen* (to last) and *gewähren* (grant, vouchsafe). *Wesen*, taken as a verb, is the same as 'to last, to continue', but it can never be established, Heidegger asserts, that enduring can rest only on the Platonic *idea* or on *essentia* in any of its forms, nor that the enduring is merely what goes on without cease. "Only what is vouchsafed endures. What has its origin in early times and so endures is the vouchsafing (that is, that which grants)." Every dispensation (*Geschick*) of disclosure into which man is cast comes from this source of all vouchsafing. Elsewhere (*Unterwegs zur Sprache*, p.

201; E.T., p. 95), Heidegger adds that *Wesen* does not mean merely to last and endure but rather to come on and be present and, while enduring, to concern us, provide us with a way, to reach out to us and sustain us.

23. The Reversal is meant to be understood in a historical sense, that is, not as a personal event (a conversion) in Heidegger's life, nor even as a revolution in 'his' philosophy, but as a happening in the history of Western thought itself. From this point of view, Heidegger's philosophy represents that historic movement, augured by Hölderlin and anticipated by Nietzsche, in which the Western philosophical tradition, having brought to the surface all its inherent possibilities, suffers a 'peripety', annuls itself and passes over into another beginning. The present century, it may be pointed out (as Heidegger has), is marked by a similar reversal in the history of science, such that its inherent will to universal and total objectivization of what is has culminated in utter 'unobjectifiability'—man's onslaught on the essent has brought science to the point of the essent's counterattack against man, to a point where what is has become utterly incapable of being represented and conceived—where it can only be calculated. The developments that have occurred in contemporary Anglo-Saxon philosophy, as the present writer interprets them, show a similar trend. Ludwig Wittgenstein, the other 'extreme' (as Erich Heller calls him) of contemporary thought, is the 'locus' of the dissolution and transformation of traditional metaphysics into something deeper and more basic. Like *Being and Time*, the *Tractatus* may be said to mark the consummation and close of a whole epoch and the *Philosophische Untersuchungen*, like the works of Heidegger in the second phase, the inauguration of a new one. Common to both Heidegger and Wittgenstein is their recognition of language as the fundamental reality for thought.

24. The following are some of the topics to which Heidegger promises, at various places in *Sein und Zeit*, to return in the omitted chapter: a consideration of the forgetting of world in European thought (p. 100); the new conception of *logos* (p. 160); the development of the Idea of Phenomenology (p. 357), of Ontology (p. 230), and of Science (p. 357); the elucidation of the connection between *Being and Truth* (p. 357); the discussion of language (p. 349); the 'as' in thinking of something as something and the nature of the copula (p. 360); the concrete working out of the structure of world (p. 316) and of everydayness (p. 372); the relation between space and time (p. 368) and the being of time (p. 406). The entire existential analysis is to be repeated in the framework of a thorough consideration of the concept of Being (pp. 333 and 436).

25. *Aus der Erfahrung des Denkens*, p. 7 (E.T., *Poetry, Language, Thought*, p. 4). The 'change in thinking' from the *Being and Time* phase to the later, rather abruptly and briefly announced in the "Letter on Humanism" after a long period of silence, caused widespread bewilderment among scholars and has given rise to conflicting interpretations of the character of this change. It has been criticized by some as a departure from the sober rationality and scientific attitude of the early phase, as an abandonment of the path of scholarly inquiry and a lapse into mysticism, and as a breakdown and failure of thought as initially planned in *Being and Time*. Others insist that there is at least a break in the movement of thought such that there is no bridge leading

from the first to the second phase. Still others, in closer sympathy with the 'way' of Heidegger's thought, see the 'reversal' as implicit in *Being and Time* itself. Karl Löwith, in his widely read and influential *Heidegger–Denker in dürftiger Zeit* (1st ed., 1953), is vehemently critical. In his remarkable discussion of the significance of "Was ist Metaphysik?" (in "Über den philosophiegeschichtlichen Ort Martin Heideggers"), Walter Schulz has shown how the way of Heidegger's thought inherently leads through the 'reversal', of which the first step is the passage from beings to Nothing and the second, more difficult than the first, from Nothing to Being. Heidegger was able to take this step, Schulz remarks, because he has remained loyal to his own starting point in *Being and Time*. Pöggeler (in "Sein als Ereignis" and in his book, *Der Denkweg Martin Heideggers*) also convincingly brings out the unity of Heidegger's way. Fridolin Wiplinger, in his elaborate exposition of Heidegger's philosophy from the perspective of the problem of truth (*Wahrheit und Geschichtlichkeit*), even characterizes Heidegger's thought as itself a "thinking of the Reversal."

Replying to Richardson's question regarding the occurrence of the 'reversal' in his thinking of Being (Richardson, *Heidegger*, pp. xvii–xxiii), Heidegger quotes from his lecture course of 1937-38, showing how his thinking was occupied with the 'reversal' (that is, with the question of 'Time and Being' as already contemplated in *Being and Time*) even a decade before the appearance of the "Letter on Humanism." As he points out here, the Reversal is in play within the matter thought about in *Being and Time* itself, demanded by it, and not something invented by himself or merely an affair concerning his thinking. He remarks further that the 'happening' of the Reversal 'is' Being (*Seyn*) as such and it can be thought only *from* the Reversal. Heidegger's elucidation of the 'reversal' in the "Preface" to Richardson's *Heidegger* should be read along with the lecture "Die Kehre" in *Die Technik und die Kehre* for a proper grasp of this complex, fluid, and ambiguous concept.

26. Quoted in Pöggeler "Sein als Ereignis."

27. And yet Heidegger, even in the *Being and Time* phase, has already gone equally beyond Greek Prometheanism and Hegelian Absolutism, as shown by the key role played by the concept of 'letting' (*Lassen*) in the writings even of this period. Heidegger recognized in *An Introduction to Metaphysics* that "the relationship to being is one of letting-be," that all willing is grounded in letting-be (p. 17). The whole of the essay, "On the Nature of Truth" is a plea for the notion of 'letting'.

28. Commenting on this passage (*Der Satz vom Grund*, p. 145), Heidegger says that it would be wrong and ungenerous to take these words as a piece of presumptuousness on the part of the person of the thinker in face of the Absolute; it is, on the contrary, expressive of a readiness to respond to the demand placed upon thought by Being manifesting itself in the form of the absolute concept.

29. *An Introduction to Metaphysics*, p. 41.

30. *Holzwege*, p. 35 (E.T., p. 67). In fairness to Heidegger it must be added that even before writing this essay—in fact, since the inception of *Being and Time* itself—he was 'on the way' to a deeper conception of willing and had

realized that man's relationship to Being can be only one of 'letting'. As against the interpretation, generally accepted, of the reversal offered here, Heidegger would, therefore, be quite justified from the point of view of his basic *intentions* to insist, as he does insist, on the continuity of his thought. Cf. the "Zusatz" to the Reclam edition (1969) of *Der Ursprung des Kunstwerkes*, where Heidegger discusses the apparent contradiction in this essay between 'positing' (willing) and 'letting'. See also *Nietzsche* and *Gelassenheit* for Heidegger's unceasing preoccupation with the problem of will and its interpretation in terms of Being.

31. "Über den philosophiegeschichtlichen Ort Martin Heideggers," *Philosophische Rundschau*, 1 (1953-1954):89.

32. *Aus der Erfahrung des Denkens*, p. 9 (E.T., *Poetry, Language, Thought*, p. 5).

33. Heidegger asserts ("Brief über den 'Humanismus'," *Wegmarken*, pp. 187-188) that already in *Being and Time*, he was attempting to "think ahead" into the truth of Being and so was in quest of a fundament for ontology. "That thinking, because of its concern with the other question (that is, the truth of Being), had from the very first emerged clear of the 'ontology' of metaphysics (including that of Kant). 'Ontology', however, whether transcendental or precritical, is open to criticism, not because it thinks about the Being of essents and, in addition, forces Being into a concept, but because it does not think the truth of Being and therefore fails to recognize that there is a kind of thinking that is more stringent than conceptual thinking. Seeking to think forward into the truth of Being, thinking (that is, in *Being and Time*), because of the difficulty of a first coming through, speaks very little of that wholly different dimension. The language is not yet true to itself, insofar as it has not yet succeeded in giving up the absurd intention of being 'science' and 'research', while holding on to the valuable help of phenomenological seeing. In order, however, to make this venture of thought within the prevailing philosophy distinguishable and at the same time intelligible, it was possible to speak only in the horizon of the prevailing (mode of thought) and by using the terminology current in it. Since then I have realized that just those terms were bound to lead, directly and unavoidably, to confusion." Cf. *Einführung in die Metaphysik*, p. 31 (E.T., p. 34); also what Heidegger says about "the ever-again undertaken attempt, since 1930, to reformulate more radically the questioning of *Being and Time*" (*Zur Sache des Denkens*, p. 61; E.T., p. 65).

34. "Brief über den 'Humanismus'," *Wegmarken*, p. 194.

35. Ibid., p. 145.

36. Ibid., pp. 147-148.

37. *Erläuterungen zu Hölderlins Dichtung*, p. 100.

38. However, as Heidegger remarks in his "Preface" to Richardson's *Heidegger* (p. xxiii), the multifold thinking of Being requires not a new language but a transformed relationship to the nature of the old.

39. *Erläuterungen zu Hölderlins Dichtung*, p. 41 (E.T. *Existence and Being*, pp. 304-305).

40. In the phrase "from man to Being" (as referring to the procedure in *Being and Time*), 'man' should be understood in the sense of the being of

man, that is, as Dasein. The phrase should not be taken to imply that in that work Heidegger aims at deriving the concept of Being from some type of anthropology or philosophy of man developed in isolation from the question of Being. As Heidegger remarks in *Was heisst Denken?* (pp. 73-74; E.T., p. 79f.), "Every philosophical, that is, thinking doctrine of the nature of man is *in itself already* a doctrine of the Being of the things that are. Every doctrine of Being is *in itself already* a doctrine of the nature of man. But neither of the two can be arrived at by a mere reversal of the other, through a dialectical maneuver. . . . No way of thinking, including that of metaphysical thinking, starts from the nature of man, passing over thence to Being or, the other way round, starting from Being returns thence to the nature of man. Every way of thinking moves rather within the whole nexus, within the totality of the relationship between Being and the human essence, otherwise it is no thinking." The difference between the approach in *Being and Time* and that after the *Kehre* is, concisely expressed, that between approaching the question of Being from the point of view of the Being of a being (in this case, human being) and interpreting the latter in terms of a new conception of Being itself. However deep it may go, a consideration of the Being of the essent still moves within 'metaphysics'; from there to Being itself there is no smooth passage but only a leap of thought.

41. See the "Einleitung" to "Was ist Metaphysik?," *Wegmarken*, pp. 201-202.

42. "Brief über den 'Humanismus'," *Wegmarken*, p. 172.

43. Ibid., p. 153.

44. Ibid., p. 168. As Heidegger remarks, this 'nearness' is the clearing of the 'there' in which man dwells as ek-sisting. The nearness of Being, the 'there' of Dasein, is called 'Home' in his address on Hölderlin's elegy, "Homecoming." The homelessness of modern man, Heidegger says, was realized by Nietzsche but he could not find any other way out of it, stuck as he was within metaphysics, than a mere inversion of metaphysics. Hölderlin's was a profounder insight into the real character of man's homecoming into his own essence, the nearness to Being.

45. Aligning himself with the school of Heidegger interpretation represented by G. Krüger and K. Löwith, Laszlo Versényi has severely criticized Heidegger for his alleged "nonhumanism" in his well-written study, *Heidegger, Being and Truth*. Entrenched securely behind a neoclassical position, he showers what he thinks are deadly barbs against Heidegger. Versényi knows, and presents briefly, the letter of Heidegger's texts very well indeed. Nevertheless, he is so completely out of sympathy with the spirit and the central direction of this philosopher's *questioning* that his criticisms appear to be aimed against a Heidegger of his own imagining. This is another confirmation of the "almost insurmountable difficulty in making oneself understood" about which Heidegger speaks in his letter to Richardson (*Heidegger*, p. viii). Surely, something has gone seriously wrong in the way Versényi introduces (p. 135, with frequent repetitions on later pages) the reference to "*das ganz Andere*" in *Unterwegs zur Sprache*, p. 128 (E.T., p. 35), and converts it into the "that which is Wholly Other" of "a negative theology and mysticism"!

46. In order to bring out the specific character of "topological thinking," Pöggeler distinguishes three different ways of understanding a matter: *Erklären, Erläutern*, and *Erörtern*. The last, Pöggeler says, constitutes the Logos of Heidegger's thinking and is an approach he traces back to the ancient discipline of Topics, the *ars inveniendi*. See his article referred to in chapter 1; also his review of books by Viehweg and by Hennis.

47. Qualifying the clear-cut distinction Richardson makes between Heidegger I and Heidegger II (that is, between the earlier and the later phases of his thought), Heidegger remarks ("Preface" to Richardson's *Heidegger*, p. xxiii) that this distinction is justified only if it is steadily borne in mind that only by way of what is thought in I is it possible to have access to what is to be thought in II, but that I becomes possible only if it is contained in II.

48. *Unterwegs zur Sprache*, p. 98 (E.T., p. 12).

49. References to *Being and Time* in Heidegger's subsequent writing and retrospective explanations and reinterpretations of particular concepts in that book are given at appropriate places in the notes to Part II of this work.

50. *Unterwegs zur Sprache*, p. 98 (E.T., p. 12).

9

Heidegger and the Western Metaphysical Tradition

Heidegger's Approach to Past Thought

All philosophical thinking, according to Heidegger, moves within the intellectual horizon opened up by a tradition. It may seek to enlarge this horizon and may attempt a critical reconstruction of that tradition by bringing into view something that has been ignored and bypassed by it. But no thinker, however original he may be, can lift himself out of the tradition that sustains him and from which the driving power and the manner of his questioning is derived. Man's knowledge of what is and his understanding of what it means to 'be' never sheds its linkage with the 'here' and the 'now', never reaches up into the *hyperouranios topos*, the heavenly region of the pure, the timeless and the Absolute. In the sense in which Heidegger raises the question of Being, the question could be raised only within the framework of the Western philosophical tradition as founded by the early Greek thinkers and only at a point in the history of that tradition where it terminates in the philosophy of Nietzsche. The question of Being is thus essentially and intrinsically a historical one, requiring both a critical, regressive analysis or "destruction" of the history of ontology as well as a reconstruction of that history in the light of the deeper and more original understanding of Being and of man in his relationship to Being acquired in the course of the inquiry. The phenomenological destruction promised for the second (unpublished) part of *Being and Time*—a task of which the nature and necessity is explained by Heidegger in section 6 of that work[1]—is an integral part of the question of Being, having the positive aim of acquiring a new perspective on the entire history of European thought and reconstructing it from the point of view of what has remained in it unsaid and unactualized.

This question is historical, further, in the sense that, as Heidegger insists, the historical destiny of Western man is bound up with the asking or failure to ask, with the manner of asking and answering, this question. Not to be content with gaining knowledge of the essent as such but, going beyond that, to inquire into the Being of essents or into Being as such may seem like verbal idolatry. Being cannot be grasped like a being and is as impalpable as Nothingness. Is it then, Heidegger asks, just an empty word, unreal vapor and an error, as Nietzsche says?[2] In *An Introduction to Metaphysics* he seeks to demonstrate that Being is neither a mere word nor empty abstraction but, with its richness of content and dynamism, holds in itself the spiritual destiny of the West. In the first place, we can meaningfully talk and think about Being because we (that is, Western thinkers) stand within a tradition which has taken its birth with the question about Being and of which the unfoldment has been determined by this origin. Second, a glance at the spiritual impoverishment of present-day Western man and at the bleakness and benightedness of his world—in Heidegger's words, "the darkening of the world, the flight of the gods, the depredation of the earth, the standardization of man, the supremacy of the mediocre"—it becomes obvious that the word 'Being' has an empty sound for us only because we have for long fallen out of Being and because our relationship to our tradition and to language has been disturbed and disrupted. What the Western world is today, it has come to be in consequence of its metaphysical foundations in early Greek thought, of the way Being revealed itself in it and of its subsequent withdrawal from the sight of Western man. To ask "What is Being?" or "Why are there essents rather than nothing?" is, therefore, not just a question of merely academic interest, remote from man's basic concerns, a professional luxury confined to the chosen few. As a philosophical question, it has arisen rather from a thinking that breaks the paths and opens the perspectives of the knowledge in which and by which a people comprehends and fulfils itself historically and culturally, of that knowledge which kindles and threatens and necessitates all questioning and valuing.[3]

Nor is this a question that concerns only the self-realization of single individuals seeking to attain philosophical truth in personal experience. Heidegger is not interested at all either in proving universally valid, eternal, and changeless verities or in an experience that is only personal and private or, for that matter, in any sort of experience in the psychological, subjective sense. His is the quest of the *koinon* (Heraclitus), the common, the suprapersonal, of the concepts, the language, and the presuppositions which provide, determine, and mold the intellectual horizon and the historical destiny of a whole people; it is the quest for the ultimate metaphysical or spiritual foundations on which the Western man's life is grounded, for the way Being has revealed itself to him and withdrawn itself from him and in so doing has shaped his nature and destiny from Greek times to the present day. The question of Being thus is not a mére intellectual pastime but one in which man's entire historical existence is involved. Nor does it seek to provide an ontology in the traditional style, much less to assess critically the past mistakes of ontology. "We are concerned," Heidegger says, "with something quite different, to restore man's historical existence—and that always includes our own future existence in the totality of the history allotted to us—to the power of Being which has to be opened up again by man for himself by going back to the origin."[4] The question of Being, far from being merely verbal, amounts to a reflection on the genesis of our *hidden history*, it is a question that points to the hidden ground of our historical existence and on the answer to which our future historical existence depends.[5] As in the case of Nietzsche, Heidegger's thinking is inspired by a passionate concern for the present, for what *is* in the world of the present, for what man, fated by Being, has made of himself and his world today, for the way he dwells in it and for the basic attitudes which dominate his way of seeing things and comprehending them. The present technological era, with its emasculation of the spirit and its restless craving for mastery over everything that is, is one in which man has become utterly blind to the Being of things and to the disclosure of all reality in them other than their calculability and amenability to manipulative control. The desiccation and hollowness of man's world today, with all weight gone out of things, and the corresponding loss of man's ability truly to dwell in it as in a home, is a consequence, Heidegger declares, of the whole Western past which has worked itself out in the present and is its living foundation. Nietzsche saw the Western spiritual horizon threatened with Nihilism—that "uncanniest of all guests, standing at the door"—and following him, Heidegger, with an even deeper insight into the hidden forces behind Western intellectual history and a more thorough familiarity with it, sees in the eclipse of Being today the relentless sway of total Nihilism, the completion of a process that has been at work at least since the time of Plato.

The question of Being is hence directly determined by the history and the present state of the human spirit on earth.

> The asking of this question is immediately and fundamentally linked up with the crucial historical question of coming to a decision. . . . What history here means, however, is not so much the past, for that is just what does not happen any longer; much less is it the merely contemporary, which also does not happen but is only a passing event, comes and goes by. History as happening is the acting and being acted upon in and right through the *present*, determined from out of the future and taking over what has been. Our asking of the basic metaphysical question is historical because it opens up the happening (*Geschehen*) of human existence in its essential relationships, that is, to essents as such in their totality, in respect of possibilities and futures never inquired into and because at the same time it binds it back to its beginnings in the living past, thus sharpening it and giving it weight in the present. In this questioning our Dasein is summoned to its history in the full sense of the word; called to it and to decision in it. . . . The basic point of view and attitude of the questioning is itself historical, standing and holding

itself in what is happening, inquiring out of this and for the sake of this. [6]

The immediate urgency of raising the question of Being comes from the fact that Being has become for us a mere word and floating mist, a fact which is not just a psychological characteristic of present-day man but one in the midst of which we stand, a state of our existence, the mode in which we are ourselves constituted in relation to Being. "The emptiness of the word 'Being', the total vanishing of its appellative force" (as Manheim happily translates) is a manifestation of that perverse and false relationship to language characterizing man today and which is itself rooted in our disrupted relationship to Being as such. Since the destiny of language itself, as Heidegger says, is grounded in the particular relationship of a people to Being in any age, even the basic words of our language no longer speak to us with their full force and with the weight of the tradition which they not only embody but of which they are themselves the wellspring.

The above considerations explain why Heidegger has ceaselessly attempted to come to grips—more strenuously than perhaps any other original philosopher—not only with the central doctrines of the great European philosophers but with the entire course of the history of Western philosophy as a whole, trying to arrive at a complete view of its inner nature and dynamism, much as only Hegel had done before him, from the perspective of the question of Being.[7] But he interprets this history not in terms of the thought that has found explicit utterance in it but from the point of view of the unexpressed presuppositions underlying it, of what has remained unsaid in it. This general principle of interpretation, laying no claim to 'scientific' history, is employed by him in the interpretation of individual philosophers, of the larger movement of philosophical history and of the basic philosophical words and concepts coming down from the early Greek origins of Western thought. Already in *Kant und das Problem der Metaphysik*, Heidegger explicitly adopts the method of interpreting past philosophers, not in terms of what they have actually said but, through a consideration of the latter, to lay bare what is implicitly presupposed in it. Every philosopher, in explicitly formulating his thoughts, leaves unexpressed the driving idea at work implicitly in his formulations and the task of *philosophical* interpretation, as opposed to that of purely historical scholarship, is to bring this to light by a creative project of thought. "Real exegesis," in Heidegger's words, "must show what does not stand in the words and is nevertheless said. To accomplish this the interpretation must use force. The essential thing is to be sought where scientific interpretation has nothing more to find, branding as unscientific everything that transcends its own preserve."[8] Explaining the procedure adopted by him in his own much disputed interpretation of the *Critique of Pure Reason*, Heidegger says,

> Now, if an interpretation merely reproduces what Kant has explicitly said, it is, from the very outset, no interpretation in the proper sense. The task before a proper interpretation is to bring expressly into view that which Kant, in his attempt to provide a foundation for metaphysics, has managed to disclose, over and above what he has explicitly formulated, but which, nevertheless, is something that Kant himself could not possibly go on to state. In all philosophical knowledge the decisive thing is not what is said in so many words but what is brought into view, through what is said, as that which still remains unsaid. . . .But, of course, in order to wrest from what the words say that which is implicitly intended in them, every interpretation must necessarily use force. Such force, however, cannot be just rambling caprice. The power of an illuminating idea must drive and guide the exposition. Only by virtue of this can an interpretation venture upon the ever audacious undertaking of putting one's trust in the hidden inner passion of a work, in order thus to be led into the unsaid in it and be constrained to say that. And that is also the way in which the guiding idea itself emerges into clarity in all its power.[9]

Such interpretation aims at reopening a basic problem at a point where historically a particular formulation and answer has been given to it, at 'repeating' the problem so as to disclose in it possibilities which have not yet been actualized. "By the repetition of a basic problem we understand the opening up of its original possibilities, hidden so long, by the elaboration of which it is transformed and so alone preserved in its substance as a problem. To preserve a problem means to hold it free and living in respect of those inner forces which render it possible as a problem in its very roots." The possible, according to Heidegger, is the wellspring of all actualized thinking and a repetition aims at retracing the path taken by the actual back to its source in the possible, in order to capture it in its moment of birth, as it were, and to see if the possible, the potential and the implicit, offers other ways in which it may be actualized in thought. Only when, starting from the present, we succeed in reaching, step by step, back to the beginnings of the historical unfoldment of the whole of European thought, to the wellspring of the possible, shall we be in a position to see that as one actualized possibility, leaving still others at the disposal of thought. Only thus will it be possible to make another beginning in thought and thus enable a renewal and regeneration of the present. As Heidegger remarks,

> To ask the question about Being means nothing less than to recapitulate (*wieder-holen*) the beginning of our historical-spiritual existence, in order to transform it into a new beginning. This is possible. It is in fact the authentic pattern of historicity, for all history takes its start in a fundamental happening. But we do not repeat a beginning by reducing it to something past and now known, which we may simply affect and ape. The beginning must be begun again, *more radically*, with all the strangeness, the darkness, the insecurity that attend a true beginning. Repetition as we understand it is anything but an improved continuation of what has been up till now by means of the same old methods.[10]

Heidegger's attitude toward history and his interpretation of the historical course of Western philosophy may be brought into sharp focus by contrasting it with the way Hegel has interpreted that history. For Hegel, the history of Western philosophy is not just a succession of diverse views and doctrines, one giving place to another, without any inner connection between them, but represents the process, in itself coher-

ent, uniform, and necessary, of the progress of the spirit towards complete consciousness of itself.[11] Philosophy as the
self-development of the spirit towards absolute knowledge is
identical with the history of philosophy; the latter is only the
externalized form of the inner dialectic of pure thought itself,
its various epochs representing the dialectical unfoldment of
one and the same truth at progressively fuller stages of its
evolution. "No other philosopher *before* Hegel," Heidegger
remarks, "has attained to such a fundamental point of view in
philosophy which both enables and requires philosophical
thinking to move within its history and at the same time
makes this movement identical with philosophy itself."[12] The
first stage in this process is represented by Greek thought, with
which philosophy proper begins and which is the stage of
thesis. Thought, at this stage, emerges into pure objectivity,
into the universal as such, but because not yet referred to a
subject and mediated by it, this is also the stage of abstraction.
The beginning, the first emergence of thought, Hegel says, is
necessarily the most abstract; it is the simplest and the poorest
or emptiest and so the earliest philosophers are the poorest of
all. In this stage, Being or the Real as the abstract universal and
pure objectivity is, as Heidegger puts it, *not yet* determined and
not yet mediated through the dialectical movement of the
spirit's absolute subjectivity and hence, for Hegel, the
philosophy of the Greeks is still in the stage of this 'not yet' and
satisfying, as he says, only to a limited extent.[13] The next
higher stage, that of antithesis, begins with Descartes in whose
philosophy the subject is posited and recognized *as* subject for
the first time, thus enabling the objectivity of the previous
stage to be grasped explicitly as objectivity. From the point of
view of the last stage as represented by his own philosophy,
Hegel quite appropriately says of Descartes, "With him we
really enter into a philosophy that stands on its own. . . .
Here, we may say, we are at home and can, like the sailor at the
end of a long voyage on a stormy sea, cry 'Land!' " The third
and highest stage, that of synthesis, in which the two earlier
stages are annulled, conserved, and taken up (*aufgehoben*, in the
threefold sense of *tollere*, *conservare*, and *elevàre*) is reached in
Hegel's own System of Speculative Idealism, "containing
within itself everything that the labor of thousands of years has

produced, the consummation and final result of all that has gone before," as he says in his *Lectures on the History of Philosophy*. This is the crowning stage of the concrete universal in which the Spirit, rich with its own self-unfolding process, comes to itself explicitly in the absolute certainty of itself as the absolute, fully self-conscious subject. As Heidegger points out, Hegel sees the nature of history in the light of Being conceived as absolute subjectivity and judging the course of philosophy before its culmination in the Spirit's absolute certainty of self-consciousness in his own system, finds in it only a movement from the less developed to the more.[14]

For Hegel, as for Heidegger, thought is concerned with something that is in itself historical in the sense of a happening (*Geschehen*). According to Hegel, thought's concern is with Being as self-thinking thought, which comes to itself only in the process of its speculative development, and the happening is understood as one whose process character is determined by the dialectic of Being.[15] Heidegger not only does not accept the subjectivistic interpretation of Being as thought but rejects the view that particular philosophies and epochs of philosophy emerge one from another, in the sense of the necessity of a dialectical process, thus differing from Hegel on both these points.[16] Heidegger also differs from Hegel in his estimate of the early thinking of a historical tradition. "The basic error," he says, "lies in the belief that history begins with the primitive and backward, the clumsy and weak. The opposite is true. The beginning is the uncanniest and mightiest. What comes after is not development but shallowness and diffusion, the failure to hold on to the beginning, rendering it ineffective and harmless and exaggerating it into a caricature. . . ." [17] Discussing the Anaximander fragment, he asks, "With what claim does the earliest address itself to us, presumably the latest of the latecomers of philosophy? . . . Does the chronological and historical remoteness of the utterance conceal in itself a historical nearness of what it leaves unsaid and which speaks, beyond the present, into coming time? . . . May it not be that what is early outstrips the late, the earliest outstripping the latest most of all?"[18]

Summarizing the main points of divergence between himself and Hegel, Heidegger says, "For Hegel, the concern of thinking is with Being in respect of essents as they are appropriated by thought (*Gedachtheit*) in and as absolute thinking. For us, the object of thinking is the same, Being, but Being in respect of its difference from beings. To put it more pointedly, for Hegel the matter of thinking is the thought (*Gedanke*) as the absolute notion. For us, the object of thinking is, provisionally expressed, the difference as difference."[19] Further, for Hegel as well as Heidegger, the criterion for a dialog with the historical heritage is the penetration into the power of the thinking of earlier thinkers. But whereas Hegel finds the specific power of thinkers in what has been thought by them, insofar as it can be taken up (*aufgehoben*, in its threefold sense) as a specific stage in the dialectic of absolute thinking, Heidegger seeks for this power not in what has already been thought, but rather in what is yet unthought and from which what has been thought receives its essential character and scope. To the more popular question whether there is any 'progress' in philosophy, Heidegger has a characteristic answer: Philosophy, insofar as it is mindful of its nature, does not move forward at all. She steps into her place and marks time so that she may ceaselessly think of one and the same thing. Moving forward, that is, away from this place, is an error that follows thinking, like a shadow thrown by thinking itself.[20] Admitting that it is what has already been thought that makes for the not-yet-thought, which comes up ever afresh in its plenitude, Heidegger continues, "The criterion of the unthought does not lead to the incorporation of what has been thought previously into still higher levels of development and systematization surpassing it, but demands that the heritage of thought be liberated in respect of what still lies in reserve in its 'has been' (*Geswesenes*). It is this which holds tradition initially in its sway and is prior to it, though without being thought about expressly and as the originative source." Finally, for Hegel the dialog with the preceding history of philosophy has the character of annulment (in the threefold sense of *Aufhebung*), whereas for Heidegger it is of the nature of taking the step back (*der Schritt zurück*). "The annulment leads into the surmounting, gathering-together sphere of absolutely posited truth in the sense of the completely developed certitude of self-knowing knowledge, while the step back opens the realm, hitherto overlooked, with reference to which the essence of truth first of all becomes something that deserves thought." The step back, Heidegger explains, does not mean taking an isolated step in thought but a particular manner of thought's movement and a long way.

> Insofar as the step back determines the character of our dialog with the history of Occidental thought, it leads our thinking in a way beyond what has hitherto been thought in philosophy. Thinking steps back before what concerns it, that is, Being, and thus brings what has been thought into a confrontation (*Gegenüber*) in which we have a view of the whole of this history and that, too, in respect of what constitutes the wellspring of this entire thinking, for it is the wellspring that alone provides the domain in which this thinking abides. This is, in contrast to Hegel, not a problem coming down to us already posed, but is rather something that has remained throughout unasked in the entire course of this history of thinking . . . the difference between Being and beings.[21]

The difference of essent and Being, itself unnoticed and unnoticeable by metaphysics, is the realm within which metaphysics, that is, Occidental thinking in the totality of its essence, can be what in fact it is. Hence, Heidegger concludes, the step back is the step that leads out of metaphysics into the essence of metaphysics, into the source and ground of its essential constitution; the step back, taking us out of the charmed circle of metaphysical thinking, alone gives the necessary distance and perspective from which one can contemplate its essential nature and meditate on the 'ontological difference' on which, as on its unthought ground, it rests.

The continuous reappropriation of a living tradition depends upon its reinterpretation from age to age. But every age necessarily interprets the past from its own dominant perspective and in terms of its own conceptual framework and language, thus transforming what it receives from the past in the very process of assimilating it. In seeking to go back—and recapture in its purity (and yet creatively, from the present perspective, in our case the perspective of the *question* of Being)—to the thinking of an age in which the foundations of this tradition were laid, we have, therefore, in a sense to reverse the process by which the original significance of the central concepts, and the sense of the basic words in which they were embodied, has been obscured by the strata of new meanings imposed upon them by later interpretation. In addition, the utmost care must be exercised to avoid interpreting earlier thinking in terms of later concepts which have evolved from them; though these alone have become historically effective, yet they only constitute one possible interpretation that might be given to the central concepts of the earlier thinkers. As Heidegger has said,[22] all later thinking that seeks a dialog with the earlier must inevitably reach out to it from its own place in history, if it is at all to bring the silence of early thought into an utterance; but this need not necessarily imply projecting later conceptions into them, so long as care is taken to enter, in an expressly inquiring spirit, into the field of vision and hearing of early thinking. No previous thinker, Heidegger asserts, has been able to reach back to the beginning of Western philosophy and to recapture its true character *as* a beginning. As he remarks, "Neither Nietzsche nor any other thinker before him—not even, and in particular, he who, before Nietzsche, for the first time thought philosophically about the *history* of philosophy, namely, Hegel—penetrate into the first beginnings; they rather see the beginning as colored by, and in the light of, what was already a falling away from the beginning and its stagnation: in the light of the Platonic philosophy."[23]

Such reinterpretation and misinterpretation, transformation and falsification has occurred repeatedly not only in the course of the transmission of ideas from one period of history to another but also continuously, within the same period, as between its different phases. In its most dramatic form however, the process can be seen at work in the historically 'fateful' translations by which Greek concepts were taken over into Latin and, later, into the vernaculars. In his quest for the unimpaired revelatory power of ancient words, Heidegger has frequently drawn attention to the havoc wrought by this translation of the Greek philosophical language into Latin, a language embodying the wholly different medieval spirit and outlook—an occurrence, Heidegger points out, by no means accidental and harmless but the first stage in the process by which we are cut off and alienated from the original essence of Greek philosophy. The translation into Latin of the Greek *physis* as *natura*, of *ousia* as *substantia*, of *logos* as *ratio*, for example, does indeed convey something of the sense embodied in the Greek terms but, as Heidegger again and again shows in his discussions of these and other terms, the Latin 'equivalents' equally stand between ourselves and what the Greek terms say, hiding from our view their original sense and obstructing entry into the genuine Greek vision and way of thinking.[24] Such translations, of course, like all milestones in the history of thought, are not just examples of capricious and avoidable misinterpretation but constitute the very stuff of a continuous historical tradition. As Heidegger has remarked, in the case of important and effective translations, "the translation is not only interpretation but is tradition, an integral part of our philosophical heritage. As tradition it belongs to the innermost movement of history. . . . An important translation corresponds, in a particular epoch of the destiny (*Geschick*) of Being, to the way in which a language, destined by Being, speaks."[25] That is why every attempt to recapture the unuttered meaning of past thinking requires a creative leap of thought and a new, all-embracing perspective, based on disillusioned, critical awareness of the present, an ear for the message of the past and a passionate concern for our destiny.[26]

The Greek Thinkers

Greek thought begins with reflection on Being, not merely in the sense of the totality of what is (*ta onta*) but with an awareness of the Being (*einai*) of all that is, of the essent in its Being. That the Being of essents claimed the thinking of the early Greeks, says Heidegger, actually is the beginning of the Occident as a historical reality and the hidden source from which its destiny springs.[27] Being (*eon, on*) revealed itself to the early Greek thinkers, the founders of the Western philosophical tradition, as *ousia*, which means, according to Heidegger, not substance as the Latin translation of this term interprets it, but constant presence (*Anwesenheit*).[28] In the light of this way of understanding Being, never explicitly considered by them, they apprehended the totality of essents as *physis*, that which emerges, unfolds itself, enters into and remains in manifestness. The central question of their inquiry, and thenceforward the main theme of Western philosophy, is concerned with the totality of essents conceived as *physis*. It is metaphysics in the sense that it is not about particular essents but about the essent as such, that is, in respect of its Being, going *beyond* essents to their Being in order, in the light of that, to understand the nature of what is. In a basic sense, as Heidegger remarks, metaphysics is physics, *episteme physike*.[29] The Greeks inquired into the Being of essents, into the truth of what is, and in this they were guided by the light of a particular conception of Being, of what it means to be, namely, the sense of Being as presence. They inquired into the Being of beings but they never asked what Being itself meant and therefore could not be aware of the particular sense of Being presupposed in their own thinking about essents as such. The history of Western philosophy, except for its earliest pre-Socratic period, is a history of 'metaphysical' thinking, that is, thinking about the Being of essents (not about Being itself) and it begins with the oblivion of Being as such and of *its* truth. The oblivion of Being is the oblivion of the difference of Being from beings which is implied in all inquiry about the Being of essents. In uncovering itself in the essent, Being withdraws itself as such and, along with that, conceals its difference from the essent. The difference breaks out in Anaximander, in Parmenides, in Heraclitus, a lightning flash in the illumination of which their thinking takes its birth; but the difference does not reveal itself *as* the difference and so remains unnamed and unthought. The history of Being begins with the oblivion of Being, of Being's own nature and of its difference from the essent.[30]

All reflection on the Being of what is, however, is itself carried on in the light of an implicit conception of Being which derives not from man but is something that comes *to* him as the destiny that holds his thinking in its grip, depending on the way Being illuminates itself in him, on the way Being dispenses and reveals itself to man. As Heidegger explains, in every age Being itself is understood in a determinate sense, disclosing itself in some aspect.[31] But all understanding, as a basic mode of disclosure, must itself move in a determinate line of vision (*Blickbahn*), a perspective which must have opened out in advance. The determinate understanding of Being moves in a predetermined perspective, not itself made by man but in which man finds himself immersed, a dispensation of Being itself, as Heidegger later calls it. Not even the Greeks did or could, due to reasons inherent in the case and not because of any human deficiency, bring this perspective to light. The history of the way man has understood and interpreted the Being of essents in their totality is, therefore, rooted in the different ways in which Being itself has, from age to age, revealed itself variously to man, in the history of Being (*Seinsgeschichte*), as Heidegger calls it. The history of Being, which is the history of the self-bestowal of Being to man and has thus an intrinsic reference to man as the seat of its illumination, is in the West the history of the way Being reveals and bestows itself in and through its own withdrawal from man. In revealing itself as the light in which essents enter into overtness, it withdraws its own essence into itself; without such revelation man could never have asked what Heidegger calls the 'leading question' (*Leitfrage*) of philosophy, the question about the Being of essents, and without this withdrawal man would not have become alienated from Being as such and, forgetting the 'fundamental question' (*Grundfrage*) of philosophy, the question about Being as such, abandoned himself to the essent as such. Being only reveals and gives itself to man as its own withdrawal and man's oblivion of Being is actually the abandonment of man by Being. The history of philosophy is the history of man's attempt to understand what is. But this understanding is itself the way Being reveals itself in Dasein and is rooted in man's relationship to Being. As Heidegger asserts, "the relationship of Being to beings can come only from Being and can have its basis only in the nature of Being."[32] The history of man's thinking of Being is thus a manifestation of the history of Being itself. And since the former is in the main a history of the way man has thought about the essent as such and as a whole, disregarding Being itself, the latter is conceived by Heidegger as the history of the self-concealment of Being. The history of philosophy, as Heidegger reads it, is thus itself grounded in the invisible, deeper history of Being, and though exhibiting, on the surface, development and advance in thinking (that is, on the level of our knowledge of and control over essents as such), it is at best a history of the progressive withdrawal of Being from man's vision and so of man's growing alienation from Being.

Traditionally, Being is contrasted with Becoming, with Seeming, with Thought, and with the Ought, fateful distinctions already latent in early Greek thought.[33] As against Becoming, Being is permanence; as against Appearance, it is the enduring prototype, the self-same; as against Thought, it is the object, what lies in front; as against the Ought, it is that which is presented to us as something to be realized. All these determinations of Being, through what the Greeks distinguished from it, at bottom mean the same; constancy of presence (*Anwesenheit*), with the notions of "contemporaneity and presence, of constancy and stability, sojourn and occurrence" included in it.[34] An examination of these contrasting pairs, however, shows that in each case Being and what is opposed to it belong intimately and inseparably together in a deeper sense, that these distinctions have emerged historically from a conception of Being in which they were originally at one with, and implicit within, Being itself. Parmenides conceived Being in sharp contrast with Becoming, thus explicitly bringing out the character of the former as the sheer fullness, gathered in itself, of the permanent, untouched by restlessness and change. Heraclitus says at bottom the same.

Being and appearance are also bound together into an original unity on the basis of which they were then distinguished from one another; the power of coming forth and abiding, *physis*, which for the Greeks constituted the Being of all that is, is at the same time a shining forth, appearing and standing out of hiddenness (*aletheia*). To be an essent is to come to light, to present and display itself; but what appears always has the possibility of appearing as what in truth it is not, of being mere appearance and illusion. As Heidegger puts it, where there is unconcealment of essents there is always the possibility of semblance and, conversely, where the essent has stood, unshaken and for long, in a certain semblance, this appearance can shatter and fall away, revealing the essent in its naked truth. Seeming and semblance are for the Greeks not subjective and imaginary but are inherent in the essent and hence, as Heidegger puts it, "they were perpetually compelled to wrest Being from appearance and preserve it against appearance . . . in the ceaseless struggle between Being and Seeming they wrested Being from the essent, bringing permanence and unconcealment to the essent."[35] As against the later falling apart of Being and Seeming with Plato, the great age of Greece was a unique creative self-assertion amid the confusion of the complex struggle between the two powers of Being and Seeming. Seeming belongs to Being itself as appearing and because of this the early Greek thinkers, Parmenides in particular, devoted their main effort to the task of rescuing Being from Seeming by distinguishing it from the latter and from non-Being—it is with this distinction that, as Heidegger says, Western man's historical existence begins. The inner unity of Being and appearance has found concise expression in Heraclitus' saying: *physis kryptesthai philei*, that is, Being, as *physis* (coming forth out of hiddenness) in itself tends to self-concealment, to a relapse into that. Being and Seeming are locked together, intrinsically, in the unity of *polemos*, of perpetual war. Becoming too, like seeming, is not sheer nothing and therefore, though opposed to Being in the sense of what stands out in permanent sameness, is yet comprehended in Being in the larger sense.

The differentiation between Being and Thought also springs from an original, inner belonging together of the two, an initial unity which itself, as Being in the profounder sense, as it were, requires its own differentiation. Logic, the science of 'thought', cannot itself explain the nature and origin of this separation because logic itself arose on the basis of this separation, after Plato's interpretation of Being as *idea* had already turned Being into an 'object' of knowledge. It can be shown, Heidegger claims, that in early Greek philosophy Being (as *physis*) and thought (as *logos*) were conceived as intrinsically belonging together, provided that we understand *logos* also in a deeper, more original sense, keeping out its later misinterpretation in terms of thinking as a subjective process, of reason, of judgment, of the Christian doctrine. Originally, *logos* meant, according to Heidegger, gathering or collection, having the sense of both collecting and collectedness; it was the primal gathering principle. "*Logos* signifies here neither meaning nor word, nor doctrine, nor the spirit of the latter but the permanent, self-abiding, original collection of gathered togetherness. . . . Logos is the permanent gathering together, the self-contained togetherness of the essent, that is,

Being."[36] *Physis* and *logos* together constitute a unity and in that sense are the same. What is is in itself gathered presence, holding together what tends to come apart; so conceived, Being is at the same time radiance and harmony, the supreme beauty.[37]

In order to show how this original unity of *physis* and *logos* is eventually broken up, Heidegger offers his own interpretation of the well-known line of Parmenides, *to gar auto noein estin te kai einai* ("thinking and being are the same" in the usual translation, no less un-Greek, Heidegger says, than the misinterpretation of *logos*) as also of his saying, *chre to legein te noein t'eon emmenai* (ordinarily translated as "It is necessary to say and to think that the essent is").[38] To understand the real meaning of *noein*, he insists, we must carefully refrain from projecting into it the modern conception of thinking as the activity of a subject, with Being as its correlate, and from interpreting it in Kantian or Hegelian terms. We should understand *noein* in the sense of *vernehmen* (to apprehend), in the double signification of taking up, accepting, letting what appears come up and of hearing a witness, questioning him and so determining how matters stand—the sense of taking on and determining.[39] Being, in the sense of *physis* or emergence into unhiddenness, and *noein* are the same in the sense of inherently belonging together; where unhiddenness occurs and Being prevails, there occurs also, as necessarily implied in it, apprehension. Further, such apprehension, far from being a power exercised by man as subject, is itself possible to man because he himself is part of Being (*physis*) and so shares in the apprehending (*noein*) that is intrinsic to Being. The being of man himself is determined by the inner unity and togetherness of *physis* and *noein*. Apprehension, Heidegger says, is here not a faculty belonging to man, with his nature already defined; apprehension is rather a happening, sharing in which alone man enters into history as an essent, appears, that is, in the literal sense, comes into being. Apprehension is not a mode of activity which man possesses as an attribute; on the contrary, man himself is a function of apprehension. What the saying of Parmenides expresses is thus a definition of the essence of man in terms of the truth of Being.

For the early Greeks, man stands in an intimate bond with

Being, deriving his own nature from that bond and existing as the locus of the self-disclosure of Being. At the same time, needed and necessitated by Being itself, he seeks to wrest the truth of Being, to make Being itself shine forth and appear by bringing it to a stand in the permanency of well-defined form, through knowledge and art, by embodying, rendering manifest, and realizing Being *in* the essent (*ins-Werk-setzen*, as, for example, when the artist incorporates the truth of Being in a 'work' of art) through the exercise of force against the order of *physis* or *dike*.[40] Knowing as apprehension (*noein*) is not mere passive reception but is an act of violence, a marching out to engage the essent in the battle for Being. Within Being itself, conceived as *physis* and *logos*, there is inherent the possibility and the necessity of *logos* (that is, *noein* as a gathering together or *legein*) differentiating itself from logos in the sense of the togetherness, the gathered character, of Being itself. Logos acquires the sense of a gathering together that makes manifest, occurring in and through man, and, as the gathering and apprehending of the being of essents, it becomes a feature of the constitutive essence of man and no longer an element in Being itself. Further, man's breakthrough into Being, but for the sake of Being and in its service, in knowledge and art, is at the same time a breakthrough into language. Language, giving form to the essent and opening it up in its being, is a collecting, gathering together and so disclosing, *logos*. It brings the essent into openness, delimitation and permanence; in primordial speech the Being of the essent is opened up in the texture of its gatheredness and maintained and preserved as such. Himself gathered together within the structure of Being, standing and acting in *logos* as gatheredness, man (as a function of *noein* or apprehension) is the gatherer charged with the task of preserving and fulfilling primarily through language (poetic creation and thought), the disclosure of Being, of guarding such disclosure against seeming and closure. *Logos* and *physis* thus split apart, facing each other as it were, but still forming a harmonious whole, the differentiation still in the service of Being. As yet this does not mean any breaking away of *logos* from Being, nor imply that *logos* stands opposed to Being in such a way as to stand in judgment (as Reason) on Being, determining and regulating what is to count as the Being of essents.

The secession of *logos* occurs, Heidegger points out, when it abandons its original essence, when Being is interpreted differently and its *physis* character is lost from view. The slow and long history of this transformation, in the midst of which Western man has long been standing, culminates in the domination of thinking as *ratio* over the Being of what is and the determination of man's essence in terms of Reason. The initial differentiation of *logos* and *physis* was followed by the breaking away of *logos* from the original unity and ultimately to its being elevated to a position of supremacy through the philosophy of Plato and Aristotle. Plato conceives Being as *idea* or *eidos*, an interpretation which then dominates the whole course of Western philosophy right up to Hegel, with whom the first phase of Western thought, as Heidegger calls it, comes to its definitive close. Idea or *eidos* means the look, the view presented by anything that confronts us, its visage. In such presentation the thing stands before us, is present, that is, *is* in the Greek sense; this is *physis* immobilized and held fast in the *aspect* presented by it. In the visage that it shows, the essent, that which is present (*Anwesende*), presents itself in its what and how, its *ousia*, which signifies at the same time the presence (*Anwesenheit*) of what is present as well as the latter in respect of its 'what'. The subsequent distinction between *existentia* and *essentia* is based on the Greek understanding of Being as constancy of presence and the Platonic interpretation of the latter as *idea*. *Idea* understood as presence, Heidegger points out, includes in itself the sense both of emerging into unhiddenness (simple *estin*) and of the *what* of the emergence (*ti estin*) and its correlate the *that* (*oti estin*). The interpretation of Being as *idea* follows from the conception of Being as *physis* (emerging and appearing), but with Plato the *idea*, instead of being recognized as the derivative that it is, usurped the position of *physis* as the sole and proper meaning of Being. What happened was nothing less than a betrayal of the original Greek insight. Being and apprehension, what is seen and seeing, belong together in one whole, but from this it does not follow that being seen alone can determine and constitute the presence (Being) of the thing seen or that Being should be conceived in terms of apprehension alone and defined as that which is apprehended by the intellect. In the interpretation of

Being as *idea*, Heidegger says, not only is a consequence of the initial conception of the nature of Being twisted and elevated to the status of that nature itself but the falsification is once again misinterpreted. Being is not only understood in the sense of *idea* (whatness or quiddity), but the latter is exalted as the real essent (*ontos on*) above the whole realm of essents, which is now degraded into the *me on*, the unreal and the imperfect, having only a share in Being (*methexis*), an imperfect copy of the ideal prototype. A chasm (*chorismos*) opens up between the *idea* as what really is and the essent as what in reality is not. The meaning of appearing, too, is transformed; it has no longer the sense of emerging or showing itself but becomes *mere* appearance, seeming—*on* and *phainomenon* fall apart. The meaning of truth, which was at the beginning the *aletheia* or unhiddenness of *physis*, also undergoes a change. Truth is understood now as the adequation (*homoiosis*) of the disclosure of essents to the ideal pattern, the idea, that is as the correctness of seeing, of apprehension in the sense of representation. The transformation of Being from *physis* to *idea* has been decisive, Heidegger claims, in giving to the history of the Occident its essential character and mold. In his essay on Plato's doctrine of truth, Heidegger brings out the Unthought in Plato's thinking through a detailed discussion of the Allegory of the Cave in the *Republic*, Book VIII. What remains unthought here, according to him, is a transformation in the conception of truth from unhiddenness to correctness of perception or knowing, from *a-letheia* to *orthotes*. The original Greek sense of truth as a wresting away from hiddenness is indeed present in the Allegory, but it is dominated and overshadowed by another conception of truth which comes into prominence. *Aletheia* comes under the domination, the yoke, of the *idea*, as Heidegger puts it, and truth as unhiddenness recedes into the background. In consequence, not only the character but also the locus of truth changes. "As unhiddenness it is still the basic feature of essents themselves. As correctness of 'seeing', it becomes a character of man's attitude toward essents,"[41] that is, a property of knowing. This change in the nature of truth goes hand in hand with the determination of the Being (*presence*) of essents as *idea*, so that presence is no longer regarded as the emergence of the hidden into unhiddenness, as it was in the beginning, but as *idea*, itself determining truth and rendering it possible. Plato's thought results, Heidegger says, from the change in the nature of truth, a change which manifests itself as the history of metaphysics, of which the final culmination begins in the thinking of Nietzsche.[42]

With the changed interpretation of *physis* there goes a corresponding transformation in the meaning of *logos*. *Logos* as gathering renders essents manifest; language is that through which the *legein* or gathering and manifesting of this *logos* occurs. But when attention is focused on the task of guarding authentic discourse against mere repetitive talk emptied of its revelatory power, the former comes to be identified with *logos* itself and becomes the locus of truth.[43] *Logos* as gathering was initially identical with the occurrence of unhiddenness (truth) and rooted in it, but now, in the sense of statement, it becomes itself the seat of truth in the sense of correctness. Originally, truth as unhiddenness was a feature of the essent and governed by gathering but now it becomes a property of *logos* (statement) not only thus shifting its locus but also changing its character from primordial unhiddenness of the essent to the correctness of statement. *Logos* thus detaches itself from its initial unity with *physis* and becomes, as statement, the arbiter of what is to count as Being, unfolding, in course, into the discipline of ontology and the doctrine of categories. The Principle of Contradiction, declaring that when two statements contradict each other, what they are about cannot *be*, embodies and illustrates this changed conception of the relationship between *physis* and *logos*. Further, since *logos* as statement is itself an objectively existing entity, it can be employed as an instrument to gain and secure truth as correctness, as an *organon*. With this final transformation of *logos* into a tool, "there arrives the hour of the birth of Logic." Ever since Aristotle, Logic, born complete in most essentials, has remained the authoritative and standard perspective for the interpretation of Being, right down to Kant and Hegel. The only thing that remains, Heidegger acidly remarks, is now "to lift it off its hinges" and effect radical changes in its very foundations.

The transformation of *physis* and *logos* and consequently

of their relation to one another is a falling off from the first beginning. As Heidegger says, "The philosophy of the Greeks conquered the Western world not on the strength of what it was in its original beginning but through what it had become towards the end of this beginning,"[44] an end which came to its final culmination with Hegel in the last century. The inner ground of the transformation of *physis* and *logos* into idea and statement lies in the change in the nature of truth from unhiddenness to correctness. The original essence of truth could not be retained and preserved and there was a "collapse of unhiddenness," of the area opened out for the appearing of the essent; from the debris 'idea' and 'statement', *ousia* and *kategoria* were salvaged, as Heidegger puts it, each existing as an objective entity, disjoined from the other and connectable only by a relation having itself the character of an objective entity. Ever since, philosophy has labored to explain and render plausible the relation between judgment (thought) and Being by all sorts of ingenious theories, in vain, because without reopening the root question of Being itself. The definitive interpretation of Being itself that emerges, in consequence of all this, is crystallized in the word *ousia*, Being in the sense of constant presence, simple givenness (*Vorhandenheit*). According to this conception of Being, henceforth to dominate European thought, only what always is, the *aei on*, counts as really being. This conception, along with the consequent interpretation of Being as *idea* also paves the way for the separation between Being and the Ought. Once Being is conceived as idea, itself in a way an essent, it no longer has its potency and its power to render something possible within itself, but becomes subordinate to something above it, to the Idea of the Good (*idea tou agathou*) which, therefore, as Plato says, stands beyond Being (*epekeina tes ousias*).[45] It is this Idea of Ideas, the Good, that endows Being (as *idea*) with the power to function as prototype. The Ought thus separates itself from Being, from within Being itself, and sets itself above it. The change in the conception of truth and the consequent interpretation of Being (presence) as *idea* converts as it were Being itself into an essent and the highest Idea, the Good, appears as the highest essent, the supersensible first cause of the existence and appearance of all sensible essents, called by Plato and, following him, by Aristotle, the divine (*to theion*). Since Plato's interpretation of Being as *idea*, Heidegger says, all thinking about the Being of essents has been metaphysical and metaphysics itself theological[46] or, as in a later formulation, ontology, theology, and logic in one, onto-theo-logic. With Plato, thinking becomes 'philosophy', that is, representational thinking, which catches only the essent in its net, or thinking in concepts, which is aimed, with its grasping and grabbing, with its calculative character, at attaining mastery over the essent. A new epoch of Being begins, not yet infected with subjectivism and still moving within the basic Greek experience, it is true, but nevertheless destined to cast its nihilistic shadow over the entire course of Western philosophy up to Nietzsche, with whom 'philosophy' runs out its course, opening out the possibility, and the necessity, of a new beginning.

In Aristotle's conception of *energeia* as the Being (*ousia*, presence) of essents, there was indeed a flash of the original spirit of Greek thought. *Energeia* in Aristotle means, according to Heidegger, coming or being brought into unhiddenness and presence and enduring so in an accomplished piece of work, a meaning which was totally lost with the Latin translation of this term into *actualitas* and its eventual transformation into Reality and Objectivity.[47]

The ontology of the *Vorhanden* (the simply given), in the language of *Being and Time*, with its conception of Being as constant presence, itself contains within it the seeds of the differentiation, and eventually of the dissension, of Becoming, Seeming, Thinking, and the Ought from Being. The original unity of Being as *physis* in its intimate relation to Truth as unhiddenness and comprehending within itself the relationship to the essence of man, flashing out for a brief historical moment in early Greek thought, could not be sustained, with consequences which have been working themselves out in the shape of the history of Western philosophy.[48] The ground for this lies, Heidegger says, in the magnitude of the beginning and in the nature of a beginning as such. "As a beginning, the beginning must in a sense leave itself behind, thus necessarily hiding itself (though this self-concealment is not nothing). A beginning can never directly preserve its power as a beginning and the only way to preserve its force and safeguard its continuation is to repeat the beginning, draw it out once again (*wieder-holen*), in its originative character, in a still deeper sense,"[49] that is, by explicitly bringing out what has remained unthought in it. That is why, in his quest for a new conception of Being, Heidegger goes back to the earliest Greek thinkers who had a glimpse of the Being of essents (*physis*) as the unity of the various elements that later fell apart and renders explicit their unuttered but presupposed conception of Being itself—Being as constant presence (*Anwesenheit, ousia*). It is this way of understanding Being, that is, the determination of the meaning and content of the infinitive 'to be' in terms of the present 'is' and not the other way round, that led to the separation of Becoming, Seeming, Thinking, and the Ought from Being, though they are themselves not sheer nothing. "But if, in these distinctions, all that is opposed to Being is *not* nothing, then it is *itself essent*, ultimately even more so (since Being itself gets its determination in opposition to them) than what the narrow conception of Being regards as essent. But then, in which sense of Being are Becoming, Seeming, Thought, and the Ought essent? In no case in the sense of Being from which they are distinguished."[50] The Greek understanding of Being, dominating the whole course of Western philosophy, is, Heidegger concludes, too narrow and "does not suffice to name everything that 'is'." It is oblivious of the one and only distinction that counts, the distinction between Being and beings, and so generates, through this oblivion, the entire unfoldment of the subsequent tradition of 'metaphysical' thinking. For this reason, Being must once again be experienced anew in its very fundament and in all the breadth of its possible nature. The Being which they (these distinctions) encircle must itself be transformed into the encompassing circle and ground of all essents, not excluding the 'terrible power of negativity' (Hegel), the Nothing. And such rethinking of Being must take cognizance of the fact, itself hidden from the Greeks and from subsequent philosophy, that from the very beginning the perspective governing the disclosure of Being was Time (Being=presence, the 'is'), though time as understood, in its turn, in the light of that narrow interpretation of Being as simple givenness (*Vorhandenheit*), as a succession of given nows.

With the arrival of Christianity, the highest essent, the Divine (*to theion*), became God the Creator, and the Being of essents as a whole was understood to lie in its createdness by God. The leading question of philosophy, namely, the question of what the essent is in its totality, appears as having been conclusively answered, the question itself being thus done away with and that, too, on an authority far superior to the chance opinions and delusions of men, as Heidegger puts it.[51] "Biblical revelation which, according to its own assertion, rests on divine inspiration, teaches that all that is, is created by a personal creator God and is sustained and ruled by Him. Through revealed truth, proclaimed by the Church doctrine as absolutely binding, the question as to what the essent is has become superfluous. The Being of the essent consists in its being created by God (*omne ens est ens creatum*)."[52] To be an essent means to belong in its particular specific position in the hierarchy of the created and, as so brought about, to correspond to the cause of creation (*analogia entis*).[53] Truth itself is understood as *homoiosis* and *convenientia*, the correspondence or adequation of things with their preconceived idea in the divine mind. To know the truth about what is, the only reliable way left for man is to devote himself to the revealed teaching, the *doctrina* of the church doctors. In its essence truth now appears in the character of 'doctrine' and its knowledge consists in the '*Summa*', the systematic collection of the whole heritage of the various doctrinal views insofar as they are consonant with the teaching of the church.

Scholars adopting this approach to the essent as a whole are called 'theologians' but, Heidegger remarks in an interesting passage, their 'philosophy' is philosophy in name only.

A 'Christian philosophy' is even more of an absurdity than the idea of a square circle. Square and circle have at least this in common that they are both spatial constructs, whereas Christian faith and philosophy are divided by an abyss. Both, it might be said, teach the truth, to which the answer is that truth here is conceived by each in wholly disparate ways. That the medieval theologians studied Plato and Aristotle, reinterpreting them in their own way, is much the same as Karl Marx using the metaphysics of Hegel for his political doctrine. Properly and strictly speaking, the *doctrina Christiana* does not mean to impart knowledge about the essent, about what is; its truth is entirely concerned with salvation, with insuring the salvation of the individual immortal soul.[54]

The Modern Age

The modern age begins with the liberation of man from the authority of the revealed truth of Christianity and church doctrine such that, standing on his own, man himself becomes his own lawgiver.[55] This liberation, however, is itself conditioned by its bond with revealed truth, through which man was assured of the salvation of his soul and made secure in that certainty. As Heidegger points out, "The liberation *from* the revelation-based certainty of salvation had, therefore, to be a liberation *into* a certainty in which man secures truth as what is known to him through his own activity of knowing. This was possible only when man himself, seeking to liberate himself, guaranteed the certainty of what is knowable, which in turn he could do only by determining, from within himself and for himself, what is to count as knowable to him and what is to be understood by knowledge and by the assurance of the known, that is, by certainty." What is of decisive importance here, Heidegger says, is not that man throws off his shackles but that with this freedom, his own essence is transmuted and he becomes a subject. For Aristotle and the Greeks, the subject (*subjectum, hypokeimenon*) was what a statement was about, that which lies before, that which underlies as its basis, the permanently present. But for Descartes, the permanently present, the given, is found in the *ego cogito*, which thus becomes the ultimate subject, the subjectness of the ego as subject lying in the certainty of self-consciousness. Man becomes an essent in whom all that is, is grounded as to the mode of its Being and its truth. Correspondingly, the nature of the essent in its totality also undergoes a change. The world turns into an image, a picture in man's grasp and at his disposal, and "the essent as a whole is set out as something which man may prepare himself to meet and which he accordingly seeks to bring in front of himself, to have and keep it, in a positive sense, before himself (*vorstellen*, taken literally)." The world is conceived as a picture and the essent as something which *is* only insofar as it is set up by the representing, producing activity of man. The Being of essents is sought and found in the representedness (*Vorgestelltheit*) of essents; the presence of the present appears, since Descartes, in the mode of objectivity. This is indeed a far cry from the early Greek conception of Being as the presence of the present, of what lies in front (the *hypokeimenon* or subject in the Greek sense), in the unhiddenness or truth of which man shares through apprehension and so *is* man. "Representation (*Vorstellen*) has no longer the character of an apprehension of what is present, in the unhiddenness of which this apprehension itself belongs, with its own mode of presence. In representation there is nothing more of the opening oneself for . . ., but only a grabbing and grasping of. . . . Here it is not what is presented that has its sway; it is the attitude of attacking that prevails." The nature of truth itself undergoes transformation, so that truth is conceived from now on, not as unhiddenness, but as the *certainty* of adequation and correctness.

Liberated from the authority of revealed truth, man has to find certitude within himself and to find a metaphysical foundation for this certitude. Such a *fundamentum absolutum inconcussum veritatis*, absolutely unshakable in its character as a foundation, Descartes provides in the *ego cogito*, in the 'I' conceived as the thinking, representing principle determining what 'being' is to mean. The *cogito ergo sum* of Descartes formulates, Heidegger points out, an intrinsic connection between *cogito*, representing, and *sum* or being, such that it is not merely *I* who am as representing but that the being of every essent consists in its being represented.[56] Further, *cogito* is always *cogito me cogitare*; every 'I think (represent)' is at the same time a representing of oneself as representing. It is of the nature of representation as such to incorporate within it the reference to the representing 'I' for which it is a representation and which itself *is* as represented in what it represents. The ego *is* as representing (*sum cogitans*) and as itself a representation of such representing. As Heidegger remarks, "*sum res cogitans* does not mean that I am a thing endowed with the property of thinking; it means that I am an essent whose mode of *being* consists in representing, such that this representing (*Vorstellen*, putting in front of oneself) puts, at the same time, the representing 'I' itself in the position of being represented."[57] Man, in quest of the certitude of what he knows and of himself as knowing, thus becomes the subject, the underlying basis and ground of everything that is, in terms of whose representing activity the Being of everything is determined and for whom everything is an object, including himself. This thorough subjectivity is at the same time extreme objectivity. The essent is objectivized by virtue of a representing which aims at holding any thing that is before oneself so that calculating man can, in his concern for certitude, secure and be certain of the essent. This conception of the Being of essents as objectivity of representation and of truth as certitude was for the first time developed in the metaphysics of Descartes, Heidegger says, and modern metaphysics in its entirety, not excluding Nietzsche, moves and keeps within the perspective opened up by Descartes in his interpretation of the essent and of truth. Descartes marks "the beginning of the consummation of Western metaphysics," a beginning of which the far-reaching metaphysical significance emerges with growing clarity and force in the views of succeeding philosophers.

The subjectivistic trend in modern metaphysics is deepened still further in Leibniz's conception of the subject as *ens percipiens et appetens*. The Being of what is (that is, the presence of the present) manifests itself not only as representation but as will, which henceforth is an essential aspect of the way Being is understood in modern times right up to Nietzsche, by whom it is explicitly recognized as the only reality. Leibniz's conception of representation, the true *subiectum*, which is at the same time force (*vis primitiva activa*) and is characterized by the synthetic function of bringing into a unity all that is (Being as unifying ground, *Logos*), prepares the way not only for Kant but is destined to constitute "the historical foundation of the modern period."[58] The Principle of Sufficient Reason, after its long period of incubation, at last emerges into clear and explicit formulation by Leibniz, and philosophy, conceiving truth as certainty, forthwith becomes a quest for the "conditions of the possibility of"; thinking comes into its own in the shape of Reason.[59] The name of

Leibniz stands, Heidegger says, not for a past system of philosophy but "designates the contemporaneity of a thinking of which the full impact has yet to be endured. . . . Only when we glance back at what Leibniz thinks can we realize how very much the present era, called the atomic age, is under the domination of the *principium reddendae rationis sufficientis*."[60] In Leibniz, Being reveals itself as Ground and as Reason, as the very principle of the calculability of essents and their subjugation by man.[61]

Plato interpreted Being (presence) as *idea*, consisting of the 'what' of anything, and the Idea as *agathon*, enabling it to be what it is; with Descartes, the *idea* becomes the *perceptum* of a *perceptio*, a representation. The *agathon* character of the *idea*, that is, Being as enabling and rendering possible, as ground, having been brought once again to light by Leibniz, manifests itself in all its power in the Kantian metaphysics. The innermost core of the history of modern philosophy, Heidegger says, consists of the process by which Being acquires its indisputable character of being essentially the condition of the possibility of essents, that is, in the modern sense, of what is represented, of what stands opposite, of objects.[62] The decisive step in this process is taken by the metaphysics of Kant, the peak or *center* to which the subjectivism of the modern period, initiated by Descartes, leads up and which points beyond to the speculative-dialectical interpretation of Being as the absolute concept by Hegel.[63] The basic metaphysical position of Kant finds expression in the fundamental principle, the "supreme principle" upon which the whole of the Transcendental Philosophy rests (as H. J. Paton describes it and as Kant himself explicitly recognizes). In its final formulation the principle runs: "The conditions of the *possibility of experience* in general are likewise conditions of the *possibility of the objects of experience*."[64] In the *Critique of Pure Reason*, Kant's aim is to discover how ontological or transcendental knowledge (the a priori synthesis) is possible. Such knowledge is concerned, not with the essent as such but, transcending that, with the possibility of a prior comprehension of its Being, with the ontological constitution of the essent, that is, with the structure of transcendence. "The supreme principle of all synthetic judgments," quoted above, sums up this structure as the unity of the two elements it mentions, experience and the objects of experience. In order that an object should be given, there must occur a prior "turning oneself toward" it, in the form of the ontological synthesis, of which the core, according to Heidegger, is constituted by the transcendental synthesis of the imagination. This turning oneself toward is the condition of the possibility of experiencing an object. In the second place, the object itself must be rendered possible by a pregiven horizon in which it may appear. This horizon is the condition of the possibility of the object in respect of its objectivity (that it can stand opposite us, confront us). As Heidegger puts it, "The turning oneself toward and letting (the object) stand opposite as such fashions the horizon of objectivity in general. . . . The transcendence is in itself ekstatic-horizonal."[65] The transcendental object, with which ontological knowledge is concerned, is not an essent hidden behind the phenomenon but is the correlate of the unity of apperception, the X as Kant calls it; it is no thing at all but sheer horizon. The X is "object in general," that is, the horizon of objectivity, the transcendence in and through which the Being of essents manifests itself a priori.

It is, Heidegger holds, the transcendental imagination which primarily renders possible such ontological knowledge by building, prior to all experience of objects, the pure schema or view of a horizon of objectivity as such, the horizon of 'constant presence' in which an object may manifest itself as present. Heidegger further suggests that it is the faculty of the imagination that constitutes the 'hidden' common root of the Sensibility and Understanding; he identifies the transcendental imagination, as Kant himself failed explicitly to do, with primordial Time, which constitutes and generates time in the modalities of past, present, and future through the operation of the threefold synthesis. Without being himself explicitly aware of it, Kant has brought together Time and the 'I think' and identified them; the pure self, that is, the finite human subjectivity, is essentially of the nature of time. Kant was bound to light upon time as the root determination of finite transcendence because the understanding of Being in Dasein, by itself as it were, projects Being in terms of time. And he was bound at the same time, Heidegger adds, to be carried back from the vulgar concept of time to the transcendental understanding of time as pure self-affection, which in its essence is one with pure apperception and in this unity renders possible the pure sensuous Reason in its wholeness. Unknown explicitly to the author, "time in its essential unity with the transcendental imagination acquires a central metaphysical function in the *Critique of Pure Reason*."[66] Had Kant realized the implications of this, the dominating position of reason and understanding, the age-old preeminence of 'Logic' in metaphysics including his own concept of a 'transcendental logic' taken as something absolute, would have been thoroughly shaken and become questionable. But in the second edition of the *Critique of Pure Reason*, Kant gives back to the Understanding its dominating place, with the consequence that metaphysics becomes, with Hegel, more radically 'Logic' than ever before.[67] If only Kant had seen that the horizon of transcendence is constituted by the pure schemata regarded as transcendental time determinations, he would have concluded, as Heidegger does in *Being and Time*, that the ontological structure of essents, that is, their Being, is essentially rooted in Time. The possibility of ontological knowledge is shown, in Kant, to be grounded in the structure of transcendence, that is, of the finite subjectivity of the human subject. Kant, "who was alive, in his philosophizing, to the problem of the possibility of metaphysics as no one before him or since," shrank back, Heidegger says, from explicitly recognizing the transcendental imagination (Time) as the ground of ontological knowledge because to have done so would have meant abandoning the firm ground of pure reason on which he himself stood and because it would have forced him to go beyond metaphysics itself to its true ground in the truth of Being as such.

"Kant is the first," says Heidegger, "to raise once again, since the philosophy of the Greeks, the question of the Being of essents as a question to be unfolded."[68] In accordance with the dominant tendency of the age, his thinking moves in the dimension of Reason, the faculty of representing something as something. It is the dimension of subjectivity, in which what is, *is* only as an object for a subject. The certifying ground, the ultimate a priori condition of the possibility of objects is the objectivity, the objectness, of objects. The conception of objectivity as constituting the Being of all essents which can be experienced, of objectivity for rational subjectivity, is the view of Being implicit in Kant's thinking, for, according to him, it is only in the light of a prior glimpse of Being as objectivity that anything can appear at all *as* an object. Being, that is, the presence of the present, reveals itself in the Kantian philosophy in the character of objectivity (standing opposite) as against the way the Greeks encountered the essent as facing them in its own character as constant presence. The original and basic conception of Being as presence is presupposed and implied in the Kantian determination of the essent as an object of experience; objectivity is the form in which the presence of the present appears in the age of subjectivity. The supreme principle of Kant's metaphysics, quoted earlier, says, according to Heidegger, "that the conditions of the possibility of representing (*vor-stellen*) what is represented are at the same time, that is, none other than, the conditions of the possibility of what is represented. They constitute the representedness which is the essence of objectivity, that is, of the Being of essents. The supreme principle says: Being is representedness. Representedness, further, is a kind of being handed over or delivered, such that the representing self can be secure of what is thus presented and brought to stand. Security is found in certitude, which is how the nature of truth is determined."[69] The connection between Being (*eon*, understood as presence) and Unity (*hen*) or the *logos* as gathering together and disclosing, left unexplained by the Greeks, appears in Kant in the form of the supreme principle of the Synthetic Unity of Apperception, which renders possible both the objectivity of the object as well as the object as such. The unity is conceived, however, as one of synthesis (*syn*=together; *thesis*=positing). The *logos* is here shifted and transferred to the 'I' as subject and yet, as apperception, it remains in contact with affection through the senses. The subjectivity of man is, with Kant, not yet absolute but still remains a subjectivity of finitude.[70]

The transcendental method is the inquiry not into objects but into the nature of their objectivity (that is, their Being) and hence into the subjectivity of Reason, for which it is objectivity and in which it is rooted. And it is further an inquiry which is itself, as Heidegger notices in his later phase, part of objectivity, a manifestation of the way Being reveals itself as the objectivity of the object of experience. The transcendental method is itself a mode of representation springing from the subjectivity of Reason in which Being itself, in revealing itself as objectivity, conceals itself *as* Being to the utmost degree.[71] The self-certitude of knowledge through representing the essent in its Being as objectivity, characteristic of modern subjectivism, finds expression in Kant's doctrine of Reason as assuring itself both of itself in its self-legislative supremacy as well as of its object by prescribing its nature to it. But in his doctrine of the transcendental imagination Kant has also for the first time seen and realized in his thinking the inventive or creative nature of Reason, as Heidegger points out, thus preparing the way for the conception of Absolute Reason in the metaphysics of the German Idealists.[72] "The categories of reason are horizons of imaginative creation (*Ausdichtung*) through which what is encountered is provided with a free and open area, placed within which, and from out of which, it becomes capable of appearing as something stable, as that which stands opposite (*Gegenstand*)." Schematization is the essential creative core of Reason, of thinking as it appears in the form of reckoning and calculation to guarantee certitude in the realm of what is by positing it as object. Kant himself speaks of Being as what is posited in transcendental reflection, in the representation of representation, thus conceiving Being in terms of an act of the human subjectivity. In this respect, Kant only follows to its logical end the central tendency of the whole history of philosophy, that is, the determination of Being regarded as presence in terms of thinking as a representation of what is.[73] But the Being of what is, not being itself an essent, cannot be grasped by representational thinking, nor itself be adequately characterized in terms of constant presence, of simple givenness, of the 'is'. Hence the need to reopen the question of Being again and to explore the possibility of giving utterance to it, not in terms of thinking, nor of an essent of any kind but in terms of its own self, that is, of the temporality that has been lying concealed within the view of Being as constant presence.

With all his subjectivism, Kant never lost sight of the finitude of Reason and of man's knowledge, a finitude which is not due merely, or primarily, to the fact that human knowledge is subject to fickleness, inaccuracy, and error. Finitude, Heidegger points out, is inherent in the very essence of knowledge, for man's knowledge is not, like divine knowledge, *intuitus originarius* (creative knowledge) but is necessarily receptive and dependent upon something given to it and, *therefore*, also in need of the activity of thinking. "Thinking as such is hence the seal of finitude."[74] The attack against the thing in itself, which Reason cannot assimilate into itself and upon which it is dependent, launched by the German Idealists, is based on a growing forgetfulness of Kant's basic insight into the finitude of man's knowledge. This forgetfulness, in turn, results in the transformation of metaphysics which is an expression of man's need for ontological knowledge, that is, of his finitude, into Logic as Hegel conceives it in the form of Absolute Knowledge: "Logic is accordingly to be conceived as the system of pure reason, as the realm of pure thought. This is the realm of Truth as it is in and for itself, without any veil. Its content, one may therefore say, is the representation of God as He is in His eternal essence before the creation of nature and of a finite spirit."[75] The quest for the real as the other to thought culminates here in the undisputed sovereignty of thought as the only reality, with nothing to limit it and completely transparent to itself and so in full possession of truth, indeed as Truth itself.

Philosophy, Hegel said, comes to port, the secure haven of self-consciousness, with Descartes.[76] But, as Heidegger remarks, it comes into full possession of the land, where it has since made itself at home, only with Hegel, who conceives the unshakable certitude of thought as the Absolute itself.[77] Philosophy, according to Hegel, is the actual knowledge of what truly is, actual being understood in the sense of the Aristotelian interpretation of presence as *energeia*, subsequently transformed into *actualitas* and objectivity and the latter understood as spirit and self-consciousness. Real or actual knowledge is absolute knowledge of the Absolute in its absoluteness, that is, the certitude of the spirit in its unconditioned self-awareness. The Absolute is not something external to knowledge, regarded as a means—instrument or medium—for grasping it. The Absolute is already present with us and our attempt to know it is already illuminated by its *parousia*. For Hegel, philosophy is science or ascertained knowledge (*Wissenschaft*), the unconditioned certitude of knowledge in self-consciousness. The subjectivity of the subject lies in its representational relation to the object and so to itself. Representation presents the object by representing it to the subject, a representation in which the subject as such presents itself. The absolute self-certitude of such presence (in presentation) is the absoluteness of the Absolute, the absolute certainty of Spirit as self-consciousness, which is realized in philosophy as absolute knowledge or science. Truth, understood previously as correspondence and so as an attribute of representation, becomes with Hegel certitude and identical with representing itself. Knowledge, with its certitude immanent in itself, severs itself from its relation to objects; representation liberates and absolves itself completely, as Heidegger puts it, from its objective reference and in this independence of self-representation attains to total absoluteness.

The *Phenomenology of Mind*, which gives an exposition of knowledge as a phenomenon (appearing in the original sense of *phainesthai*), does not describe so much the passage of the mind from the natural consciousness to absolute knowledge and is not so much, Heidegger says, an *itinerarium mentis in Deum* as itself a manifestation of ascertained knowledge, as the emergence of Science itself. Hegel's distinction between the natural consciousness and real knowledge does not imply, according to Heidegger, that the former is 'mere' appearance; it is the consciousness which is untrue, not in the sense of being false or illusory, but as the not yet perfectly true, being driven forward towards its own truth by the power of the will of the Absolute. The natural consciousness is itself a mode of knowledge (*Bewusstsein*=being in the state of having known) and as consciousness, it is presence (Being) in the mode of a gathering together of representations, that is, as subjectivity. It is not real knowledge in the sense that it represents only the essent, paying no heed to the essent in its Being. But the natural consciousness is able to represent the essent only because, without explicitly knowing it, it has already represented to itself the Being of essents in a general and indeterminate way. As opposed to actual knowledge, which has the Being of essents as its object, it is only, as Hegel says, a notion of knowledge, not real knowledge assured of the actuality of the actual. The natural consciousness, Heidegger asserts, is not necessarily coincident with the sensuous consciousness; it is a confinement, not to the perceptual, but to *any* kind of immediate object it may represent, be it the nonsensible entities of logic and reason, be it the supersensible entities of the spirit. Representation as such is the hallmark of the natural consciousness. Consciousness itself is neither the natural consciousness taken by itself nor real knowledge taken by itself but the original unity of both, in and for itself. Consciousness itself is the unrest of its own self-differentiation into natural and real knowing and thus contains in itself, itself *is*, the principle of its movement beyond the natural.

The object of consciousness, as immediately present in representation and without any reference to the act or agent of the representation is called by Hegel Being, which for him means the essent. Being in this sense is for him what is not yet, really and in truth. Being has for him always this narrow sense of 'mere Being' because what truly is, is the *ens actu*, the actual, of which the actuality consists in the knowledge of the certitude fully aware of itself; the latter alone 'is' the true and the whole Reality. Being, supposed to have been left behind in absolute knowledge thus comes back again, though, as Heidegger comments, Hegelian 'Science' takes no notice of this fact. In contradistinction to Hegel's usage, Heidegger uses the word 'Being' for what Hegel calls objectivity, with Kant, as well as for what he conceives to be the truly actual and what he calls the actuality of the spirit. As he remarks, "We interpret the *einai*, Being, of the Greeks not like Hegel in terms of its view as the objectivity of the immediate representation of a subjectivity that has not yet found itself, that is, not in terms of subjectivity, but in terms of the Greek *aletheia*, as presence in and through unhiddenness,"[78] a presence (*ousia, Anwesen*) which has its basis in an as yet unthought character of time of which the true nature has yet to reveal itself. As Heidegger remarks, according to his own usage Hegel should not, strictly speaking, apply the word Being, as he is inevitably led to do, to the reality of the real, to the spirit which, for him, is self-consciousness (*Selbst-bewusstsein, being* self-conscious). Being, in Heidegger's sense, discloses itself in Hegel, at the same time concealing its own truth, as the absoluteness of the Absolute.

Hegel realizes that the distinctions between knowing and its object, between the object and its objectivity, between knowing and the knowledge of this knowing, all fall within consciousness itself. But, Heidegger points out, because Hegel's thinking moves within the sphere of metaphysical representation, he is unable to grasp the real significance of these distinctions, ultimately traceable to the unnoticed ambiguity of the *on* (which means both the essent and its Being) on which metaphysics itself is based. In terms of his own distinction between the ontic and the ontological, Heidegger designates the natural consciousness as the ontic consciousness, primarily concerned with representing the essent, its immediate object. "But," he says, "representing the object is at the same time representing it, though without explicit a- wareness, *as* object. This consciousness has gathered together the object in its objectivity and is therefore ontological. But, while representing the object it does not direct itself to objectivity as such; the natural consciousness is ontological and yet not quite such. We may, therefore, describe the ontic consciousness as preontological. As such, the natural consciousness *is* the implicit distinction between the ontically true and ontological truth."[79] Consciousness *is* itself as this distinction and hence, as natural, not cut off from the ontological but resting on it, and yet confined mostly to the ontic, not going behind to the truth of its true object, the essent. This truth, underlying its true immediate object, is indeed not something hidden behind or under the object, as Heidegger puts it, but is rather the prior, fore-given horizon of light within which objects can at all show themselves and be known as such. What Hegel calls the self-examination of consciousness is the process of continuous comparison between the ontic and the preontological by which consciousness comes to its own real Being as fully manifest ontological consciousness. This is the dialectical movement which consciousness executes on itself—on its knowledge as well as on its object—in the sense that out of it the new and true object arises, which Hegel calls experience.[80] This is Hegel's term for the Being of what is, the full presence, appearance or epiphany of consciousness, of the subjectivity of the subject. The basic feature of consciousness is to be already what, at the same time, it is not yet, to hold itself in the not yet of the already, to be on its way to that. As Heidegger puts it, "The Being (presence) of consciousness consists in its self-moving character. The Being which Hegel conceives as experience is fundamentally characterized by movement."[81] This movement is dialectical in the sense of a continuing dialog between the natural and the real, between the ontic and the ontological knowledge, through and as which consciousness gathers itself together and realizes itself in its complete truth, the absolute notion. The movement culminates in experience, the self-manifestation of consciousness as self-representation, "the presentation of the absolute subject as representation, and thus as absolving itself fully." Experience, Heidegger continues, "is the subjectivity of the absolute subject. Experience is the presentation of absolute representation and as such the *parousia* (complete presence) of the Absolute. Experience is the absoluteness of the Absolute," the way consciousness *is* as presence and appearance. Experiencing is the mode in which consciousness sets forth on its ascent to its own notion—as what it truly is—reaching out for and attaining to its truth, in which consummation its own nature as appearance shines forth. "Experiencing is a mode of presence, that is, of Being. Through experience, emergent consciousness comes into its own presence, abiding in itself as thus emerging forth. Experience gathers consciousness together into the collectedness of its own essence . . . the truth of what is true, the Being of what is, the shining forth of what emerges."[82] In experience thus conceived, there is a reversal (*Umkehrung*, turning round) of consciousness from the habitual representation of what appears to its appearance, from the essent to its Being, a reversal or conversion which is due to our own agency (*unsere Zutat*) in the sense that, setting aside our private opinions and predilections, we *let* that which appears (consciousness) shine forth by itself and appear as it is in its own Being, impelled by the Absolute which, as Will, realizes itself in experience. The exposition of the experience of consciousness in the *Phenomenology of Mind* is itself the fulfillment of the Absolute's will, a manifestation of the way man is related in his essence to the Absolute, as fulfilling its will, part of the Absolute's *parousia*.

According to Heidegger, the exposition of the emergence

of absolute knowledge in the *Phenomenology* represents Hegel's ontology of the actual consciousness in its actuality, of the subject as subject, that is, of the true essent as Hegel conceives it in its wholeness. The Science or absolute knowledge of which this is only a part leads on to its proper completion in his *Science of Logic*, which exhibits, Heidegger says, not the self-manifestation of the Absolute, but how the Absolute is present to itself in its absoluteness, the self-comprehension of the Absolute in absolute notion. This is the theology (or theiology, as Heidegger prefers to call it) of the Absolute. The Science of the Absolute, Heidegger says, is for Hegel, about the time when the *Phenomenology of Mind* was first published, "the ontotheiological knowledge of the true essent as essent. In its entirety, it unfolds itself in its two aspects in the *Science of the Phenomenology of Mind* and in the *Science of Logic*. Hegel's *Science of Logic* is at this time conceived as the Theology of the Absolute and not as Ontology. The form taken by the latter is the *Science of the Experience of Consciousness* (the title under which the *Phenomenology* was first published in 1807). The *Phenomenology* is the 'first Science', the *Logic* the Science proper, within the first philosophy, constituting the truth of essents as such. This Truth is of the essence of metaphysics."[83] Hegel dropped the first title of the *Phenomenology*, Heidegger suggests, perhaps because he shrank back from acknowledging the original force of the word 'experience', with its suggestion of reaching out and arriving, a mode of presence, of *einai*, of Being. The term 'phenomenology', which was substituted for it, carries, nevertheless, the same meaning: the *phainesthai*, the self-emergence or appearance of the absolute subject, the spirit. The Phenomenology of the Mind is the appearance of the Spirit, as gathered together in the dialog between the ontic and the ontological consciousness, in its *parousia*.

Both the *Phenomenology* and the *Logic* are, Heidegger points out, theologies of the Absolute, the first, of the Absolute in its *parousia* (that is, its presence with us) and the second, of the Absolute in its absoluteness. And both are ontologies, worldly, inasmuch as they represent the worldliness of the world, the essent (conceived as subjectivity) in its totality. But, as Heidegger remarks, "the science of absolute knowledge is not the worldly theology of the world because it secularizes the Christian, church theology but because it is itself implied in the very essence of ontology." Hegel's metaphysics demonstrates the metaphysical character of theology itself and provides confirmation of the essentially onto-theological character of metaphysics, as it has developed since the age of the Greeks. True to the metaphysical tradition, Hegel's thinking is concerned, as Heidegger points out elsewhere, with the essent as such and as a whole, with the movement of Being from its emptiness and abstraction to its concrete fullness.[84] Like all metaphysics, it thinks the essent as such, that is, in general, and the Being of the essent as the unity of the most general, conceived as the most universal basis to which one can penetrate; and it thinks the essent in its totality and its Being as the unity of this whole, conceived as the foundation on which all that is can be grounded, that is as the highest Being. It is ontology and theology in one—the *logos* of the most universal Being and of the highest (*theion*). For Hegel, the true Science or metaphysics is 'Logic', not because it has thought for its theme, but because for him, too, the main concern of thinking is with Being, as presence, in the form of the ancient *Logos*, the ground which provides the foundation, with Being conceived as ground.

Hegel declares that the goal of philosophy, in its dialectical progress from the abstract universal, Being, to the full concreteness of Absolute spirit, is truth, finally reached in his own Science.[85] Taking truth in the sense of the absolute certitude of the self-knowledge of the absolute subject, Hegel does not realize that just this certitude itself is dependent upon truth in a more fundamental sense, upon truth understood as disclosure or unhiddenness, *aletheia*. Whether in the initial emergence and manifestation of Spirit as pure Being or in the final self-manifestation of Spirit as Absolute Idea, truth as prior disclosure or unhiddenness must already be presupposed. And this leads, Heidegger says, to "the further question whether the unhiddenness has its seat in spirit, conceived as absolute subject, or whether, on the contrary, unhiddenness is itself the locus and a pointer to the location in which alone such a thing as a representing subject can 'be' what it is."[86] Thinking of historical reality in terms of Being conceived as absolute subjectivity and approaching it in the speculative, dialectical manner, Hegel, despite his taking 'the kingdom of pure truth' as the goal of philosophy, is debarred from the awareness that truth in the primordial sense of unhiddenness (*aletheia*) still remains the Unthought of philosophy, the mystery that it has always been. "Hegel takes Being, when he conceives it as indeterminate immediacy, as what is posited by the determining, conceiving subject. Accordingly, he cannot allow Being, in the Greek sense of *einai*, to be detached from its connection with the subject and set it free in its own essence. The latter, however, is presence, that is, a coming out of concealment into unhiddenness, into presence."[87] *Aletheia*, which has its sway even before philosophy proper begins, still remains a mystery. Being can reveal itself as presence only with the prior occurrence of unhiddenness. But the latter, *aletheia*, still remains unthought in its essence.[88]

According to Heidegger, Schelling's thinking does not represent just a stage in the development of German Idealism from Kant to Hegel, and it is time that we stopped judging it from the Hegelian perspective. His treatise on freedom is one of the profoundest works of German as well as Western philosophy. It is true that this treatise exhibits Schelling's ceaseless quest to give adequate expression and form to his innermost problem as again suffering shipwreck. This was bound to happen, Heidegger points out, because the general standpoint of philosophy during that period did not allow his real question to unfold itself from an appropriately conceived center. Such shipwreck, however, is not really a personal failure, nor something negative, but, on the contrary, an indication that something novel is in the process of emerging, heralding a new beginning. This treatise, Heidegger says, is one of those very rare works in which a cloud, eventually to send forth the lightning flash of a new vision, is beginning to form. For this reason Schelling must be regarded as the truly creative and the most far-reaching thinker of the entire age of the philosophy of German Idealism, so much so indeed that he pushes it to a point where it is forced to surrender its own basic standpoint. What is hidden at the core of this work, the new beginning, cannot be grasped in terms of any philosophy thus far, not even Schelling's own. For, as Heidegger says, every philosophical work, insofar as it is truly philosophical, drives philosophy beyond the standpoint adopted in the work itself, and the true significance of a philosophical work lies in the fact that it opens up a whole new realm, starts off new beginnings and endeavors, through which its own approach and way are shown to have been inadequate and superseded. Heidegger's interpretation of Schelling, as we have it in the lecture course of 1936 and later notes included in his *Schelling*, cannot be summarized as part of a general account of his interpretation of the Western metaphysical tradition; what is significant in this thinker is the incipience of something new and different, not so much the metaphysical matrix which seems to quicken it. Heidegger's own continued wrestling with Schelling's treatise on freedom represents rather the means by which he sought to emerge into the open, beyond and clear of the metaphysical tradition, and, by appropriating what is seminal in Schelling, to attempt a truly and explicitly new beginning in his own thinking. This is also largely true of Heidegger's relationship with the thought of Nietzsche, who is as much the harbinger of the new beginning as he is a prisoner of the metaphysical tradition.

Hegel's metaphysics of absolute knowledge as Spirit, according to Heidegger, marks the beginning of the last stage in the development of metaphysical thought but not yet its final consummation. Although unconditioned certitude has come into its own in Hegel as absolute actuality, the will, implicit in the conception of Reality since Leibniz and implied in Kant's as well as Hegel's concept of Reason, is yet to emerge explicitly and be acknowledged expressly as the Being of what is.[89] The consummation of metaphysics, the ultimate stage of its development, occurs in the thinking of Nietzsche, with whom the possibilities latent in metaphysics since its Platonic inception are fully explored and exhausted. The full implications of the awareness, present in Leibniz, Kant, Fichte, Schelling, Hegel, and Schopenhauer, that the Will constitutes the Being of all that is, are drawn out and carried to their logical conclusion by Nietzsche, who saw, and thought through, as no thinker before him, the dark shadow cast over the present and the coming world history by the Nihilism inherent in the metaphysical (that is, the Platonic-Christian) tradition of the West. He conceived his own work as a reaction against and an overcoming of metaphysics, a fight against Platonism. But, like all counter movement, like everything 'anti-', as Heidegger puts it, it remains itself necessarily stuck up in what it attacks. "Nietzsche's countermove against metaphysics is, as its mere inversion, itself ensnared in metaphysics, inextricably and without a way out left; it has cut itself off from its own essence and, as itself metaphysical, become incapable of recognizing its own essential nature."[90] Nietzsche's philosophy is itself a manifestation of the last epoch of metaphysics, the entire history of which is itself one long-drawn-out epoch in the history of Being and of the way Being has revealed and dispensed itself to man through its own withdrawal.

Seeking to take Nietzsche seriously as a thinker, not just as one who philosophized existenzielly (which, Heidegger says, he never did), Heidegger finds that his thinking is no less pointed, detached, and stringent than the thinking of Aristotle. "The customary, but none the less questionable, juxtaposition of Nietzsche with Kierkegaard," Heidegger remarks, "fails to recognize, due to a failure to appreciate the true nature of thinking, that as a metaphysical thinker Nietzsche has his place secure near Aristotle,"[91] which cannot be said about Kierkegaard, although the latter refers to Aristotle more frequently. It is widely held that Nietzsche is not a strict thinker but a poet-philosopher; that he cannot be counted among the philosophers, who excogitate only abstractions, shadowy and remote from life; that if he is to be called a philosopher at all he must be regarded as a 'philosopher of life' (*Lebensphilosoph*) who has at last done away with abstract thinking. This estimate of Nietzsche, Heidegger holds, is utterly mistaken. It was Nietzsche who said, "Abstract thinking is, for many, hard and a torture—for me, on favorable days, it is a feast and an intoxication." Nietzsche's philosophy, despite its aphoristic style and unsystematic form, is metaphysics and has its place on "the long course of the age-old leading question of philosophy: What is the essent?"[92] The divers themes which recur in his thought are linked together by an inner unity and, Heidegger believes, constitute a meaningful pattern which in essence is metaphysical. This, of course, can be seen only if we look at Nietzsche's thought from the perspective of the history of Being, a perspective which was not available to Nietzsche and which, in fact, is accessible only to a thinking that has taken the leap out of metaphysical thinking and so can see in Nietzsche the final culmination of such thinking.

Heidegger sums up the central concepts of Nietzsche's philosophy in five basic key terms in his thinking.[93] These are: the Will to Power; Nihilism; the Eternal Recurrence of the Same; the Superman; Justice. Metaphysics is the truth of essents as such in their totality. This truth is the unhiddenness of the 'what' of the essent (the *essentia* or *Seiendheit*, beingness) as well as of its 'that' (the *existentia*, that and how the essent as a whole is). Further, the truth of essents appears in varying forms, depending on the way the essent is conceived from time to time, being thus historical in its very nature. Finally, according to the way truth appears in any period of its history, it requires a type of humanity which corresponds to it, establishes it, makes it known, and preserves it. In Nietzsche's metaphysics, Heidegger says, "The Will to Power names the Being of essents as such, the *essentia* of essents. 'Nihilism' is the name for the history of the truth of essents as thus determined. The 'Eternal Recurrence of the Same' is the way the essent as a whole is, the *existentia* of essents. The 'Superman' refers to the type of man demanded by this whole (as conformable and adequate to it). 'Justice' is the essential character of the truth of essents as Will to Power."[94] Each of these concepts involves the others and must be understood with reference to them. They constitute, in their unity, Nietzsche's metaphysics, his vision of the truth of essents as such in their totality.

The Will to Power, Nietzsche says, is "the innermost essence of Being."[95] Will here must be understood, hence, not in the psychological sense of a mental faculty, but metaphysically, as the basic character, the Being, of the essent as such, in terms of which Nietzsche comprehends all essents, physical or mental. The will is not any sort of wishing or striving but, fundamentally and in essence, commanding. It is again not something separate and external to power, and the latter is not a goal which the will seeks to attain as something outside it. Both together constitute an indivisible unity, the will to power being the essential character of power itself, which is never a final possession but ceaselessly tends to exceed itself, which *is* as such constant self-enhancement. Power is always, therefore, for more power, power over power, and the will essentially the Will to will. Concerned with its own preservation and increase, the will to power prescribes for itself the conditions which render this possible. The process of Becoming, the movement toward more power inherent in the will to power, secures itself by setting up 'points of view', outlooks, which can be counted upon, and must be reckoned with—the will to power is, as Nietzsche calls it, intrinsically 'perspectivistic'. These points of view are measures and quantities, that is, values; the 'seeing' characteristic of the will to power is by its very nature a reckoning with values. Value is essentially the point of view employed by "the commanding-calculating seeing of the will to power." Such points of view condition the complex fabric of science (knowledge), art, politics, and religion, shapes taken by the will to power, which may, in turn, be themselves called value structures. "The Will to Power is, in accordance with its innermost nature, a perspectivistic reckoning with the conditions of its possibility, which are as such set up by itself. The Will to Power is in itself value-positing."[96] It is a will that wills values and is itself the valuational principle, and hence the thinking which takes the truth of things as will to power is necessarily a thinking in terms of values. "The metaphysics of the Will to Power—and only that—is properly and necessarily a thinking in terms of values. . . . In such value-thinking consists the self-consciousness of the Will to Power. . . . Value-thinking is implied in the way the Will to Power is itself, the subiectum. . . . The Will to Power reveals itself as the subjectivity of which the distinctive mark is evaluative thinking."[97]

Plato, with whom metaphysics begins, conceived the Being of the essent as idea, the principle of the unity of what is diverse, and at the same time the good, the enabling or the condition of the possibility of what is.[98] The ideas, which alone truly are, belong to the supersensible realm, and viewed from Nietzsche's metaphysical position they are values. The essent as such in its totality is comprehended in terms of the supersensible—whether understood as the God of Christianity, as the moral law, as Reason, as progress or as the happiness of the many—the Ideal or, from Nietzsche's point of view, the highest values. All metaphysics is Platonism for the people.

Taking the concept of value as the clue to his historical reflection on metaphysics, the basis of Western history, Nietzsche interprets and examines metaphysics in terms of the Will to Power as the sole principle of valuation. He regards all metaphysics as a system of values, but without explicit recognition of the Will to Power as the supreme principle. Hence he conceives his own metaphysics of the Will to Power as providing the "principle of a new scheme of values," involving a "revaluation of past values." Such revaluation constitutes the ultimate character of Nihilism. According to Nietzsche, Nihilism means the devaluing of the highest values. In Heidegger's words, "Nihilism is the process of the devaluation of the highest values prevailing hitherto. The annulment of these values is the collapse of what has hitherto been taken as the truth about the essent as such in its totality . . . the fundamental happening in the history of the West, a history of which metaphysics has been the foundation and guiding principle. Insofar as metaphysics has received its peculiar theological mold through Christianity, this devaluation must also be expressed theologically, in the words, 'God is dead'."[99] 'God' means here the supersensible realm in general, the true eternal world, beyond this earthly one, as the real and only goal, both as conceived by Christian faith and in its secularized form (Conscience, Reason, Progress, the Social Instinct). But though the devaluation of the highest values, the vanishing of all value from the world, is part of the Nihilistic process and the fundamental happening in the history of the West, it does not yet exhaust the full essence of Nihilism. The collapse of the highest values prevailing hitherto demands the setting up of new ones, a revaluation of all values. Hence, Nihilism does not stop short at mere nullity but has a liberating, affirmative character. As a historical process, "Nihilism is a devaluation of the hitherto highest values, aiming at the thorough revaluation of all values"; it implies the total rejection of past values and a grounding of the essent as a whole on entirely different conditions. But, Heidegger points out, "even with this recognition of the affirmative character of European Nihilism we do not come to its innermost core; for Nihilism is neither just *one* historical occurrence nor even the *central* feature of Western history, but is itself the law of this history, its 'logic'."[100] As such, Nihilism manifests itself in a series of stages, beginning with Pessimism, the preliminary form of Nihilism, with its two subforms, the pessimism of the weak and the pessimism of the strong. 'Incomplete Nihilism' denies indeed the values hitherto taken as the highest, but only puts new ideals in the place of the old (Communism in place of primitive Christianity; Wagner's music in place of dogmatic Christianity), without abandoning that 'place', the self-subsisting supersensible dimension, itself. For 'extreme' or complete Nihilism there are no self-subsistent eternal truths whatever. Extreme Nihilism, insofar as it remains content with such negation, remains 'passive', whereas 'active' Nihilism, rejecting both this world as well as the ideal, supersensible world, goes on to affirm a new principle of valuation and, as truly liberating man from the bondage of the old, is characterized by Nietzsche as 'ecstatic Nihilism'. "Despite the appearance of being merely negative, it affirms, neither anything given nor an ideal, but rather the 'principle of valuation' itself, the Will to Power,"[101] thus becoming full-fledged and complete, 'classical' Nihilism, as which Nietzsche understands his own metaphysics. Revaluation for Nietzsche does not mean, Heidegger remarks, "that in the old and the same place of the hitherto prevailing values new ones are set up; the term means, in the first place and always, *that the place itself is determined anew*."[102] It is through the "revaluation" that, for the first time, values are conceived *as* values, that is, as the conditions of the Will to Power. The revaluation is, strictly speaking, a rethinking of the essent as such in its totality in terms of 'values'.

According to Nietzsche's doctrine, the total worth of the world cannot be evaluated, for it makes no sense to speak of the total value of the essent as a whole which, as Will to Power, sets up values as the condition of its own maintenance and increase.[103] In itself it is worthless, having no intrinsic meaning, aim, or purpose. This, however, must be understood not in a merely negative sense but as asserting something positive about *how* the essent as a whole is: The Eternal Recurrence of the Same. This "most difficult of all thought." as Nietzsche calls it, must be grasped in its inseparable connection with the Will to Power, as characterizing, together with the latter, the essent as a whole. As Heidegger expresses it, "The essent, which *as such* has the fundamental nature of the Will to Power, can be, *as a whole*, only the Eternal Recurrence of the Same. And conversely, the essent, which *as a whole* is the Eternal Recurrence of the Same, must *as essent* have the fundamental character of the Will to Power."[104] The values or ends set up by the Will to Power are not something "in themselves," outside this Will, with the attainment of which it can come to rest; these ends, points of resistance or hindrance essential for the operation of power, are set up by the will and are immanent in it. The Will to Power as power beyond power is intrinsically a perpetual return into itself, giving thus to the essent as a whole, that is, to the process of Becoming, its unique state of movement, not directed towards any ultimate goal extraneous to itself, and yet ceaselessly moving towards self-imposed ends and so ever returning to itself. Further, the essent as a whole, conceived in its Being as Will to Power, must be a fixed quantity because power, with ceaseless increment inherent in it, cannot increase infinitely in the absence of any surplus, as Heidegger puts it, beyond itself, from which it can feed itself. The world, as power, must not be conceived, Nietzsche says, as unlimited, for it *cannot* be so conceived, the concept of infinite power being self-contradictory. The world is incapable of eternal novelty. Since the essent as such is conceived as Will to Power and hence as eternal becoming which advances towards no predetermined goal beyond it, and since this eternal becoming is limited as to the possible forms and power structures in which, as Will, it can manifest itself, therefore, the essent regarded as the Will to Power must be, as a whole, a perpetual return of the same. This circular movement, "the primordial law of the essents as a whole," is the mode of presence (Being) of what is as such ever varying or becoming, but in a way that guarantees the utmost constancy and invariability as a whole. As Heidegger remarks, the Eternal Return is the most unvarying perpetuation of what is ceaselessly varying. In Nietzsche's doctrine, the conception of Being as constant presence, as old as metaphysics, appears in the guise of the Eternal Recurrence of the Same. "To set the stamp of Being on Becoming—in this lies the highest Will to Power," as Nietzsche says, adding, "that everything returns is the utmost approximation of a world of Becoming to one of

Being." The conception of the Eternal Recurrence of the Same, the summit of Nietzsche's metaphysical vision, is, as the truth about the essent in its totality, neither a merely personal experience of this thinker, with its validity confined within the limits of a personal view, nor is it amenable to scientific, empirical demonstration. The Will to Power itself, the basic character of the essent as such, and not a 'Mr. Nietzsche', as Heidegger puts it, sets up and determines the thought of the Eternal Recurrence of the Same.[105]

Nietzsche's conception of the Superman or Overman (as Walter Kaufmann translates *Übermensch* in his *Nietzsche*, finding the English 'superman' misleading) has nothing to do with a supersensible ideal of humanity, nor does it announce the impending emergence somewhere of a 'suprahuman' personality.[106] It is not, Heidegger says, the product of the arrogance of a 'Mr. Nietzsche' and it does not mean the crudely magnified capriciousness of the deeds of violence in the manner common to humanity so far. As against a mere inflating and carrying beyond all bounds of man in his existing character, the Overman marks a reversal of the hitherto prevailing nature of man. The Overman, in Heidegger's words, is man nihilistically reversed. He is the type of man who corresponds metaphysically to Nietzsche's vision of the essent, which is as such the Will to Power and in its totality the Eternal Return of the Same. The Overman is the complete negation of the man of the past, of man as shaped by the Platonic world view and Christian morality, but it is a negation that springs from the affirmation of the Will to Power. In the epoch of 'metaphysics', man is conceived as, and is, in consequence of the way he is related to Being, the rational animal. The Overman represents a denial of this nature of man, but it is a nihilistic denial of this nature in the sense that it merely reverses the relative positions of rationality and animality, making Reason a mere tool in the service of the latter. The metaphysical emergence, in Hegel, of Reason as absolute subjectivity, that is, as the Being of what is, prepares the ground for the total, nihilistic inversion of the role of Reason in Nietzsche. "The nihilistic denial of the metaphysical primacy, determining what is to count as being, of unconditioned Reason—not its complete rejection—is the affirmation of the unconditioned role of the body as the warrant and point of reference for all interpretation of the world."[107] The will, inherent previously in Reason as representing and in its service, now emerges as dominant, with Reason subservient to it as calculative thought and evaluation. It is transformed into the Will to Power, its own sole lawgiver and the Being of all that is. The subjectivity of the Absolute spirit, though unconditioned, was yet incomplete, but the inversion of rational subjectivity into the subjectivity of the Will is its final consummation. The reversal of the subjectivity of unconditioned representation into the subjectivity of the Will to Power is the overthrow of the primacy of Reason as the guiding principle and arbiter for the conception of what is, a phenomenon described by Nietzsche as the death of the God of Christian morality. The Overman is the necessary consequence of this ultimate, completed subjectivity. With the collapse of the supersensible realm in general, there remains, in the midst of essents as such and as a whole, only man who, as the ultimate subject and sole embodiment of representing, value-positing Will, must offer himself to the Will to Power as the abode of its pure presence. The Overman, going beyond the man of the past, is the subject in whom the pure essence of the Will to Power finds its dwelling; in willing itself, the Will to Power must will its own highest condition, the Overman. Man as he was up till now was characterized by Reason as his distinctive mark and was therefore 'the animal not yet fixed in his nature', but as the Overman, with his animality as itself the very essence of the Will to Power, he is at last defined and established in his true nature, the prototype of a humanity in accord with the essent conceived as the unconditioned, completed subjectivity of the Will to Power, fit for absolute mastery over the earth. The Overman is the guardian and the repository of the truth of the essent as such and in its totality, as this truth is determined by the Will to Power and the Eternal Recurrence of the Same.

In Nietzsche's subjectivistic thinking, Truth retains its character of certitude and permanence but in conformity with his nihilistic revaluation, it ceases to be a supersensible light and becomes, as a condition of the Will to Power, a value.[108] Truth, for him, is a value necessary for the Will to Power and, as producing the illusion of permanence in what is ever a becoming, it is a kind of error. As the condition of the maintenance of the Will to Power, truth is necessary but not sufficient, for the Will to Power is primarily the will, not merely to the retention of power but to its incessant enhancement. For the latter, art alone suffices and hence, for Nietzsche, "art is of greater value than Truth." As 'error', truth also continues to be understood in his thinking as a kind of correspondence. But the original character of truth as *aletheia*, unrecognized but still implicitly present in all modern thought in a changed, perverted and disguised form, also shines through in Nietzsche's conception of art. The modern liberation of man from truth as certitude of salvation, leading man to seek assurance in himself, shows its real, full nature in the metaphysics of the Will to Power. We see here the final overthrow of creative Reason bearing the stamp of the logos—the divine creative power—of Christian theology. Man's new freedom now finds assurace and justification in a new kind of righteousness or justness, a manifestation of the Will to Power itself as setting up conditions of its own preservation and enhancement. In Nietzsche, as Heidegger puts it, Righteousness (*Gerechtigkeit*), "because it is the highest mode of the Will to Power, is the real basis for the determination of the nature of truth. In the metaphysics of the unconditioned and complete subjectivity of the Will to Power, truth exhibits itself as 'righteousness'."[109] In Nietzsche's sense of this term, however, all its associations deriving from Christian, humanistic morality must be excluded. Keeping in view the fact that in the metaphysics of the Will to Power the right can only be what the Will sets up for its own perpetuation, we must understand righteousness as a pure function of Power. "Looking out beyond the petty and narrow perspectives of good and bad," prevailing thus far, righteousness opens out the wholly new point of view from which man is seen as pushing on to absolute mastery over the earth. Nietzsche himself, Heidegger points out, never explicitly realized that and how righteousness is the aspect in which he conceives truth, that is, the unhiddenness by virtue of which the essent manifests itself as such and in its totality as the Will to Power and the Eternal Recurrence of the Same. "The metaphysics of unconditioned and complete subjectivity, without explicitly saying it, thinks its own nature, that is, the nature of truth, as righteousness. The truth of essents as such as a whole is accordingly truth about the essent but such that its own nature is determined by the basic character of the essent, that is, by the Will to Power as its highest form."[110] Nietzsche's metaphysics is, as all metaphysics necessarily is, the truth of essents as such and as a whole in a double sense: truth about the essent because truth which itself derives from the Being of essents. Such truth is essentially historical in character, each of its historical manifestations depending upon the way Being reveals itself to thinkers in different ages.

With Nietzsche's philosophy, in which the tradition of Western thinking comes, in an important sense, to a focus and fulfills itself, we come to the end of the metaphysical epoch in the history of that tradition. "The decisive question," Heidegger says, "for him who still can, indeed must, raise a philosophical question at all at the end of Western philosophy, is not the question about the basic character of the essent, how the Being of essents is to be characterized; the question rather is: What is this Being itself? It is the question about 'the sense of Being', not merely about the Being of essents; and 'sense', moreover, is defined precisely as that in terms of which and by virtue of which Being can at all reveal itself as such and become manifest in its truth."[111] It is to what Heidegger has to say on this question that we therefore turn now.

Notes

1. See chapter 2, "The Twofold Task of the Investigation."
2. For a contemporary echo of Nietzsche's verdict, see the amusing "Discussion" between Marjorie Grene and Stuart Hampshire in *Encounter*, April 1958, arising out of a review by Hampshire of Marjorie Grene's book on Heidegger. She "heartily" agrees with her critic that Heidegger's ontology "is indeed empty and arrogant nonsense."
3. *Einführung in die Metaphysik*, p. 8 (E.T., p. 9).
4. Ibid., p. 32 (E.T., p. 34). As Werner Marx says ("Heidegger's New Conception of Philosophy," see also *Heidegger und die Tradition*, passim), Heidegger's philosophy is the quest of a second, new beginning. "Today when we say of any particular thing, that 'it is' or 'is not', that 'it is' or is only 'becoming', that 'it is true, genuine' or only 'sham' or when we say that man is 'in truth' or 'in error', we are still thinking under the influence of the first conception of the 'essence of Being and Man' as poetically composed by these first thinkers. In this sense the pre-Socratics set a 'beginning', and a

'first beginning'. The ultimate aim of Heidegger's 'new conception of philosophy' during his second phase is to attain a 'second beginning'—to compose anew the Essence of Being and the Essence of Man."

5. *Einführung in die Metaphysik*, pp. 70, 71 (E.T., pp. 77, 79).

6. Ibid., pp. 33-34 (E.T., pp. 35-37).

7. This concern with the historical tradition and with the Greek world whose foundations still sustain the Western world is inspired by Heidegger's passionate concern for the future destiny of man on earth and for man's regeneration through a new relationship to Being. As he remarks, "Just because we have ventured upon the great and long task of pulling down a world grown old and of rebuilding really and truly anew, that is, historically, we must know the tradition. We must know more, that is, in a manner more stringent and binding than all ages and times of upheaval before us. Only the most radical historical knowledge can make us alive to the extraordinary character of our tasks and preserve us from a new wave of mere restoration and uncreative imitation." Ibid., p. 96 (E.T., p. 106).

8. Ibid., p. 124 (E.T., p. 136).

9. *Kant und das Problem der Metaphysik*, p. 182f. (E.T., p. 206f.). See also *Einführung in die Metaphysik*, p. 134 (E.T., p. 147f.) where, referring to the already "proverbial farfetched and onesided character of the Heideggerian method of exegesis," Heidegger remarks, "Nevertheless, we may and, indeed, must ask here: which interpretation is the true one? Is it the one that simply takes over the perspective into which it happens to find itself already and because it presents itself as familiar and obvious, or is it rather the interpretation which questions the customary perspective in its very roots, because it could be, and in fact is so, that this line of vision does not lead to what needs to be seen?" The latter kind of exegesis, Heidegger adds, needs a leap that is possible only if we really *ask* a question and through such questioning first create our perspectives. "But then, this is done not in a rambling, capricious way nor by clinging to a system taken as a norm, but in and out of historical necessity, out of the exigency of our historical existence."

10. Ibid., p. 29f. (E.T., p. 32).

11. In Heidegger's Being-centered Thought, the place of this is taken by the dispensation or destiny (*Geschick*) of Being. Explaining the role of the individual thinker and the suprapersonal character of the history of thought, Heidegger says in *Der Satz vom Grund* (pp. 144-146), that of all that is difficult to grasp in this world, what is most difficult to grasp, because it lies closest to us inasmuch as we ourselves are that, is the idea that the history of thought rests on the dispensation of Being. This history is not the story of the personal views of individual thinkers thinking original thoughts but of the way thinkers respond to the claim of Being itself. We all stand in the clearing of Being, in the area of openness and light brought about by the way Being dispenses itself, in its own withdrawal, to us. But we do not just stand round unconcerned in this clearing; we stand in it as appropriated by the claim of Being, owned and charged by Being and in its service. The thinker is charged and endowed with the gift appropriate to the task of putting into words the Being of what is, of building and forming in the clearing of Being, of taking care of being.

12. "Hegel und die Griechen," in *Wegmarken*, p. 172.

13. Ibid., p. 266.

14. Ibid., p. 269. Referring to Hegel's approach to history, Heidegger says ("Brief über den 'Humanismus'," *Wegmarken*, pp. 166-167), "The happening of history occurs as, and arises from, the destiny (dispensation) of the truth of Being, in which Being gives itself and, in giving itself, also withdraws itself. Nevertheless, Hegel's conception of history as the development of the 'Spirit' is not untrue. It is also not partly right and partly wrong. It is as much true as metaphysics, which in Hegel's system achieves for the first time an expression of its absolutely conceived essence. Along with its inversion by Marx and Nietzsche, absolute metaphysics is part of the history of the truth of Being. What is generated by that is not touched or disposed of by refutations of any sort. It can only be taken in and assimilated by retrieving its truth so that it is conceived more deeply, as embedded in Being itself and is withdrawn from the sphere of merely human views."

15. Cf. *Identität und Differenz*, p. 40 (E.T., p. 45).

16. Cf. *Was ist das—die Philosophie?*, p. 29 (E.T., p. 63).

17. *Einführung in die Metaphysik*, p. 119 (E.T., p. 130).

18. *Holzwege*, p. 300.

19. "Die Onto-theo-logische Verfassung der Metaphysik," in *Identität und Differenz*, p. 42f. (E.T., p. 47).

20. "Brief über den 'Humanismus'," *Wegmarken*, p. 166.

21. "Die Onto-theo-logische Verfassung der Metaphysik," in *Identität und Differenz*, p. 46 (E.T., p. 50).

22. *Vorträge und Aufsätze*, p. 238f.

23. *Nietzsche I*, p. 469.

24. See *An Introduction to Metaphysics*, passim.

25. *Der Satz vom Grund*, p. 164.

26. On Heidegger's approach to the history of philosophy, see W. Szilasi, "Interpretation und Geschichte der Philosophie." Helmuth Plessner compares ("Offene Problemgeschichte") Heidegger's approach with that of Hartmann. Werner Marx (*Heidegger und die Tradition*) discusses critically Heidegger's new determination of Being in relation to the traditional conception as represented by Aristotle and Hegel. For excellent summaries of Heidegger's interpretation of the Western philosophers, see P. Fürstenau, *Heidegger—das Gefüge seines Denkens*, pp. 101-168 and K. Kanthack, *Das Denken Martin Heideggers*. See also Richardson, *Heidegger*, pp. 301-382, for a presentation of Heidegger's views on Plato, Aristotle, Descartes, Hegel, and Nietzsche.

Durchblicke, a collection of essays edited and published by Vittorio Klostermann on the occasion of Heidegger's eightieth birthday, contains the following studies relevant to Heidegger's interpretations of past philosophers: Klaus Held, "Der Logos-Gedanke des Heraklit"; Walter Hirsch, "Platon und das Problem der Wahrheit"; Fr.-W. von Herrmann, "Sein und cogitationes—Zu Heideggers Descartes-Kritik"; Wolfgang Janke, "Die Zeitlichkeit der Repräsentation—Zur Seinsfrage bei Leibniz"; Hansgeorg Hoppe, "Wandlungen in der Kant-Auffassung Heideggers"; Jacques Taminiaux, "Dialectique et différence"; Eckhard Heftrich, "Nietzsche im Denken Heideggers". Gérard Granel and Rudolf Boehm have articles on Heidegger in relation, respectively, to Husserl and to Merleau-Ponty.

This volume also includes two valuable articles dealing with the general theme of Heidegger and Marx. Jan Patočka's "Heidegger vom anderen Ufer" examines the response of Marxist thinkers like Georg Luckács and Karel Kośik to Heidegger's thought. Gajo Petrović's "Der Spruch des Heidegger" examines the possibility of a "productive dialog" between Heidegger's thinking and Marxism on the basis of Heidegger's remarks on Marx in the "Letter on Humanism." On this whole subject, see Kostas Axelos, *Einführung in ein künftiges Denken—über Marx und Heidegger.*

27. *Vorträge und Aufsätze*, p. 227.

28. Heidegger has devoted a long essay to Anaximander of Samos, in which he gives an elaborate interpretation of the oldest philosophical utterance of Western thought ("Der Spruch des Anaximander" in *Holzwege*). Discussing the word *chreon* ('necessity' in the usual translation; Heidegger renders it as need or use—*Brauch*), he shows that with Anaximander already an awareness of the Being of what is and of the distinction between Being and beings had flashed out. "*To chreon* is the oldest name in which thinking gives utterance to the Being of essents, in which also the nature of the relationship between Being as presence and essents (what is, as present) finds the first expression, a relationship with essents that springs from the nature of Being itself. *To chreon*, anticipating the *logos* of Heraclitus, expresses the way Being itself *is* as the relation with essents.

29. "Vom Wesen und Begriff der Physis," *Wegmarken*, p. 311.

30. *Holzwege*, p. 336.

31. *Einführung in die Metaphysik*, p. 89 (E.T., p. 99).

32. *Holzwege*, p. 334.

33. The following account of Heidegger's interpretation of early Greek philosophy is based on *Einführung in die Metaphysik* (chap. 4). For an elaborate account of Heidegger's treatment of Parmenides and Heraclitus, see the book by G. J. Seidel mentioned in note 65 to chapter 1. Seidel has also an excellent chapter on "The Meaning of Language for Heidegger."

34. See *Was heisst Denken?*, 143f. (E.T., pp. 235-238) for further discussion of the Greek conception of Being as presence.

35. *Einführung in die Metaphysik*, p. 80 (E.T., p. 89).

36. Ibid., p. 98 (E.T., p. 108).

37. Heidegger has also dealt at length with his interpretation of *logos* and *legein* in an independent essay in *Vorträge und Aufsätze*. Discarding all later interpretations of *logos* as "ratio, as word, as cosmic order, as the logical and the necessity in thought, as meaning, as reason," as derivative he goes back to its original meaning: laying down, collecting and gathering, and as such, speech. *Logos*, as Heidegger explains it (p. 227), is the gathering principle, the *hen panta* (all is one) of Heraclitus. "The *logos* names that which gathers together all that is present (that is, the essent) in its presence (that is, Being), laying it out in such gathering. The Logos names that within which the presence of the present takes place. . . . In the thinking of Heraclitus the Being (presence) of essents manifests itself as the Logos, the gleaning,

gathering, laying out (*lesende Lege*)." Heidegger also shows here how, for the first time, Heraclitus determines the nature of man in terms of his belongingness to Being.

For Heidegger's approach to the interpretation of Heraclitus, see Martin Heidegger and Eugen Fink, *Heraklit*.

38. For a detailed discussion of this line, see *Was heisst Denken?*, pp. 106–117 (E.T., pp. 172–193); also see the essay, "Moira" (in *Vorträge und Aufsätze*). For Parmenides also the nature of man and his relationship to Being comes from Being itself.

39. See also *Was heisst Denken?*, p. 125, (E.T., p. 203) where *noein* is rendered as 'being mindful of' or 'taking care of'.

40. For an elaboration of the Greek tragic conception of man, as the *deinotaton*, the uncanny agent of acts of violence, see Heidegger's interpretation of the first chorus song in the *Antigone* of Sophocles in *An Introduction to Metaphysics*, where he speaks of "the creative man, who marches out into the unsaid, who breaks into the unthought, enforces what has never happened, makes what has never been seen to appear." See also "Der Ursprung des Kunstwerkes" in *Holzwege*, for elucidation of the concept of setting into a work (Sich-ins-Werk-Setzen).

41. "Platons Lehre von der Wahrheit," *Wegmarken*, 136f.

42. See also the illuminating discussion of Plato's theory of art in *Nietzsche I*, chapter 1, and comments on Plato scattered throughout the work.

43. As Heidegger points out in a discussion of the *homo mensura* doctrine of Protagoras (*Holzwege*, p. 94f.; also *Nietzsche II*, p. 135f.), the change in the interpretation of what is, including man, came about as a result of the Platonic struggle against the Sophists and, in that sense, in dependence upon them.

44. *Einführung in die Metaphysik*, p. 144 (E.T., p. 158).

45. On *agathon*, see "Vom Wesen des Grundes," *Wegmarken*, p. 56–57 (E.T., pp. 93, 95); "Platons Lehre von der Wahrheit," *Wegmarken*, pp. 132–135; also *Nietzsche II*, pp. 223–233.

46. "Platons Lehre von der Wahrheit," *Wegmarken*, p. 141.

47. See also the next chapter for Aristotle's doctrine of *energeia*. As already remarked, scattered discussions of Aristotle are to be found throughout Heidegger's writings. Except for a commentary on Aristotle's *Physics* B 1 ("Vom Wesen und Begriff der *Physis*") dealing with the Aristotelian concepts of *physis*, *ousia*, and *kinesis*, nothing by way of a systematic treatment has, however, been published. Hence the meager treatment of Aristotle here.

48. Already by the time of Aristotle, *physis* had come to denote a particular region of essents, distinguished from the sphere of *ethos* and *logos* and no longer having the broad meaning of the totality of essents. See *Holzwege*, p. 298.

49. *Einführung in die Metaphysik*, p. 145f. (E.T., p. 160).

50. *Ibid.*, p. 155 (E.T., p. 170).

51. *Nietzsche I*, p. 131.

52. *Ibid.*, p. 132.

53. *Holzwege*, p. 83.

54. Ibid., p. 132.

55. For this account of Descartes and the rise of modern philosophy see "Die Zeit des Weltbildes" in *Holzwege*; also *Nietzsche II*, pp. 131-192.

56. *Nietzsche II*, p. 162.

57. Ibid., p. 164.

58. Ibid., p. 442.

59. See *Der Satz vom Grund*, passim; the whole of this book is devoted, by way of a continuous discussion of the Principle of Sufficient Reason, to the philosophy of Leibniz and is important also for the elucidation of Heidegger's conception of the destiny of Being (*Seinsgeschick*) and of the history of Being (*Seinsgeschichte*) in relation to the history of thought.

60. Ibid., p. 65.

61. Heidegger's essay "Aus der letzten Marburger Vorlesung" is an examination of Leibniz's monadology, dating back to 1928. This was first published in *Zeit und Geschichte* and was subsequently included in *Wegmarken*.

62. *Nietzsche II*, p. 230f.

63. See *Nietzsche II*, p. 231; also "Kants These über das Sein," *Wegmarken*, p. 307. The central place (*die Mitte*) that Heidegger assigns to Kant in the history of modern thought is reflected in his unceasing preoccupation with Kant in his own thinking. Apart from the major work *Kant und das Problem der Metaphysik*, written during the *Being and Time* phase, scattered discussions of Kant's views can be found in most of his later writings. "*Kants These über das Sein*," an essay, and *Die Frage nach dem Ding*, a full-sized book, are devoted entirely to Kant. See also the report of the discussion with Ernst Cassirer at the Davos conference in: *Ergänzungen zu einer Heidegger-Bibliographie* by Guido Schneeberger. H. J. Pos gives an interesting account of the encounter between the two philosophers at Davos in his "Recollections of Ernst Cassirer." A less biased and more detailed account was provided by Carl Hamburg ("A Cassirer-Heidegger Seminar"), who also gives a full translation of the discussion report in Schneeberger. *Die Frage nach dem Ding* is subtitled *Zu Kants Lehre von den Transzendentalen Grundsätzen* ("On Kant's doctrine of Transcendental Principles") and is in the main a study of chapter 2 ("System of all Principles of Pure Understanding") of Book II (Analytic of Principles) of the Transcendental Analytic in the *Critique of Pure Reason*, thus making good what was lacking in *Kant und das Problem der Metaphysik*, as Heidegger says. In the perspective of the inquiry into the thingness of a thing, that is, of the a priori determination of the most general characteristics of the Being of an essent, Heidegger considers this as the very heart and core of the whole work, in accordance with Kant's own innermost intentions. Heidegger's procedure in this book is one of straightforward exegesis; but an exegesis that nevertheless seeks to go beyond the one-sidedness and bias of the Idealistic and the neo-Kantian interpretations.

64. *Critique of Pure Reason*, A 158, B 197. About this sentence Heidegger writes (*Die Frage nach dem Ding*, p. 143; E.T., p. 183), "He who grasps this sentence, grasps Kant's *Critique of Pure Reason*. He who grasps the latter, knows not just a book in the literature of philosophy but has a grasp of the

basic attitude characterizing our historical existence, which we can neither circumvent, nor leap over, nor disavow in any other way. We must, on the contrary, by appropriating and transforming it, bring it to a decision in the future."

65. *Kant und das Problem der Metaphysik*, p. 111 (E.T., p. 123).

66. Ibid., p. 219 (E.T., p. 252).

67. From another direction this is also the conclusion of Heidegger's second book on Kant. Kant determines the nature of human knowledge so that thought becomes subservient to intuition, thus losing its old supremacy. This radically transforms the nature of thinking and hence of logic. But as Heidegger remarks, it was not within the power of Kant to realize fully and work this out, for that would have meant nothing short of jumping over his own shadow. "This no one can do. But the uttermost exertion in making this forbidden attempt—this is the decisive and basic movement of the act of thinking. In Plato, in Leibniz, above all in Kant, finally in Schelling and Nietzsche, we can observe in different ways this basic movement. Hegel alone has apparently succeeded in jumping over this shadow—but only by eliminating the shadow, that is, the finitude of man, and leaping into the sun itself. Hegel has passed over the shadow which does not mean that he has leapt over it. And yet every philosopher *must* want to do this. In this 'must' lies his vocation. The longer the shadow, the more far-reaching is the spring." (*Die Frage nach dem Ding*, p. 117f.; E.T., p. 150f.).

68. *Der Satz vom Grund*, p. 131.

69. *Nietzsche II*, p. 231.

70. "Kants These über das Sein," *Wegmarken*, pp. 287-289.

71. *Der Satz vom Grund*, p. 137.

72. *Nietzsche I*, p. 584.

73. "Kants These über das Sein," in which Heidegger discusses Kant's statement that Being is not a real predicate but the pure positing of a thing (*Critique of Pure Reason*, A 598, B 626).

74. *Kant und das Problem der Metaphysik*, p. 31 (E.T., p. 30).

75. *Wissenschaft der Logik I*, p. 31.

76. The following account is based on Heidegger's essay "Hegels Begriff der Erfahrung" in *Holzwege*, a commentary on the sixteen paragraphs of Hegel's "Introduction" to his *Phenomenology of Mind*.

77. *Holzwege*, p. 118 (E.T., p. 27).

78. Ibid., p. 142 (E.T., p. 67).

79. Ibid., p. 163 (E.T., p. 108).

80. See *The Phenomenology of Mind*, trans. Baillie, p. 142.

81. *Holzwege*, p. 167 (E.T., p. 116).

82. Ibid., p. 170 (E.T., p. 120).

83. Ibid., p. 184 (E.T., p. 142f.).

84. *Identität und Differenz*, pp. 53-55 (E.T., pp. 56-58).

85. See for this paragraph, "Hegel und die Griechen" in *Wegmarken*.

86. *Wegmarken*, p. 268.

87. Ibid., p. 269.

88. As with all the other philosophers considered in this chapter, only an outline of the way Heidegger interprets Hegel is given here. The wider

question of his relation to Hegel, to Plato and Aristotle, to medieval thought and Christianity, to Kant, Schelling, and Nietzsche cannot be dealt with here. How much of the thought of the past, and in what form, is alive in Heidegger's own philosophy is also a question for the future. For Heidegger's relation to Hegel in particular, see Jan van der Meulen, *Heidegger und Hegel*. See also Heidegger's comments on Hegel in *Heraklit*, and H.-G. Gadamer's critical essay "Anmerkungen zu dem Thema 'Hegel und Heidegger'." This essay appears under the title "Heidegger und die Sprache der Metaphysik" in Gadamer, *Kleine Schriften III*.

89. Cf. *Vorträge und Aufsätze*, pp. 76, 114.

90. *Holzwege*, p. 200; cf. "Platons Lehre von der Wahrheit," *Wegmarken*, p. 133: "The concept of value emerging in the 19th century as the inner consequence of the modern conception of truth, is the latest as well as the weakest offspring of the *agathon*. . . . Insofar as Nietzsche's thought is dominated by the idea of value . . . without awareness of its metaphysical origin, Nietzsche is also the most unbridled Platonist in the history of Western metaphysics."

91. *Holzwege*, p. 230.

92. *Nietzsche I*, pp. 12 and 14.

93. The following account is based on the essay entitled "Nietzsches Metaphysik" in *Nietzsche II*.

94. *Nietzsche II*, p. 260.

95. See chapters 1 ("Der Wille zur Macht als Kunst") and 3 ("Der Wille zur Macht als Erkenntnis") of *Nietzsche I* for detailed treatment of the Will to Power.

96. *Nietzsche II*, p. 272.

97. Ibid.

98. On Nihilism, see *Nietzsche II*, chapters 5 ("Der Europäische Nihilismus") and 7 ("Die Seinsgeschichtliche Bestimmung des Nihilismus"); also the essay "Nietzsches Wort 'Gott ist Tot' " (in *Holzwege*) and "Zur Seinsfrage."

99. *Nietzsche II*, p. 275f. Cf. Karl-Heinz Volkmann-Schluck, "Zur Gottesfrage bei Nietzsche" in *Anteile*.

100. *Nietzsche II*, p. 277f.

101. Ibid., p. 281.

102. Ibid., p. 282.

103. On the Eternal Recurrence, see the detailed treatment in chapter 2 ("Die Ewige Wiederkehr des Gleichen") and in chapter 4 ("Die Wiederkunft des Gleichen und der Wille zur Macht") of *Nietzsche* (in Vols. 1 and 2, respectively).

104. *Nietzsche II*, p. 284.

105. For a more detailed account of this central concept of Nietzsche's philosophy, see the brilliant chapter 2 of *Nietzsche I*. As Heidegger remarks there (pp. 257-258), "'Nietzsche's doctrine of the Eternal Recurrence of the Same is not just one theory about what is among others. It has developed as a result of the most bitter argument with the Platonic-Christian mode of thinking and with the way the latter has worked itself out and developed in the modern age. This mode of thinking is at the same time judged by

Nietzsche as the distinctive feature of Western thought and of its history in general." For a criticism of Heidegger's views on this doctrine, see Karl Löwith, *Nietzsches Philosophie der Ewigen Wiederkehr des Gleichen*, pp. 222-225.

106. On the Superman, see also "Wer ist Nietzsches Zarathustra?" in *Vorträge und Aufsätze*.

107. *Nietzsche II*, p. 300.

108. See *Nietzsche I*, pp. 612-616, for Nietzsche's conception of Truth, where righteousness is also discussed in the section entitled, "Die Wahrheit als Gerechtigkeit."

109. *Nietzsche II*, p. 325.

110. Ibid., p. 332.

111. *Nietzsche I*, p. 26.

IO
The Question of Being

"In the treatise *Being and Time*, the question about the sense of Being is posed and developed, *as a question*, for the first time in the history of philosophy."[1] Negatively, it has been shown there that to 'be' is not merely to be simply given or to be the object for a knowing subject, these being themselves derivative modes of Being presupposing a more fundamental sense of the term. Positively, it has been suggested that not merely the being of man but Being as such is inseparably bound up with time. How far and in what sense the notions of truth, of nothingness, of transcendence, of ground, and of language are interlinked with that of Being is discussed in subsequent works and answered with some finality. In the writings of the second phase, there is a determined, self-conscious attempt to shed the vestiges of the metaphysical way of conceiving Being, that is, in terms of and from the point of view of the essent. *An Introduction to Metaphysics* attacks the question of Being directly and may be taken, as Heidegger suggests in the foreword to the eighth edition (1957) of *Being and Time*, as complementary to that work, approaching as it does the question mainly from its historical aspect. Like *Being and Time*, it is introductory, leading on to the problem only, and incomplete, in the sense that it confines itself to showing, in its historical part, how the prevailing conception of Being as "constancy of presence," coming down from the Greeks, is inadequate.

Traditional metaphysics, taking the generality and emptiness of the concept of Being for granted, occupies itself with the essent as such, with the essent in its Being (the *Seiendheit* or beingness of a being) rather than with Being as such, seeking to fill up the emptiness of Being with notions derived from the side of the essent. Heidegger seeks to demonstrate in this work that 'Being' is not just a universal, the most general concept, and therefore empty of all content but, as the light in which all that is discloses itself to us, is inexhaustible in the richness of its meaning, strangely complex in its structure and a power determinative of man's historical existence. He does this, first, by showing that even the word 'Being', in its grammar and etymology is not so empty as it sounds. Second, by entering into a detailed examination of the Greek conception of Being, he shows how highly determinate it is in its contrast with the notions of Seeming, Becoming, and the Ought.

The main reason for the fact that the word 'Being' (German, *Sein*; Greek, *einai*; Latin, *esse*) sounds empty and nebulous in its meaning lies, Heidegger explains,[2] in the character of its grammar and etymology. The German *das Sein* (Being) is a verbal substantive based on the infinitive *sein* (to be). The infinitive is a word form that, as it were, cuts off what is meant in it from all determinate relationships of signification, that abstracts from all particular relations. It is an abstract verbal concept, designating only the most general, indeterminate meaning of a verb. And when the abstract infinitive, in the present case *sein* (to be), is transformed into a substantive *das Sein* (Being), this indefiniteness is further aggravated, and the emptiness lying within the infinitive is as it were still more firmly established and stabilized. In addition, the substantive form carries the ineradicable suggestion that what is called 'Being' itself *is*, though obviously only the essent is and not, over and above that, Being also. Thus the term becomes a name for something utterly indeterminate. A consideration of the etymology of the term, however, is more rewarding. Etymologically, the various inflections of the verb *sein* (as also of the English 'be') are derived, Heidegger says, from three different roots: (1) *es*, (Sanskrit *asu*, be, live, that which stands and moves and rests in itself, the living, self-standing; compare Sanskrit *asti*; Greek *estin*; Latin *esse*; German *ist*; English *is*). (2)

bhu (Sanskrit, arise, emerge, by itself come to stand; compare Greek *phuo, phuein*, shine forth, appear; Latin *fuo*; German *bin*; English *be*). (3) *vas* (Sanskrit, dwell; compare Sanskrit *vasami*; German *wesan, gewesen, wesen*; Latin *vesta*; English *was*). Three concrete meanings have thus entered originally into 'Being': to live, to emerge, to dwell; but today these have become extinct and only the abstract sense of 'to be' remains. The three meanings have got mixed up, effacing one another, so that no determinate sense stands out explicitly. These, however, are mere facts of linguistic science and however suggestive as such, they contribute little to the question about Being itself; the question of Being is not a matter of etymology and grammar.

From the point of view of linguistic usage, however, two important facts about 'Being' and 'is' stand out as philosophically relevant. First, when we say that something 'is'—really meaning it, and as determined by a particular situation, aim and mood, and not merely as just a propositional specimen—the 'is' may be variously meant. In the 'is' Being discloses itself in a variety of ways—*to on legetai pollachos*, as Aristotle said, but in a deeper sense.[3] But this diversity of meanings, far from being arbitrary, shows a single determinate trait running through them all, holding our understanding of 'Being' within a definite horizon of sense, that of constant presence (*ständige Anwesenheit*), as which the Greeks initially experienced Being. This is further indicated by the fact that the verbal substantive *Sein* (Being) is understood by us in terms of the infinitive, which in turn we comprehend, "involuntarily and almost as if there were no alternative," in terms of 'is', with all its diversity of use. "The specific verb form 'is', the third person singular of the present indicative, has here a preeminent status." The sense in which we understand 'Being' today is thus historically determined, suggesting that the inquiry into the sense of Being cannot dispense with the historical dimension. It is true, in the second place, that we are concerned neither with the word as such nor with its 'meaning' but with what they are about, the thing itself, that is, with Being. The latter, however, is no entity. No thing corresponds to the word 'Being' and its meaning, from which it by no means follows that Being consists only of the word and its meaning. This points, Heidegger concludes, to the peculiar fact about 'Being' that here the word and its meaning are more profoundly dependent on what is meant (that is, the thing itself) than in the case of other words. And, conversely, Being also is itself dependent on the word in a quite different and deeper sense than any essent. "In each of its inflections the word 'Being' bears an essentially different relation to Being itself from that of all other nouns and verbs of the language to the essent which they denote." Hence, the inquiry into Being is inextricably bound up with a reflection on language, the shrine of Being. As explained earlier, the Greek conception of Being, determining ours, is inadequate and so is the way the Greeks looked upon language, its logic and its grammar, which were themselves molded by that conception of Being and have in turn given their stamp to the way *we* talk now. And once this is realized, it becomes imperative to make a fresh start and seek, by means of more appropriate language, to come closer to the true nature of Being. The path to this, however, lies through a consideration of the various ways in which metaphysics, by its very character as essent-centered, represents, not Being itself, but the Being of essents and the way it conceives the relation between what is and its Being.

Being and Metaphysical Thought

Metaphysics determines the nature of man in terms of his relationship to essents.[4] But since metaphysics is concerned with the essent in view of its Being, man's relationship to essents itself requires that he should be conceived in terms of the more basic relationship with Being. Metaphysical thinking, however, unaware of its own foundation, can hardly recognize the latter relationship as such, except in terms of the former. And yet, in all our dealings with the essent we necessarily and inevitably stand in some kind of relationship with Being. As Heidegger puts it, "We have dealings with essents and at the same time hold ourselves in the relationship to Being. Only so do we have a footing in the essent as a whole and our sojourn in it." We always stand, in other words, in the midst of the distinction between beings and Being, the distinction on which, in fact, our relationship both to Being and to essents is dependent. "We cannot evade the distinction between Being and beings, not even when we presumably cease thinking metaphysically. Everywhere and always, we stand and move on the narrow path of this distinction which carries us from essents to Being and from Being to essents in all our relationship with essents, of whatever kind or rank, of whatever degree of certainty or accessibility it may be. . . . Perhaps the distinction is the real core of that natural disposition of the human mind for metaphysics (of which Kant speaks)." What man is and what his relationship to Being is, are grounded, Heidegger holds, on this distinction. This distinction, far from being a mere invention and a mental construct, is the very ground on which metaphysics itself can originate, for it alone renders possible any thinking about the essent as such, that is, in its Being. It is the unrecognized and unacknowledged but nonetheless constantly employed foundation of all metaphysics. This distinction, further, is not 'made' by anybody, is not the result of an 'act' of a distinguishing 'subject' and yet it *is*. Heidegger therefore prefers to designate this distinction by the more impersonal phrase "Ontological Difference" or just "Difference," meant to suggest that essents and Being are somehow held apart, separated and yet kept together in their relationship with each other, in and by themselves and not merely as a distinction of the intellect. (In conformity with this dynamic conception of Being, the Difference also is not just a static 'relation' but is to be conceived dynamically, as differentiation, as an 'issue' for settlement (*Austrag*) between the two 'terms' of the relation.) Though based as to its own possibility upon the Difference, metaphysics cannot recognize it *as such* and so remains shut out from the possibility of thinking about Being *as* Being.[5]

The perennial question of metaphysics, as Aristotle explicitly laid down, is: "What is the essent (*ti to on*)?" The answer that the Aristotelian First Philosophy gives to this question is that "a being is spoken of in many ways" or, in Heidegger's translation, that the essent, in respect of its being, becomes manifest in many ways. But Aristotle does not inquire why and how and to what extent the Being of beings unfolds itself in the four modes which he merely asserts without seeking to determine their common origin. What is the common meaning of Being as expressed in these four ways of regarding Being: Being as property, Being as possibility and actuality, Being as truth, Being as schema of the categories? "What is the sense of Being expressing itself in these four headings? How can they be brought into a comprehensible harmony?" We cannot become aware of this unified sense, Heidegger asserts, without first raising and clearing up the question: From where does Being as such (not merely the essent as such) get its determination?[6] But this question metaphysics is not in a position even to raise. As concerned with the essent as such and in entirety (that is, in its Being), metaphysics presupposes, and bases itself upon, the Ontological Difference. It seeks to conceive Being, but it does so not as Being, not in its difference from beings, but always in terms of the essent and as subserving its concern with the essent. Metaphysics is the movement of thought away from and beyond the essent as a whole toward its Being but it is at the same time a movement that comes back to the essent as its ultimate destination. In the direction *away* from the essent, it conceives Being as the most general determination of the essent and in the direction *towards* the essent, its ground and generative principle (*arche*, as, for example, in the Christian conception of the creation of everything that is by a First Cause or in the Enlightenment idea of governance by cosmic reason.) All the time, it is the essent that is in the forefront, as requiring explanation, as the measure and the goal, as the realization and fulfilment of Being; even while the latter is conceived as an 'Ideal', and thus higher in rank than the essent, it is still in a way in the service of the essent. For metaphysics, the essent as a whole thus has the preeminence, a position of supremacy over Being. Going beyond the essent to its Being, here, is itself oriented to the eventual movement back from Being to the essent. The awareness or light of Being itself is never absent in our dealings with essents, but to metaphysical thinking it always appears as *their* Being and determined by its relationship to *them*. As a form of presence (the presence of what is present), Being reveals itself as *chreon*, as *moira*, as *logos*, as *idea*, as *energeia*, the latter afterwards progressively deformed into *actualitas*, reality (or actuality) and objectivity, culminating, in its extreme subjectivistic form, in the Will to Power.[7] Looking from the point of view of essents and conceiving Being under the limited temporal horizon of the present, metaphysics characterizes Being in a variety of ways. Some of the principal ways in which metaphysics thus conceives Being (as presence) may be reviewed briefly here.

The question, "What is the essent as such?" is a question about the Being of essents. The nature of this is determined in terms of its "what" and its "that," which together make up the essent in its Being. The "what" is determined by Plato as *idea*, and when later this is termed "essence (*wesen*)," this only means that the Being of beings is conceived in terms of its 'whatness', to the neglect of its 'that'. The Being of beings is here approached from the side of essents and conceived in its relation to essents as the genus and the universal from which they derive their character as essents. The *essentia* is the quiddity, the *genos* in the double sense of origin and genus, the one (*hen*) in the many (*polla*), the universal (*koinon*). It is the 'what' of anything, irrespective of whether that thing exists, and is thus pure possibility. As against this, the 'that' is the *existentia*, the existence or actuality of what is. *That* the essent is, is its *existentia* which, according to Plato, is to be found in what truly answers to the 'what', the real Being, the Idea as the *ontos on*, as opposed to the essent which, properly speaking, 'is' not, for Plato. Being is differentiated into what anything is and that it is. With this differentiation (Aristotle) and the preparation for it (Plato), Heidegger says, begins the history of Being as metaphysics. Since Aristotle, who first explicitly formulated the distinction between the *ti estin* (the 'what') and the *oti estin* (the 'that'), however, it is in the actuality of the actual, in existence, that the real and proper Being of anything is thought to lie, *existentia* being, as Heidegger puts it, the commonest metaphysical name for Being. For Aristotle, what is present (that is, the essent) is that which, having come forth into unhiddenness, stands there as the invariant 'this', the particular (*tode ti*). The movement of coming forth or of production comes to a rest in this and hence the presence or Being of the present is characterized by motion and its consummated mode, rest, which is the fulfilment and gathering together, the *telos* or end of motion. As such consummation of motion, the essent, tarrying there in the steadiness of the 'look' or aspect (*eidos*) it presents, is conceived by Aristotle as *ergon*, as a work. The presence (Being or *ousia*) of a particular 'this' has for him, therefore, the character of *energeia* or, as he also calls it, *entelecheia*. On the basis of this general conception of *ousia* as *energeia*, there arises then the distinction between *ousia* in the primary sense of the particular 'this' and in the secondary sense of the look presented by it, its 'what', which is common to all the particular instances of its manifestation.

This distinction between existence and essence, Heidegger points out, is not coincident with the distinction between Being and essents but falls within Being itself. Plato takes one term of the pair (essence) as identical with Being, whereas Aristotle emphasizes the other (existence). Aristotle's conception of Being as *energeia*, embodied in the particular 'this', is, according to Heidegger, more comprehensive and nearer the original Greek spirit, the view of Being as *physis*, in the sense that though the *eidos* (the 'look' of the 'this') can be conceived in terms of *energeia* as a mode of presence, the *tode ti*, the particular essent, remains, as *me on*, inconceivable in terms of the Platonic idea. The two modes of *ousia*, *idea* and *energeia*, constitute, in the interplay of their distinction, the basic framework of all metaphysics as it unfolds itself in the course of its history. Sometimes one of them comes to the forefront as the basic character of Being and sometimes the other, each undergoing radical modification with the development of metaphysical thought. The history of metaphysics is the history of the modification of *idea* into idea and representation, of *energeia* into *actualitas*, existence, actuality, and objectivity, but it is a history in which the primal nature of Being as the unity underlying these two remains hidden. Since the transformation of the Aristotelian *energeia* into *actualitas*—later, *existentia*—this remains the dominant conception of Being and hence, as Heidegger puts it, the history of Being reveals itself primarily in the history of *energeia*. The essent is conceived henceforth as what is actual (as against the merely potential or possible), that which possesses causal efficacy, its actuality (Being) lying not merely in its being the ground (*arche*) of what is but primarily in its character as cause (*aition*). From this the theological conception of Being as the highest essent or God, itself present in complete actuality as *actus purus* and supreme cause, follows inevitably.

As its very name suggests, metaphysics goes beyond the

essent to its Being. The latter is for it 'sheer transcendence', as Heidegger expressed it in *Being and Time*. Metaphysics rises above the essent to its what-ness, its *essentia*. This ascent to the *essentia* is transcendence in the transcendental sense of Kant. At the same time, transcendence means the transcendent in the sense of the first existing ground of the essent as existing, that is, in respect of its *existentia*. Ontology, Heidegger says, represents transcendence as the transcendental; theology represents it as the transcendent. This twofold ascent of metaphysics, however, is only for the sake of representing the essent itself, that is, of an eventual return to it. In its upward movement metaphysics does not stop to contemplate Being itself but passes it by, as Heidegger puts it, "for it has already conceived Being in its own way, namely, as the essent insofar as it, the essent, is" (that is, as the is-ness of what is). All transcendence, ontological or theological, according to him, is conceived relatively to the subject-object relation, in terms of which man understands himself and his world in the era of subjectivity.

The Platonic conception of Being as *ousia*, that is, the Being of essents regarded merely as their being-ness or is-ness (*Seiendheit*), also leads to its being taken as the abstract universal. Being in this view, is the most general (*to koinaton*), the highest universal arrived at by a process of abstraction from the particular essents. It is, therefore, utterly empty, carrying no other meaning except that of subsuming all that is under itself. In later philosophy, indeed, this is established as logically obvious. But, as Heidegger points out, this characterization of Being as the most general concept says nothing about the nature of Being, a nature which every metaphysical doctrine understands in a specific, concrete sense of its own. At the most, it describes how we arrive at the concept through the process of generalization. "Through the interpretation of Being as the most general, nothing whatever is said about Being itself; it says only how metaphysics thinks about the *concept* of Being." Evidently this is only a way of refusing, on the part of metaphysics, to notice the difference between Being and beings while yet making use of it all the time.[8]

Being in the sense of the is-ness of what is, in the next place, is not regarded merely as the highest universal but also as what comes before, the Apriori or the '*Prius*'. Plato, and following him, Aristotle, have determined the *ousia* of the essent as the *proteron*. Plato has demonstrated that to see two things as having the same color, for example, we must already know sameness. The two colored things, of course, come first in our experience—they are first in relation to us (*pros hemas*) and the sameness comes later. But in respect of its own Being (*te physei*), sameness comes first and the particular essents later. Sameness, as enduring presence (the Being of what is the same) must have already come in our view (as *idea*) before two things can show themselves as having the same color; as the Being of these it is also prior to them. The knowledge of what is thus Apriori is therefore, from the point of view of essents, metaphysics. Since Plato, this conception of Being as the Apriori is dominant throughout the whole history of Western philosophy, which may thus be rightly described as the history of Platonism. Actually, Heidegger remarks, the Apriori is not just a property of Being but Being itself in its unhiddenness, though with the interpretation of truth (*aletheia*) in terms of apprehension (*noein*), it afterwards came to be regarded as a property of knowing. In conceiving Being as the Apriori, as coming before essents, metaphysics conceives it exclusively from the point of view of the essent and as referring back to that, irrespective of whether the Apriori is taken to mean what is prior in itself or in the order of knowing or as determining the possibility of objects. "So long as the Being of essents is conceived as the Apriori, this way of determining Being itself prevents a consideration of Being as Being, a consideration which could perhaps enable us to realize how far Being as Being enters into this apriori relationship with essents and whether this relationship is merely incidental to Being, only following in its wake, or whether Being itself is this relation."[9]

Another consequence of the Platonic doctrine of Ideas is the conception of Being as a condition of the possibility of what is. Plato conceived Being, in the sense of the is–ness (*Seiendheit*) of what is, as *idea* and the essential nature of all Ideas, the Idea of Ideas, as the *agathon*, the good in the sense of the enabling and the empowering. The *idea tou agathou* is *epikeina tes ousias*, beyond even the is–ness of what is, in the sense that the enabling character of the Idea is what really constitutes the is–ness or Being of all that is. Since Plato, Being has thus been understood not only as apriori but also as that which enables essents to be, renders them possible. Being means the condition of the possibility of whatever is. In modern philosophy, with the transformation of the Platonic *idea* into representation, the enabling character of Being comes under the sway of subjectivity. Being is conceived as the representedness of what is represented, the former being regarded as the condition of the possibility of the latter. In Kant, the is-ness of the essent, conceived as object, is its objectivity and the latter is the *a priori* condition of the possibility of objects in general. As Heidegger remarks, "through Kant's interpretation of Being, the is-ness (*Seiendheit*) of what is is for the first time expressly conceived in the sense of the condition of the possibility, which then leaves the way open for its unfoldment into the conception of value in the metaphysics of Nietzsche."[10] This way of conceiving Being, like those mentioned before, is primarily concerned with the essent in its character as essent, with the essent in its Being and not with Being as such, and therefore remains confined within the metaphysical sphere of the truth of essents, without access to the truth of Being itself.

It lies in the very nature of metaphysics as representational thinking to represent the Being of essents as their ground. In representing anything to ourselves, we represent it *as* this or that. With this "as this or that," we accommodate the thing represented somewhere, deposit it there, as it were, provide it with a ground.[11] Only what is brought to a stand in a representation for which adequate ground has been provided, that is, is an 'object' in the modern sense, counts as an essent, as something that is. The enormous power of the demand made on us by the *principium reddendae rationis* (the Principle of Sufficient Reason), incubating so long, has, in the modern phase of the history of Being, emerged with Leibniz to the surface and the man of today is completely in its grip, as Heidegger shows in *Der Satz vom Grund*. Metaphysics seeks to ground essents in Being but, in doing so, it turns Being itself into an essent, be it the highest essent in the sense of a first cause, be it the preeminent essent in the sense of the subject (of subjectivity regarded as the condition of the possibility of all objectivity) or, as a combination of the two, the highest essent as the Absolute in the sense of unconditioned subjectivity. The question of Leibniz, later taken up by Schelling, "Why are there essents at all and not rather nothing?" is a question that asks for a first cause and for the highest ground, itself essent, of all that is. It is the question, as old as Plato and Aristotle, about the *theion*, the Divine, which for metaphyics is necessarily the essent ground of essents. Metaphysics is not only ontology, the inquiry into the essent as such in respect of its *essentia* but also theology, the inquiry into the highest essent. The metaphysical concept of Being as ground converts Being into a being and, because of its concern with essents, thinks of it in terms of these. How far is it possible to think of Being as Being and yet as Ground, how far and in what sense Being itself can be thought as Ground and not merely from the point of view of essents, how far the Being-centered conception of Ground can itself be understood in terms of play is, Heidegger suggests, still a task for the future. Nevertheless, the beginnings of an answer to these questions are suggested by Heidegger in his conception of *Ereignis*.

The above mentioned ways of characterizing Being are metaphysical in the sense that they approach Being from the perspective of beings, seeking to grasp *their* truth and not letting Being itself shine forth in its truth. For metaphysics, Being is always the essent in its Being, never Being in its own truth. In thinking about the essent as such it has a fleeting glimpse of Being, in passing and on its way to the essent. It thinks indeed of the essent as such but it does not ponder the "as such" itself, as Heidegger puts it. This "as such" is the unhiddenness of the essent, which metaphysics ignores. Being itself is the unhiddenness in which the essent has its presence. But this unhiddenness itself remains hidden to metaphysics. This is so, not because of a failure of thought on the part of metaphysics but because Being itself stays away. The illumination which lights up the essent itself remains inaccessible to metaphysics in its own nature as such illumination. Metaphysics thus does not think of Being *as* Being, does not let it 'be' itself, but always understands it from the point of view of its own concern with the essent and so in terms of the latter. For it, Being as such is a nullity and for this reason, as Heidegger asserts, "metaphysics, as metaphysics, is the real

Nihilism . . . The metaphysics of Plato is no less nihilistic than the metaphysics of Nietzsche. In the former, the Nihilistic essence is still hidden, in the latter it comes fully into view."[12]

Being itself is none of the things metaphysics conceives it as being. As Heidegger puts it, "It is itself. To realize and to say this is what the thinking of the future must learn. 'Being'—that is not God and not a World ground. Being is farther away than all that is, whether it be a rock, an animal, a work of art, a machine, an angel, or God. Being is the nearest. And yet the nearest is what remains remotest from man."[13] As mentioned before, metaphysics by its very nature is not only ontology but also theology, for it is concerned not only with the essent as such but also with the essent as a whole. Its wholeness constitutes the unity of essents, unifying by virtue of being the generative ground. In the essay "The Onto-Theo-Logical Structure of Metaphysics" (in *Identität und Differenz*), Heidegger has gone more deeply into this question than in his earlier discussion in the introduction to "What is Metaphysics?," seeking to delve into the unitary essence of metaphysics and discover the single source in which this triple character of metaphysics has its origin.[14] Having had experience of theology, both that of religious faith as well as of philosophy, in his own origin and development, he "prefers now to be silent about God in the sphere of thinking."[15] The onto-theological character of metaphysics, he says, has become questionable for thought, not because of any sort of atheism but because of a realization that onto-theo-logy is itself rooted in an as yet unthought unity of the essence of metaphysics. The question how God comes into philosophy must, therefore, be explicitly raised. And to do this is to ask, taking the 'step back', what the source of the onto-theological structure of metaphysics is.

Metaphysics is 'Logic', in the first place, not because its theme is thinking, but because it is concerned with the Being of essents as originally revealed in the shape of *Logos* (gathering together and laying down as a unity, the *hen panta*), the self-fathoming and self-substantiating Ground, and which therefore takes into its service thinking as proving and grounding. Metaphysics is Ontology because, concerned with the essent as such, it thinks Being as the unity of the utmost generality, as the unity to be found at the bottom of things. And it is Theology in the sense that it thinks Being as the unity of the essent as a whole, that is, as the highest above all, as the unity which provides the ground and establishes. In each case, the Being of essents is taken as Ground and metaphysics may, therefore, be described as being concerned, basically and radically, with the grounding of essents, "giving an account of the Ground, accounting for it and in the end calling it to account." The Being of essents as such manifests itself as having the character of a ground and this is such in a complete sense only when conceived as the first Ground, *prote arche*. For metaphysics, the primary concern of thought is thus with Being conceived as Ground in the sense of a self-caused First Cause (*causa prima, ultima ratio*) or *causa sui*. This is the God of metaphysics, irrespective of whether its character as Ground appears in the form of *logos* or *hypokeimenon*, substance or subject, in the course of its historical unfoldment. The Ontological Difference, on the basis of which Being and essents get differentiated, is the ultimate source of the onto-theological structure of metaphysics. In the course of this dynamic 'Differentiation', Being appears as Ground (*Logos*) and the essent as the grounded, the two being held apart in an intimacy of relationship such that "not only does Being as Ground provide a foundation for the essent but the latter (in its wholeness), on its part and in its own way, grounds and generates Being." In the light of Being as Ground, the grounding itself appears as something that is, an essent, and therefore itself in need of being accounted for in terms of a highest essent conceived as the first cause. "Because Being reveals itself as Ground, the essent is the grounded and, as the highest essent, itself the grounding first cause. As metaphysics thinks the essent in respect of its Ground as that which is common to every essent as such, it is 'Logic' in the shape of Onto-logic. As metaphysics thinks the essent as such in its totality, that is, in regard to the highest, all-grounding essent, it is 'Logic' in the form of Theo-logic." The happening of Differentiation, through which Being reveals itself as Ground or *Logos*, is itself generative of metaphysics and the ultimate 'explanation', if it may be called such, for the fact that the essent appears both as grounded and, representing to itself (as 'Logic') its own ground as something that is (that is, itself as its own utmost generality and totality), the self-caused First Cause. This is how God comes into, and is the way He is known to, philosophy. But, as Heidegger remarks, "To this God, man can neither pray nor make offerings and sacrifices. Man can neither kneel down in awe before the *causa sui* nor can he sing and dance before this God. Accordingly, the godless thinking which is compelled to give up the God of philosophy, God conceived as *causa sui*, is perhaps closer to the (really) godly God, freer for Him, than (metaphysics as) onto–theo–logic would like to admit."[16]

Truth of Being—*Ereignis* and *Geviert*

The step back out of metaphysics into the source which generates the whole sphere in which metaphysical thinking can function leads to that which makes the central question of metaphysics—What is the essent in its Being?—itself possible. This is the 'Difference', so termed "provisionally and unavoidable in the language of tradition,"[17] between Being and beings, the twofoldness (*Zwie-falt*) of essents and Being. The participation (*methexis*) of the essent in Being (as idea), of which Plato speaks and into which, following him, the entire history of philosophy inquires, already *presupposes*, Heidegger says, such twofoldness of Being and beings. To speak of Being is to speak of the Being of essents and to speak of the essent is to speak of the essent in its Being. The one is implied in the other. "We speak," as Heidegger says, "always on the basis of the twofoldness. It is always already given, for Parmenides as much as for Plato, for Kant as much as for Nietzsche. The twofoldness has already laid open the sphere within which it becomes possible to represent the relation between essents and Being,"[18] either as the Platonic *chorismos* or as transcendence—both of these presuppose the distinction or twofoldness and therefore cannot themselves generate it. Accordingly, Heidegger argues, Being should be thought in its difference from the essent and the latter in its difference from Being. For, "Being as well as the essent, in their different ways, emerge from and through the Difference."[19] When we

thus think of Being in terms of Difference, of Being as Difference, Being shows itself in the character of going over to the
essent, as coming down to it and revealing it and the essent
appears as that which, through such descent of Being, comes
into unhiddenness and appears as if it were by itself unhidden.
As against the traditional conception of transcendence as the
movement from Dasein to Being (in terms of which he mentioned the Ontological Difference earlier), Heidegger thinks
of the Difference now as the interplay and resolution (*Austrag*)
of Being's descent into beings and the latter's emergence into
unconcealedness. Being is the revealing descent (*entbergende
Überkommnis*) and the essent is the coming into and enduring
in the haven of unhiddenness, the arrival (*sich bergende Ankunft*)
which hides its own self in this unconcealedness. Both
emerge, as thus differentiated, from the Difference, their identical source. The Difference between Being and essents is not
just a static and formal 'relation' between two terms but the
interplay, the working out or the process of resolution
(*Austrag*) of the two opposed movements of revealing (descent) and concealing (arrival). This conception of *Austrag* carries Heidegger into a dimension more basic than the differentiation of Being and the essent on which metaphysical thought
rests, "beyond Being" (the Platonic *epikeina*, but in a more
fundamental sense!), a dimension into which entry is rendered
almost insuperably difficult by the inherently 'metaphysical'
character of the Western languages themselves. As Heidegger
remarks, "What is called here *Austrag*, leads our thinking into
a realm, to speak about which the principal terms of
metaphysics, Being and essent, Ground and the grounded, do
not any longer suffice. For what these words name, what the
mode of thinking governed by them conceives, originates, as
the Different (that is, the Being of what is in general and as the
highest), from the Difference, of which the genesis is beyond
the purview of metaphysics and cannot be thought in its
language."[20]

Just as a consideration of the Difference leads Heidegger
beyond the 'Being' of metaphysics, so also does reflection on
the Identity between the essence of man (as a thinking being)
and Being itself.[21] The unity of a thing with itself, its identity
(which is never a bare, abstract unity but is always self-

mediated and complex) constitutes, according to the whole tradition of European thought, a principal feature of the Being of all that is.[22] But, as Heidegger points out, the earliest Greek utterance in which this Being is expressly mentioned, namely, the saying of Parmenides that Being and apprehension (thought) are the same (*to gar auto noein estin te kai einai*), expresses something entirely different. As against the traditional doctrine of metaphysics, according to which Identity belongs to Being, Parmenides suggests that Being inheres in an Identity, that thinking and Being belong in the Self-same, that they belong together through this Self-same. The sameness of *to auto*, the Self-same, lies, according to Heidegger, in a belonging–together, though a belonging–together which must be interpreted otherwise than in terms of the later metaphysical conception of Identity as a feature of Being, for here Being itself is regarded as a feature of this Identity. Without taking the Parmenidean conception of belonging–together as the last word on the identity of thought and Being, Heidegger proceeds to consider what belonging–together in the sense of mediated Identity means.

Belonging-together in the customary sense is a belonging-*together* in which the sense of belonging is determined by the 'together', that is, in terms of its unity. Here, to 'belong' means, Heidegger says, to be coordinated and incorporated into the order of a 'together', given its place in the unity of a manifold, put together into the unity of a system mediated through the unifying center of an effective synthesis. "Philosophy conceives such belonging-together as *nexus* and *connexio*, as the necessary connection between one thing and another." On the other hand, belonging-together may also be understood as *belonging*-together, such that the 'together' is determined in terms of belonging. "Belonging-together" can yield a sense in which it is not the unity of togetherness that determines the sense of 'belonging' but in which togetherness itself is understood in the light of belonging. It is in this sense that thought and Being belong together in the Self-same. Man (with thinking as his distinctive character) and Being *belong* together; they are held together in a unity, but not in the sense of being coupled together, as the traditional concepts of man and Being represent. May it not be, Heidegger asks, that this togetherness or unity is rather one of mutuality, of belonging *to* each other? In fact, as he points out, even in the traditional concepts of man and Being there is an inkling of this mutuality of the two. As himself an essent, man is included within the order of Being. But his distinction lies in the fact that, as a thinking being who is open to Being, he faces Being, remains related to it and thus corresponds (is responsive) to it. Properly speaking, man *is* only this relationship of correspondence or responsiveness. "In man there prevails a belongingness to Being, a belongingness which is receptive to Being because it is delivered up and entrusted (*übereignet*) to the latter."[23] Similarly, Heidegger asserts, Being in the sense of presence *is* and endures only as, through its claim, it solicits man and is of concern to him; man, open to Being, alone lets it come as presence. Such occurrence of presence wants the open area of a clearing (*Lichtung*) and because of this need remains delivered up to the nature of man. Man and Being are, as Heidegger puts it, entrusted to each other and belong to each other. It is on the basis of this conception, not further examined, of the belonging-together of man and Being that the nature of each was later given its metaphysical determination. But so long as we represent everything, as metaphysics does, in terms of system and mediation, with or without dialectic, this relationship can only be conceived as one of connection and interlinking, brought about either from the side of man or of Being. Access to this *belonging*-together, a deeper insight into it, is possible, Heidegger asserts, only when we break loose from the attitude of representational thinking, when we take the spring away both from the current conception of man as *animal rationale*, a subject for his objects, as well as from Being conceived as the Ground of all essents as such. The *belonging*-together of man and Being can properly be realized only by such a leap. "This leap has the abruptness of an unbridged entry into that belongingness which alone bestows the interrelation of man and Being and hence the 'constellation' of the two. The leap is the sudden entrance into that realm which has enabled man and Being to have ever already reached each other in their essence, by virtue of both being entrusted to each other out of a mutual sufficiency."[24]

The present-day constellation of man and Being, the way

they concern each other, is that of technology, regarded not as merely a production of man but as manifesting in its essence the way in which Being addresses itself to us and claims us. The claim or demand under which today not only man but all essents, including nature and history, stand in respect of their Being is that of planning and calculation. In our very depths we are today challenged to apply ourselves in every sphere to planning and calculation: the essent as such addresses itself to us in respect of its calculability. Being is itself subject to the challenge of letting the essent manifest itself under the aspect of calculability and, in the same measure, man is challenged to treat the essent as an object of his planning and reckoning. The gathered complex of this challenge, which delivers man and Being to each other so that they challenge each other in this fashion is called by Heidegger the *Ge-Stell* (configuration, mutual 'placing'; coined analogously to *Ge-setz*, what is laid down, the Law). The constellation in which our age stands is determined by this mutual challenging of Being and man, claiming us in the mode of the *Ge-Stell*. The *Ge-Stell* is not something that can be encountered within the horizon of representational thinking, through which we think the Being of essents as presence, and it is not itself something ultimate but only a secret hint of that which has the real sway over the constellation of Being and man. "The *belonging*-together of man and Being in the manner of reciprocal challenging brings dismayingly home to us that and how man is taken up into the ownership (*vereignet*) of Being and, on the other hand, how Being is dedicated (*zugeeignet*) to the nature of man and is taken up into that.[25] In the *Ge-Stell* there prevails a singular owning and being owned (dedication). It is important to realize, in a simple, straightforward manner, this relationship (of mutual fittingness and owning, *eignen*) in which man and Being belong (*ge-eignet*) to each other (and are so in harmony with each other), that is, to meditate on what we call the *Ereignis*." (This word ordinarily means 'event', but Heidegger uses it in its etymological sense of *Er-eignis*, the occurrence of owning.)[26] The configuration of man and Being in the modern world of technology, the *Ge-Stell*, is itself one manifestation of a deeper mutuality of man and Being, a prelude, as Heidegger calls it, to the primordial *Er-eignis*. This conception hence opens out a possibility of the *Ge-Stell* being overcome and transformed into a deeper 'owning' through the *Er-eignis*, thus retrieving the technological world from its position of domination and taking it back into that of servitude within the realm which enables man to reach up truly into the *Er-eignis*.[27]

What the term *Er-eignis* aims at disclosing is the nearest, the most intimate, of all that is close to us and in which we are already held; for, as Heidegger puts it, "Could anything be closer to us than what brings us nearer that to which we belong and within which we *are* as the 'belonged', the *Er-eignis?*" The *Er-eignis* is that domain, suspended in itself, which enables man and Being to reach one another in their essence and, by shedding those determinations which metaphysics has given to them, to attain to their real nature. The Self-same (*to auto*) from which Being and Thought derive their mutual belongingness and in which they themselves belong is the real Identity which metaphysics conceives as an attribute of Being. Heidegger, on the contrary, seeks to show how "Being belongs, along with thought, in an Identity of which the nature has its source in that letting belong-together which we call the *Er-eignis*." The essence of Identity, he asserts, is a property of the *Er-eignis*. The Principle of Identity, which presupposes Identity as a trait of Being, is thus no longer a principle in the ultimate sense but, interpreted in terms of the *Er-eignis*, is transformed into a leap, "a spring which breaks away from Being as the ground of essents and so becomes a leap in the abyss.[28] This abyss, however, is neither an empty Nothingness nor dark chaos but—the *Er-eignis*." A consideration of what Being in its difference from beings means has thus led to the Difference as fundamental to both and the nature of Difference has been determined in terms of the *Austrag*. The latter leads into the sphere "beyond Being,"[29] the sphere of the *Er-eignis*, the primordial Identity (not to be thought as a static state of affairs but as event, or rather, as eventuation) from which man and Being both derive not only the intimacy of their mutual relationship but also their own respective natures. The *Austrag* (referring to the dynamic character of the relation between Being and beings), with its interplay of revelation (of beings) and concealment (of Being), is itself consequent upon the coming together of man and Being, which does not exclude their drawing apart, withdrawal itself being a mode of being-with through the *Er-eignis*. Heidegger's quest for the "sense," or essence, of Being thus terminates in the conception of *Er-eignis* as the ultimate, in terms of which Being itself can be understood.[30] The essent in its Being, the essence of Being itself and the nature of man must indeed be so understood, if we are not to remain imprisoned within the representational thinking of metaphysics, if we are to enter once again, surrendering our self-will, into the simplicity and the translucent depth of what is and to prepare thus a shrine into which the light of the Holy may descend, so rendering possible the manifestation of the Divine.

From the very beginning of Western thought until today Being has signified presence (*Anwesen*), and from presence speaks the present (*Gegenwart*). As presence, Being gets its determination from time, even though Being is not a thing and is, therefore, not in time. Time, in turn, is determined by Being (has being), though it too is not a thing, for in its ceaseless passing away, it remains as time and so has presence (*Anwesenheit*). Being, as well as time, is a matter (*Sache*) for thought, though the former is not itself an entity and the latter is itself not temporal. The relationship between these two matters (*Sachen*) is that which holds them together, binds them, and is the *Sachverhalt*, the state of affairs, to which the "and" in "Being and Time" and "Time and Being" points. It is this "and," this relationship, primordial and ultimate, which holds Heidegger's thinking in thrall and which requires being brought into view.[31]

We cannot say that Being is, or that Time is; we should say rather that "it gives" Being, "it gives" Time (*Es gibt* = there is, as in the sentence 'It rains'), that Being is granted, Time is granted. What is the manner in which Being is granted and in which Time is granted? How are we to understand this "giving" and the "It" that gives Being as well as Time? What is Being itself in its very own, and Time itself in its very own? Being is given or granted in the sense that presence is enabled, rendered possible. In the beginning of Western thinking (in the *esti gar einai* of Parmenides), Being was thought but not the "It gives" as such. The latter remains hidden, withdrawing itself in favor of the gift that has been given; which gift is henceforth thought and conceptualized as Being, as a view to providing a ground for beings. Being is sent forth on its vicissitudes (its historical determinations from the pre-Socratics to Nietzsche and later), but in this fateful movement of destiny (*Geschick*), both the giving or sending and what sends it forth remain hidden as such. In the sending forth of this giving lies what is the very own of Being and not in its Being-character, for when we think of Being as such the matter itself in a way leads us away from Being, from the gift to the giving.

What is the It that grants Being, sends it forth? Is it the time-character that lies hidden in Being as presence? But time itself, even when thought in terms of what is its very own as the reaching out to each other of past, future, and present in their unity, time itself is the gift of a giving; it is granted, It gives Time. Time cannot be the It that gives Being. This giving of the "It gives" is, further, twofold: giving as the sending forth, the destiny, of Being and giving as the lighting-clearing (*lichtende*) reaching over of Time. In both these ways of granting, sending forth and extending, there is evident a dedicating, an entrusting—of Being as presence and of Time as the realm of the open—of each to the other in what is their very own. What thus determines both Time and Being, in their very own, that is, in their mutual belongingness, is the *Ereignis*. That which lets both matters (*Sachen*, Being and Time) belong together, which not only brings them into their own inmost nature but preserves and holds them in their togetherness, is the *Ereignis*, the relationship of the holding together of these two. It is this primordial relationship that is the ultimate state of affairs (*Sach-Verhalt*), which releases, lets forth, and brings about both Being and Time in their own individual characters. The "It" in "It gives Being, It gives Time" is thus seen to be the *Ereignis*. The giving of this "It gives" is, however, at the same time a keeping to itself, a denial, a withholding—the It that grants, the *Ereignis*, withdraws itself while sending forth Being, denies itself in the reaching over of Time. The *Ereignis* is the Self-same which guards itself from total unhiddenness; and it is nothing new but the Self-same that is the oldest of the old in Western thought, the ancient secret hiding itself in the name *A-letheia*.

Being thus derives its sense or nature from something

more fundamental, the *Ereignis*, and from the point of view of its essence, therefore, it can no longer be called "Being." As Heidegger expresses it, when Being is thought in its truth it undergoes a transformation and in consequence loses its name;[32] in the *Ereignis* Being itself is "got over."[33] This possibility, it may be pointed out, already lay inherent in the original asking of the question about the *sense* of Being in *Being and Time*. The very asking of the question was to move away from metaphysics, exposing oneself to the possibility that what metaphysics conceives as "Being," and through such conceiving itself develops *as* metaphysics, is in its essence something different and profounder. As Heidegger remarks,

> Metaphysics does not acknowledge Being *as* Being. 'Acknowledging' this, however, means to let Being, in regard to the origin to its essence, have free play in all its dubiousness. It means to endure the question of Being, to persist in asking it. And this implies meditating on the origin of presence and perpetuity and so leave open for thought the possibility that 'Being' may, on the way to 'as Being', give up its own character in favor of a more fundamental determination. The talk of 'Being itself always bears a question mark.[34]

It drives, he says elsewhere,[35] the attempt to represent it from one predicament to another, while the source of this perplexity remains hidden. Nothingness goes with Being as a possible manifestation of that; in essence it is nothing other than Being. Nihilism is itself rooted in the metaphysical revelation of Being as the truth of things, in the metaphysical conception of Being itself, and for this reason, to go beyond "Being," and only that, is to go beyond Nothingness. The overcoming of Nihilism depends upon the surmounting or surpassing (*Verwindung*) of metaphysics.[36]

Being is turned towards man, gives itself to him, but this does not mean that "Being" is something by itself and then occasionally also turns towards man. "Perhaps this 'turning towards' itself is, in a way that is still obscure, that which we call, awkwardly enough and vaguely, 'Being' "—of which the turning away or withdrawal, in the age of Nihilism, is itself a mode of turning toward. The turning toward and the turning away of Being are not to be thought as if man came upon them only now and then and for the moment. The nature of man rather rests on this that at all times he abides, in this fashion or that, in this turning toward and turning away. "We say of 'Being itself' ever *too little* when, in saying 'Being', we leave out the presence *to* (as entering into) the nature of man and so fail to recognize that this nature (*Wesen*) itself is a constituent of 'Being'. We also say of man ever *too little* when, in saying 'Being' (not being human), we set man apart and only subsequently bring what is thus set up into relation with 'Being'. And we say *too much* if, on the other hand, we think of Being as the all-encompassing, thereby representing man as only a special kind of being among others (plants, animals) and then putting the two into a relation. This is so because in the essence of man himself lies the relation to Being, which is determined as such by virtue of the relationship of resorting to in the sense of needing (*Brauchen*), and which is thus drawn out of its alleged 'in and for itself'." The talk of a "turning-toward (or bestowal) of Being" remains, Heidegger says, a makeshift and thoroughly questionable, because Being depends on this turning-towards, which therefore can never be just added on to "Being." To be present ("Being") is as such to be present for a human being always, a call that addresses man in his essence. And man's nature is in itself receptive to this call, for it belongs in the call of this behest, in this coming to be (*An-wesen*). The ultimate, in each case, is the Self-same, the belonging-together of call and hearing. Can this still be called "Being"? It is, Heidegger says, no longer "Being" at all in the sense in which it has revealed itself traditionally, namely, as presence. This isolating, disconnecting word "Being" has to be abandoned as also the name "Man." Once the belonging-together is seen to be the more basic truth, the whole question about the relation between the two reveals itself as inadequate, for it is incapable of entering the realm of that which it aims at inquiring into. As Heidegger remarks, we cannot, in fact, even say that "Being" and "man" "are" the same in the sense that they belong together; for when we speak in *this* manner, we turn each of them into independently existing entities.

If the turning-toward is intrinsic to "Being," so that the latter rests on the former, then "Being" is dissolved into the turning-toward, as Heidegger puts it. This now becomes the main thing to be inquired into; Being henceforth is considered as that questionable something "which has reverted and been absorbed into its own essence." Accordingly, a preliminary attempt to explore this realm of the "turning-toward" of what has been called *Ereignis* above and which constitutes the "sense," the "truth" or "essence" of Being ("Being itself"),[37] can refer to "Being," Heidegger says, only by writing it as crossed out.[38] The striking out of the word by means of a cross is intended, in the first place, to have the defensive function of keeping off the almost ineradicable habit of representing "Being" as something that stands over against man, existing by itself and only at times reaching up to man. According to this way of conceiving, man has the appearance of being excepted or excluded from "Being." Actually, Heidegger remarks, he is not only not left out, that is, he is not only included in "Being," but "Being," needing man in his essence, is obliged to give up the appearance of being a separate, independent reality (*Für-sich*). And for this reason it is also something having quite a different nature than the conception of a totality comprehending the subject-object relation would like to admit.[39] Being present ("be-ing," *An-wesen*, as Heidegger now writes the word for "being present," *Anwesen*, to mark the departure from the traditional concept, at the same time avoiding the word "being") as such turns towards man's essence in which (or where) through man's mindfulness of it, the turning-toward is consummated. Man in his very essence is the remembrance of Being in the sense of 'Being' crossed out and intrinsically part of it. Be-ing (*An-wesen*) is grounded in the turning-toward, which as such uses the being of man so that the latter may expend himself for that.

Obviously, the cross mark over Being cannot, as Heidegger points out, be merely a negative sign of cancellation; it, in fact, hints at the positive content of the conception of a Being beyond Being, the *Ereignis*. "It points rather," Heidegger says, "into the four regions of the Square (*Geviert*) and their gathering at the place of intersection."[40] The four regions of the Fourfold are Earth, the Heavens, Gods, and Mortals. The Earth is that which serves and supports, out of which everything emerges. As Heidegger says elsewhere, "This coming forth and emerging itself, as a whole, was called in ancient times *physis* by the Greeks. . . . We call it the Earth. . . . The Earth is that into which the emergence of all that comes forth is as such referred back,"[41] in which it remains embedded as its sustaining principle. It is the hiddennness involved in all un-hiddenness, the closure out of which all disclosure arises and in which it is rooted and preserved; it is that which manifests itself as the hidden in all unhiddenness, recalcitrant to all disclosure, intrinsically shut up in itself. The celestial region of Heaven is the pure principle of light, in which everything that emerges into unhiddenness shines forth as what it is. It is the wide horizon of openness—the sun in its course, the changing faces of the moon, the round of the seasons, of day and night—overarching the Earth as its necessary correlate. The Immortals are "the beckoning messengers of Divinity"; they bring with them the area of holiness in which God may appear, even though as His own absence. This is the dimension of the Holy, invoked by the great poets, which once made it possible for the world to be filled with the gods and with God; the forsakenness of the world, the absence of the gods, is itself something positive both as reminder and as promise.[42] The Mortals are men; they are called so not because their life on earth is terminable but because they alone are capable of dying (*sterben*), of taking, in the midst of life, death upon themselves *as* death. Accepting death as 'the shrine of Nothingness' and as part of life, they embody, as mortals, the relationship to Being as Being (for Nothingness is, as the "veil of Being," Being itself experienced as the sheer other to what is, from the point of view of the latter). Each of these four is involved in the other and together they constitute an indissoluble unity. Each, in itself at one with the other, belongs to the other and together they are united in the simple unity of the Fourfold. Each of the four reflects in its way the nature of the other and each is in its way mirrored back into its very own within the artless unity of the four. The Fourfold represents the happening of a mutual owning and acknowledging of each by each and of each into the unity of the *Geviert*, such that each is at the same time expropriated into the freedom of its own nature. This owning-expropriating fourfoldness in its unity is called by Heidegger the mirror game (*Spiegel-Spiel*) of the Fourfold, its play of reflection, play, because not explicable by anything outside itself. In "Hölderlins Erde und Himmel," Heidegger speaks of the interrelationship of earth and heaven, God and man as the "infinite relation," following Hölderlin's usage The relation which holds these together is called infinite because, standing within it, each of the four is freed of its onesidedness and finitude. The mediating center or core of this relation, its intimacy (*Innigkeit*), is itself neither earth nor Heaven, neither God nor man. It is the *Ereignis*, or what Heidegger here calls *Geschick*, which holds the four together in their intimacy and thus constitutes the heart of "the in-finite relation."[43]

This play of earth and heaven, gods and mortals is called, in its unity, the World by Heidegger. Earlier, in "Der Ursprung des Kunstwerkes," Heidegger had conceived world, the area of openness for the play of man's historical existence, as the polar opposite of the earth, the impenetrable and the closed, in order to show how truth comes to pass through the warring of these antagonistic principles as they are embodied in a work of art and to emphasize, further, how truth comprehends in itself hiddenness as well as unhiddenness, resulting in what Heidegger calls "the strange opponency of presence" in everything that is. The world is not caused and has no ground; it happens or opens out as its own "world-ing." This means that, as he puts it, it can neither be explained in terms of something else nor does it have a foundation outside itself. Concepts like those of cause and ground are inappropriate in the context of the "world-ing" of the world. 'World', Heidegger points out, has no longer a metaphysical sense here and means neither the secularized conception of a *universum* of Nature and History nor the theological conception of creation (*mundus*), nor does it mean simply the totality of all that is (*kosmos*).[44] The mirror game of the world, the play of the Fourfold in its unity, is the round dance of the occurrence of owning (*Ereignen*).[45] The being-in-the-world which was described in *Being and Time* as constitutive of Dasein is now characterized simply as 'dwelling', which is the way mortals have their sojourn on earth. Man is man insofar as he has his home on the earth, under the heavens, in front of the gods, with his fellowmen. Mortals *are* in the Fourfold in the sense that they truly dwell in the world, that they take care of, cherish, and tend the Fourfold by saving the earth and leaving it free in its essence as earth, by receiving the heaven as heaven, by awaiting the arrival of the gods, by shepherding themselves, in their own essence, toward death. But for mortals, the sole way of dwelling in this fourfold manner in the *Geviert* is through their sojourn with things (*Dinge*). Only in such sojourn with things is it possible for men to enter into relation with Being and the world. "We are," as Heidegger puts it, "in the strict sense of the term, the be-thinged [*die Be-Dingten*, that is, conditioned by our relationship with things]. We have left behind the arrogance of being in any way unconditioned."[46] Dwelling in the Fourfold and with things, man tends the former by drawing its essence into the things. And the Fourfold is preserved in the things only when they are allowed to unfold their own nature as things through the cultivating building care of man. Man dwells insofar as he builds and the essence of building is to permit true dwelling—with things.

A thing, for example, a bridge or a jug, gathers together in itself earth and heaven, gods and mortals. It is not merely a symbol for such gathering but, as a thing, it is itself the gathering together of the quadrate (*Geviert*) of the four in its unity. The thing 'in itself', the reality of the thing, is such gathering together (as the old High German word 'thing' literally means). A thing is such because it 'things', gathers together, bringing to pass the Fourfold and making it abide for a while in this or that thing. An essent is a thing neither in the Roman sense of *res*, nor in the sense of the medieval *ens*, nor at all in the modern sense of an object. It is a thing, as Heidegger puts it, insofar as it 'things'. The presence of a present thing, for example, a jug (that is, the being of this essent), in fact, comes to pass and is determined out of (in terms of) the 'thing-ing' (gathering) of a thing. In bringing the quadrate of earth, heaven, gods, and mortals to bide together in its simple unity for a while in itself, the thing, any and every thing, 'things' the world, gathering it together into itself. The four regions of the quadrate, constituting the world, are gathered together at the point of intersection of the cross over 'Being', the point which thus represents the thing. All that a thing is, is granted to it by world. Only when we let the thing *be* as the gathering together of the world in its 'worlding', do we think, Heidegger says, of the thing as thing, the thing as it is in itself. In their turn, things unfold, by virtue of their gathering character, the world in which they are as this or that thing for a while.[47] Things bear, bring forth world, conjuring it into existence, as it were. Manifesting themselves through and out of the world, they bring this world to man and so provide him with his world.[48] World and things are not two separate entities but are held apart in a relationship of intimacy through the Difference (which Heidegger now writes as *Unter-Schied*, corresponding to the change from the language of 'Being' and 'essent' to that of 'world' and 'thing'). The Difference, from which world and thing derive their respective natures, lets things rest in the favor of world, in what it grants to them, and it lets the world acquiesce in the way in which and the extent to which the thing gathers it together. And as with the difference between Being and beings, the difference between world and thing, the 'between' itself, is the self-mediation of an Identity in which things and world (which include men or 'mortals') both belong. This is the *Er-eignis*, the togetherness of man's owning and being owned within the *Geviert*, the Fourfold of the world, for which Being has always remained a 'provisional name'.[49]

Language, Truth, Time, and Thought

The interplay of world and thing in their difference and mutuality as well as the happening of Identity (*Ereignis*) are bound up with language in the most intimate fashion. "Language is the softest and also the most vulnerable vibration, holding everything in place, in the swaying edifice of the *Ereignis*. Insofar as our nature is owned in language, we dwell in *Ereignis*. . . . The *Er-eignis* is vibrant with the essence of that which speaks as language, once called the house of Being."[50] Language, Heidegger says, is something more than an activity of man, more than expression or a means to it, more than a representation of the actual or the imaginary. Primarily, it is language itself which 'speaks', not man; *his* speaking is only an echo of and response to that, depending upon how he hears what language itself says. The essence of language lies in stillness—the rest in which all motion is gathered together—the stillness which the Differentiation, the 'between', brings to the thing as a thing in the world, enabling it to be itself, and to world in its world-ing intimacy with thing. Language is the chime of stillness (*Geläut der Stille*), itself nothing human in its essence. Man's essence, on the other hand, lies in speech and he realizes his own nature insofar as, needed by the still essence of language, he gives himself over to that. "Men are capable in *their* way, of uttered speech only insofar as they belong in the chime of stillness."[51] The speech of mortals is a call and an invitation to things and to world, invoking them by giving them names, to emerge from the pristine simplicity of the 'between' of their togetherness; it is out of this originally poetic character of speech that man's everyday language develops through a process of degeneration. Man speaks only insofar he hears, insofar as he listens to the silent call of the 'between', that is, to what language itself speaks. "Man speaks, insofar as he co-responds to language. To co-respond is to hear. And to co-respond is to hear because it is to be owned by the call of the silent."[52]

It is the word that gives its Being to everything. "No thing is, where the word fails," as Stefan George's poem has it. Everything that is, that and how it is, depends upon the word. The relationship between word and thing is not an external relation between two independent entities, the word itself is the relationship which sustains in itself the thing so that it 'is' a thing, which holds everything in Being and preserves it so. Everything, as the essent that it is, owes its 'is' to the word which, hence, does not merely stand in relation to the thing but is itself the relationship. But the word itself is not a thing, nothing that is; in the sense in which it is itself a thing, it cannot either constitute or generate the 'is' or things. The word has no Being and the 'is', likewise, is no essent. Neither the word nor Being 'are', nor, in consequence, the relationship between them. And yet, 'it gives' (*es gibt*) both, the word even in a profounder sense than Being, which makes every essent 'be'. The word, which 'it gives', itself gives Being and so is itself never something given but is ever itself the giver, pure and simple. The essence of language—of which thinking and composing (*Dichten*) are the two modes, most near to each other and yet distinct, lies in what Heidegger terms Saying (*Sage*, from *sagan*).[53] Saying in this primary sense is showing something, letting it appear, be heard and seen, emancipating it into its own, in a manner both revealing and concealing, the dispensing of that which has been called world above (that is, 'Being' in Heidegger's earlier usage).

According to the classical view of language as laid down for posterity by Aristotle (in his *Peri Hermeneias* or *De Interpretatione*) language is made up of written words, which indicate vocal sounds, themselves the indications of the happenings of the soul and these in turn indicate things. Language here is conceived, Heidegger remarks, in terms of vocal utterance, that is, in physical terms. But the physical (metaphysically conceived as belonging to the realm of the 'sensible') is itself rooted in what has been called Earth above. It is therefore more appropriate to speak of language, with Hölderlin, as the flower of the mouth. "In language the Earth opens out to the blossoming of Heaven."[54] The word thus points to the region, is itself the region, in which Earth and Heaven, the flow of the deep and majestic height, meet together. The manifestation of language as vocal sound, the earthy in language, cannot be explained in physiological or physical terms or in terms of phonetics but derives from the silent chime, from the evocative call of the Saying that gathers together world and lets it manifest itself in things. The four regions of the fourfold, Earth, Heaven, God, and Man, are brought and held together in their mutuality by what Heidegger calls the Nearness (*Nähe*, the source of all nearing), the still center from which all movement flows, the temporalization of time, the spatialization of space, the interplay of the four world regions—the World Play. The Nearness, the unmoving but dynamic core of this interplay, is the chime of stillness and is identical with that Saying which dispenses and makes manifest the world (that is, the 'Being' of metaphysics). Language as the Saying of the world quadrate is not something to which man bears some relationship; it is itself rather "the relationship of all relationships," the very principle of relationship, within which man is held and which sustains him. "It [language] holds together, sustains, gives to each and enriches, the mutuality of the world regions, keeps and tends it, and it does so by keeping itself to itself."⁵⁵ Just as Being, in revealing essents, conceals its own self, so also the *Sage*, in revealing world, keeps its own essence hidden. Not the spoken word—itself a thing—but the Saying (*die Sage*), as the chime of stillness of which the spoken word is but an echo, bestows world and hence also "that which we call by the little word 'is'." Word and thing, Saying and Being, are bound together in a unity. The ancient *logos*—meaning both the saying which discloses the essent in its 'is' as well as Being, the presence of the present—bears testimony to this hidden unity.⁵⁶

The attempts to penetrate the mystery of language, beginning with Greek antiquity, and seeking to grasp it in terms of speech and so as a mode of human activity, converge to their pinnacle, according to Heidegger, in Wilhelm von Humboldt's reflections on language, as finally expressed in the great "introduction" to this work on the Kawi language of Java, separately published (1836) under the title, *Über die Verschiedenheit des menschlichen Sprachbaues und ihren Einfluss auf die geistige Entwicklung des Menschengeschlechts*. This work has decisively influenced, directly or indirectly, the whole of linguistic science and philosophy of language that have developed since its publication. Language as the embodiment of speech is, according to Humboldt, not merely a means of communication but "a true *world*, which the *spirit* has to set up between itself and *objects* through the inner labor of its energy." Despite his profound insight into the deeper nature of language, in particular its dynamic character, Humboldt's views do not reach into its essence. Language for him is *one* type and form (among others, though the most significant) of the world views built up by human subjectivity. And his thoughts on it are formulated, moreover, in the language of the metaphysics of his age, that of Leibniz in particular. Humboldt is concerned with language, Heidegger says, not *as* language, not with language as it is in itself, but with language a manifestation of the spiritual (intellectual) development of the human race. Such attempts to comprehend language in terms of something other than itself—energy, activity, power of the spirit, world view, expression—do indeed say something true *about* language, but, seeking to have a grasp on it through something else, they fail to touch its essence.

Saying something (as distinguished from speaking, for much may be spoken but nothing said and, contrariwise, nothing be spoken and yet a great deal said) is showing or exhibiting it. And such showing is not primarily or exclusively a human activity. "Showing or letting something manifest itself characterizes, as appearing, the presence or absence of every kind and level of essents. Even where the showing is done by our saying, this showing, as a pointing-to, is preceded by a letting-itself-be-shown."[57] Speaking, further, is at the same time, hearing, primarily so, in fact. Hearing does not merely accompany and envelop speaking, as in the case of a conversation. Speaking, Heidegger says, is in itself intrinsically a hearing; it is listening to the language that we speak. We speak only insofar as we listen to what language itself says, that is, shows, and we can hear what language says only insofar as we are in our very essence taken up into the essence of language, belong to it. There is no such thing as *the* language, but only particular languages, into which particular peoples and races are born, in which they are nurtured and have their dwelling. Language is essentially mother tongue, dialect, the language of home and, so regarded, itself a home for man. In this sense, language is, in what it says, creative and revelatory in its very essence. Language opens up to man his world, determining the way in which he is integrated and taken up into the unity of the Fourfold, whether and how he dwells in the world as in a home.[58] Saying (*Sage*), that is, language in its essence, is the still stream that unites, while itself generating them, its two banks: what it says and our speech echoing that. Saying does not constitute merely the subsequent expression of what is already manifest; all shining forth and its cessation depend rather upon Saying as a showing. Saying governs and directs the free area of that clearing (*Lichtung*) in which appearing and disappearing occur. What is it that stirs and quickens, that gives its motion, to Saying, that makes it open out a path to speech and thus renders anything manifest? This unknown and yet intimate moving principle is insusceptible of being 'placed' by means of a topological discussion (logical topography, *Erörterung*), for it is the place, the locality, of all locations and of the play of time and space. It can barely be named as a kind of fittingness, a kind of owning (*Eignen*, which carries both meanings, appropriation as well as appropriateness). This is what has been described above as the happening of Identity, of mutual owning, adequacy and unity—the *Ereignis*, which bestows the free area of a clearing in which anything can manifest itself as present or absent. The *Ereignis* grants to mortals, as Heidegger puts it, the sojourn in their own essence, so that they become capable of speaking. Because the manner in which Saying shows is an appropriating (in the double sense indicated above), the ability to listen, and so belong, to Saying also rests upon the *Ereignis*. The owning of man, as one who can hear, in Saying, emancipates man into his own, solely in order that, as one who can speak, he may respond to Saying out of his very own, thus bringing the soundless Saying into the utterance of language. The *Ereignis* enables Saying to emerge into speech; it is the *Ereignis* that, forging paths from Saying to speech, moves the former toward the latter. Itself resting in the *Ereignis*, Saying, as showing or bringing into view, is the most specific and proper mode of appropriating (*Ereignen*). The *Ereignis* is inherently self-saying, language-generating. In its essence, language can therefore be described, with Heidegger, as the melody of the *Ereignis*. In consequence, the way language itself speaks at any particular time, the relationship in which we stand to language and the way we respond to it, depends upon the way and the extent to which the *Ereignis* reveals or withdraws itself from epoch to epoch. Language was described by Heidegger in the writings of his middle phase as "the house of Being" because all being-present (that is, Being) is in its guardianship. But the shining forth of the latter is itself "consigned to the care of the appropriating showing of saying. Language is the house of Being because, as Saying, it is the mode (as song) of the *Ereignis*."[59]

The *Ereignis*, not resulting from anything else, is itself the source of all giving, the giving of which the ampleness even grants anything like an 'it gives (*es gibt*)', of which even 'Being' has need in order to come into its own as presence. It is the ultimate, irreducible to anything more basic, inexplicable in terms of anything reaching further back. "The *Ereignis* is the most inconspicuous of all that is inconspicuous, the simplest of all that is simple, the nearest of all that is near and the farthest of all that is far; it is that within which we mortals reside for life. . . . If law means that which lets everything abide in its very own nature, which lets everything belong in what is fit and proper to it, then the *Ereignis* is the simplest and gentlest of all laws, indeed, *the* Law, in that it gathers mortals into the adequateness to their own essence and into being owned by it and keeps them within that."[60] In this "realm of all realms," this swaying edifice of the *Ereignis*, suspended in itself, also lies hidden the mystery of *aletheia*, of truth in the sense of unhiddenness, with the concealment and disclosure necessarily implied in it. Truth in the primordial sense is not a property of statements, neither does it reside in things or even in the "Being" of what is. Truth as *aletheia* is the happening of the *Ereignis* itself. Being as presence itself depends upon the prior occurrence of unhiddenness, of a clearing (*Lichtung*), an open, lit-up area in which anything can manifest itself and *be*. This lit-up area is what has been called World above.[61] Man's relationship to the clearing is nothing other than this clearing itself; as part of the world quadrate, man is owned in it, needed by it and in turn himself tends it. The happening of disclosure (*Entbergung*), through which anything comes into manifestness and is, occurs, as explained above, through Saying. Such disclosure or entry into the clearing (*Lichtung*) does not merely illuminate or bring to light something that already is but rather grants it its presence and gathers and contains it in it. But the showing or disclosure brought about by Saying, the chime of stillness, does not itself generate the *Lichtung* but rather presupposes such occurrence of overtness in and through the *Ereignis* itself. Both *aletheia*, Truth, and Saying, the light and the vibration, have their source in the *Ereignis*, the coming together, the mutual owning of man and Being, the supreme identity. As inherently self-saying the *Ereignis* is also the illuminating; it is the former because it is the latter, for, as Heidegger says, "the whole essence of language rests on disclosure, on the sway of *aletheia*."[62] The "realm of all realms," the *Ereignis*, is also the realm of Truth as the primordial happening of openness—*aletheia* itself. Being itself rests in its truth (that is, in the *Ereignis* as described above) and "the truth of Being *is* as the Being of truth."[63] In this happening of Truth, man, belonging together with Being in the *Ereignis*, has an ineliminable share, for it is through his responsive gesture that

Truth is embodied and "descends" (thereby truly "ascending" into its own), "trues" itself and is "trued," into a "work" (art, poetic utterance, thought). The primary form of this is the human word, thinking in the basic sense. As a thinking being, man is owned, claimed, used, and called upon to fulfil and realize the Truth, watch over it and so let the Truth prevail.

Contrary to the traditional conception (mainly religious) which regards Truth as sheer transparency and pure light, Heidegger insists that the unhiddenness characterizing truth as *aletheia* is inseparably bound up with hiddenness—the two together constitute the full nature of Truth, which is hence called "the Mystery" by Heidegger. The essent or thing, as earth, is at bottom itself opaque and inscrutable, never surrendering its full secret. In disclosing the essent (or thing), Being, as the twofoldness of the Differentiation (or World), itself remains hidden; in revealing World and Thing in their togetherness, the Saying (the chime of silence) itself remains hidden; in generating the last, the *Ereignis* itself remains hidden. All disclosure and overtness, in bringing about unhiddenness, itself remains hidden.[64] But the concealment (*Verbergung*) that attends upon disclosure (*Entbergung*) and constitutes its matrix is, as Heraclitus divined, not sheer antagonism to the latter but remains ever "turned towards" it; concealment and disclosure "love" each other (*physis kryptesthai philei*), are inclined towards and friendly to each other, together constituting a unity. Concealing itself is not mere closing itself up but, as Heidegger says, a sheltering and guarding, in which the possibility of emerging into light is essentially preserved, in which such emergence belongs.[65] "Self-concealment guarantees to self-disclosure its essence." Truth, as such interplay of covertness and overtness, is not something eternally abiding in its fulness in some remote Empyrean but a happening, and one in which we are most intimately involved. It is in the main a happening of the withdrawal of Being, its self-concealment from man, and of the revelation of beings—the destiny of Nihilism as reflected in the rise and development of the Western metaphysical tradition. Historically, the light of truth has taken possession of the Western mind in various forms from one epoch to another—as *a-letheia*, as *homoiosis*, as *doctrina*, as certitude, as the Eternal

Recurrence of the Same, as *Ge-Stell*. Truth is therefore not only history but destiny (*Geschick*), in the sense that, from epoch to epoch, man finds himself thrown into and in the grip of the particular form in which truth prevails in a particular epoch, so that all his thinking and doing, the way things show themselves to him, the way he comports himself towards them and what and how he thinks about them, the way he *is* in the world, is determined by the particular epochal light of truth in which he happens to live. But this dependence of man is not a one-sided determination of man by the concealing-revealing light of Truth. Truth, as determinative of man's existence, needs being tended and cherished by man in order to prevail *as* truth. As Heidegger remarks, "Some day we shall learn to think our worn-out word truth (*Wahrheit*) in terms of guarding and watching over (*die Wahr, wahren*) and realize that truth is the tendance of Being and that Being as presence belongs in it."[66] The step back from metaphysical thinking into the remembrance of the truth of Being and so of the true nature of Truth itself is, in Heidegger's eyes, a preparation for a future which will permit this pristine truth to prevail in all its liberating power.[67]

The basic trait of that which revealed itself to Western thought as Being is manifested in presence and representation. "From the early days of the Greeks up to the late period of our century 'Being' means being present. Every sort of presence and presentation has its origin in the happening of presence" (that is, the revelation of Being as presence).[68] Western thought in its entire course does not even say clearly and fully what presence itself means, far from bringing into view that on which the presence of what is present depends. "It would, therefore," Heidegger says, "be falling into an error to suppose that the Being of what is must mean, solely and for all times, the presence of the present."[69] Once the conception of time as made up of a succession of 'nows' is seen to be derivative and its true nature is realized, presence also reveals itself in its real character, being itself understood now in terms of the integral essence of Time, as the arrival (*Ankunft*), the coming, of the "has been" in the form of the yet to be—as the Moment. The conception of Being as presence and that of time as a series of 'nows' go together, one implying the other. And both together involve the conception of thinking as representation and a kind of grasping (*Be-greifen*).

Of all Western thinkers, Nietzsche, and he alone, had a glimpse into this profound truth about the way presence, 'now' time and representation are linked together.[70] In *Thus Spake Zarathustra* (Part II), he characterizes the thinking of man hitherto as inspired by the spirit of vengeance. Vengeance, as such, is vengeance against Time, Nietzsche says, "this, and this alone, is revenge itself: the Will's revolt against time and its 'it was'." What Nietzsche himself sought and longed for was a way out that might bring to man deliverance from this spirit and from the way of thinking inspired by that. "That man might be redeemed from vengeance, this is for me the bridge to the ultimate hope and a rainbow after prolonged foul weather." In his dealings with essents, man represents the essent in respect of the fact that it is, what and how it is, that is, in respect of its Being. Such representation is the nature of metaphysical thinking and of man's relationship to what is. In accordance with the manifestation of Being as Will (explicitly so in the modern age), man also appears to himself as essentially willing. His relationship to Being, that is, thinking, is also thus willing in the form of representing essents. All representing is willing, a kind of pursuing, chasing, ambushing; a defiance and derogation of what is. Such representing finds in Time its greatest stumbling block, for time in its essence (as 'now' time) is a passing away. As Heidegger puts it, "Time passes. And it passes so that it passes away. The passage of time is, of course, also a coming but it is a coming that is inevitably a going away into the past. The coming of time (that is, the future) never comes to stay but only to go."[71] Hence, transitoriness or vanishing into the past is the very essence of time. Time *is* what Nietzsche calls the "it was" of time. "Representation, with the willing intrinsic to it, tosses and knocks in vain against this irrevocable 'it was', unable to prevail against it, an 'it was' stiff and frozen in its finality, in which the passing of time itself passes away into the deadness of the past. The redemption from this need to say "no" to time, this great misery of the Will's own revolt, cannot lie for Nietzsche in a liberation from all willing, as in Schopenhauer and Buddhism,[72] for this will mean a lapse into utter nothingness (since Being=Will) and it cannot be a liberation from time as such, for it is the 'now', the present in which alone anything 'is' (since Being=presence). For him the redemption from the refractory and the contrary in time, its ineluctable pastness, can only be through a perpetuation of what "goes" into a "coming" again, so that the passing away sheds its deadness and comes ever anew—the Eternal Recurrence of the Same. If the Being of all that is is willing,[73] if time is taken in the Aristotelian sense of being a flow of 'nows', if the 'now', that is, the presence of the present, is what to "be" means and if, in consequence, thinking consists in representing and conceiving, then the doctrine of the Eternal Recurrence is the only way out for the Will, the only way in which the Will can heal itself, through such representation, of the wound that Time inflicts upon it. And so long as Time is understood in the Aristotelian sense and Eternity as the 'now' brought to a stand (*nunc stans*), Being, as *presence* can never be liberated from its thraldom to time, nor can the Eternity of which Schelling speaks, nondependence upon time, ever belong to Being.

In *Being and Time*, Heidegger developed a way of thinking about time which enables us to regard its three ecstasies, past, present, and future, as manifestations of a deeper temporality of which these are 'temporalizations'. Time in this sense was described there as the transcendental horizon of the comprehension of Being, as that in which Dasein's transcendence itself is rooted. As against the traditional conception, according to which time, consisting of a flow of 'nows' that is, as basically the present, is itself something that is present in the present, that is, as essent, it was suggested that time in the primordial sense is that in terms of which Being itself may be understood, in terms, that is, not of presence only but of the integral unity of future, past, and present. As against the traditional conception, moreover, emphasis was placed on the 'futuristic', the future-oriented, character of time rather than on the past, with the 'going' of the latter incorporated into the 'coming' of the future. In *Kant und das Problem der Metaphysik*, still approaching time from the point of view of Dasein's transcendence, Heidegger identified primordial time with the transcendental imagination (the faculty of synthesis in the general, as he interprets it), in which pure sensibility and pure understanding are themselves rooted and united and which generates, through pure intuition, time as a series of 'nows'.[74] Time in this sense thus constitutes, as self-affection, the basis of the specific finitude of the human subject—rationality dependent upon sensibility—and so man's finite self-hood itself. Transcendental time and the "I think," the I, neither of them 'in time' themselves, are the same and constitute the ultimate horizon in which anything can appear as present. Time is the being of Dasein and, as the ultimate horizon for the manifestation of anything as essent, identical with Being itself. Being in its truth is for Heidegger pure happening; it is, as he says, nothing other than its own happening, the happening of primordial disclosure as the *Ereignis*, in which, while lighting up or opening out world, Being in its essence withholds its own self. The 'history of Being' (that is, Being in the sense of *Ereignis*) begins with its *epoche*, its keeping itself to itself, and the epochs of this history are the epochs of man's progressive oblivion and falling out of his relationship to Being. This falling out is itself, however, something positive and a manifestation of his relatedness to Being, a relatedness which even in the extremity of man's alienation remains big with the promise of a revelation of Being in its truth, of a transmutation or absorption of Being in its own true essence, the *Ereignis*. This is what Heidegger once called the eschatology of Being.[75] As *Ereignis*, the truth of Being is itself the happening of the belonging-together of man and Being (the 'is'), the happening of truth as concealing-revealing illumination. To what extent this belonging-together reveals itself to man, in which light of truth man stands in a particular epoch, how Being (presence) discloses itself to him in its difference from beings, is the dispensation (*Geschick*), varying from age to age, of the truth of Being, that is, of the *Ereignis* itself. The history of Being is not a series of events 'in time' but "Being itself" and the 'it gives' of Time with its still source in that togetherness out of which man and Being (presence) both emerge.

True Time, Heidegger says, is not a mere flow of duration but "the arrival" of what has been. This is not something that has vanished into the past but is the gathering together of what continues to be; it is prior to all arrival because, as such gathering, it withholds itself preserved in its own beginning.[76]

What is early, in other words, in generating the later, does not as it were pour itself out fully into that and itself vanish into the nothingness of a dead and petrified past but remains quick with its rich essence, a treasure hidden and held in trust, as the hiddenness sustaining and nourishing the unhiddenness of all that comes into the present as presence.[77] The hidden treasure lying thus suspended in what has been releases itself, so to speak, in what is yet to come, approaching the present from the direction of the future, as the future. Space and Time, Heidegger remarks further, are not what they appear to be for calculating, representational thought, mere parameters for measuring off nearness and remoteness conceived as intervals of distance.[78] In this age of the peculiar constellation of man and Being characterized as the *Ge-Stell* above, they appear so but their true nature is revealed when we think nearness and remoteness, temporal or spatial, in terms of the Self-same, the togetherness of man and Being as itself the principle of all nearing. The nearness which is true neighborliness can never depend upon space and time in their character as parameters. Facing and being turned towards each other, mutuality (*Gegen-einander-über*), characteristic of neighborliness, is the way earth and heaven, God and man are united together into true nearness in the world quadrate. Here, each, open in its self-concealment, opens out to the other, the one extending and yielding itself to the other and so each remaining itself; each guards and tends the other and at the same time covers it over. Nearness in this sense is closed to time (as also space) as a parameter because its 'nows' never open out to each other; they cannot even be said to shut each other out, for such closure itself is a mode of mutuality and presupposes it.[79] The parametrical, only possible in a world dominated by technology, is the devastation of all mutuality and a standing denial of true nearness.

"We can say of Time that it temporalizes (*zeitigt*), of space that it spatializes," keeping in mind that the meaning of Identity is letting-belong-together, mutual owning.[80] Time temporalizes, in the sense of ripening, bringing on and bringing forth. It brings on, in unified fashion and contemporaneously, what it has 'matured' equally, the has been, presence, and what we await, the future. Thus temporalizing, it transports us all at once into its threefold ecstasy, at the same time bringing back to us, through the opening up of each, the concordant unity of has been, presence, and awaiting. Carrying away and bringing to, in this fashion, time gives its motion to the triple ecstasy. Time itself in the entirety of its essence does not move but rests in stillness. Both the carrying away and bringing back of Time and (in a similar way) the rooming in, letting in and out of Space, belong together in the Self-same, the play of Stillness, which Heidegger admits, is for the present recalcitrant to further thought. The Self-same, holding time and space gathered together in their essence, gives motion and direction to the mutuality of the four world regions, thus bringing to pass the Play of the World.

In the lecture on "Zeit und Sein," Heidegger has sought further to explicate the nature of true Time in terms of the sort of present (*Gegenwart*) exhibited in it and of the *Ereignis* which "gives" or grants Time.[81] True Time is the unity of present, past, and future, which until now has been conceived in terms of the present regarded as a 'now'. But present also signifies presence (*Anwesenheit*), which cannot itself be determined in terms of the 'now', and this character of presence may itself be the key to an understanding of the present. What does understanding the present in terms of presence imply? Presence is something that concerns us and the present is that which awaits us out there (*Gegenwart*). Man stands within the solicitation of presence, in such fashion that he receives as a gift the presence (Being) which "It gives" by becoming aware of what is manifested in all letting-be-present. What is no longer present in the sense of the 'now', the has-been and the yet-to-come, also concerns or solicits us; in the has-been and the coming also, presence is thus reached out to us.

In the present, the has-been and the to-be, there is at play a reaching over of presence to us, soliciting us. And this reaching over is in itself a unity of reaching out, of giving itself over, of present, past, and future to one another, the unity which alone should properly be called Time and which in itself is not temporal. This reaching to one another by present, past, and future of the kind of presence characteristic of each brings about the clearing (*Lichtung*) of an openness. In this consists the primordial dimensionality of Time, which is prior to space and has nothing to do with measurable moments of time. Authentic time, thought in terms of this threefold reaching out, is three dimensional. The unity of these three dimensions itself rests in the mutuality at play among them and may be called the fourth dimension of true time. Properly speaking, this is the first and basic dimension, for it is this which holds the other three apart in their interplay and is the nearness (*Nähe*) that brings near. This nearing nears by holding apart. It holds the has-been open by denying its arrival as the present; it holds the arriving from the future open by withholding the present in the coming. The nearing of this nearness has the character of denial and withholding. Like Being itself, Time is not. But "It gives" Time, in which the way it is given is determined by the denying-withholding Nearness. The giving in which time is granted is the reaching over, clearing and covering at once, in which an openness occurs but the giving itself remains concealed. Authentic time is the Nearness of presence out of the present, the has-been and the future, the Nearness which unifies its reaching out in a threefold clearing; true time is this fourfold reaching or passing of openness, what is given in the giving of the "It gives Time." But the It that "grants" Time is the *Ereignis*.

The step back from metaphysics into its origins leads to a transmutation of 'Being' into something more fundamental. This contains within itself the unity of being with the essence of man and is such that its meaning is not confined to the unhiddenness of a mere "constancy of presence" but includes within it the 'not' of hiddenness as well as the 'has been' and the 'waiting' of past and future in their indivisible unity with the present. Such Being is not Will, implicitly or explicitly, for it is neither Ground nor Creator when thought about in terms of itself rather than from the point of view of essents. The *Ereignis* is rather a 'letting be' (*Lassen*), the Play of a belonging-ness that unites together earth and heaven, gods and men within the Fourfold of World, uniting world and things into each other's favor, uniting Word and Being through a permissive letting be. Since Being or Truth in the primordial sense of the *Ereignis* is not something that can ever 'present' itself or be given as an object to thought, it cannot be grasped within a concept, cannot be represented, whether as subject, object, or substance. Thinking in the traditional sense of conceiving and representing, in all its various historical forms, is no longer adequate to it. The step back has led, further, to a conception of man in which man is not an independent entity 'having' a relationship to Being but 'is' in his essence this relationship itself. Man also in this sense cannot be brought within the grip of a concept. In consequence, the relationship between man and Being, that is thinking, cannot itself be a concept or representation. Time itself, as it emerges into view when we step out of representational thinking, is no longer a succession of presented 'nows', mere sempiternity, but a gathering together of what has been and the coming, an 'arrival' charged with the inexhaustible yet to be, lying within the has been. As one with Being, time, like the former, is never itself presented in the present of a bare now but is the integral unity of the has been and the coming that arrives in a concrete present no longer shorn of its riches but equally incapable of conceptual representation.[82]

Throughout the entire history of Western philosophy, Being has been approached from the point of view of and interpreted in terms of its relationship to thinking. And thinking, as an activity of the human subject, has been understood as serving the double purpose of providing the horizon, the setting, for the interpretation of Being and also the organon or tool for it.[83] But, as we have seen, the original Greek revelation of Being as presence itself constitutes the basis on which thinking in the form of representation can manifest itself. In consequence, not only can thinking in this sense not provide the prior horizon for the interpretation of Being but it can also not be regarded as a neutral instrument, self-validating and self-evident in its universality, for such interpretation. "Logic" as the theory of thinking cannot, hence, be taken as the measure and starting point, whether as horizon or as organon, for the interpretation of Being. Being (*einai*) and thinking (*noein*) belong together in an Identity (*to auto*) prior to both; it is the happening (*Ereignis*) of primordial Truth (*Lichtung*) which determines both the form in which Being (presence) reveals itself as well as the mode of thinking corresponding to it. Neither "Being" nor "Thinking" are entities with a permanently fixed character and the historicity of forms in which the former manifests itself is reflected in a corresponding transformation in the way "thinking" itself is understood. Throughout the history of Western philosophy, not only has the conception of Being as presence (with its various historical forms) remained an unexamined presupposition but also, along with that, the conception of thinking as representation (*Vorstellen*)—the "oblivion" of Being is at the same time oblivion of the true character of thinking. It follows from this that all "criticisms" of thought (empiricistic or rationalistic, including the Kantian critique of thinking understood as Reason) which have been offered from time to time, have taken a particular form of thinking as embodying the universally valid nature of thought and then proceeded to determine its powers and functions. Heidegger's quest for the truth of Being may be described, therefore, as being also the quest for the true essence of thinking, presupposed in all its historical manifestations but never itself brought to light. It is the most radical "critique" not only of metaphysics but also of the representational thinking that necessarily goes with it and, unlike all previous critiques, it is not destructive but seeks only to uncover the unacknowledged truth or essence of both metaphysics and thought, the source from which both arise and into which they both revert in Heidegger's conception of Identity.[84] The determination of the positive essence of thinking, like that of man (and thinking *is* man in his relationship to Being), must be attempted, according to Heidegger, in terms of the truth of Being, and not the other way round, for, as Heidegger never tires of repeating, the relationship to Being is determined from the side of Being and so must be described in terms of Being itself rather than of man, as metaphysics invariably does.

Thinking in the primary sense is mindfulness, minding or remembrance, the *noein* which, in Parmenides' sentence, belongs together with "Being" in the *to auto*, the Self-same. Thinking as such, as distinguished from the unthinking calculation of science and the "philosophy" about essents, is thinking *of* the Self-same, of Being (where Being is both subject and object), demanded and brought to pass by Being and in turn a cherishing of it. Thinking in this primordial sense is cherishing, holding in memory, unceasing and collected abiding, not merely with what is past but equally with the present and the coming. It is a gathered-together mindfulness of the has been, the is, and the coming in their unity, the remembrance of Be-ing (*An-wesen*, that is, Being in the nonmetaphysical sense, not confined to presence), entirely at the disposal and behest of the *Ereignis* in which it is owned.[85] As such cherishing and dependence, thinking is man's responsive relationship to Being, a kind of thanking. It is a thanksgiving for the gift of our own essence, for the relationship of belongingness in the truth of Being. Being itself, as itself this relationship, claims our remembrance and we, as intrinsically belonging in the Identity, are the mortals that we are in virtue of such remembrance. It is remembrance in and through which what is in itself thought-worthy, that is, Being in its truth, is preserved, "trued" and liberated in its "it gives" and in its coming to us as a gift entrusted to our care. Such cherishing is not something different from and external to Truth but the latter itself in the way in which it gives itself to us as what is most worthy and needy of thought.[86]

Thinking in the above sense is nothing psychological, no "act" of a supposedly independent agent called man and directed towards or against some entity standing over against him. With the emergence of Being (*einai*) as presence (*physis*), itself needing (*chre*) letting-lie-in-front (*legein, Vorliegen-lassen*) as well as mindfulness of taking care of (*noein, in-die-Acht-nehmen*), as Parmenides has it, there arises a conception of thinking which eventually developed into the logical concept of thinking as judgment. The initial coupling together of *noein* (*Vernehmen*, apprehension) and *legein* (stating), however, had as yet nothing in it of Reason (*Vernunft*, from *Vernehmen*) and Judgment (*logos*). As yet, thinking is "not a grasping, neither a grabbing at what lies in front, nor an attack on it. What lies in front is not, in *legein* and *noein*, molded into shape by gripping and handling. Thinking is not (as yet) comprehending."[87] It is only with the falling out of *legein* and *noein*, originally interwoven and resting on and determined in their unity by the differentiation, the twofoldness (*Zwiefalt*), of Being and beings, from their dependence on Being (as Difference) that they appear later in the form of *ratio*. Thinking is thus transformed into logic; Reason and its concepts (representation) are only *one* mode of thinking, not self-determined but dependent upon the way the Greek *logos* was transformed into *ratio* as European man's specific response to the way the Being of essents disclosed itself to him and claimed him. For such rational, representational thinking, everything turns into an essent, is objectivized and rendered amenable to the taming, subjugating Will of a Subject. Being in its truth eludes its grasp, as also man, world, and thing in their essence. It is this inaccessibility of the truth of Being to such thinking that Heidegger strikingly formulates in the statement, "Thinking only begins when we have realized that Reason, elevated for centuries into a position of supremacy, is the most pertinacious opponent of thinking."[88] Thinking, as man's relationship to "the region of all regions," must, like all true relationships, maintain and preserve both man and Being in their real nature, and it can do so only when it ceases to be representational and conceptual, when it sheds itself of its volitional character and becomes a serene "letting," beyond willing and beyond the will not to will. Thinking in the sense in which alone it is adequate to man's belongingness in the *Ereignis* can only be, as Heidegger says in his dialog on serenity,[89] a kind of waiting (not an awaiting, which always has an object), a surrender, a tranquil resignation to the Self-same. Such thinking is not a self-assertive act of man but is the expression of his repose in Being; it is not a going beyond or an ascent to something remote from man but is the Instancy (*Inständigkeit*, standing within) in what is nearest, in the nearing region of the *Ereignis* which, as primordial Truth, is nearness (*Nähe*) itself. This thinking does not argue and prove, gives nothing that might be kept as a possession, brings no final conceptual "clarity"; it only points and shows, letting the "region" to which it belongs exhibit itself in all its mystery. And language is not its tool or expression but this thinking itself, its very motion and chant.

The Saving Leap

For Heidegger, the Western metaphysical tradition has been a ladder which has enabled him to climb up to the place and moment of its birth and to see this point as pregnant with the entire development which, through its culmination in the scientific and technological mode of thinking dominating the man of today, has assumed a planetary importance, far exceeding the limits of a geographically or historically localized 'culture' or 'civilization'. In this "Europeanization of the earth," Edmund Husserl, the Husserl of the last *Krisis* phase, sees the abiding and universal significance of Western 'philosophy' in its Greek origins, for it is this essentially Greek phenomenon that constitutes the foundation of the rise and development of modern science.[90] Heidegger likewise insists on the basically Greek character of Western European philosophy (and there is no other, either Chinese or Indian, as he puts it),[91] which for him is an essentially Western phenomenon, as distinguished from the 'thinking' of the East and from the 'thinking' which has found expression, outside the central 'philosophical' mainstream, within the literary, the religious, and the mystical tradition of the West itself. As he remarks, the phrase "Western European philosophy" is in truth a tautology, because 'philosophy' is in essence Greek; even though it is dominated in its modern form by Christian conceptions, it still remains true that "the West and Europe, and only they, are, in the innermost movement of their history, basically 'philosophical'.[92] This is testified by the rise and dominance of the sciences. Because they originate from the innermost dynamic core of Western European history, namely the philosophical, they are in a position today to give its specific contemporary stamp to the history of mankind upon the whole earth."[93] Unlike Husserl, however, Heidegger sees this "complete Europeanization of the earth and of mankind" eating away all substance from things, drying up the very wellsprings of reality.[94] He sees this because, having climbed back to the source from which Western metaphysical thought has sprung up, he not only finds in this source a wellspring hiding in itself much that has remained the Unthought though sustaining foundation of Western philosophy but, taking the step back, leaps from this point into a region which is above the opposition of East and West, beyond the clash of traditions and the conflict of religions. This "region of all regions," suspended in itself, is itself above all regional loyalties and the Babel of conflicting tongues. It is the realm of that universality and simplicity of primordial truth, the happening of *aletheia*, of overtness, in the belongingness of man and Being in the Self-same, where alone divergent traditions, disfranchised of their exclusive claims and yet without losing their own identity, can meet together as one, as belonging-together in the Self-same. If there is any hope of an ultimate unity of divergent philosophies and religions, it lies not in the throwing of dubious bridges across them, not in questionable syntheses and compromises, but solely, through a going back of each to its own origins, in the leap into this swaying region, vibrant with the possibility of giving voice to its primordial word in a multiplicity of tongues.[95]

This realm is inaccessible to representational thinking; 'philosophy', as conceptual thought, has no entry into this sphere of the *Ereignis*. But neither is it accessible only in the ineffable immediacy of the 'personal' experience of individual men. This realm opens out and reveals itself, Heidegger believes as a thinker, to the unpretentious simplicity and humility of plain 'Thinking', dwelling in the neighborhood of poetic utterance as a mode of pure saying, itself no more than the spoken echo of the chime of Stillness, to that thinking which is an utterance, revealing and so in a true sense realizing, of man's belongingness, with all that is, in the Self-same. The leap out of metaphysical thinking, away from the separateness of man and Being, is not an abdication of thought, not a leap into the 'mystical', into some kind of intuitive, unmediated cognitive experience, but, as a leap of thought, only a transformation of its own nature, such that, surrendering its conceptuality, its will to grasp, it becomes a simple co-respondence to the *Ereignis*, content in its function of *letting* what is reveal itself, of *letting* Truth shine forth in all its obscuring-revealing mystery. As a European, Heidegger has only the ladder of his own central 'philosophical' tradition by which to climb over to its earliest germination and to take from there the leap that might, as he hopes,[96] convert "this Land of the Evening, away beyond Occident and Orient and cutting straight through the European, into a place from which there may emanate a new historical destiny (a history governed by the mutuality of man and Being rather than by the withdrawal of the latter, as thus far) in the time to come." Perhaps other traditions have other ladders enabling them to go up to the spring-board, perhaps a ladder is not indispensable.[97] But the leap by which one can alight on this region, and from there have a complete view of the birth and development of one's tradition in its entirety, is by itself not enough. The leap is a renunciation of the might of conceptual, representational thinking—from the point of view of the latter a renunciation of thought itself—but like all renunciation, it does not impoverish but gives, bestows upon the thinker "the inexhaustible power of the simple." All that metaphysical thought has sought, in vain, to catch in its conceptual net, the Soul, the World, God (the subject-matter of the three branches of *metaphysica specialis*, Psychology, Cosmology, and Theology) comes back in its truth to a thinking that has reverted to its own humble essence. To such renunciation and surrender to the Self-same, Soul, World, and God all speak with the true eloquence of simplicity.[98] And the thinker's task, like the poet's, far from being consummated in the transforming leap that enables him to listen to the voice of silence, only *begins* here, for the realm of the *Ereignis* needs, to be truly and effectively the realm of Truth that it is, man's guarding, tending, and realizing response. In order that man's collective historical existence should become a true 'dwelling' in this region, it is necessary that he should work unwearyingly, with all self-will transmuted into tranquil resignation (*Gelassenheit*), at building, by means of the inexhaustible wealth of material that language puts at his disposal, a home for humanity on this region.

It is towards such planetary construction (which might be described, in the idiom of contemporary linguistic philosophy, as the construction of a universal, basic language of Truth from which the languages of different philosophical and religious traditions can be derived) that Heidegger seeks to take the first pioneering steps, leaving to the future a task no less vast in its magnitude than it is supreme in its urgency. In this endeavor at planetary thinking, Heidegger realizes, a 'dialog' with East Asiatic thought is inescapable. Neither side, he believes, is as yet equal to the impending encounter between the ways in which the European and East Asiatic languages speak. And this is no less true about the sphere of a possible dialog between them for, as he says, "Neither of the two is capable, by itself, to lay open and establish this sphere."[99] The central tradition of Indian thought, with its clear vision of the realm of Identity and of the intimacy of man's belongingness in what Heidegger calls the *Ereignis*, has surely a vital contribution to make to this venture at cooperative building.[100] But in an age in which the "Europeanization of the Earth and of humanity" is no longer a mere threat but has become a harsh reality, when his way of thinking is in most respects taken up into and dominated by the universal sway of the metaphysical, the rational, the scientific, and the technological, the thinking Indian faces a challenge to which he was never exposed before: the compulsion of belonging, irretrievably and inescapably, to this 'one world' of the *Ge-Stell*, to a world 'one' only in the desolation of being enveloped within the Nihilistic metaphysical heritage of the West. The present spiritual situation and its challenge is utterly new in history because of its universal and all-enveloping character, because there is neither escaping it nor a possibility of directly attacking it and because no strategy of defense can be enduringly effective against it. Its "compulsion" lies in this that there is no other way open, to us in the East, but to go along with this Europeanization and to go *through* it. Only through this voyage into the foreign and the strange can we win back our own self-hood; here as elsewhere, the way to what is closest to us is the longest way back.[101] This challenge demands a bold, freely undertaken marching out into the alien, the questionable and the unhomelike. And it demands a profounder rethinking of our Indian tradition in terms of its own original beginnings, of what was originally 'heard' in it, a more searching and critical analysis of its historical unfoldment, a clearer vision of the nature, significance, and limitations of metaphysical thinking (that is, representational, conceptual, logical, scientific thinking in the Western sense, as also of allied manifestations within our own tradition), a greater sensitiveness to the silent message of language. As a powerful stimulus to such rethinking—which alone is true appropriating and safe-guarding—of the basic truth of our tradition and as a summons inviting us to participate in the cooperative endeavor of planetary building, Heidegger's thinking, single-minded and yet polyphonic in its beauty, passionate and yet commanding in the sweep of its vision, may not be without some relevance.

As remarked at the very outset, Heidegger's philosophy is not a finished system, lying ready to be submitted to a final critical scrutiny. It is neither a system (being itself an investigation into the implicit basis of all Western philosophical systems) nor something finished and complete. Itself "on the way," it only opens out an unexplored "way" for future thought. Moreover, Heidegger is too close to us in time to afford the distance requisite for an impartial, objective assessment—the contemporary, as Heidegger has himself remarked, is the least understood, being always "untimely."[102] Nevertheless, from the perspective of the exposition of the nature of Being given above, we may address a few questions to Heidegger as a thinker of Being, for whom the "essence" of Time, too, cannot itself be temporal nor eternity a mere word.

It has been suggested here that Heidegger's thinking carries him beyond the limitation of his own tradition into a region of "pure" thinking, the region of Being in *its* truth, unconditioned by the particular tradition *from* which one happens to leap into it, unconditioned by the particular form of representational thinking—Western "philosophy" or metaphysics—which has historically preceded the leap. In *Gelassenheit*, Heidegger in fact roundly speaks of two "kinds" of thinking, suggesting that it lies in the very nature of man's relationship to Being to bifurcate into these two modes. He says (p. 15; E.T. p. 46), "Thus there are two kinds of thinking, each of which is in its way legitimate and necessary: calculative thinking and meditative (recollective) thoughtfulness." And yet one does not find in Heidegger an explicit recognition of the possibility that such a universal, historically unconditioned level of thinking, valid for all traditions and yet leaving room for individual variations (as regards the form assumed by both the essent-centered as well as the Being centered thought), might actually have been realized in some other tradition. Heidegger admits that thinking in "the manner of conceptual representation all too easily creeps into every type of human experience, even where (as in the case of the Japanese) thinking is in a certain sense nonrepresentational" and that hence "the metaphysical mode of representation . . . is in some respect inevitable."[103] If this is true of man in general, the origin of such representational thinking cannot lie in the Western destiny of Being. May it not be that man *as* man (irrespective of whether he is Greek, or Chinese, or Indian) has some comprehension of Being insofar as, as man, he has dealings with essents? May it not be that, *as* man—Oriental or Occidental—he has the inherent tendency toward becoming forfeit to the world and, losing himself in it, to interpret Being in terms of the essent; that, always and everywhere, in becoming forfeit to the world, man relates himself to the essent, to world and to Being by representing and conceptualizing it? May this truth not have been realized already in another tradition?

It may be admitted that the thinking of the *Ereignis*, the reaching up to this realm, is mediated in the case of the Western man by the history of his own metaphysical tradition. Does it follow from this that such dwelling in the "Region of all regions" must always be mediated? Does not Heidegger himself admit that it is Being in its truth that is the all empowering, in which all dispensation has its source? And even if it is in some sense necessarily mediated, must its mediation have the unique character of the Western metaphysical destiny? Further, the findings of the analytic of Dasein are presumably not restricted to the *Dasein* of Western man or to a particular epoch in history nor, by the same logic, is what Heidegger later says about the belongingness of man and Being in the Self-same. What Heidegger says about the human state as one of confusion, delusion, and error (*Irren, Irre, Irrtum*) in *Vom Wesen der Wahrheit* is not itself a historical manifestation but a characterization of the way history itself (that is, man's historical existence) always, everywhere *is*. Is it not possible that it is a universal character of thought to lapse into the "metaphysical" and to develop into a tradition of the oblivion of Being as such? Is not the tradition of Indian thought one in which the lapse into representational thinking—of a different complection than that in the West, to be sure—has already come under the scrutiny of thought, is it not a tradition in which an awareness of the "Difference," of the "Identity," and of the necessity of a "reversal" are present from its earliest beginnings? Perhaps, it is "the Thinker's profound loyalty to his inner limits" of which Heidegger speaks in *Nietzsche* that prevents him from a precipitate and premature answer.

In a letter published immediately after the first world war under the title "La Crise de l'esprit," Paul Valéry asked, "This Europe, will it become *what it is in reality*, that is, a little cape of the Asiatic continent? Or will this Europe remain rather *what it seems*, that is, the priceless part of the whole earth, the pearl of the globe, the brain of a vast body?" Quoting these sentences, Heidegger remarks that perhaps Europe has already become what it is, a mere cape, yet it remains, at the same time, the brain of the entire body of the earth, the brain that carries out our technological-industrial, planetary-interstellar computations.[104] The contemporary world situation is, in respect of its essential source, through and through European-Western-Greek, and if it is to change, the resources for this must lie, and be sought, in the untapped abundance of this origin, of that great beginning to which there cannot be any mere return but which preserves in itself the saving possibility that may yet in its coming fulfil and heal the present. That is why Heidegger inquires into this 'great beginning', asking whether Europe, this cape and brain, must first become "the land of a sunset," from which the morning of another world history may prepare to dawn. This new dawn, Heidegger admits, cannot remain in its Western isolation but "opens itself to the few other great beginnings which, in what is their very own, belong in the Self-same of the source of that Infinite Relation which sustains and holds the earth."[105] The *Upanishadic*, mystical tradition of Indian religious and philosophical thought, by going back to its own unspent origins and opening itself out at the same time to the 'unthought' in that other great beginning in the West, can perhaps contribute more substantially towards the preparation of a new dawn than has seemed possible so far.

Notes

1. *Einführung in die Metaphysik*, p. 64 (E.T., p. 70).
2. Ibid.
3. For example, see ibid. p. 75; also *Nietzsche II*, p. 246.

4. For the following, see *Nietzsche II*, pp. 203-256.

5. According to Max Müller (*Existenzphilosophie im geistigen Leben der Gegenwart*, 2d ed., p. 73), during the preliminary drafting of Division III of *Being and Time* (which was to bear the title, "Time and Being"), Heidegger sought to distinguish three kinds of Difference: the 'transcendental', or Ontological Difference in the narrower sense—the difference between the essent and its beingness (*Seiendheit*); the 'transcendence-having', or Ontological Difference in the wider sense—the difference between the essent and its beingness on the one hand and Being itself on the other; the 'transcendent', or Theological Difference in the strict sense—the difference of God from the essent, from its beingness and from Being. This attempt was, however, given up as a merely speculative construction, not based on the experience of thought.

6. See Richardson's *Heidegger*, p. x. Pöggeler illustrates the multiple speakability of being with reference to the 'transcendentals' of scholastic philosophy: *res, unum, aliquid, bonum*, and *verum*.

7. Also as substance. Sections 19-21 of *Being and Time* are devoted to a discussion of the Cartesian determination of the Being of beings as substance. In "Aus der letzten Marburger Vorlesung" (*Wegmarken*, pp. 373-395), Heidegger offers a revised extract from a lecture course on Leibniz given at Marburg in 1928. He discusses here Leibniz's conception of the substantiality of substance as monad and of *vis activa* (with its character as *perceptio* and *appetitus*) as its unifying essence.

8. See also *Identität und Differenz*, pp. 63-64 (E.T., pp. 65-68). In speaking of it as a universal, we conceive Being in a manner in which It, Being, is never given. It is utterly impossible to conceive 'Being' (infinitely more so, Heidegger says, than the reality of a universal, as illustrated in Hegel's story of the man who found that only fruits were to be bought but never fruit) as the universal corresponding to particular essents. Being only appears in this or that historical form (that is, as it dispenses itself from epoch to epoch), as *Physis, Logos, Hen, Idea, Energeia*, Substantiality, Objectivity, Subjectivity, Will to Power, Will to Will. But what comes as such historical destiny is not to be found laid out neatly like apples, pears, and peaches, on the counter of the historian's representation. The description (below) of Being in terms of the Difference and of the latter in terms of an issue for resolution (*Austrag*), Heidegger says, perhaps brings into view something common and pervasive which runs through the entire destiny (dispensation) of Being from beginning to end. But it still remains difficult, Heidegger admits, to say how this universality is to be thought, if it is neither a universal valid for all particulars nor a law secure of the necessity characteristic of a dialectical process.

9. *Nietzsche II*, p. 347.

10. Ibid., p. 232.

11. *Der Satz vom Grund*, p. 39.

12. *Nietzsche II*, p. 343.

13. "Brief über den 'Humanismus'," *Wegmarken*, p. 162.

14. For the following, see "Die Onto-theo-logische Verfassung der Metaphysik" in *Identität und Differenz*.

15. For Heidegger's "experience" of theology, see chapter 1, "The De-

velopment of Heidegger's Thought." In his article, "Martin Heidegger und die Marburger Theologie," already referred to, H.-G. Gadamer gives a fascinating picture of the theological climate at Marburg during the twenties, of the young Heidegger in theological debate, of "the breathtaking radicalism of Heidegger's questioning, which drew even theology under its sway." This article vividly brings out the significance of his preoccupation with Aristotle at this time, the theological relevance of many of his ideas in *Being and Time*, and his influence on Bultmann's theology and beyond it on the hermeneutic philosophy of Gadamer himself. From the very beginning, Gadamer says, the questions which clamored within him were theological ones. "The *Urform* of *Being and Time*" was an address given at a gathering of Marburg theologians in 1924.

16. See on this whole problem, W. Schultz, *Der Gott der Neuzeitlichen Metaphysik*. As Pöggeler has remarked, the question of God has been there on Heidegger's path of thought from the very beginning and so also his wrestling with the claims and credentials of theology. In the pre-*Sein-und-Zeit* years he gave lecture courses, none of which have been published, on the philosophical foundations of medieval mysticism (1919-20), on the phenomenology of religion (1920-21) and on Augustine and neo-Platonism (1921), held a colloquium, with Ebbinghaus, on the theological foundations of Kant's *Religion Within the Limits of Pure Reason* (1923), and gave a lecture on phenomenology and theology (1927). His views, expressed in conversation, have been reported by H. H. Schrey (in *Martin Heideggers Einfluss auf die Wissenschaften*) and by H. Noack (*Anstösse I*, 1954). In 1959, Heidegger conducted a day-long seminar (unpublished) on "Christian Faith and Thinking" at a meeting of the "Old Marburgers," of which the impact on theologians is recorded in *The Later Heidegger and Theology*, edited by Robinson and Cobb. Heidegger's address on "Time and Being" was also given at a meeting of the "Old Marburgers" in 1962.

17. *Identität und Differenz*, p. 46 (E.T., p. 50).

18. *Was heisst Denken?*, p. 174 (E.T., p. 227).

19. See "Die Onto-theo-logische Verfassung der Metaphysik" in *Identität und Differenz* for the whole of this paragraph.

20. *Identität und Differenz*, pp. 69-70 (E.T., p. 71).

21. For the following, see "Der Satz der Identität" in *Identität und Differenz*. This lecture, Heidegger points out in his "Foreword," glances both forward and backward: ahead into the sphere with which the lecture on "The Thing" is concerned and back into the sphere of the Difference from which metaphysics derives its essential character.

22. The Principle of Identity does not, Heidegger claims, merely say that every A is itself the same but rather that every A is with itself the same (*idem, to auto, das Selbe; Identity* as distinguished from sameness). In self-sameness there lies the relation of 'with', hence a mediation, a union, a synthesis, unification into a unity. This is the reason why, throughout the history of Western thought, Identity appears in the character of Unity. But this Unity is by no means the monotonous vacuity of what, in itself without relation, persists unwearyingly in its indifferent oneness. But Western thought needs more than two thousand years until the relation of the same with itself, lying

within Identity and already glimmering in the beginning, comes to light definitely and in its characteristic form. Only the philosophy of Speculative Idealism, prepared by Leibniz and Kant, gives accommodation, through Fichte, Schelling, and Hegel, to the intrinsically synthetic nature of Identity. After the epoch of Speculative Idealism it is no longer permissible for thought to conceive the unity of Identity as mere sameness and to ignore the mediation inherent in unity. Where this happens, Identity is conceived only abstractly. According to Heidegger, it may be added, the Principle of Identity, like the Principle of Sufficient Reason, refers primarily to the Being of what is and only consequentially to thought. "The Principle holds as a law of thought only insofar as it is a Law of Being." See Heidegger's essay "Grundsätze des Denkens" (in *Jahrbuch für Psychologie und Psychotherapie* 6 (1958), for an examination of the laws of thought in relation to the dialectical thought of Hegel and Marx.

23. *Identität und Differenz*, p. 22 (E.T., p. 31).

24. Ibid., p. 24 (E.T., p. 33).

25. Kurt F. Leidecker's translation of *Vereignen* by "alienation" (in his translation of *Identität und Differenz*, entitled *Essays in Metaphysics: Identity and Difference*) is not the only incredible rendering in this translation. The *Ereignis* as the source of the relationship between Being and man has a doubly positive character—viewed from the side of man, it is *Vereignen* and from the side of Being, it is *Zueignen*. My own understanding here is based on the (oral) explanations of Dr. Walter Biemel and has the sanction of Dr. Otto Pöggeler's account in his article "Sein als Ereignis."

26. The original meaning of the word, Heidegger points out, is: eyeing, seeing, beckoning with the glance, appropriating (*aneignen*, taking into possession). He intends the term to be taken as "a leading word in the service of thought . . . as little amenable to translation as the Greek *Logos* and the Chinese *Tao*."

27. See the lecture "Die Frage nach der Technik" (in *Vorträge und Aufsätze*) for a discussion of the Greek concept of *techne* as a mode of 'knowing' or, more precisely, of disclosure and unhiddenness and, in terms of that, for an elucidation of the *Ge-stell*. The latter is the mode in which truth—the aspect in which everything discloses itself to us—prevails in the present age, which is not of our making but within which we move and have our being. As Heidegger says here (pp. 28-29), both the Greek *poiesis* and the present-day *Ge-stell*, are "modes of disclosure, or *aletheia*. The *Ge-stell* manifests the occurrence of unhiddenness, such that modern technology in its functioning discloses the real in the character of an enduring quantity at our disposal (*Bestand*, used technically here). It is therefore neither a merely human doing nor indeed a mere means for such doing. The purely instrumental and anthropological determination of technology falls to the ground; it cannot be rendered viable by being propped up with the help of metaphysical and religious interpretations." In "Hölderlins Erde und Himmel," Heidegger remarks that the *Ge-stell* is the disguise in which the *Ereignis* manifests itself in the present age, holding within it, thus, a promise of the advent, of a possible coming, of the primordial, true belongingness in the future

(*Erläuterungen zu Hölderlins Dichtung*, p. 153). See also the lecture "Die Kehre" in *Die Technik und die Kehre*.

28. For a similar interpretation of the Principle of Sufficient Reason, passing from the principle regarded as a *Satz* in the sense of statement (about the essent) to the principle considered as a *Satz* in the sense of a leap (into the nature of Being as Ground), see *Der Satz vom Grund*, p. 96.

29. This Platonic phrase, it should be noted, is never used by Heidegger himself.

30. This is not quite equivalent to saying, as Otto Pöggeler does (in his article, "Sein als Ereignis"), that "with the determination of Being as *Ereignis*, Heidegger reaches the goal he set before himself in *Being and Time*. . . . The occurrence of such mutuality of relationship in history *is* Being." See Heidegger's remarks in *Unterwegs zur Sprache*, p. 260 (E.T., p. 129)," . . . it may appear unbelievable to many that the author has been using in his manuscripts the word *Ereignis* . . . for more than twenty-five years. What it refers to, though in itself something simple, continues for the time being difficult to think. For thought must first disaccustom itself from slipping back into the idea that here it is "Being" that is conceived as *Ereignis*. The *Ereignis* is intrinsically different in its richness from any conceivable metaphysical determination of Being. Being, on the other hand, can be thought, as regards the derivation of its essence, in terms of *Ereignis*. See also "Zeit und Sein" (in *Zur Sache des Denkens*, p. 22; E.T., p. 21f.). Heidegger here points out, further, that *Ereignis* is not to be regarded as a higher, more comprehensive concept under which Being and Time can be subsumed. Rather, "being turns out to be the gift of the destiny of presence, granted through the reaching over of Time. The gift of presence is the property of the happening of owning. Being disappears in the *Ereignis*."

In his book on Heidegger, Pöggeler quotes frequently from an unpublished work of Heidegger entitled, *Beiträge zur Philosophie* (written during 1936–38) which deals at length with *Ereignis*. Other unpublished works from which he also quotes are: *Die Überwindung der Metaphysik* (1938–39), *Das Ereignis* (1941), *Hölderlins Hymnen* (lectures course, 1942) and *Einblick in das, was ist* (four addresses given at Bremen in 1949, entitled "Das Ding," "Das Gestell," "Die Gefahr," and "Die Kehre," of which only the third remains unpublished). For these references, see also Orlando Pugliese: *Vermittlung und Kehre*. The whole question of the relation between man and Being in Heidegger has been discussed critically by R. Pflaumer in his article "Sein und Mensch im Denken Heideggers."

31. See "Zeit und Sein" (*Zur Sache des Denken*) for this paragraph and the next two.

32. *Nietzsche II*, p. 336.

33. *Vorträge und Aufsätze*, p. 71.

34. *Nietzsche II*, p. 338.

35. See "Zur Seinsfrage," passim, for the following.

36. Curiously enough, Kluback and Wilde (in their English translation of this essay, entitled *The Question of Being*) translate *Verwindung* as 'restoration', which completely distorts the sense of the text and contravenes

Heidegger's express rejection of the notion of a *Restauration* (that is, restoration), a few lines below, in this context.

37. In his latest writing Heidegger prefers to speak of the "essence" or nature (*Wesen*) of Being, whereas in the *Being and Time* phase he speaks of the "sense," and later, of the "truth" of Being.

38. Earlier, Heidegger also tried for a time the device of spelling "*Sein*" in the old fashion as *Seyn*.

39. Cf. Karl Jaspers' conception of the Encompassing (*das Umgreifende*).

40. See Heidegger's account of these, all too brief, in "Bauen Wohnen Denken" and "Das Ding" in *Vorträge und Aufsätze*; also "Hölderlins Erde und Himmel." In English, Vycinas (*Earth and Gods*) and Richardson (*Heidegger*) give good expositions; more perceptive and lucid is James M. Demske's "Heidegger's Quadrate and Revelation of Being," selected and translated from his book, *Sein, Mensch und Tod*, a finely written study of the concepts of death and mortality in Heidegger's earlier as well as later thought.

41. Cf. "Der Ursprung des Kunstwerkes" in *Holzwege*, p. 31 (E.T., *Poetry, Language, Thought*, p. 42).

42. Apart from the incidental remarks in the Hölderlin essays, there is very little in Heidegger's published writings that can throw further light on his conception of the Holy and of "God and the gods." W. Schulz has pointed out ("Über den philosophiegeschichtlichen Ort Martin Heideggers," *Philosophische Rundschau* 1, 1953-1954, p. 222) that in these essays the Holy has been determined as the Unmediated and the poet as the mediator. But the poet himself needs the mediation of the gods to give utterance to the Holy. The gods are the intermediaries, upon whom the poet depends and who in turn depend upon the poets. See also W. Schulz *Der Gott der Neuzeitlichen Metaphysik* (pp. 54-58). Vincent Vycinas, in his *Earth and Gods*, discusses Heidegger's view with reference to the Greek conception of divinity. However, as Demske points out in the article mentioned above, it would be misguided to interpret Heidegger's talk of the 'Immortals', inspired by Hölderlin's usage and by his spiritual quest, as an attempted revival of paganism: "The use of the category 'the Immortals' here, far from constituting a decision for Greek paganism as opposed to Christianity, seems to fit smoothly into a Judaeo-Christian framework which includes the legitimate 'pagan' insight of the presence of the Divine, however hazy and ill defined this idea may be, in the things of human experience." See in this connection, the criticism offered by Hans Jonas in his article on Heidegger and theology.

Keeping clear of the way of faith as also of the metaphysical conceptualizations of speculative theology, and seeking to think of the Divine in terms of the truth of Being, not of the truth of beings as Western religious thought has done so far, Heidegger finds in Hölderlin a poet who directs the thinker to the future which is open for a nonmetaphysical experience of Divinity and its arrival. The metaphysical-moralistic God, as Nietzsche saw, is dead but not so Divinity, which lives on and abides as a task for future thought. The absence of God, like all absence, is not nothing; "it is just the presence, which still remains to be appropriated, of the hidden fullness of that which has been and which therefore is ever a gathered together abiding of the Divine in the Greek, in prophetic Judaism, in the Sermon of Jesus. This no-longer is itself a not-yet of the veiled arrival of its inexhaustible essence." (*Vorträge und Aufsätze*, p. 183). Hölderlin's poetry was for Heidegger a pointer in the direction of a rethinking about God in terms of the Holy and of Truth, of the arrival of the Divine as an event to be awaited and prepared for by a deeper insight into the meaning of Truth and Being. The Godlessness of the present is due neither to a mere failure of belief among men nor to a moral incapacity, but is part of the history of Being itself. We can begin to overcome this when we realize, with Hölderlin, that primordial Truth (*Aletheia*), is the Holy, itself above gods and mortals. The Holy is the necessary element or medium for the manifestation of Divinity. The Holy, in itself pure immediacy, finds expression in the poetic word and is revealed through the mediation of a god, a being in whom the light of the Holy is gathered as in a single ray which claims and addresses mortals. See Pöggeler (*Der Denkweg*, pp. 193-95, 215-35 and 260-67) for the relevance of Hölderlin in this regard and Richardson's *Heidegger* for summaries of the first four Hölderlin essays.

The most thorough discussion of this subject to date is provided by Helmut Danner in *Das Göttliche und der Gott bei Heidegger*, 1971.

43. *Erläuterungen zu Hölderlins Dichtung*, pp. 163 and 170-171.

44. Commenting on Heidegger's preoccupation with "World," W. Marx says, "We can see here Heidegger's attempt to help in building a new cosmos to take the place of the traditional one that Cartesianism had destroyed. It is not a cosmos of immutable Essences, teleologically ordered as conceived by the Greeks, nor is it the meaningful order and hierarchy of divine Essences of medieval times. It is rather a cosmos, a world, of an ever-active manifestation of the ways that Being *west*." ("Heidegger's New Conception of Philosophy.")

45. For further explanation of *Gering, Ring, reigen,* and so forth, see, besides "Das Ding," "Hölderlins Erde und Himmel."

46. *Vorträge und Aufsätze*, p. 179.

47. *Unterwegs zur Sprache*, p. 22 (E.T., *Poetry, Language, Thought*, p. 199-200).

48. Cf. the account, in "Der Ursprung des Kunstwerkes," of how a work of art, a temple, for example, represents the occurrence of truth or unhiddenness and as such opens out and sets up a world, from which then all things derive their character and which determines man's attitudes and decisions.

49. *Vorträge und Aufsätze*, p. 229.

50. *Identität und Differenz*, pp. 30, 32 (E.T., pp. 38, 39). In *Being and Time*, language is touched upon within the limits of the existenzial analytic and described in terms of the ontological constitution of Dasein. In *Erläuterungen zu Hölderlins Dichtung* the mode of being of language is then more explicitly hinted at as the house in which man dwells in the neighborhood of Being. *Unterwegs zur Sprache*, finally, thinks of language in terms of the *Geviert* and the *Ereignis*, completing, as it were, the "step back" from the representational thinking of metaphysics to the meditative, reminiscent thinking which alone is appropriate in this "realm of all realms," the *Ereignis*.

51. *Unterwegs zur Sprache*, p. 30 (E.T., *Poetry, Language, Thought*, p. 208).

52. Ibid., p. 33 (E.T., *Poetry, Language, Thought*, p. 210).

53. Cf. "Sprache und Heimat" (in *Dauer im Wandel*, p. 186); also the essay "Moira" in *Vorträge und Aufsätze* for the derivation of 'Saying' (*die Sage*) from the *phacis* of Parmenides and the *logos* of Heraclitus.

54. *Unterwegs zur Sprache*, p. 206 (E.T., p. 99).

55. Ibid., p. 215 (E.T., p. 107).

56. See also the essay "Logos" in *Vorträge und Aufsätze*.

57. *Unterwegs zur Sprache*, p. 254 (E.T., p. 123).

58. Cf. "Sprache und Heimat."

59. *Unterwegs zur Sprache*, p. 267 (E.T., p. 135).

60. Ibid., p. 259 (E.T., p. 128).

61. Cf. *Vorträge und Aufsätze*, p. 276.

62. "Hegel und die Griechen" in *Wegmarken*, p. 271. Heidegger's approach to the phenomenon of language and his reflections on it have stimulated considerable rethinking in philosophical circles. This is represented at its best in the writings of H.-G. Gadamer and Karl Otto Apel. The latter seeks, in addition, to mediate between the approaches to language of Heidegger and Wittgenstein. See also Stephen A. Erickson's *Language and Being*. Incidentally, in the field of psychiatry, Heidegger's thinking on language has profoundly influenced the distinguished French psychoanalyst Jacques Lacan (*The Language of the Self*, translated, with notes and commentary, by Anthony Wilden, Baltimore: Johns Hopkins, 1968).

63. *Was ist Metaphysik?*, p. 40 (E.T., p. 302). The key word in Heidegger's later thinking is not so much Being as Truth in the sense of *Lichtung*. In response to my request in 1958 for advice regarding the best way I could approach his thought, Professor Heidegger suggested the problem of Truth as the most fruitful. Lack of confidence in my ability to do so then, however, made me shy away from taking his advice and led me into the present attempt at a *Gesamtdarstellung*. The interpretation of Heidegger's final view of the question of Being offered in this chapter is, as the critical reader will have noticed, hesitant, faltering, and not always appropriately expressed. But in its basic intention it diverges from Pöggeler's in not laying as much stress on historicity as he does. I find myself in greater sympathy, in this respect, with Alfredo Guzzoni's critical remarks in his review of Pöggeler's "Der Denkweg Martin Heideggers" (in *Philosophisches Jahrbuch*, 1964) and ask with him if the idea of history (not only in the vulgar sense but even in Heidegger's deeper view), despite the all-important role it has played in his thinking, is not rather part of all that to which he seeks to bid farewell in a thinking for which meditation on the *Ereignis* has become the main task.

Two books dealing with the nature of Truth and its close inter connectedness with historicity and Being in Heidegger's thought are: *Wahrheit und Geschichtlichkeit* by Fridolin Wiplinger (referred to earlier) and *Sein und Wahrheit* by Willy Bretschneider (the latter is a doctoral dissertation). *The Anatomy of Disillusion* by W. B. Macomber is the fullest study in English of Heidegger's notion of Truth. Walter Biemel is the first to see clearly that Heidegger's inquiry into Being is at the same time inquiry into Truth in the sense of *aletheia*, and it is the special merit of his monograph *Heidegger* that it exhibits this twofold character of the *leitmotiv* of Heidegger's thinking from *Being and Time* to the latest writings.

64. Cf. "Der Ursprung des Kunstwerkes" (*Holzwege*, p. 42; E.T., *Poetry, Language, Thought*, p. 53f.), where Heidegger speaks of the hiddenness pervading all that is (that is, is unhidden), while itself remaining hidden, as having a twofold character: denial (*Versagen*) and dissembling (*Verstellen*). The essent, Heidegger says, denies itself to us (that is, does not manifest itself to us in all the richness of the "thing" that it truly is) up to the very limit where we can barely say that it is; and it dissembles by showing itself as other than what it is and so deludes us.

65. *Vorträge und Aufsätze*, p. 271.

66. *Holzwege*, p. 321.

67. It may be doubted whether Heidegger's conception of truth as unhiddenness or disclosure, with its necessary reference to hiddenness, is purely Greek in origin. Similarly, the conception of truth as happening and as "truing" is not so much Greek as Judaic in origin. See Otto Pöggeler's remarks in *Philosophischer Literaturanzeiger* 15, 7 (Review of *Index zu Sein und Zeit*). During the course of a conversation with the author (on 15 July 1958), Professor Heidegger explained the hiddenness necessarily involved in Being (as *Anwesen*) as follows: We could not be aware of this pencil as a pencil at all unless its thing character (that is, its Being) remained hidden. When we are aware of the pencil as an object, the *being* ascribed to it, that is, being an object for a subject, remains hidden. This is also true of all types of interpretation, metaphysical or otherwise. In Hegel's metaphysics of the Absolute, for example, when the Absolute is conceived as a sort of full transparency of unhiddenness of Being, the origin of Hegel's own philosophy in subjectivism remained hidden.

68. "Zur Seinsfrage," *Wegmarken*, p. 228 (E.T., p. 63).

69. *Was heisst Denken?*, p. 143 (E.T., p. 235).

70. For the following, see *Was heisst Denken?* passim, and *Vorträge und Aufsätze*, pp. 101-128; also *Nietzsche I*, chapter 2.

71. *Was heisst Denken?*, p. 39 (E.T., p. 96).

72. *Vorträge und Aufsätze*, p. 117.

73. Heidegger quotes (ibid., p. 113) the following sentences from Schelling's treatise on Human Freedom (*Philosophischen Untersuchungun über das Wesen der Freiheit und die damit zusammenhängenden Gegenstände*, 1809) as the classical formulation of this conception, (followed by Schopenhauer's *Die Welt als Wille und Vorstellung*, 1818) in which the conception of representation finds a similar classical utterance: "In the last and ultimate instance there is no other Being whatsoever except Will. Will is primal Being and to it alone (that is, Will) are applicable all the predicates of that (that is, primal Being): Unfathomability (having no ground outside itself), Eternity, independence from time, self-affirmation. The whole of philosophy is only an effort aiming at giving expression to this sovereign Being."

74. See also *Die Frage nach dem Ding*, pp. 115, 154-157 (E.T., pp. 147, 197-201) for a discussion of Space and Time as pure intuitions.

75. See "Der Spruch des Anaximander" in *Holzwege*.

76. *Unterwegs zur Sprache*, p. 58 (E.T., p. 176f.).

77. *Vorträge und Aufsätze*, p. 143.

78. For this paragraph see *Unterwegs zur Sprache*, pp. 213-214 (E.T., p. 106).

79. See Hegel's account of the 'now' in chapter 7 above.

80. *Unterwegs zur Sprache*, p. 213 (E.T., p. 106).

81. For this paragraph and the next, see *Zur Sache des Denkens*, pp. 11-18 (E.T., pp. 11-17). Summaries of "Zeit und Sein" were given, before this lecture was published in 1968, by Heinrich Rombach (in *Die Gegenwart der Philosophie*), in *Philosophy Today*, 10 (1966), and by Orlando Pugliese (*Vermittlung und Kehre*). See also Heidegger's "Preface" in Richardson's *Heidegger*, Kockelmans "Heidegger on *Time and Being*," and Schuwer, "Prolegomena to 'Time and Being': Truth and Time" (John Sallis, ed., *Heidegger and the Path of Thinking*). The "Protokoll zu einem Seminar über den Vortrag 'Zeit und Sein' " in *Zur Sache des Denkens*, pp. 27-60 (E.T., pp. 25-54), provides an indispensable commentary on the lecture.

82. It must be pointed out, expressly and emphatically, that the above account of Difference and Identity (*Ereignis*), World and Thing, Language, Truth, and Time, that is, the account of Heidegger's thinking about the truth of Being, belongs to the sphere of "what is to be thought" (*das Zu-Denkende*). All that Heidegger seeks to accomplish is to open up a sphere, so long closed, for future thought, himself taking only the first preparatory steps. Moreover, this thinking does not and cannot result in a set of sharply defined 'concepts', but only in a simple 'saying' which discloses something of a realm which never finally sheds its mysteriousness.

83. See "Kants These über das Sein," *Wegmarken*, pp. 302-306.

84. See L. Landgrebe, "Husserl, Heidegger, Sartre," where he shows how these three philosophers have contributed, each in his own way, to such a critique and towards the emergence of a new conception of thinking (*pensée méditative*, as Landgrebe calls it) which alone can do justice to the fundamental problems of our epoch.

85. Heidegger refers in this context to the myth of Mnemosyne, daughter of Earth and Heaven, the bride of Zeus, and the mother of the nine muses. See *Was heisst Denken?*, p. 7 (E.T., p. 11).

86. For this paragraph and the following one, see *Was heisst Denken?* passim, and the essay with this title in *Vorträge und Aufsätze*.

87. *Was heisst Denken?*, p. 128 (E.T., p. 211).

88. *Holzwege*, p. 247.

89. Cf. *Gelassenheit*, p. 44 (E.T., p. 68). The term *Gelassenheit* (serenity, calmness, collectness; translated by Richardson as 'release') belongs to the vocabulary of German mysticism. Heidegger employs it to indicate man's true relation to the Region, a "nay-saying to willing" which is a "higher kind of action that is yet no activity." The corresponding term in *Being and Time* is *Entschlossenheit* ('resoluteness'). For a summary of the dialog, *Zur Erörterung der Gelassenheit*, see Richardson (*Heidegger*, pp. 502-510); also Versényi (*Heidegger, Being, and Truth*, pp. 142-146) for a brief discussion of both the dialog and the address entitled *Gelassenheit*.

90. See *Die Krisis der europäischen Wissenschaften*, p. 4, and the whole of section 6. So also, in his own way, does Bertrand Russell. See the "Introduction" to his *Wisdom of the West*.

91. *Was heisst Denken?*, p. 136 (E.T., p. 224).

92. See *Was ist das—die Philosophie?*, p. 13 (E.T., p. 31).

93. Specifically, the universal sway of technology, and of science as its expression, is a historical consequence and manifestation of the notion of Being as presence underlying it. As Heidegger has said, "Once modern technology has extended its sway over the entire earth, it is not just the sputniks and their offshoots that circle around our planet. It is Being as presence, in the sense of a calculable quantity, that forthwith begins to address and lay its claim equally on all dwellers of the earth. Those who live in non-European parts of the earth are not expressly aware of this; moreover, they may be unable to know the origin of this determination of Being and may not wish to do so. Obviously, such knowledge is least of all desired by those busy developers who are today dragging the so-called underdeveloped people within the range of hearing of that demand which speaks from the inmost core of modern technology" (*Zur Sache des Denkens*, p. 7; E.T., p. 7).

94. See *Unterwegs zur Sprache*, p. 103 (E.T., p. 15f.). As Karlfried Gründer remarks, the problem of the essence, possibility and limitations of science pervades all of Heidegger's writings. Cf. "M. Heideggers Wissenschaftskritik in ihren geschichtlichen Zusammenhängen." This article, a translation of which appeared in *Philosophy Today*, is valuable for an understanding of Heidegger's attitude towards science, as it is also for the role which Hölderlin has played in his thinking.

95. Cf. the remarks of H.-G. Gadamer on the extent to which Western philosophy can be synthesized with Eastern (in "Vorwort" to *Grundriss der allgemeinen Geschichte der Philosophie* by W. Dilthey, Frankfurt, 1949; quoted by Glasenapp in *Das Indienbild deutscher Denker*): "Obwohl die Forschung auf dem Gebiete der Philosophie des Ostens inzwischen weiter gefördert worden ist, glauben wir uns heute eher weiter von ihrem philosophischen Verständnis entfernt: die Schärfung unseres historischen Bewusstseins hat die Übersetzungen oder Übertragungen der Texte . . . von Grund auf problematisch gemacht . . . Von einer aneignung dieser Dinge durch die abendländische Philosophie kann nicht die Rede sein. Nur die negative Einsicht kann als gesichert gelten, dass unsere eigenen, durch die Griechen geprägten Grundbegriffe das Fremde in der Substanz verändern." To be sure, these remarks are made from a perspective quite different from that of intellectual and cultural "ambassadors," professionally engaged in bridging cultural gulfs. But they deserve more serious attention and a more philosophical response than defenders of the Indian cultural heritage like Helmuth von Glasenapp have been able to offer. Similar doubts were expressed by Professor Heidegger in conversation.

96. *Holzwege*, p. 300. Cf. in this connection Egon Vietta's observations in his *Die Seinsfrage bei Martin Heidegger* (pp. 93-94): "Indian princes in particular have ever again sought for a religion which should be equally valid for all

men and above all creeds. The quest of a religion for which all dogmatic differences become untenable engages every thoughtful east Asiatic. The East also knows the sage for whom the various religious communities coexist as of equal value in the eyes of God. But in Oriental thinking the sages themselves have not been able to find a way of realizing this demand in thought. For that reason, we may suggest, at least as a question, whether Heidegger's philosophizing does not offer such a way. Heidegger's thinking is world historical, very much as the thinking of Plato and Kant has determined the course of Western history." (See also *Erläuterungen zu Hölderlins Dichtung*, pp. 176-177.)

97. Cf. *Gelassenheit*, p. 51 (E.T., p. 73).

98. *Der Feldweg*, p. 7.

99. "Zur Seinsfrage," *Wegmarken*, p. 252 (E.T., p. 10). Cf. Heidegger's remarks in "From a Dialogue on Language" (*Unterwegs zur Sprache*, pp. 93-94; E.T., p. 8):". . . even today the appropriate word is still to be found. The outlook for the thinking that labors to prove adequate to the essence of language still remains obscure in its full scope. For this reason, I cannot as yet see whether the nature of language as I am attempting to think, *also* suffices to express the nature of east Asiatic language, whether in the end—which would be at the same time the beginning—it is at all possible to realize in thought an essence of language which might guarantee that European-Western and east Asiatic ways of talking ('saying') can enter into a mutual dialog in such a manner that a music flowing from a single source can be heard in it." This dialog between Heidegger and a Japanese scholar brings home the need of extreme caution in every kind of 'comparative' philosophizing and in the employment of Western metaphysical terms to express ideas rooted in another linguistic soil. One consequence of the "all-consuming Europeanization" mentioned above is that even Eastern scholars are tempted to adopt, even outside the scientific sphere, European conceptual thinking as the measure by which to judge, and naturally find deficient, their own nonrepresentational ways of saying, that is, showing, the truth of things.

In his challenging essay "Über den paradigmatischen Charakter der griechischen Kultur," Johannes Lohmann takes the extreme position that even among the Indo-European languages, the demythologization of language and the conceptualization of the verb 'is' has been accomplished only in Greek. He says, "So Kommt nur in Griechenland der Samen, den die indogermanische Sprache . . . hervorgebracht hat, zum Wachstum, zur Blüte und zur Reife. In Indien geht das *esti* als 'copula' des Satzes . . . praktisch wieder verloren." Perhaps a greater familiarity with the Indian thinkers' discovery of *Vak* and their labors to conceptualize the 'is'—with a history covering the period from 500 B.C. to A.D. 1600—would have enabled Lohmann to see that there is more to Indian thought than a mere elevation of the magic word *Brahman* to a world principle. In what specific sense the Greek 'concept' is yet unique and in this uniqueness dominates the world today, is an open question which Heidegger has been the first to explore in all its implications. Lohmann's investigations, published in a series of articles in *Lexis* and in his book, *Philosophie und Sprachwissenschaft*, constitute a valuable application of Heidegger's insights to linguistic science and a first attempt at analyzing how and why different languages speak differently. An English translation of his important essay "M. Heidegger's 'Ontological Difference' and Language" is included in *Heidegger and Language*, edited and translated by Joseph J. Kockelmans (Evanston: Northwestern University Press, 1972).

100. The task envisaged here is something quite different from "comparative philosophy." Suggestions towards an interpretation of early Indian philosophy, stimulated by Heidegger's mode of thinking, have been made by Leo Gabriel (*Vom Brahma zur Existenz*. But as against such attempts, in themselves not without value, what Heidegger speaks about is a "dialog" between the *languages* of the East and the West, an inquiry into the different ways in which they speak. A good example of the first, comparative type of 'dialog' is an article by the Japanese philosopher Hajime Tanabe entitled "Todesdialektik." Tanabe approaches Heidegger's philosophy from the point of view of Mahāyāna Buddhism, especially Zen, and interprets Heidegger's analysis of death and his conception of *Ereignis* from this point of view. Heidegger, it may be added, has deeply influenced contemporary Japanese thinking and, ever since the twenties, has been in intimate contact with Japanese scholars and, through them, with Buddhist thought.

On the theme of Heidegger and Eastern thought, see the contributions of Elisabeth F. Hirsch, Takeshi Umehara, and J. L. Mehta in the symposium on this subject in *Philosophy East and West*, 20 (1970):3; also Koichi Tsujimura in Richard Wisser, *Martin Heidegger im Gespräch*.

101. As Heidegger has remarked ("Hölderlins Hymnen," quoted by Pöggeler in *Denkweg*, p. 226), the appropriation of what is our very own occurs only as a homecoming, as a return from a journey into the alien and the other; this is the law of being at home as a making oneself at home. See also the motto placed at the beginning of this work.

102. As will have become evident by now, Heidegger's regular practice, on his 'way' of thought, has been to look back constantly at what he has already thought and interpret it from his present position, while going beyond it all the time. The 'later' Heidegger is thus always, explicitly or implicitly, a commentator and critic of his own former self. Among his explicitly autobiographical statements are the remarks in "Aus einem Gespräch von der Sprache" (in *Unterwegs zur Sprache*), the "Preface" in Richardson's *Heidegger*, remarks in his address to the Heidelberg Academy of Sciences (in *Jahresheft der Heidelberger Akademie der Wissenschaften, 1957/58*, Heidelberg, 1959, and in the "Vorwort" to *Frühe Schriften*), and "Mein Weg in die Phänomenologie" in *Zur Sache des Denkens*. For the controversial problem of the nature and justification of his self-interpretations, see F. W. von Herrmann's *Die Selbstinterpretation Martin Heideggers*.

103. *Unterwegs zur Sprache*, p. 116 (E.T., p. 25). Cf. Heidegger's "suggestions" on the problem of a nonobjectifying thinking and speaking in contemporary theology in *Phänomenologie und Theologie*. Heidegger remarks here (pp. 42-45) that our everyday experience of things is not objectifying; nor does it even necessarily imply turning what is experienced into something thematically represented. It is only the natural scientific thinking and

speaking that is objectifying; outside the field of natural science and technology, thinking and speaking are by no means objectifying. The saying of language is not necessarily a statement of propositions about objects, but is rather a co-responding to what shows itself, to what manifests itself and addresses us.

104. *Erläuterungen zu Hölderlins Dichtung*, p. 176-177.

105. The new beginning can emerge only as a transformation of the first, great beginning. As Heidegger remarks in *Schelling* (p. 175), "There remains only the possibility that we may transform history (*Geschichte*), that is, really fulfill the hidden necessity of history, into which neither knowledge nor deeds reach down. Transformation, truly accomplished, is real creativity. For the great beginning of Western philosophy too did not come out of nothing. Rather, it became great because it successfully faced the challenge of overcoming (*Überwinden*), that is, bringing within the framework of a truth of Being, what was its diametrical opposite, the mythical in general and the Asiatic in particular." In the new beginning, as Heidegger envisages it, the mythical and the Asiatic are no longer experienced as opposites to be overcome and a mutual reaching out and meeting becomes a real possibility. After "the end of philosophy," it is now "the task of thinking" to accomplish this meeting and this togetherness, from both sides, in the medium of language.

Bibliography

I. Heidegger's Writings
(In chronological sequence)

1. "Das Realitätsproblem in der modernen Philosophie." *Philosophisches Jahrbuch der Görres-Gesellschaft* 25 (1912).
2. "Neuere Forschungen über Logik." *Literarische Rundschau für das katholische Deutschland* 38 (1912).
3. Review of *Kants Briefe* by F. Ohmann. *Literarische Rundschau für das katholische Deutschland* 40 (1914).
4. Review of *Zeitlichkeit und Zeitlosigkeit* by N. Bubnoff. *Literarische Rundschau für das katholische Deutschland* 39 (1913).
5. Review of *Von der Klassifikation psychischer Phänomene* by Franz Brentano. *Literarische Rundschau für das katholische Deutschland* 40 (1914).
6. Review of *Kant und Aristoteles* by C. Sentroul. *Literarische Rundschau für das katholische Deutschland* 40 (1914).
7. Review of *Kant-Laienbrevier* by F. Gross. *Literarische Rundschau für das katholische Deutschland* 40 (1914).
8. *Die Lehre vom Urteil im Psychologismus: Ein kritisch-positiver Beitrag zur Logik* (Leipzig: Barth, 1941). Freiburg Dissertation, 1914.
9. "Der Zeitbegriff in der Geschichtswissenschaft." *Zeitschrift für Philosophie und philosophische Kritik* 161 (1916). Freiburg Probevorlesung, 1915.
10. *Die Kategorien- und Bedeutungslehre des Duns Scotus* (Tübingen: Mohr, 1916). Freiburg Habilitationsschrift, 1915.
11. "Abendgang auf der Reichenau." *Das Bodenseebuch* 4 (1917).
12. "Selbstanzeige" of *Die Kategorien- und Bedeutungslehre des Duns Scotus*. *Kant-Studien* 21, 4 (1917).
13. "Zur Geschichte des philosophischen Lehrstuhls seit 1866." *Die Philipps-Universität zu Marburg 1527-1927* (Marburg: N. G. Elwert'sche Verlagsbuchhandlung [G. Braun], 1927).

14. *Sein und Zeit, Erste Hälfte*. In *Jahrbuch für Philosophie und phänomenologische Forschung*, 8 (Halle: Niemeyer, 1927). Simultaneously published separately: 7th edition, with "Vorbemerkung," and with "Erste Hälfte" left out (Tübingen: Niemeyer, 1953). Variations in reading, as between earlier and later editions, noted by Macquarrie and Robinson in the English translation. Lecture courses on "Hermeneutik der Faktizität" date back to 1919-1920; lecture course on "Ontologie oder Hermeneutik der Faktizität," 1923; lecture course on Descartes, Marburg, 1923-1924; address on "Die Zeit," 1924; and address to Marburg theologians, 1924.

15. " 'Anmerkungen' zu Husserl," in part in W. Biemel's "Husserls Encyclopaedia Britannica Artikel und Heideggers Anmerkungen dazu"; complete in *Husserliana*, vol. 9 (The Hague: Nijhoff, 1962), pp. 237-301 and 590-600.

16. " 'Brief' (22 Oct. 1927) an Husserl." *Husserliana*, vol. 9, pp. 600-602.

17. Review of *Philosophie der symbolischen Formen*, 2 Teil, by Ernst Cassirer. *Deutsche Literaturzeitung für Kritik der Internationalen Wissenschaft* (Berlin), Neue Folge, 5 (1928).

18. "Vorbemerkung des Herausgebers," in "Edmund Husserls Vorlesungen zur Phänomenologie des inneren Zeitbewusstseins." In *Jahrbuch für Philosophie und phänomenologische Forschung* 9 (Halle: Niemeyer, 1928).

19. *Was ist Metaphysik?* (Bonn: Cohen, 1929). Freiburg Inaugural Lecture, 1929; conceived, 1928. Fourth edition, with "Nachwort," and fifth edition, with "Einleitung" (Frankfurt: Klostermann, 1943 and 1949, respectively).

20. *Vom Wesen des Grundes*. Supplementary volume, *Jahrbuch für Philosophie und phänomenologische Forschung* (Halle: Niemeyer, 1929). Simultaneously published separately: 3d. edition, with "Vorwort" (Frankfurt: Klostermann, 1949). Conceived, 1928.

21. *Kant und das Problem der Metaphysik* (Bonn: Cohen, 1929). Second edition, with new "Vorwort" (Frankfurt: Klostermann, 1951).

22. *Die Selbstbehauptung der deutschen Universität* (Breslau: Korn, 1933).

23. "Hölderlin und das Wesen der Dichtung." *Das innere Reich* 3 (München: Langen and Müller, 1936). Published separately (München: Langen and Müller, 1937). Speech at Rome, 1936.

24. "Wege zur Aussprache." In *Allemannenland. Ein Buch von Volkstum und Sendung* (Stuttgart: Engelhorns Nachf., 1937). Also in Schneeberger's *Nachlese zu Heidegger* (see Schneeberger, Guido, below).

25. "Lettre à M. J. Wahl." *Bulletin de la Société française de Philosophie* 37 (1937). Also in Jean Wahl, *Existence Humaine et Transcendence* (Neuchâtel: Editions de la Baconnière, 1944).

26. "Prologue." In *Qu'est-ce que la métaphysique?* Translated and edited by Henry Corbin (Paris: Gallimard, 1938).

27. *Hölderlins Hymne 'Wie wenn am Feiertage'* (Halle: Niemeyer, 1941). Speech delivered 1939.

28. "Platons Lehre von der Wahrheit." In *Geistige Überlieferung* (Berlin) 2 (1942). Also in *Platons Lehre von der Wahrheit, mit einem "Brief über den Humanismus"* (Bern: Francke, 1947). Conceived 1930-1931.
29. *Vom Wesen der Wahrheit* (Frankfurt: Klostermann, 1943). Second edition, with enlarged "Schlussanmerkung," 1949. Delivered as address since 1930; lecture course, 1937-1938.
30. "Andenken." In *Hölderlin Gedenkschrift*. Edited by P. Kluckhohn (Tübingen: Mohr, 1943).
31. "Nachwort zu: *Was ist Metaphysik?*," 1943. Added to the fourth edition of no. 19 (above).
32. *Erläuterungen zu Hölderlin* (Frankfurt: Klostermann, 1944). Containing "Heimkunft an die Verwandten" (address, 1943) and no. 23 (above).
33. "Brief über den Humanismus." In *Platons Lehre von der Wahrheit* (Bern: Francke, 1947). Published separately as *Über den Humanismus* (Frankfurt: Klostermann, 1949).
34. "Einleitung zu: *Was ist Metaphysik?*," 1943. Added to the fourth edition of no. 19.
35. "Der Zuspruch des Feldweges." *Sonntagsblatt* (Hamburg) 23 October 1949. Also in *Wort und Wahrheit* (Wien) 5 (1950). Second edition, with the title *Der Feldweg* (Frankfurt: Klostermann, 1956).
36. *Holzwege* (Frankfurt: Klostermann, 1950). Contains
"Der Ursprung des Kunstwerkes," dating back to address delivered during 1935-1936; published separately, with "Zusatz" (1956) (Stuttgart: Reclam, 1960).
"Die Zeit des Weltbildes," dating back to address in 1938.
"Hegels Begriff der Erfahrung," dating back to seminars and addresses during 1942-1943.
"Nietzsches Wort 'Gott ist tot'," dating back to Nietzsche lecture courses during 1936-1940, and address in 1943.
"Wozu Dichter?," address, 1946.
"Der Spruch des Anaximander," part of a treatise written in 1946.
37. *Erläuterungen zu Hölderlins Dichtung* (Frankfurt: Klostermann, 1951). Second edition of no. 32, containing all the four Hölderlin essays mentioned above.
38. "Seinsverlassenheit und Irrnis." In *Ernst Barlach* (Darmstadt: Herausgegeben von der Kulturverwaltung der Stadt Darmstadt und dem Landestheater Darmstadt, 1951). Included in "Überwindung der Metaphysik" in *Vorträge und Aufsätze* (no. 52 below). Written during 1936-1946.
39. " 'Briefe' an Emil Staiger." *Zu einem Vers von Mörike. Ein Briefwechsel mit Martin Heidegger* by Emil Staiger. *Trivium* (Zürich) 9 (1951). Also separately Zürich: Atlantis Verlag, n.d.).
40. "Das Ding." *Jahrbuch der Bayerischen Akademie der Schönen Künste* (München) 1 (1951). With "Nachwort," in *Vorträge und Aufsätze* (no. 52 below). Address, 1950.
41. "Logos." In *Festschrift für Hans Jantzen* (Berlin: Mann, 1951). Dates back to lecture course on "Logik," 1944.

42. "Bauen Wohnen Denken." In *Mensch und Raum* (Darmstadter Gespräch, 2) (Darmstadt: Neue Darmstadter Verlagsanstalt, 1952). Address, 1951.
43. "Was heisst Denken?" *Merkur* (München) 6 (1952).
44. "Georg Trakl." *Merkur* (München) 7 (1953). Also under the title "Die Sprache im Gedicht" in *Unterwegs zur Sprache*.
45. *Einführung in de Metaphysik* (Tübingen: Niemeyer, 1953). Lecture course, 1935.
46. " 'Brief' an die Redaktion." *Die Zeit* (Hamburg) 39 (24 September 1953).
47. "Die Frage nach der Technik." *Jahrbuch der Bayerischen Akademie der Schönen Künste* 3 (1954). Also in *Die Künste im Technischen Zeitalter* (München) 1956. Address, 1953; enlarged form of address on "Das Gestell" in 1949.
48. "Anmerkungen über die Metaphysik." *Festschrift für Emil Preetorius* (Wiesbaden) 1954. Included in "Überwindung der Metaphysik" in *Vorträge und Aufsätze* (no. 52 below). Written during 1936-1946.
49. "Wissenschaft und Besinnung." *Börsenblatt für den Deutschen Buchhandel* (Frankfurt) 13 April 1954. Address, 1953.
50. ". . . dichterisch wohnet der Mensch . . ." *Akzente, Zeitschrift für Dichtung* (München) 1 (1954). Address, 1951.
51. "Heraklit." *Festschrift der 350. Jahresfeier des Humanistischen Gymnasiums in Konstanz* (Konstanz) 1954. Under the title "Aletheia" in *Vorträge und Aufsätze* (no. 52 below). Dates back to lecture course on Heraclitus, 1943.
52. *Vorträge und Aufsätze* (Pfullingen: Neske, 1954). Contains nos. 40, 41, 42, 43, 47, 49, 50, and 51; also "Überwindung der Metaphysik" (incorporating nos. 38 and 48), "Wer ist Nietzsches Zarathustra?" (address, 1953) and "Moira" (from lecture course on "Was heisst Denken?" 1951-1952).
53. *Aus der Erfahrung des Denkens* (Pfullingen: Neske, 1954). Written 1947.
54. *Was heisst Denken?* (Tübingen: Niemeyer, 1954). Lecture course, 1951-1952.
55. "Über 'Die Linie'," in *Festschrift für Ernst Jünger* (Frankfurt: Klostermann, 1955). Separately as *Zur Seinsfrage* (Frankfurt: Klostermann, 1956).
56. *Was ist das—die Philosophie?* (Pfullingen: Neske, 1956). Address, 1955.
57. "Encuentros con Ortega y Gasset." *Clavileño—Revista de la Asociación Internacional de Hispanismo* (Madrid) 7, 39 (1956).
58. *Der Satz vom Grund* (Pfullingen: Neske, 1957). Contains lecture course of 1955-1956 and address, 1956.
59. *Hebel—der Hausfreund* (Pfullingen: Neske, 1957).
60. *Identität und Differenz* (Pfullingen: Neske, 1957). Contains "Der Satz der Identität," an address of 1957, and "Die onto-theo-logische Verfassung der Metaphysik," the concluding lecture of a seminar on Hegel's *Wissenschaft der Logik* in 1956-1957.
61. "Vom Wesen und Begriff der *physis*, Aristoteles *Physik* B 1." *Il Pensiero* (Milan) 3 (1958). Seminar lectures, 1940.

62. "Grundsätze des Denkens." *Jahrbuch für Psychologie und Psychotherapie* (Freiburg) 6 (1958).
63. *Unterwegs zur Sprache* (Pfullingen: Neske, 1959). Contains
     "Die Sprache." Address, 1950.
     "Die Sprache im Gedicht." No. 44 above.
     "Aus einem Gespräch von der Sprache." Written during 1953-1954.
     "Das Wesen der Sprache." Three addresses in 1957-1958.
     "Das Wort." Address, 1958.
     "Der Weg zur Sprache." Address, 1959, published also in *Die Sprache* (Darmstadt) 1959.
64. "Aufzeichnungen aus der Werkstatt." *Neue Zürcher Zeitung* (Zürich) 26 September 1959.
65. "Antrittsrede." *Jahresheft der Heidelberger Akademie der Wissenschaften* 1957-1958 (Heidelberg) 1959; also *Wissenschaft und Weltbild* (Wien) 12 (1959).
66. *Gelassenheit* (Pfullingen: Neske, 1959). Contains "Gelassenheit," address, 1955; and "Zur Erörterung der Gelassenheit, aus einem Feldweggespräch über das Denken." Written, 1944-1945.
67. "Ein Wort des Dankes." In *Martin Heidegger 26. September 1959* (Messkirch: Acker, 1959).
68. "Hegel und die Griechen." In *Die Gegenwart der Griechen im neueren Denken* (Tübingen: Mohr, 1960).
69. "Hölderlins Erde und Himmel." In *Hölderlin-Jahrbuch*, 1958-1960. (Tübingen: Mohr, 1960). Address, 1960.
70. *Nietzsche*, 2 vols (Pfullingen: Neske, 1961). Contains
     A. Lecture course on Nietzsche, consisting of
        "Der Wille zur Macht als Kunst," 1936-1937.
        "Die ewige Wiederkehr des Gleichen," 1937.
        "Der Wille zur Macht als Erkenntnis," 1939.
        "Die ewige Wiederkehr des Gleichen und der Wille zur Macht," 1949.
        "Der europäische Nihilismus," 1940.
        "Nietzsches Metaphysik," 1940.
     B. Treatises
        "Die seinsgeschichtliche Bestimmung des Nihilismus," 1944-1946.
        "Die Metaphysik als Geschichte des Seins," 1941.
        "Entwürfe zur Geschichte des Seins als Metaphysik," 1941.
        "Die Erinnerung in die Metaphysik," 1941.
71. "Sprache und Heimat." *Hebbel Jahrbuch* (Heide) 1960. Also, in an abridged version, in *Dauer im Wandel: Festschrift für Carl J. Burckhardt* (München: Callwey, 1961).
72. *Die Frage nach dem Ding. Zu Kants Lehre von den transzendentalen Grundsätzen* (Tübingen: Niemeyer, 1962). Lecture course, 1935-1936.
73. "Kants These über das Sein." In *Festschrift für Erik Wolf, Existenz und Ordnung* (Frankfurt: Klostermann, 1962). Separately (Frankfurt: Klostermann, 1963).

74. "Ansprache zum Heimatabend." In *700 Jahre Stadt Messkirch* (Messkirch: Privately printed, 1962).
75. "Aus einer Erörterung der Wahrheitsfrage." In *Zehn Jahre Neske Verlag* (Pfullingen: Neske, 1962). From lecture course 1937-1938.
76. *Die Technik und die Kehre* (Pfullingen: Neske, 1962). Contains "Das Gestell." Address, 1949, published in enlarged form as no. 47. "Die Kehre." Address, 1949.
77. "Mein Weg in die Phänomenologie." In *Hermann Niemeyer zum achtzigsten Geburtstag, 16 April 1963* (Privately printed, 1963).
78. "Vorwort" (1962), in William J. Richardson, *Heidegger* (The Hague: Nijhoff, 1963).
79. "Aus der letzten Marburger Vorlesung." In *Zeit und Geschichte: Festschrift für Rudolf Bultmann zum 80. Geburtstag* (Tübingen: Mohr, 1964). From lecture course on Leibniz, 1928.
80. "Adalbert Stifters 'Eisgeschichte'." In *Wirkendes Wort* (Zürich: Schweizerische Bibliophilien Gesellschaft, 1964).
81. *Über Abraham a Santa Clara* (Messkirch: Acker, 1964).
82. "Das Ende der Philosophie und die Augfabe des Denkens," French translation: *Kierkegaard vivant* (Paris: Gallimard, 1966).
83. " 'Leserbrief' zu 'Mitternach einer Weltnacht'." *Der Spiegel* (Hamburg) 22, 7 (7 February 1966): 110-113.
84. " 'Brief' an Max Kommerell" (4 August 1942). In *M. Kommerell, Briefe und Aufzeichnungen 1919-1944*. Herausgegeben von Inge Jens (Freiburg: Walter, 1967).
85. *Wegmarken* (Frankfurt: Klostermann, 1967). Contains nos. 19, 20, 28, 29, 31, 33, 34, 55, 61, 68, 73, and 79, with a "Vorbemerkung" added.
86. "Zeit und Sein." In *L'endurance de la pensée: Pour saluer Jean Beaufret* (Paris: Plon, 1968). Lecture, 1962.
87. "A Letter from Heidegger, with Commentary by W. J. Richardson, S.J." In *Heidegger and the Quest for Truth*, edited by Manfred S. Frings (Chicago: Quadrangle, 1968).
88. *Zur Sache des Denkens* (Tübingen: Niemeyer, 1969). Contains nos. 77, 82, 86, and "Protokoll zu einem Seminar über den Vortrag 'Zeit und Sein'," prepared by Alfredo Guzzoni.
89. "Phänomenologie und Theologie" and "Einige Hinweise auf Hauptgeschichtspunkte für das theologische Gespräch über 'Das Problem eines nichtobjektivierenden Denkens und Sprechens in der heutigen Theologie'." *Archives de Philosophie* (Paris) 32 (1969). The first a lecture, 1927, and the second a letter, 1964.
90. *Martin Heidegger zum 80. Geburtstag: Von seiner Heimatstadt Messkirch* (Frankfurt: Klostermann, 1969). Contains "Vom Geheimnis des Glockenturms" (written 1956), and nos. 35, 66 ("Gelassenheit"), 67, 74 (under the title "700 Jahre Messkirch"), and 81; also a "Geburtstagsbrief" by the philosopher's brother, Fritz Heidegger.
91. "Die Kunst und der Raum." In *Die Kunst und der Raum—L'art et l'espace* (St. Gallen: Erker Verlag, 1969).
92. "Dankansprache." In *Ansprachen zum 80. Geburtstag—Martin Heidegger 26 September 1969* (Messkirch: Stadt Messkirch, 1969).

93. "Über das Zeitverständnis in der Phänomenologie und im Denken der Seinsfrage." In *Phänomenologie—lebendig oder tot?*, ed. H. Gehrig (Karlsruhe: Badenia Verlag, 1969).

94. "Martin Heidegger in Gespräch." In *Martin Heidegger in Gespräch*, ed. Richard Wisser (Freiburg/München: Alber, 1970). Television interview.

95. *Phänomenologie und Theologie* (Frankfurt: Klostermann, 1970). Contains no. 89, with a "Vorwort" added.

96. *Heraklit* (Frankfurt: Klostermann, 1970). Seminar, jointly with Eugen Fink, 1966-1967.

97. "Letter." *Philosophy East and West* 20, 3 (1970). Heidegger issue.

98. "A Letter from Heidegger" (1966). In *Heidegger and the Path of Thinking*, ed. John Sallis (Pittsburgh: Duquesne University Press, 1970).

99. *Schellings Abhandlung über das Wesen der menschlichen Freiheit (1809)*, ed. Hildegard Feick (Tübingen: Niemeyer, 1971). Contains lecture course, 1936; selected pieces from a seminar, 1941; and extracts from seminar notes, 1941-1943.

100. *Erläuterungen zu Hölderlins Dichtung*. Enlarged fourth edition (Frankfurt: Klostermann, 1971). Contains the four essays in no. 37, no. 69, and "Das Gedicht," address, 1968.

101. *Frühe Schriften* (Frankfurt: Klostermann, 1972). Contains nos. 8, 9, 10, 12, and a "Vorwort" which includes no. 65.

102. "Anmerkungen zu Karl Jaspers' *Psychologie der Weltanschauungen*." In Hans Saner, Hg., *Karl Jaspers in der Diskussion* (München: Piper, 1973).

103. *Kant und das Problem der Metaphysik*. Enlarged fourth edition (Frankfurt: Klostermann, 1973). The new additions are: a "Vorwort" and an "Anhang." The latter includes: I. Davoser Vorträge ("Kants Kritik der reinen Vernunft und die Aufgabe einer Grundlegung der Metaphysik") and II. Davoser Disputation ("Davoser Disputation zwischen Ernst Cassirer und Martin Heidegger").

104. The following volumes of Heidegger's Marburg lectures in "II. Abteilung: Vorlesungen (1923-1944)" of *Martin Heidegger: Gesamtausgabe* (Frankfurt: Vittorio Klostermann) were announced in 1975, marking the commencement of a new phase in Heidegger scholarship:

Vol. 21, *Logik (Aristotles)*, Walter Biemel, ed.

Vol. 24, *Die Grundprobleme der Phänomenologie*, Friedrich-Wilhelm von Herrmann, ed.

Vol. 26, *Logik (Leibniz)*, Klaus Held, ed.

II. English Translations of Heidegger's Writings
(*In chronological sequence*)

"Remembrance of the Poet" ("Heimkunft/An die Verwandten") and "Hölderlin and the Essence of Poetry" ("Hölderlin und das Wesen der Dichtung"), Douglas Scott, trans. In Werner Brock, *Existence and Being*. See Part III below. These are two of the six essays on Hölderlin in *Erläuterungen zu Hölderlins Dichtung*. See Part I above, no. 37.

"On the Essence of Truth" (*Vom Wesen der Wahrheit*) and "What is Metaphysics?" (*Was ist Metaphysik?*), R. F. C. Hull and Allan Crick, trans. In Werner Brock, *Existence and Being*. See Part III below.

"The Age of the World View" ("Die Zeit des Weltbildes" in *Holzwege*), Marjorie Grene [Glicksman], trans. *Measure*, 2 (1951).

"The Way Back into the Ground of Metaphysics" ("Einleitung," *Was ist Metaphysik?*), Walter Kaufmann, trans. *In* Walter Kaufmann, *Existentialism from Dostoiewski to Sartre* (New York: Meridian, 1957).

What is Philosophy? (Was ist das—die Philosophie?), William Kluback and Jean T. Wilde, trans. With German text (New York: Twayne, 1958).

The Question of Being (Zur Seinsfrage), William Kluback and Jean T. Wilde, trans. With German text (New York: Twayne, 1958).

An Introduction to Metaphysics (Einführung in die Metaphysik), Ralph Manheim, trans. (New Haven: Yale University Press, 1959).

Being and Time (Sein und Zeit), John Macquarrie and Edward Robinson, trans. (New York: Harper & Row, 1962).

Kant and the Problem of Metaphysics (Kant und das Problem der Metaphysik), James S. Churchill, trans. (Bloomington, Ind.: Indiana University Press, 1962).

"Plato's Doctrine of Truth" (*Platons Lehre von der Wahrheit*), John Barlow, trans.; and "Letter on Humanism" (*Brief über den 'Humanismus'*), Edgar Lohner, trans. Both in William Barrett and Henry D. Aiken, *Philosophy in the Twentieth Century* (New York: Random House, 1962).

Discourse on Thinking (Gelassenheit), John M. Anderson and E. Hans Freund, trans. (New York: Harper & Row, 1966).

What is a Thing? (Die Frage nach dem Ding), W. B. Barton, Jr., and Vera Deutsch, trans. (Chicago: Regnery, 1967).

What is Called Thinking? (Was heisst Denken?), Fred D. Wieck and J. Glenn Gray, trans. (New York: Harper & Row, 1968).

"The Problem of Non-Objectifying Thinking and Speaking," in *Philosophy and Religion*, Jerry Gill, ed. Minneapolis: Burgess Publishing Co., 1968

The Essence of Reasons (Vom Wesen des Grundes), Terrence Malick, trans. With German text (Evanston, Ill.: Northwestern University Press, 1969).

Identity and Difference (Identität und Differenz), Joan Stambaugh, trans. With German text (New York: Harper & Row, 1969).

Hegel's Concept of Experience ("Hegels Begriff der Erfahrung" in *Holzwege*) (New York: Harper & Row, 1970).

"Martin Heidegger: A Recollection" ("Antrittsrede," Akademie der Wissenschaften, Heidelberg) Hans Siegfried, trans. *Man and World* 3, 1 (1970).

On the Way to Language (Unterwegs zur Sprache). All essays except "Die Sprache," Peter D. Hertz, trans. "Words," Joan Stambaugh, trans. (New York: Harper & Row, 1971).

Poetry, Language, Thought, Albert Hofstadter, trans. (New York: Harper & Row, 1971). Contains translations of *Aus der Erfahrung des Denkens*; "Der Ursprung des Kunstwerkes" and "Wozu Dichter?" (*Holzwege*); "Bauen Wohnen Denken," "Das Ding," and ". . . dichterisch wohnet der Mensch . . ." (*Vorträge und Aufsätze*); "Die Sprache" (*Unterwegs zur Sprache*).

"The Turning" ("*Die Kehre*"), Kenneth Maly, trans., in *Research in Phenomenology*, Vol. 1 (1971).

On Time and Being (*Zur Sache des Denkens*), Joan Stambaugh, trans. (New York: Harper & Row, 1972).

The End of Philosophy, Joan Stambaugh, trans. (New York: Harper & Row, 1973). Contains translations of "Die Metaphysik als Geschichte des Seins," "Entwürfe zur Geschichte des Seins als Metaphysik" and "Die Erinnerung in die Metaphysik" (*Nietzsche II*), and "Überwindung der Metaphysik" (*Vorträge und Aufsätze*).

"Art and Space" (*Die Kunst und der Raum*), Charles H. Seibert, trans. *Man and World* 6, I (1973).

"The Problem of Reality in Modern Philosophy" ("Das Realitätsproblem in der modernen Philosophie"), Philip J. Bossert, trans. *Journal of the British Society for Phenomenology* 4, I (1973).

The Pathway (*Der Feldweg*), Thomas F. O'Meara, O.P., trans. (Revisions: Thomas J. Sheehan). *Listening—Journal of Religion and Culture* 8, I-3 (1973).

"Messkirch's Seventh Centennial" ("700 Jahre Messkirch"), Thomas J. Sheehan, trans. *Listening—Journal of Religion and Culture* 8, I-3 (1973).

Early Greek Thinking, David Farrell Krell and Frank A. Capuzzi, trans. (New York: Harper & Row, 1975). Contains translations of "Der Spruch des Anaximander" (*Holzwege*), and of "Logos," "Moira,"' and "*Aletheia*" (*Vorträge und Aufsätze*).

III. Books and Articles about Heidegger

Adamczewski, Zygmunt. "On the Way to Being (Reflecting on Conversations with Martin Heidegger)." In John Sallis, ed., *Heidegger and The Path of Thinking* (See Sallis, John, below). Other articles of this author, not listed here, are equally important for a meticulous study of Heidegger's texts.

Allemann, Beda. *Hölderlin und Heidegger* (Zürich: Atlantis, 1956).

———. "Martin Heidegger und die Politik." *Merkur* (München) 21, 10, 1967; also Otto Pöggeler, ed., *Heidegger* (See Pöggeler, Otto, ed., below).

Anteile. Martin Heidegger zum 60. Geburtstag (Frankfurt: Klostermann, 1950).

Apel, K. O. "Wittgenstein und Heidegger. Die Frage nach dem Sinn von Sein und der Sinnlosigkeitsverdacht gegen alle Metaphysik." In *Philosophisches Jahrbuch* 75, 1 (1967).

Arendt, Hannah. "Martin Heidegger ist achtzig Jahre alt." In *Merkur* 23, 10 (1969).

Astrada, Carlos, et al. *Martin Heideggers Einfluss auf die Wissenschaften. Aus Anlass seines 80. Geburtstages* (Bern: Francke, 1949).

Axelos, Kostas. *Einführung in ein künftiges Denken: Über Marx und Heidegger* (Tübingen: Niemeyer, 1966).

Biemel, Walter. "Heideggers Begriff des Daseins." *Studia Catholica* 24 (1949).

————. *Le Concept de Monde chez Heidegger* (Louvain: Nauwelaerts, 1950).
————. "Husserls Encyclopaedia Britannica Artikel und Heideggers Anmerkungen dazu." *Tijdschrift voor Philosophie* 12 (1950).
————. "Dichtung und Sprache bei Heidegger." *Man and World* 2 (1969).
————. *Martin Heidegger* (Hamburg: Rowohlt, 1973).
————. "Heidegger und die Metaphysik." In *Symposion Heidegger* (Madrid: Colectia Destin, 1971).
Birault, Henri. "Heidegger et la pensée de la finitude." *Revue Internationale de la Philosophie*, no. 52 (1960). Heidegger issue.
Bock, I. *Heideggers Sprachdenken* (Meisenheim: Hain, 1966).
Brechter, Joseph. *Geschichtliche Transzendenz bei Heidegger* (Meisenheim: Hain, 1972).
Bretschneider, Willy. *Sein und Wahrheit* (Meisenheim: Hain, 1965).
Brock, Werner. *Existence and Being* (Chicago: Regnery, 1949).
Bröcker, Walter. "Heidegger und die Logik." *Philosophische Rundschau* 1 (1953).
Bucher, A. J. *Martin Heidegger: Metaphysikkritik als Begriffsproblematik* (Bonn: Grundmann, 1972).
Buddeberg, Else. *Denken und Dichten des Seins, Heidegger/Rilke* (Stuttgart: Metzlersche Verlagsbuchhandlung, 1956).
Caputo, John D. "Meister Eckhart and the Later Heidegger: The Mystical Element in Heidegger's Thought." *Journal of the History of Philosophy* 12, 4 (1974) and 13, 1 (1975). Other articles by this author, not listed here, are equally valuable.
Cassirer, Ernst. "Kant und das Problem der Metaphysik." *Kant-Studien* 36 (1931).
Danner, Helmut. *Das Göttliche und der Gott bei Heidegger* (Meisenheim: Hain, 1971).
Deeley, John M. *The Tradition via Heidegger* (The Hague: Nijhoff, 1971).
Deely, John M., and Novak, Joseph A. "The Idea of Phenomenology." *The New Scholasticism* 44, 3 (1970).
Demske, J. M. *Sein, Mensch und Tod: Das Todesproblem bei Heidegger* (Freiburg/München: Alber, 1963).
————. "Heidegger's Quadrate and Revelation of Being." *Philosophy Today* 8 (1964).
De Waelhens, A. *La Philosophie de Martin Heidegger* (Louvain: Nauwelaerts, 1942).
De Waelhens, A., and Biemel, W. "Heideggers Schrift 'Vom Wesen der Wahrheit'." *Symposion* 3 (1952).
Doherty, Joseph E. *Sein, Mensch und Symbol. Heidegger und die Auseinandersetzung mit dem Neukantianische Symbolbegriff* (Bonn: Bouvier, 1972).
Duda, Sibylle. *Selbstwerdung und Sprache bei Heidegger* (Wien: Verlag Notring, 1971).
Eliade, Mircea, et al. *Symposion Heidegger. Omagiu Românescu lui Martin Heidegger* (Madrid: Colectia Destin, 1971).
Fay, Thomas A. "Heidegger on Logic: A Genetic Study of His Thought on Logic." *Journal of the History of Philosophy* 12, 1 (1974).
Feick, Hildegard. *Index zu "Sein und Zeit,"* 2d rev. ed. (Tübingen: Niemeyer, 1968).

Fink, Eugen. "Dank an den Denker." In *Martin Heidegger 26. September 1969. Ansprachen zum 80. Geburtstag* (Messkirch: Stadt Messkirch, 1970).

Frings, Manfred. "Heidegger and Scheler." *Philosophy Today* 12, 1 (1968).

———, ed. *Heidegger and the Quest for Truth* (Chicago: Quadrangle, 1968).

Fürstenau, P. *Heidegger: Das Gefüge seines Denkens* (Frankfurt: Klostermann, 1958).

Gabriel, Leo. "Gespräche mit Martin Heidegger." *Wissenschaft und Weltbild* 9 (1956).

Gadamer, H.-G. "Zur Einleitung." In *Heidegger: Der Ursprung des Kunstwerkes* (Stuttgart: Reclam, 1960).

———. "Martin Heidegger und die Marburger Theologie." *In* H.-G. Gadamer, *Kleine Schriften I*, 1967.

———. "Heidegger und die Sprache der Metaphysik." In Gadamer, *Kleine Schriften III*, 1972. (Stuttgart: Kohlhammer, 1968 [with the title "Anmerkungen zu dem 'Thema Hegel und Heidegger' "]).

———, ed. *Die Frage Martin Heideggers. Beiträge zu einem Kolloquium mit Heidegger aus Anlass seines 80. Geburtstages* (Heidelberg: Winter, 1969).

———. "Der Denker Martin Heidegger." Gadamer, ed., *Die Frage Martin Heideggers* (Heidelberg: Winter, 1969).

———. "Hegel und Heidegger." *In* Gadamer, *Hegels Dialektik* (Tübingen: Mohr, 1971).

———. "Martin Heidegger." *In* Gadamer, *Kleine Schriften III* (Tübingen: Mohr, 1972).

Gadamer, H.-G., et al. *Hegel, Hölderlin, Heidegger* (Karlsruhe: Badenia Verlag, 1971).

Gelven, Michael. *A Commentary on Heidegger's "Being and Time"* (New York: Harper & Row, 1970).

Glicksman [Grene], Marjorie. "A Note on the Philosophy of Heidegger." *Journal of Philosophy* 35 (1938).

Gray, Glenn J. "The Splendor of the Simple." *Philosophy East and West* 20, 3 (1970). Heidegger issue. Gray's other articles on Heidegger, not listed here, are equally illuminating.

Grene, Marjorie [Glicksman]. *Martin Heidegger* (New York: Hillary House, 1957).

Gründer, Karlfried. "M. Heideggers Wissenschaftskritik in ihren geschichtlichen Zusammenhängen." *Archiv für Philosophie* 11 (1962).

Hamburg, Carl. "A Cassirer-Heidegger seminar." *Philosophy and Phenomenological Research* 25 (1964).

Harries, Karsten. "Heidegger's Conception of the Holy." *The Personalist* 47 (1966).

Henrich, Dieter. "Über die Einheit der Subjektivität." *Philosophische Rundschau* 3 (1955).

Herrmann, F. W. v. *Die Selbstinterpretation Martin Heideggers* (Meisenheim: Hain, 1964).

Huch, Kurt Jürgen. *Philosophiegeschichtliche Voraussetzungen der Heideggerschen Ontologie* (Frankfurt: Europaische Verlagsanstalt, 1967).

Hühnerfeld, Paul. *In Sachen Heidegger* (München: List, 1961).

Ijsseling, S. "Van en over Heidegger. Kronieck van de Heideggerliteratur 1955-1965." *Tijdschrift voor Filosofie* 27 (1965).
Ilting, K. H. "Sein als Bewegtheit." *Philosophische Rundschau* 10 (1962).
Jonas, Hans. "Heidegger and Theology." *Review of Metaphysics* 18 (1964).
Kanthack, K. *Das Denken Martin Heideggers* (Berlin: de Gruyter, 1959).
King, Magda. *Heidegger's Philosophy: A Guide to His Basic Thought* (New York: Macmillan, 1969).
Klostermann, Vittorio, Hg. *Durchblicke: Martin Heidegger zum 80. Geburtstag* (Frankfurt: Klostermann, 1970).
Kockelmans, Joseph J. *Martin Heidegger: A First Introduction to His Philosophy* (Pittsburgh: Duquesne, 1965).
———. "Heidegger on Time and Being." *The Southern Journal of Philosophy* 8, 4 (1970). Special issue on Heidegger.
———, ed. *On Heidegger and Language* (Evanston: Northwestern University Press, 1972).
Krüger, Gerhard. "M. Heidegger und der Humanismus." *Studia Philosophica* 9 (1969); also, *Theologische Rundschau* 18 (1950).
Landgrebe, Ludwig. "Husserl, Heidegger, Sartre." *Revue de Metaphysique et de Morale* 6 (1964).
Langan, T. *The Meaning of Heidegger: A Critical Study of an Existentialist Phenomenology* (New York: Columbia, 1961).
Levy, H. "Heidegger's Kant-Interpretation." *Logos* 21 (1932).
Liebrucks, Bruno. "Idee und ontologische Differenz." *Kant-Studien* 48 (1956/57).
Lohmann, Johannes. "M. Heidegger's Ontological Difference and Language." In Kockelmans, Joseph J., ed., *On Heidegger and Language*. (See Kockelmans, Joseph J., ed., above.)
Löwith, Karl. *Heidegger—Denker in dürftiger Zeit*, 3d ed. (Göttingen: Vandenhoek, 1964).
Lübbe, Hermann. *Bibliographie der Heidegger-Literatur 1917-1955* (Meisenheim: Hain, 1957).
Macomber, W. B. *The Anatomy of Disillusion* (Evanston: Northwestern University Press, 1967).
Macquarrie, John. *An Existentialist Theology* (London: SCM Press, 1955).
———. *Martin Heidegger* (Richmond: Knox, 1968).
Martin Heidegger zum siebzigsten Geburtstag (Pfullingen: Neske, 1959).
Martin Heidegger 26. September 1969. Ansprachen zum 80. Geburtstag (Messkirch: Stadt Messkirch, 1970).
Marx, Werner. "Heidegger's New Conception of Philosophy." *Social Research* 22 (1955).
———. *Vernunft und Welt. Zwischen Tradition und anderem Anfang* (The Hague: Nijhoff, 1970).
———. *Heidegger und die Tradition* (Stuttgart: Kohlhammer, 1961). English translation, *Heidegger and The Tradition* (Evanston: Northwestern, 1971).
Mehta, J. L. *The Philosophy of Martin Heidegger* (Varanasi, India: Banaras Hindu University Press, 1967).
———. Abridged paperback version of the Banaras Press edition (New York: Harper & Row, 1971).

————. "Heidegger and the Comparison of Indian and Western Philosophy." *Philosophy East and West* 20, 3 (1970).

Meulen, J. van der. *Heidegger und Hegel* (Meisenheim: Hain, 1954).

Meyer, H. *Martin Heidegger und Thomas von Aquin* (München: Schöningh, 1964).

Moehling, Karl A. "Martin Heidegger and the Nazi Party: An Examination." Ph.D. dissertation, Northern Illinois University, Dekalb, 1972.

Müller-Lauter, W. *Möglichkeit und Wirklichkeit bei Martin Heidegger* (Berlin: de Gruyter, 1960).

Nishitani, Keiji. "Two Addresses by Martin Heidegger—Preliminary Remark." *The Eastern Buddhist* (Kyoto), New Series, 1, 2 (1966).

Noack, Hermann. "Gespräch mit Martin Heidegger." *Anstösse* 1. Evangelischer Akademie, Hofgeismar, 1954.

Noller, Gerhard, Hg. *Heidegger und die Theologie* (München: Kaiser, 1967).

Ortega y Gasset, J. "Heidegger und die Sprache der Philosophie." *Universitas* 7 (1952).

Ott, Heinrich. *Denken und Sein: Der Weg Martin Heideggers und der Weg der Theologie* (Zollikon: Evangelischer Verlag, 1959).

Otto, Walter F. "Die Zeit und das Sein." In *Anteile: Martin Heidegger zum 60. Geburtstag.*

Palmier, Jean-Michel. *Les Écrits politiques de Heidegger* (Paris: Éditions de l'Herme, 1968).

Pereboom, M. Dirk. "Heidegger-Bibliographie, 1917-1966." *Freiburger Zeitschrift für Philosophie und Theologie*, Freiburg (Schweiz) 16 (1969).

Perotti, James L. *Heidegger on the Divine* (Ohio: Ohio University Press, 1974).

Perpeet, Wilhelm. "Heideggers Kunstlehre." *Jahrbuch für Aesthetik und allgemeine Kunstwissenschaft* (Kohr) 8 (1963).

Pflaumer, R. "Sein und Mensch im Denken Martin Heideggers." *Philosophische Rundschau* 13 (1966).

Pöggeler, Otto. "Jean Wahls Heidegger-Deutung." *Zeitschrift für philosophische Forschung* 12 (1958).

————. "Sein als Ereignis." *Zeitschrift für philosophische Forschung* 13 (1959).

————. "Metaphysik und Seinstopik bei Heidegger." *Philosophisches Jahrbuch* 70 (1962).

————. "Review of *Index zu 'Sein und Zeit'.*" *Philosophischer Literaturanzeiger* 15 (1962).

————. *Der Denkweg Martin Heideggers* (Pfullingen: Neske, 1963).

————, ed. *Heidegger* (Köln/Berlin: Kiepenheuer & Witsch, 1969).

————. "Heidegger Heute." In Pöggeler, ed., *Heidegger*, 1969.

————. "Heideggers Topologie des Seins." *Man and World* 2 (1969).

————. *Philosophie und Politik bei Heidegger* (Freiburg/München: Alber, 1972).

Pugliese, Orlando. *Vermittlung und Kehre: Grundzüge des Geschichtsdenkens bei Martin Heidegger* (München: Alber, 1965).

Richardson, William J. *Heidegger: Through Phenomenology to Thought* (The Hague: Nijhoff, 1963).

————. "Heidegger's Critique of Science." *The New Scholasticism* 42, 4,

(1968). Heidegger issue. Richardson's other articles on Heidegger, not listed here, are equally valuable.

Robinson, James M., and Cobb, John B., Jr. *The Later Heidegger and Theology* (New York: Harper & Row, 1963).

Rosales, Alberto. *Transzendenz und Differenz: Ein Beitrag zum Problem der ontologischen Differenz beim frühen Heidegger* (The Hague: Nijhoff, 1970).

Ryle, Gilbert. "Critical Notice of *Sein und Zeit*." *Mind* 38 (1929).

Sallis, John, ed. *Heidegger and The Path of Thinking* (Pittsburgh: Duquesne, 1970).

Sass, Hans-Martin. *Heidegger-Bibliographie*. 2d enl. ed. (Meisenheim: Hain, 1968).

Sass, Hans-Martin, et al. *Materialien zu einer Heidegger-Bibliographie* (Meisenheim: Hain, 1975).

Schmitt, Richard. *Martin Heidegger on Being Human: An Introduction to* Sein und Zeit (New York: Random House, 1969).

Schneeberger, Guido. *Ergänzungen zu einer Heidegger-Bibliographie* (Bern: Privately printed, 1960).

————. *Nachlese zu Heidegger* (Bern: Privately printed, 1961).

Schöfer, Erasmus. *Die Sprache Heideggers* (Pfullingen: Neske, 1962).

Schrey, H-H. "Die Bedeutung der Philosophie Martin Heideggers für die Theologie." In Astrada, et al., *Martin Heideggers Einfluss auf die Wissenschaften* (See Astrada, Carlos, et al., above).

Schulz, Walter. "Über den philosophiegeschichtlichen Ort Martin Heideggers." *Philosophisches Jahrbuch* 1 (1953/54).

Schuwer, André. "Prolegomena to 'Time and Being': Truth and Time." In John Sallis, ed., *Heidegger and the Path of Thinking* (See Sallis, John, ed., above).

Schwann, Alexander. *Politische Philosophie im Denken Heideggers* (Köln/Opladen: Westdeutscher Verlag, 1965).

Seidel, G. J. *Martin Heidegger and the Pre-Socratics* (Lincoln: University of Nebraska Press, 1964).

Sherover, Charles M. *Heidegger, Kant and Time* (Bloomington: Indiana University Press, 1971).

Sinn, Dieter. "Heideggers Spätphilosophie." *Philosophische Rundschau* 14, 2 (1967).

Sitter, Beat. "Zur Möglichkeit dezisionistischer Auslegung von Heideggers ersten Schriften." *Zeitschrift für philosophische Forschung* 24 (1970).

Stassen, Manfred. *Heideggers Philosophie der Sprache in* Sein und Zeit (Bonn: Bouvier, 1973).

Szilasi, Wilhelm. "Interpretation und Geschichte der Philosophie." In Astrada, et al., *Martin Heideggers Einfluss auf die Wissenschaften* (see Astrada, Carlos, et al., above).

Tsujimura, Koichi. "Martin Heideggers Denken und die Japanische Philosophie." In *Martin Heidegger 26. September 1969. Ansprache zum 80. Geburtstag* (Messkirch: Stadt Messkirch, 1970).

Tugendhat, Ernst. *Der Wahrheitsbegriff bei Husserl und Heidegger* (Berlin: de Gruyter, 1967).

Vail, L. M. *Heidegger and Ontological Difference* (University Park and London: The Pennsylvania State University Press, 1972).

Versényi, Laszlo. *Heidegger, Being, and Truth* (New Haven: Yale, 1965).

Vietta, Egon. *Die Seinsfrage bei Martin Heidegger* (Stuttgart: Schwab, 1950).

Vycinas, Vincent. *Earth and Gods: An Introduction to the Philosophy of Martin Heidegger* (The Hague: Nijhoff, 1961).

Wild, John. "An English Version of Martin Heidegger's *Being and Time*." *Review of Metaphysics* 16 (1962).

Wiplinger, Fridolin. *Wahrheit und Geschichtlichkeit: Eine Untersuchung über die Frage nach dem Wesen der Wahrheit im Denken Martin Heideggers* (Freiburg/München: Alber, 1961).

———. "Würdigung eines Denkers? Martin Heideggers 80. Geburtstag." *Wissenschaft und Weltbild* 22, 3 (1969).

Wisser, Richard. *Martin Heidegger im Gespräch* (Freiburg/München: Alber, 1970).

Wyschogrod, Michael. *Kierkegaard and Heidegger* (London: Allen & Unwin, 1954).

IV. Other Works

Becker, Oskar. *Dasein und Dawesen: Gesammelte philosophische Aufsätze* (Pfullingen: Neske, 1963).

Biemel, Walter. "Die Bedeutung von Kants Begründung der Aesthetik für die Philosophie der Kunst." *Kant-Studien*, Ergänzungsheft, 77 (1960).

Bollnow, O. F. *Dilthey* (Stuttgart: Kohlhammer, 1955).

Brentano, Franz. *Von der mannigfachen Bedeutung des Seienden nach Aristoteles* (Hildesheim: Olms, 1960).

Brock, Werner. *Introduction to Contemporary German Philosophy* (Cambridge: Cambridge University Press, 1935).

Bröcker, Walter. *Aristoteles*, 2d ed. (Frankfurt: Klostermann, 1957).

De Waelhens, A. "Die phänomenologische Idee der Intentionalität." In *Husserl und das Denken der Neuzeit* (The Hague: Nijhoff, 1959).

Dilthey, Wilhelm. *Gesammelte Schriften*, V, VII and VIII (Stuttgart: Teubner, 1958–1961).

Dilthey, Wilhelm, and Yorck, Paul. *Briefwechsel zwischen Wilhelm Dilthey und dem Grafen Paul Yorck v. Wartenburg, 1877-1897* (Halle: Niemeyer, 1923).

Farber, Marvin. *Foundations of Phenomenology* (Albany: State University of New York Press, 1967).

Fink, Eugen. *Zur ontologischen Frühgeschichte vom Raum-Zeit-Bewegung* (The Hague: Nijhoff, 1957).

———. *Sein, Wahrheit, Welt* (The Hague: Nijhoff, 1958).

———. *Alles und Nichts* (The Hague: Nijhoff, 1959).

———. *Spiel als Weltsymbol* (Stuttgart: Kohlhammer, 1960).

———. *Nietzsches Philosophie* (Stuttgart: Kohlhammer, 1960).

———. *Epiloge zur Dichtung* (Frankfurt: Klostermann, 1971).

Friedländer, Paul. *Platon*, vol. I, 2d ed. (Berlin: Walter de Gruyter, 1954).

Gabriel, Leo. *Von Brahma zur Existenz*, 2d ed. (München: Herold, 1956).

Gadamer, H.-G. "Vorwort." In W. Dilthey, *Grundriss der allgemeinen Geschichte der Philosophie* (Frankfurt: Klostermann, 1949).

———. "Einleitung." In R. G. Collingwood, *Denken: Eine Autobiographie* (Stuttgart: Kohlhammer, 1955).

———. *Wahrheit und Methode* (Tübingen: Mohr, 1960; 3d enl. ed., 1972).

———. "Hermeneutik und Historismus." *Philosophische Rundschau* 9 (1961); also in *Wahrheit und Methode* (1972).

———. "Die phänomenologische Bewegung." *Philosophische Rundschau* 11 (1963); also in *Kleine Schriften* III (1972).

———. "Die Universalität des hermeneutischen Problems." *Philosophisches Jahrbuch* 73 (1966); also in *Kleine Schriften* I (1967).

———. *Hegels Dialektik: Fünf hermeneutische Studien* (Tübingen: Mohr, 1971).

———. *Kleine Schriften* I, II and III (Tübingen: Mohr, 1967 and 1972).

Hartmann, Nicolai. *Ethics*, vol. I (London: Allen & Unwin, 1932).

Heller, Erich. *The Disinherited Mind* (New York: Meridian, 1959).

Henrich, Dieter, et al., eds. *Die Gegenwart der Griechen im neueren Denken: Festschrift für Hans-Georg Gadamer zum 60. Geburtstag* (Tübingen: Mohr, 1960).

Hodges, H. A. *The Philosophy of Wilhelm Dilthey* (London: Kegan Paul, 1952).

Husserl, Edmund. *Ideen* I, II and III (The Hague: Nijhoff, 1950-1952).

———. *Die Krisis der europaischen Wissenschaften* (The Hague: Nijhoff, 1954).

———. *Phänomenologische Psychologie* (The Hague: Nijhoff, 1962).

———. *Logische Untersuchungen*, 3 vols. (Tübingen: Niemeyer, 1968).

Jaspers, Karl. *Psychologie der Weltanschauungen* (Heidelberg: Springer, 1950).

Kanthack, K. *Nicolai Hartmann und das Ende der Ontologie* (Berlin: de Gruyter, 1962).

Kaufmann, Walter. *Nietzsche* (Princeton: Princeton University Press, 1968).

Kuhn, H. "The phenomenological concept of 'horizon'." In *Philosophical Essays in Memory of Edmund Husserl*, ed. Marvin Farber (Cambridge, Mass.: Harvard University Press, 1960).

Landgrebe, Ludwig. *Phänomenologie und Metaphysik* (Hamburg: Von Schröder, 1949).

———. *Philosophie der Gegenwart* (Bonn: Athenäum-Verlag, 1952).

———. "Husserls Abschied vom Cartesianismus." *Philosophische Rundschau* 9 (1961); also in *Der Weg der Phänomenologie*.

———. *Der Weg der Phänomenologie* (Gütersloh: Mohn, 1963).

Lipps, Hans. "Pragmatismus und Existentialismus." In *Die Wirklichkeit des Menschen* (Frankfurt: Klostermann, 1954).

Lohmann, Johannes. "Über den paradigmatischen Charakter der griechischen Kultur." In *Die Gegenwart der Griechen im neueren Denken* (Gadamer-Festschrift) (Tübingen: Mohr, 1960).

———. *Philosophie und Sprachwissenschaft.* (Berlin: Duncker & Humboldt, 1965).

Löwith, Karl. *Nietzsches Philosophie der ewigen Wiederkehr des Gleichen* (Stuttgart: Kohlhammer, 1958).

Manasse, E. M. "Bücher über Platon, I." *Philosophische Rundschau* 5, Beiheft I (1957).

Misch, Georg. "Lebensphilosophie und Phänomenologie." *Philosophischer Anzeiger* 3 & 4, 1929-1930.

———. "Einleitung." *In* W. Dilthey, *Gesammelte Schriften* V (Stuttgart: Teubner, 1957).

Möller, Joseph. *Existenzial Philosophie und katholische Theologie* (Baden-Baden: Verlag für Kunst und Wissenschaft, 1952).

Müller, Max. *Existenzphilosophie im geistigen Leben der Gegenwart*, 2d ed. (Heidelberg: Kerle, 1958).

Oltmanns, K. *Meister Eckhart*, 2d ed. (Frankfurt: Klostermann, 1958).

Paton, H. J. *Kant's Metaphysic of Experience*, 2 vols. (London: Allen & Unwin, 1936).

Plessner, Helmuth. "Offene Problemgeschichte." In Robert Heiss, et al., *Nicolai Hartmann—Der Denker und sein Werk* (Berlin: de Gruyter, 1952).

Pöggeler, Otto. "Das Wesen der Stimmungen." *Zeitschrift für philosophische Forschung* 14 (1960).

———. "Zur Deutung der Phänomenologie des Geistes." In *Hegel-Studien*, I (Bonn: Bouvier, 1961).

———. "Review of books by Viehweg and by Hennis." *Philosophischer Literaturanzeiger* 18 (1965).

———. "Hermeneutische und mantische Phänomenologie." *Philosophische Rundschau* 13 (1965).

Pos, H. J. "Recollections of Ernst Cassirer." In *The Philosophy of Ernst Cassirer*, ed. P. A. Schilpp (Evanston, Ill.: The Library of Living Philosophers, Inc., 1949).

Robinson, James M., and Cobb, John B., Jr. *The New Hermeneutic* (New York: Harper & Row, 1964).

Rombach, Heinrich. *Die Gegenwart der Philosophie* (München: Alber, 1962).

Sartre, J. P. *Being and Nothingness* (London: Methuen, 1956).

Scheler, Max. *Der Formalismus in der Ethik und die materiale Wertethik* (Bern: Francke, 1954).

———. *The Nature of Sympathy* (New Haven: Yale University Press, 1954).

Schleiermacher, F. *Hermeneutik*, ed. H. Kimmerle (Heidelberg: Winter, 1959).

Schmitt, Richard. "In search of Phenomenology" (a review of Spiegelberg). *Review of Metaphysics* 15, 4 (1962).

Schulz, Walter. *Die Vollendung des deutschen Idealismus in der Spätphilosophie Schellings* (Stuttgart: Kohlhammer, 1955).

———. *Der Gott der neuzeitlischen Metaphysik* (Pfullingen: Neske, 1957).

Siewerth, G. *Das Schicksal der Metaphysik von Thomas zu Heidegger* (Einsiedeln: Johannes, 1959).

Spiegelberg, Herbert. *The Phenomenological Movement*, 2 vols. (The Hague: Nijhoff, 1960).

Tanabe, Hajime. "Todesdialektik." *Martin Heidegger zum siebzigsten Geburtstag* (Pfullingen: Neske, 1959).

Tillich, Paul. *Systematic Theology*, vol. I (Chicago: University of Chicago Press, 1951).

Volkmann-Schluck, K-H. *Plotin als Interpret der Ontologie Platos*, 2d ed. (Frankfurt: Klostermann, 1957).

———. "Zur Gottesfrage bei Nietzsche." In *Anteille: Martin Heidegger zum 60. Geburtstag* (Frankfurt: Klostermann, 1950).

Wild, John. *The Challenge of Existentialism* (Bloomington: Indiana University Press, 1959)

———. "Man and His Life-World." In *For Roman Ingarden* (The Hague: Nijhoff, 1959).

Wisser, Richard. *Verantwortung im Wandel der Zeit* (Mainz: Hase & Koehler, 1967).

Wittgenstein, Ludwig. *Notebooks 1914-1916* (Oxford: Blackwell, 1961).

Index

Absolute, the, 389-90, 393-95
Ad-tension (*Gewärtigen*), 255, 262-63, 273n.9, 292-94
Agathon, 23, 348n.15, 384, 411n.45, 414n.90, 425-26
Aletheia, 22, 70n.28, 101, 190, 192, 197n.3, 203n.30, 203-4n.31, 329, 370, 375, 391, 395-96, 406, 437, 450-52, 472n.27, 475n.42, 476-77n.63. *See also* Truth
Allemann, Beda, 60, 74n.61
Anaximander, 34, 37, 38, 334, 363, 368, 410n.28
Andenken, see Remembrance
Anticipation (*Vorlaufen,* running ahead), 179, 213, 219-21, 240, 242-43, 250-53
Anwesen (-heit), see Presence
Anxiety, 175-78, 200-1n.16, 220-21, 225, 257-58, 317
Apel, K. O., 476n.62
Apophainesthai (apophansis), 101, 162-64, 190
Appearance, 99-100. *See also* Phenomenon
A priori, 136, 146-47n.5, 195. *See also* Being, as
Aquinas, St. Thomas, 88, 148n.9, 188
Arche, 198n.6, 320-1, 347n.13, 421, 423. *See also* Ground
Arendt, Hannah, 39
Aristotle, 11, 12, 22, 23, 24, 29, 34, 36, 37, 49, 54, 57, 61, 66n.5, 70n.28,

72n.46, 72-73n.49, 75n.65, 81n.116, 87, 88, 94, 98, 100, 101, 105, 129, 149n.12, 171, 185, 187, 190, 193, 197n.3, 197-98n.6, 237n.3, 257, 298, 301, 302, 303, 306, 320, 322, 331, 338, 374, 378, 380, 381, 398, 409n.26, 411n.47, 411n.48, 414n.88, 418, 420, 422, 423, 425, 427, 446, 417n.15
Art (aesthetics), 74-75n.63
Augustine, St., 11, 12, 72n.49, 148n.9, 171, 197n.6, 200n.16, 301, 471n.16
Austrag, see Issue
Authenticity (inauthenticity), 111, 142-44, 158, 172-74, 176-78, 200n.14, 217-18, 211-22, 238-39n.10, 249-50
Axelos, Kostas, 410n.26

Beaufret, J., 61, 341
Becker, Oskar, 274n.15
Bedeutsamkeit, see Significance
Befindlichkeit, see Disposition
Being: and becoming, 370; and beings, *see* Ontological Difference; and language, *see* Language and Being; and man, 340-42, 352-53n.40, 353n.44, 353n.45, 372-73, 431-36, 439-40. *See also Ereignis*; and the Ought, 377; and seeming, 370-71; and thought, 78n.94, 371-72, 377, 459-62; and time, 94-95, 307, 379, 436, 452-458; as *a priori*, 424-25; as condition of possibility (*agathon*), 377, 384, 425-26; as crossed

Luther, Martin, 11, 12, 200n.16

MacMurray, John, 198n.6
Macomber, W. B., 476n.63
Macquarrie, John, 68n.15
Macquarrie, J., and Robinson, E., 79n.107
Man, das, see Everyman
Man, interpretation of, in Being and Time, 31; Greek view of, 372-73, 411n.40; traditional theory of, 432-33; and Being, see Being and man
Manasse, E. M., 75n.65
Manheim, Ralph, 69n.23, 78n.78, 359
Marx, Karl, 380, 409n.14, 410n.26, 472n.22
Marx, Werner, 66n.5, 75n.65, 79n.103, 150n.18, 196n.3, 407-8n.4, 409n.26, 475n.44
Meaning, see Sense
Medieval philosophy, 10, 423-24
Mehta, J. L., 481n.100
Merleau-Ponty, M., 79n.107, 410n.26
Metaphysical tradition, the Western, 12, 66n.5, 67-68n.11, 343, 462-63
Metaphysics, 24-26, 333-36, 338-39, 419-30, 438; and God, 428-30, 471n.16; overcoming of, 27-28, 67-68n.11, 331, 438; Aristotle's view of, 420-21; Hegel's, 394-95; Nietzsche's, 399
Method, concept of, 44-48; phenomenological, 98-99, 101-4
Meulen, van der, J., 75n.65, 414n.88
Misch, Georg, 70n.33, 289
Mitsein, see Being-together-with
Moehling, Karl A., 74n.61
Möller, Joseph, 68n.15
Moment, the, 255, 260, 273-74n.10, 274n.12, 283, 301, 309n.13, 452
Mood (attunement), 154-56, 197n.5, 198n.6
Mörike, E., 33
Mortals, 440-43
Müller, Max, 67n.10, 68n.15, 345n.5, 470n.5
Müller-Lauter, W., 309n.5
Mutuality (of man and Being), see Ereignis
My-ownness, see Ipseity
Mysticism, 10, 49, 63, 81n.121, 464

Nähe, see Nearness
Nearness, 132, 134-35, 341, 353n.44, 446, 456, 458
Newton, I., 193-94
Nietzsche, F., 6, 22-24, 33, 36, 37, 57, 58, 72n.47, 73n.49, 74n.63, 75n.65, 80n.111, 145n.1, 236n.1, 288, 309n.13, 316, 334, 337, 343, 350n.23, 353n.44, 355, 356, 357, 358, 366, 378, 383, 384, 397-407, 409n.14, 409n.26, 413n.67, 414n.88, 414n.90, 414-15n.105, 415n.108, 426, 430, 437, 453-54, 474n.42
Nihilism, 358, 397, 401-402, 414n.8, 428, 438, 451
Noack, H., 471n.16
Noein, 49, 98, 372-73, 411n.39, 425, 459, 460-61
Noller, Gerhard, 68n.15
Nothingness (the nothing), 32, 177, 200-1n.16, 221, 237n.5, 316-19, 326, 344n.3, 344n.4, 345n.5, 345-46n.6, 346n.11
Nullity (the "not"), 227-230. See also Nothingness

Object (objectivity), 46-47, 319, 326, 328, 383, 386-88, 392
Oltmanns, K., 73n.49
One, the, see Everyman
Ontic vs. ontological, 40, 42, 91-92, 106n.6, 181, 291, 392-93
Ontological Difference, 89, 321, 325, 345n.5, 346n.11, 365, 419-20, 429, 430-31, 444, 470n.5
Ontological (existenzial) interpretation, 42-43, 244-47
Ontology, 102, 104, 107n.8, 427-30. See also Fundamental ontology, history of, 95-98
Onto-theo-logy, 393-95, 427, 428-30
Ortega y Gasset, J., 60, 64
Ott, Heinrich, 52, 68n.15
Otto, Walter F., 309-10n.13
Ousia (parousia), 29, 70n.28, 98, 151n.24, 366, 367, 374, 377, 390, 391, 393-394, 423, 424, 425. See also Presence
Overman, 404-5, 415n.106
Overtness (Erschlossenheit), see Dasein, overtness of
Owning (being owned), see Ereignis

About the Author

J. L. Mehta, at present visiting professor at Harvard University, is a foremost interpreter of the philosophy of Heidegger. Thoroughly acquainted with the German philosophical tradition and language, Dr. Mehta is equally at home in the rich Hindu tradition, and brings to the investigation of Heidegger an insightful viewpoint quite different from that of other interpreters. His work has been ranked along with that of Pöggeler and Marx among the outstanding studies of Heidegger's thought.

In 1963 Dr. Mehta received the Ph.D. degree at Banaras Hindu University, Varanasi, India, and taught there for several years before teaching at the University of Hawaii from 1971 to 1973. He was a Fulbright Visiting Lecturer at Mount St. Mary's College, Emmitsburg, Pennsylvania, and Yale University from 1964 to 1965. As an Alexander von Humboldt Foundation Fellow in 1957-1958, he studied at the universities of Cologne and Freiburg with such Heidegger experts as Eugen Fink, Ludwig Landgrebe, Walter Biemel, and Johannes Lohmann, and was privileged to have several meetings with Heidegger himself.

Dr. Mehta has contributed to several journals, including *Philosophy East and West, Visva Bharati Journal of Philosophy,* and *Foundations of Language.*